PRAISE FOR THE BEST RECIPE SERIES AND OTHER AMERICA'S TEST KITCHEN TITLES

"An instant classic."
CHICAGO SUN-TIMES on AMERICA'S BEST LOST RECIPES

"This tome definitely raises the bar for all-in-one, basic, must-have cookbooks. . . . Kimball and his company have scored another hit."
PORTLAND OREGONIAN on THE AMERICA'S TEST KITCHEN FAMILY COOKBOOK

"A foolproof, go-to resource for everyday cooking."
PUBLISHERS WEEKLY on THE AMERICA'S TEST KITCHEN FAMILY COOKBOOK

"A timesaving tome."
THE CHICAGO TRIBUNE on 834 KITCHEN QUICK TIPS

"A moderate approach to lightening everyday dishes for the family."
THE CHICAGO TRIBUNE on THE BEST LIGHT RECIPE

"Further proof that practice makes perfect, if not transcendent. . . . If an intermediate cook follows the directions exactly, the results will be better than takeout or Mom's."
THE NEW YORK TIMES on THE NEW BEST RECIPE

"Exceptional renditions with thorough instruction . . ."
PUBLISHERS WEEKLY on COOKING AT HOME WITH AMERICA'S TEST KITCHEN

"Like a mini-cooking school, the detailed instructions and illustrations ensure that even the most inexperienced cook can follow these recipes with success."
PUBLISHERS WEEKLY on BEST AMERICAN SIDE DISHES

"Makes one-dish dinners a reality for average cooks, with honest ingredients and detailed make-ahead instructions."
THE NEW YORK TIMES on THE BEST COVER & BAKE RECIPES

"[The Best Meat Recipes] conquers every question one could have about all things meat."
THE SAN FRANCISCO CHRONICLE on THE BEST MEAT RECIPES

"The best instructional book on baking this reviewer has seen."
LIBRARY JOURNAL (STARRED REVIEW) on BAKING ILLUSTRATED

"A must-have for anyone into our nation's cooking traditions—and a good reference, too."
LOS ANGELES DAILY NEWS on THE BEST AMERICAN CLASSICS

"If you've always wanted to make real Italian dishes as close to the Italian way as we can make them in America, here's a cookbook that shows you how."
PITTSBURGH POST-GAZETTE on THE BEST ITALIAN CLASSICS

"Cook's Illustrated to the rescue. . . . The Best Vegetable Recipes belongs on every cooking reference shelf. Here's to our health."
PITTSBURGH TRIBUNE-REVIEW on THE BEST VEGETABLE RECIPES

WELCOME TO AMERICA'S TEST KITCHEN

THIS BOOK HAS BEEN TESTED, WRITTEN, AND edited by the folks at America's Test Kitchen, a very real 2,500-square-foot kitchen located just outside of Boston. It is the home of *Cook's Illustrated* magazine and *Cook's Country* magazine and is the Monday-through-Friday destination for more than three dozen test cooks, editors, food scientists, tasters, and cookware specialists. Our mission is to test recipes over and over again until we understand how and why they work and until we arrive at the "best" version.

We start the process of testing a recipe with a complete lack of conviction, which means that we accept no claim, no theory, no technique, and no recipe at face value. We simply assemble as many variations as possible, test a half dozen of the most promising, and taste the results blind. We then construct our own hybrid recipe and continue to test it, varying ingredients, techniques, and cooking times until we reach a consensus. The result, we hope, is the best version of a particular recipe, but we realize that only you can be the final judge of our success

(or failure). As we like to say in the test kitchen, "We make the mistakes, so you don't have to."

All of this would not be possible without a belief that good cooking, much like good music, is indeed based on a foundation of objective technique. Some people like spicy foods and others don't, but there is a right way to sauté, there is a best way to cook a pot roast, and there are measurable scientific principles involved in producing perfectly beaten, stable egg whites. This is our ultimate goal: to investigate the fundamental principles of cooking so that you become a better cook. It is as simple as that.

You can watch us work (in our actual test kitchen) by tuning in to *America's Test Kitchen* (www.americastestkitchen.com) or *Cook's Country from America's Test Kitchen* (www.cookscountrytv.com) on public television, or by subscribing to *Cook's Illustrated* magazine (www.cooksillustrated.com) or *Cook's Country* magazine (www.cookscountry.com). We welcome you into our kitchen, where you can stand by our side as we test our way to the "best" recipes in America.

THE BEST SLOW & EASY RECIPES

A BEST RECIPE CLASSIC

THE
BEST
SLOW & EASY
RECIPES

A BEST RECIPE CLASSIC

BY THE EDITORS OF

COOK'S ILLUSTRATED

PHOTOGRAPHY
KELLER + KELLER, CARL TREMBLAY, AND DANIEL J. VAN ACKERE

ILLUSTRATIONS
JOHN BURGOYNE

America's
TEST KITCHEN

BROOKLINE, MASSACHUSETTS

America's Test Kitchen
17 Station Street
Brookline, MA 02445

ISBN 13: 978-1-933615-24-0
ISBN 10: 1-933615-24-9

Library of Congress Cataloging-in-Publication Data
The Editors of *Cook's Illustrated*

The Best Slow & Easy Recipes: More Than 250 Foolproof,
Flavor-Packed Roasts, Stews, Braises, Sides, and Desserts That Let the Oven Do the Work

1st Edition
ISBN 13: 978-1-933615-24-0
ISBN 10: 1-933615-24-9
(hardcover): U.S. $35 CAN $38
I. Cooking. I. Title
2008

Manufactured in the United States of America

10 9 8 7 6 5 4 3 2 1

Distributed by America's Test Kitchen, 17 Station Street, Brookline, MA 02445

Editorial Director: Jack Bishop
Executive Editor: Elizabeth Carduff
Senior Food Editor: Julia Collin Davison
Associate Editors: Elizabeth Wray Emery, Louise Flaig, Rachel Toomey, and Sarah Wilson
Editorial Assistant: Elizabeth Pohm
Test Cooks: Suzannah McFerran, Bryan Roof, and Megan Wycoff
Assistant Test Cook: Adelaide Parker
Design Director: Amy Klee
Art Director: Greg Galvan
Designer: Erica Lee
Staff Photographer: Daniel J. van Ackere
Additional Photography: Keller + Keller, Carl Tremblay
Food Styling: Marie Piraino and Mary Jane Sawyer
Illustrator: John Burgoyne
Production Director: Guy Rochford
Senior Production Manager: Jessica Lindheimer Quirk
Traffic and Project Manager: Alice Cummiskey
Color and Imaging Specialist: Andrew Mannone
Production and Imaging Specialist: Lauren Pettapiece
Copyeditor: Cheryl Redmond
Proofreader: Debra Hudak
Indexer: Elizabeth Parson

Pictured on front of jacket: Pork Roast en Cocotte with Apples and Shallots (page 66)

Pictured on back of jacket: Chicken en Cocotte with Garlic and Rosemary (page 59), Slow-Roasted Beef Eye Round (page 6), Oven-Barbecued Pulled Pork (page 38), Creamy Baked Polenta (page 269), Pan-Roasted Peaches (page 334)

CONTENTS

PREFACE

TWENTY YEARS AGO, MY WIFE AND I purchased an AGA stove for our farmhouse. It was the large four-oven model and we had to have the kitchen floor reinforced to handle 1200 pounds of cast iron. I quickly learned that the AGA is not about stovetop cooking since the two burners lose heat fairly quickly, as does the entire stovetop if the insulating covers are left up for more than 10 or 15 minutes. This is a stove that is designed for long, slow cooking, and once I adjusted to that notion, a whole new world of cookery was revealed. I loved two things about it. First, the oven does most of the work. You can get things going and then just walk away. Second, the food tastes better when cooked low and slow. Over time, I have come to describe this form of culinary endeavor as "slow and easy" cooking.

When I was a kid in Vermont, there were a lot of things that were interminably slow. To make a phone call, you had to crank up the phone and then the call was connected through an operator on a party line. This meant, of course, that she knew everything about everybody. Our ice cream maker was also hand-cranked, which required a half-hour of my sister Kate and me sitting on the floor churning fresh peach ice cream. Floyd Bentley always mowed hay with his team, walking steadily, almost lazily, around the huge bottom fields by the Green River. (The only time they picked up the pace was when he mowed over a yellow-jacket nest.) And I spent thousands of hours in the front parlor of the yellow farmhouse (the center of our town's farming and cooking activity) with farmers who might go a full five minutes without saying anything at all. Everything else was just as slow. Country people never run or even walk quickly, not even when a thunderstorm is moving in. Cows are slower than slow as are rainy afternoons, the lazy wet dog asleep underneath the Kalamazoo wood stove in winter, and the wait for the maple syrup to sheet off the skimmer.

These days I remember slow times with great affection. "Slow and easy" is no longer a term of derision, as in slow traffic or slow service. If you visit Calvin Coolidge's homestead in Plymouth Gap you can see the front parlor where the 30th President of The United States took the oath of office, the church he attended (right across the street), his father's general store (just down the road), and the huge two-level barn. You can stand there and drink in "slow and easy" until time stops, you exhale a long, slow breath, and the world seems just a wee bit simpler and better.

In the kitchen, slow and easy seems to me the ideal way to cook. Let me give you an example. Take a seasoned browned chicken, throw it in a pot, add a small onion, a few cloves of garlic, a bay leaf, and some fresh thyme. Cover and roast at 250 degrees for about an hour and a half until done. The chicken creates its own "jus," which is rich in flavor since it has not been adulterated with stocks or other liquids. It is simple, delicious, easy. And we have adapted this approach for fish, beef, pork, turkey, even eggs.

The premise is time-tested. Let slow cooking do the work and enhance the flavor. We oven-roast, we oven-braise, we use a slow cooker, and we turn stovetop recipes into oven recipes (braises are much better in the oven since the pot heats evenly—on the stovetop, the bottom is hotter than the sides, which often results in burning or overcooking). We even investigate slow-cooking vegetables and fruits and have come up with some fresh approaches including slow-braised carrots and pan-roasted peaches.

Slow isn't hard. Slow isn't complicated. Slow is walk-away cooking, it's letting an oven do the work for you.

Time is all we have and we don't have much of it. We can fight time and rush around creating "meals in minutes" or we can use time to our advantage. The latter philosophy is simpler, it's smarter, and it's better. It's slow and easy.

CHRISTOPHER KIMBALL
Founder and Editor,
Cook's Illustrated and *Cook's Country*
Host, *America's Test Kitchen* and
Cook's Country from America's Test Kitchen

1
OVEN-ROASTING

OVEN-ROASTING

ROASTING IS ONE OF THE MOST BASIC and simple ways to cook large cuts of meat; a moderate oven temperature and extended cooking time can build rich, concentrated flavor and yield tender, juicy meat. And few cooking methods can beat roasting for ease—although roasting takes a relatively long time compared to other cooking methods, the process is largely unattended.

Roasting typically occurs at temperatures in the range of 350 to 400 degrees, but we were intrigued by a number of recipes that use a much lower temperature (and longer cooking time) to slow roast a variety of meat, poultry, and even fish. Whether it was a leg of lamb roasted for seven hours or a tough cut of beef cooked for an entire day in a 130-degree oven, the result was incredibly juicy, meltingly tender meat. We set out to explore this lower, slower approach to roasting to find out just how far we could take it: Could we use it for everything from beef, lamb, and pork to poultry and fish? And are there some instances where a more traditional method of roasting is truly best?

What we found was that in many cases, a lower oven temperature and longer cooking time do indeed produce more tender meat. The reasons are simple. For one, a low temperature provides gentle heat, which means that the meat (especially the outer portion) is less likely to dry out. And large tough cuts of meat in particular benefit from long cooking, which gives the connective tissue time to break down, rendering the meat tender.

While most home ovens don't go below 200 degrees and most home cooks aren't going to slowly roast anything for 24 hours, we were happy to discover that you can still get great results with a more moderate approach. Our Pomegranate-Glazed Roast Bone-In Leg of Lamb (page 17) cooks (for the majority of the time) at 250 degrees and takes about two hours. The same goes for our Walk-Away Roast Chicken (page 41), which has an added bonus: by roasting the chicken at such a low temperature, we found we were able to eliminate the step of turning the bird multiple times, making it much more convenient than a typical roast chicken. The only downside to roasting at low temperatures is the lack of a nicely browned exterior, but this is easily solved by either searing the meat prior to going in the oven (as with our Prime Rib on page 9), or cranking up the oven heat toward the end of cooking for a brief period (as we do for the leg of lamb and chicken).

With some recipes, such as our Herb-Crusted Pork Loin (page 30) and Roast Duck with Port-Cherry Sauce (page 52), we found that a more traditional approach was the way to go. For these, we had the best results with a higher temperature of 350 degrees and found no benefit in going any lower. The same goes for Cuban-Style Roast Pork (page 26)—even when roasted at 325 degrees, this hefty cut still requires six hours in the oven to become juicy and fork-tender.

Testing the limits of roasting even further, we wondered what would happen if we brought another slow cooking technique—barbecuing—indoors. After much trial and error, we discovered an unlikely method (tea smoking) that allowed us to replicate the smoke flavor that usually comes from hours spent on the grill. The result? Oven-Barbecued Spareribs (page 37) and Oven-Barbecued Pulled Pork (page 38) that taste so authentic you might be fooled into thinking they're the real thing.

And what about fish? Of course it's a given that the oven is great for roasting salmon or firm-fleshed white fish like cod or halibut. But the best results are usually with a high or moderate oven temperature for a short period of time. We did, however, come up with a handy method of oven poaching a whole side of salmon at a low temperature that yields incredibly moist and tender fish and couldn't be easier (no special equipment or water required—wrapped in foil, the salmon sits right on the oven rack).

What all of these recipes have in common, regardless of whether the method is traditional or unusual, is that they deliver meat or fish with little hands-on attention, perfectly roasted, and—with a short rest—ready for the table.

Slow-Roasted Beef Eye Round

FOR MOST FAMILIES, SUNDAY ROAST BEEF isn't prime rib; it's a lesser cut that's sometimes good, sometimes not. Our goal was to let the oven do the work for us, using low, slow heat to transform a bargain cut into a tender, juicy roast that can stand on its own at dinner.

First we needed to zero in on the most promising cut of beef. After a week in the kitchen testing a slew of low-cost cuts, we had a clear winner: the eye round roast. Though less flavorful than fattier cuts from the shoulder (the chuck) and less tender than other meat from the back leg (the round), the eye roast had one key attribute the others lacked: a uniform shape from front to back. This was a roast that would not only cook evenly but look good on the plate as well.

We were pretty sure this inexpensive cut of meat would be well-suited to a low and slow cooking approach—tough cuts of meat benefit from an extended cooking time because the connective tissue has time to break down, rendering the roast more tender. But before heading down the low-temperature path, which normally involves roasting meat in an oven set between 250 and 325 degrees, we wanted to try something more extreme. To extract maximum tenderness from meat, the popular 1960s nutritionist Adelle Davis advocated cooking it at the temperature desired when it was done. For a roast to reach an end temperature of 130 degrees for medium-rare, this process could involve 20 to 30 hours of cooking. Davis's advice wasn't new. Benjamin Thompson, the 18th-century physicist who invented the roasting oven, observed that leaving meat to cook overnight in an oven heated by a dying fire resulted in exceptional tenderness.

Tossing aside practical considerations like food safety and the gas bill, we decided we had to replicate these two experts' findings. We set the one oven in the test kitchen capable of maintaining such a low temperature to 130 degrees and popped in an eye round. Twenty-four hours later, we pulled out a roast with juicy, meltingly tender meat that tasters likened to beef tenderloin. What special beef magic was going on here?

Beef contains enzymes that break down its connective tissues and act as natural tenderizers. These enzymes work faster as the temperature of the meat rises—but just until it reaches 122 degrees, at which point all action stops. Roasting the eye round in an oven set to 130 degrees allowed it to stay below 122 degrees far longer than when cooked in the typical low-temperature roasting range, transforming this lean, unassuming cut into something great.

But given that most ovens don't heat below 200 degrees—and that most home cooks don't want to run their ovens for a full day—how could we expect others to re-create our results? We would have to go as low as we could and see what happened. To accommodate the widest possible range of ovens, we settled on 225 degrees as our lowest starting point. We also decided we would brown the meat first to give it nice color and a crusty exterior. (While tender, our 130-degree roast had an unappetizing gray exterior.)

When we took the roast out of the oven, however, we were disappointed. It was tender, but nothing like the texture of the eye round cooked at 130 degrees. What could we do to keep the meat below 122 degrees longer? A new idea occurred to us: Why not shut off the oven just before the roast reached 122 degrees? As the oven cooled, the roast would continue to cook even more slowly.

Using a meat-probe thermometer to track the internal temperature of the roast, we shut off the oven when the meat reached 115 degrees. Sure enough, the meat stayed below 122 degrees 30 minutes longer, allowing its enzymes to continue the work of tenderizing, before creeping to 130 degrees for medium-rare. Tasters were certainly happy with this roast. It was remarkably tender and juicy for a roast that cost so little.

With the tenderness problem solved, it was time to tackle taste. So far we'd simply sprinkled salt and pepper on the roast just before searing it. Perhaps the flavor would improve if the meat were salted overnight or even brined. Brining—normally reserved for less fatty pork and poultry—certainly pumped more water into the beef and made it very juicy, but it also made it taste bland, watery, and less beefy. Next we tried salting the meat for first four, then 12, and finally 24 hours. As might be expected, the roast benefited most from the longest salting. Because the process of osmosis causes salt to travel from areas of higher to lower concentration, the full 24 hours gave it the most time to penetrate deep into the meat. There was another benefit: Salt, like the enzymes in meat, breaks down proteins to further improve texture.

At last we had tender, flavorful beef for a Sunday roast that anyone would be proud to serve their family. The leftovers—if there are any—would have no need for mayonnaise or mustard to taste good.

Slow-Roasted Beef Eye Round

SERVES 6 TO 8

For a smaller roast (2½ to 3½ pounds), reduce the amount of kosher salt to 3 teaspoons (or 1½ teaspoons table salt); for a larger roast (4½ to 6 pounds), cut the meat in half crosswise to create 2 smaller roasts before cooking. Because this cut of meat is one muscle group with a fairly tight structure, tying the roast isn't necessary. If you prefer your meat more or less cooked than medium-rare, see "Testing Meat for Doneness" on page 7. Open the oven door as little as possible and remove the roast from the oven when taking its temperature. Serve with Simple Beef Jus (page 10) or any of the fresh herb sauces on page 11.

> 4 teaspoons kosher or 2 teaspoons table salt
> 1 (3½- to 4½-pound) boneless beef eye round roast (see note)
> 2 tablespoons vegetable oil
>   Ground black pepper

1. Sprinkle the salt evenly over the roast. Place the roast on a large plate, cover with plastic wrap, and refrigerate for 18 to 24 hours.

2. Pat the roast dry with paper towels, rub with 1 tablespoon of the oil, and season with pepper. Cover the meat loosely with plastic wrap and let sit at room temperature for 1 to 2 hours.

3. Adjust an oven rack to the middle position and heat the oven to 225 degrees. Set a wire rack inside a large rimmed baking sheet lined with foil. Heat the remaining 1 tablespoon oil in a 12-inch skillet over medium-high heat until just smoking. Brown the roast on all sides, 12 to 14 minutes, reducing the heat if the pan begins to scorch. Transfer the roast, fat side up, to the prepared wire rack and roast until the very center registers 115 degrees on an instant-read thermometer, 1¼ to 1¾ hours.

4. Turn the oven off and let the roast continue to cook in the oven, without opening the door, until the very center of the meat registers 130 degrees (for medium-rare), 30 to 35 minutes longer. (If the roast has not reached the desired temperature in the time specified, heat the oven to 225 degrees for 5 minutes, shut it off, and continue to cook the roast to the desired temperature.)

5. Transfer the roast to a cutting board, tent loosely with foil, and let rest for 30 minutes. Slice the roast thin and serve.

➤ VARIATION

Slow-Roasted Garlicky Beef Eye Round

For a smaller roast (2½ to 3½ pounds), reduce the amount of kosher salt to 3 teaspoons (or 1½ teaspoons table salt); for a larger roast (4½ to 6 pounds), cut the meat in half crosswise to create 2 smaller roasts before cooking. Because this cut of meat is one muscle group with a fairly tight structure, tying the roast isn't necessary. If you prefer your meat more or less cooked than medium-rare, see "Testing Meat for Doneness" on page 7. Open the oven door as little as possible and remove the roast from the oven when taking its temperature. Serve with Simple Beef Jus (page 10) or any of the fresh herb sauces on page 11.

BEEF AND GARLIC RUB

2 tablespoons vegetable oil

3 medium garlic cloves, minced or pressed through a garlic press (about 1 tablespoon)

4 teaspoons kosher or 2 teaspoons table salt

1 teaspoon minced fresh thyme leaves

1 (3½- to 4½-pound) boneless beef eye round roast (see note)
   Ground black pepper

GARLIC PASTE

¼ cup olive oil

20 large garlic cloves, peeled and halved lengthwise

2 sprigs fresh thyme

2 bay leaves

½ teaspoon salt

1. FOR THE BEEF AND GARLIC RUB: Mix 1 tablespoon of the oil, garlic, salt, and thyme together, then rub the mixture evenly over the roast. Place the roast on a large plate, cover with plastic wrap, and refrigerate for 18 to 24 hours.

2. Wipe off the garlic mixture with paper towels. Rub the roast with the remaining 1 tablespoon oil and season with pepper. Cover the meat loosely with plastic wrap and let sit at room temperature for 1 to 2 hours.

3. FOR THE GARLIC PASTE: Meanwhile, cook the oil, garlic, thyme, bay leaves, and salt together in a small saucepan over medium-high heat until bubbles start to rise to the surface. Reduce the heat to low and cook until the garlic is softened, about 30 minutes. Cool the garlic oil completely, then strain through a fine-mesh strainer. Transfer the garlic to a small bowl, discarding the herbs, and mash to a paste with 2 tablespoons of the garlic oil. Set the garlic paste and remaining 2 tablespoons garlic oil aside.

4. Adjust an oven rack to the middle position and heat the oven to 225 degrees. Set a wire rack inside a large rimmed baking sheet lined with foil. Heat 1 tablespoon of the garlic oil in a 12-inch skillet over medium-high heat until just smoking. Brown the roast on all sides, 12 to 14 minutes, reducing the heat if the pan begins to scorch.

5. Transfer the roast, fat side up, to the prepared wire rack. Brush the roast with the remaining garlic oil, spread the garlic paste along the top, and roast until the very center registers 115 degrees on an instant-read thermometer, 1¼ to 1¾ hours.

6. Turn the oven off and let the roast continue to cook in the oven, without opening the door, until the very center of the meat registers 130 degrees (for medium-rare), 30 to 35 minutes longer. (If the roast has not reached the desired temperature in the time specified, heat the oven to 225 degrees for 5 minutes, shut it off, and continue to cook the roast to the desired temperature.)

7. Transfer the roast to a cutting board, tent loosely with foil, and let rest for 30 minutes. Slice the roast thin and serve.

TESTING MEAT FOR DONENESS

A thermometer takes the guesswork out of knowing when a roast is done. To ensure that the probe stays in the roast, insert the thermometer at an angle. To get an accurate reading, push the probe deep into the roast and then slowly draw it out until you locate the center of the meat (indicated by the lowest temperature). Avoid bones and pan surfaces. And take more than one reading.

The ideal serving temperatures for optimal flavor and juiciness are listed below. If food safety is your primary concern, cook all meat until well-done. Note: The meat should come off the heat 5 to 10 degrees below the desired final temperature, as the internal temperature will continue to rise as the meat rests. (The exception to this is the Slow-Roasted Beef Eye Round on page 6—it should be cooked to the desired doneness as its temperature won't rise once removed from the oven.)

TYPE OF MEAT	RARE	MEDIUM-RARE	MEDIUM	MEDIUM-WELL	WELL-DONE
BEEF	125	130	140	150	160
LAMB	125	130	140	150	160

PRIME RIB

PRIME RIB IS NOT AN EVERYDAY DISH—YOU may only cook it once a year, usually for a holiday or other special occasion—so when you do cook it, you want to be sure to get it right. Most people tend to stick with the same straightforward cooking technique of roasting the meat in a 350-degree oven for a set amount of time based on the weight of the roast. Other recipes we've found use much hotter ovens, up to 425 degrees. Then there is the approach that many restaurants use: They slowly roast the meat at a low temperature for a long period of time. Intrigued by this low and slow technique, we decided to head into the kitchen to find out if it would indeed produce a better, more tender roast.

We immediately encountered a problem. Most restaurants roast their meat using special ovens that can be set at an unusually low temperature—the meat is initially roasted at 250 degrees, then the oven heat is decreased to 140 degrees. But most home ovens don't go below 200 degrees. We wondered if we could get the same results by holding the oven temperature steady at 250 degrees the entire time.

Before we tested a lower temperature, we decided to roast prime ribs at higher temperatures as a basis for comparison. All of the prime ribs roasted

TYING PRIME RIB

It is imperative to tie prime rib before roasting. If left untied, the outer layer of meat will pull away from the rib-eye muscle and overcook. To prevent this problem, tie the roast at both ends, running the string parallel to the bone.

at oven temperatures exceeding 300 degrees (all the way up to 425) looked pretty much the same. Each slice of carved beef was well-done around the exterior, medium toward the center, and a beautiful, pink medium-rare at the center. We might have been tempted to report that roasting temperature doesn't much matter if we hadn't tried cooking prime rib at less than 300 degrees. The results surprised us, although it certainly wasn't love at first sight.

INGREDIENTS: Two Rib Roasts

A whole rib roast (aka prime rib) consists of ribs 6 through 12. Butchers tend to cut the roast in two. We prefer the cut further back on the cow, which is closest to the loin. This cut is referred to as the first cut, the loin end, or sometimes the small end because the meat and ribs get larger as they move up toward the shoulder. The first cut can include anywhere from two to four ribs. Sometimes we like a large roast for the holidays and in this case we prefer a roast with four ribs. At other times, a slightly smaller roast, with just three ribs, is fine. When ordering the former, be sure to specify the first four ribs from the loin end—ribs 9 through 12—to receive the first cut. When ordering a three-rib roast, ask for the first three ribs from the loin end—ribs 10 through 12.

Either way, the first cut is more desirable because it contains the large, single rib-eye muscle and is less fatty. The less desirable cut, which is still an excellent roast, is closer to the chuck (or shoulder) end and is sometimes called the second cut. The closer to the chuck, the less tender the roast becomes.

FIRST CUT

SECOND CUT

FRESH HERB SAUCES

Salsa Verde

MAKES ABOUT 1 CUP

Salsa verde is an all-purpose parsley sauce that tastes excellent with roasted meats and poultry.

1	slice high-quality white sandwich bread
½	cup extra-virgin olive oil
2	tablespoons juice from 1 lemon
2	cups lightly packed fresh parsley leaves
2	medium anchovy fillets
2	tablespoons capers, drained and rinsed
1	small garlic clove, minced or pressed through a garlic press (about ½ teaspoon)
⅛	teaspoon salt

1. Toast the bread in a toaster at a low setting until the surface is dry but not browned, about 15 seconds. Cut the bread into rough ½-inch pieces (you should have about ½ cup).

2. Process the bread pieces, oil, and lemon juice together in a food processor until smooth, about 10 seconds. Add the parsley, anchovies, capers, garlic, and salt and pulse until the mixture is finely chopped (the mixture should not be smooth), about 5 pulses, scraping down the sides of the bowl as needed. Transfer the mixture to a small bowl and let stand at room temperature until the flavors meld, about 30 minutes, or up to 4 hours, before serving.

Chimichurri

MAKES ABOUT 1 CUP

Chimichurri is a fresh Argentinean parsley sauce that tastes great with beef, pork, poultry, and fish.

1	cup minced fresh parsley leaves
½	cup extra-virgin olive oil
¼	cup finely minced red onion
¼	cup red wine vinegar
2	tablespoons water
5	medium garlic cloves, minced or pressed through a garlic press (about 5 teaspoons)
1	teaspoon salt
¼	teaspoon red pepper flakes

Stir all of the ingredients together in a small bowl and let stand at room temperature until the flavors meld, about 30 minutes, or up to 4 hours, before serving.

Fresh Cilantro Sauce

MAKES ABOUT 1 CUP

We prefer the mild flavor of regular olive oil in this sauce. Serve with pork, poultry, fish, and even vegetables.

¼	cup walnuts
2	medium garlic cloves, unpeeled
2½	cups lightly packed fresh cilantro leaves and stems, tough stem ends trimmed
½	cup olive oil (see note)
2	tablespoons water
4	teaspoons juice from 1 lemon
1	scallion, sliced thin
	Salt and ground black pepper

1. Toast the walnuts in a small dry skillet over medium heat, stirring frequently, until just golden and fragrant, about 5 minutes; set aside. Toast the garlic cloves in the skillet over medium heat, stirring frequently, until fragrant, and the color of the cloves deepens slightly, about 7 minutes. Let the garlic cool slightly, then peel and chop.

2. Process the toasted walnuts, toasted and chopped garlic, cilantro, oil, water, lemon juice, scallion, ½ teaspoon salt, and ⅛ teaspoon pepper in a food processor, scraping down the sides of the bowl as needed, until smooth, about 1 minute. Season with salt and pepper to taste and let stand at room temperature until the flavors meld, about 30 minutes, or up to 4 hours, before serving.

ROAST BONELESS LEG OF LAMB

AT ITS BEST, BONELESS LEG OF LAMB IS PLEAS-antly tender and juicy, with a deeply browned exterior that is the perfect contrast to a rosy-pink interior. But all too often it emerges from the oven overcooked and tough, with a rubbery texture and "gamey" flavor—hardly appealing. Knowing that many recipes call for roasting lamb at temperatures of up to 400 degrees, we suspected that high heat might be to blame for mediocre lamb, and we wondered what effect a lower temperature might have. But before we could get started in the kitchen, we need to look at the cut of meat itself.

A whole boneless leg can weigh 8 to 9 pounds; great for a crowd, but we wanted something better suited to a small, elegant dinner. A better choice was a boneless half leg, which weighs 3 to 5 pounds. Obviously, there are two halves to choose from: the sirloin (from the top of the leg) and the shank (from the bottom of the leg). After roasting each, we found little difference in terms of flavor or tenderness between the sirloin and the shank, but ultimately decided to use the shank end simply because it's so much easier to find. (That said, if you can find the sirloin end, it can be used as well.)

At first glance, it seems that roasting a boneless leg of lamb should a relatively simple affair—after all, the butcher has done all the work of removing the bone and wrapping the meat into a nice bundle, so it stands to reason that all this roast requires is a little seasoning before going into a hot oven. But we quickly learned that no matter how tidy they look at the store, boneless legs of lamb require further trimming and retying once you get them home. Often, the roast is simply shoved into an elastic netting; this not only lends an off-flavor to the meat during roasting, but prevents any sort of crust from forming, resulting instead in an unattractive quilted pattern. We also discovered that the netting allows butchers to hide all sorts of problems such as multiple pieces of meat or large pieces of gristly fat. We recommend asking the butcher to remove the netting so you can inspect the roast before purchasing. Once the netting has been removed, it is crucial to trim away any large pieces of fat left on the inside of the roast; the extra fat, we learned, renders during roasting and results in the unappealing gamey flavor so typical of lamb. Before retying the roast with twine, we found it helpful to quickly pound it to ensure an even thickness.

With a well-trimmed, securely tied shank-end boneless leg of lamb in hand, we began to experiment with various oven temperatures. Roasting in ovens ranging from 250 to 450 degrees, we noted significant differences. When the lamb was roasted at the high end of the range (between 400 and 450 degrees), it developed a nice crust,

BONELESS LEG OF LAMB

There are two basic methods butchers use to remove the bone from a shank end leg of lamb—known as corkscrew and butterfly—and these methods produce distinctly different roasts. A corkscrew boneless leg of lamb is more common and the roast has an awkward, corkscrew-like shape. This awkward shape doesn't matter if you are making a simple lamb roast, such as Leg of Lamb en Cocotte with Garlic and Rosemary (page 71), but can be troublesome if you want to stuff your roast, or even spread a simple paste on it, as in our Garlic-Herb-Crusted Roast Boneless Leg of Lamb (page 13). A butterflied boneless leg of lamb is slightly less common, but has a more regular shape and works best with any sort of filling. A common problem with butterflied legs of lamb, however, is that they are butchered poorly and often cut into several pieces. This can be hard to detect at the supermarket, because poorly butchered butterflied legs of lamb are often hidden within elastic netting. If buying a butterflied leg of lamb that is wrapped inside netting, have the butcher cut open the netting for you to inspect the meat before purchasing.

CORKSCREWED　　BUTTERFLIED

but when sliced, the roast had a large gray ring of overcooked meat that was tough and dry—exactly what we were trying to avoid. Roasting the lamb at more moderate temperatures of 300 and 350 degrees produced decent results with an acceptable crust and fairly tender, moist meat. But as we had hoped, a low 250-degree oven produced the best meat yet—exceptionally tender with a rosy interior.

The exterior of this low-roasted lamb, however, was unappealingly pallid. This problem was easily solved by browning the meat in a skillet on the stovetop prior to roasting. The direct heat jump-started the cooking of the lamb's exterior, producing a crisp, flavorful crust in a matter of minutes.

With the cooking method established, we focused our attention on flavor. We found that a simple rub of aromatics—just a little bit of herbs and garlic—spread over the meat before retying the roast enhanced the flavor of the lamb without overpowering it. A savory bread crumb crust also proved to be a welcome addition to the exterior, turning our roast into a company-worthy dish. To prevent the crumb crust from falling off the roast when trying to remove the twine, we found it necessary to cut the twine and place the crust on the lamb towards the end of cooking, after the roast had roasted long enough to hold its shape. Cranking the heat up to 425 degrees for the remainder of the cooking ensured that the crumbs would brown and crisp. While our roast leg of lamb takes a little more effort than simply tossing it in the oven and walking away, we think the results are well worth it.

Garlic-Herb-Crusted Roast Boneless Leg of Lamb

SERVES 4 TO 6

A butterflied boneless leg of lamb is the easiest cut to work with here; however, make sure that the meat is in a single piece. If the meat is packaged in elastic netting, have the butcher cut open the netting for you to inspect before purchasing (see page 12 for more information). If necessary, a corkscrewed leg of lamb can be substituted; however, the roast will require a bit more trimming in order to lie flat. If you prefer your meat more or less cooked than medium-rare, see "Testing Meat for Doneness" on page 7.

I	slice high-quality white sandwich bread, quartered
⅓	cup lightly packed fresh parsley leaves
3	tablespoons olive oil
2	tablespoons minced fresh rosemary
3	medium garlic cloves, minced or pressed through a garlic press (about I tablespoon)
I	ounce Parmesan cheese, grated (½ cup)
I	(3½- to 4-pound) butterflied boneless half leg of lamb (see note)
	Salt and ground black pepper
I	tablespoon Dijon mustard

1. Pulse the bread in a food processor to fine crumbs, about 16 pulses; transfer to a medium bowl and set aside. Process the parsley, 1 tablespoon of the oil, rosemary, and garlic together in the food processor until finely minced, about 1 minute. Measure out and reserve 1½ tablespoons of the herb mixture separately. Toss the remaining herb mixture with the bread crumbs, Parmesan, and 1 more tablespoon oil.

2. Lay the lamb with the rough interior side (which was against the bone) facing up and trim away any fat and gristle. Press the meat flat to the counter and, following the illustration on page 14, cover the meat with plastic and pound to a uniform ¾-inch thickness.

3. Remove the plastic wrap and season the lamb with salt and pepper. Spread the reserved 1½ tablespoons herb mixture evenly over the meat, leaving a 1-inch border around the edge, then roll and tie the roast. Pat the roast dry with paper towels and season with salt and pepper.

4. Adjust an oven rack to the lower-middle position and heat the oven to 250 degrees. Set a wire rack inside a large rimmed baking sheet lined with foil. Heat the remaining 1 tablespoon oil in

a 12-inch skillet over medium-high heat until just smoking. Brown the roast on all sides, including the ends, 12 to 14 minutes, reducing the heat if the pan begins to scorch.

5. Transfer the roast to the prepared wire rack, seam side down, and roast until the very center of the meat registers 100 degrees on an instant-read thermometer, 50 to 70 minutes.

6. Remove the lamb from the oven and increase the oven temperature to 425 degrees. Remove the twine from the lamb, coat the top and sides of the roast with the mustard, then press the bread crumb mixture into the mustard to adhere. Continue to roast the lamb until the crumbs are browned and the center of the meat registers 125 degrees (for medium-rare) on an instant-read thermometer, 25 to 30 minutes longer. (If the topping becomes brown before the meat is done—especially if cooking the meat past medium-rare—lightly cover the roast with foil and continue to roast until the meat registers the desired doneness.)

7. Transfer the roast to a cutting board and let rest, uncovered, for 30 minutes. Slice the roast into ¼-inch-thick slices and serve.

PREPARING A ROAST BONELESS LEG OF LAMB

1. Cover the lamb with plastic wrap and pound to a uniform ¾-inch thickness.

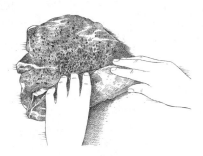

2. Season the meat with salt and pepper, then spread the reserved 1½ tablespoons herb mixture evenly over the meat, leaving a 1-inch border around the edge. Roll the meat lengthwise, around the filling, into a roast.

3. Tie the roast with kitchen twine to secure. (For more information on how to tie a lamb roast, see the illustrations on page 72.)

4. To brown the ends of the roast, hold the roast upright with tongs.

5. When the lamb is almost midway through cooking, remove it from the oven and carefully remove the twine.

6. Coat the lamb with the mustard and the herb and bread crumb mixture, pressing it on well to ensure that it sticks.

> VARIATION

Indian-Spiced Roast Boneless Leg of Lamb

A butterflied boneless leg of lamb is the easiest cut to work with here; however, make sure that the meat is in a single piece. If the meat is packaged in elastic netting, have the butcher cut open the netting for you to inspect before purchasing (see page 12 for more information). If necessary, a corkscrewed leg of lamb can be substituted; however, the roast will require a bit more trimming in order to lie flat. If you prefer your meat more or less cooked than medium-rare, see "Testing Meat for Doneness" on page 7. Garam masala is a blend of Indian spices found in specialty food stores and well-stocked grocery stores.

¼	cup lightly packed fresh mint leaves
¼	cup lightly packed fresh cilantro leaves
2	tablespoons olive oil
3	medium garlic cloves minced or pressed through a garlic press (about 1 tablespoon)
1	tablespoon minced or grated fresh ginger
1	teaspoon garam masala (see note)
¼	teaspoon ground coriander
¼	teaspoon ground cumin
¼	cup slivered almonds
¼	cup raisins
1	tablespoon plain yogurt
1	(3½- to 4-pound) butterflied boneless half leg of lamb (see note)
	Salt and ground black pepper

1. Process the mint, cilantro, 1 tablespoon of the oil, garlic, ginger, ½ teaspoon of the garam masala, ⅛ teaspoon of the coriander, and ⅛ teaspoon of the cumin together in a food processor until finely minced, about 1 minute. Measure out and reserve 1½ tablespoons of the herb mixture separately, leaving the rest of the mixture in the food processor.

2. Add the almonds and raisins to the herb mixture in the food processor and continue to process until finely ground, about 45 seconds; transfer to a small bowl and set aside. Combine the yogurt with the remaining ½ teaspoon garam masala, ⅛ teaspoon coriander, and ⅛ teaspoon cumin and set aside.

3. Lay the lamb with the rough interior side (which was against the bone) facing up and trim away any fat and gristle. Press the meat flat to the counter and, following the illustration on page 14, cover the meat with plastic and pound to a uniform ¾-inch thickness.

4. Remove the plastic wrap and season the lamb with salt and pepper. Spread the reserved 1½ tablespoons herb mixture evenly over the meat, leaving a 1-inch border around the edge, then roll and tie the roast. Pat the roast dry with paper towels and season with salt and pepper.

5. Adjust an oven rack to the lower-middle position and heat the oven to 250 degrees. Set a wire rack inside a large rimmed baking sheet lined with foil. Heat the remaining tablespoon oil in a 12-inch skillet over medium-high heat until just smoking. Brown the roast on all sides, including the ends, 12 to 14 minutes, reducing the heat if the pan begins to scorch.

6. Transfer the roast to the prepared wire rack, seam side down, and roast until the very center of the meat registers 100 degrees on an instant-read thermometer, 50 to 70 minutes.

7. Remove the lamb from the oven and increase the oven temperature to 425 degrees. Remove the twine from the lamb, coat the top and sides of the roast with the yogurt mixture, then press the almond-raisin mixture into the yogurt to adhere. Continue to roast the lamb until the nut mixture is browned and the center of the meat registers 125 degrees (for medium-rare) on an instant-read thermometer, 25 to 30 minutes longer. (If the topping becomes brown before the meat is done—especially if cooking the meat past medium-rare—lightly cover the roast with foil and continue to roast until the meat registers desired doneness.)

8. Transfer the roast to a cutting board and let rest, uncovered, for 30 minutes. Slice the roast into ¼-inch-thick slices and serve.

ROAST BONE-IN LEG OF LAMB

A ROAST BONE-IN LEG OF LAMB MAKES AN impressive centerpiece to the holiday table. When properly cooked, this hefty cut sports a browned, crusty exterior and juicy, ultra-rich meat. But this cut of meat has its challenges, the biggest of which is its tendency to cook unevenly. This is largely due to the unevenness of the leg. We searched the test kitchen library for recipes and discovered that the methods for roasting a bone-in leg of lamb vary widely. Some recipes tout the virtues of roasting at high temperatures, while others swear by low temperatures and slow roasting. But before we could determine the best temperature for roasting, we needed to look at the actual cut of meat.

At the thicker sirloin end, the meat surrounding the flat, twisting hipbone is very thin. The center of the leg, which consists of the top half of the thigh, is fleshy, but the thigh tapers dramatically toward the knee joint, and the shank itself is just a tiny bit of meat. The only way to deal with this problem is to remove the hipbone and aitchbone entirely. Fortunately, most butchers take care of this for you, and the roast is sold as a semi-boneless leg of lamb.

Our first question was whether tying the roast was an essential step. After much trial and error, we did find a way to tie this large, awkward piece of meat and found that it did indeed produce a more evenly cooked roast. But since this roast serves eight to 12 people, having some variation in the doneness of the meat seemed like a good idea, so we nixed the idea tying our leg of lamb. Happy about our streamlined process thus far, we moved on to test a variety of roasting temperatures.

In our research, we found that recipes recommend a range of roasting temperatures from 250 to 450 degrees. We decided to cover the range, roasting legs of lamb at 250, 300, 350, 400, and 450 degrees. Those roasted at the higher temperatures had a nice crust, but a thick gray ring of overcooked meat towards the exterior. They were tough, dry, and gamier in flavor. The two roasted at 300 and 350 degrees, weren't bad, but weren't great either. The one roasted at 250 yielded exceptionally tender meat, rich in flavorful juices. This was undoubtedly the best yet, except for one problem—the exterior of the meat was unappealingly pallid.

Searing the leg of lamb before roasting it was out of the question due to its awkward shape and size. Some of the recipes we had come across touted "oven-searing" as a solution, wherein the oven temperature is cranked up (to 450 degrees) either at the beginning or end of the roasting time to crisp up the exterior. We tested both options and found a significant difference. The crust that formed when the oven was cranked at the beginning not only took longer but was also a bit flabby compared to the crust that formed when the oven was cranked up at the end of cooking. The reason for this difference is that the fat from the roast renders during its low-temperature roasting time, and getting a crust using the heat of the oven (as opposed to the direct heat of searing) is faster and more effective after the majority of the fat has already been rendered. As a precaution, we added ¼ cup of water to the roasting pan during this high heat finish to prevent the drippings from burning and smoking out the kitchen.

Finally, we set about flavoring the lamb. We tried inserting slivers of garlic into slits that we cut into the meat, but this technique yielded unevenly flavored meat, harsh and garlicky in one bite, faintly flavored in the next. We tried rubbing the lamb with garlic paste (both raw and roasted) and marinating for various intervals, but the flavor remained superficial and failed to permeate the big, thick roast. Our next attempt was to spread garlic-rosemary oil over the leg of lamb halfway through the final high-heat roasting.

BUYING LEG OF LAMB

When you go to the supermarket, you will probably be able to buy either a whole leg (which we use for this recipe) or a half leg. When buying half, you can get either the sirloin (upper half) or the shank (lower half). We prefer the shank end simply because it's easier to find.

 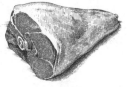

SIRLOIN END   **SHANK END**

While tasters liked this more pungent flavor, it was difficult to gauge when to spread it on the roast—if added too soon, it would burn during the final blast of oven heat. We finally tried spreading it on the lamb as it came out of the oven. The residual heat from the meat "cooked" the garlic and rosemary just enough to take away any raw bite for superb flavor. Also, the flavors drip down over the meat as your carve the roast, so that every slice has some flavor. Finally, for a Middle Eastern–inspired variation, we brushed the lamb with a pomegranate glaze.

Roast Bone-In Leg of Lamb with Garlic and Rosemary

SERVES 8 TO 12

This recipe actually uses a semi-boneless leg of lamb, which is what you most commonly find at the market; if, by chance, the leg has the full bone, have the butcher remove the hipbone and aitchbone for you. The leg of lamb should be well trimmed with just a thin layer of fat on the top; in our experience, most lamb sold at the market is already well trimmed. If you prefer your meat more or less cooked than medium-rare, see "Testing Meat for Doneness" on page 7.

LAMB
1   (6- to 8-pound) semi-boneless leg of lamb, trimmed (see note)
1   tablespoon olive oil
    Salt and ground black pepper

GARLIC OIL
2   tablespoons olive oil
5   medium garlic cloves, minced or pressed through a garlic press (about 5 teaspoons)
2   teaspoons minced fresh rosemary
½   teaspoon salt

1. FOR THE LAMB: Pat the lamb dry with paper towels, rub with the oil, and season with salt and pepper. Cover the roast loosely with plastic wrap and let sit at room temperature for 1 to 2 hours.

2. FOR THE GARLIC OIL: Combine all of the ingredients in a small bowl and set aside.

3. Adjust an oven rack to the lowest position

and heat the oven to 250 degrees. Set a wire rack inside a large rimmed baking sheet lined with foil. Transfer the lamb to the prepared wire rack, fat side up, and roast until the thickest part of the meat registers 100 degrees on an instant-read thermometer, about 1 hour and 40 minutes.

4. Pour ¼ cup water into the baking sheet, increase the oven temperature to 450 degrees, and continue to roast until the meat closest to the bone registers 125 degrees (for medium-rare) on an instant-read thermometer, about 20 minutes longer.

5. Transfer the lamb to a cutting board and brush with the garlic oil. Tent the lamb loosely with foil and let rest for 30 minutes. Carve the lamb following the illustration on page 18 and serve.

➤ VARIATION

Pomegranate-Glazed Roast Bone-In Leg of Lamb

This recipe actually uses a semi-boneless leg of lamb, which is what you most commonly find at the market; if, by chance, the leg has the full bone, have the butcher remove the hipbone and aitchbone for you. The leg of lamb should be well trimmed with just a thin layer of fat on the top; in our experience, most lamb sold at the market is already well trimmed. If you prefer your meat more or less cooked than medium-rare, see "Testing Meat for Doneness" on page 7.

LAMB
1   (6- to 8-pound) semiboneless leg of lamb, trimmed (see note)
1   tablespoon olive oil
    Salt and ground black pepper

POMEGRANATE GLAZE
2   cups pomegranate juice
⅓   cup sugar
3   sprigs fresh thyme

1. FOR THE LAMB: Pat the lamb dry with paper towels, rub with the oil, and season with salt and pepper. Cover the roast loosely with plastic wrap and let sit at room temperature for 1 to 2 hours.

2. FOR THE POMEGRANATE GLAZE: Meanwhile, simmer all of the glaze ingredients together in a small saucepan over medium heat until thickened

CARVING BONE-IN LEG OF LAMB

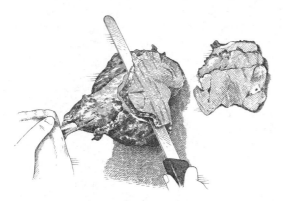

Grasp the shank bone with a kitchen towel and hold the leg at an angle to the cutting board. Using a long, thin slicing knife, cut ¼-inch-thick slices of meat, slicing parallel to the bone and turning the leg as needed.

and the mixture measures about ½ cup, about 20 minutes. Discard the thyme sprigs and divide the glaze evenly into two separate bowls (half of the glaze will be used during cooking, while the other half is reserved for serving).

3. Adjust an oven rack to the lowest position and heat the oven to 250 degrees. Set a wire rack inside a large rimmed baking sheet lined with foil. Transfer the lamb to the prepared wire rack, fat side up, and brush with about half of the glaze reserved for cooking. Roast the lamb until the thickest part of the meat registers 100 degrees on an instant-read thermometer, about 1 hour and 40 minutes.

4. Brush the lamb with the remaining glaze reserved for cooking and pour ¼ cup water into the baking sheet. Increase the oven temperature to 450 degrees and continue to roast the lamb until the meat closest to the bone registers 125 degrees (for medium-rare) on an instant-read thermometer, about 20 minutes longer.

5. Transfer the lamb to a cutting board and brush with half of the glaze reserved for serving. Tent the lamb loosely with foil and let rest for 30 minutes. Brush with the remaining glaze reserved for serving, carve the lamb following the illustration above, and serve.

SPIRAL-SLICED HAM

IT'S EASY TO UNDERSTAND WHY HAM IS served at just about every major holiday. Since it is already cooked and cured, all it needs is a glaze and some time in the oven and you're basically good to go. So why is it that all too often, we are served ham that is dried-out and leathery and tastes like salty jerky with a sticky, saccharine exterior? Ideally, ham is moist and tender and the glaze complements but doesn't overwhelm the meat. We've cooked hundreds of hams in the test kitchen over the years and have had our share of disasters, so we decided to reexamine this topic to learn what really works—and what doesn't.

Hams come in five forms: boneless, semiboneless, bone-in, whole, and half. Each of these types is available unsliced or presliced (often labeled "spiral-sliced"). We favor bone-in hams that have been spiral-sliced, as they offer the best flavor with the least amount of post-cooking carving. We also found that, as a rule of thumb, you should allow about ½ pound of ham per person. This takes into consideration any weight lost during cooking as well as the weight of the bone.

CHOOSING A SPIRAL-SLICED HAM

For easy carving, look for a shank-end ham, which has a tapered, pointed end opposite the cut side. The sirloin, or butt, end has a rounded, blunt end.

SHANK END

SIRLOIN END

A whole ham is the entire leg of the animal, so unless you are feeding a very large crowd, we recommend a half ham. Half hams are available in two distinct cuts: shank end (the bottom part of the leg) and sirloin end (the portion of the leg closer to the rump). If labeling is unclear, it's easy to identify half hams by their shape—shank hams have a pointed end much smaller than the larger end, whereas the sirloin (or butt) end is rounded. We recommend the shank end for ease of carving, since the bone is relatively straight compared with the odder-shaped bones in the sirloin end.

Reading labels is also very important when shopping for ham. Typically, supermarket hams are wet-cured, a process that involves soaking the ham in brine. During this process, the ham will absorb water and gain weight. Not surprisingly, we found hams that gained the least water weight (labeled "ham with natural juices") taste the best. Avoid labels that read "ham with water added" or "ham and water products."

Now, we know what you're thinking: If a spiral-sliced ham is already cooked, why do you have to cook it? Well, truth be told, there is nothing you have to do to serve a cured and cooked ham other than cut it off the bone. When ham is the centerpiece of a holiday dinner, however, most people prefer to have it served warm, and often with a glaze. After roasting many hams to temperatures ranging from 100 to 160 degrees, we found the ideal temperature to be between 110 and 120 degrees. This was enough to take the chill off the meat without drying it out. Cooking the ham to a higher internal temperature (as many sources suggest) guarantees dry meat.

Most recipes cook the ham at 350 degrees for the entire time, but we realized that even at this relatively modest temperature the resulting ham will be tough, with a parched exterior. After numerous tests, we found that a ham cooked in a 250-degree oven was best, since it lessens the temperature differential between the exterior and the interior as the ham cooks. Placing the ham in hot tap water for 90 minutes prior to cooking further ensures that it will heat evenly by taking the chill off the exterior of the ham.

TRIMMING THE OVEN BAG

Use scissors to trim the oven bag, leaving 1 inch above the tie.

Next, we discovered that roasting the ham in an oven bag reduces the amount of moisture lost. Compared with a cold ham shoved into a 350-degree oven, this method reduces moisture loss in a 10-pound ham by 50 percent. If an oven bag is unavailable, aluminum foil will work, but you will have to add three to four minutes of cooking time per pound of meat (between 21 and 40 minutes for a 7- to 10-pound ham).

Almost all spiral hams come with a packet of premixed glaze and instructions to brush it on the ham while cooking. Glaze is a good idea, but the stuff in the packets tastes awful. We think it's more than worth the 10 minutes it takes to make your own glaze. Since we were cooking our ham inside an oven bag, we needed to figure out a new approach to glazing. Once the internal temperature of the ham reached 100 degrees, we cut open the bag and increased the oven temperature to 350 degrees. We then applied the glaze and baked the ham for 10 minutes. After removing the ham from the oven, we applied more glaze, and then made a quick sauce with the remaining glaze and the drippings in the oven bag.

Lastly, we tested whether or not to rest the ham before serving. We found that a 15-minute rest allowed the internal temperature to increase by 5 to 15 degrees, which meant we could bake the ham less in order to reach the ideal serving temperature of 110 to 120 degrees.

CARVING A SPIRAL-SLICED HAM

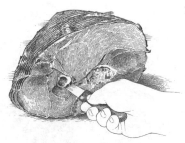

1. With the tip of a paring or carving knife, cut around the bone to loosen the attached slices.

2. Using a long carving knife, slice horizontally above the bone and through the spiral-cut slices, toward the back of the ham.

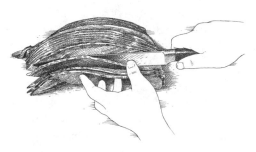

3. Pull the cut portion away from the bone and cut between the slices to separate them fully.

4. Beginning at the tapered end, slice above the bone to remove the remaining chunk of meat. Flip the ham over and repeat the procedure for the other side.

Glazed Spiral-Sliced Ham
SERVES 16 TO 20

Make sure the plastic or foil covering the ham is intact and waterproof; if there is a hole in the covering, wrap the ham in several layers of plastic wrap. Instead of using the plastic oven bag in step 2, the ham may be placed cut side down in the roasting pan and covered tightly with foil, but you will need to add 3 to 4 minutes per pound to the heating time in step 3. If using an oven bag, be sure to cut slits in the bag so it does not burst.

1	(7- to 10-pound) spiral-sliced bone-in half ham, preferably shank end, plastic or foil covering intact (see note)
1	large plastic oven bag
1	recipe glaze (see page 22)

1. Place the covered ham in a stockpot or large container, cover with hot tap water, and let stand for 45 minutes. Drain, cover again with hot tap water, and let stand for 45 minutes longer.

2. Adjust an oven rack to the lowest position and heat the oven to 250 degrees. Unwrap the ham, discarding the plastic disk covering the bone. Place the ham in the oven bag. Gather the top of the bag tightly so the bag fits snugly around the ham, tie the bag, and trim the excess plastic following the illustration on page 19. Transfer the ham, cut side down, to a large roasting pan and cut 4 slits in the top of the bag.

3. Bake the ham until the meat closest to the bone registers 100 degrees on an instant-read thermometer, 1 to 1½ hours (about 10 minutes per pound).

4. Remove the ham from the oven and increase the oven temperature to 350 degrees. Cut open the oven bag and roll back the sides to expose the ham. Brush the ham with one-third of the glaze and return to the oven until the glaze becomes sticky, about 10 minutes longer.

5. Remove the ham from the oven, transfer to a cutting board, and brush with another third of the glaze. Tent the ham loosely with foil and let rest for 15 minutes.

6. While the ham rests, cook the remaining third of the glaze with 4 to 6 tablespoons of the ham juices in a small saucepan over medium-high

heat until thickened and saucy. Carve the ham following the illustrations on page 20 and serve, passing the sauce separately.

ROAST FRESH HAM

ALTHOUGH THIS ROAST IS CALLED A HAM, it gains much of its undeniable appeal from the fact that it's not really a ham at all—or at least not what most of us understand the term to mean. It's not cured and hasn't already been cooked when you purchase it, the way a spiral-sliced ham is. It's not salted and air-dried like prosciutto or smoked like a country ham. In fact, the only reason this cut of pork is called a ham is because it comes from the pig's hind leg. We imagined that this large cut would be well suited to slow roasting.

Even before we began roasting, we had decided that a full fresh ham, weighing in at about 20 pounds, was too much for all but the very largest feast. So we decided to use one of the two cuts into which the leg is usually divided—the sirloin, which comes from the top of the leg, or the shank, from the bottom of the leg (see below for more information). After further research, we decided to go with the shank end, simply because its straightforward bone composition simplifies carving. We also decided that we wanted our ham skin-on (we couldn't see giving up the opportunity for cracklings—crisp pieces of rendered fat). Fortunately, this is how these roasts are typically sold.

From our experiences with other large roasts, we knew what the big problem would be: making sure the roast cooked all the way through while the meat stayed tender and moist. So our first goal would be straightforward—we needed to determine the best oven temperature and cooking time.

Early on in this process, we determined that the roast needed to be cooked to a lower final internal temperature than some experts recommend. We found that we preferred the roast pulled from the oven at 145 to 150 degrees—at this point, the meat is cooked to about medium-well but retains a slight blush. While the roast rests, its residual heat brings the temperature up to approximately 155 to 160 degrees. (This roast is cooked to a higher temperature than most; otherwise, the resulting meat will be mushy.)

That determined, we started testing different oven temperatures. First to come out of the oven was a ham that we had roasted at 400 degrees for the entire time. The cracklings were leathery and the meat was extremely dry. We then tried roasting at a low heat the whole way through. This ham tasted like a wrung-out washcloth, with no cracklings in sight. It was clear that we had our work cut out for us.

Next we started the ham at a lower temperature (350 degrees) and finished it at a higher one (500 degrees), hoping to end up with both moist meat and crisp cracklings. To our dismay, this ham was also rather dry, which we attributed to the ham's long stay in the oven—made necessary by the low cooking temperature. What's more, the brief hike in temperature at the end of cooking didn't help to crisp the skin.

Reversing this process, we then tried starting the ham at the high temperature to give the meat a head start and get the skin on its way to crisping, then turned down the heat for the remainder of the roasting time to cook the meat through. Although meat cooked according to this method was slightly chalky and dry, the skin was close to ideal—nice and crisp. Since this high heat to low

BUYING FRESH HAM

Ham comes from the pig's hind leg. Because a whole leg is too large for most occasions, it is usually cut into two sections. The sirloin, or butt, end is harder to carve than our favorite, the shank end. Either way, make sure to buy a fresh ham with skin, which will protect the meat and keep it moist.

SHANK END   **SIRLOIN END**

heat method was the most promising approach we had tried, we decided that this would be our master roasting method.

Hoping to solve the dry meat dilemma, we brined the ham, immersing it in a solution of salt water and spices to tenderize and flavor it. The salt in a brine causes the protein structure in meat to unravel and trap water in its fibers; brining also encourages the unwound proteins to gel, forming a barrier that helps seal in moisture. Together, these effects allow the cook to increase the roasting temperature, thus speeding the roasting

process without fear of drying out the meat. The results were just what we hoped: The brined ham emerged from the oven succulent, flavorful, and incredibly tender.

Just when we thought the ham couldn't possibly get any better, we decided to try roasting one face-down on a rack set in a roasting pan rather than letting it sit directly in the pan. This adjustment kept the cut end from becoming tough and leathery from the direct contact with the hot pan. Using a rack also allowed the heat to circulate around the ham, promoting more even cooking.

GLAZES FOR HAM

Cherry-Port Glaze

MAKES I GENEROUS CUP, ENOUGH TO GLAZE I SPIRAL-SLICED OR FRESH HAM

½	cup ruby port
½	cup cherry preserves
I	cup packed dark brown sugar
I	teaspoon ground black pepper

Simmer the port in a small saucepan over medium heat until reduced to 2 tablespoons, about 5 minutes. Add the remaining ingredients and cook, stirring occasionally, until the sugar dissolves and the mixture is thick and syrupy, 5 to 10 minutes. (The glaze will thicken as it cools between bastings; rewarm over medium heat as needed to loosen.)

Coca-Cola Glaze with Lime and Jalapeño

MAKES I GENEROUS CUP, ENOUGH TO GLAZE I SPIRAL-SLICED OR FRESH HAM

2	cups packed brown sugar
I	cup Coca-Cola
¼	cup juice from 2 limes

2	medium jalapeño chiles, stemmed, seeded, and cut crosswise into ¼-inch-thick slices

Cook all of the ingredients together in a small saucepan over medium heat, stirring occasionally, until the mixture is thick and syrupy, 5 to 10 minutes. (The glaze will thicken as it cools between bastings; rewarm over medium heat as needed to loosen.)

Maple-Orange Glaze

MAKES I GENEROUS CUP, ENOUGH TO GLAZE I SPIRAL-SLICED OR FRESH HAM

¾	cup maple syrup
½	cup orange marmalade
2	tablespoons unsalted butter
I	tablespoon Dijon mustard
I	teaspoon ground black pepper
¼	teaspoon ground cinnamon

Cook all of the ingredients together in a small saucepan over medium heat, stirring occasionally, until the mixture is thick and syrupy, 5 to 10 minutes. (The glaze will thicken as it cools between bastings; rewarm over medium heat as needed to loosen.)

With our cooking method firmly in place, we turned to tweaking the flavor of the roast. We first looked to spice and herb rubs. Fresh thyme, sage, rosemary, garlic, brown sugar, cloves, dry mustard, juniper berries, peppercorns, and salt were all given an equal opportunity to complement the pork. We liked the combination of sage's earthy sweetness and garlic's pungent bite as well as the addition of fresh parsley, ground black pepper, and kosher salt. Since our rub didn't lean strongly on any one particular spice, we were left with a wide-open field of glazing options.

While some recipes we tried called for simply basting the roast in its own drippings, we veered in the direction of a sugary glaze, which would help crisp, caramelize, and sweeten the skin. But the intermittent encounters between glaze, brush, and ham were still under negotiation: Exactly when should we glaze? Throughout the roasting period? If so, at what intervals? Since part of the beauty of this pork roast is that it can be left in the oven mostly unattended, we didn't want glazing to complicate the process. Starting the ham at 500 degrees prevented us from glazing it at the outset—the sugary glaze would definitely char black before the roast had been in the oven very long. We decided to let the roast cook unglazed at 500 degrees for the first 20 minutes. We then turned the oven temperature down to 350 degrees and began to brush it liberally with glaze. We continued to do so at 45-minute intervals, which amounted to three bastings during the roasting period. This ham was the one: flavorful meat with sweetened, crunchy skin.

SCORING THE SKIN

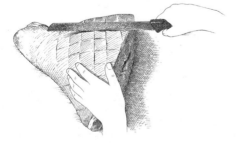

Without cutting into the meat, slice through the skin and fat with a serrated knife, making a 1-inch diamond pattern.

More than one person in the test kitchen proclaimed this ham to be the best roast pork they'd ever eaten—rich and tender, with an underlying hint of sweetness. Perhaps even better is the sweet, slightly salty, crisp and crunchy skin that intensifies to a deep crimson by the time the roast is done.

Roast Fresh Ham
SERVES 8 TO 10

A whole ham (which is the entire leg) is too large for most occasions, and it is often cut into two sections: the sirloin end and the shank end. We find the shank end much easier to work with; however, a sirloin end can be substituted. To use kosher salt in the brine, see page 24 for conversion information. If the pork is "enhanced" (see page 28 for more information), skip the brine in step 2 and don't rinse the pork in step 4. If you don't have room in your refrigerator, you can brine the ham in a large insulated cooler; add 5 or 6 freezer packs to the brine to keep it chilled.

HAM AND BRINE
1   (6- to 8-pound) fresh bone-in half ham with skin, preferably shank end
3   cups packed brown sugar
2   cups table salt (see note)
2   medium garlic heads, cloves separated and crushed
10 bay leaves
½   cup black peppercorns, crushed

HERB RUB
1   cup lightly packed fresh sage leaves
½   cup lightly packed fresh parsley leaves
¼   cup olive oil
8   medium garlic cloves, peeled and chopped coarse (about 8 teaspoons)
1   tablespoon kosher salt
1½ tablespoons ground black pepper

1   recipe glaze (see page 22)

1. FOR THE HAM AND BRINE: Following the illustration at left, carefully slice through the skin and fat on the ham with a serrated knife, making a 1-inch diamond pattern; be careful not to cut into the meat.

2. Dissolve the sugar and table salt in 2 gallons water in a stockpot or large container. Stir in the garlic, bay leaves, and peppercorns, submerge the ham in the brine, cover, and refrigerate for 18 to 24 hours.

3. FOR THE HERB RUB: Process the sage, parsley, oil, garlic, kosher salt, and pepper together in a food processor to a smooth paste, about 30 seconds.

4. Set a wire rack inside a roasting pan. Remove the ham from the brine and rinse. Pat the ham dry with paper towels. Transfer the ham, wide cut side down, to the prepared wire rack. (If using the sirloin end, place the ham skin side up.) Rub the garlic and herb mixture all over the ham, cover loosely with plastic wrap, and let sit at room temperature for 1 to 2 hours.

5. Meanwhile, adjust an oven rack to the lowest position and heat the oven to 500 degrees. Roast the ham for 20 minutes. Reduce the oven temperature to 350 degrees and brush the ham with the glaze. Continue to roast the ham, brushing it with the glaze every 45 minutes, until the meat closest to the bone registers 145 to 150 degrees on an instant-read thermometer, about 2½ hours longer.

6. Transfer the ham to a cutting board, tent loosely with foil, and let rest until the meat closest to the bone registers 155 to 160 degrees, 30 to 40 minutes. Carve the ham following the illustrations below and serve.

➤ VARIATION

Cola Ham

Follow the recipe for Roast Fresh Ham, substituting 6 liters Coke Classic for the water in the brine, omitting the brown sugar, and reducing the salt to 1½ cups. (Be sure to use a large container, because this mixture will be very bubbly.) Proceed as directed, rubbing the ham with the garlic and herb mixture and brushing it with Coca-Cola Glaze with Lime and Jalapeño (page 22).

TWO TYPES OF SALT FOR BRINING

You can use either kosher or regular table salt for brining. Kosher salt is ideal because its large airy crystals dissolve so quickly in water. Unfortunately, the salt crystals of the two major brands of kosher salt—Morton and Diamond Crystal—are not equally airy, and therefore measure differently. This inconsistency between the two brands makes precise recipe writing a challenge. Because there's no way to tell which brand of kosher salt you might have on hand, we list table salt in our brining recipes. If you use kosher salt in your brine, keep the following in mind when making the conversions from table salt in our brining recipes:

¼ cup Table Salt = ½ cup Diamond Crystal Kosher Salt
OR ¼ cup plus 2 tablespoons Morton Kosher Salt

CARVING THE TWO CUTS OF FRESH HAM

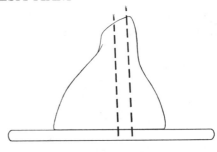

SHANK END

1. Transfer the ham to a cutting board and carve it lengthwise alongside the bone, following the 2 dotted lines in the illustration above.

2. Lay the large boneless pieces that you have just carved flat on the cutting board and slice into ½-inch pieces.

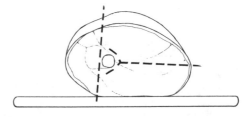

SIRLOIN END

1. Transfer the ham to a cutting board and carve into 3 pieces around the bones along the dotted lines in the illustration above.

2. Lay the large boneless pieces that you have just carved flat on the cutting board and slice into ½-inch pieces.

CUBAN-STYLE ROAST PORK

BOLDLY FLAVORED, SLOW-COOKED MEATS are typical fare in the Caribbean. One of the best examples is *lechón asado*, or roast pork marinated in a flavorful mixture of citrus, garlic, olive oil, and spices. Tradition calls for a whole pig slowly cooked on a spit over a wood fire, but many modern versions use a suckling pig, fresh ham, or pork shoulder instead—and some recipes even bring the meat indoors to be roasted in the oven.

Our goal was to create a foolproof recipe for this bold-flavored, slow-cooked dish, complete with crackling-crisp skin, tender meat, and a bracing garlic-citrus sauce. And we wanted a recipe that could be made indoors (great for any time of the year). After testing half a dozen recipes in various cookbooks, we realized we had our work cut out for us. Burnt skin that peeled off, chewy meat so dry even the sauce couldn't save it, and marinades that failed to impart much flavor were common problems. This recipe is a project, so if the texture and flavor aren't great, why bother?

Cuban-style roast pork should have a texture somewhere between that of a juicy, sliceable American pork roast and fall-apart-when-you-touch-it pulled pork. The best authentic recipes we sampled called for an internal temperature of around 190 degrees, at which point the collagen and fat have mostly broken down and rendered but not quite to the extent they would in pulled pork. As for the cut, we went with the picnic shoulder (often simply labeled "pork shoulder"), an inexpensive, fatty, bone-in cut that comes with a generous amount of skin attached; the crispy skin, after all, is a hallmark of this dish. (See "Picking the Perfect Pork Roast" below.)

The recipes we found for Cuban pork were a varied lot, but most followed the same sequence: Infuse the raw pork with flavor (using a marinade or wet paste), cook for several hours, cut into small pieces, then toss with a mojo sauce, a garlicky vinaigrette that often serves double duty as a marinade. We would deal with flavor infusion later. First, we wanted to figure out the best way to roast the pork.

After letting the pork sit overnight in a working marinade of citrus juice, garlic, and olive oil, we proceeded to roast it on a rack set over a rimmed baking sheet in the oven. After testing various oven temperatures, we found 325 degrees was best—it provided gentle heat that produced pork that was equally juicy and tender throughout. It took the interior of the roast a total of six hours to reach our target 190 degrees. To ensure even cooking and crisp skin, we started the pork in the oven skin side down and flipped it halfway through cooking.

Half the recipes we had collected called for marinating the pork shoulder overnight (or even for two or three days); the other half went with a coating of wet paste. Each method had its advantages. The marinade penetrated deep into the meat, while the paste held fast to the exterior of the pork throughout cooking, yielding an assertively flavored crust. For the best of both worlds, we opted for a combination.

Unfortunately, the wimpy marinade we were using—two or three fresh-squeezed oranges, plus a

PICKING THE PERFECT PORK ROAST

What's the best cut for Cuban-style pork? We tried them all. Widely available Boston butt (the upper portion of the front leg) was an attractive option thanks to its high fat content. But it comes with no skin attached, and the crisp, flavorful skin is one of the highlights of this dish. Fresh ham (from the rear leg) has skin but is usually too lean. We settled on the picnic shoulder (also called pork shoulder), a flavorful cut from the lower portion of the front leg with a fair share of fat and skin.

BOSTON BUTT
Fatty but skinless

FRESH HAM
Great skin but too lean

PICNIC SHOULDER
Our choice: great skin, great fat

few minced garlic cloves—just wasn't cutting it. We gradually increased the citrus and garlic until we were up to two heads of garlic and almost two dozen oranges. (With this more powerful formula, we found that we could get away with marinating the pork for just 12 hours rather than two or three days.)

As for the exterior paste, the usual blend of mashed garlic, kosher salt, pepper, oregano, cumin, olive oil, and orange juice, plus a shot of white vinegar for extra kick (basically, the components of a mojo sauce), worked just fine. Cutting fairly wide slits all over the pork proved to be the most effective method for trapping the paste's flavors.

We now had a solid (and fuss-free) cooking method and a great two-pronged technique for infusing flavor. The only problem remaining was an inconsistent texture. The sections of the meat closest to the crust (and, thus, near the exterior layer of fat) always came out moist and tender, but the leaner interior was less predictable. On a bad day, it could turn out so dry that even a generous slathering of mojo sauce barely saved it.

The test kitchen often relies on the magic of brining (soaking in a solution of salt, water, and sometimes sugar) to remedy lean-meat texture problems, but we were already spending 12 hours soaking the pork in a marinade. The answer was simple: We took the test kitchen's basic formula for a brine, replaced some of the water with orange juice, and created a hybrid brine-marinade. We compensated for the diluted flavor (courtesy of the added water) by upping the soaking time from 12 hours to between 18 and 24 hours. The result was flavorful meat that came out tender even close to the bone.

Most large cuts of meat benefit from resting after cooking, which allows the juices to redistribute evenly throughout the meat. Our Cuban pork roast was no exception. Compared side by side, a roast rested for 30 minutes was much juicier than one we sliced into immediately after cooking. Even more interesting is what happened when the roast rested for an entire hour: As expected, the exterior and the portions bordering knobs of fat were delicious, but now the lean interior portions were every bit as moist.

All the pork needed now was a final splash of mojo sauce, which could be quickly mixed and cooled to room temperature while the pork rested. Made with many of the same ingredients used in the brine and paste, the mojo provided another bright, fresh hit of flavor. As we took bites of the tangy, garlicky pork and sips from an icy mojito, we knew our efforts had been worth it: this dish had finally gotten its mojo back.

Cuban-Style Roast Pork
SERVES 8 TO 10

To use kosher salt in the brine, see page 24 for conversion information. If the pork is "enhanced" (see page 28 for more information), skip the brine in step 1 and don't rinse the pork in step 2. Letting the cooked roast rest for a full hour before serving is crucial for tender meat. This roast has a crispy skin that should be served along with the meat.

PORK AND BRINE
- 3 cups sugar
- 2 cups table salt
- 4 cups orange juice
- 2 medium garlic heads, unpeeled cloves separated and crushed
- 1 (7- to 8-pound) bone-in, skin-on pork picnic shoulder

GARLIC-CITRUS PASTE
- 12 medium garlic cloves, peeled and chopped coarse (about ¼ cup)
- 2 tablespoons ground cumin
- 2 tablespoons dried oregano
- 1 tablespoon salt
- 1½ teaspoons ground black pepper
- 6 tablespoons orange juice
- 2 tablespoons distilled white vinegar
- 2 tablespoons olive oil

- 1 recipe Mojo Sauce (page 27)

1. FOR THE PORK AND BRINE: Dissolve the sugar and salt in 6 quarts water in a stockpot or large container. Stir in the orange juice and garlic, submerge the pork in the brine, cover, and refrigerate for 18 to 24 hours.

2. FOR THE GARLIC-CITRUS PASTE: Pulse the garlic, cumin, oregano, salt, and pepper together in a food processor to a coarse paste, about 10 pulses.

With the machine running, add the orange juice, vinegar, and oil through the feed tube and process until smooth, about 20 seconds.

3. Remove the pork from the brine and rinse. Pat the pork dry with paper towels and cut 1-inch-deep slits (about 1 inch long) all over the pork, spaced about 2 inches apart. Rub the paste all over the pork and into the slits. Cover the pork loosely with plastic wrap and let sit at room temperature for 1 to 2 hours.

4. Adjust an oven rack to the lower-middle position and heat the oven to 325 degrees. Set a wire rack inside a large rimmed baking sheet lined with foil. Transfer the pork to the prepared wire rack, skin side down, and roast for 3 hours.

5. Flip the pork skin side up and continue to roast until the meat closest to the bone registers 190 degrees on an instant-read thermometer, about 3 hours longer. (If the pork skin begins to get too dark, lightly cover the pork with foil.)

6. Transfer the pork to a cutting board, tent loosely with foil, and let rest for 1 hour. Remove the skin in one large piece. To serve the skin, scrape the excess fat from the underside and cut into strips. Scrape off and discard the top layer of fat from the pork, then cut the meat away from the bone in 3 or 4 large pieces. Slice each piece of meat against the grain into ¼-inch-thick slices and serve with the mojo sauce.

Mojo Sauce
MAKES ABOUT 1 CUP

The sauce can be refrigerated in an airtight container for up to 1 day. If chilled, bring to room temperature before serving. If using table salt, reduce the amount to ½ teaspoon.

4	medium garlic cloves, minced (about 4 teaspoons)
1	teaspoon kosher salt (see note)
½	cup olive oil
½	teaspoon ground cumin
¼	cup distilled white vinegar
¼	cup orange juice
¼	teaspoon dried oregano
⅛	teaspoon ground black pepper

Following the illustrations at left, mince the garlic and salt into a smooth paste. Heat the oil in a medium saucepan over medium heat until shimmering. Stir in the garlic paste and cumin and cook until fragrant, about 30 seconds. Off the heat, whisk in the remaining ingredients. Transfer the sauce to a bowl and cool to room temperature. Whisk the sauce to recombine before serving.

MINCING GARLIC TO A PASTE

There are times when you want minced garlic to be absolutely smooth. Sprinkling minced garlic with a little salt can help this process along. If possible, use kosher or coarse salt; the larger crystals do a better job of breaking down the garlic than fine table salt.

1. Mince the garlic on a cutting board. Sprinkle the minced garlic with salt.

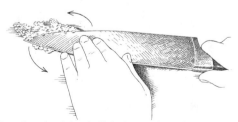

2. Drag the side of the chef's knife over the garlic-salt mixture to form a fine paste. Continue to mince and drag the knife as necessary until the paste is smooth.

EASIER CITRUS PRESSING

A citrus press can be a handy tool, but using one to press the juice from several lemons or oranges can be a pain. Try cutting the fruit into quarters rather than halves. Juicing a quarter is not only easier than juicing a half, but it also yields more juice.

ROAST PORK LOIN

UNASSUMING AND SIMPLE TO PREPARE, A boneless pork roast is hearty fare for a casual family feast. The practical advantages of this supermarket cut are many: It is affordable and widely available; the mild, sweet flavor of roast pork pairs well with most any side dish; and leftovers make great sandwiches. Roasting this cut slowly for an extended period of time is key; when cooked at high temperatures, pork loin becomes dried out near the edges long before the center is done. But how low does the oven temperature need to be? We set out in search of juicy, evenly cooked meat.

The two types of boneless roasts from the loin are the common center loin roast, which contains a lean, unbroken eye of meat, and the blade-end loin roast, which has a section of the shoulder's blade muscle attached. Both are fine, although tasters slightly preferred the flavor and juiciness of the blade-end roast, which benefits from a deposit of fat that separates the two muscles.

As we typically do in our test kitchen, we tried brining the pork (soaking it in a saltwater solution to season and boost juiciness), and brining did, indeed, yield tender, juicy, well-seasoned pork. The unbrined pork was tough and dry by comparison.

Today's leaner pork may be pleasing to health-conscious carnivores, but its low fat content makes it exceptionally prone to overcooking. Pork is best served at a temperature of 150 degrees, rather than the 160 degrees (or higher) recommended by many older recipes. If, however, you take the roast out of the oven once it reaches this temperature, it will be overcooked. The temperature of the roast will continue to rise, by as much as 10 degrees, once it has been taken out of the oven. The thing to do is to remove the roast when it registers 140 to 145 degrees, and then let it rest on the cutting board before slicing.

Just as important as the final temperature of the roast is how quickly it gets there. We roasted pork loins at a variety of oven temperatures, starting at the higher end and working our way down. Roasts cooked at the high end of the spectrum (up to 450 degrees) developed tough, leathery exteriors while the centers remained undercooked. We gradually decreased the heat, and finally found that a moderate 325-degree oven proved ideal; even large roasts (where the disparity in cooking rates between the exterior and interior is greatest) were tender and juicy throughout when cooked at this temperature, and we saw no advantage to going lower.

Innumerable tests have proven that roasts with a deep brown, caramelized crust both look and taste better than those without. Trying to brown the meat using high oven heat at the beginning or end of the roasting produced marginal results, so we decided to sear it on the stovetop. Because we had already tied the meat into a neat bundle (to ensure even cooking), it fit well in a skillet on the stovetop, which gave us great browning and lots of control over the process. Tying a roast may seem fussy to some, but we discovered that this small investment of time is amply rewarded.

After we had our basic recipe down, we decided to develop some variations, and a glazed pork loin seemed like a simple and attractive option. After

INGREDIENTS:
Enhanced or Unenhanced Pork?

Because modern pork is remarkably lean and therefore somewhat bland and prone to dryness if overcooked, a product called "enhanced" pork has overtaken the market. In fact, it can be hard to find unenhanced pork in some areas. Enhanced pork has been injected with a solution of water, salt, sodium phosphates, sodium lactate, potassium lactate, sodium diacetate, and varying flavor agents to bolster flavor and juiciness, with the total amount of enhancing ingredients adding 7 to 15 percent extra weight. Pork containing additives must be so labeled, with a list of the ingredients. After several taste tests, we have concluded that while enhanced pork is indeed juicier and more tender than unenhanced pork, the latter has more genuine pork flavor. Some tasters picked up unappealingly artificial, salty flavors in enhanced pork. Enhanced pork can also leach juices that, once reduced, will result in overly salty sauces. In the test kitchen, we prefer natural pork, but the choice is up to you. It should be noted however, that if you buy enhanced pork you should not brine it, as it has essentially already been brined.

transferring the browned roast to the oven, we made a quick glaze in the now-empty skillet with apricot preserves, orange juice, dried apricots, and lemon juice, and then we simply brushed the glaze on the pork during the final 15 minutes of roasting. Finally, we developed an herb-crusted pork loin; rubbed with a simple herb paste and covered with a light coating of bread crumbs, this variation is packed with flavor and makes for an elegant presentation.

Simple Roast Pork Loin

SERVES 4 TO 6

We left a ¼-inch-thick layer of fat on top of the roast; if your roast has a thicker fat cap, trim it back to be about ¼ inch thick. To use kosher salt in the brine, see page 24 for conversion information. If the pork is "enhanced" (see page 28 for more information), skip step 1, don't rinse the pork in step 2, and season the roast with salt in step 2.

½	cup sugar
½	cup table salt
1	(2½- to 3-pound) boneless pork loin roast, trimmed and tied at 1½-inch intervals
	Ground black pepper
1	tablespoon vegetable oil

1. Dissolve the sugar and salt in 2 quarts water in a large container. Submerge the pork in the brine, cover, and refrigerate for 1 to 1½ hours.

2. Remove the roast from the brine and rinse. Pat the roast dry with paper towels, season with pepper, cover loosely with plastic wrap, and let sit at room temperature for 30 to 60 minutes.

3. Adjust an oven rack to the middle position and heat the oven to 325 degrees. Set a wire rack inside a large rimmed baking sheet lined with foil. Heat the oil in a 12-inch skillet over medium-high heat until just smoking. Brown the roast on all sides, 8 to 10 minutes, reducing the heat if the pan begins to scorch.

4. Transfer the pork to the prepared wire rack and roast until the very center of the meat registers 140 to 145 degrees on an instant-read thermometer, 50 to 75 minutes.

5. Transfer the pork to a cutting board, tent loosely with foil, and let rest until the very center registers 150 degrees, about 10 minutes. Remove the twine, slice the roast into ½-inch-thick slices, and serve.

➤ VARIATIONS

Apricot-Orange Glazed Pork Loin

We left a ¼-inch-thick layer of fat on top of the roast; if your roast has a thicker fat cap, trim it back to be about ¼ inch thick. To use kosher salt in the brine, see page 24 for conversion information. If the pork is "enhanced" (see page 28 for more information), skip step 1, don't rinse the pork in step 2, and season the roast with salt in step 2.

½	cup sugar
½	cup table salt
1	(2½- to 3-pound) boneless pork loin roast, trimmed and tied at 1½-inch intervals
	Ground black pepper
1	tablespoon vegetable oil
1	cup apricot preserves
½	cup orange juice
¼	cup dried apricots, quartered
3	tablespoons juice from 1 lemon
	Warm water, as needed

1. Dissolve the sugar and salt in 2 quarts water in a large container. Submerge the pork in the brine, cover, and refrigerate for 1 to 1½ hours.

2. Remove the roast from the brine and rinse. Pat the roast dry with paper towels, season with pepper, cover loosely with plastic wrap, and let sit at room temperature for 30 to 60 minutes.

3. Adjust an oven rack to the middle position and heat the oven to 325 degrees. Heat the oil in a 12-inch skillet over medium-high heat until just smoking. Brown the roast on all sides, 8 to 10 minutes, reducing the heat if the pan begins to scorch. Transfer the roast to a 13 by 9-inch baking dish and roast until the very center registers about 110 degrees on an instant-read thermometer, 35 to 60 minutes.

4. Meanwhile, pour off any fat left in the skillet and add the apricot preserves, orange juice, dried

apricots, and lemon juice to the skillet. Simmer over medium heat, scraping up any browned bits, until slightly thickened and fragrant, about 3 minutes. Transfer the glaze to a small bowl.

5. Brush the glaze over the pork and continue to roast, turning the pork often to coat it with glaze, until the very center of the meat registers 140 to 145 degrees on an instant-read thermometer, about 15 minutes longer. (If the glaze begins to dry out and burn in the oven, stir in up to ¼ cup warm water.)

6. Transfer the pork to a cutting board, pour the glaze left in the baking dish over the roast, tent loosely with foil, and let rest until the very center registers 150 degrees, about 10 minutes. Remove the twine, slice the roast into ½-inch-thick slices, and serve.

Herb-Crusted Pork Loin

We left a ¼-inch-thick layer of fat on top of the roast; if your roast has a thicker fat cap, trim it back to be about ¼-inch thick. To use kosher salt in the brine, see page 24 for conversion information. If the pork is "enhanced" (see page 28 for more information), skip step 1, don't rinse the pork in step 4, and season the roast with salt in step 4.

PORK AND BRINE

½	cup sugar
½	cup table salt
1	(2½- to 3-pound) boneless pork loin roast, trimmed

HERB CRUST

1	slice high-quality white sandwich bread, quartered
1	ounce Parmesan or pecorino cheese, grated (½ cup)
5	tablespoons olive oil
1	medium shallot, minced (about 3 tablespoons)
	Salt and ground black pepper
⅓	cup lightly packed fresh parsley or basil leaves
2	tablespoons minced fresh thyme leaves
1	teaspoon minced fresh rosemary, or ½ teaspoon dried
1	medium garlic clove, minced or pressed through a garlic press (about 1 teaspoon)

1. FOR THE PORK AND BRINE: Dissolve the sugar and salt in 2 quarts water in a large container. Submerge the pork in the brine, cover, and refrigerate for 1 to 1½ hours.

2. FOR THE HERB CRUST: Meanwhile, pulse the bread in a food processor to fine crumbs, about 16 pulses. Toss the bread crumbs with 2 tablespoons of the Parmesan, 1 tablespoon of the oil, shallot, ⅛ teaspoon salt, and ⅛ teaspoon pepper and set aside.

3. Process the parsley, thyme, rosemary, garlic, remaining 6 tablespoons Parmesan, 3 more tablespoons of the oil, ⅛ teaspoon salt, and ⅛ teaspoon pepper, together in the food processor to a smooth paste, about 20 seconds. Transfer the herb paste to a small bowl.

4. Remove the roast from the brine and rinse. Pat the roast dry with paper towels. Following the illustrations on page 31, carefully slice through the fat cap with a serrated knife, making a ¼-inch diamond pattern; be careful not to cut into the meat. Cut a pocket into the side of the roast and spread ¼ cup of the herb paste inside the pocket. Using kitchen twine, tie the roast at 1½-inch intervals. Season the roast with pepper, cover loosely with plastic wrap, and let sit at room temperature for 30 to 60 minutes.

5. Adjust an oven rack to the lower-middle position and heat the oven to 325 degrees. Set a wire rack inside a large rimmed baking sheet lined with foil. Heat the remaining tablespoon oil in a 12-inch skillet over medium-high heat until just smoking. Brown the roast on all sides, 8 to 10 minutes, reducing the heat if the pan begins to scorch.

6. Remove the twine, coat the top and sides of the roast with the remaining herb paste, then press the bread crumb mixture into the herb paste to adhere. Transfer the pork to the prepared wire rack and roast until very center of the meat registers 140 to 145 degrees on an instant-read thermometer, 50 to 75 minutes.

7. Transfer the pork to a cutting board, taking care not to squeeze any juices out of the center pocket of the roast, and let rest, uncovered, until the very center registers 150 degrees, about 10 minutes. Slice the roast into ½-inch-thick slices and serve.

PREPARING HERB-CRUSTED PORK LOIN

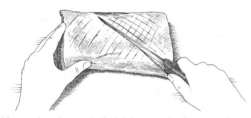

1. Using a sharp boning knife, lightly score the fat cap on the roast to make a ¼-inch crosshatch pattern.

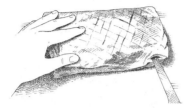

2. Starting ½ inch from the end of the roast, insert the knife into the middle of the roast, with the blade parallel to the work surface.

3. Cut along the side of the pork, stopping ½ inch short of the other end. Pull open the roast and use gentle strokes to cut a deeper pocket.

4. Spread ¼ cup of the herb paste evenly into the pocket, using a spatula and your fingers to make sure the paste reaches the corners of the pocket.

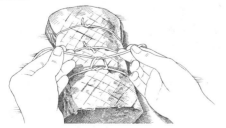

5. Fold the roast over to its original shape and tie at even intervals along its length with kitchen twine.

CHINESE BARBECUED PORK

WITH ITS RUBY-RED COLOR, DEEPLY BROWNED and crusty edges, and sticky glazed exterior, Chinese barbecued pork (aka *char siu*) is irresistible. In Chinatown, these burnished strips of meat hang in storefront windows, enticing hungry passersby. But since we don't get to Chinatown all that often, we wondered if we could replicate this classic Chinese dish at home. After all, isn't it just barbecued meat?

Unlike American barbecue, where large cuts are cooked with smoke on outdoor cookers until they achieve a fall-apart tenderness, Chinese barbecued meats are usually cut into strips and cooked in an oven. Once the exterior is slightly charred, the meat is brushed with honey and cooked until a lacquered glaze forms. It's like having barbecue with almost all crust. Sounds simple enough.

Traditional recipes cut pork butt into long strips. When we cut the meat into thicker steaks, it was much too fatty and tough. We concluded that cutting the meat into strips is a must, as it helps render fat during the relatively short cooking time. We tried using country-style ribs, because they are already cut into strips, but found that they were more dry and chewy than strips cut from a pork butt. Working with a boneless pork butt, we cut the pork in half lengthwise and then into eight long strips, removing some of the hard fat between the individual muscles. We marinated the meat in a classic mixture of light and dark soy sauces, Chinese rice wine, hoisin sauce, spices, and either fermented red bean curd or red food coloring (red foods are seen as bringing good fortune in Chinese cuisine). There was just one hook—actually, more like eight hooks.

Traditional recipes call for cutting the meat into thin strips and hanging the strips on metal rods that go inside refrigerator-sized ovens. The idea is that the heat can attack the meat from all sides and create a thick crust. We tried fabricating S-shaped hooks out of metal hangers and suspending the meat from the top rack of a test kitchen oven, but our forearms were soon covered with battle scars caused by our failed attempts to rescue dangling pieces of meat before they fell onto the floor of the oven. No meat—no matter how delicious—is worth second-degree burns. We needed to develop a cooking method suited to a home oven.

Suspending the meat from hooks was out, but what if we placed the strips of meat on a rack set over a baking sheet? Wouldn't an all-over crust form? We ran a series of tests with oven temperatures ranging from 350 to 500 degrees. The pork roasted in the cooler ovens remained moist and was less fatty, but it never achieved the characteristic browning and intense flavor; the meat cooked in the hotter ovens browned beautifully, but it was still too tough, with pockets of unrendered fat. Choosing the middle road (roasting at 425 degrees) didn't work, so we were left with one option—cooking the meat at a low temperature to render the fat and then cranking up the heat to develop a burnished crust.

For our next tests, we lost the rack and placed the strips of meat on a big sheet of aluminum foil, poured the marinade over the top, and then tightly sealed the foil. After two hours, we opened the foil packet and browned the pork under the broiler. All the fat had been rendered, but the meat reminded tasters of slightly charred pot roast—it simply fell apart at the approach of a fork.

We returned to cooking the meat on a rack set over a baking sheet, but this time we covered the pan with foil. After an hour at 300 degrees, we removed the foil and turned the oven to broil. The meat had a better crust, but it was still too soft. Eventually, we discovered that covering the meat for only 20 minutes during the initial hour of cooking was all that we needed to render excess fat and keep the meat tender. We then removed the foil and continued to cook the

meat until a thick crust formed. A final blast of heat from the broiler produced a thick, slightly charred crust, and the meat was now tender but chewy.

All the pork needed was a final adjustment of flavor in the marinade and glaze. First, we needed to tinker with the traditional marinade ingredients— light and dark soy sauces, rice wine, red fermented bean curd, hoisin sauce, and five-spice powder. In the end, tasters were happy with just regular soy sauce (rather than the light and dark) and saw no harm in replacing the rice wine with sherry. (That said, if you can find Chinese rice wine, we recommend using it.) The red bean curd was just too hard to find so we omitted it. Instead, we boosted the flavor of the marinade with ginger, garlic, toasted sesame oil, and white pepper.

Marinades are all about flavor penetration, but how long does that take? After four hours, the meat had soaked up the potent flavors of the marinade. Times in excess of four hours caused the meat to become too salty. But four hours was a long time to wait. Could we speed up this process? Pricking the meat with a fork before marinating enhanced the penetration of the marinade so much that just 30 minutes was sufficient.

To achieve a lacquered appearance, char siu requires the application of a honey glaze during the last few minutes of cooking. To create the traditional red color, we supplemented the honey with ketchup. We simmered the honey and ketchup (along with some reserved marinade) to give it a syrupy consistency. We had finally replicated one of our favorite Chinese dishes at home.

PREPARING PORK FOR CHINESE BARBECUED PORK

Pork butts are usually about 4 inches thick. If using a pork butt that is thinner than 4 inches, cut it into 6 pieces instead of 8.

1. Cut the roast in half lengthwise.

2. Turn each half on the cut side and slice lengthwise into 4 equal pieces.

3. Trim the excess hard, waxy fat, leaving some fat to render while cooking.

Chinese Barbecued Pork

SERVES 6

Do not use a drawer broiler in step 5 because the heat source will be too close to the meat and will burn the glaze. Instead, increase the oven temperature in step 5 to 500 degrees and cook the pork for 8 to 12 minutes before glazing, then about 6 to 8 minutes once the glaze has been applied (on both sides). Chinese rice cooking wine, also known as Shaoxing, can be found in the international aisle of large supermarkets or specialty Asian markets, but sherry makes a suitable substitute.

I	(4-pound) boneless pork butt, cut into 8 strips and trimmed (see the illustrations on page 32)
½	cup sugar
½	cup soy sauce
6	tablespoons hoisin sauce
¼	cup Chinese rice cooking wine or dry sherry (see note)
2	tablespoons minced or grated fresh ginger
2	medium garlic cloves, minced or pressed through a garlic press (about 2 teaspoons)
I	tablespoon toasted sesame oil
I	teaspoon five-spice powder
¼	teaspoon ground white pepper
⅓	cup honey
¼	cup ketchup

1. Poke each strip of pork with a fork 10 to 12 times on each side and place in a large zipper-lock bag. Whisk the sugar, soy sauce, hoisin sauce, wine, ginger, garlic, sesame oil, five-spice powder, and pepper together in a medium bowl. Measure out and reserve ½ cup of the marinade. Pour the remaining marinade into the bag with the pork. Seal the bag, pressing out as much air as possible, and refrigerate for at least 30 minutes or up to 4 hours, flipping the bag occasionally to ensure that the pork marinates evenly.

2. While the meat marinates, cook the honey, ketchup, and reserved ½ cup marinade together in a small saucepan over medium heat, whisking occasionally, until syrupy and measures about 1 cup, 4 to 6 minutes; set aside.

3. Adjust an oven rack to the middle position and heat the oven to 300 degrees. Set a wire rack inside a large rimmed baking sheet lined with foil and coat the rack with vegetable oil spray.

4. Remove the pork from the marinade, letting any excess drip off. Transfer the pork to the prepared wire rack and pour ¼ cup water into the bottom of the pan. Cover the pan with heavy-duty aluminum foil, crimping the edges tightly to seal. Roast the pork for 20 minutes. Remove the foil and continue to roast the pork until the edges begin to brown, 40 to 45 minutes.

5. Turn the oven to broil and broil the pork, leaving it on the same oven rack, until evenly browned, 7 to 9 minutes. Being careful of the hot juices in the pan bottom, remove the pan from the oven, brush the pork with half of the glaze, then continue to broil until the meat is a deep mahogany color, 3 to 5 minutes.

6. Using tongs, flip the meat over and continue to broil until the second side is evenly browned, 7 to 9 minutes. Being careful of the hot juices in the pan bottom, remove the pan from the oven, brush the pork with the remaining glaze, then continue to broil until the meat is a deep mahogany color, 3 to 5 minutes. Transfer the pork to a cutting board and let rest, uncovered, for 10 minutes. Cut the pork into thin strips and serve.

OVEN BARBECUE

THE BARBECUE SEASON FOR MUCH OF THE country is cruelly short. When the temperature plunges as fall drifts into winter, it's virtually impossible to maintain the modest grill temperatures required to turn tough cuts of meat tender. When the craving strikes for crisp-crusted, smoky spareribs or tender pulled pork in midwinter, many of us have just two options: Head to the local barbecue shack or attempt barbecueing in the oven. But is it really possible to replicate outdoor barbecue inside using the low, slow heat of an oven?

Barbecue is as much cooking method as flavoring agent. The low temperature and steady blanket of hardwood smoke work almost like braising, rendering the collagen—a protein in meat's tough connective tissue—to rich-tasting, silky gelatin. The low temperatures and moist environment are easy to replicate in the oven; the smoke, by contrast, is not.

We wanted to develop indoor recipes for two of our barbecued favorites, spareribs and pulled pork. We started with the ribs. The indoor barbecued-rib recipes we found were a dubious lot. Most smothered racks in smoke-flavored sauce and baked them slowly. Sure, the ribs tasted OK—slather an old shoe in smoky sauce and it will taste good—but none possessed the deep, rich flavor of true barbecue. Others slicked the ribs with liquid smoke, smearing on a dry rub just before baking—not much better. As it turns out, there's a fundamental difference between ribs that taste of smoke and ribs that are smoked.

There was a third option: indoor smoking. Indoor smokers are essentially roasting pans fitted with a wire rack and a tight-fitting lid. Shredded wood chips are sprinkled across the pan bottom, the food is set on the rack, and the pan is sealed. The pan is heated on the stovetop to ignite the chips, after which it enters the oven to finish cooking. Some indoor smokers we tested worked fairly well, but the designs are so basic that we opted to rig one up from equipment we had on hand.

Before we got ahead of ourselves, we had to choose the ribs. For outdoor barbecue, we favor St. Louis–style spareribs—pork spareribs (located near the belly) trimmed of skirt meat and excess cartilage—and saw no reason to change.

Squeezing the ribs onto a wire rack in the kitchen's biggest roasting pan, we tossed a handful of hickory chips into the bottom of the pan and sealed it with foil. We slid the pan over a burner set on high and waited. And waited. Smoke finally began seeping out from the foil long after we were afraid the pan would melt from such heat. Once the alarm sounded, we guessed the ribs were smoky enough and transferred the pan to a 250-degree oven to finish.

The ribs tasted smoky alright, but this method certainly had flaws: It was hard finding a pan large enough to fit the ribs, it took us three trips to find wood chips (during off-season, most hardware stores switch out grilling paraphernalia for snow shovels), and the billowing smoke made the test kitchen reek of hickory for days.

Could we move the entire process to the oven, thereby containing the smoke? With no direct high heat, we could also switch to a rimmed baking sheet, which had enough room for the ribs to lie flat. We cranked the oven to 400 degrees, placed the ribs on a wire rack set over the baking sheet, added the wood chips, and, once again, waited for smoke. An hour passed without the faintest whiff. After 1½ hours, we pulled the pan out and found gray, greasy, gristly-looking ribs without a hint of smoke flavor.

Higher heat? After turning up the temperature in 25-degree increments, we finally smelled smoke at 500 degrees. Where there's smoke, there should be flavor, but no such luck. The oven still wasn't hot enough to ignite the wood.

Just when we were getting desperate, a colleague suggested another option: tea smoking. Chinese cooks smoke a variety of foods over smoldering black tea. So we replaced the wood chips with loose tea, closed the oven door, and—while the leaves didn't burn—the distinct aroma of tea that filled

REMOVING THE RIB MEMBRANE

1. Insert a spoon handle between the membrane and the ribs to loosen slightly.

2. Using a paper towel, grasp the loosened membrane and pull away gently to remove.

BARBECUE SAUCES
FOR SPARERIBS AND PULLED PORK

Lexington Barbecue Sauce

MAKES ABOUT 2½ CUPS

This tart, vinegary sauce, a standard in Lexington, Kentucky, has a potent flavor and thin texture that perfectly balances the richness of slow-cooked, smoky barbecue. It should be served on the side or spooned sparingly over the meat before serving.

I	cup water
I	cup cider vinegar
½	cup ketchup
I	tablespoon sugar
¾	teaspoon salt
½	teaspoon ground black pepper
½	teaspoon red pepper flakes

Mix all of the ingredients together in a medium bowl until the sugar dissolves.

Classic Barbecue Sauce

MAKES ABOUT 2½ CUPS

This is our own, homemade version of a classic store-bought barbecue sauce—thick, sweet, and slightly tangy with a hearty tomato-molasses flavor.

2	tablespoons vegetable oil
I	medium onion, minced
I	medium garlic clove, minced or pressed through a garlic press (about I teaspoon)
I	teaspoon chili powder
¼	teaspoon cayenne pepper
I ¼	cups ketchup
½	cup water
⅓	cup light or dark molasses
3	tablespoons cider vinegar

3	tablespoons Worcestershire sauce
3	tablespoons Dijon mustard
I	teaspoon hot sauce
	Salt and ground black pepper

1. Heat the oil in a large saucepan over medium heat until shimmering. Add the onion and cook until softened, 5 to 7 minutes. Stir in the garlic, chili powder, and cayenne and cook until fragrant, about 30 seconds.

2. Stir in the remaining ingredients and simmer over medium-low heat, stirring occasionally, until the sauce is thickened, about 15 minutes. Season with salt and pepper to taste and strain the sauce (if desired) before serving.

Mid-South Carolina Mustard Sauce

MAKES ABOUT 2½ CUPS

This barbecue sauce hails from central South Carolina, where most barbecue sauce is yellow (not red), with a strong mustard flavor and thinner consistency. Spoon it sparingly over cooked meat, serving additional sauce at the table.

I	cup cider vinegar
I	cup vegetable oil
6	tablespoons Dijon mustard
2	tablespoons maple syrup or honey
4	teaspoons Worcestershire sauce
2	teaspoons salt
I	teaspoon hot sauce
	Pinch ground black pepper

Mix all of the ingredients together in a medium bowl.

the kitchen surprised us. The ribs tasted faintly of it, too. Perhaps outright combustion wasn't necessary—"roasting" was enough to unlock the tea's flavor. Smoky-tasting Lapsang Souchong tea leaves, cured over smoldering pine or cypress boughs, seemed like the perfect candidate.

With the oven set to high heat, we could smell smoke in minutes. After 30 minutes, the ribs tasted decidedly smoky. Using powdery tea from tea bags or grinding loose tea leaves to a fine powder (thereby maximizing the tea-to-baking-surface ratio) imbued the ribs with an even deeper flavor. Neither as sweet as hickory nor as sharp as mesquite, the tea perfumed the ribs with a rich smokiness far deeper than that lent by barbecue sauce or liquid smoke.

The ribs were smoky, but the high heat required to "roast" the tea had also made them inedibly tough. We found two solutions. One was to set the baking sheet on a baking stone to jump-start the smoking process. The other was to chill the rib racks in the freezer as the oven preheated—this cooled them enough that they could withstand a very high heat and quickly absorb "smoke" without toughening. After just half an hour at 500 degrees, our prechilled ribs had absorbed as much of the smoky flavor as possible and we could decrease the oven temperature dramatically.

To cook the ribs, we experimented with temperatures ranging between 200 and 300 degrees; 250 degrees proved best—the ribs were now fork-tender, though moist and gummy. A pass under the high heat of the broiler quickly turned the wet exterior into a crisp yet chewy crust. Adding some liquid to the pan further improved things, creating a moist environment similar to braising and making the ribs even more tender. Water worked fine but added no flavor; beer and apple juice—both common "mops" used to keep the meat moist in outdoor barbecue—were better options. Beer brought a slightly boozy taste to the meat, but the juice added welcome sweet depth.

Smoky and tender but slightly bland, the ribs were ready for some spice. Barbecued ribs can be cooked "dry"—coated with spices and served as is—or "wet," brushed with sauce shortly before serving. We've always had a weakness for the latter, but tasters argued that the big-flavored sauce masked the tea's smokiness.

We knew we wanted to keep the rub simple to make way for the ribs' smoky pork flavor so we started with the basics: salt, pepper, paprika, and brown sugar. We added some chili powder and a little cayenne for heat. Finally, a thin slathering of mustard brought just the right tangy, sharp kick to the pork and, as an added bonus, helped the spices stick fast. For an extra level of flavor, we added a few cloves of minced garlic and a spoonful of ketchup.

Next, we hoped to apply all we had learned from our indoor ribs to pulled pork. After testing bone-in shoulder roasts (also called Boston butt), fresh ham, and picnic roasts, we determined that the shoulder roast, which has the most fat, also retains the most moisture and flavor during a long, slow cook.

We rubbed the roast with a spice mixture, then froze it before smoking, just as we had done with the ribs. We found that because the roast was so large, the smoke didn't penetrate the interior of the meat as well as it did the racks of ribs. Opting for a boneless pork butt (a cut that is readily available and easy to shred once cooked) and cutting it in half solved the problem, increasing the surface area of the meat and thereby allowing more smoke flavor to permeate the pork. After the 30-minute smoking period, we added the apple juice to the pan and let the pork cook for 4 hours at 250 degrees, until it yielded moist, tender meat. We were happy to find that our technique for indoor barbecued ribs translated so easily to pulled pork. Now, all we needed to do was shred the pork and toss it with sauce—since barbecue fans all have their favorite, we decided to create three sauce recipes, a classic tomato-based sauce, a mustard sauce, and a vinegar sauce.

All that our barbecue lacked now was the rosy, smoke-colored evidence of live-fire barbecue—but one taste of our ribs or pulled pork and no one missed this small detail. Smoky-tasting, tender to a fault, and judiciously spicy, these indoor barbecued ribs and pulled pork are so good we might even make them in midsummer.

Oven-Barbecued Spareribs

SERVES 4

Some brands of tea are ground coarser than others and loose tea is often not ground at all; if necessary, grind the tea to a fine powder in a spice grinder before measuring. Be careful when opening the crimped foil to add the juice, as hot steam and smoke will billow out. Serve with one of the barbecue sauces on page 35, if desired.

6	tablespoons yellow mustard
2	tablespoons ketchup
3	medium garlic cloves, minced or pressed through a garlic press (about 1 tablespoon)
3	tablespoons brown sugar
1½	tablespoons kosher salt
1	tablespoon sweet paprika
1	tablespoon chili powder
2	teaspoons ground black pepper
½	teaspoon cayenne pepper
2	racks St. Louis–style spareribs (2½ to 3 pounds each) trimmed of surface fat, membrane removed (see the illustrations on page 34), and each rack cut in half
¼	cup finely ground Lapsang Souchong tea (from about 12 tea bags)
½	cup apple juice

1. Combine the mustard, ketchup, and garlic in a small bowl. In a separate small bowl, combine the sugar, salt, paprika, chili powder, black pepper, and cayenne. Spread the mustard mixture evenly over both sides of the ribs, then coat both sides with the spice mixture. Wrap the ribs in plastic wrap and refrigerate for at least 8 or up to 24 hours.

2. Transfer the ribs to the freezer and freeze until well chilled, about 45 minutes. Adjust the oven racks to the lowest and upper-middle positions (the upper rack should be least 5 inches below the broiler). Place a baking stone on the lower rack and heat the oven to 500 degrees.

3. Line a large rimmed baking sheet with foil. Sprinkle the tea evenly over the bottom of the baking sheet and top with a wire rack. Unwrap the ribs, transfer to the prepared wire rack with the meat side facing up, and cover with heavy-duty aluminum foil, crimping the edges tightly to seal. Place the baking sheet on the baking stone and roast the ribs for 30 minutes.

4. Reduce the oven temperature to 250 degrees, leaving the oven door open for 1 minute to cool. While the oven is open, carefully open one corner of the foil and pour the apple juice into the bottom of the baking sheet; reseal the foil. Continue to roast until the meat is very tender and begins to pull away from the bones, about 1½ hours longer. (Begin to check the ribs after 1 hour; leave loosely covered with foil for the remaining cooking time.)

5. Remove the foil, gently flip the racks bone side up, and move the baking sheet to the upper-middle oven rack. Turn on the broiler and broil the ribs until well browned and crisp in spots, 5 to 10 minutes. Flip the ribs meat side up and cook until well browned and crisp, 5 to 7 minutes longer. Transfer the ribs to a cutting board and let cool 10 minutes before slicing apart the individual ribs and serving.

CHOOSING THE RIGHT PORK RIBS

SPARERIBS
Ribs from near the pig's fatty belly. An acceptable choice, but needs a fair amount of home trimming.

ST. LOUIS–STYLE
Spareribs that have been trimmed of skirt meat and excess cartilage. Minimal fuss—our top choice.

BABY BACK
Smaller, leaner ribs from the (adult) pig's back. Tender, but the meat dries out too quickly for our recipe.

Oven-Barbecued Pulled Pork

SERVES 8

Some brands of tea are ground coarser than others and loose tea is often not ground at all; if necessary, grind the tea to a fine powder in a spice grinder before measuring. Be careful when opening the crimped foil to add the juice, as hot steam and smoke will billow out. Store-bought barbecue sauce works fine here, but for the best flavor, use one of the barbecue sauces on page 35. Serve the pulled pork on white bread with dill pickle chips.

3	tablespoons sweet paprika
2	tablespoons dark brown sugar
4	teaspoons chili powder
I	tablespoon salt
2	teaspoons ground cumin
2	teaspoons ground black pepper
I	(5-pound) boneless pork butt, cut in half widthwise
¼	cup finely ground Lapsang Souchong tea (about 12 tea bags)
½	cup apple juice
2½	cups barbecue sauce (see page 35), at room temperature or slightly warm (see note)

1. Mix the paprika, sugar, chili powder, salt, cumin, and pepper together, then rub the mixture evenly over the pork. Wrap the pork in plastic wrap and refrigerate for at least 8 or up to 24 hours.

2. Transfer the pork to the freezer and freeze until well chilled, about 45 minutes. Adjust the oven racks to the lowest and upper-middle positions (the upper rack should be least 5 inches below the broiler). Place a baking stone on the lower rack and heat the oven to 500 degrees.

3. Line a large rimmed baking sheet with foil. Sprinkle the tea evenly over the bottom of the baking sheet and top with a wire rack. Unwrap the pork, transfer to the prepared wire rack, and cover with heavy-duty aluminum foil, crimping the edges tightly to seal. Place the baking sheet on the baking stone and roast the pork for 30 minutes.

4. Reduce the oven temperature to 250 degrees, leaving the oven door open for 1 minute to cool. While the oven is open, carefully open one corner of the foil and pour the apple juice into the bottom of the baking sheet; reseal the foil. Continue to roast the pork until the meat is very tender and meets little resistance when poked with a fork, about 4 hours longer. (Begin to check the pork after 3 hours; leave loosely covered with foil for the remaining cooking time.)

5. Remove the foil and move the baking sheet to the upper-middle oven rack. Turn on the broiler and broil the pork until well browned and crisp in spots, 5 to 10 minutes. Flip the meat over and continue to broil until well browned and crisp, 5 to 7 minutes longer.

6. Transfer the pork to a cutting board, and let rest, uncovered, until just cool enough to handle, about 30 minutes. Shred the meat into thin shreds, discarding the large pieces of fat. Toss the shredded meat with ½ cup of the sauce and serve, passing the remaining sauce separately.

WALK-AWAY ROAST CHICKEN

WITH ITS HALLMARK CRISP, BROWNED SKIN and tender, juicy meat, roast chicken is an eminently satisfying dish. But it is usually a complicated one to prepare. The main problem is that roasting a chicken requires constant attention—the chicken has to be basted and turned multiple times during cooking. Basting a chicken every few minutes is a time-consuming task, and although turning a chicken several times while it roasts can produce good results, it requires a lot of hands-on time. Could we streamline the process and still get a really great roast chicken, one that doesn't require constant monitoring while in the oven? We aimed to develop a true hands-off walk-away roast chicken and wondered if oven temperature might play a role—would a low, slow roasting time keep the meat moist without all the fuss?

If we were going to give our chicken little to no attention once it was in the oven, we wanted to concentrate our efforts on ensuring optimal flavor before going in the oven. Over the years, the test kitchen has learned that brining chicken in a sugar and salt solution produces better flavor, texture, and caramelization (thanks to the sugar) of the skin. Brining ensures that the meat is seasoned through to the bone and also adds moisture that is retained when the chicken is cooked, resulting in a more flavorful, juicy piece of meat.

Once the chicken was brined and patted dry, we turned our attention to the skin. Most recipes brush the bird with either butter or oil to help brown and crisp the skin. We tried both. We started with butter and basted every 15 minutes. Basting with butter produced poor results. Despite a nice brown color, the skin was chewy and greasy. The next bird was basted with oil, which turned out a crisper skin that was more of a golden-brown color. We then tried simply brushing the bird with

olive oil before roasting and letting it cook undisturbed in the oven without any further basting. This was the best method—great color and crisp texture, with minimal fuss.

We also knew from earlier tests that separating the skin from the meat allows hot air to circulate more freely under the skin, renders more fat, and produces crisper skin. Since we were separating the skin from the meat anyway, we though we'd slip a little butter between the skin and meat—this helped keep the delicate breast meat juicy while adding flavor.

Trussing is another technique that is often recommended when roasting a whole bird, as it is said to promote more even cooking. We trussed a bird according to the best French method and found that it took one and a half hours to cook. The white meat was overcooked, but the dark meat

EQUIPMENT: Roasting Pans

Though most cooks haul out their roasting pan infrequently, when you do need this large pan, nothing else will do. This is especially true when cooking a whole bird. A roasting pan should promote deep, even browning of food. It should be easy to maneuver in and out of the oven. And it should be able to travel from oven to stovetop, so that you can deglaze the pan and loosen drippings.

Roasting pans can be made from stainless steel, enameled steel, nonstick-coated aluminum, or anodized aluminum, all of which we tested. We decided not to test pans lined with copper, which are prohibitively expensive; cast-iron pans, which when loaded with food are too heavy to lift; and pans made from Pyrex, ceramic, or stoneware, all of which seem better suited to lasagna and casseroles because they can't be used on top of the stove.

We tested eight roasting pans and preferred the materials we like in other cookware—stainless steel and anodized aluminum. These materials are heavy (though not excessively so) and produce good browning. Although nonstick coatings made cleanup easier, roasting racks slid around in these pans.

Roasting pans generally come in two different styles—they either have upright handles or they have side handles. Upright handles tend to be square in shape, while side handles are generally oval loops. We found upright handles to be easier to grip. The problem with side handles is that their position, coupled with the large size of the pan, can cause you to bring

your forearms perilously close to the hot oven walls. We tested one pan without handles, which was by far the most difficult to take out of the oven.

We tested pans ranging in length from 16 to 20 inches and in width from 11 to 14 inches. We preferred pans that measured about 16 inches long and 12 to 14 inches across. Larger pans made for an awkward fit in the oven and, because of their large surface area, tended to burn pan drippings more easily.

Our favorite pan is the Calphalon Contemporary Stainless Steel Roasting Pan ($100). It has all the features of more expensive pans (including its own V-rack). It's hefty enough for even the biggest bird, is easy to get into and out of the oven, and is widely available.

THE BEST ROASTING PAN
The Calphalon Contemporary Stainless Steel Roasting Pan ($100) is sturdy enough to support the weight of a large bird, has easy-to-grip upright handles, and has a bottom that is heavy enough to prevent burning.

CALPHALON

FLAVORED BUTTERS FOR ROAST CHICKEN AND TURKEY

USING FLAVORED BUTTERS, ALSO CALLED COMPOUND BUTTERS, IS AN EASY WAY TO ADD flavor to a simple roast chicken or turkey breast. All of these recipes make enough for one recipe Walk-Away Roast Chicken (page 41), but you will need to double these recipes if making Easy Roast Turkey Breast (page 44).

Lemon-Thyme Butter
MAKES ABOUT 2 TABLESPOONS

2 tablespoons unsalted butter, softened
1 tablespoon minced fresh thyme leaves
2 medium garlic cloves, minced or pressed
  through a garlic press
  (about 2 teaspoons)
1 teaspoon grated zest from 1 lemon

Combine all of the ingredients in a small bowl.

Orange-Rosemary Butter
MAKES ABOUT 2 TABLESPOONS

2 tablespoons unsalted butter, softened
2 medium garlic cloves, minced or pressed
  through a garlic press
  (about 2 teaspoons)
2 teaspoons minced fresh rosemary
1 teaspoon grated zest from 1 orange

Combine all of the ingredients in a small bowl.

Southwestern-Flavored Butter
MAKES ABOUT 2 TABLESPOONS

2 tablespoons unsalted butter, softened
2 medium garlic cloves, minced or pressed
  through a garlic press
  (about 2 teaspoons)
2 teaspoons minced fresh oregano leaves
2 teaspoons ground cumin
2 teaspoons chili powder
¾ teaspoon cocoa powder
½ teaspoon cayenne pepper

Combine all of the ingredients in a small bowl.

Asian-Flavored Butter
MAKES ABOUT 2 TABLESPOONS

2 tablespoons unsalted butter, softened
1 tablespoon minced or grated
  fresh ginger
1 medium garlic clove, minced or pressed
  through a garlic press
  (about 1 teaspoon)
1 teaspoon five-spice powder

Combine all of the ingredients in a small bowl.

was just right. We concluded that trussing makes it more difficult to cook the inner part of the thigh properly—because it is less exposed to the heat, it needs more oven time. With an untrussed bird, the white and dark meat were both nicely roasted. With our chicken preparation complete, it was time to look into roasting temperatures.

A typical recipe for roast chicken calls for roasting the chicken at 375 degrees for about one hour. But these recipes also call for turning the chicken multiple times, and we wanted our recipe to allow us to simply place the bird in the oven and walk away until it was done. Could we lower the temperature (giving us a longer period of walk-away time) and get away with leaving the bird untouched once it went into the oven? Roasting the chicken at a much lower temperature—250 degrees—without turning it did indeed produce moist meat, but it also resulted in pale, flabby skin. Since we wanted a classic roast chicken, crisp skin was a must. We reasoned that cranking the heat toward the end of roasting—after the fat from the skin had a chance to render—would brown and crisp the skin.

We knew the chicken would need to roast at a higher heat for a fair amount of time to achieve the crisp skin we were after, so we would need to turn the heat up well before the chicken was done. Chicken is fully cooked when the breast meat registers 160 to 165 degrees and the thigh meat 170 to 175 degrees. We tried turning the oven temperature up to 425 degrees once the chicken registered an internal temperature of 130 degrees. This gave the bird about 30 minutes of high heat, and the results were impressive—tender, juicy meat, with crisp golden skin. And we didn't have to turn it once.

For variations we decided to add vegetables to the pan for a complete meal. We developed one with just potatoes (because sometimes that is all you want), another with root vegetables, and a third with spring vegetables. The only difference in the cooking was that we returned the vegetables to the oven to caramelize while the chicken rested.

Walk-Away Roast Chicken
SERVES 4

To use kosher salt in the brine, see page 24 for conversion information. If using a kosher chicken, skip step 1 and don't rinse the chicken in step 3. We recommend using a V-rack (see page 49) to roast the chicken.

½	cup sugar
½	cup table salt
I	(4½- to 5-pound) whole chicken, giblets discarded
2	tablespoons unsalted butter or flavored butter (see page 40), softened
I	tablespoon olive oil
	Ground black pepper

1. Dissolve the sugar and salt in 2 quarts water in a large container. Submerge the chicken in the brine, cover, and refrigerate for 1 to 1½ hours.

2. Adjust an oven rack to the lower-middle position and heat the oven to 250 degrees. Coat a V-rack with nonstick cooking spray and set inside a roasting pan.

3. Remove the chicken from the brine and rinse. Pat the chicken dry with paper towels, then following the illustrations below, carefully separate the chicken skin from the breast meat, being careful not to break the skin. Place the butter underneath the skin, then gently massage the skin to distribute the butter evenly over the breast.

APPLYING THE BUTTER

 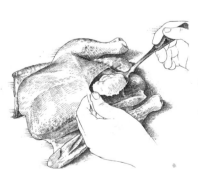 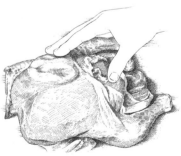

1. With your fingers, carefully loosen the skin over the breast.

2. Spoon I tablespoon of the butter under the skin on each side of the breast.

3. With your fingers on top of the skin, work the butter to distribute it evenly over the breast.

4. Following the illustration on page 58, tuck the wings behind the back. Brush the chicken with the oil and season with pepper. Place the chicken, breast side up, in the prepared V-rack and roast until the thickest part of the breast registers 125 to 130 degrees on an instant-read thermometer, 1½ to 1¾ hours.

5. Increase the oven temperature to 425 degrees and continue to roast the chicken until the thickest part of the breast registers 160 to 165 degrees and the thickest part of the thigh registers 170 to 175 degrees on an instant-read thermometer, about 30 minutes longer.

6. Transfer the chicken to a cutting board and let rest, uncovered, for 10 minutes. Carve the chicken following the illustrations below and serve.

➤ VARIATIONS

Walk-Away Roast Chicken with Potatoes

Toss 2½ pounds red potatoes, scrubbed and cut into 1-inch pieces, and ½ pound large shallots, peeled and halved, with 3 tablespoons olive oil and season with salt and pepper. Follow the recipe for Walk-Away Roast Chicken, spreading the vegetables evenly in the roasting pan underneath the V-rack in step 2; roast the chicken as directed. While the chicken rests in step 6, return the vegetables to a 500-degree oven and continue to roast, stirring occasionally, until fully cooked and golden, 5 to 10 minutes. Serve the vegetables with the chicken.

CARVING A WHOLE CHICKEN, TURKEY, OR DUCK

After brining and roasting the perfect bird, you still have one last task before bringing it to the table—carving it. And while carving isn't difficult, there is definitely a way to approach it that will yield nicely portioned chicken parts and slices of boneless breast—portions that look attractive on a platter and are easy to serve. While the illustrations below are of a chicken, the same carving technique can be used for turkey or duck.

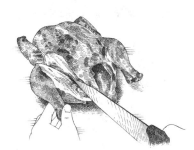

1. Cut the chicken where the leg meets the breast.

2. Pull the leg quarter away from the carcass. Separate the joint by gently pressing the leg out to the side and pushing up on the joint.

3. Carefully cut through the joint to remove the leg quarter.

4. Cut through the joint that connects the drumstick to the thigh. Repeat on the second side to remove the other leg.

5. Cut down along one side of the breastbone, pulling the breast meat away from you as you cut.

6. Remove the wing from the breast by cutting through the wing joint. Slice the breast into attractive slices.

Walk-Away Roast Chicken with Root Vegetables

Toss 1 pound red potatoes, scrubbed and cut into 1-inch pieces, 1 pound carrots, peeled and cut into 1-inch pieces, and 4 medium parsnips, peeled and cut into 1-inch pieces, with 3 tablespoons olive oil and season with salt and pepper. Follow the recipe for Walk-Away Roast Chicken, spreading the vegetables evenly in the roasting pan underneath the V-rack in step 2; roast the chicken as directed. While the chicken rests in step 6, return the vegetables to a 500-degree oven and continue to roast, stirring occasionally, until fully cooked and golden, 5 to 10 minutes. Serve the vegetables with the chicken.

Walk-Away Roast Chicken with Spring Vegetables

Toss 1 pound small potatoes, scrubbed and quartered, ½ pound shallots, peeled and halved, 1 pound asparagus, tough ends trimmed and cut into 2-inch lengths, and 1 (9-ounce) box frozen artichokes, thawed and patted dry, with 3 tablespoons olive oil and season with salt and pepper. Follow the recipe for Walk-Away Roast Chicken, spreading the vegetables evenly in the roasting pan underneath the V-rack in step 2; roast the chicken as directed. While the chicken rests in step 6, return the vegetables to a 500-degree oven and continue to roast, stirring occasionally, until fully cooked and golden, 5 to 10 minutes. Serve the vegetables with the chicken.

EASY ROAST TURKEY BREAST

ROASTING A WHOLE TURKEY BREAST SHOULD be easy. The biggest challenge with the holiday bird is that the dark meat takes longer to cook than the white meat; this is neatly avoided by the all-white breast. And the stuffing, which slows down the whole process and makes it much more cumbersome, is a nonissue. You have no choice but to bake the holiday dressing separately. So why is this seemingly easy recipe often so troublesome?

Sometimes lean white turkey meat is moist and juicy, but more often than not the meat comes out chalky and dry. The layers closest to the skin get especially parched as the meat near the bone takes its time coming up to temperature, and the skin is never as crisp as we'd like.

Over the years, the test kitchen has discovered that brining (soaking in a salt and sugar water solution for several hours) makes turkey moister. The salt changes the protein structure in the meat and helps it hold on to more moisture. Brining is especially helpful with delicate white meat, so it came as no surprise that brined turkey breasts were clearly juicier than unbrined turkey breasts. But brining is not enough. The right roasting technique is a must, too.

To get crisp skin we looked to several recipes in the test kitchen archives that call for loosening

PREPARING A TURKEY BREAST FOR ROASTING

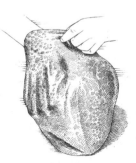

1. Using your hands, separate the skin from the meat, taking care to not tear the membrane around the perimeter of the breast; release the skin on either side of the breastbone.

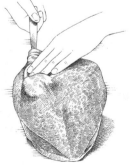

2. Using a spoon, work half of the softened butter under the skin on one side of the breast. Repeat with the remaining butter on the other side of the breast.

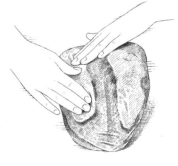

3. Using your hands, gently rub the turkey skin to evenly distribute the butter over the entire breast.

poultry skin and rubbing the meat with softened butter. Loosening the skin helps it to lift and separate from the meat, which promotes even browning and creates crisper skin. The fat in the butter also keeps the breast meat moist and adds much-needed flavor. To test this with our turkey breast, we loosened the skin, rubbed the meat with butter, and set the breast skin side up in a V-rack inside a roasting pan. At 450 degrees, the turkey skin scorched and the meat was much too dry. We then tried reducing the oven temperature to 325 degrees, and our turkey breast emerged with flabby, straw-colored skin. But although the skin lacked crispness and was unacceptably pale, the meat was tender and flavorful.

After testing several more oven temperature combinations, we finally found the best method— starting the turkey breast in a 425-degree oven for the first half hour of cooking and then reducing the heat to 325 degrees for the remaining hour. The initial blast of heat kick-starts the browning, ensuring the skin is beautifully golden by the end of the cooking time. (Because a turkey breast is all white meat, there is less fat that needs time to render—as is the case with a whole bird—so we found no benefit to waiting until the end of the cooking time to turn up the heat.) And the low temperature gently finishes the turkey meat, helping it stay moist and tender.

However, there was one minor problem: During the high-heat roasting, the minimal drippings in the pan burned, smoking up the oven and, eventually, the test kitchen. A quick solution was to add water to the roasting pan before cooking. A cup was the perfect amount; any more and too much steam formed, preventing parts of the skin from browning properly.

We had one last round of tests to conduct. We were adding salt and pepper to the 4 tablespoons of butter we were rubbing over the turkey meat and wondered what other flavors might work. Fresh herbs, citrus zest, garlic, and even ground spices were easy to incorporate into the softened butter mixture and gave the turkey a significant flavor boost. In order to make sure these flavors didn't overwhelm small patches of the turkey breast, we found it imperative to massage the butter evenly into the meat. Dividing the butter mixture in half and working each portion over one side of the breast guaranteed that the butter and seasonings were evenly applied.

Our recipe isn't any harder than the failed recipes we tried. But the butter and dual oven temperatures ensure that the skin is really crisp and the meat is flavorful and moist.

Easy Roast Turkey Breast
SERVES 8 TO 10

Many supermarkets are now selling "hotel-style" turkey breasts. Try to avoid these if you can, as they still have the wings attached. If this is the only type of breast you can find, you will simply need to remove the wings before proceeding with the recipe. To use kosher salt in the brine, see page 24 for conversion information. If using a kosher or "self-basting" turkey breast, skip step 1 and don't rinse the turkey in step 3. Serve with All-Purpose Gravy (page 10) or one of the fresh herb sauces on page 11.

½	cup sugar
½	cup table salt
1	(6- to 7-pound) whole bone-in, skin-on turkey breast, trimmed
4	tablespoons (½ stick) unsalted butter or flavored butter (see page 40), softened
1	tablespoon olive oil
¼	teaspoon ground black pepper

1. Dissolve the sugar and salt in 4 quarts water in a large container. Submerge the turkey in the brine, cover, and refrigerate for 3 to 6 hours.

2. Adjust an oven rack to the middle position and heat the oven to 425 degrees. Coat a V-rack with nonstick cooking spray and set inside a roasting pan.

3. Remove the turkey breast from the brine and rinse. Pat the turkey dry with paper towels, then following the illustrations on page 41, carefully separate the turkey skin from the breast meat, being careful not to break the skin. Place the butter underneath the skin, then gently massage the skin to distribute the butter evenly over the breast.

4. Brush the turkey with the oil and season with pepper. Transfer the turkey, breast side up, to the prepared V-rack and pour 1 cup water into the roasting

pan. Roast the turkey breast for 30 minutes.

5. Reduce the oven temperature to 325 degrees and continue to roast the turkey until the thickest part of the breast registers 160 to 165 degrees on an instant-read thermometer, about 1 hour longer.

6. Transfer the turkey to a cutting board and let rest, uncovered, for 20 minutes. Carve the turkey breast following the illustrations on page 62 and serve.

ULTIMATE ROAST TURKEY AND GRAVY

THERE'S A SIMPLE REASON SO MANY PEOPLE have trouble roasting a whole turkey: The white and dark meat cook at different rates. This almost always results in dry, overcooked breast meat and undercooked leg and thighs. You have some leeway with the dark meat, which is almost impossible to dry out during normal roasting times. The problem is that the breast, which is exposed to direct heat and finishes cooking at a lower temperature, becomes parched, while the legs and thighs take their time creeping to doneness. We were determined to find a cooking method that would finish both the white and dark meat simultaneously.

We already knew that the first step to a really great bird is brining (soaking the bird in a solution of salt, sugar, and water). Brining results in firm yet juicy meat that's fully seasoned. We experimented with the brining time and found that 12 to 14 hours in the refrigerator produces a nicely seasoned turkey without overly salty pan juices.

Our first roasting experiments used the method most frequently promoted by the National Turkey Federation, the U.S. Department of Agriculture, and legions of cookbook authors and recipe writers. This method features a moderately low roasting temperature of 325 degrees, a breast-up bird, and an open pan. We tried this method twice, basting one turkey and leaving the other alone. The basted turkey acquired a beautifully tanned skin, while the unbasted bird remained quite pale. Both were cooked to 170 degrees in the leg/thigh. This meant the breasts reached an unpalatably dry temperature of 180 degrees.

We quickly determined that almost all turkeys roasted in the traditional breast-up manner produced breast meat that was 10 degrees ahead of the leg/thigh meat. Recipes that use the technique of tenting the bird's breast and upper legs with foil fared a little better. The foil deflects some of the oven's heat, reducing the ultimate temperature differential between white and dark meat from 10 to 6 degrees. Most of the recipes we found that used this technique roasted the bird at a consistent 325-degree temperature. During the last 45 minutes of roasting the foil is removed, allowing enough time for browning. But because the result is essentially the same as other recipes that cook that bird breast side up (the white meat is still slightly overcooked by the time the dark meat is done), we determined that roasting turkeys with their breasts up is a losing proposition.

HIDDEN INSIDE THE TURKEY

Tucked neatly inside a turkey are the neck and a small bag of giblets, which can be added to the gravy for extra flavor. The giblets are three small organs that have been washed and are ready go: the heart, the gizzard, and the liver. We recommend using the heart and gizzard in the gravy, but not the liver—its flavor is just too strong and overpowering.

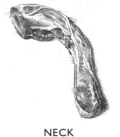

NECK

HEART

GIZZARD

LIVER

We also discovered that stuffing a bird makes overcooked meat more likely. This is because stuffing slows interior cooking—our tests showed a difference of nearly 30 degrees in internal temperature after an hour in the oven between an unstuffed and a stuffed bird. Slower cooking means a longer oven time, which can translate to bone-dry surface meat. If the turkey is your priority, we recommend cooking the dressing separately.

INGREDIENTS:
Supermarket Chicken Broth

Which chicken broth should you reach for when you haven't got time for homemade? We recommend choosing a mass-produced, lower-sodium brand and checking the label for evidence of mirepoix ingredients (carrots, celery, onion, and herbs). In a tasting of all the widely available brands, Swanson Certified Organic was a clear winner. And if you don't mind adding water, Better Than Bouillon Chicken Base came in a very close second and was the favorite of several tasters. Swanson's less-expensive Natural Goodness Chicken Broth was just about as good as the winner, though some tasters thought it tasted "overly roasted."

THE BEST CHICKEN BROTHS

SWANSON CERTIFIED ORGANIC FREE RANGE CHICKEN BROTH
Swanson's newest broth won tasters over with "very chickeny, straightforward, and honest flavors," a hearty aroma, and restrained "hints of roastiness."

BETTER THAN BOUILLON CHICKEN BASE
We're not ready to switch to a concentrated base for all our broth needs (you have to add water), but the 18-month refrigerator shelf life means it's a good replacement for dehydrated bouillon.

SWANSON NATURAL GOODNESS CHICKEN BROTH
Swanson's standard low-sodium broth was full of chicken flavor, but several tasters noted an out-of-place, overly roasted flavor.

Our most successful attempt at achieving equal temperatures in leg and breast came when we borrowed James Beard's technique of turning the turkey as it roasts. In this method, the bird begins breast side down on a V-rack, then spends equal time on each of its sides before being turned breast side up. The V-rack is important not just to hold the turkey in place but also to elevate it, affording it some protection from the heat of the roasting pan. This combination of rack and technique produced a turkey with a breast temperature that ran only a few degrees behind the leg temperature. But we quickly realized that the size of the turkey can make a difference in the oven temperature. We found that large turkeys get nicely browned with an initial high-heat roast (400 degrees), followed by a moderate temperature of 325 degrees. But our turkeys were in the 12- to 14-pound range and were cooking in as little as two hours, yielding quite pale skin. Clearly, we needed higher heat for the entire cooking time. We also remembered that in our earlier tests, the basted turkeys had beautifully browned skin. Sure enough, by keeping the heat to 400 degrees, then basting and turning our turkey, we got just what we wanted. But turning the bird several times and continually basting it makes for a fussy recipe. Could we streamline the process?

Instead of basting, we brushed the bird with melted butter only at the outset. This eliminated the extra work and produced a beautifully golden bird. Next, we wondered if we could get away with only turning the bird once, from breast side down to breast side up. Indeed we could—this turkey was just as evenly cooked as ones that had been turned twice as much.

All that was left to do was fine-tune the flavorings. Some aromatics (onions, carrots, and celery) added to the pan yielded flavorful pan juices from which we could build a rich gravy. Once the turkey was removed from the oven, we set it aside to rest while we made our sauce. A combination of the pan-roasted vegetables and juice, along with some butter, flour (for thickening), wine, bay leaves, and thyme gave us a simple but classic gravy that was the perfect complement to our turkey.

Ultimate Roast Turkey and Gravy

SERVES 10 TO 12

To use kosher salt in the brine, see page 24 for conversion information. If you don't have room in your refrigerator, you can brine the turkey in a large insulated cooler; add 5 or 6 freezer packs to the brine to keep it chilled. If you're roasting a kosher or self-basting turkey, skip the brine in step 2, and don't rinse the turkey in step 4. For extra-crisp skin, consider air-drying the turkey following the instructions on page 48. Including the giblets in the gravy is optional; see page 45 for more information on giblets. Ignore the pop-up timer (but do not remove it until the turkey is done); they are notoriously unreliable and the turkey will be overcooked by the time it pops.

TURKEY

1	(12- to 14-pound) turkey, thawed if necessary (following the instructions on page 50)
1	cup sugar
1	cup table salt
3	medium onions, chopped coarse
1½	medium carrots, chopped coarse
1½	celery ribs, chopped coarse
3	tablespoons unsalted butter, melted
1	cup low-sodium chicken broth, as needed

GRAVY

5–6	cups low-sodium chicken broth
6	tablespoons (¾ stick) unsalted butter or reserved turkey fat from step 7
¾	cup unbleached all-purpose flour
1	cup dry white wine
2	bay leaves
4	sprigs fresh thyme, or ½ teaspoon dried
	Salt and ground black pepper

1. FOR THE TURKEY: Following the illustrations at right, remove the giblet package from the body cavity and the neck from the neck cavity. Remove and discard any plastic or metal trussing device holding the drumsticks together. Trim the tailpiece. If using giblets in the gravy, remove the heart and gizzard from the giblet package and discard the liver. Refrigerate the turkey neck, tailpiece, and reserved giblets (if using) until needed.

PREPARING A TURKEY FOR ROASTING

1. Remove the giblet package from the body cavity and the neck from the neck cavity.

2. Cut off the tailpiece and reserve with the neck and giblets (if using) to help flavor the gravy.

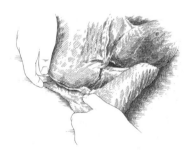

3. Tucking the wings under the bird will prevent the wingtips from burning. Simply twist the wing tip back behind the back of the bird—it should stay in place by itself.

4. Remove any plastic trussing, and discard. Secure the legs by tucking the ankles of the bird into the band of skin at the tail of the bird. If the band is missing, tie the legs together at the ankles with kitchen twine.

TECHNIQUE: Air-Drying Turkey

For the crispest skin on a roast turkey, we suggest air-drying. By air-drying the bird, uncovered in the refrigerator, the moisture is wicked away from the skin so that it browns more quickly and deeply when roasting in the oven. To air-dry a turkey, set a wire rack inside a rimmed baking sheet. Remove the turkey from the brine and rinse. Pat the turkey dry, inside and out, with paper towels. Transfer the turkey, breast side up, to the prepared wire rack. Refrigerate the turkey, uncovered, until the skin is very dry and taut, 8 to 16 hours; prep and roast the turkey as directed.

2. Dissolve the sugar and salt in 2 gallons water in a large stockpot or container. Submerge the turkey in the brine, cover, and refrigerate for 12 to 14 hours.

3. Adjust an oven rack to the lowest position and heat the oven to 400 degrees. Toss the onions, carrots, celery, turkey neck, tailpiece, and reserved giblets (if using) together with 1 tablespoon of the butter, then spread into a large roasting pan. Line a large V-rack with heavy-duty foil and use a paring knife or skewer to poke 20 to 30 holes in the foil. Set the V-rack inside the roasting pan.

4. Remove the turkey from the brine and rinse. Pat the turkey dry, inside and out, with paper towels. Following the illustrations on page 47, tuck the wings behind the back and tie the turkey legs together. Brush the breast side of the turkey with 1 more tablespoon butter. Place the turkey, breast side down, in the V-rack, then brush the backside of the turkey with the remaining 1 tablespoon butter. Roast the turkey for 45 minutes. (If, at any point, the drippings begin to burn, add the chicken broth to the roasting pan.)

5. Remove the turkey from the oven and, using clean potholders or kitchen towels, flip the turkey breast side up. Continue to roast the turkey until the thickest part of the breast registers 160 to 165 degrees and the thickest part of the thighs registers 170 to 175 degrees on an instant-read thermometer, 50 to 60 minutes longer.

6. Tip the turkey so that the juice from the cavity runs into the roasting pan. Transfer the turkey to a cutting board and let rest, uncovered, while making the gravy.

7. FOR THE GRAVY: Using a slotted spoon, transfer the roasted vegetables, turkey neck, tail-piece, and reserved giblets (if using) to a bowl and reserve. Transfer the roasting juices into a liquid measuring cup or fat separator, scraping up any browned bits from the pan. Defat the liquid, reserving the fat (if desired). Add enough broth to the defatted juices to measure 7 cups.

8. Melt the butter (or heat the turkey fat) in a large saucepan over medium heat. Stir in the flour and cook, stirring often, until dark brown, 10 to 15 minutes. Slowly whisk in the wine, followed by the broth until smooth. Stir in the bay leaves, thyme, and reserved roasted vegetables, giblets (if using), neck, and tailpiece. Simmer the gravy until thickened and no longer tastes of flour, 20 to 30 minutes.

9. Strain the gravy through a fine-mesh strainer into a serving pitcher, pressing hard on the vegetables to extract as much liquid as possible. Season the gravy with salt and pepper to taste and cover to keep warm. Remove the twine holding the drumsticks and carve the turkey following the illustrations on page 42. Serve, passing the gravy separately.

➤ VARIATION

Ultimate Roast Turkey and Gravy for a Crowd
SERVES 20 TO 22

To use kosher salt in the brine, see page 24 for conversion information. If you don't have room in your refrigerator, you can brine the turkey in a large insulated cooler; add 5 or 6 freezer packs to the brine to keep it chilled. If you're roasting a kosher or self-basting turkey, skip the brine in step 2, and don't rinse the turkey in step 4. For extra-crisp skin, consider air-drying the turkey following the instructions above. Whether or not you include the giblets (for the gravy) is optional; see page 45 for more information on giblets. This turkey will be quite big and heavy, and if you are reluctant to flip it during roasting, skip the step of lining the V-rack with foil and simply roast the bird breast side up for the full time. Ignore the pop-up timer (but do not remove it until the turkey is done); they are notoriously unreliable and the turkey will be overcooked by the time it pops.

TURKEY

1	(18- to 22-pound) turkey, thawed if necessary (following the instructions on page 50)
1½	cups sugar
1½	cups table salt

3	medium onions, chopped coarse
1½	medium carrots, chopped coarse
1½	celery ribs, chopped coarse
3	tablespoons unsalted butter, melted
1	cup low-sodium chicken broth, as needed

GRAVY

9–10	cups low-sodium chicken broth
12	tablespoons (1½ sticks) unsalted butter or reserved turkey fat from step 7
1½	cups all-purpose flour
1½	cups dry white wine
4	bay leaves
4	sprigs fresh thyme, or ½ teaspoon dried
	Salt and ground black pepper

1. FOR THE TURKEY: Following the illustrations on page 47, remove the giblet package from the body cavity and the neck from the neck cavity. Remove and discard any plastic or metal trussing device holding the drumsticks together. Trim the tailpiece. If using giblets in the gravy, remove the heart and gizzard from the giblet package and discard the liver. Refrigerate the turkey neck, tailpiece, and reserved giblets (if using) until needed.

2. Dissolve the sugar and salt in 3 gallons water in a large stockpot or container. Submerge the turkey in the brine, cover, and refrigerate for 12 to 14 hours.

3. Adjust an oven rack to the lowest position and heat the oven to 400 degrees. Toss the onions, carrots, celery, turkey neck, tailpiece, and reserved giblets (if using) together with 1 tablespoon of the butter, then spread into a large roasting pan. Line a large V-rack with heavy-duty foil and use a paring knife or skewer to poke 20 to 30 holes in the foil. Set the V-rack inside the roasting pan.

4. Remove the turkey from the brine and rinse. Pat the turkey dry, inside and out, with paper towels. Following the illustrations on page 47, tuck the wings behind the back and tie the turkey legs together. Brush the breast side of the turkey with 1 more tablespoon butter. Place the turkey, breast side down, in the

---

EQUIPMENT: Roasting Racks

A roasting rack (also known as a V-rack) raises poultry and roasts out of the drippings, while giving the oven's heat easy access to the whole surface—a good start toward a well-rendered exterior and even cooking. We recommend purchasing a fixed V-rack (as opposed to an adjustable one) because we've found that the adjustable V-racks are not as sturdy as the fixed ones and are prone to collapse, especially after turning the bird. But which brand of V-rack is best? We brought several into the test kitchen to find out.

Right away, we noted that not all V-racks are actually V-shaped. The slight bend on some roasting racks barely qualifies as a "V" and leaves no room for roasting vegetables underneath. The innovative Cuisipro Roast and Serve ($28.95) is shaped like a trough with a hinge at the center. Remove the dowel from the hinge and the rack comes apart, dropping the roast onto a platter or cutting board. While it worked fine, this rack was another that didn't elevate the roast enough, and its size (15 inches by 11½ inches) makes it a tight squeeze in all but the largest pan.

In addition to shape, handles were a decisive factor. Tall, vertical handles make removing the rack easy, even with bulky oven mitts. Horizontal handles, or no handles at all, make removal nearly impossible. In our tests, we also noticed that handle position matters. When located on the short sides of a rectangular rack they can get in the way of the roasting pan's handles. We prefer handles positioned on the long side of the rack.

The All-Clad Nonstick Roasting Rack ($24.95) is our top choice. It's large enough to hold two small chickens and has the features we like. With its handles on the short side, the Norpro ($9.75) is a distant runner-up. If you're also in the market for a new roasting pan, you should consider our favorite roaster, the Calphalon Contemporary Stainless Steel Roasting Pan ($100), which includes a rack that's just as good as the All-Clad model.

THE BEST ROASTING RACK

All-Clad's Nonstick Roasting Rack ($24.95) is our favorite for its large capacity and easy-to-grasp handles.

ALL-CLAD

V-rack, then brush the backside of the turkey with the remaining 1 tablespoon butter. Roast the turkey for 1 hour. (If, at any point, the drippings begin to burn, add the chicken broth to the roasting pan.)

5. Remove the turkey from the oven and, using clean potholders or kitchen towels, flip the turkey breast side up. Reduce the oven temperature to 325 degrees and continue to roast the turkey until the thickest part of the breast registers 160 to 165 degrees and the thickest part of the thigh registers 170 to 175 degrees on an instant-read thermometer, about 2 hours longer.

6. Tip the turkey so that the juice from the cavity runs into the roasting pan. Transfer the turkey to a cutting board and let rest, uncovered, while making the gravy.

7. FOR THE GRAVY: Using a slotted spoon, transfer the roasted vegetables, turkey neck, tailpiece, and reserved giblets (if using) to a bowl and reserve. Transfer the roasting juices into a liquid measuring cup or fat separator, scraping up any browned bits from the pan. Defat the liquid, reserving the fat (if desired). Add enough broth to the defatted juices to measure 11 cups.

8. Melt the butter (or heat the turkey fat) in a large saucepan over medium heat. Stir in the flour and cook, stirring often, until dark brown, 10 to 15 minutes. Slowly whisk in the wine, followed by the broth until smooth. Stir in bay leaves, thyme, and reserved roasted vegetables, giblets (if using), neck, and tailpiece. Simmer the gravy until thickened and no longer tastes of flour, 20 to 30 minutes.

9. Strain the gravy through a fine-mesh strainer into a serving pitcher, pressing hard on the vegetables

---

TECHNIQUE: How To Thaw Turkey

There are two ways to thaw a turkey: both take time, but one is a little faster (which helps if you're in a pinch). For a slow thaw, place the frozen turkey in a large disposable roasting pan supported by a baking sheet, and let thaw in the refrigerator; count on 1 day of defrosting for every 4 pounds of bird. For a quicker thaw, place the frozen turkey in a bucketful of cold tap water; count on 30 minutes per pound and change the water every 30 minutes to avoid bacterial growth.

---

to extract as much liquid as possible. Season the gravy with salt and pepper to taste and cover to keep warm. Remove the twine holding the drumsticks and carve the turkey following the illustrations on page 42. Serve, passing the gravy separately.

ROAST DUCK

DUCK IS AN IDEAL CANDIDATE FOR SLOW cooking—it has thick, fatty skin that needs plenty of time in the oven to properly render and crisp. And because duck has a good amount of fat, the breast meat can survive prolonged exposure to the heat of the oven and be cooked to a relatively high temperature without drying out, unlike chicken or turkey. Our goal for this recipe was simple: We wanted to determine the best method for roasting duck that would give us fully cooked meat (that would still be moist and flavorful) and crisp skin—without the grease. And, since an average duck serves just 2 or 3 people, we wanted to use two ducks, which could serve a larger group.

Pekin ducks (also called Long Island ducks) are the type mostly commonly found in the supermarket, so we started our testing there. Our initial tests demonstrated the need to start getting rid of fat from the outset. We found that unless the skin rests directly on meat or bone it will never crisp properly. So we began by removing the large clumps of fat that line the body and neck cavity, something that is easily done by hand. We then tucked the wings behind the breasts, and the legs into the flap of skin at the end of the body so that the duck remained in a tidy shape during roasting—this resulted in more even cooking.

With our duck prepped, we turned our attention to the roasting method. Every source we consulted agreed that a roasting rack is necessary to keep the duck elevated, thus keeping it from cooking in a pool of its own rendered fat. After that, there was little agreement. Many recipes suggest pricking the skin to encourage further rendering. We used a fork as well as the tip of a paring knife to prick the duck all over and both worked moderately well.

Taking this concept a step further, we tried scoring the skin directly over the biggest fat pockets. We scored the top of each breast five times, and also scored the bottom of the duck. The fat on these ducks was very well rendered, producing the most crispy skin so far.

As for roasting temperature, some restaurants start duck in a 500-degree oven to render the fat quickly and then reduce the heat to 350 degrees to finish cooking the duck through. Our instincts told us this approach was problematic, and the billows of smoke that filled the test kitchen confirmed our doubts—this is a method that only works in a kitchen equipped with an extremely powerful exhaust fan.

Next we tried roasting the duck at a very low 250 degrees, thinking that the cooking time would be long enough to allow most of the fat to render, while the low temperature would keep the meat tender and moist. After three hours of roasting, we found that the duck had actually rendered less fat than at the higher temperature, the skin was flabby and unappetizing, and the meat was dry. It was evident that we needed some sort of compromise—a high enough temperature to melt the thick layer of fat, but not so high that the skin would burn before the fat rendered.

Looking for a happy medium, we then tried roasting the duck in a moderately hot 350-degree oven, then finishing with a higher temperature of 425 degrees to crisp the skin. This was an improvement—the skin was crisp—but the breast meat was still on the dry side and the legs still had pockets of fat under the skin.

We now wondered if brining the ducks would solve the dry meat problem. The test kitchen typically brines lean cuts of meat (such as pork, turkey, and chicken) to yield moist and tender meat and so we originally thought this step would be unnecessary for duck, which is quite fatty. However, when we compared a brined duck with an unbrined one, the results surprised us. The brined bird was much juicier, very flavorful and far more tender—and we noticed that the sugar in the brine helped encourage more crispy skin.

After a few more temperature adjustments, we settled on roasting the duck at 350 degrees until the breast meat reached 160 degrees, then turning the oven up to 450 degrees, and roasting the duck until the breast meat reached 180 degrees to get perfectly crisp skin. Tasters devoured this duck with its thin, golden, crisp skin and moist and tender meat. Now all we needed was a sauce to complement the rich roast duck. For a classic accompaniment, we combined some chopped dried cherries for tartness, some balsamic vinegar for an acidic note, thyme sprigs for freshness, and port to sweeten and combine the mixture. We reduced it all together until syrupy, stirred in a little butter before serving, and drizzled it over the duck.

PREPARING DUCKS FOR ROASTING

1. Using a sharp knife, make 5 shallow slashes diagonally across each breast half, about an inch apart, being careful not to cut into the flesh.

2. Make 6 shallow slashes across the backside of each duck, being careful not to cut into the flesh.

Roast Duck with Port-Cherry Sauce

SERVES 4 TO 6

To use kosher salt in the brine, see page 24 for conversion information. If using kosher ducks, skip step 1 and don't rinse the ducks in step 3. Port comes in many styles, but we prefer to use an inexpensive Tawny port here. Make sure the ducks are not hanging over the rim of the baking sheet or they will drip hot fat onto the bottom of the oven and make a smoky mess.

DUCKS

½   cup sugar
½   cup table salt
2   (3½- to 4-pound) whole ducks, neck, giblets, and excess fat removed
    Ground black pepper

SAUCE

2   cups port (see note)
¾   cup balsamic vinegar
¼   cup dried tart cherries, chopped coarse
1   medium shallot, minced (about 3 tablespoons)
2   sprigs fresh thyme
2   tablespoons unsalted butter
    Salt and ground black pepper

1. FOR THE DUCKS: Dissolve the sugar and salt in 4 quarts water in a large container. Submerge the ducks in the brine, cover, and refrigerate for 3 to 6 hours.

2. Adjust an oven rack to the middle position and heat the oven to 350 degrees. Set a wire rack on top of a rimmed baking sheet lined with foil.

3. Remove the ducks from the brine and rinse. Pat the ducks dry with paper towels. Following the illustrations on page 51, make 5 shallow slashes diagonally across each breast half of each duck, about 1 inch apart, being careful not to cut into the flesh. Make 6 shallow slashes across the backside of each duck, being careful not to cut into the flesh. Following the illustration on page 58, tuck the wings behind the back. Season the ducks with pepper and place them breast side up on the prepared wire rack.

4. Roast the ducks until the thickest part of the breast registers 160 degrees on an instant-read thermometer, about 45 minutes.

5. Increase the oven temperature to 450 degrees and continue to roast the ducks until the skin is golden and crisp and the thickest part of the breast registers 180 degrees, about 20 minutes longer.

6. FOR THE SAUCE: Meanwhile, bring the port, vinegar, cherries, shallot, and thyme to a simmer in a medium saucepan over medium heat until thickened and measures about 1¼ cups, 35 to 40 minutes. Off the heat, discard the thyme sprigs, cover, and set aside.

7. Transfer the ducks to a cutting board and let rest, uncovered, for 10 minutes. Reheat the sauce over medium heat, then stir in the butter, and season with salt and pepper to taste. Carve the ducks, following the illustrations on page 42, and serve, passing the sauce separately.

OVEN-POACHED SIDE OF SALMON

POACHED SALMON IS A VERSATILE DISH AND it is especially great for serving a crowd. Light and cool, with a hint of fresh lemon and herbs, it is excellent over a simple salad, with a piece of crusty bread, or on its own, perhaps with a dollop of creamy horseradish sauce. But poaching a side of salmon presents one big problem: Unless you own a fish poacher, it is nearly impossible to fit such a large piece of fish into a pot. Not wanting to spend money on such a specific piece of equipment, we headed into the kitchen to find a solution.

When pressed, most of the test kitchen staff admitted that in the past they have cheated when poaching salmon. One test cook confessed to cutting a beautiful 4-pound side of salmon into several large sections—whatever was necessary to get the fish to fit into his largest pot. He'd then filled the pot with water and seasonings, added the fish, brought it to a boil, covered it, and turned off the heat. About 30 minutes later, the fish was done.

MAKING OVEN-POACHED SALMON

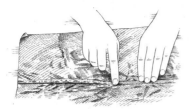

1. Cut 3 sheets of heavy-duty foil about a foot longer than the fish. Using 2 of the sheets, overlap their edges by 1 inch, and fold to secure the seam.

2. Lay the third sheet of foil over the seam and coat the sheets with vegetable oil spray.

3. Run your fingers over the surface of the fish to feel for pinbones, and then remove them with tweezers or needle-nosed pliers.

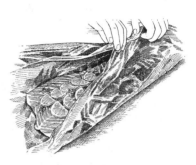

4. Hold a sharp chef's knife at a slight downward angle to the flesh and cut off and discard the whitish, fatty portion of the belly.

5. Lay the salmon down the center of the foil, sprinkle with the vinegar, and arrange the herbs and lemon slices on top.

6. Bring the edges of the foil up over the salmon. Fold the edges together to secure the seam, but do not crimp too tightly.

We liked this method, but it only works if your style of entertaining is like that of the above-mentioned test cook: You don't really care how things look, only how they taste. Hacking the side of salmon up into two or three pieces simply won't do if presentation is any concern. How, then, to fit a whole side of salmon into a pot that's clearly too small? The answer seemed simple enough: Make the fish fit the pot. If you fill a large pot with water and seasonings and gently bend the side of salmon to fit inside, the fish obediently curves along the pot's sides, cooks evenly, and tastes great. But the problem of presentation remains: The curved fish looks incredibly odd and the flesh flakes apart at the bend.

We then wondered what would happen if we got rid of the water altogether and instead simply steamed the salmon in its own moisture. Sure, it wouldn't truly be poaching, but if it looked and tasted like poached salmon, would it really matter?

We plopped the side of salmon down on three sheets of heavy-duty foil, seasoned it, and

wrapped it up. We baked the fish on a baking sheet at 300 degrees, poking a trusty instant-read thermometer right through the foil every 20 minutes or so. Our first couple of tries were near-disastrous failures—it seemed to take about two hours to go from 33 degrees to 110 degrees, and then about two minutes to go from 110 degrees to 140 degrees. The salmon we cooked at this temperature had three problems: It was overcooked, with a chalky, throat-clogging texture; the skin stuck to the foil; and the flavor was bland.

In an attempt to gain more control over the cooking process, we lowered the oven temperature to 250 degrees. This meant a relatively long cooking time, but that was OK since we knew it would be largely unattended. Still, we had problems with overcooking; the internal temperature of the fish, like that of a roast, continued to rise after we removed it from the oven. And, like many roasts that are an odd shape—think of leg of lamb—the thinner side became overcooked before the thicker side was done. We could compensate for the overcooking of the thinner end by removing the fish from the oven before it was done (that was easy enough) but then wouldn't the thicker portion be undercooked?

We gained more control by cooking the foil packet directly on the oven rack; this kept the bottom from cooking more rapidly than the top. But in the end, all we could really do was undercook the thickest part slightly in hopes of keeping the tail end palatable. And, indeed, that was a fine solution; because fully cooked salmon is somewhat chalky, some people like it when it's slightly translucent, anyway. Serve from the thick end of the fish and if there are any leftovers, they'll be from the overcooked tail (use them to make salmon salad, cakes, or croquettes).

Solving the sticky skin was easy: We just coated the aluminum foil with vegetable oil spray. All we needed to do to spark the fish's flavor was give it a dose of vinegar and lemon juice. When we served it with lemon wedges and a cool dill sauce, we had everyone fooled into thinking our oven-poached salmon was the real thing.

Oven-Poached Side of Salmon with Lemon-Dill Sour Cream

SERVES 8

If serving a big crowd, you can oven-poach two individually wrapped sides of salmon in the same oven (on the upper-middle and lower-middle racks) without altering the cooking time. White wine vinegar can be substituted for the cider vinegar. Be sure to follow our directions for wrapping the salmon in foil (see page 53); otherwise, the fish's juices may leak onto the bottom of your oven, creating a pesky mess. To test the fish for doneness, simply poke an instant-read thermometer right through the foil.

SALMON

1	(4-pound) side of salmon
	Salt
2	tablespoons cider vinegar
6	sprigs fresh tarragon or dill
2	lemons, sliced thin
2	tablespoons minced fresh tarragon or dill leaves (for serving)
1	lemon, cut into wedges (for serving)

LEMON-DILL SOUR CREAM

1	cup sour cream
1	medium shallot, minced (about 3 tablespoons)
1	tablespoon minced fresh dill
1½	teaspoons juice from 1 lemon
	Salt and ground black pepper

1. FOR THE SALMON: Adjust an oven rack to the middle position and heat the oven to 250 degrees. Following the illustrations on page 53, assemble 3 sheets of foil and coat them with vegetable oil spray.

2. Remove any pinbones from the salmon and, using a sharp knife, trim any whitish fat from the belly, following the illustration on page 53. Pat the fish dry with paper towels and season both sides with salt. Lay the salmon, skin side down, on top of the foil. Sprinkle with the vinegar, lay the tarragon sprigs over the fish, and top with the lemon slices. Crimp the foil down over the fish into a tight packet.

3. Lay the foil-wrapped fish directly on the oven rack (without a baking sheet) and cook until the color of the flesh has turned from pink to orange and the thickest part of the fish registers 135 to 140 degrees on an instant-read thermometer, 45 to 60 minutes.

4. Remove the fish from the oven, open the foil packet, and discard the lemon slices and herbs. Let the salmon cool at room temperature, on the foil, for 30 minutes.

5. Pour off any accumulated liquid, reseal the salmon in the foil, and refrigerate until cold, about 1 hour. (The poached salmon can be refrigerated for up to 2 days. Let the salmon sit at room temperature for 30 minutes before serving.)

6. FOR THE LEMON-DILL SOUR CREAM: Combine all of the ingredients in a medium bowl and season with salt and pepper to taste. Cover and refrigerate until the flavors meld, about 30 minutes, or up to 4 hours.

7. TO SERVE: Unwrap the salmon and brush away any gelled poaching liquid. Slide your hands under both ends of the salmon and carefully transfer the fish to a serving platter. Sprinkle the salmon with the minced tarragon and serve with the lemon wedges.

2

COOKING EN COCOTTE

Cooking en Cocotte

COOKING EN COCOTTE, OR CASSEROLE-roasting, is a common cooking method in France that is typically used for chicken, lamb, and even eggs. The approach is simple: Place a seasoned piece of meat in a pot, scatter in a small handful of chopped vegetables, cover, and bake. This technique has many similarities to braising: it utilizes a covered pot, low oven temperature, and extended cooking time to yield tender, flavorful meat. But unlike braising, no liquid is added to the pot. Instead, juices are drawn from the meat and into the pot, and the meat cooks in its own juices. These juices eventually create a moist-heat environment, so that the meat cooks gently and its flavors are concentrated. The result is unbelievably tender and flavorful meat undiluted by additional liquid. Not having much experience with this cooking method, but intrigued by its possibilities, we were eager to uncover the secrets to success.

Since *poulet en cocotte* is a Parisian bistro classic, we decided to start our testing with chicken. We quickly learned a few things about the proper equipment for cooking en cocotte. It's important to use a vessel large enough to hold the piece of poultry or meat that you're cooking—for most of these recipes you'll need a 7- to 8-quart Dutch oven. We also found that heavy stainless-steel or enameled cast-iron Dutch ovens fared better than lightweight versions, with better heat retention and more even heating. Also, a tight-fitting lid was key to preventing steam from escaping. To compensate for pots with loose-fitting lids, we found it necessary to seal the pot with foil before adding the top.

Aside from the proper equipment, we discovered that the right oven temperature is another key factor in the success of cooking en cocotte. We tested a range of temperatures below 400 degrees. Temperatures from 325 to 375 degrees produced decent results, but even lower temperatures—around 250 degrees—yielded incredibly tender meat, thanks to the delicate heat and longer cooking time. Sure, some of these low-temperature versions took up to an hour and 45 minutes to cook, but it was all walk-away time and tasters raved about the meat's rich, concentrated flavor.

Due to the low oven temperature we did find it beneficial to sauté or sweat the aromatics on the stovetop first before making our way to the oven.

This not only developed their flavor and softened their texture, but also gently warmed the pot so it wasn't completely cold when transferred to the oven (which would have unnecessarily extended the cooking time). We also occasionally found that the addition of a small amount of wine greatly enhanced the flavor of the aromatics, but we made sure to allow time for the liquid to cook off before adding the meat to the pot. Besides adding flavor during the cooking process, we found that the aromatics could serve double duty, forming the base of a flavorful relish or sauce for the finished dish.

With a basic recipe in place, we tested a couple of different variables to see if we could extract even more flavor with this cooking method. We tried basting the meat, but opening the oven every 20 minutes was a hassle that had little impact on the flavor of the finished dish. We then tried browning the meat on the stovetop before placing it in the oven. This step requires a little extra effort, but we think the result—deeper, richer flavor—is well worth the time. We did find that small variances in the weight of a piece of meat could greatly affect the cooking time. To compensate for this, we provide a range of times in our recipes that correspond with weight ranges given for the meat.

Now that we had a very successful technique for meat, we wondered if this method of cooking en cocotte would work with fish. Initial tests were promising, but we realized some changes were necessary. Notably more delicate, fish didn't require the initial searing that the poultry and meat did. Fish is typically quick cooking, so we were surprised at how long fish could spend in the oven and still remain incredibly moist. Its buttery texture and clean flavor impressed tasters. Finally we turned to eggs en cocotte, a classic dish that requires a technique of its own. Although this dish is usually baked in a water bath in the oven, we found a completely different way of making it on the stovetop that results in perfectly cooked whites and tender, runny yolks.

Wherever you choose to dive in, these casserole-roasted recipes are sure to impress you with their delicate texture and intense flavor. We're certain this cooking technique will soon become a staple in your repertoire.

CHICKEN EN COCOTTE

POULET EN COCOTTE IS A PARISIAN BISTRO classic. The dish typically features a whole chicken baked with a smattering of vegetables in a covered pot. At first glance, this chicken is nothing to rave about—it has pale, soft skin very unlike the crisp exterior of the roasted poultry we are used to. But the first time we tried this dish, one bite confirmed that it was something very special indeed—the meat was incredibly tender and juicy, with a rich, soul-satisfying flavor.

The basic method for chicken en cocotte is simple: Place a seasoned chicken in a pot, scatter in a small handful of chopped vegetables, cover, and bake. Unlike braising, little or no liquid is added to the pot, resulting in a drier cooking environment. Many of the recipes we found called for adding additional ingredients such as potatoes, onions, carrots, bacon, mushrooms, or tomatoes. But when we tried piling in these extras, we found they served only to cover up what we were really after: great chicken flavor, pure and simple. It occurred to us that our piles of vegetables were creating a steamy environment that could be washing out the chicken flavor. What if we actually decreased the humidity inside the pot? Would that give us the result we were looking for?

For our next go-round we cooked a chicken with nothing more than a little oil to prevent it from sticking. When we pulled the pot from the oven and removed the lid, a tiny puff of steam emerged—not the great whoosh that had been escaping from the tests with vegetables. This bird had a great flavor that won tasters over. And with no vegetables to soak them up, the flavorful juices remained in the pot. After defatting the liquid, we had a simple, richly flavored jus to accompany our chicken—a huge bonus. Still, the bird was not quite perfect. Tasters complained that the breast meat was a tad tough and fibrous, and we had to agree. We wondered what a lower oven temperature would do.

After testing a half dozen chickens at varying temperatures, we settled on 250 degrees as the ideal oven temperature because it yielded the most tender breast meat. While these birds took longer to cook than an average roasted chicken, the results were well worth the time invested.

Though most recipes did nothing to the chicken except season it before placing it in the pot to bake, we decided extra measures were necessary. Browning the top and bottom of the chicken on the stovetop before placing it in the oven was our first thought. Tasters liked the effects as the flavors deepened, but we still had a problem with the dark meat not cooking quickly enough. By the time the breast meat was perfectly cooked to 160 degrees, the dark meat (which needs to be cooked to 175 degrees) still wasn't ready. Placing the rack on the lowest position to situate the bird closer to the heat source, combined with browning the dark meat for an extra minute or two, solved the problem.

With the cooking process under control, we decided it was time to finesse the flavors. While we did not want to fill the pot with vegetables, we discovered that we could get away with adding a small amount of potently flavored aromatic vegetables—chopped onion, whole garlic cloves, and a few thyme sprigs. Lightly browning them along with the chicken helped remove any excess moisture, while the caramelization of the vegetables added rich color and flavor to the sauce. Stirring in a little fresh lemon juice to finish the sauce

PROTECTING THE WINGS

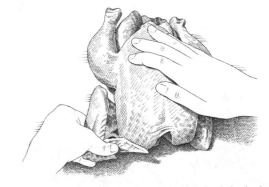

Tucking the wings of a chicken (or duck) behind the back will keep them out of the way and prevent the wingtips from burning. Simply twist the wing back behind the back and close the joints of the wing tightly. The tension of the closed, tucked wing will help to keep it in place.

brightened and balanced all of its flavors. We then experimented with a few variations on the aromatic vegetables and arrived at a simple garlic-rosemary version, one flavored with small pieces of chorizo and a pinch of saffron, and, finally, one flavored with ginger and shiitake mushrooms.

This simple French-style chicken in a pot will never place first in a beauty contest, of course, if a browned roast bird is the standard. But its tender, juicy, intensely flavored meat is sure to be a winner every time.

Chicken en Cocotte with Thyme and Lemon

SERVES 4

If using a smaller or larger chicken, adjust the cooking time as necessary.

1	(4½- to 5-pound) whole chicken, giblets discarded
	Salt and ground black pepper
2	tablespoons olive oil
1	small onion, peeled, halved, and sliced thin (see the illustration at right)
6	medium garlic cloves, peeled and crushed (see the illustration on page 63)
1	bay leaf
2	sprigs fresh thyme
½–1	teaspoon juice from 1 lemon

1. Adjust an oven rack to the lowest position and heat the oven to 250 degrees. Pat the chicken dry with paper towels, tuck the wings behind the back following the illustration on page 58, and season with salt and pepper.

2. Heat the oil in a large Dutch oven over medium-high heat until just smoking. Add the chicken, breast side down, and scatter the onion, garlic, bay leaf, and thyme around the chicken. Cook until the chicken breast is lightly browned, about 5 minutes. Flip the chicken breast side up and continue to cook until the back of the chicken and the vegetables are well browned, 6 to 8 minutes, reducing the heat if the pot begins to scorch.

3. Off the heat, place a large sheet of foil over the pot and press to seal, then cover tightly with the lid. Transfer the pot to the oven and cook until the thickest part of the breast registers 160 to 165 degrees and the thickest part of the thigh registers 170 to 175 degrees on an instant-read thermometer, 80 to 110 minutes.

4. Remove the pot from the oven. Transfer the chicken to a cutting board, tent loosely with foil, and let rest for 20 minutes. Strain the juices from the pot into a fat separator, reserving the strained vegetables. Let the juices settle for about 5 minutes.

5. Add the defatted juices back to the pot, add the strained vegetables and any accumulated juices from the chicken, and cook over low heat until hot. Discard the bay leaf and thyme and season to taste with lemon juice, salt, and pepper. Carve the chicken following the illustrations on page 42 and serve, passing the sauce separately.

➤ VARIATIONS

Chicken en Cocotte with Garlic and Rosemary

Follow the recipe for Chicken en Cocotte with Thyme and Lemon, increasing the amount of crushed garlic to 12 cloves and substituting 2 sprigs fresh rosemary for the thyme. Before returning the strained vegetables to the pot in step 5, mash the cooked garlic with the back of a spoon to create a paste, then whisk into the sauce.

SLICING ONIONS THIN

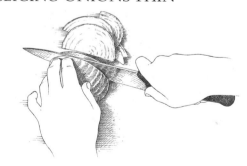

To slice an onion thin, halve it pole to pole, peel it, set it on a cut side, and then slice crosswise.

Chicken en Cocotte with Chorizo, Onion, and Saffron

Follow the recipe for Chicken en Cocotte with Thyme and Lemon, substituting a generous pinch of saffron for the thyme and 1 to 2 teaspoons sherry vinegar for the lemon juice. Before browning the chicken in step 2, brown 4 ounces chorizo, cut into ¼-inch pieces, in the hot oil until golden, about 5 minutes; transfer the chorizo to a small bowl, leaving the fat in the pot. Continue with the recipe as directed, returning the browned chorizo to the pot before covering with the foil in step 3.

Chicken en Cocotte with Ginger and Shiitake Mushrooms

Follow the recipe for Chicken en Cocotte with Thyme and Lemon, substituting 1 to 1½ teaspoons rice wine vinegar for the lemon juice. Add 4 ounces shiitake mushrooms, stemmed, wiped clean, and diced fine, and 1 tablespoon minced or grated fresh ginger to the pot with the onions in step 2. Continue with the recipe as directed, adding 1 more teaspoon minced or grated fresh ginger and 1 tablespoon soy sauce to the sauce in step 5.

TURKEY BREAST EN COCOTTE

COOKING A TURKEY BREAST IS A GREAT alternative to tackling the whole bird. For one thing, many people prefer the white meat of a breast to the dark meat of legs and thighs. It's also much easier to handle (a whole bird can be very unwieldy), yet still provides a substantial amount of meat. Having successfully developed a recipe for chicken en cocotte, we wondered if we could use this same method (cooking the poultry in a covered pot over low heat for an extended period of time) to get the same great results with a turkey breast—perfectly cooked, incredibly moist and tender meat.

Inspecting the variety of turkey breasts available at our local supermarket, we first found ourselves making the decision between bone-in and boneless breasts. Previous experience with other meats led us to believe that bone-in breasts would be more flavorful, and a simple side-by-side test confirmed this. Boneless breasts lacked the depth of flavor of their bone-in counterparts, and they also had a tendency to dry out during cooking. Bone-in turkey breasts tend to vary in size, weighing anywhere from 5 to 10 pounds. After several initial tests, we decided that a 6- to 7-pound turkey breast was ideal—it's large enough to feed a small crowd (up to eight people), but small enough to fit in our 7-quart Dutch oven. To further ensure that a breast of this size easily fit into the pot, we found it helpful to trim the rib bones.

As with chicken, we found that browning the turkey breast was an essential step in developing deep flavor. Adding some aromatics to the pot further rounded out the flavor, and we settled on a combination of onion, carrot, celery, garlic, thyme, and bay leaf. After 1 hour and 45 minutes, our turkey breast was done—the skin was definitely not crisp, but that was not our goal. Instead, we had an extremely tender, juicy, and moist piece of meat.

We knew we could make a simple jus by defatting the juices left in the pot, but we wondered if we could take it a step further and turn it into a quick gravy for a more impressive sauce. Initially, we tried straining and defatting the jus, then thickening it with a roux. This technically left us with gravy, but it lacked the richness and complexity of a gravy made from well-roasted turkey bones.

Left scratching our heads, we took a new approach. After removing the turkey from the pot, we reduced the jus until it had all but evaporated. This did two things. First, it concentrated the turkey flavor and produced a mahogany fond on the bottom of the pot. Second, it separated the fat from the jus. It was into this rendered fat that we stirred flour to make a roux. And by leaving the aromatics in the pot during the whole reduction process we were sure to extract as much flavor from them as possible. We then added a full quart of chicken broth to the pot, brought it to a simmer, and reduced it to a proper gravy consistency, which we strained as tasters waited in anticipation. The result was a deeply flavored gravy reminiscent of Thanksgiving dinner.

With the success of our gravy in hand, we decided to develop a couple of sauce variations that would also complement our turkey breast, including an orange-chipotle sauce and a mole. These simple yet flavorful recipes are easy to prepare and are a great alternative to the whole bird you might make only once a year.

Turkey Breast en Cocotte with Pan Gravy

SERVES 6 TO 8

Many supermarkets are now selling "hotel-style" turkey breasts. Try to avoid these if you can, as they still have the wings attached. If this is the only type of breast you can find, you will simply need to remove the wings before proceeding with the recipe. Be sure to use a 7- to 8-quart Dutch oven here. Don't buy a turkey breast larger than 7 pounds; it won't fit in the pot. For a smaller turkey breast, reduce the cooking time as necessary.

I	(6- to 7-pound) whole bone-in turkey breast
	Salt and ground black pepper
2	tablespoons olive oil
I	medium onion, chopped medium
I	medium carrot, chopped medium
I	celery rib, chopped medium
6	medium garlic cloves, peeled and crushed (see the illustration on page 63)
2	sprigs fresh thyme
I	bay leaf
¼	cup unbleached all-purpose flour
4	cups low-sodium chicken broth

1. Adjust an oven rack to the lowest position and heat the oven to 250 degrees. Using kitchen shears or a chef's knife, trim the rib bones and any excess fat from the turkey, following the illustration at right. Pat the turkey dry with paper towels and season with salt and pepper.

2. Heat the oil in a large Dutch oven over medium-high heat until just smoking. Add the turkey, breast side down and scatter the onion, carrot, celery, garlic, thyme, and bay leaf around the turkey. Cook, turning the breast on its sides and stirring the vegetables as needed, until the turkey and vegetables are well browned, 12 to 16 minutes, reducing the heat if the pot begins to scorch.

3. Off the heat, place a large sheet of foil over the pot and press to seal, then cover tightly with the lid. Transfer the pot to the oven and cook until the thickest part of the breast registers 160 to 165 degrees on an instant-read thermometer, 1½ to 1¾ hours.

4. Remove the pot from the oven. Transfer the turkey to a cutting board, tent loosely with foil, and let rest while making the gravy.

5. Place the pot with the juices and vegetables over medium-high heat and simmer until almost all of the liquid has evaporated, 15 to 20 minutes. Stir in the flour and cook, stirring constantly, until browned, 2 to 5 minutes. Slowly whisk in the chicken broth, bring to a simmer and cook, stirring often, until the gravy is thickened and measures about 2½ cups, 10 to 15 minutes.

6. Strain the gravy through a fine-mesh strainer and season with salt and pepper to taste. Carve the turkey following the illustrations on page 62 and serve, passing the gravy separately.

TRIMMING A TURKEY BREAST

To ensure the turkey breast will fit in the pot, use kitchen shears to trim the rib bones on both sides of the breast following the vertical line of fat.

➤ VARIATIONS

Turkey Breast en Cocotte
with Orange-Chipotle Sauce

Many supermarkets are now selling "hotel-style" turkey breasts. Try to avoid these if you can, as they still have the wings attached. If this is the only type of breast you can find, you will simply need to remove the wings before proceeding with the recipe. Be sure to use a 7- to 8-quart Dutch oven here. Don't buy a turkey breast larger than 7 pounds; it won't fit in the pot. For a smaller turkey breast, reduce the cooking time as necessary.

I	(6- to 7-pound) whole bone-in turkey breast
	Salt and ground black pepper
2	tablespoons olive oil
I	medium onion, chopped medium
6	medium garlic cloves, peeled and crushed (see the illustration on page 63), plus I medium garlic clove, minced or pressed through a garlic press (about I teaspoon)
2	sprigs fresh thyme
I	bay leaf
2	cups orange juice
½	cup sugar
¼	cup white wine vinegar
2	tablespoons minced fresh cilantro leaves
1–2	teaspoons minced chipotle in adobo sauce

1. Adjust an oven rack to the lowest position and heat the oven to 250 degrees. Using kitchen shears or a chef's knife, trim the rib bones and any excess fat from the turkey, following the illustration on page 61. Pat the turkey dry with paper towels and season with salt and pepper.

2. Heat the oil in a large Dutch oven over medium-high heat until just smoking. Add the turkey, breast side down and scatter the onion, crushed garlic, thyme, and bay leaf around the turkey. Cook, turning the breast on its sides and stirring the vegetables as needed, until the turkey and vegetables are well browned, 12 to 16 minutes, reducing the heat if the pot begins to scorch.

3. Off the heat, place a large sheet of foil over the pot and press to seal, then cover tightly with the lid. Transfer the pot to the oven and cook until the thickest part of the breast registers 160 to 165 degrees on an instant-read thermometer, 1½ to 1¾ hours.

4. Remove the pot from the oven. Transfer the turkey to a cutting board, tent loosely with foil, and let rest while making the sauce. Strain the juices from the pot into a fat separator, discarding the strained vegetables. Let the juices settle for about 5 minutes then defat the juices.

5. Add the defatted juices back to the pot and stir in the orange juice, sugar, vinegar, and any accumulated juices from the turkey. Simmer the

CARVING A TURKEY BREAST

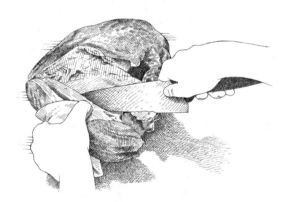

1. Run a carving knife or chef's knife along one side of the breastbone. Use your other hand (with a towel to protect it from the heat) to pry the entire breast half from the bone while cutting, being mindful to keep the skin intact.

2. Once the breast half is completely removed from the bone, lay it flat on the cutting board and slice it on the bias. Repeat the process with the meat on the other side of the breastbone.

sauce over medium-high heat until it is thickened and measures about 1 cup, 10 to 12 minutes.

6. Stir in the cilantro, chipotle, and minced garlic and season the sauce with salt and pepper to taste before serving. Carve the turkey following the illustrations on page 62 and serve, passing the sauce separately.

Turkey Breast en Cocotte with Mole

Many supermarkets are now selling "hotel-style" turkey breasts. Try to avoid these if you can, as they still have the wings attached. If this is the only type of breast you can find, you will simply need to remove the wings before proceeding with the recipe. Be sure to use a 7- to 8-quart Dutch oven here. Don't buy a turkey breast larger than 7 pounds; it won't fit in the pot. For a smaller turkey breast, reduce the cooking time as necessary.

1	(6- to 7-pound) whole bone-in turkey breast
	Salt and ground black pepper
5	tablespoons vegetable oil
1	medium onion, chopped medium
6	medium garlic cloves, peeled and crushed (see the illustration at right), plus 3 medium garlic cloves, minced or pressed through a garlic press (about 1 tablespoon)
2	sprigs fresh thyme
1	bay leaf
2	tablespoons chili powder
2	tablespoons cocoa powder
½	teaspoon ground cinnamon
⅛	teaspoon ground cloves
1	(14.5-ounce) can diced tomatoes, drained
¼	cup raisins
2	tablespoons creamy peanut butter

1. Adjust an oven rack to the lowest position and heat the oven to 250 degrees. Using kitchen shears or a chef's knife, trim the rib bones and any excess fat from the turkey, following the illustration on page 61. Pat the turkey dry with paper towels and season with salt and pepper.

2. Heat 2 tablespoons of the oil in a large Dutch oven over medium-high heat until just smoking.

Add the turkey, breast side down and scatter the onion, crushed garlic, thyme, and bay leaf around the turkey. Cook, turning the breast on its sides and stirring the vegetables as needed, until the turkey and vegetables are well browned, 12 to 16 minutes, reducing the heat if the pot begins to scorch.

3. Off the heat, place a large sheet of foil over the pot and press to seal, then cover tightly with the lid. Transfer the pot to the oven and cook until the thickest part of the breast registers 160 to 165 degrees on an instant-read thermometer, 1½ to 1¾ hours.

4. Remove the pot from the oven. Transfer the turkey to a cutting board, tent loosely with foil, and let rest while making the sauce. Strain the juices from the pot into a fat separator, reserving the strained vegetables. Let the juices settle for about 5 minutes, then defat the juices; set aside.

5. Meanwhile, add the remaining 3 tablespoons oil, minced garlic, chili powder, cocoa powder, cinnamon, and cloves to the pot and cook over medium heat until fragrant, about 1 minute. Stir in the defatted juices, strained vegetables, any accumulated juices from the turkey, tomatoes, raisins, and peanut butter and simmer over medium-high heat, stirring occasionally, until slightly thickened, 8 to 10 minutes.

6. Discard the thyme and bay leaf, then puree the sauce in a blender until smooth, about 20 seconds. Season with salt and pepper to taste. Carve the turkey following the illustrations on page 62 and serve, passing the mole separately.

CRUSHING GARLIC

Crush the garlic cloves with the side of a large chef's knife and discard the loosened skin.

Cooking en Cocotte 101

Cooking en cocotte shares some similarities with braising—both techniques use covered pots and low-temperature ovens to yield tender, flavorful meat. But unlike braising, where lots of liquid is added to the pot, with this method meat or fish is placed in a dry pot and left to cook in nothing more than the essence of its own juices (and some aromatics). The result is moist and tender meat with a deep flavor undiluted by additional liquid. Here are the key things to remember when cooking en cocotte:

1. Include Just a Few Aromatics and No Liquid: Add a small amount of potently flavored aromatics to help flavor the sauce—too many vegetables create a steamier environment which washes out the flavor of the meat. Resist the temptation to add liquid to the pot—again, liquid creates too much steam and dilutes the flavors. Instead, the meat or fish cooks in its own juices—when the juices are released by the meat, a moist environment is created so that the meat cooks gently and its flavors are concentrated. You will be surprised by the amount of flavorful liquid left behind in the pot.

2. Brown the Meat: We brown meat (but not fish) on the stovetop to enhance its flavor. Due to the low oven temperature, we also find it beneficial to sauté the aromatics on the stovetop with the meat. This step develops their flavor and softens their texture, evaporates any excess moisture, and, finally, warms the pot so it is not completely cold when it goes into the oven. You need a large (7- to 8-quart) Dutch oven to ensure that large pieces of meat will fit.

3. Seal the Pot Tightly: Cover the pot with aluminum foil before adding the lid to ensure that the juices stay in the pot while cooking. Loose-fitting lids, with no foil, allow too much steam to escape, which will weaken the flavors and extend the cooking time unnecessarily.

4. Cook in a 250-Degree Oven: After testing a range of oven temperatures below 400 degrees, we found that lower was in fact better, yielding incredibly tender meat thanks to the delicate heat. Cooking in a low oven ensures a steady heat environment, which allows the internal temperature of the meat to rise slowly. This extended cooking at 250 degrees produces moist, flavorful meat with concentrated flavors.

5. Cook the Meat (or Fish) Until Just Done: Unlike braising, where the meat is generally cooked until tender and falling off the bone, meat cooked en cocotte is cooked until it is just done—we like to take the temperature of the meat to ensure it is not overcooked or undercooked. Beef and lamb are cooked until medium rare, pork and chicken until they are just cooked through, and fish until it is opaque and flakes apart when gently prodded with a paring knife.

6. Let It Rest: Transfer the meat (or fish) to a cutting board and let it rest while you finish making the sauce. This is especially important for meat, since resting allows the juices to redistribute within the meat. This step also gives you time to finish the sauce or jus in the pot to spoon over the top of the meat or fish before serving.

PORK ROAST EN COCOTTE

ROASTING PORK EN COCOTTE AT FIRST SEEMED like a dicey proposition to us. Our options for roasts were obviously limited to the big (and fatty) pork shoulder roast (also known as Boston butt) and pork loins of various cuts. Both options seemed to have issues that would make them unsuitable for this particular cooking method: The pork shoulder is well marbled with fat and we suspected that this cut, though perfect for braising, would release lots of unwanted oil into the pot, while lean pork loins would virtually steam to inedible toughness in a covered pot. But we were willing to give it a try anyway and of the two options we thought the loin would be the least problematic.

We knew we wanted a boneless cut, which would be much easier to fit into the pot than a bone-in option, but there is more than one choice. Tasters slightly preferred the blade-end loin to the center-cut loin for its flavor and juiciness, which is due in part to the fat that separates the two muscle sections at one end of the roast. But both types of pork loin roasts will work in this recipe—it's the size of the loin that's most important. Pork loins can come in different shapes and sizes depending on how they've been butchered. Pieces that weigh the same can be long and thin or short and wide (see page 67 for more information). For practical purposes, a shorter, wider piece (about 7 to 8 inches long and 4 to 5 inches wide) is ideal simply because it fits into the pot. We also found that tying the meat made for easier browning and more even cooking.

We browned the meat on the stovetop in a large Dutch oven, added a handful of aromatics, covered the pot, and cooked it slowly in a 250-degree oven. The result was just what we had hoped—an incredibly juicy, tender roast. We were surprised to learn that, at such a low oven temperature, a mere extra half-pound can add 15 to 20 minutes to the cooking time.

It was now time to focus on adding flavor to the pork. We decided to try adding herbes de Provence, which is a mixture of dried herbs used frequently in the south of France and typically includes basil, fennel seed, lavender, marjoram, rosemary, sage, summer savory, and thyme. We seasoned the pork with the herbs along with salt and pepper before browning it. Tasters enjoyed the subtle flavors that the herbs lent the finished dish; as the herbs simmered in the juices slowly being released as the pork cooked, their flavor bloomed and intensified.

But the herbs alone weren't delivering enough flavor. Since fruit is a traditional pairing with pork, we decided to try adding apples to the mix. But we also knew the apples would release a considerable amount of liquid which, as we had learned from other en cocotte recipes, would dull the flavor of the meat. In addition, we knew the apples would take up a fair amount of space in the pot, preventing the pork from browning evenly. To combat these problems, we removed the browned pork to a plate and cooked the apples separately on the stovetop to allow some of their juices to evaporate. We then added the pork back to the pot to let the dish finish in the oven. We were pleasantly surprised with the results—we now had a rustic, chunky applesauce to accompany our pork. To streamline the process, we decided to add the aromatics to the pot with the apples. Some shallots not only helped offset the sweetness of the dish but they also gave the mixture an appealing texture.

To finish, we created a variation, substituting a flavorful spice rub for the herbes de Provence. Tasters liked a combination of coriander, paprika, cumin, and anise, as well as a pinch of cayenne for heat and a touch of brown sugar for sweetness. These spices have a tendency to burn, however, so we found it best to brown the roast lightly over a more moderate heat. We replaced the apples and shallots with a few sliced onions, which we caramelized, providing a sweet contrast to the potent spice rub.

Pork Roast en Cocotte with Apples and Shallots

SERVES 4 TO 6

This recipe works best with a pork roast that is about 7 to 8 inches long and 4 to 5 inches wide. We found that leaving a ¼-inch-thick layer of fat on top of the roast is ideal; if your roast has a thicker fat cap, trim it back to be about ¼ inch thick. You can find herbes de Provence in most large grocery stores; however, 1 teaspoon each dried thyme, dried rosemary, and dried marjoram can be substituted.

1	(2½- to 3-pound) boneless pork loin roast, trimmed and tied at 1½-inch intervals
1	tablespoon herbes de Provence (see note)
	Salt and ground black pepper
3	tablespoons vegetable oil
8	medium shallots, peeled and quartered
1	pound Golden Delicious or Granny Smith apples (2 to 3 medium), peeled, cored, and cut into ½-inch-thick wedges
¼	teaspoon sugar
1	tablespoon unsalted butter

1. Adjust an oven rack to the lowest position and heat the oven to 250 degrees. Pat the pork dry with paper towels, sprinkle the herbes de Provence evenly over the pork, and season with salt and pepper.

2. Heat 2 tablespoons of the oil in a large Dutch oven over medium-high heat until just smoking. Brown the pork well on all sides, 7 to 10 minutes, reducing the heat if the pot begins to scorch. Transfer the pork to a large plate.

3. Add the remaining 1 tablespoon oil to the pot and heat over medium heat until shimmering. Add the shallots and cook, stirring often, until golden, about 3 minutes. Stir in the apples and sugar and cook, stirring often, until golden, 5 to 7 minutes.

4. Off the heat, nestle the pork, along with any accumulated juices, into the pot. Place a large sheet of foil over the pot and press to seal, then cover tightly with the lid. Transfer the pot to the oven and cook until the very center of the roast registers 140 to 145 degrees on an instant-read thermometer, 35 to 55 minutes.

5. Remove the pot from the oven. Transfer the pork to a cutting board, tent loosely with foil, and let rest until the center of the roast registers 150 degrees on an instant-read thermometer, about 20 minutes. Stir the butter into the apple-shallot mixture, season with salt and pepper to taste, and cover to keep warm.

6. Remove the twine, slice the pork thin, and transfer to a serving platter. Spoon the apple-shallot mixture over the pork and serve.

➤ VARIATION

Spice-Rubbed Pork Roast en Cocotte with Caramelized Onions

This recipe works best prepared with a pork roast that is about 7 to 8 inches long and 4 to 5 inches wide. We found that leaving a ¼-inch-thick layer of fat on top of the roast is ideal; if your roast has a thicker fat cap, trim it back to be about ¼ inch thick. To prevent the spices from burning when browning the pork in step 2, be sure to use medium heat.

1	(2½- to 3-pound) boneless pork loin roast, trimmed and tied at 1½-inch intervals
5	teaspoons ground coriander
2	teaspoons paprika
1	teaspoon salt
1	teaspoon brown sugar
¾	teaspoon ground anise seeds
¾	teaspoon ground cumin
	Pinch cayenne pepper
3	tablespoons vegetable oil
2	medium onions, peeled, halved, and sliced thin (see the illustration on page 59)
3	medium garlic cloves, minced or pressed through a garlic press (about 1 tablespoon)
1	tablespoon unsalted butter

1. Adjust an oven rack to the lowest position and heat the oven to 250 degrees. Pat the pork dry with paper towels. Toss the coriander, paprika, salt, brown sugar, anise, cumin, and cayenne together in a small bowl, then rub the mixture evenly over the pork.

2. Heat 2 tablespoons of the oil in a large Dutch oven over medium heat until just smoking. Lightly brown the pork on all sides, 5 to 7 minutes, reducing the heat if the pot begins to scorch or the spices begin to burn. Transfer the pork to a large plate.

3. Add the remaining 1 tablespoon oil to the pot and heat over medium heat until shimmering. Add the onions, cover, and cook until softened and wet, about 5 minutes. Remove the lid and continue to cook the onions, stirring often, until dry and well browned, 10 to 12 minutes. Stir in the garlic and cook until fragrant, about 30 seconds.

4. Off the heat, nestle the pork, along with any accumulated juices, into the pot. Place a large sheet of foil over the pot and press to seal, then cover tightly with the lid. Transfer the pot to the oven and cook until the very center of the roast registers 140 to 145 degrees on an instant-read thermometer, 35 to 55 minutes.

THE RIGHT ROAST

Buying the right pork loin will make all the difference in these en cocotte recipes because the pork needs to fit inside the pot. Look for 2½- to 3-pound pork loin roasts that are wide and short and steer clear from those that are long and narrow. We prefer a roast cut from the blade end, however a center-cut roast (which is more common) works just fine.

LONG AND NARROW

At 12 inches long and 3 inches wide, this pork loin will not fit in a large Dutch oven.

WIDE AND SHORT

At 8 inches long and nearly 5 inches wide, this pork loin fits comfortably in a large Dutch oven.

5. Remove the pot from the oven. Transfer the pork to a cutting board, tent loosely with foil, and let rest until the center of the roast registers 150 degrees on an instant-read thermometer, about 20 minutes. Stir the butter into the onions, season with salt and pepper to taste, and cover to keep warm.

6. Remove the twine, slice the pork thin, and transfer to a serving platter. Spoon the onions over the pork and serve.

BEEF EN COCOTTE

COOKING BEEF EN COCOTTE, WE HOPED, would combine the best of both braising and roasting. If it worked, it would allow us to take an inexpensive cut of beef and make it tender in much the same way that braising does—the low, slow heat allows the fibers time to break down, rendering a tough piece of meat tender. But like roasting, cooking beef en cocotte would allow us to cook the meat to the desired doneness (such as medium-rare) without having to spend a lot of money on an already-tender, prime piece of meat. Three inexpensive roasts immediately came to mind as possibilities for this method: eye round roast (a lean cut from the leg that usually becomes tender when cooked slowly), chuck roast (the popular choice for stews and pot roast, which contains a higher than usual amount of sinew and collagen), and top sirloin roast (which is lean with a bold, beefy flavor and ideal for grill-roasting and roasting to medium-rare).

To determine which roast we liked best, we seared each in a Dutch oven, then placed the covered pot in the oven at 250 degrees. We were surprised to discover how quickly these roasts cooked—they all took about 25 minutes to reach medium-rare. This was not enough time for the chuck roast to become tender; instead, it was unbearably chewy, with strands of sinew throughout. The eye round roast was a bit more promising, but was still tough despite its rosy interior. Top sirloin was far and away the best option as it was noticeably more tender, with concentrated beef flavor.

Sticking with top sirloin, we settled on a 3- to 4-pound roast, which we trimmed of excess fat and then tied prior to searing to help ensure even cooking. With our cut of meat and cooking time settled, all we needed to do was work on building other flavors to complement the beef.

Onions are a classic accompaniment to beef and we thought the sweetness of caramelized onions would provide a nice balance of flavors. We had the best results caramelizing the onions in the pot after the beef was seared. To boost the flavor of the onions we added some garlic and then deglazed the pot with sherry, scraping up the fond as the liquid reduced. (Since we didn't want liquid in the pot when it went into the oven, we made sure to let the sherry reduce before adding the seared beef back in.) We placed the beef on top of the onions, covered the pot, and then into the oven it went. Once the meat was cooked to medium-rare, we let it rest while we completed our sauce. We added chicken broth to the onions and reduced the mixture slightly to concentrate the flavors, then finished the sauce with a little butter for richness. For another classic pairing, we decided to create a variation with a boldly flavored mushroom sauce. We were pleased with the results—cooking beef en cocotte allowed us to take an inexpensive cut of meat and turn it into a tender, perfectly cooked roast.

Beef en Cocotte with Caramelized Onions

SERVES 6 TO 8

Be sure to trim the meat well or you'll wind up with a greasy sauce; feel free to ask your butcher to trim and tie the roast for you. If you prefer beef either more or less cooked than medium-rare, see "Testing Meat for Doneness" on page 7.

1   (3- to 4-pound) top sirloin beef roast, trimmed and tied once around the middle (see the illustration on page 69)
    Salt and ground black pepper
3   tablespoons vegetable oil
3   medium onions, peeled, halved, and sliced thin (see the illustration on page 59)
3   medium garlic cloves, peeled and crushed (see the illustration on page 63)
¼   cup dry sherry
2   cups low-sodium chicken broth
1   tablespoon unsalted butter

1. Adjust an oven rack to the lowest position and heat the oven to 250 degrees. Pat the beef dry with paper towels and season with salt and pepper.

2. Heat 2 tablespoons of the oil in a large Dutch oven over medium-high heat until just smoking. Brown the beef well on all sides, 7 to 10 minutes, reducing the heat if the pot begins to scorch. Transfer the beef to a large plate.

3. Add the remaining 1 tablespoon oil to the pot and heat over medium heat until shimmering. Add the onions and garlic, cover, and cook until softened and wet, about 5 minutes. Remove the lid and continue to cook the onions, stirring often, until dry and well browned, 10 to 12 minutes. Stir in the sherry, scraping up any browned bits, and cook until almost all of the liquid has evaporated, about 1 minute.

4. Off the heat, nestle the beef, along with any accumulated juices, into the pot. Place a large sheet of foil over the pot and press to seal, then cover tightly with the lid. Transfer the pot to the oven and cook until the very center of the roast registers 125 degrees on an instant-read thermometer (for medium-rare), 20 to 30 minutes.

5. Remove the pot from the oven. Transfer the beef to a cutting board, tent loosely with foil, and let rest for 20 minutes. Stir the chicken broth into the onions and simmer over medium-high heat until slightly thickened, about 2 minutes. Off the heat, whisk in the butter, season with salt and pepper to taste, and cover to keep warm.

6. Remove the twine, slice the meat against the grain into ¼-inch-thick slices, and transfer to a serving platter. Spoon the sauce over the meat and serve.

➤ VARIATION

Beef en Cocotte with Mushroom Sauce

If you can't find cremini mushrooms, feel free to substitute button, shiitake, or finely chopped portobello mushrooms. Be sure to trim the meat well or you'll wind up with a greasy sauce; feel free to ask your butcher to trim and tie the roast for you. If you prefer beef either more or less cooked than medium-rare, see "Testing Meat for Doneness" on page 7.

1	(3- to 4-pound) top sirloin beef roast, trimmed and tied once around the middle (see the illustration at right)
	Salt and ground black pepper
3	tablespoons vegetable oil
5	ounces cremini mushrooms, trimmed, wiped clean, and sliced ¼ inch thick (see note)
1	medium onion, minced
3	medium garlic cloves, peeled and crushed (see the illustration on page 63)
½	ounce dried porcini mushrooms, rehydrated, liquid strained and reserved, and mushrooms minced
2	sprigs fresh tarragon
1	tablespoon tomato paste
¼	cup dry white wine
2	tablespoons cognac
1½	cups low-sodium chicken broth
1	tablespoon unsalted butter

1. Adjust an oven rack to the lowest position and heat the oven to 250 degrees. Pat the beef dry with paper towels and season with salt and pepper.

2. Heat 2 tablespoons of the oil in a large Dutch oven over medium-high heat until just smoking. Brown the beef well on all sides, 7 to 10 minutes, reducing the heat if the pot begins to scorch. Transfer the beef to a large plate.

3. Add the remaining 1 tablespoon of oil to the pot and heat over medium heat until shimmering. Add the cremini mushrooms, onion, garlic, porcini mushrooms, and tarragon, cover, and cook until the mushrooms are softened and wet, about 5 minutes. Remove the lid and continue to cook,

stirring often, until the mushrooms are dry and well browned, 10 to 12 minutes.

4. Stir in the tomato paste and cook until lightly browned, about 30 seconds. Stir in the reserved porcini soaking liquid, wine, and cognac, scraping up any browned bits, and cook until almost all of the liquid has evaporated, about 5 minutes.

5. Off the heat, nestle the beef, along with any accumulated juices, into the pot. Place a large sheet of foil over the pot and press to seal, then cover tightly with the lid. Transfer the pot to the oven and cook until the very center of the roast registers 120 to 125 degrees on an instant-read thermometer (for medium-rare), 20 to 30 minutes.

6. Remove the pot from the oven. Transfer the beef to a cutting board, tent loosely with foil, and let rest for 20 minutes. Stir the chicken broth into the vegetables and simmer over medium-high heat until slightly thickened, about 2 minutes. Off the heat, remove the tarragon, whisk in the butter, season with salt and pepper to taste, and cover to keep warm.

7. Remove the twine, slice the meat against the grain into ¼-inch-thick slices, and transfer to a serving platter. Spoon the sauce over the meat and serve.

TYING TOP SIRLOIN

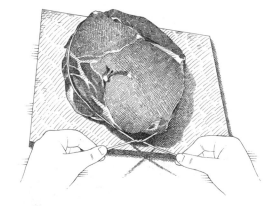

To correct for an unevenly cut or oddly shaped top sirloin roast, and to ensure even cooking, tie a piece of kitchen twine around the center of the roast.

EQUIPMENT: Dutch Ovens

A good Dutch oven (variously called a stockpot, round oven, or casserole by manufacturers) is absolutely a kitchen essential. It is heavier and thicker than a real stockpot, allowing it to retain and conduct heat more effectively, and deeper than a skillet, so it can handle large cuts of meat and cooking liquid. Dutch ovens are the best choice for braises, en cocotte cooking, stews, and chilis, as they can go on the stovetop to sear foods and then into the oven to finish with steady, slow cooking. Their tall sides also make them useful for deep-frying, and many cooks press Dutch ovens into service for jobs like boiling pasta. But with prices for these kitchen workhorses ranging from $40 to six times that price, we wondered if more money buys you a better pot. We rounded up nine Dutch ovens and brought them into the test kitchen to find out.

For our first test, we prepared a beef stew that starts on the stovetop and then moves to the oven. In each pan we browned cubes of beef in batches and observed whether the pan heated evenly and consistently without burning the drippings. After the long, slow cooking in the oven, we tasted the stew to see if the meat had become fork-tender and the broth had reduced to an intense flavor. Of all the tests we did, this was the most important, because it focused on the unique abilities of Dutch ovens. As expected, the pricey All-Clad and Le Creuset pots sailed through with flying colors. Surprisingly, so did a few of the others.

We noticed a few trends. Our favorite pots from All-Clad and Le Creuset measure 9¾ inches across, enabling them to brown 3½ pounds of beef in three batches, something narrower pots couldn't do—the narrowest one necessitated browning the beef in five batches, a serious flaw. A couple of the pots were also too lightweight and browned the meat unevenly.

Next we tested heat transfer and retention by frying a pound of frozen French fries. The best pans retained heat well enough to prevent the temperature of the oil from dropping too precipitously when the fries were added. Those whose oil temperature dropped too much or took too long to recover produced soggy, greasy fries. An unexpected issue emerged during this test. Fries cooked in uncoated cast-iron pans tasted rusty. Cast iron is a great choice for a Dutch oven because it holds heat so well. But cast iron will react with many foods. Some manufacturers (such as Le Creuset, Tramontina, and Mario Batali) coat their cast iron with a layer of enamel to avoid this.

For our last test, we cooked a triple batch of white rice in each Dutch oven to see how they simmered on very low heat. All but one pot made fluffy rice with intact grains.

When all the smoke and steam and sizzling fry oil cleared, the most expensive pots came out on top. Other than price, it's hard to argue with the pots made by All-Clad and Le Creuset. (Some of our test cooks prefer the sturdiness of the latter, while others opt for the lighter, easier-to-manage All-Clad pot.)

Although we weren't surprised by our winners, we were shocked at their narrow margin of victory. The $40 Tramontina 6.5-quart Cast-Iron Dutch Oven held its own and kept up with the winners in almost every test. While our test cooks are not ready to trade in their favorite Dutch ovens, the Tramontina is a real find for budget-minded cooks.

If you're willing to spend $100 on a Dutch oven, and you have the biceps to handle it, the 6-quart Mario Batali pot performs nearly as well as the Le Creuset and All-Clad pots. (It should be noted, however, that while this size works for most recipes in this book, the recipes in this chapter require a 7- to 8-quart Dutch oven.) Yes, the browning wasn't perfect, but that seems like a minor quibble that most cooks would never notice. These are two good choices, both reasonably priced. Now that's good news.

THE BEST DUTCH OVENS

The All-Clad Stainless 8-quart Stockpot ($260) and the 7¼-quart Le Creuset Round French Oven ($260) are our top choices. (The All-Clad is the best choice for cooks who prefer a lighter pot.) For those looking for a less-expensive alternative, the Tramontina Cast-Iron Dutch Oven ($40) and the Mario Batali Italian Essentials Pot by Copco ($100) are both solid choices and are our best buys.

ALL-CLAD STAINLESS
STOCKPOT

LE CREUSET ROUND
FRENCH OVEN

TRAMONTINA CAST-IRON
DUTCH OVEN

MARIO BATALI ITALIAN
ESSENTIALS POT
BY COPCO

LEG OF LAMB EN COCOTTE

LIKE CHICKEN, LAMB IS COMMONLY COOKED en cocotte in France. In particular, we found many recipes for leg of lamb en cocotte, so we started our testing there. A bone-in leg of lamb makes for a dramatic presentation, but we also knew we had no chance of fitting one in our Dutch oven, so we turned to boneless. We could buy one of two portions into which the leg is traditionally divided: the shank end (the middle part of the leg) and the sirloin end (the top part of the leg). In terms of flavor and tenderness, tasters found little difference from section to section. The shank end, however, is much easier to work with and tie into a tidy roast, and also tends to be meatier. The sirloin end, by comparison, is often a little lopsided and unevenly cut.

We found that the particular technique used to remove the bone from the meat is quite important. Most butchers use one of two methods—butterflying or corkscrewing—and they produce distinctly different roasts. A corkscrew boneless leg of lamb is more common but the roast has a somewhat awkward, corkscrew-like shape. A butterflied boneless leg of lamb is slightly less common, but has a more regular shape. However, butterflied legs of lamb tend to be butchered poorly and cut into several pieces—something you don't notice until you get home because a boneless leg of lamb (both butterflied

and corkscrewed) usually comes wrapped in elastic netting. Though either will work, we decided to go with the corkscrew leg of lamb since it's readily available, and once it's tied the awkward shape isn't really an issue (see page 12 for more information).

Since lamb's gamey flavor comes mostly from the fat, we found it necessary to trim as much as possible before cooking. This gave the finished roast a milder flavor that tasters appreciated. With our leg of lamb trimmed, tied, and ready to go, the recipe was simply a matter of following our en cocotte method. We seared the lamb on all sides, removed the pot from the heat, and discarded any accumulated fat in the pot. Garlic and rosemary are traditional flavorings for lamb, and we saw no reason to deviate from this classic combination, so we simply added a couple of sprigs of rosemary and a handful of sliced garlic cloves to the pot with the lamb just before it went into the oven. In just an hour we had a simple yet boldly flavored dish to add to our en cocotte repertoire.

Leg of Lamb en Cocotte with Garlic and Rosemary

SERVES 6 TO 8

We prefer the shank end of the boneless leg of lamb here (rather than the sirloin end). There are two methods butchers use to remove the bone from the meat, referred to as corkscrewed and butterflied; we find the corkscrewed type much easier to work with but a butterflied leg of lamb will also work. For more information on buying lamb, see page 12. If you prefer lamb either more or less cooked than medium-rare, see "Testing Meat for Doneness" on page 7.

1	(4- to 5-pound) shank end, boneless leg of lamb, trimmed and tied (see the illustrations on page 72) Salt and ground black pepper
2	tablespoons olive oil
8	medium garlic cloves, peeled and sliced thin (see the illustration at left)
2	sprigs fresh rosemary

1. Adjust an oven rack to the lowest position and heat the oven to 250 degrees. Pat the lamb dry with paper towels and season with salt and pepper.

SLICING GARLIC

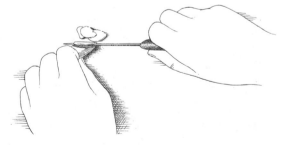

Slicing garlic is a nice alternative to mincing or pressing it through a garlic press because the slices add both textural and visual appeal—it's a technique often used in rustic Italian cooking. To slice a clove of garlic, simply peel the clove, then slice it thin with a paring knife. Whether you slice it widthwise or lengthwise is up to you—cutting it widthwise is certainly easier, but the long oval slices from cutting it lengthwise are a bit more attractive in the finished dish.

2. Heat the oil in a large Dutch oven over medium-high heat until just smoking. Brown the lamb well on all sides, 7 to 10 minutes, reducing the heat if the pot begins to scorch. Transfer the lamb to a large plate.

3. Pour off all of the fat from the pot. Add the garlic and rosemary and nestle the lamb, with any accumulated juices, into the pot. Place a large sheet of foil over the and press to seal, then cover tightly with the lid. Transfer the pot to the oven and cook until the very center of the lamb registers 125 degrees on an instant-read thermometer (for medium-rare), 45 to 60 minutes.

4. Remove the pot from the oven. Transfer the lamb to a cutting board, tent with foil, and let rest for 20 minutes. Remove the rosemary from the jus in the pot, then cover to keep the jus warm.

5. Remove the twine, slice the lamb into ¼-inch-thick slices against the grain, and transfer to a serving platter. Spoon the jus over the lamb and serve.

➤ VARIATION

Moroccan-Spiced Leg of Lamb en Cocotte with Olives

Follow the recipe for Leg of Lamb en Cocotte with Garlic and Rosemary, omitting the rosemary. Add ½ cup pitted green olives, 4 strips lemon zest (see at right), 1½ teaspoons coriander seeds, 1 cinnamon stick, and ½ teaspoon cumin seeds to the pot with the garlic. Stir 1 teaspoon lemon juice into the jus before serving.

REMOVING STRIPS OF CITRUS ZEST

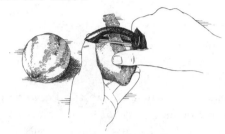

Run a vegetable peeler from pole to pole to remove long, wide strips of zest.

FISH EN COCOTTE

FISH IS WELL SUITED TO A VARIETY OF PREPARATIONS, from pan-searing, baking, and steaming to grilling and oven-roasting. Some types of fish have a high fat content and some are quite lean, but they all have one trait in common: They tend to cook fairly quickly. Since the whole premise of cooking en cocotte is to slow down cooking to concentrate flavor, we were skeptical that this technique would successfully translate to fish. Nevertheless, we decided to head into the kitchen to find out just how far we could push the limits of cooking en cocotte.

Salmon is the fish most often found on home dinner tables, so we started there. We knew it would be important to have uniform pieces of fish that would cook evenly, so we settled on using a whole

TYING A BONELESS LAMB ROAST

1. Slip a 5-foot piece of twine under the lamb roast and tie a double knot, then loop the long end of twine under and around the roast.

2. Run the long end through the loop. Repeat this procedure down the length of the roast.

3. Roll the roast over and run the twine under and around each loop.

4. Once finished, tie the end of the twine to the original knot.

center-cut fillet that we could cut ourselves into four individual servings. (That said, if only individual fillets are available, just be sure that they are of even size and thickness.) We also found it best to remove the skin from the salmon so the actual flesh of the fish would pick up the flavors of the aromatics. Removing the skin also made our final sauce less greasy. As we had done with our other en cocotte recipes, we started by searing the fish to develop a crust and deepen its flavor. Leeks, with their delicate, onion-like sweetness, are a nice complement to salmon so we decided to use them as our aromatic. After we seared the salmon, we sautéed the leeks (along with some thyme and garlic) until they softened, then placed the seared

fish on top of the leeks, and placed the covered pot in a 250-degree oven, where the fish took about 30 minutes to cook through.

The results were promising, but we wondered if we could streamline the process even further: Was it really necessary to sear the salmon? For our next test we skipped the searing and were happy to discover that this extra step was not necessary with fish. By not searing the fish, we got just what we wanted: perfectly cooked, moist salmon that flaked apart into large buttery chunks. After removing the salmon from the pot we added a healthy dose of white wine to the leeks and simmered the mixture until it had reduced slightly, then whisked in some butter for

EQUIPMENT: Instant-Read Thermometers

In the test kitchen, we always use an instant-read thermometer to determine when meat is optimally cooked. (We also use it to check the temperature of bread, caramel sauce, and candy, and to test the temperature of oil when frying.) Our favorite instant-read thermometer is the ThermoWorks Super-Fast Thermapen, a test kitchen workhorse that quickly provides accurate readings across a broad range of temperatures. But at $89, the Thermapen isn't cheap. And in the past, the only inexpensive instant-read thermometers available were mediocre dial-face models. Dial-face thermometers are hard to read, and their sensors are in the wrong place—more than an inch up the stem. In contrast, digital instant-read thermometers have their sensors on the very tip of the probe, making them easy to use in both shallow liquids and deep roasts.

But in recent years, cheaper digital instant-read thermometers have become available. Could any of them approach the performance of our trusty Thermapen? We purchased eight digital instant-read thermometers, all priced under $25, and put them through their paces in the kitchen. Three of the models we tested (Cooper-Atkins, CDN Candy, and Polder 363-90) weren't totally accurate in boiling water and/or ice water. What's more, none of the offenders featured a calibrating function.

In our next test—taking the temperature of hot oil—testers' hands became uncomfortably hot with the slower models. Fast response time proved to be an especially important factor in our ratings.

Does the size of the thermometer make a difference? Bigger is better, but only to a point. With its mammoth 8¼-inch probe, the CDN Candy thermometer had no trouble finding the center

of our biggest roast, but it was cumbersome with smaller items. At the other end of the spectrum, the probes on the CDN Q2-450, Cooper-Atkins, and Polder 371 were too short (just 2¾ inches) to reach the center of a big roast. The ideal probe length is 4 to 5 inches.

Some of the thermometers include "extra" features—such as auto shutoff and minimum/maximum temperature memory—but these were deemed nonessential. Testers did value thermometers that could be calibrated. They also liked thermometers that registered a wide range of temperatures, from below zero (for frozen items) to 400 degrees.

In the end, none of our cheap contenders could match the speed, temperature range, or accuracy of the Thermapen, but the CDN ProAccurate Quick Tip Digital Cooking Thermometer came pretty close, and for a fraction of the price.

THE BEST INSTANT-READ THERMOMETERS

The ThermoWorks Super-Fast Thermapen 211-476 is fast, accurate, and easy to use. The Thermapen also has the widest temperature range (−58 to 572 degrees), but note its hefty price tag—$89. The CDN ProAccurate Quick Tip Digital Cooking Thermometer DTQ450 was not quite as fast as the mighty Thermapen, but fast enough, and its low price, $17.95, puts it in reach of most cooks.

THERMOWORKS

CDN PROACCURATE

richness before spooning it over the salmon.

Pleased with the results of our salmon en cocotte, we turned our attention to two other popular fish: halibut and swordfish. For the halibut, we settled on using steaks rather than fillets. But steaks vary considerably in size depending on the weight of the particular fish. Our advice is this: Inspect the steaks in the fish case and choose the two that are closest in size. This approach ensures that the steaks will cook at the same rate. We found the ideal size steak to be between 10 and 12 inches in length and roughly 1¼ inches thick. Steaks do have cartilage at either end that contains small bones. Cutting off this cartilage ensures that the steaks will fit neatly in the pot and diminishes the likelihood that the small bones located there will end up on your dinner plate.

The halibut took a little longer to cook through than the salmon (about 10 minutes longer), but the results were just as satisfying. After trying a variety of relishes, salsas, flavored butters, and vinaigrettes, tasters all agreed that a simple combination of olive oil, gar-lic, and tomatoes best complemented the lean halibut. Pan roasting sliced garlic in extra-virgin olive oil drew out its flavor, and once the garlic was golden brown, we stirred in some cherry tomatoes and placed the halibut on top. As the fish cooked, the tomatoes began to break down, releasing their juices and helping to build a sauce. For a final hit of bold flavor, we added some capers, thyme, and red pepper flakes. Finishing with another splash of extra-virgin olive oil rounded out the flavors and completed the dish.

Finally, we turned our attention to the swordfish. Swordfish is relatively meaty, so we knew it could

stand up to a boldly flavored sauce, and we thought that chermoula might be just what this dish needed. Chermoula is a traditional Moroccan sauce or paste that is usually used as marinade for fish and typically consists of generous amounts of cilantro, lemon, garlic, and olive oil. Carrots are a nice complement to chermoula, so we decided to incorporate them into our dish. We grated the carrots (for quicker cooking) and after sautéing them we added the chermoula, nestling the swordfish on top. When the fish was done, we transferred it to a platter and spooned the sauce on top. Tasters raved about the combination of flavors and the moist, tender fish.

Elegant enough for a dinner party, yet simple enough for a weeknight, these flavorful dishes will undoubtedly become instant classics.

Salmon en Cocotte with Leeks and White Wine

SERVES 4

To ensure uniform pieces of fish that cook at the same rate, we prefer to buy a whole center-cut fillet and cut it into evenly sized individual fillets ourselves. If buying individual fillets, make sure they are the same size and thickness. If the fillets are thicker or thinner than 1¼ inches, you may need to adjust the cooking time slightly. If you can only find skin-on fillets, be sure to remove the skin before cooking or the sauce will be greasy; have the fishmonger do this for you, or see the illustration at left. You can substitute artic char or cod fillets for the salmon.

1	(1¾- to 2-pound) skinless salmon fillet, about 1½ inches at thickest part (see note)
	Salt and ground black pepper
2	tablespoons extra virgin olive oil
2	medium leeks, white and light green parts only, halved lengthwise, sliced thin, and rinsed thoroughly (see the illustrations on page 107)
2	sprigs fresh thyme
2	medium garlic cloves, minced or pressed through a garlic press (about 2 teaspoons)
½	cup dry white wine
2	tablespoons unsalted butter, cut into 2 pieces

1. Adjust an oven rack to the lowest position and heat the oven to 250 degrees. Following the

SKINNING SALMON FILLETS

Starting at one end of the fillet, slide the knife between the skin and flesh, until you can grab hold of the skin with paper towel. Holding the skin firmly, continue to cut the flesh from the skin until it is completely removed.

illustration on page 53, trim any whitish fat from the belly of the fillet, then cut the fish into 4 equal pieces. Pat the salmon dry with paper towels and season with salt and pepper.

2. Heat the oil in a large Dutch oven over medium-low heat until shimmering. Add the leeks, thyme, and a pinch of salt, cover, and cook until softened, 8 to 10 minutes. Stir in the garlic and cook until fragrant, about 30 seconds. Remove the pot from the heat.

3. Lay the salmon, skinned side down, on top of the leeks. Place a large sheet of foil over the pot and press to seal, then cover tightly with the lid. Transfer the pot to the oven and cook until the salmon is opaque and flakes apart when gently prodded with a paring knife, 25 to 30 minutes.

4. Transfer the fish to a serving platter and tent loosely with foil. Stir the wine into the leeks in the pot and simmer over medium-high heat until slightly thickened, about 2 minutes. Off the heat, whisk in the butter, and season with salt and pepper to taste. Spoon the sauce over the salmon and serve.

➤ VARIATION
Salmon en Cocotte with Celery and Orange
Follow the recipe for Salmon en Cocotte with Leeks and White Wine, adding 2 ribs celery, sliced thin, and 1 teaspoon minced fresh orange zest along with the garlic in step 2. Substitute ½ cup orange juice for the wine, and add 1 orange, segmented when thickening the sauce in step 3.

INGREDIENTS: **Salmon**

In season, we've always preferred the more pronounced flavor of wild-caught salmon to farmed Atlantic salmon, which has traditionally been the main farm-raised variety for sale in this country. But with more species of wild and farmed salmon available these days, we decided to see what distinguishes one from the next. We tasted three kinds of wild Pacific salmon alongside two farmed kinds; they ranged in price from $9 to $20 per pound. While we loved the generally stronger flavor of the wild-caught fish, our tasting confirmed two things: If you're going to spend the extra money on wild salmon, make sure it looks and smells fresh, and realize that high quality is available only from late spring through the end of summer.

FARMED SPECIES
ATLANTIC $9/LB.
SEASON: YEAR-ROUND
The sedentary, farm-bound lifestyle of
this fish gave it a "buttery" texture enjoyed by some tasters, but its farm diet may account for the "bland," "vegetal" flavors noted by others. Tasters were divided on texture: Some praised its "supple" consistency, but others called it "squishy" or "mushy."

TEST KITCHEN FAVORITE
KING $12/LB.
SEASON: YEAR-ROUND
Tasters loved this variety's "custardy"
texture and "rich" yet "mild" flavor that "tasted of the sea." But this farmed species is not as widely available as its Atlantic counterpart and may require a trip to a specialty store.

WILD SPECIES
COHO $12/LB.
SEASON: JULY THROUGH
SEPTEMBER

This species of wild salmon has never enjoyed the popularity of king or sockeye, perhaps due to its far leaner constitution. Many of our tasters found it to be "mealy," comparing its texture to that of canned fish. Coho was praised, however, for a flavor that was "just right"—neither too fishy nor too mild.

KING $20/LB.
SEASON: MAY THROUGH
SEPTEMBER
This prized variety winds up on the
menus of many top restaurants, which pushes the retail price to about $20 per pound. Wild king has to travel father than coho salmon to reach its spawning grounds, and thus boasts far fattier flesh. Tasters found the fish to have a strong flavor and a "meaty" texture. However, the firmness of this fish's flesh was considered by some to be overly "rubbery."

TEST KITCHEN FAVORITE
SOCKEYE $13/LB.
SEASON: MAY THROUGH
SEPTEMBER
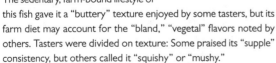
In great demand in Japan, the sockeye (its name is a corruption of an American Indian word and has nothing to do with the fish's eyes) was distinguished by its "clean, briny" notes and deep reddish color—the darkest of all the species. Some found the "big flavor" off-putting, but others praised the same assertiveness. Tasters also liked the "smooth," "firm" texture that gave the sockeye a "good bite."

Substitute 2 tablespoons extra-virgin olive oil for the butter.

Halibut en Cocotte with Roasted Garlic and Cherry Tomatoes
SERVES 4

Using a high-quality extra-virgin olive oil here is important; for more information on buying extra-virgin olive oil, see page 78. Make sure your halibut steaks are of equal size to ensure even cooking; if your steaks are thicker or thinner than 1¼ inches, the cooking time may vary slightly. You can substitute swordfish steaks for the halibut.

¼	cup extra-virgin olive oil (see note)
2	medium garlic cloves, sliced thin (see the illustration on page 71)
⅛	teaspoon red pepper flakes
	Salt
2	cups (12 ounces) cherry tomatoes, quartered
1	tablespoon capers, rinsed
1	teaspoon minced fresh thyme leaves
2	(1¼-pound) halibut steaks, each about 1¼ inches thick and 10 to 12 inches long, and trimmed of cartilage at both ends (see the illustration at right)
	Ground black pepper

1. Adjust an oven rack to the lowest position and heat the oven to 250 degrees. Cook 2 tablespoons of the oil, the garlic, red pepper flakes, and

TRIMMING CARTILAGE

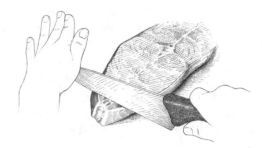

Cutting off the cartilage at the ends of the steaks ensures that they will fit neatly in the pan and diminishes the likelihood that the small bones located there will end up on your dinner plate.

a pinch of salt together in a large Dutch oven over medium-low heat until the garlic is light golden, 2 to 4 minutes. Off the heat, stir in the tomatoes, capers, and thyme.

2. Pat the halibut dry with paper towels and season with salt and pepper. Lay the halibut on top of the tomatoes. Place a large sheet of foil over the pot and press to seal, then cover tightly with the lid. Transfer the pot to the oven and cook until the halibut is opaque and flakes apart when gently prodded with a paring knife, 35 to 40 minutes.

3. Transfer the halibut to a serving platter and tent loosely with foil. Bring the tomato mixture in the pot to a simmer over medium-high heat until slightly thickened, about 2 minutes. Off the heat, stir in the remaining 2 tablespoons olive oil, and season with salt and pepper to taste. Spoon the sauce over the halibut and serve.

THREE KINDS OF HALIBUT STEAKS

Most halibut steaks consist of four pieces of meat attached to a central bone (left). It is not uncommon, however, to encounter a steak with just two pieces, both located on the same side of the center bone (center). These steaks were cut from the center of the halibut, adjacent to the belly cavity. The belly, in effect, separates the two halves. We slightly preferred full steaks with four meat sections; each full steak serves two people. If you can find only the belly steaks, you will have to purchase four steaks instead of two to make the recipe. Avoid very small, boneless steaks (right) cut entirely free from the bone and each other. Most boneless steaks won't serve even one person.

FULL STEAK
4 sections

BELLY CUT
2 sections

BONELESS STEAK
1 section

SERVING HALIBUT STEAKS

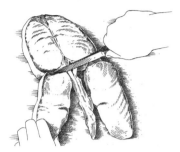

Remove the skin from the cooked steaks and separate each quadrant of meat from the bones by slipping a spatula or knife gently between them.

➤ VARIATION

Halibut en Cocotte with Fennel and Saffron

Pernod is a French anise-flavored liqueur available at most liquor stores. You can substitute dry sherry for the Pernod; however, the flavor of the sauce will be quite different.

Follow the recipe for Halibut en Cocotte with Roasted Garlic and Cherry Tomatoes, adding 1 bulb fennel, trimmed of stalks, cored, and cut into ½-inch-thick strips (see the illustrations on page 108), and a pinch of saffron to the pot after the garlic has lightly browned in step 1; cover and cook over medium-low heat until the fennel is tender, 8 to 10 minutes, then continue with the recipe as directed. Stir 1 tablespoon Pernod into the pot when thickening the tomato mixture in step 3.

Swordfish en Cocotte with Carrots and Chermoula

SERVES 4

Chermoula is a traditional Moroccan sauce made by pureeing generous amounts of cilantro, garlic, and lemon together. Using a high-quality extra-virgin olive oil here is important; for more information on buying extra-virgin olive oil, see page 78. Make sure your swordfish steaks are of equal size to ensure even cooking; if your steaks are thicker or thinner than 1¼ inches, the cooking time may vary slightly. You can substitute halibut steaks for the swordfish.

- ¾ cup packed fresh cilantro leaves
- 5 tablespoons extra-virgin olive oil
- 2 tablespoons juice from 1 lemon
- 4 medium garlic cloves, minced or pressed through a garlic press (about 4 teaspoons)
- 1 teaspoon ground cumin
- 1 teaspoon paprika
- ¼ teaspoon cayenne pepper
  Salt
- 2 medium carrots, peeled and grated
- 4 (6- to 8-ounce) swordfish steaks about 1¼ inches thick
  Ground black pepper

1. Adjust an oven rack to the lowest position and heat the oven to 250 degrees. Process the cilantro, 3 tablespoons of the oil, lemon juice, garlic, cumin, paprika, cayenne, and ¼ teaspoon salt together in a food processor until smooth, about 20 seconds.

2. Heat the remaining 2 tablespoons oil in a large Dutch oven over medium-low heat until shimmering. Add the carrots, cover, and cook, stirring occasionally, until softened, 4 to 6 minutes. Off the heat, stir in the pureed cilantro mixture.

3. Pat the swordfish dry with paper towels and season with salt and pepper. Lay the swordfish on top of the carrot-chermoula mixture. Place a large sheet of foil over the pot and press to seal, then cover tightly with the lid. Transfer the pot to the oven and cook until the swordfish is opaque and flakes apart when gently prodded with a paring knife, 35 to 40 minutes.

4. Transfer the swordfish to a serving platter. Season the carrot-chermoula mixture with salt and pepper to taste, then spoon it over the swordfish and serve.

➤ VARIATION

Swordfish en Cocotte with Shallots, Cucumbers, and Mint

Follow the recipe for Swordfish en Cocotte with Carrots and Chermoula, substituting 3 shallots, sliced thin, for the carrots. Substitute ¾ cup packed fresh mint leaves and ¼ cup packed fresh parsley leaves for the cilantro and omit the paprika. Add 1 medium cucumber, peeled, seeded, and sliced thin, to the pot with the pureed herb mixture in step 2.

INGREDIENTS: High-End Extra-Virgin Olive Oils

Our favorite inexpensive supermarket brand of olive oil is DaVinci, and it has continued its dominance in the test kitchen over other mass-market brands. But what if price isn't your first consideration? Does more money buy better olive oil?

When Americans want extra-virgin olive oil, we generally buy Italian. But a growing number of extra-virgin olive oils from other countries now fill store shelves, including more offerings from Spain, the top olive-growing nation, and Greece. There are even oils from California. Gathering 10 best-selling boutique extra-virgin olive oils from a variety of countries, priced at $20 to $56 per liter, we stripped them of their stylish labels and put them through the rigors of a blind tasting.

Sipped straight up from little cups, the extra-virgin olive oils in our lineup offered a pleasingly wide range of flavors, from fruity and "olive-y" to mild, buttery, and mellow to powerfully green, grassy, and pungent. Why does olive oil have such a wide-ranging flavor profile? Experts agree that the type of olive, the time of harvest (earlier means greener, more bitter, and pungent; later, more mild and buttery), and processing are the biggest factors. As one expert pointed out, olive oil is really just olive juice, and the quickest, gentlest extraction yields the truest flavors. The best-quality oil comes from olives picked at their peak and processed as quickly as possible without heat (which can coax more oil from the olives but at the expense of flavor).

The big loser in our tasting was DaVinci, our favorite inexpensive oil, which finished dead last. Although disappointed, we weren't really surprised. This oil may be better than the other inexpensive options, but it couldn't compete with high-end products. At least when it comes to olive oil, high prices buy more than just pretty bottles.

We were surprised, however, that tasters were not impressed with the high-end Italian oils, which finished in fifth through eighth place. Our two top finishers came from Spain, the third from Greece. We needed to explain these unexpected findings.

As we tallied our tasting results, we realized that our two favorite oils—both praised by tasters for their fairly assertive yet well-balanced flavor—were made with a blend of olives. The Columela and Núñez de Prado oils are a mix of intense Picual and mild Hojiblanca olives (the Núñez also adds delicate-flavored Picudo olives), creating a "fruity" olive oil with no elements that were perceived as too strong tasting—or too mild. By contrast, the other two Spanish oils we tasted, L'Estornell and Pons, were made with only the mild-mannered Arbequina olive, and they rated much less favorably.

Darrell Corti, owner of Corti Brothers store in Sacramento, California, and chairman of olive-oil judging at the Los Angeles County Fair (the top domestic and international olive oil competition in the United States), told us that producers often blend extra-virgin oils from olives with distinct flavors to create the overall flavor profile they want. According to Corti, the best oil is often made from a blend of varietals; the blend may consist of several oils, each one made from a single varietal (known as monocultivar, or single-olive, oils), or from a "field blend," in which different types of olives are picked and then processed together to create a single oil.

Was blending the answer we sought? Maybe not. Ranking nearly as high as the top Spaniards was a Greek oil, Terra Medi, made only with Koroneiki olives. It is not a blend, yet its balanced character and fruity, rounded flavor, with no harsh notes, made it similar in profile to the two top oils. Additionally, while some of the so-so Italian oils were made from single varietals, others were blends. So blending alone doesn't guarantee great oil.

The choice of olives is one factor that makes a particular oil more or less appealing. With their characteristic green, intense olive flavor and peppery aftertaste, the Italian oils had a few vocal supporters, but the majority of tasters felt that the oils' harsh pungency overwhelmed the olive flavor.

In the end, balance turned out to be the key factor that determined the winners of our tasting, and we found it in Spanish oils, not Italian oils. Our tasters preferred oils of medium-fruity intensity. Italian oils generally fall into the intense category.

For everyday use (particularly for recipes where olive oil is heated or must compete with strong flavors), we'll stick with DaVinci, but for drizzling over foods just before serving, the test kitchen is ready for an oil change. The top-ranked Columela is our new test-kitchen favorite when we want an extra-virgin olive oil with high-end flavor but don't want to break the bank to pay for it.

THE BEST EXTRA-VIRGIN OLIVE OIL

A blend of intense Picual and mild Hojiblanca olives, Columela Extra-Virgin Olive Oil ($35.90 per liter) took top honors for its fruity flavor and excellent balance.

Eggs en Cocotte

OUEFS EN COCOTTE IS A CLASSIC FRENCH DISH of eggs cooked in individual ramekins that are usually baked in a water bath in the oven. It is a unique and elegant way to serve eggs for a crowd. We envisioned the ideal eggs en cocotte to have perfectly set whites with soft, runny yolks, enriched with a splash of cream. Most of the recipes we found for this dish followed the same basic formula: Crack one or two eggs into a buttered ramekin, season with salt and pepper, add some cream, place the ramekins in a water bath, and bake until set. Simple enough, right? Wrong. After cooking our way through dozens of eggs, we were faced with the same problem time and again: whites that were not cooked all the way through and yolks that were hard and overcooked—a far cry from the eggs en cocotte we imagined. Determined to find a way to make this recipe work, we decided to take a closer look at the method.

The majority of recipes we found in our research used a water bath. The ramekins that hold the eggs are placed in a shallow pan of water, which then goes into the oven—the idea being that the gentle heat and humidity created by the water keeps the eggs from overcooking at the edges or drying out. To see if the water bath was necessary, we compared a batch of eggs en cocotte cooked in a water bath against a batch cooked simply on a baking sheet. While both batches of eggs suffered the same issues—soupy, transparent whites and overcooked yolks—the eggs cooked on the baking sheet had notably harder edges. So the water bath was indeed creating a gentler cooking environment for our eggs. We pressed on to solve what was clearly our fundamental problem: getting the whites to cook through without overcooking the yolks.

Up to this point we had been putting two eggs in each ramekin. We wondered if using only one egg per ramekin would ensure more even cooking. We quickly determined there was no difference between one and two eggs, and since two eggs is a typical serving, we decided to develop our recipe with two eggs in each ramekin.

We then tested a number of different variables: oven temperature (300 all the way up to 400 degrees); room-temperature eggs versus cold eggs; preheating the ramekins; and resting the eggs in the water bath after cooking. No luck. Almost ready to throw in the towel, we gave the water bath some more thought. It was definitely providing a gentle cooking environment, but maybe it was too gentle. What about covering the pan with foil to trap some of the steam created by the water?

We loaded up another batch of ramekins with eggs and cream, placed them in a water bath in the oven, and covered them with foil. This was definitely an improvement—clearly, covering the eggs was important and the steam was making a significant difference—but the whites were still too soupy to eat. After a few more rounds of tests, we were still frustrated. We could not get a consistent cooking time, and the more we opened the oven door to check the eggs, the harder it was for the whites to cook through. Having watched us cook our way through literally hundreds of eggs, a fellow test cook turned to us and said, "Why not steam the eggs on the stovetop?" Intrigued by the possibility, we quickly cracked another dozen eggs into ramekins, placed them in a roasting pan of simmering water on the stovetop, and covered them with foil. Now we were getting somewhere—these egg whites were the most thoroughly cooked yet.

To eliminate boiling water splashing onto the eggs and the task of checking eggs under foil, we switched from the roasting pan to a large Dutch oven. We filled it with about an inch of water, placed a rack in the bottom of the pan, and brought it to a boil. We gently placed four ramekins, each with two eggs, on the rack and covered the pot with a tight-fitting lid, and then reduced the heat to medium. The rack allowed us to create a hotter steaming environment and all but eliminated the risk of splashing the eggs. In less than seven minutes, our eggs emerged with the whites creamy and set and the yolks soft and runny. We had finally solved the mystery of perfectly cooked eggs en cocotte.

Now that we had achieved perfectly cooked eggs, we focused on the cream and some flavorings. Most recipes called for adding a tablespoon or two of cream to the eggs. During our testing we realized the pooling cream on top was obscuring any visual clue we might have that the whites were properly cooked—and since timing was essential in this dish, not having that visual clue was a real hindrance.

Why not simply spoon some hot cream over the eggs when they had finished cooking? This worked wonders and enabled us to cook our eggs en cocotte consistently and perfectly time and again.

To add a bit of flavor, we sautéed some minced shallots in a little butter, poured in the cream, reduced it slightly to thicken it, and stirred in a pinch of fresh thyme. We spooned this over our next batch of eggs en cocotte—we had arrived. These were the simple, yet elegant eggs we had hoped for. A bit untraditional, yes, as our recipe steams the eggs rather than bakes them in a water bath. But we think this divergence is justified by every perfectly cooked bite.

Eggs en Cocotte

SERVES 4

You will need a rack that fits inside your Dutch oven. If you do not have a rack, see the illustration at right for making your own foil rack. We find it easiest to use tongs and a sturdy, flat spatula to transfer the ramekins into and out of the pot. The eggs can overcook quickly so check them often after 5 minutes of cooking. If you are serving this dish for company, you may want to practice once or twice to get your timing down.

2	tablespoons unsalted butter
1	medium shallot, minced (about 3 tablespoons)
½	cup heavy cream
½	teaspoon minced fresh thyme leaves
	Salt and ground black pepper
8	large eggs

1. Melt 1 tablespoon of the butter in a small saucepan over medium heat. Add the shallot and cook until softened, about 3 minutes. Stir in the cream and simmer, stirring occasionally, until thickened, 3 to 5 minutes. Stir in the thyme and season with salt and pepper to taste. Remove the cream mixture from the heat and cover to keep warm.

2. Meanwhile, place a rack in the bottom of a large Dutch oven and fill with water until it sits just below the rack. Cover the pot and bring the water to a boil over high heat. Rub the inside of four 4- to 5-ounce ramekins with the remaining tablespoon of butter. Crack 2 eggs into each ramekin and season with salt and pepper.

3. When the water is boiling, gently place the ramekins on the rack in the pot and cover. Reduce the heat to medium and cook the eggs until the whites are set but the center jiggles slightly when shaken, and the yolks are pale yellow and covered with a light film, 5 to 7 minutes, checking the eggs every 30 seconds after 5 minutes of cooking.

4. Spoon 1 tablespoon of the warm cream mixture into each ramekin and serve immediately.

➤ VARIATIONS

Eggs en Cocotte with Parmesan Cream
Follow the recipe for Eggs en Cocotte, stirring 1 ounce grated Parmesan cheese (½ cup) into the cream mixture with the thyme in step 1.

Eggs en Cocotte with Mushroom Cream
Be sure that the porcini mushrooms are thoroughly rehydrated and softened before using here.

Follow the recipe for Eggs en Cocotte, adding ¼ ounce dried porcini mushrooms, rehydrated and minced (soaking liquid discarded), to the saucepan with the shallot in step 1.

MAKING A FOIL RACK

Fold a 12- to 14-foot sheet of aluminum foil in half lengthwise and then in half lengthwise again; gently roll and scrunch it into a narrow tube. Coil the foil tube into a tight disk about 6 inches across. Flatten slightly to allow the ramekins to sit evenly.

3

CHILIS, STEWS, AND SAUCES

CHILIS, STEWS, AND SAUCES

CHILIS, STEWS, AND MANY SAUCES ARE SLOW cooking by nature. And after the initial preparation, they require very little attention; time and gentle simmering do the work, allowing flavors to slowly build in the pot. Better yet, you can take inexpensive, everyday ingredients and turn them into something extraordinary—a tough cut of meat becomes incredibly tender or a simple combination of beans, ground meat, and spices melds to create a rich, thick, boldly flavored chili. This method of cooking is as old as cooking itself, but with our society's barrage of "instant this" and "quick that," it's easy to forget all the wonderful aspects of allowing a collection of flavors to slowly build and coalesce in one simmering pot.

But although making a chili or stew is fairly simple and straightforward, that's not to say you can just dump everything in a pot and put the lid on—the way you prepare each individual ingredient and the order in which you add them are important. For our Classic Beef Chili (page 86), we found that adding the spices to the oil at the beginning along with the aromatics is the key to unlocking their flavor. We also found that adding the beans early in the cooking process allowed them to meld into the flavor of the chili.

For our beef stews (such as Beef Carbonnade, page 99), we made some important observations that apply to many of the recipes in this chapter. First, we discovered the merits of cooking them in the oven rather than on the stovetop. When we prepared two identical beef stews, one cooked on top of the stove and one cooked in the oven, both produced moist tender meat in 2½ hours, but the textures of the braising liquids differed dramatically. The stovetop stew produced a thin sauce more like soup, while the oven-braised stew yielded a silky and luxurious sauce. Why so different? At moderate temperatures, the flour in a braising liquid gradually absorbs water, thus thickening the sauce. If the liquid gets too hot, however, the starch breaks down and loses its thickening properties, resulting in a thinner sauce. Because stovetop cooking heats from the bottom only, the flour closest to the heat source loses its thickening ability.

The gentle, lengthy oven simmer also gives the collagen in the meat plenty of time to break down, resulting in unbelievably tender beef. Finally, the oven method allows the cook more control in the cooking process. With a gentle oven simmer, you don't have to worry about the liquid cooking off over the course of a couple of hours and making your stew too thick. You can also rest assured that the bottom of the pot will not be scorched at the end of cooking—a typical by-product of longer stovetop simmering and one that can ruin the flavor of your dish. Slow, gentle, moist heat cooking in the oven helps to make our meat stews as complex in flavor as they are foolproof.

We also learned a few lessons about building flavor in these dishes. Browning the meat creates a flavorful fond upon which you can build a base for the sauce along with the aromatics. Staggering the addition of other ingredients—such as vegetables—based on the amount of time they need to cook, effectively adds complex layers of flavor into these dishes. We found this simple approach to building layers of flavor is an essential component of most every stew, from Pork Stew with Fennel and Prunes (page 108) to our Hearty Chicken Stew with Leeks, Potatoes, and Saffron (page 115) to the French classic, Cassoulet (page 112).

Hopefully you'll find some stews in this chapter that are new to you, such as Lamb Tagine (page 106), a Moroccan specialty that combines lamb with olives, lemon, and apricots for an assertive and unique dish, or Mediterranean Calamari Stew with Garlic and Tomatoes (page 121), a seafood stew bursting with the flavors of garlic, tomatoes, olives, capers, and parsley. We also offer some vegetable stews, which are a surprisingly satisfying alternative to meat-based ones. Our Hearty Root Vegetable and Mushroom Stew (page 125) gets much of its flavor from the fond, as meat stews do, but in this case the fond comes from sautéing the aromatics and mushrooms for an extended period of time until a dark brown coating develops on the bottom of the pan. And when developing the recipe for Tuscan White Bean Stew (page 123), we uncovered the secret to perfectly cooked beans: by soaking the dried beans in salted water overnight—rather than cooking them in salted water—the beans turned out tender and creamy every time.

We have also included a couple of slow cooked meat sauces in this chapter, such as Classic Bolognese Sauce (page 129). Here ground meat cooks for hours at the barest simmer along with milk, wine, and tomatoes. The result is exceptionally tender meat coated in a rich, complex sauce. As with all the recipes in this chapter, the results are worth the wait.

BEEF CHILI

LIKE POLITICS, CHILI PROVOKES HEATED debate. Some purists insist that a chili that contains beans or tomatoes is just not chili. Others claim that homemade chili powder is essential or that ground meat is taboo. But there is one kind of chili that almost every American has eaten (or even made) at one time or another. It's the kind of chili you liked as a kid and still see being served at Super Bowl parties. Made with ground meat, tomatoes, beans, and chili powder, this thick, fairly smooth chili is spiced but not spicy—and it's not intended to fuel impassioned exchanges over the merits of ancho versus New Mexican chiles.

Although this simple chili should come together easily, it should not taste as if it did. The flavors should be rich and balanced, the texture thick and hearty. Unfortunately, many "basic" recipes yield a pot of underspiced, underflavored chili reminiscent of Sloppy Joes. Our goal was to develop a no-fuss chili that tasted far better than the sum of its common parts.

Most of the recipes for this simple chili begin by sautéing onions and garlic. Tasters liked red bell peppers added to these aromatics but rejected other options, including green bell peppers, celery, and carrots. After this first step, things became less clear. The most pressing concerns were the spices (how much and what kind) and the meat (how much ground beef and whether or not to add another meat). There were also the cooking liquid (what kind, if any) and the proportions of tomatoes and beans to consider.

Our first experiments with these ingredients followed a formula we had seen in many recipes: 2 pounds ground beef, 3 tablespoons chili powder, 2 teaspoons ground cumin, and 1 teaspoon each red pepper flakes and dried oregano. Most recipes add the spices after the beef has been browned, but we have usually found that ground spices develop a deeper flavor when they have direct contact with the hot cooking oil.

To see if these results would apply to chili, we set up a test with three pots of chili—one with the ground spices added before the beef, one with the spices added after the beef, and a third in which we toasted the spices in a separate skillet and added them to the pot after the beef. The batch made with untoasted spices added after the beef tasted weak. The batch made with spices toasted in a separate pan was better, but the clear favorite was the batch made with spices added directly to the pot before the meat. In fact, subsequent testing revealed that the spices should be added at the outset—along with the aromatics—to develop their flavors fully.

Although we didn't want a chili with killer heat, we did want real warmth and depth of flavor. Commercial chili powder is typically 80 percent ground dried red chiles, with the rest a mix of garlic powder, onion powder, oregano, ground cumin, and salt. To boost flavor, we increased the amount of chili powder from 3 to 4 tablespoons, added more cumin and oregano, and tossed in some cayenne for heat. We tried some more exotic spices, including cinnamon (which was deemed "awful"), allspice (which seemed "out of place"), and coriander (which added some "gentle warmth"). Only the coriander became part of our working recipe.

It was now time to consider the meat. Two pounds of ground beef seemed ideal when paired with two 15-ounce cans of beans. Tests using 90 percent, 85 percent, and 80 percent lean ground beef showed that there is such a thing as too much fat. Pools of orange oil floated to the top of the chili made with ground chuck (80 percent lean beef). At the other end of the spectrum, the chili made with 90 percent lean beef was a tad bland—not bad, but not as full-flavored as the chili made with 85 percent lean beef, which was our final choice.

We wondered if another type of meat should be used in place of some of the ground beef. After trying batches of chili made with ground pork, diced pork loin, sliced sausage, and sausage removed from its casing and crumbled, tasters preferred the hearty flavor and texture of an all-beef chili.

Next we tried adding various liquids to our chili. Some of us have always made chili with beer and been satisfied with the results. But when we tried beer, we were surprised to find that it subdued that great beefy flavor. We then tried batches made with water (too watery), chicken broth (too chickeny and dull), beef broth (too tinny), wine (too acidic), and no liquid at all except for that in the tomatoes. This no-liquid chili was beefy-tasting and by far the best.

Tomatoes were definitely going into the pot, but we had yet to decide on the type and amount. We first tried two small (14.5-ounce) cans of diced tomatoes, which was clearly not enough. What's more, the tomatoes were too chunky, and they were floating in a thin sauce. We tried two 28-ounce cans of diced tomatoes, pureeing the contents of one can in the blender to thicken the sauce. Although the chunkiness was reduced, the sauce was still watery. Next we paired one can of tomato puree with one can of diced tomatoes and, without exception, tasters preferred the thicker consistency. Though we usually don't like the slightly cooked flavor of tomato puree, we decided that this recipe needed the body it provided. In any case, after the long simmering time, any such flavor was hard to detect.

We tried cooking the chili with the lid on, with the lid off, and with the lid on in the beginning and off at the end. The chili cooked with the lid on was too soupy, that cooked with the lid off too dense. Keeping the lid on for half of the cooking time and then removing it was ideal—the consistency was rich but not too thick. Two hours of gentle simmering was sufficient to meld the flavors; shorter cooking times yielded chili that was soupy or bland—or both.

Most recipes add the beans toward the end of cooking, the idea being to let them heat through without causing them to fall apart. But this method often makes for very bland beans floating in a sea of highly flavorful chili. After testing several options, we found it best to add the beans with the tomatoes. The more time the beans spent in the pot, the better they tasted and we found that they held their shape just fine, especially dark red kidney beans, black beans, and pinto beans (the other common choice for chili, light red kidney beans, does tend to break down more).

It was now time to try some of those offbeat additions to the pot that other cooks swear by, including cocoa powder, ground coffee beans, mushrooms, olives, and lima beans. Our conclusion? Each of these ingredients was either weird tasting or too subtle to make much difference. A sprinkling of garnishes was all our chili needed—tasters liked any combination of cilantro, scallions, onion, avocado, cheese, and sour cream, as well as a squeeze of fresh lime juice. Satisfied that we'd created a basic chili

good enough to silence any debate, we had some fun with variations using bacon, Moroccan spices, Southwestern flavors, and even turkey. Now we truly had a chili to suit every taste.

Classic Beef Chili

SERVES 6 TO 8

Serve with lime wedges, chopped fresh cilantro, sliced scallions, minced onion, diced avocado, shredded cheddar or Monterey Jack cheese, and/or sour cream. The flavor of the chili improves with an overnight rest; if possible, make it a day or two in advance and reheat before serving.

2	tablespoons vegetable oil
2	medium onions, minced
1	red bell pepper, stemmed, seeded, and cut into ½-inch pieces
6	medium garlic cloves, minced or pressed through a garlic press (about 2 tablespoons)
¼	cup chili powder
1	tablespoon ground cumin
2	teaspoons ground coriander
1	teaspoon red pepper flakes
1	teaspoon dried oregano, preferably Mexican
½	teaspoon cayenne pepper
	Salt
2	pounds 85 percent lean ground beef
2	(15-ounce) cans dark red kidney beans, drained and rinsed
1	(28-ounce) can diced tomatoes
1	(28-ounce) can tomato puree

1. Heat the oil in a large Dutch oven over medium heat until shimmering. Add the onions, bell pepper, garlic, chili powder, cumin, coriander, pepper flakes, oregano, cayenne, and 1 teaspoon salt and cook, stirring often, until the vegetables are softened, 8 to 10 minutes.

2. Increase the heat to medium-high. Stir in the beef, 1 pound at a time, and cook while breaking up the chunks with a wooden spoon until no longer pink, about 3 minutes per pound.

3. Stir in the beans, diced tomatoes with their juice, and tomato puree and bring to a boil. Cover, reduce the heat to low, and simmer, stirring occasionally, for 1 hour.

4. Uncover and continue to simmer, stirring occasionally, until the beef is tender and the chili is dark, rich, and slightly thickened, about 45 minutes longer. (If at any time the chili begins to stick to the bottom of the pot, stir in ½ cup water.) Season with salt to taste before serving.

➤ VARIATIONS

Beef Chili with Bacon and Pinto Beans

Cook 8 ounces (about 8 slices) bacon, cut into ½-inch pieces, over medium heat until rendered and crisp, about 8 minutes. Pour off all but 2 tablespoons of the bacon fat and leave the bacon in the pot. Follow the recipe for Classic Beef Chili, omitting the oil, and adding the vegetables and spices to the pot with the bacon and remaining bacon fat; continue to cook as directed. Substitute 2 (15-ounce) cans pinto beans, drained and rinsed, for the kidney beans.

Beef Chili with Moroccan Spices and Chickpeas

Serve with chopped fresh cilantro, sliced scallions, minced onion, and/or sour cream.

Follow the recipe for Classic Beef Chili, omitting the chili powder and red pepper flakes and adding 4 teaspoons sweet paprika, 1 tablespoon ground

---

INGREDIENTS : Chili Powder

While there are numerous applications for chili powder, its most common use is in chili. Considering that most chili recipes rely so heavily on chili powder (ours uses a whopping ¼ cup), we thought it was necessary to gather up as many brands as possible to find the one that made the best chili. To focus on the flavor of the chili powder, we made a bare-bones version of our chili and rated each chili powder for aroma, depth of flavor, and level of spiciness. Tasters concluded that Spice Islands Chili Powder was the clear winner. This well-known supermarket brand was noted by one taster as having "a big flavor that stands out from the others."

THE BEST CHILI POWDER
Spice Islands Chili Powder is our favorite chili powder, with its perfect balance of chili flavor and spiciness.

---

ginger, and ½ teaspoon ground cinnamon with the other spices in step 1. Substitute 2 (15-ounce) cans chickpeas, drained and rinsed, for the kidney beans. Add 1 cup raisins (if desired) to the pot with the beans and tomatoes. Stir in 1 tablespoon lemon juice and 1 teaspoon grated lemon zest before serving.

Smoky Southwestern Chili with Chipotle, Black Beans, and Corn

Follow the recipe for Classic Beef Chili, omitting the red pepper flakes and cayenne pepper and adding 1 tablespoon minced chipotle chile in adobo sauce with the spices in step 1. Substitute 1 (15-ounce) can black beans, drained and rinsed, for all of the kidney beans. After the chili is thickened in step 4, stir in 2 cups frozen corn kernels and continue to simmer until heated through, about 2 minutes. Stir in 1 to 2 more tablespoons minced chipotle to taste before serving.

Classic Turkey Chili

The technique for adding the ground turkey to the pot is a little different, and makes the ground turkey appear crumbled, like ground beef; otherwise, the turkey will have a stringy appearance.

Follow the recipe for Classic Beef Chili, substituting 2 pounds 93 percent lean ground turkey for the beef; add only 1 pound of the ground turkey in step 2. Add the remaining pound of turkey, pinched in teaspoon-sized pieces (see the illustration below), to the chili after uncovering the chili in step 4. Continue to cook as directed.

GETTING THE RIGHT TEXTURE FROM GROUND POULTRY

Pack the meat together in a ball, then pinch off teaspoon-sized pieces of meat and stir them into the chili. This technique makes the ground turkey appear crumbled, like ground beef, rather than stringy.

CHILI CON CARNE

CHILI CON CARNE IS A STRICTLY TEXAN chili that consists primarily of beef and chiles—no tomatoes, onions, or beans to be found. And after much research on this type of chili, we had our work cut out for us: We wanted a chili that would be hearty, heavy on the meat, and spicy but not overwhelmingly hot. It should have a creamy consistency somewhere between soup and stew, and its flavors should be balanced so that no single spice or seasoning stood out or competed with the chiles or beef.

Because chiles are the heart of chili con carne, we had to learn about the different types. After considerable testing and tasting, we settled on a combination of ancho and New Mexican for the dried chiles (for more information on dried chiles, see below), with a few jalapeños added for their fresh flavor and bite. Chilis made with toasted and ground whole dried chiles tasted noticeably fuller and warmer than those made with chili powder. The two main toasting methods are oven and skillet and, after trying both, we went with the oven simply because it required less attention and effort than skillet toasting. The chiles will puff in the oven, become fragrant, and dry out sufficiently after five to six minutes. Because chiles can take on a distinctly bitter flavor if toasted too long, we made sure to remove them from the oven promptly—six minutes in a 350-degree oven was enough to develop their flavor.

With the chiles chosen and toasted, the next big question was how best to prepare them. The two options here are to rehydrate the toasted chiles in liquid and process them into a puree or to grind them into a powder. It didn't take long for us to select grinding as the preferred method. It was easier, faster, and much less messy than making the puree, which tasters felt produced a chili that was too rich, more like a Mexican enchilada sauce than a bowl of chili.

With the chiles prepared, it seemed like the right time to determine the best ratio of chile to meat. Many of the recipes we looked at in our research suggested that a tablespoon of ground chiles per pound of meat was sufficient, but we found these chilis to be bland and watery. Three tablespoons per pound of meat, on the other hand, produced chili with too much punch and richness. Two tablespoons per pound was the way to go.

There was little agreement in the recipes we had collected as to how the ground chiles should be added. After running several tests, we found that sautéing the spices, including the chiles, is key to unlocking their flavor. We also discovered that blending the ground chiles with water to make a paste keeps them from scorching in the pot.

INGREDIENTS: Dried Chiles

For the most part, chili con carne is based on fairly mild dried chiles. The most common of these are dark, mahogany red, wrinkly-skinned ancho chiles, which have a deep, sweet, raisiny flavor; New Mexican red chiles, which have a smooth, shiny, brick-red skin and a crisp, slightly acidic, earthy flavor; California chiles, which look like New Mexican reds but have a slightly milder flavor; and long, shiny, smooth, dark brown pasilla chiles, which are a little hotter than the other three varieties and have a grapey, herby flavor.

We sampled each of these types, as well as a selection of preblended commercial powders, alone and in various combinations in batches of chili. Though the chilis made with individual chiles tasted much more pure and fresh than any of the premixed powders, they nonetheless seemed one-dimensional on their own. When all was said and done, the two-chile combination we favored was equal parts ancho, for its earthy, fruity sweetness and the stunning deep red color it imparted to the chili, and New Mexican, for its lighter flavor and crisp acidity.

Chile heat was another factor to consider. Hotter dried chiles that appear regularly in chili include guajillo, de árbol, pequín, japones, and cayenne. Though we did not want to develop a fiery, overly hot chili, we did want a subtle bite to give the dish some oomph. We found that minced jalapeños, added with the garlic to the chili pot, supplied some heat and a fresh vegetal flavor.

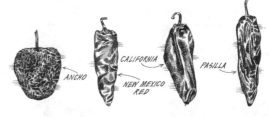

ANCHO   CALIFORNIA   PASILLA   NEW MEXICO RED

Chuck is a common choice for the meat in chili con carne, and we saw no reason to deviate here. Most of the recipes we looked at specified that the meat should be cut into ¼-inch cubes; however, we found that larger 1-inch chunks gave the chili a satisfying heartiness. In addition, cutting a chuck roast into larger chunks was much faster and easier than breaking it down into fussy ¼-inch dice.

Next we set out to determine the best type, or types, of liquid for the chili. Our research indicated that the main contenders were water, chicken broth, beef broth, beer, black coffee, and red wine. We tried each one on its own, as well as in a variety of combinations. The surprise result was that we liked plain water best simply because it didn't compete with the flavor of the chiles.

Though common in other chili recipes, tomatoes and onions are left out of Texas chili. Including these two ingredients may break with tradition, but we found both to be essential. The acidity of the tomato and the sweetness of the onion, both used in small amounts, add interest and dimension to the chili. The batches we tested without them were decidedly dull. After experimenting with various tomato products, we settled on one small can of tomato sauce—its texture didn't interfere with that of our smooth chili sauce. Five cloves of fresh garlic were also a welcome addition, as were some cumin and a little oregano.

We found that bacon lends the chili a subtly sweet, smoky essence that tasters appreciated. Other "secret" ingredients fell by the wayside. Coke imparted a sourish, off-taste. Brown sugar cut the heat of the chiles too much. And while an ounce of unsweetened chocolate gave the chili a slightly rounder, deeper flavor, and 2 tablespoons of peanut butter made the sauce a bit creamier, we decided they were not essential.

Chili con carne typically employs a thickener to tighten the sauce and make it smoother. Flour, roux (a paste of flour and melted butter), cornstarch, and masa harina (a flour ground from corn treated with lime, or calcium oxide) are the most common options. Dredging the meat in flour before browning and adding a roux along with the liquid were both effective, but these approaches made it more difficult to finesse the consistency of the finished product because both were introduced early in the cooking

process. A roux added at the end of the cooking left a taste of raw flour. We did prefer thickening at the end of cooking, though, because we could control the consistency by adding thickener gradually until the chili reached the right consistency. We like chili thick enough to coat the back of a wooden spoon.

Our first choice for thickening was masa harina, added at the end of cooking. Masa both thickened and imparted a slightly sweet, earthy corn flavor to the chili. If masa harina is not available, you can substitute cornstarch—although it brings no flavor to the chili, it is predictable, easy to use, and gives the sauce a silky consistency and attractive sheen.

All our con carne needed now was a sprinkling of garnishes for color and freshness and we had a chili that was simple yet utterly satisfying.

Chili con Carne

SERVES 6

For a spicier chili, include the jalapeño seeds and ribs or add a pinch of cayenne or a dash of hot sauce near the end of cooking. Serve with chopped fresh cilantro, sliced scallions, minced onion, diced avocado, shredded cheddar or Monterey Jack cheese, and/or sour cream. The flavor of the chili improves with an overnight rest; if possible, make it a day or two in advance and reheat before serving.

3	medium ancho pods (about ½ ounce), toasted and ground (see page 90) or 3 tablespoons ancho chili powder
3	medium New Mexican pods (about ¾ ounce), toasted and ground (see page 90) or 3 tablespoons New Mexican chili powder
2	tablespoons ground cumin
2	teaspoons dried oregano, preferably Mexican
7½	cups water, plus extra as needed
8	ounces (about 8 slices) bacon, cut into ¼-inch pieces
1	(3½- to 4-pound) boneless beef chuck eye roast, trimmed and cut into 1-inch pieces Salt and ground black pepper
1	medium onion, minced
5	medium garlic cloves, minced or pressed through a garlic press (about 5 teaspoons)
4	small jalapeño chiles, seeds and ribs removed, chiles minced (see note)

1   (8-ounce) can plain smooth tomato sauce
2   tablespoons juice from 1 lime
5   tablespoons masa harina or 3 tablespoons
    cornstarch

1. Mix the ground chiles, cumin, and oregano together in a small bowl, then stir in ½ cup of the water to form a thick paste; set aside. Fry the bacon in a large Dutch oven over medium-low heat until rendered and crisp, about 8 minutes. Transfer the bacon to a paper towel–lined plate with a slotted spoon and reserve the fat separately in a small bowl.

2. Pat the beef dry with paper towels and season with salt and pepper. Return 1 tablespoon of the reserved bacon fat to the pot and heat over medium-high heat until just smoking. Add half of the meat and cook, stirring occasionally, until well browned, 7 to 10 minutes, reducing the heat if the pot begins to scorch. Transfer the browned beef to a medium bowl. Repeat with 1 more tablespoon reserved bacon fat and the remaining beef; transfer to the bowl.

3. Add 1 more tablespoon reserved bacon fat to the pot and heat over medium heat until shimmering. Add the onion and cook, stirring often, until softened, 5 to 7 minutes. Stir in the garlic and jalapeños and cook until fragrant, about 30 seconds. Stir in the spice paste and cook, stirring often, until fragrant, 2 to 3 minutes.

4. Stir in the cooked bacon, browned beef, tomato sauce, lime juice, and remaining 7 cups water, scraping up any browned bits. Bring to a simmer and continue to cook, uncovered, stirring occasionally and adjusting the heat as necessary to maintain a steady simmer, until the meat is tender

TECHNIQUE:
Toasting and Grinding Chiles

To ensure the best chile flavor, we recommend toasting whole dried chiles and grinding them yourself. Buy dried chiles that are moist and pliant, like dried fruit, then toast them on a baking sheet in a 350-degree oven until fragrant and puffed, about 6 minutes. Let the chiles cool, then remove the stem seeds. Tear the chiles into small pieces and process in a spice grinder until powdery, 30 to 45 seconds.

and the juices are dark, rich, and starting to thicken, about 2 hours.

5. Mix the masa harina with ⅔ cup water (or the cornstarch with 3 tablespoons water) to form a smooth paste, stir it into the chili, and continue to simmer until thickened, 5 to 10 minutes. Season with salt and pepper to taste before serving.

WHITE CHICKEN CHILI

WHITE CHICKEN CHILI IS A FRESHER, LIGHTER cousin of the thick red chili most Americans know and love. While its origins date back to the health and Southwestern crazes of the 1980s, white chicken chili has since shown up in a number of Midwestern family cookbooks and has become a regular on the chili cook-off circuit. Its appeal is not surprising. First, because the recipe uses chicken rather than beef, many folks appreciate it for being healthier. Next, because there are no tomatoes to mask the other flavors, the chiles, herbs, and spices take center stage. Unlike red chili, which uses any combination of dried chiles, chili powders, and cayenne pepper, white chicken chili gets its backbone from fresh green chiles. So much so, in fact, that the recipe is sometimes called chili verde, or green chili.

The ingredients in white chicken chili are fairly consistent: diced or ground chicken, green chiles (usually fresh but sometimes canned or pickled), onions, white beans, garlic, spices, and chicken broth. But most of the recipes we tried were too watery and bland, bearing a closer resemblance to chicken and bean soup than actual chili. While the floating bits of mushy beans and overcooked chicken were hard to overlook, the chiles themselves were often barely noticeable. But amid all these bad recipes, we saw the possibility of creating something great—a rich, stew-like chili with moist, tender chicken, perfectly cooked beans, and a complex flavor profile.

The basic procedure for making white chicken chili is fairly simple. Most recipes start by browning the chicken. Next, the browned chicken is set aside and the chiles, onion, garlic, and spices are sautéed in the same pot. Finally, the chicken is added back in along with chicken broth and white beans and simmered until the chicken has cooked through.

Ground chicken was moist but had a chewy, spongy texture and an unattractive crumbly appearance so we ruled it out. The choice between white and dark meat was a close call. Chicken thighs tasted richer and meatier, but they tended to compete with the fresh flavors of the chiles and seasonings. Boneless, skinless chicken breasts were attractive but lent little flavor to the broth. We had better luck with bone-in, skin-on breasts. We browned the pieces first to help develop fond (the flavorful bits on the bottom of the pot) and render fat, which we saved to cook with the aromatics.

We were ready to move on to the main order of business: the chiles. Some recipes rely solely on canned or jarred green chiles. While offering convenience, they were also too vinegary and pickled. That left us with six widely available fresh chiles to choose from: poblanos, Anaheims, banana peppers, Italian peppers, jalapeños, and serranos. Banana peppers and Italian peppers were uninspiring. Extremely hot serranos were also out. We hoped to find a one-size-fits-all chile but discovered that more than one variety was necessary to provide the complexity and modest heat we were looking for. A trio of poblanos, Anaheims, and jalapeños did just that, with each chile bringing its own inimitable characteristics (see "The Chosen Chiles" below) to the table.

We briefly sautéed the chopped chiles along with diced onions, garlic, and spices over relatively high heat before adding the broth, beans, and chicken. This technique yielded chiles that didn't soften much and had a flat, vegetal flavor. Roasting softened the chiles but provided an unwanted smokiness that muddied the dish. We found the solution back on the stovetop by lowering the heat and covering the pot. In 10 minutes, the chiles and onions were softened, and the flavors of the garlic and spices were nicely bloomed. As for the spices, tasters liked the standard cumin but preferred aromatic coriander to the more commonly used dried oregano.

At this point, we were ready to deal with the chicken. After removing the skin, we poached the breasts until they were just done (about 20 minutes) and set them aside while the base continued to cook. Canned beans were simple to use, and tasters favored larger cannellini beans over navy beans.

To fix the wateriness problem that had plagued so many of our test recipes, we tried adding a small amount of masa harina (a corn flour product), which we had used to thicken our Chili con Carne (page 89). While it technically worked, the "corny" flavor came through too strongly here. We wondered if pureeing some of the ingredients would give us the results we wanted. Pureeing a cup each of the sautéed chile-onion mixture, beans, and broth not only gave the chili a nicely thickened consistency but also ensured that chile flavor was present in every drop.

With a host of complex Southwestern flavors, interesting textures, and filling but not heavy ingredients, this white chicken chili had come full circle.

THE CHOSEN CHILES

We found that using a combination of poblanos, Anaheims, and jalapeños was the key to achieving vibrant chile flavor in our White Chicken Chili. Here's what each chile brings to the table.

JALAPEÑO
This small smooth-skinned, forest green chile provides heat and a bitter, green bell pepper–like flavor.

ANAHEIM
This long medium green, mildly spicy chile has an acidic, lemony bitterness.

POBLANO
This large heart-shaped, blackish green chile is mild to medium-hot and packs a rich, vegetal, slightly sweet flavor.

White Chicken Chili

SERVES 6 TO 8

For more heat, include the jalapeño seeds and ribs when mincing. If you can't find Anaheim chiles, add an additional poblano and jalapeño to the chili. Serve with sour cream, tortilla chips, and lime wedges.

3	jalapeño chiles, seeds and ribs removed (see note)
2	medium onions, chopped coarse
3	poblano chiles, seeds and ribs removed, chiles chopped coarse
3	Anaheim chiles, seeds and ribs removed, chiles chopped coarse (see note)
3	pounds bone-in, skin-on split chicken breasts (about 4 split breasts), trimmed
	Salt and ground black pepper
2	tablespoons vegetable oil
6	medium garlic cloves, minced or pressed through a garlic press (about 2 tablespoons)
1	tablespoon ground cumin
1½	teaspoons ground coriander
2	(15-ounce) cans cannellini beans, drained and rinsed
4	cups low-sodium chicken broth
¼	cup minced fresh cilantro leaves
4	scallions, sliced thin
3	tablespoons juice from 2 limes
1	tablespoon minced fresh oregano leaves

1. Coarsely chop 2 of the jalapeño chiles and pulse them, together with the onions, in a food processor to the consistency of chunky salsa, about 12 pulses. Transfer the mixture to a bowl. Pulse the poblano and Anaheim chiles together in the food processor to the consistency of chunky salsa, about 12 pulses; transfer to the bowl with the onions and jalapeños.

2. Pat the chicken dry with paper towels and season with salt and pepper. Heat 1 tablespoon of the oil in a large Dutch oven over medium-high heat until just smoking. Brown half of the chicken on both sides, 5 to 8 minutes per side, reducing the heat if the pot begins to scorch. Transfer the chicken to a plate, leaving the fat in the pot. Repeat with the remaining tablespoon oil and chicken.

3. Pour off all but 2 tablespoons of the fat left in the pot. Add the chopped chile-onion mixture, garlic, cumin, coriander, and 1 teaspoon salt and cook over medium heat, stirring occasionally, until the vegetables are softened, 8 to 10 minutes.

4. Remove the pot from the heat and transfer 1 cup of the cooked vegetables to the food processor. Process the cooked chile mixture with 1 cup of the beans and 1 cup of the broth until smooth, about 20 seconds. Return the pureed mixture to the pot.

5. Stir in the remaining 3 cups of the broth, scraping up any browned bits. Add the chicken with any accumulated juices and bring to a simmer. Cover, turn the heat to medium-low, and simmer until the thickest part of the breast registers 160 to 165 degrees on an instant-read thermometer, about 20 minutes.

6. Transfer the chicken to a cutting board. Stir in the remaining beans and continue to cook the chili over medium heat until the beans are heated

SEEDING FRESH CHILES

Using a knife to remove the seeds and ribs from a hot chile pepper takes a very steady hand. Fortunately, there is a safer alternative.

1. Cut the pepper in half lengthwise with a knife.

2. Starting opposite the stem end, run the edge of a small melon baller scoop down the inside of the pepper, scraping up seeds and ribs.

3. Cut off the core with the scoop.

through and the chili has thickened slightly, about 10 minutes.

7. When the chicken is cool enough to handle, remove the meat from the bones and shred into bite-sized pieces (see the illustrations on page 116); discard the skin and bones. Return the shredded chicken to the chili and continue to cook until heated through, about 2 minutes.

8. Mince the remaining jalapeño and stir it into the chili with the cilantro, scallions, lime juice, and oregano. Season with salt and pepper to taste before serving.

BEEF STEW

BEEF STEW SHOULD BE RICH AND SATISFYING. Unfortunately, many recipes for beef stew result in tough, dry meat and a watery, bland sauce. In addition, the classic vegetables for beef stew—potatoes, carrots, and peas—can often become mushy and flavorless during the long simmer. Our goals for this recipe then were clear: We wanted tender meat and a rich, smooth sauce; and we wanted to coordinate the cooking times of the vegetables to prevent their flavors and textures from being compromised. Once we mastered a basic beef stew, we also hoped to create some new and interesting variations for a modern spin on this hearty classic.

Starting with the beef itself, we set out to determine the ideal cut. We browned 12 different cuts of beef, marked them for identification, and cooked them in the same kind of pot. The biggest disappointment came from the packages labeled "stew meat," because they contained misshapen and small bits of meat along with scraps from various parts of the animal—basically, the butcher's leftovers. We needed to handpick the beef that was just right for this slow cooking technique. Chuck proved to be our cut of choice—flavorful, tender, and juicy with a moderate price tag. The names given to different cuts of chuck vary, but the most commonly used names for retail chuck cuts include boneless chuck eye roasts, cross rib roasts, blade steaks and roasts, shoulder steaks and roasts, and arm steaks and roasts. We particularly like chuck eye roast, but all

chuck cuts work well when trimmed and braised.

We next focused on braising liquids. We tried water, wine, homemade beef stock, store-bought beef broth, store-bought chicken broth, and combinations of these liquids. Water made the stews taste, well, watery. Stew made with homemade beef stock tasted great, but we decided that beef stew has plenty of other hearty ingredients to give it flavor and therefore doesn't require such a time-consuming ingredient. Using all store-bought beef broth was a little overpowering, but cutting it with some store-bought chicken broth balanced the flavors nicely. A little wine was also a welcome addition.

As for building the stew itself, the traditional method involves first browning the meat, then using the leftover browned bits as a base for building the sauce along with aromatics like onions, garlic, and tomato paste, as well as a little flour for thickening. The meat is then cooked in the sauce with vegetables and flavorings until it's tender (and the sauce is thick and rich). We've tested this method enough to know it needed little revision from us as it is already quite sensible and streamlined; we were more interested in the actual cooking of the stew once everything was in the pot.

After a little testing, we noted that the temperature of the stewing liquid during cooking is crucial. We found it essential to keep the temperature of the liquid below boiling (212 degrees Fahrenheit) as boiled meat turns tough and the exterior of the meat becomes especially dry. Keeping the liquid at a simmer allows the internal temperature of the meat to rise slowly. By the time the meat is fork-tender, much of the connective tissue will have turned to gelatin. The gelatin, in turn, helps to thicken the stewing liquid. Simmering the stew in the oven—rather than on the stovetop—gave us the most consistent results. We found that putting a covered Dutch oven in a 325-degree oven ensured that the temperature of the stewing liquid remained below the boiling point, at about 200 degrees. (The oven must be kept at a temperature higher than 200 degrees because ovens are not completely efficient in transferring heat; a cooking temperature of 325 degrees recognizes that some heat will be lost as it penetrates through the pot and into the stew.)

Finally, we looked at the vegetables. The peas

tasted best when stirred in just a few minutes before serving. The carrots and potatoes, on the other hand, weren't so simple and required further testing. We ultimately determined that they both should be added halfway through the stew's cooking time. Any longer and they fell apart.

With our recipe for classic beef stew mastered, we focused our attention on creating some unique and unexpected variations. Borrowing some of the flavors we love from Asian cuisine, our first variation included shiitake mushrooms, cabbage, and water chestnuts. The mushrooms enhanced the meaty flavor of the dish, as did a modest amount of soy sauce. Cabbage is a traditional pairing with beef and we found that cutting it into substantial 1½-inch pieces and adding it toward the end of cooking helped it remain intact and retain its color. Scallions and ginger completed this Asian-inspired stew.

For our second variation we paired mushrooms (we liked porcini, portobello, and cremini) with creamy parsnips—the parsnips have a natural sweetness that complements the rich, earthy flavor of both the beef and mushrooms. And finally, we developed a beef stew that highlighted two classic holiday ingredients: chestnuts and pears. We found that both fresh and jarred chestnuts worked in our stew, while either Bosc or Bartlett pears were ideal. Tasters felt the red wine from our master recipe overpowered the delicate pears so we tried white wine. This was an improvement, but dry sherry was even better, offsetting the sweetness of the pears.

Classic Beef Stew
SERVES 6 TO 8

A $7 to $10 bottle of medium-bodied red table wine made from a blend of grapes, such as a Côtes du Rhône, will work well here.

1	(3½- to 4-pound) boneless beef chuck eye roast, trimmed and cut into 1½-inch pieces
	Salt and ground black pepper
3	tablespoons vegetable oil
2	medium onions, minced
3	medium garlic cloves, minced or pressed through a garlic press (about 1 tablespoon)
1	tablespoon minced fresh thyme leaves, or 1 teaspoon dried
3	tablespoons unbleached all-purpose flour
1	tablespoon tomato paste
1	cup dry red wine
1¼	cups low-sodium chicken broth
1¼	cups low-sodium beef broth
2	bay leaves
1½	pounds red potatoes (about 5 medium), scrubbed and cut into 1-inch pieces
1	pound carrots (about 6 medium), peeled and sliced 1 inch thick
1	cup frozen peas, thawed
¼	cup minced fresh parsley leaves

1. Adjust an oven rack to the lower-middle position and heat the oven to 325 degrees. Pat

CUTTING BEEF STEW MEAT

You simply can't make good stew from bad meat. And to get the best stew meat possible (regularly shaped, evenly cut, and all from the chuck), you should really cut it up yourself. We like to use a beef chuck eye roast, but any boneless beef roast from the chuck will work. The trick is not to cut the pieces of meat too small while trimming away the fat—the fat will render into the stew and be easy to skim off later. That said, however, don't be surprised if you have a good amount of trim—count on roughly ½ pound trim for every 4 pounds of meat.

1. Pull apart the roast at its major seams (delineated by lines of fat and silver skin); use a knife as necessary.

2. With a sharp, thin-tipped knife, trim off the excess fat and silver skin.

3. Cut the meat into pieces as directed in specific recipes.

the beef dry with paper towels and season with salt and pepper. Heat 1 tablespoon of the oil in a large Dutch oven over medium-high heat until just smoking. Add half of the meat and cook, stirring occasionally, until well browned, 7 to 10 minutes, reducing the heat if the pot begins to scorch. Transfer the browned beef to a medium bowl. Repeat with 1 tablespoon more oil and the remaining beef; transfer to the bowl.

2. Add the remaining 1 tablespoon oil to the pot and place over medium-low heat until shimmering. Add the onions and ¼ teaspoon salt and cook, stirring often, until softened, 5 to 7 minutes. Stir in the garlic and thyme and cook until fragrant, about 30 seconds. Stir in the flour and tomato paste and cook, stirring constantly, for 1 minute. Slowly whisk in the wine, scraping up any browned bits. Gradually whisk in the broths until smooth and bring to a simmer.

3. Stir in the browned meat with any accumulated juices and the bay leaves and bring to a simmer. Cover, place the pot in the oven, and cook for 1 hour. Stir in the potatoes and carrots and continue to cook in the oven, covered, until the meat is tender, 1 to 1½ hours longer.

4. Remove the stew from the oven and remove the bay leaves. Stir in the peas, cover, and let stand for 5 minutes. Stir in the parsley and season with salt and pepper to taste before serving.

➤ VARIATIONS

Asian Beef Stew with Shiitakes, Cabbage, and Water Chestnuts

The soy sauce is a salty addition to this stew, so season the stew meat and finished stew carefully. Chinese rice cooking wine, also known as Shaoxing, can be found in Asian markets or the international aisle of large supermarkets. Serve with steamed white rice.

1	(3½- to 4-pound) boneless beef chuck eye roast, trimmed and cut into 1½-inch pieces
	Salt and ground black pepper
3	tablespoons vegetable oil
12	ounces shiitake mushrooms, stemmed, wiped clean, and sliced ¼ inch thick
6	scallions, white and green parts separated, whites minced and greens sliced thin
6	medium garlic cloves, minced or pressed through a garlic press (about 2 tablespoons)
3	tablespoons minced or grated fresh ginger
2	tablespoons unbleached all-purpose flour
1	cup Chinese rice cooking wine or dry sherry (see note)
1	cup water
¾	cup low-sodium chicken broth
¾	cup low-sodium beef broth
⅓	cup soy sauce
1	pound green cabbage (½ medium head), cored and cut into 1½-inch pieces
2	(8-ounce) cans sliced water chestnuts, drained

1. Adjust an oven rack to the lower-middle position and heat the oven to 325 degrees. Pat the beef dry with paper towels and season lightly with salt and pepper. Heat 1 tablespoon of the oil in a large Dutch oven over medium-high heat until just smoking. Add half of the meat and cook, stirring occasionally, until well browned, 7 to 10 minutes, reducing the heat if the pot begins to scorch. Transfer the browned beef to a medium bowl. Repeat with 1 tablespoon more oil and the remaining beef; transfer to the bowl.

2. Add the remaining 1 tablespoon oil to the pot and place over medium-low heat until shimmering. Add the mushrooms and cook, stirring often, until softened and beginning to brown, 5 to 7 minutes. Stir in the scallion whites, garlic, and ginger and cook until fragrant, about 30 seconds. Stir in the flour and cook, stirring constantly, until golden, about 1 minute. Slowly whisk in the wine, scraping up any browned bits. Gradually whisk in the water, broths, and soy sauce until smooth and bring to a simmer.

3. Stir in the browned meat with any accumulated juices and bring to a simmer. Cover, place the pot in the oven, and cook until the meat is mostly tender, 1¾ to 2¼ hours. Stir in the cabbage and continue to cook in the oven, covered, until the cabbage is wilted, about 15 minutes longer.

4. Remove the stew from the oven. Stir in the water chestnuts and let stand for 5 minutes. Stir in the scallion greens and season with salt and pepper to taste before serving.

Beef Stew with Parsnips and Mushrooms

If the tops of the parsnips are much thicker than the ends, cut the tops in half lengthwise to make the pieces more consistent. You can substitute white button mushrooms for the cremini mushrooms in this recipe. A $7 to $10 bottle of medium-bodied red table wine made from a blend of grapes, such as a Côtes du Rhône, will work well here.

1	(3½- to 4-pound) boneless beef chuck eye roast, trimmed and cut into 1½-inch pieces
	Salt and ground black pepper
5	tablespoons vegetable oil
2	medium onions, minced
¾	ounce dried porcini mushrooms, rinsed and minced
3	medium garlic cloves, minced or pressed through a garlic press (about 1 tablespoon)
1	tablespoon minced fresh thyme leaves, or 1 teaspoon dried
3	tablespoons unbleached all-purpose flour
1	cup dry red wine (see note)
1¼	cups low-sodium chicken broth
1¼	cups low-sodium beef broth
2	bay leaves
1	pound parsnips, peeled and cut into 1-inch pieces (see note)
12	ounces portobello mushroom caps (2 medium), wiped clean and cut into ¼-inch pieces
1	pound cremini mushrooms, stemmed, wiped clean, and quartered
¼	cup minced fresh parsley leaves

1. Adjust an oven rack to the lower-middle position and heat the oven to 325 degrees. Pat the beef dry with paper towels and season with salt and pepper. Heat 1 tablespoon of the oil in a large Dutch oven over medium-high heat until just smoking. Add half of the meat and cook, stirring occasionally, until well browned, 7 to 10 minutes, reducing the heat if the pot begins to scorch. Transfer the browned beef to a medium bowl. Repeat with 1 tablespoon more oil and the remaining beef; transfer to the bowl.

2. Add 1 tablespoon more oil to the pot and place over medium-low heat until shimmering. Add the onions, porcini mushrooms, and ¼ teaspoon salt and cook, stirring often, until softened, 5 to 7 minutes. Stir in the garlic and thyme and cook until fragrant, about 30 seconds. Stir in the flour and cook, stirring constantly, until golden, about 1 minute. Slowly whisk in the wine, scraping up any browned bits. Gradually whisk in the broths until smooth and bring to a simmer.

3. Stir in the browned meat with any accumulated juices and the bay leaves and bring to a simmer. Cover, place the pot in the oven, and cook for 1 hour. Stir in the parsnips and continue to cook in the oven, covered, until the meat is tender, 1 to 1½ hours longer.

4. Meanwhile, heat 2 teaspoons more oil in a 12-inch nonstick skillet over medium-high heat until shimmering. Add the portobello mushrooms and cook, stirring often, until lightly golden, about 8 minutes. Transfer the mushrooms to a medium bowl. Repeat twice more with the remaining 4 teaspoons oil and cremini mushrooms, cooking them in two batches.

5. Remove the stew from the oven and remove the bay leaves. Stir in the cooked mushrooms, cover, and let stand for 5 minutes. Stir in the parsley and season with salt and pepper to taste before serving.

Beef Stew with Chestnuts and Pears

We like to use Bosc or Bartlett pears here because they maintain their shape nicely when cooked in the stew. You can either use jarred, peeled chestnuts or fresh chestnuts that you peel yourself; see page 97 for how to peel fresh chestnuts.

1	(3½- to 4-pound) boneless beef chuck eye roast, trimmed and cut into 1½-inch pieces
	Salt and ground black pepper
3	tablespoons vegetable oil
2	medium onions, minced
3	medium garlic cloves, minced or pressed through a garlic press (about 1 tablespoon)
1	tablespoon minced fresh thyme leaves, or 1 teaspoon dried
3	tablespoons unbleached all-purpose flour
1	cup dry sherry
1¼	cups low-sodium chicken broth
1¼	cups low-sodium beef broth
2	bay leaves

1½ pounds Bosc or Bartlett pears
    (about 4 pears), peeled, cored and cut into
    1-inch pieces
10 ounces (about 1¾ cups) peeled chestnuts
    (see note)
¼ cup minced fresh parsley leaves

1. Adjust an oven rack to the lower-middle position and heat the oven to 325 degrees. Pat the beef dry with paper towels and season with salt and pepper. Heat 1 tablespoon of the oil in a large Dutch oven over medium-high heat until just smoking. Add half of the meat and cook, stirring occasionally, until well browned, 7 to 10 minutes, reducing the heat if the pot begins to scorch. Transfer the browned beef to a medium bowl. Repeat with 1 tablespoon more oil and the remaining beef; transfer to the bowl.

2. Add the remaining 1 tablespoon oil to the pot and place over medium-low heat until shimmering. Add the onions and ¼ teaspoon salt and cook, stirring often, until softened, 5 to 7 minutes. Stir in the garlic and thyme and cook until fragrant, about

PEELING FRESH CHESTNUTS

1. Using a paring knife, score a large X into the outer shell.

2. Roast the scored nuts on a rimmed baking sheet in a 350-degree oven until the outer shell peels away where scored, 10 to 15 minutes. Let the nuts cool, then peel the shell and the inner paper-like skin away from the nut.

30 seconds. Stir in the flour and cook, stirring constantly, until golden, about 1 minute. Slowly whisk in the sherry, scraping up any browned bits. Gradually whisk in the broths until smooth and bring to a simmer.

3. Stir in the browned meat with any accumulated juices and the bay leaves and bring to a simmer. Cover, place the pot in the oven, and cook for 1 hour. Stir in the pears and continue to cook in the oven, covered, until the meat is tender, 1 to 1½ hours longer.

4. Remove the stew from the oven and remove the bay leaves. Stir in the chestnuts, cover, and let stand for 5 minutes. Stir in the parsley and season with salt and pepper to taste before serving.

BEEF CARBONNADE

A BASIC BEEF STEW CAN BE ALTERED IN dozens of ways, usually by adding more ingredients to the pot. But can you go the other way and strip beef stew down to its bare bones (or, to be more precise, to its beef)? If you trade the carrots and potatoes for a mess of onions and add a good dose of beer as part of the braising liquid, you've created a simple Belgian beef stew called *carbonnade à la flamande*. In a carbonnade, the heartiness of the beef melds with the soft sweetness of sliced onions in a lightly thickened broth that is rich, deep, and satisfying, with the malty flavor of beer.

We made several versions of carbonnade and discovered that making a poor one is easy. Some stews were so gussied up that it was hard to notice all but the most serious flaws. But stews stripped down to the three main ingredients were primed for failure—any mistake really stood out. After several trials, we wound up with batches of tasteless beef and onions in a pale, one-dimensional broth.

Backing up, we decided on the basic stew method that would serve as a springboard for arriving at an improved recipe: Cubed chuck eye roast is browned and set aside, onions are sautéed in the empty pot, flour is sprinkled over the onions, liquid is added, the beef is returned to the pot, and the stew simmers in the oven. With the basics in place, we now had to figure out the particulars—the best way to cook the onions, the right type of beer, and what additional flavors (if any) we wanted.

Onions—and lots of them—go into a traditional carbonnade. Two pounds was the right amount for a generous pot of stew (made with 3½ to 4 pounds of beef). After trying white, red, and yellow onions, we decided that thinly sliced yellow onions tasted the best. We found that the onions should be just lightly browned before being incorporated into the stew— if they are overcaramelized, they have a tendency to disintegrate after two hours of stewing.

To deepen the gentle sweetness of the onions, we tried adding a bit of brown sugar, a traditional ingredient in carbonnade, but tasters found it too sweet. We then thought to add a spoonful of tomato paste while sautéing the onions, a trick we had used in other recipes. This simple (if untraditional) ingredient dramatically improved the flavor. A sprinkling of salt helped the onions release their moisture, which kept the flavorful fond (browned bits) from burning and helped to loosen it from the pot during deglazing. Garlic is not an ingredient in all carbonnade recipes, but we liked it, adding two minced cloves to the onions only after the onions had cooked to make sure the garlic didn't burn.

An essential component of Belgian cuisine is beer, Belgium's national drink. Belgians routinely pour beer into dishes at times when other cooks might uncork a bottle of wine. Cooking with wine is fairly straightforward; most reasonable choices work just fine in a stew. Cooking with beer is a different story. Beers of the light, lager persuasion lacked potency and resulted in a pale, watery-tasting stew. We tried a number of dark beers and found that moderately dark ales, very dark ales, and stouts made the richest and best-tasting carbonnades (see below for more information).

While the braising liquid for carbonnade is typically beer, beef stock is sometimes added. We made carbonnades with beer as the only liquid, but they lacked backbone and were sometimes overwhelmingly bitter, depending on the type of beer used. A combination of beef and chicken broth (a staple of our other beef stews) added along with the beer was a hit. Fresh thyme and ground nutmeg were natural additions and cider vinegar perked things up with sweet-and-sour tones. With the right cut of beef, plenty of yellow onions, and a rich, dark beer, we made the simplest of all stews, carbonnade, come to life.

INGREDIENTS: Beer for Carbonnade

When making carbonnade, purists will settle for nothing less than a traditional copper-colored Belgian ale with fruity, spicy aromas and a pleasant hoppy bitterness. But is it the only choice?

To find out, we pulled together nine different styles of beer, ranging from a dark, full-bodied stout to a nonalcoholic brew. After a few hours in the oven, the flavors you taste straight from the bottle are concentrated and easily recognized in this stew. Our tasters preferred beers that possessed plenty of sweetness matched with moderate bitterness. Light-bodied beers, like Bud Light, were noted for a mild sweetness but lacked the contrasting bitterness to make a balanced, full-flavored stew. On the other hand, brews with a high degree of bitterness often did not have enough sweetness. This was the case with Sierra Nevada's Pale Ale, which came across as singularly bitter.

Not surprisingly, our top choice was Chimay Pères Trappistes Ale-Première. This traditional Belgian Trappist ale was "rich and robust" and brought out a "very deep flavor" with a "dark

chocolate finish." But we also found a couple of good alternatives: Newcastle Brown Ale, an English ale low on both sweetness and bitterness, which allowed for "lots of malt" flavor; and surprisingly, O'Doul's Amber—a nonalcoholic beer with a fruity sweetness brought out the stew's "rich beefiness."

THE BEST BEERS FOR CARBONNADE

Beef Carbonnade

SERVES 6

We recommend serving this stew with buttered egg noodles or mashed potatoes. See page 98 for more information about the type of beer to use for this recipe.

1	(3½- to 4-pound) boneless beef chuck eye roast, trimmed and cut into 1½-inch pieces
	Salt and ground black pepper
3	tablespoons vegetable oil
4	ounces (about 4 slices) bacon, cut into 1-inch pieces
2	pounds onions (about 4 medium), halved and sliced ¼ inch thick
2	medium garlic cloves, minced or pressed through a garlic press (about 2 teaspoons)
1	tablespoon minced fresh thyme leaves, or 1 teaspoon dried
⅛	teaspoon ground nutmeg
3	tablespoons unbleached all-purpose flour
1	tablespoon tomato paste
¾	cup low-sodium chicken broth
¾	cup low-sodium beef broth
2	cups beer (see note)
2	bay leaves
1	tablespoon cider vinegar

1. Adjust an oven rack to the lower-middle position and heat the oven to 325 degrees. Pat the beef dry with paper towels and season with salt and pepper. Heat 1 tablespoon of the oil in a large Dutch oven over medium-high heat until just smoking. Add half of the meat and cook, stirring occasionally, until well browned, 7 to 10 minutes, reducing the heat if the pot begins to scorch. Transfer the browned beef to a medium bowl. Repeat with 1 tablespoon more oil and the remaining beef; transfer to the bowl.

2. Add the bacon to the pot and cook over medium heat until rendered and beginning to brown, about 5 minutes. Stir in the remaining 1 tablespoon oil, onions, and ¼ teaspoon salt and cook, stirring often, until softened, 5 to 7 minutes. Stir in the garlic, thyme, and nutmeg and cook until fragrant, about 30 seconds. Stir in the flour and tomato paste and cook, stirring constantly, for

1 minute. Slowly whisk in the broths, scraping up any browned bits. Gradually whisk in the beer until smooth and bring to a simmer.

3. Stir in the browned meat with any accumulated juices, bay leaves, and vinegar and bring to a simmer. Cover the pot partially (the lid should be just off center to leave about 1 inch open), place the pot in the oven, and cook until the meat is tender and the sauce is thickened and glossy, 2 to 2½ hours.

4. Remove the stew from the oven and remove the bay leaves. Season with salt and pepper to taste before serving.

DAUBE PROVENÇAL

DAUBE PROVENÇAL, ALSO KNOWN AS DAUBE niçoise, is a beef stew from the city of Nice that makes use of many of its local ingredients. It is traditionally cooked in an earthenware pot called a *daubière* (hence the name) and nestled into the fireplace surrounded by the burning embers to cook long and slow, transforming chunks of beef, red wine, and aromatics (such as garlic, olives, anchovies, oranges, dried mushrooms, and tomatoes) into a rich, deep, and flavorful stew.

But few of these ingredients made it into the large stack of "authentic" recipes we uncovered in our research. When tested, many of these recipes were one-note wonders—beef stew with olives or beef stew with oranges. We would have to find a way to incorporate the strong, independent flavors of Provence into a robust but cohesive stew.

Having developed a reliable set of techniques to turn tough beef into tender stew (see Classic Beef Stew on page 94) we saw no reason to deviate: Brown the beef (to ensure the richest, meatiest flavor); add the aromatic vegetables; sprinkle some flour in the pan (to thicken the braising liquid); deglaze with the predominant cooking liquid; add the meat back to the pot; and, finally, cover and cook in a low to medium oven until tender. Our choice of meat for stew is cut from the chuck, or shoulder, which is notoriously tough (the meat softens nicely during long, slow cooking) but also flavorful. While various chuck cuts are appropriate for this recipe, we found that the chuck eye roast offered the best flavor and texture.

Most beef stews have a personality-defining ingredient, like the wine in beef Burgundy or the beer in carbonnade. In contrast, daube Provençal relies on a complex blend of ingredients, which we methodically began to test. Tasters loved the earthiness of dried cèpes (the mushrooms known more commonly by their Italian name, porcini). Niçoise olives lent a briny and authentic local flavor and tomatoes brought brightness and texture. Orange peel contributed a subtle floral element, while herbs, particularly thyme and bay leaves, are a natural addition in anything from Provence.

Tasters weren't enthusiastic about every authentic ingredient we tried. When we broached the subject of anchovies, some tasters claimed that these pungent fish have no place in beef stew. When we made our stew without the anchovies, though, tasters complained that the stew lacked depth of flavor. Over the next couple of days, we quietly added the anchovies back in one at a time and stopped at three fillets, at which point tasters praised the rich, earthy flavors of the dish and noticed a complexity that had been missing without them. (They never knew the secret.)

Pig's trotters, a standard ingredient in many older recipes, contribute body to the sauce in the form of gelatin and flavor from the pork meat and fat. But the protests against a foot in the stew were too much, and this time we caved in. We substituted salt pork, a salt-cured cut from the pig's belly, and adjusted the amount of salt in the stew to accommodate it. The salt pork, like the anchovies, added a richness of flavor that was unmistakably absent when it was not included. We added it in a single piece that we removed and discarded just before serving, once the pork had given up its flavor to the stew.

We had been following the French technique of adding a small amount of flour in the form of a roux, a butter and flour thickener, but up to this point we weren't satisfied with the consistency of the sauce. The butter sometimes ended up floating to the top of the stew, making it look greasy, and the sauce was still too thin. We returned to our established technique and omitted the step of making a roux. Instead, we sprinkled flour into the pot to cook with the vegetables and tomato paste. We also increased the amount

of flour to ⅓ cup. The result was immediately noticeable. The extra flour created a braising liquid that thickened to the consistency of a luxurious sauce.

What started as a key ingredient in daube Provençal, the red wine, had now been relegated to a mere afterthought, barely discernible amid the other ingredients. Our recipe contained a half bottle. Could we add more? Conservatively, we began adding more wine, careful not to sacrifice the integrity of the other flavors. In the end, we discovered that this stew was bold enough to accommodate an entire bottle—at least in theory. The wine tasted a bit raw, so we put the stew back into the oven for additional 15-minute increments until the total cooking time approached three hours. The resulting sauce was just what we wanted, with rich round flavors and a velvety texture.

What was good for the sauce wasn't so good for the meat. We had been cutting the chuck roast into 1-inch cubes, a standard size for beef stew. But with the longer cooking time, the meat was drying out and losing its distinct character. By cutting the chuck roast into 2-inch pieces, we were able to keep the longer braising time and create a truly complex sauce. The beef was now tender and flavorful, and the larger pieces added to the rustic quality of this dish—an ideal rendition of a Provençal classic.

Daube Provençal
SERVES 6 TO 8

There are many salty ingredients in this stew, so season it carefully. We tie the salt pork with twine in order to make it easy to identify after cooking; otherwise, it looks exactly like a piece of stew meat. Cabernet Sauvignon is our favorite wine for this recipe, but Côtes du Rhône and Zinfandel also work. If niçoise olives are not available, kalamata olives, though not authentic, can be substituted.

1   (3½- to 4-pound) boneless beef chuck eye roast, trimmed and cut into 2-inch pieces
    Salt and ground black pepper
3   tablespoons olive oil
2   medium onions, halved and sliced ⅛ inch thick
¾   ounce dried porcini mushrooms, rinsed and minced

1   tablespoon minced fresh thyme leaves,
    or 1 teaspoon dried

⅓   cup unbleached all-purpose flour

2   tablespoons tomato paste

1   (750-ml) bottle dry red wine

1   cup water

¾   cup low-sodium chicken broth

¾   cup low-sodium beef broth

5   ounces salt pork, rind removed, tied tightly
    with butcher's twine

4   (3-inch-long) strips orange zest from one
    orange (see the illustration on page 72),
    cut into thin matchsticks

1   cup pitted niçoise olives, patted dry
    and chopped coarse

4   medium garlic cloves, peeled and sliced thin

3   anchovy fillets, rinsed and minced
    (about 1 teaspoon)

2   bay leaves

1   pound carrots (about 6 medium), peeled
    and sliced 1 inch thick

1   (14.5-ounce) can whole tomatoes, drained
    and cut into ½-inch pieces

2   tablespoons minced fresh parsley leaves

1. Adjust an oven rack to the lower-middle position and heat the oven to 325 degrees. Pat the beef dry with paper towels and season with salt and pepper. Heat 1 tablespoon of the oil in a large Dutch oven over medium-high heat until just smoking. Add half of the meat and cook, stirring occasionally, until well browned, 7 to 10 minutes, reducing the heat if the pot begins to scorch. Transfer the browned beef to a medium bowl. Repeat with 1 tablespoon more oil and the remaining beef; transfer to the bowl.

2. Add the remaining 1 tablespoon oil to the pot and heat over medium-low heat until shimmering. Add the onions, mushrooms, thyme, and ¼ teaspoon salt and cook, stirring often, until softened, 5 to 7 minutes. Stir in the flour and tomato paste and cook, stirring constantly, for 1 minute. Slowly whisk in the wine, scraping up any browned bits. Gradually whisk in the water and broths until smooth and bring to a simmer.

3. Stir in the browned meat with any accumulated juices, salt pork, orange zest, half of the olives, garlic, anchovies, and bay leaves and bring to a

simmer. Cover the pot partially (the lid should be just off center to leave about 1 inch open), place the pot in the oven, and cook for 1½ hours. Stir in the carrots and continue to cook in the oven, partially covered, until the meat is tender and the sauce is thickened and glossy, 1 to 1½ hours longer.

4. Remove the stew from the oven and remove the salt pork and bay leaves. Stir in the tomatoes and remaining olives, cover, and let stand for 5 minutes. Stir in the parsley and season with salt and pepper to taste before serving.

BEEF BURGUNDY

IF THE LOUVRE WERE JUST A MUSEUM, THEN *boeuf à la bourguignonne* might be just beef stew. Both are French and utterly extraordinary, but only one can be enjoyed at home. We liken beef Burgundy more to a fabulous prime steak napped with a rich, silken red wine reduction sauce than to a mundane beef stew. The beef in beef Burgundy is cut into satisfyingly large chunks that become utterly tender. The braising liquid, brimming with voluptuous wine and infused with aromatic vegetables, garlic, and herbs, is finessed into a sauce of burgundy velvet studded with mushrooms and pearl onions. Beef Burgundy is earthy, big, robust, warm, and welcoming in a brooding sort of way.

At least that's what it is at its best. We have had versions that fell far short of this ideal, with tough meat or a dull sauce with no flavor complexity. We wanted to find a way to bring this classic dish to its full potential in a home kitchen.

Recipes for beef Burgundy are very much alike. Aromatic vegetables (onions, garlic, and carrots), red wine, stock, herbs, mushrooms, and pearl onions are all requisite ingredients; their combinations and proportions and the variations in preparation and technique are where the recipes diverge.

After testing a few recipes, we quickly made a couple of important observations. First, marinating the beef in the red wine and herbs that will later go into the braise—a common recommendation in recipes—does not improve the flavor of the cooked meat. Second, the braising liquid requires straining to rid it of bits of aromatic vegetables and herbs so that it may become a silky sauce. We found that bundling these ingredients in cheesecloth made their extraction possible in one easy step. The aromatics cannot be sautéed when bundled in cheesecloth, but we were happy to discover that this did not affect the flavor of the finished stew. For good measure we used generous amounts of chopped onions, carrots, and garlic, as well as parsley, thyme, and bay leaves, to create a balanced mélange of flavors.

The cut of beef best suited to the long braise of beef Burgundy is a chuck eye roast. It's the cut that almost every recipe calls for and the one we prefer in a regular beef stew because of its rich, meaty flavor. Because the beef in a beef Burgundy is cut into chunks larger than those in a beef stew—we liked 2-inch pieces—we found it necessary to take extra care to trim off as much fat and silver skin as possible; larger pieces of beef also mean larger, more detectable bites of these undesirables.

Every recipe we uncovered in our research began with either salt pork or bacon cut into lardons, or small strips, and fried to a crisp; the fat that results is used to brown the beef chunks. The crisped pork is added to the pot to simmer alongside the beef so that it can contribute its flavors to the braise. We tried both bacon and salt pork and favored the cleaner, purer flavor of salt pork. Classically, the salt pork is served in the stew as "garnish" but some tasters objected to the fatty pieces dotting this otherwise elegant dish. Instead of fishing out pieces of pork fat before serving, we decided to add it to the cheesecloth bundle along with the aromatics, after it had given up its fat in sautéing.

Wine was the next issue. Beef Burgundy does not exist without a healthy dose of it. We concluded after several batches that anything less than a whole bottle left the sauce lacking and unremarkable. After numerous experiments, we had determined that a Burgundy, or at least a decent Pinot Noir, is indeed the wine of choice. Though most recipes indicate that all of the wine should be added at the outset, one recipe, as well as one wine expert, recommended saving just a bit of the wine to add at the very end, just before serving. This late embellishment of raw wine vastly improved the sauce, brightening its flavor and giving it resonance. A

combination of chicken and beef broth, along with a little water, rounded out the liquid component.

We also found that just a small amount of dried porcini mushrooms wrapped into the cheesecloth package brought the meatiness and savory quality that homemade beef stock would conceivably have added. A modicum of tomato paste added color.

With everything assembled in the pot, into the oven it went, where the constant, all-encompassing heat produced an even simmer that required little attention. Focusing finally on the mushroom and pearl onion garnish, we noted that it was impossible to cook them in the stew alongside the beef because they turned mushy. The convenience of already peeled frozen pearl onions was too great to ignore, and a brisk simmer in a separate pan (a skillet) with some water, butter, and sugar was all they needed to take on some flavor and life. Giving the mushrooms a quick sauté also worked well and created glazed beauties that were ready to grace the

MAKING THE AROMATIC BOUQUET

1. Lay a double layer of cheesecloth (14-inch square) in a medium bowl. Place the designated ingredients in the cheesecloth-lined bowl.

2. Gather together the edges of the cheesecloth and fasten them securely with kitchen twine. Trim any excess cheesecloth with scissors if necessary.

stew, along with a sprinkling of fresh parsley. Once we added the final flourish, a little brandy for richness and warmth, we finally had a beef Burgundy elegant enough for company.

Beef Burgundy

SERVES 6 TO 8

If not enough fat is rendered from the salt pork for browning the meat, add vegetable oil. Serve with boiled potatoes, mashed potatoes, or buttered noodles.

AROMATIC BOUQUET

4	ounces salt pork, cut into ¼-inch-thick matchsticks
10	sprigs fresh parsley, torn into pieces
6	sprigs fresh thyme
2	medium onions, chopped coarse
2	medium carrots, chopped coarse
1	medium head garlic, cloves separated and crushed
2	bay leaves, crumbled
½	ounce dried porcini mushrooms, rinsed

STEW

1	(3½- to 4-pound) boneless beef chuck eye roast, trimmed and cut into 2-inch pieces
	Salt and ground black pepper
3	tablespoons unsalted butter, cut into 3 pieces
⅓	cup unbleached all-purpose flour
1	tablespoon tomato paste
1	(750-ml) bottle red Burgundy or Pinot Noir
1½	cups low-sodium chicken broth
1¼	cups low-sodium beef broth

GARNISH

7	ounces frozen pearl onions
½	cup water
2	tablespoons unsalted butter
1	tablespoon sugar
1	pound white mushrooms, wiped clean and halved if small or quartered if large
	Salt
2	tablespoons brandy
3	tablespoons minced fresh parsley leaves
	Ground black pepper

1. FOR THE BOUQUET: Cook the salt pork in a large Dutch oven over medium heat until lightly browned and crisp, about 12 minutes. With a slotted spoon, transfer the salt pork to a plate. Pour off and reserve the fat. Following the illustrations on page 102, assemble the salt pork and remaining bouquet ingredients into a double-layer cheesecloth pouch and tie securely with kitchen twine.

2. FOR THE STEW: Adjust an oven rack to the lower-middle position and heat the oven to 325 degrees. Pat the beef dry with paper towels and season with salt and pepper. Heat 1 tablespoon of the rendered pork fat in a large Dutch oven over medium-high heat until just smoking. Add half of the meat and cook, stirring occasionally, until well browned, 7 to 10 minutes, reducing the heat if the pot begins to scorch. Transfer the browned beef to a medium bowl. Repeat with 1 tablespoon more rendered pork fat and the remaining beef; transfer to the bowl.

3. Add the butter to the pot and melt over medium-low heat. Stir in the flour and tomato paste and cook, stirring constantly, for 1 minute. Slowly whisk in all but 2 tablespoons of the wine, scraping up any browned bits. Gradually whisk in the broths until smooth and bring to a simmer.

4. Stir in the browned meat with any accumulated juices, submerge the aromatic bouquet in the liquid, and bring to a simmer. Cover, place the pot in the oven, and cook until the meat is tender, 2½ to 3 hours.

5. FOR THE GARNISH: Bring the pearl onions, water, butter, and sugar to a boil in a large nonstick skillet over medium-high heat. Reduce the heat to medium, cover, and cook until the onions are fully thawed and tender, 5 to 8 minutes. Uncover, increase the heat to medium-high, and cook until all the liquid evaporates, 3 to 4 minutes. Add the mushrooms and ¼ teaspoon salt and cook, without stirring, for 2 minutes. Stir and continue to cook, stirring often, until the vegetables are browned and glazed, 8 to 12 minutes. Remove from the heat and set aside.

6. Remove the stew from the oven and remove the aromatic bouquet. Stir in the mushroom and onion garnish, cover, and let stand for 5 minutes. Stir in the remaining 2 tablespoons wine, brandy, and parsley and season with salt and pepper to taste before serving.

Stews 101

The making of stew is a sort of kitchen alchemy that turns a modest cut of meat and some basic vegetables into something rich, flavorful, and much more interesting. Even better, stews generally require little preparation or effort; time and gentle simmering do all the work. That said, we've all had (or made) stews with tough meat, listless vegetables, and dull, watery broth. Here are the steps necessary for producing a superior stew.

1. Cut Your Own Meat:

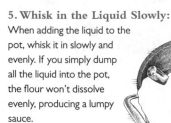

Packages of precut "stew meat" consist of variously sized scraps from the butcher that will cook at different rates. By cutting your own stew meat, you not only guarantee that the chunks of meat will be the same size, but you can pick the best cuts for stewing. It is very important to use fatty, flavorful cuts of meat, such as cuts from the shoulder area for beef, pork, and lamb, or thigh meat for chicken. These cuts of meat are well marbled with fat, which means they won't dry out during long, slow stewing time.

2. Brown the Meat Properly:

Browning the meat is key to developing a deep, meaty flavor in the stew. There are three things to keep in mind when browning meat: Get the pot hot (the oil should be just smoking over medium-high heat); don't crowd the meat (or it will steam rather than brown); and turn the heat down if the pan begins to scorch (if the flavorful browned bits left in the pot burn, the stew will have a burnt taste).

3. Sauté Aromatics to Enhance Flavor:

Recipes that call for dumping spices and aromatics, such as garlic and onion, into the pot at the same time as the liquid fail to maximize their flavor. So hold the liquid and sauté these flavor-enhancing ingredients first.

4. Add Flour Early to Thicken the Stew:

Many recipes call for thickening a stew at the end of cooking by leaving the lid off, but this method risks overcooking and produces a thin, jus-like broth. Instead, thicken the stew at the beginning of the cooking process by sprinkling flour into the pot (usually over the sautéed aromatics); this method yields a consistently thickened sauce with a silky texture more akin to gravy. When adding the flour to the pot, be sure to cook it for a minute or so to remove the raw flour taste, before whisking in the liquid.

5. Whisk in the Liquid Slowly:

When adding the liquid to the pot, whisk it in slowly and evenly. If you simply dump all the liquid into the pot, the flour won't dissolve evenly, producing a lumpy sauce.

6. Cover and Cook in the Oven:

To ensure a steady, gentle simmer that allows the internal temperature of the meat to rise slowly and eliminates the risk of scorching the pot bottom, cook the stew in a covered Dutch oven at a moderate oven temperature (between 300 and 325 degrees). This will keep the temperature of the stewing liquid below the boiling point (212 degrees) and ensure meat that is tender, not tough.

7. Add the Vegetables Partway Through Cooking:

When vegetables are dumped indiscriminately into the pot at the outset of cooking, they not only lose flavor and turn mushy, but also water down the stew. Adding them partway through the cooking time ensures that they will be fully cooked but not mushy.

8. Cook Until the Meat Is Fall-Apart Tender:

When meat is undercooked, its fat and connective tissue have not had the chance to break down sufficiently and it will taste rubbery and tough. Cook meat to the point where collagen has melted down into gelatin. This yields tender meat that separates easily when pulled apart with two forks.

LAMB TAGINE

TAGINES, EXOTICALLY SPICED, ASSERTIVELY flavored stews, are a specialty of Morocco. Typically slow cooked in earthenware vessels of the same name, tagines can include all manner of meats, vegetables, and fruit, though one of our favorites combines lamb with olives, lemon, and apricots. The briny bite of the olives and clarifying tartness of the lemon bring out the best in the meat and the spices, while the sweetness of the apricots provides a pleasing contrast.

While we love tagine, it's not a dish we ever conceived of as American home cooking. Why? The few traditional recipes we had seen required time-consuming, labor-intensive cooking methods (some that were entirely foreign to us), a special pot (the tagine), and hard-to-find ingredients (preserved lemon). Although usually game for a day in the kitchen or a hunt for exotica, we realized that tagine, at its most elemental level, is just stew.

A little research proved that we weren't the first to take a stab at making tagine accessible. We collected a number of recipes for lamb with olives and lemon, and although most lacked the depth of an authentic tagine, they held promise nonetheless. They proved that, first, a western cooking method—braising (brown the meat, sauté the aromatics, add broth, and simmer)—was a serviceable substitution. Second, a Dutch oven worked fine—no special equipment necessary. And finally, the flavors associated with Moroccan cooking weren't necessarily "exotic"— they were more a strategic blending of common ingredients and spices already in most cupboards.

When making lamb stews in the past, we have used both the meat and the bones from lamb shoulder chops for maximum flavor. But given the abundance of flavors in this recipe, we wondered if we could simplify the process and use boneless lamb shoulder meat instead. We were happy to find that no one missed the subtle complexity provided by the bones. Although we find it necessary to pat beef dry with paper towels before browning it, when we tried doing so with lamb the paper towels stuck to the meat, so we skipped this step.

A few sliced onions and a healthy dose of garlic rounded out the basic flavors of our tagine, and so we were ready to tackle the defining ingredients: spices, olives, and lemon. Many recipes called for a spice blend called *ras el hanout*, which may contain upward of 30 spices. As with many spice blends, ras el hanout is more a matter of taste than rigid formula. We experimented with a broad range of spices until we landed on a blend that was short on ingredients but long on flavor. Cumin and ginger lent depth, cinnamon brought warmth to temper a little cayenne heat, and citrusy coriander boosted the stew's lemon flavor. Paprika added sweetness and, perhaps more important, colored the broth a deep, attractive red. Thoroughly toasting the spices brought out the full depth of flavors.

Finding the right olive proved harder than we anticipated. Big meaty, green Moroccan olives were the obvious choice, but they were a rarity at any of our local supermarkets. Other big green olives, like Manzanilla, Cerignola, or Lucques, were the right size, but the flavors were either too mild or too assertive to match the other flavors in the tagine. Greek "cracked" olives, however, tasted great and were easy to find. But when we added the olives to the stew too soon, their flavor leached out into the broth, rendering them bitter. Stirring in the olives at the end of the stew's simmering time (with the apricots) proved a much better approach, as they retained more of their flavor and firm texture.

The lemon flavor in authentic tagines comes from preserved lemon, a long-cured Moroccan condiment that's hard to find outside of specialty stores. "Quick" preserved lemons can be produced at home in a few days, but we wanted to keep the tagine simple and fast. Part tart citrus, part pickled brine, preserved lemon provides a taste that is impossible to imitate. So we chose not to try; instead, we aimed to add a rich citrus background note to the broth. We added a few broad ribbons of lemon zest along with the onions, and the high heat coaxed out the zest's oils and mellowed them. Adding two lemons' worth of juice just before serving reinforced the bright flavor. A couple spoonfuls of honey further balanced the broth, and minced cilantro freshened things, but we felt the stew still lacked a certain spark. A last-minute addition of raw garlic and finely chopped lemon zest seemed to clinch it, as the sharpness brought out the best in each of the stew's components.

Lamb Tagine

SERVES 6 TO 8

If you cannot find pitted green olives, substitute pimiento-stuffed green olives; if the olives are particularly salty, give them a rinse. A variety of dried fruits, including pitted prunes, dark raisins, golden raisins, or currants, can be substituted for the apricots. Serve with couscous. Be sure to zest both lemons before juicing them.

1	(3½- to 4-pound) boneless lamb shoulder roast, trimmed and cut into 1½-inch pieces
	Salt and ground black pepper
3	tablespoons olive oil
3	medium onions, halved and sliced ¼ inch thick
4	(2-inch-long) strips lemon zest from 1 lemon (see page 72)
8	medium garlic cloves, minced or pressed through a garlic press (about 8 teaspoons), plus 2 medium garlic cloves, minced to a fine paste (see the illustrations on page 27)
2½	teaspoons sweet paprika
1	teaspoon ground cumin
½	teaspoon ground ginger
½	teaspoon ground coriander
½	teaspoon ground cinnamon
¼	teaspoon cayenne pepper
¼	cup unbleached all-purpose flour
4	cups low-sodium chicken broth
2	tablespoons honey
1	pound carrots (about 6 medium), peeled and sliced 1 inch thick
2	cups pitted Greek green olives, halved (see note)
1	cup dried apricots, chopped
¼	cup minced fresh cilantro leaves
¼	cup juice from 2 lemons
½	teaspoon grated lemon zest from 1 lemon

1. Adjust an oven rack to the lower-middle position and heat the oven to 325 degrees. Season the lamb with salt and pepper. Heat 1 tablespoon of the oil in a large Dutch oven over medium-high heat until just smoking. Add half of the meat and cook, stirring occasionally, until well browned, 7 to 10 minutes, reducing the heat if the pot begins to scorch. Transfer the browned lamb to a medium bowl. Repeat with 1 tablespoon more oil and the remaining lamb; transfer to the bowl.

2. Add the remaining 1 tablespoon oil to the pot and place over medium-low heat until shimmering. Add the onions, lemon zest strips, and ¼ teaspoon salt and cook, stirring often, until the onions are softened, 5 to 7 minutes. Stir in the minced garlic, paprika, cumin, ginger, coriander, cinnamon, and cayenne and cook until fragrant, about 30 seconds. Stir in the flour and cook, stirring constantly, until golden, about 1 minute. Slowly whisk in the broth, scraping up any browned bits, until smooth, and bring to a simmer.

3. Stir in the browned meat with any accumulated juices and the honey and bring to a simmer. Cover, place the pot in the oven, and cook for 1 hour. Stir in the carrots and continue to cook in the oven, covered, until the meat is tender, 1 to 1½ hours longer.

4. Remove the tagine from the oven and remove the lemon zest strips. Stir in the olives and apricots, cover, and let stand for 5 minutes. Stir in the cilantro, lemon juice, mashed garlic, and grated lemon zest and season with salt and pepper to taste before serving.

CHOPPING DRIED FRUIT

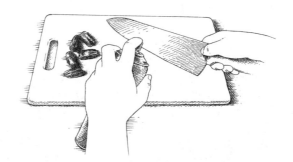

Dried fruit, especially apricots (or dates), very often sticks to the knife when you try to chop it. To avoid this problem, coat the blade with a thin film of vegetable cooking spray just before you begin chopping any dried fruit. The chopped fruit won't cling to the blade, and the knife will stay relatively clean.

PORK STEW

THOUGH LESS COMMON HERE IN THE UNITED States, pork stews are popular in many parts of the world, and one of our favorites is a dish from France that combines braised pork with carrots, prunes, brandy, and a touch of cream. The pork is fall-apart tender, its flavor enhanced by the sweetness of the carrots and the prunes, yet savory with a stock and cream broth—a luxurious blend of flavors and textures. Elegant without being fussy, it's the perfect dish for entertaining. We wanted a rich, satisfying pork stew with a careful balance of savory and sweet.

We already knew from our experience with stewing beef that the shoulder, or chuck, is the best cut for braising, and so we assumed that pork shoulder would also make the best, most flavorful pork stew. To test this proposition, we stewed various cuts of pork from both the shoulder and loin, including several kinds of chops. The shoulder cuts were indeed far superior to those from the loin. Like beef chuck, pork shoulder has enough fat to keep the meat tender and juicy during the long cooking process.

But which cut from the shoulder works best? Pork shoulder is called Boston butt or Boston shoulder in most markets. The picnic roast also comes from the shoulder, but includes the skin and bone, which means more prep work. As with beef, we recommend buying a boneless roast and cutting it into cubes yourself (you can use a picnic roast, but the bone, skin, and thick layer of fat will need to be removed with a knife and discarded). Once the pork was cubed and seasoned with salt and pepper, we browned it to enhance its flavor and that of the overall stew. After setting aside the meat, we added leeks to the pot, cooking them until they softened, which provided a sweet, aromatic backdrop for the stew.

With the cut of meat and the choice of aromatic settled, we moved on to the braising liquid. We needed a full 5 cups of liquid to properly braise the pork and provide ample liquid for serving the stew. Brandy would be the defining flavor of our braising liquid, complemented by chicken broth for a savory element and cream for richness. We knew this would require a careful balancing act. Starting with 1 cup of brandy (enough to generously deglaze the pan and shine through the other ingredients in this flavorful braise without overwhelming them), we added 2 cups each of the chicken broth and cream. But this was too heavy. And because this stew requires a significant amount of time in the oven, the sweetness of the cream was also now a bit cloying, which in turn dulled the flavor of the brandy. (Like our beef stews, this pork stew is started on the stovetop to brown the meat and start cooking the vegetables, but the bulk of the cooking happens in the oven for gentle, all-encompassing heat.) The obvious fix was to decrease the amount of cream (to 1 cup) and increase the amount of chicken broth (to 3 cups). This was an

PREPARING LEEKS

1. Trim and discard the roots and the dark green leaves.

2. Slice the trimmed leek in half lengthwise, then cut it into ¼-inch pieces.

3. Rinse the cut leeks thoroughly in a bowl of water to remove the dirt and sand.

PREPARING FENNEL

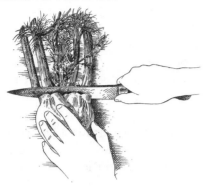

1. Cut off the stalks and feathery fronds (the fronds can be minced and used for a garnish).

2. Trim a very thin slice from the base and remove any tough or blemished outer layers from the bulb.

3. Cut the bulb in half through the base. Use a small, sharp knife to remove the pyramid-shaped core.

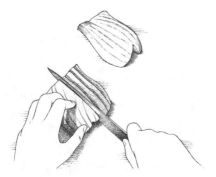

4. Lay the cored fennel flat on the cutting board and slice into ½-inch-thick strips.

improvement, but the cream still had that overly sweet, "cooked" flavor. Holding the cream and adding it at the end of cooking worked best: the cream retained its fresh flavor without overpowering the other ingredients.

We already knew prunes and carrots would play an integral role in our stew, but we thought another vegetable might further round out the flavors. We settled on fennel—with its subtle anise notes, it perfectly complemented the other flavors of the stew. Combined with the cream, the brandy, and the pork, it was a hit. Because fennel and carrots cook at a much faster pace than pork, we added them halfway through cooking so they could coast to the finish line together. The prunes were best added at the very end of cooking to prevent them from breaking down and disintegrating into the stew. Freshly minced tarragon and parsley, as well as some lemon juice, all added a welcome complexity to the finished dish.

Pork Stew with Fennel and Prunes
SERVES 6 TO 8

Boneless pork butt roast is often labeled as boneless Boston butt in the supermarket. Don't substitute dried tarragon or parsley here. While 1 cup of brandy may seem like a lot for this recipe, we recommend using an inexpensive brand and not skimping on the amount—it provides just the right balance of flavors. Serve with buttered noodles or rice pilaf.

1   (3½- to 4-pound) boneless pork butt roast, trimmed and cut into 1½-inch pieces (see note)
     Salt and ground black pepper
3   tablespoons vegetable oil
1   large leek, white and light green parts only, halved lengthwise, sliced ¼ inch thick, and rinsed thoroughly (see the illustrations on page 107)
3   medium garlic cloves, minced or pressed through a garlic press (about 1 tablespoon)
3   tablespoons unbleached all-purpose flour

1 cup brandy (see note)

3 cups low-sodium chicken broth

2 bay leaves

1 pound carrots (about 6 medium), peeled and sliced 1 inch thick

1 large fennel bulb (about 1 pound), trimmed of stalks, cored, and cut into ½-inch-thick strips (see the illustrations on page 108)

1 cup heavy cream

1 cup prunes, halved

2 tablespoons minced fresh tarragon leaves

2 tablespoons minced fresh parsley leaves

1 tablespoon juice from 1 lemon

1. Adjust an oven rack to the lower-middle position and heat the oven to 325 degrees. Pat the pork dry with paper towels and season with salt and pepper. Heat 1 tablespoon of the oil in a large Dutch oven over medium-high heat until just smoking. Add half of the meat and cook, stirring occasionally, until well browned, 7 to 10 minutes, reducing the heat if the pot begins to scorch. Transfer the browned pork to a medium bowl. Repeat with 1 tablespoon more oil and the remaining pork; transfer to the bowl.

2. Add the remaining 1 tablespoon oil to the pot and place over medium-low heat until shimmering. Add the leek and ¼ teaspoon salt and cook, stirring often, until wilted and lightly browned, 5 to 7 minutes. Stir in the garlic and cook until fragrant, about 30 seconds. Stir in the flour and cook, stirring constantly, until golden, about 1 minute. Slowly whisk in the brandy, scraping up any browned bits. Gradually whisk in the broth until smooth and bring to a simmer.

3. Stir in the browned meat with any accumulated juices and the bay leaves and bring to a simmer. Cover, place the pot in the oven, and cook for 1 hour. Stir in the carrots and fennel and continue to cook in the oven, covered, until the meat is tender, about 1 hour longer.

4. Remove the stew from the oven and remove the bay leaves. Stir in the cream and prunes, cover, and let stand for 5 minutes. Stir in the tarragon, parsley, and lemon juice and season with salt and pepper to taste before serving.

➤ VARIATION
Veal Stew with Fennel and Prunes
Follow the recipe for Pork Stew with Fennel and Prunes, substituting a 3½- to 4-pound boneless veal shoulder roast, trimmed and cut into 1½-inch pieces, for the pork roast.

PORK VINDALOO

VINDALOO IS A COMPLEX, SPICY DISH THAT originated in Goa, a region on India's western coast. Because Goa was once a Portuguese colony, much of the local cuisine incorporates Indian and Portuguese ingredients and techniques. In fact, the word vindaloo comes from the Portuguese words for wine vinegar (*vinho*) and garlic (*alhos*). In addition to these two ingredients, vindaloo gets its warm, pungent flavor from a mixture of spices (such as cumin and cardamom), chiles (usually in the form of cayenne and paprika), tomatoes, and mustard seeds. As for the main ingredient, although there are versions made with chicken, beef, or lamb, vindaloo is most often made with pork.

A well-prepared vindaloo features tender meat in a thick, reddish-orange sauce with a delicately balanced flavor. The heat of the chiles is tamed by the sweetness of the aromatic spices and the acidity of the tomatoes and vinegar. Onions and garlic add pungency, while the mustard seeds lend their unique flavor and crunch.

Most vindaloo recipes we tested were pretty good but we noticed two recurring problems—tough and/or dry meat and muddied flavors. We decided to start with the meat component in this dish and then focus on the flavoring options.

Given our experience stewing beef, we figured that pork shoulder would make the best stew. To test this proposition, we stewed various cuts of pork from the shoulder and loin, including several kinds of chops. The shoulder cuts were far superior to the loin. Like beef chuck, pork shoulder has enough fat to keep the meat tender and juicy during the long cooking process.

Pork shoulder is often called Boston butt or Boston shoulder in markets. The picnic roast also comes from the shoulder. For vindaloo, a boneless Boston butt is your best option because there is less waste. (You can use a picnic roast, but the bone, skin, and thick layer of fat will need to be discarded.) As with beef, we recommend buying a boneless roast and cutting it into pieces yourself. When we purchased precut pork labeled "stew meat," the results were disappointing. The pieces were irregularly sized and seemed to have come from several parts of the animal. The resulting stew had pieces that were dry and overcooked.

We browned the pork to enhance its flavor and that of the stewing liquid. We left a little room in the pot between the pieces of meat and cooked them for at least seven minutes to get each pork cube well browned.

Spices are the cornerstone of this stew. We used a classic combination of sweet and hot spices and found that we got the best flavor from small amounts of many spices, rather than larger amounts of fewer spices. For chile flavor, we used sweet paprika and cayenne. To give the stew its characteristic earthy qualities, we added cumin, along with sweet, aromatic cardamom and cloves. Mustard seeds, a spice used frequently in the cooking of South India, added pungency. Bay leaves rounded out the flavor of this stew and a sprinkling of cilantro just before serving lent the final fresh note.

Our next area of concern was the stewing liquid. Most traditional recipes simply use water. The theory is that water is a neutral medium that allows the flavors of the meat and spices to come through as clearly as possible. We wondered, though, if chicken broth would add richness and body to the stewing liquid. We prepared two batches—one with water, the other with chicken broth. Tasters felt that the chicken broth added complexity and fullness without calling attention to itself.

A hallmark of pork vindaloo is its interplay of sweet and sour flavors. Two tablespoons of red wine vinegar and 1 teaspoon of sugar provided the right balance. In order to give it time to soften and mix with the other flavors, we added the vinegar at the beginning of cooking. For further acidity, diced canned tomatoes, with their juice, were far

less work than fresh tomatoes (which needed to be peeled and seeded) and performed admirably in taste tests.

Pork Vindaloo

SERVES 6

Boneless pork butt roast is often labeled as boneless Boston butt in the supermarket. Serve with basmati rice.

1	(3½- to 4-pound) boneless pork butt roast, trimmed and cut into 1½-inch pieces (see note)
	Salt and ground black pepper
3	tablespoons vegetable oil
3	medium onions, minced
8	medium garlic cloves, minced or pressed through a garlic press (about 8 teaspoons)
1	tablespoon sweet paprika
¾	teaspoon ground cumin
½	teaspoon ground cardamom
¼	teaspoon cayenne pepper
¼	teaspoon ground cloves
3	tablespoons unbleached all-purpose flour
1½	cups low-sodium chicken broth
1	(14.5-ounce) can diced tomatoes
2	bay leaves
1	teaspoon sugar
2	tablespoons red wine vinegar
1	tablespoon mustard seeds
¼	cup minced fresh cilantro leaves

1. Adjust an oven rack to the lower-middle position and heat the oven to 325 degrees. Pat the pork dry with paper towels and season with salt and pepper. Heat 1 tablespoon of the oil in a large Dutch oven over medium-high heat until just smoking. Add half of the meat and cook, stirring occasionally, until well browned, 7 to 10 minutes, reducing the heat if the pot begins to scorch. Transfer the browned pork to a medium bowl. Repeat with 1 tablespoon more oil and the remaining pork; transfer to the bowl.

2. Add the remaining 1 tablespoon oil to the pot and place over medium-low heat until shimmering. Add the onions and ¼ teaspoon salt and cook, stirring often, until softened, 5 to 7 minutes. Stir in

the garlic, paprika, cumin, cardamom, cayenne, and cloves and cook until fragrant, about 30 seconds. Stir in the flour and cook, stirring constantly, until golden, about 1 minute. Slowly whisk in the broth, scraping up any browned bits, until smooth, and bring to a simmer.

3. Stir in the browned meat with any accumulated juices, tomatoes with their juice, bay leaves, sugar, vinegar, and mustard seeds and bring to a simmer. Cover, place the pot in the oven, and cook until the meat is tender, about 2 hours.

4. Remove the stew from the oven and remove the bay leaves. Stir in the cilantro and season with salt and pepper to taste before serving.

CASSOULET

CASSOULET IS PERHAPS FRANCE'S MOST revered stew. The dish typically is composed of garlicky white beans, pork sausage, duck confit, and a variety of other meats such as lamb and pork loin—the whole capped with a buttery bread crumb topping. Unlike a simple beef stew, which requires just one type of meat, cassoulet contains a host of meats, all of which meld together into one rich and hearty meal. While this classic French peasant dish can be replicated at restaurants, it is usually not regarded as a dish for the casual home cook. The time investment alone is impractical and it can be difficult to achieve a perfect balance of flavors. On more than one occasion we have eaten cassoulets that were overwhelmed by salt or swimming in fat, most often because of the confit and sausages. But we love this dish so much that we decided it would be worth the effort to try to streamline it without compromising its fundamental nature.

We started our testing with the duck confit—an essential component of cassoulet. You can purchase confit by mail order or in some specialty shops, but we wanted to also try our hand at making our own. To make confit, duck legs are placed in a large container, sprinkled heavily with salt, and cured for 24 to 48 hours. The salt draws the juices out, which both preserves and tenderizes the meat. After this sojourn in salt, the meat is slowly simmered in

its own fat, so that the flavor of the fat penetrates the spaces previously occupied by the juices. The finished confit may be used immediately or stored in an airtight container. We felt we could cut this time down considerably—after all, the salt cure used to be for preserving, which we can now do in our modern refrigerators. We wanted to salt the duck just long enough to allow the salt to penetrate the meat, in order to make the flavors more pronounced. A couple of hours wasn't long enough, but overnight was perfect. With an overnight salt cure and two hours in a moderately low oven, our duck confit was ready.

Our next test involved figuring out which meats to use. We knew that we wanted to be true to the original recipe and use either fresh pork or lamb. We decided to try stewing the meat in liquid on top of the stove rather than roasting it. This method yielded great results in terms of tenderness, but the meat had none of the depth of flavor that occurs with roasting. Searing the meat first took care of that problem. Because we were now stewing the meat, we needed to use cuts that were appropriate for this method. We tried pork loin, the choice in so many cassoulet recipes, but the loin became waterlogged and tasteless during stewing. We also tried pork butt, which is actually part of the shoulder. This cut, which has more internal fat than the center loin, retained the moisture and flavor that was lost with the other cut. But we needed less than two pounds, and a pork butt that small can be hard to find. We settled on country-style pork ribs as a good substitute; cut from near the shoulder, they had enough fat to stay moist and tender.

Next we focused on the topping. Tradition dictates fresh bread crumbs, but tasters disliked the way they made the meaty broth of our cassoulet gritty. Our solution? Croutons. We buttered and seasoned cubes of bread and baked them in the oven until golden brown and crisp. Once added to the cassoulet, the bottoms soaked up the meaty juices while the tops stayed buttery and crisp.

Now for the heart and soul of this dish—the beans. In all the discussions over what ingredients should go into a cassoulet, everyone agreed on at least one thing: the dish must be made with white kidney-shaped beans. The two kinds of white beans from this region in France are the *tarbais* (a large flat bean with a kidney shape) and the *lingot* (a smaller and rounder bean). Which of these beans to use is a debate of great importance to the French, but since neither bean is available stateside, we needed to find a close facsimile. Our criteria were that the beans would retain their shape and add a soft texture to the dish. Canned beans fell apart quickly, so we opted for dried beans. We tested four varieties, and the winner was the pale green flageolet bean. These small, French kidney-shaped beans have a creamy, tender texture and delicate flavor that perfectly enhanced the cassoulet. (Flageolets can be hard to find outside of specialty markets and gourmet shops, in which case cannellini or navy beans can be substituted.)

After soaking the beans in salt water, which allowed them to firm up and "set" the skins, making the beans less prone to breaking and bursting during cooking, we rinsed and drained the beans, then cooked them. (For more information on soaking beans in salt water, see our Tuscan White Bean Stew story on page 122.) While we usually cook beans in just water, this dish requires a slightly richer sauce, so we swapped the water for low-sodium chicken broth.

The traditional sausage used in cassoulet is garlic pork sausage, one that we had much difficulty finding in our markets. If you can find it, we recommend using it, but we found that garlic chicken sausage or sweet Italian sausage (without fennel seeds if possible) made the best substitutes. We browned these while the beans were cooking (although you can brown them in the same pot as the beans as a first step—just remove the browned sausages before adding the beans) in order to render as much of the fat as possible and obtain a rich golden color. Once the sausages were browned, we set them aside to await the assembly of the cassoulet.

We started with the beans and braised pork, adding them to our baking dish in great spoonfuls. Into this mixture we nestled the browned sausages and then arranged the duck confit legs on top in order to allow the skin to crisp and brown during the baking process. In order to prevent the croutons from burning, we cooked the cassoulet

for 50 minutes, then sprinkled the croutons on top, and 10 minutes later our cassoulet emerged from the oven browned, bubbling, and perfect. This isn't a quick dish, but with a little time management, the process moves swiftly. At last we had it: a homemade cassoulet that was worthy of its reputation.

Cassoulet
SERVES 6 TO 8

We strongly prefer the flavor of garlic pork sausage here (sometimes called Irish sausage), but other flavors of sausage, including garlic chicken sausage or sweet Italian sausage can be substituted; the flavor of sausage you use will affect the flavor of the finished dish. You can either buy duck confit at a high-end grocery store or butcher shop or make it yourself (see page 182).

PORK AND BEANS

2	pounds dried flageolet beans (or cannellini or navy beans) rinsed, picked over, and salt-soaked overnight or quick salt-soaked (see page 122)
1–1½	pounds boneless country-style pork ribs, trimmed and cut into 1-inch cubes
1	tablespoon vegetable oil
1	medium onion, minced
9	medium garlic cloves, minced or pressed through a garlic press (about 3 tablespoons)
2	tablespoons minced fresh thyme leaves, or 2 teaspoons dried
1	cup dry white wine
1	tablespoon tomato paste
10	cups low-sodium chicken broth, plus extra as needed
1	(28-ounce) can diced tomatoes, drained

CASSOULET AND CROUTONS

6–8	(4- to 6-inch-long) garlic pork sausage links (about 1 pound, see note)
5	slices high-quality white sandwich bread, cut into ½-inch cubes
3	tablespoons unsalted butter, melted Salt and ground black pepper
6–8	confit duck legs, scraped clean of confit fat (see note)

1. **FOR THE PORK AND BEANS:** Drain the beans, discarding the soaking liquid, and rinse well. Pat the ribs dry with paper towels. Heat the oil in a large Dutch oven over medium-high heat until just smoking. Add the pork and cook, stirring occasionally, until well browned, 7 to 10 minutes, reducing the heat if the pan begins to scorch.

2. Stir in the onion and cook, stirring often, until softened, 5 to 7 minutes. Stir in the garlic and thyme and cook until fragrant, about 30 seconds. Stir in the wine and tomato paste, scraping up any browned bits. Stir in the drained beans, chicken broth, and tomatoes and bring to a boil. Reduce to a gentle simmer and cook, uncovered, stirring occasionally, until the beans and pork are just tender, about 1 hour.

3. **FOR THE CASSOULET AND CROUTONS:** Meanwhile, brown the sausages in a 12-inch non-stick skillet over medium heat until golden on all sides, 5 to 8 minutes; transfer to a paper towel–lined plate.

4. Adjust an oven rack to the middle position and heat the oven to 400 degrees. Toss the bread cubes with the butter, ¼ teaspoon salt, and ⅛ teaspoon pepper and spread out over a rimmed baking sheet. Bake until light golden and crisp, about 15 minutes; set aside and leave the oven on.

5. When the beans are just tender, the level of the broth and beans should be equal; if necessary add more broth. Nestle the sausages into the bean mixture, and lay the duck legs, skin side up, on top of the beans (the duck skin should be exposed; do not nestle into the beans).

6. Bake the cassoulet, uncovered, until the duck skin is golden and crisp, and the casserole is bubbling around the edges, about 50 minutes. Sprinkle the croutons over the top and continue to bake until they form a crust, about 10 minutes longer. Let the cassoulet rest and absorb some of the liquid, 15 to 20 minutes, before serving.

➤ VARIATION
Cassoulet with Lamb
Follow the recipe for Cassoulet, substituting 1 to 1½ pounds boneless lamb shoulder for the pork.

CHICKEN STEW

CHICKEN STEW IS A BIT HARD TO DEFINE. Say "beef stew" and most everyone can imagine large boneless chunks of browned beef floating in a rich, dark sauce along with some vegetables. But what, exactly, is chicken stew? We imagine tender, substantial chunks of chicken, accompanied by potatoes, carrots, and peas, enveloped in a glossy, flavorful gravy-like sauce. We think a bowl of chicken stew should be a hearty, comforting meal in and of itself.

Our research of chicken stew yielded recipes with a range of complexity. Some started with a whole chicken that was cut up, browned, and then simmered in water to make stock. The liquid was then strained and the meat was removed from the bones before composing the rest of the stew. The result was pretty tasty, but it seemed like an excessive amount of work. On the other end of the spectrum were recipes that simply poached cubed, boneless skinless breasts and some vegetables in a quick "sauce" made of canned soup. These versions tasted like bad cafeteria food—we knew more simmering time would be needed to develop the rich flavor we were after.

Starting in on our own recipe for chicken stew, we based it loosely on our method for making beef stew—brown the meat, make a sauce with aromatics, flour, wine, and store-bought broth, then simmer the meat and vegetables until they are tender. We set out using a whole chicken, cut up into pieces, but we quickly encountered several problems. The breasts cooked through more quickly than the thighs and drumsticks and tasted dried out, bland, and stringy—a far cry from the tender pieces of stew meat we had in mind. Additionally, the wings contained mostly inedible skin and very little meat. But the dark meat, the thighs and drumsticks, produced wonderfully tender chunks of meat—perfect for stew.

Making the stew again using whole chicken legs we noted that tasters preferred the meatier thighs to the drumsticks. Also, we found the bones undesirable in the finished stew. Thinking that boneless, skinless thighs would be the answer, we were disappointed when a stew made with boneless thighs produced a weaker broth and tough meat. The bone-in thighs, on the other hand, produced a deeply flavored stew with tender pieces of meat—the bones deepen the flavor of the sauce, while the skin acts as a cushion between the meat and the pan, preventing it from getting tough during the browning stage (we removed the skin after browning to prevent a greasy sauce).

Our final tests with the chicken focused on the cooking method. Like beef stew, chicken stew is best when gently simmered, and the temperature for simmering is easier to maintain in a low oven than on the stovetop. On the stovetop, the cooking time varied and even though we set the flame at the same heat level every time, the heat transfer was not uniform. Stewing in a 300-degree oven was much more reliable, producing a predictably even, consistent level of heat. Next, we tested the optimal stewing time. After 30 minutes of stewing, the thighs were cooked through and no longer pink. Unfortunately, they were not as meltingly tender as we desired, and the chicken did not have enough flavor. What if we were to cook them longer?

After gradually increasing the cooking time, we ended up keeping the dish in the oven for 1¼ hours. At this point, the meat was nearly falling off the bone; it was exceedingly tender and flavorful, and the thighs did not seem overcooked. Why does this long cooking time work? The long stay in the oven breaks down the connective tissue in the thighs, much as it does in a pot roast, yielding more tender meat. (White meat contains little connective tissue, so there's no benefit to cooking it longer.) We removed the bones and shredded the meat before adding it back into the stew.

Longer simmering time also quieted some initial reservations a few tasters had expressed about having to remove the meat from the bone before serving: the thighs were so tender it only took a few minutes to pull it into large chunks before returning it to the pot. With the simple addition of some peas, carrots, and potatoes and a sprinkling of fresh herbs, we had our ideal comfort food—a hearty, satisfying stew that didn't take all day to make.

Hearty Chicken Stew
SERVES 6 TO 8
Do not substitute boneless chicken thighs here.

4	pounds bone-in, skin-on chicken thighs (10 to 12 thighs), trimmed
	Salt and ground black pepper
2	tablespoons vegetable oil
2	medium onions, minced
4	medium garlic cloves, minced or pressed through a garlic press (about 4 teaspoons)
1	teaspoon minced fresh thyme leaves, or ¼ teaspoon dried
3	tablespoons unbleached all-purpose flour
½	cup dry white wine
3½	cups low-sodium chicken broth
1	pound carrots (about 6 medium), peeled and chopped medium
1½	pounds red potatoes (about 5 medium), scrubbed and cut into ¾-inch chunks
2	bay leaves
1	cup frozen peas
¼	cup minced fresh parsley leaves

1. Adjust an oven rack to the lower-middle position and heat the oven to 300 degrees. Pat the chicken dry with paper towels and season with salt and pepper. Heat 1 tablespoon of the oil in a large Dutch oven over medium-high heat until just smoking. Add half of the chicken and brown on both sides, 5 to 8 minutes, reducing the heat if the pot begins to scorch. Transfer the chicken to a medium bowl. Repeat with the remaining 1 tablespoon oil and the remaining chicken; transfer to the bowl. When the chicken is cool enough to handle, remove and discard the skin.

2. Pour off all but 2 tablespoons of the fat left in the pot and place over medium heat until shimmering. Add the onions and ¼ teaspoon salt and cook, stirring often, until softened, 5 to 7 minutes. Stir in the garlic and thyme and cook until fragrant, about 30 seconds. Stir in the flour and cook, stirring constantly, until golden, about 1 minute. Slowly whisk in the wine, scraping up any browned bits. Gradually whisk in the broth until smooth and bring to a simmer.

3. Add the chicken with any accumulated juices, the carrots, potatoes, and bay leaves and bring to a simmer. Cover, place the pot in the oven, and cook until the chicken is very tender but not quite falling off the bone, about 1¼ hours.

4. Remove the pot from the oven, transfer the chicken to a cutting board, and remove the bay leaves. When the chicken is cool enough to handle, remove the meat from the bones and shred into large pieces following the illustration on page 116; discard the bones.

5. If the sauce is too thin, continue to simmer the stew over medium-high heat as needed to thicken. Off the heat, stir in the shredded chicken and the peas, cover, and let stand for 5 minutes. Stir in the parsley and season with salt and pepper to taste before serving.

➤ VARIATION

Hearty Chicken Stew with Leeks, Potatoes, and Saffron

Saffron gives this stew a yellow-orange hue and a rich, earthy flavor.

Follow the recipe for Hearty Chicken Stew, substituting 4 large leeks, white and light green parts only, halved lengthwise, sliced ½ inch thick, and rinsed thoroughly (see the illustrations on page 107), for the onions; cook the leeks with the salt over medium heat as directed, until softened, 4 to 5 minutes. Add ¼ teaspoon saffron threads, crumbled, to the pot with the garlic and thyme.

CHICKEN AND DUMPLINGS

DESPITE AMERICA'S ONGOING LOVE AFFAIR with comfort food, chicken and dumplings, unlike its baked cousin, chicken pot pie, hasn't made a comeback. After making several dozen batches of this dish, we think we know why. It has to do with the dumplings—as tricky as it can be to make pie pastry or biscuits for pot pie, dumplings are far more temperamental. With pot pie, dry oven heat and a rich sauce camouflage minor flaws in biscuits or pastry, whereas moist, steamy heat highlights gummy or leaden dumplings. But the idea of this classic one-pot meal is immensely appealing to us—light yet substantial, tender yet durable dumplings accompanying a rich, hearty sauce of chicken and vegetables—and we were determined to uncover the secret.

In different parts of the country, dumplings come in different shapes. They may be rolled thin and cut into strips, rolled thick and stamped out like biscuits, or simply dropped into the stew in rounds. Most flour-based dumplings are made of flour and salt, plus one or more of the following: butter, eggs, milk, and baking powder. Depending on the ingredient list, dumplings are usually mixed in one of three ways. The most common is a biscuit or pastry style in which cold butter is cut into the dry ingredients, then cold milk and/or eggs are stirred in just until mixed. Other dumplings are made by simply mixing wet into dry ingredients. Many of the eggier dumplings are made like pâte à choux (a type of French pastry), adding flour to hot water and butter, then whisking in eggs one at a time.

Using our Hearty Chicken Stew (page 114) as the base, we spent a full day making batch after batch of dumplings in some combination of the ingredients and three mixing methods outlined above. By the end of the day, after sampling dumplings that ranged from tough and chewy to fragile and disintegrated, we finally found a method for producing light and fluffy dumplings that held up beautifully during cooking. To make these dumplings, we cut butter into a mix of flour, baking powder, and salt. Then, instead of adding cold liquid to the dry ingredients, we added hot liquid to the flour-butter mixture. This type of dumpling is a success because hot liquids, unlike cold ones, expand and set the starch in the flour, keeping it from absorbing too much of the cooking liquid. We took the process a step further—instead of cutting the butter into the flour, we simply melted it and mixed it into the dry ingredients with the warm liquid. These were the firm yet tender dumplings we were looking for, and better yet, they were easy to make.

Although we were pretty sure that dumplings made with vegetable shortening wouldn't taste as good as those made with butter, we had high hopes for the ones made with chicken fat. After a side-by-side test of dumplings made with butter, shortening, and chicken fat, we selected those made with chicken fat (butter was a close second). The shortening dumplings tasted flat, like cooked flour and chicken broth, while the ones made with chicken fat tasted chickeny and rich. Liquids were simple. Dumplings made with chicken broth tasted too similar to the stewing liquid. Those made with water were dull. Because buttermilk tends to separate and even curdle when heated, we ruled it out. Whole milk dumplings were tender, with a rich flavor—our first choice.

With the dough resolved, we tested the formula by shaping it. After fussing with a rolling pin, biscuit cutters, and the like, we decided that the simpler route of dropping spoonfuls of dough into the stew actually yielded better-textured dumplings.

We then turned our attention to tweaking the stew. Overall, this dish needed more sauce than our hearty chicken stew in order to accommodate all of the dumplings, so we increased the amount of broth and flour. Swapping dry sherry for wine, adding a little milk, and omitting the garlic and

potatoes also pleased the tasters and made the dish more traditional. With the secret to tender dumplings uncovered, we finally had a hearty and satisfying stew.

Old-Fashioned Chicken and Dumplings
SERVES 6 TO 8

Don't use low-fat or nonfat milk for this dish. After pouring the fat from the pan in step 2, you should have 3 tablespoons for making the dumplings; if there is not enough fat, supplement it as needed with butter. Also, don't make the dumpling dough until you are ready to drop them into the stew.

STEW

4 pounds bone-in, skin-on chicken thighs (10 to 12 thighs), trimmed
  Salt and ground black pepper
2 tablespoons vegetable oil
3 tablespoons unsalted butter
2 celery ribs, sliced ¼ inch thick
1 medium onion, minced
6 tablespoons unbleached all-purpose flour
¼ cup dry sherry
4½ cups low-sodium chicken broth
¼ cup whole milk
4 medium carrots, peeled and sliced ¼ inch thick
1 teaspoon minced fresh thyme leaves, or ¼ teaspoon dried
2 bay leaves
1 cup frozen peas
3 tablespoons minced fresh parsley leaves

DUMPLINGS

2 cups (10 ounces) unbleached all-purpose flour
1 tablespoon baking powder
1 teaspoon salt
1 cup whole milk
3 tablespoons reserved chicken fat or unsalted butter (see note)

SHREDDING CHICKEN

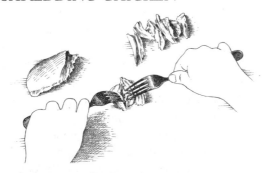

Hold a fork in each hand, with the tines facing down. Insert the tines into the chicken meat and gently pull the forks away from each other, breaking the meat apart. Depending on the recipe, you can shred the chicken into small pieces (for chili) or large pieces (for stew).

1. FOR THE STEW: Adjust an oven rack to the lower-middle position and heat the oven to 300 degrees. Pat the chicken dry with paper towels and season with salt and pepper. Heat 1 tablespoon of the oil in a large Dutch oven over medium-high heat until just smoking. Add half of the chicken and brown on both sides, 5 to 8 minutes, reducing the heat if the pot begins to scorch. Transfer the chicken to a medium bowl. Repeat with the remaining 1 tablespoon oil and the remaining chicken; transfer to the bowl. When the chicken is cool enough to handle, remove and discard the skin.

2. Pour off and reserve any chicken fat. Add the butter to the pot and melt over medium heat. Add the celery, onion, and ¼ teaspoon salt and cook, stirring occasionally, until softened, 5 to 7 minutes. Stir in the flour and cook, stirring constantly, until golden, about 1 minute. Whisk in the sherry, scraping up any browned bits. Gradually whisk in the broth and milk until smooth and bring to a simmer.

3. Add the chicken with any accumulated juices, carrots, thyme, and bay leaves and bring to a simmer. Cover, place the pot in the oven, and cook until the chicken is very tender but not quite falling off the bone, about 1¼ hours.

4. Remove the pot from the oven, transfer the chicken to a cutting board, and remove the bay leaves. When the chicken is cool enough to handle, remove the meat from the bones and shred into large pieces (see page 116); discard the skin and bones. Stir the shredded chicken, peas, and parsley into the pot and season with salt and pepper to taste.

5. FOR THE DUMPLINGS: Stir the flour, baking powder, and salt together in a large bowl. Microwave the milk and reserved chicken fat in a microwave-safe bowl until just warm (do not overheat), about 1 minute. Stir the warmed milk mixture into the flour mixture with a wooden spoon until incorporated and smooth.

6. Return the stew to a simmer over medium heat. Following the illustrations at right, drop golf-ball-sized dumplings into the stew, leaving about ¼ inch of space around each dumpling (you should have about 18 dumplings). Reduce the heat to low, cover, and cook until the dumplings have doubled in size, 15 to 18 minutes. Serve.

➤ VARIATION

Chicken and Dumplings with Leeks and Tarragon

Follow the recipe for Old-Fashioned Chicken and Dumplings, substituting 2 leeks, white and light green parts only, halved lengthwise, sliced 1 inch thick, and rinsed thoroughly (see the illustrations on page 107), for the carrots and celery, and minced fresh tarragon leaves for the parsley.

MAKING DUMPLINGS

1. Gather a golf-ball-sized portion of the dumpling batter onto a soupspoon, then push the dumpling into the stew using a second spoon.

2. Cover the stew with the dumplings, leaving about ¼ inch of space around each dumpling to allow room to expand. Cover the pot and cook for about 15 to 18 minutes.

3. When fully cooked, the dumplings will have doubled in size.

CAJUN-STYLE CHICKEN, SAUSAGE, AND CORN STEW

LOOKING FOR AN ALTERNATIVE TO CLASSIC chicken stews, we turned to the Deep South for inspiration. We wanted to capture the flavors of Louisiana cuisine in a hearty, boldly flavored chicken stew.

Using our Hearty Chicken Stew (page 114) as a jumping-off point and adding some corn, we made our first batch of stew. As with the chicken stew, we found that bone-in thighs worked great, especially when we removed the meat from the bone and shredded it before serving. We then thought to add some andouille sausage, a type commonly found in Louisiana, and liked the smoky, meaty flavor it added to the sauce. An unfortunate side effect of simmering the andouille in the stew for over an hour, however, was that it became dry and tough. Giving kielbasa a try, we found it lent a similar smoky, meaty flavor, but was able to retain a tender, juicy texture. Slicing the sausage into bite-sized pieces before cooking made it easy to incorporate into the stew. Browning the chicken and sausage before adding them to the stew deepened their flavor (and also left behind browned bits in the pot that added flavor to the sauce) and we found it best to brown them separately.

The addition of cayenne, red bell peppers, onion, celery, and some fresh herbs pumped up the flavor of the sauce and gave the stew a decidedly Louisiana kick. The only complaint now was that the corn was hard to taste. Testing the difference between using fresh and frozen corn, we learned that frozen simply doesn't work—it withers into wrinkly bits during the long simmering time and contributes little flavor to the stew. Fresh corn, cut off the cob, is an absolute must for this recipe

Wanting an even heartier corn flavor in this stew, we tried the obvious solution of simply adding more corn to the pot; but this just bulked up the stew with more corn kernels rather than adding more corn flavor. We then tried scraping the corn pulp out of the cobs and found the potent, sweet, fragrant corn flavor we were looking for. We also noted that the corn pulp—rich with cornstarch—thickened the sauce nicely and eliminated the need to add any flour. Depending on how juicy your corn is, you can thicken the stew as needed by simmering a few extra minutes while you're shredding the cooked chicken before serving.

⚘

Cajun Chicken, Sausage, and Corn Stew

SERVES 6 TO 8

The flavor of this stew really depends on good fresh corn. Don't forget to scrape the pulp out of the cobs or the stew will be watery and a little bland. This homey dish is usually served with a crusty, rustic loaf of bread to help sop up the sauce and plenty of hot sauce; you can also serve this over plain steamed rice.

6	ears corn, husks and silk removed
3	pounds bone-in, skin-on chicken thighs (8 to 10 thighs), trimmed
	Salt and ground black pepper
2	tablespoons vegetable oil
1	pound kielbasa sausage, sliced ¼ inch thick
2	red bell peppers, stemmed, seeded, and cut into ½-inch pieces
2	medium onions, minced
2	celery ribs, minced
¼	teaspoon cayenne pepper
4	medium garlic cloves, minced or pressed through a garlic press (about 4 teaspoons)
1	teaspoon minced fresh thyme leaves, or ¼ teaspoon dried
3½	cups low-sodium chicken broth
2	bay leaves
¼	cup minced fresh cilantro leaves

1. Adjust an oven rack to the lower-middle position and heat the oven to 300 degrees. Working with one ear of corn at a time, stand the corn on end inside a large bowl. Following the illustrations on page 119, use a paring knife to cut the kernels off the cob. Using the back of a butter knife, scrape any remaining pulp off the cob and into the bowl. Discard the cobs.

2. Pat the chicken dry with paper towels and season with salt and pepper. Heat 1 tablespoon of

the oil in a large Dutch oven over medium-high heat until just smoking. Add half of the chicken and brown on both sides, 5 to 8 minutes, reducing the heat if the pot begins to scorch. Transfer the chicken to a medium bowl. Repeat with the remaining 1 tablespoon oil and the remaining chicken; transfer to the bowl. When the chicken is cool enough to handle, remove and discard the skin.

3. Pour off all but 1 tablespoon of the fat left in the pot. Add the kielbasa and cook over medium heat until it begins to brown, about 2 minutes. Stir in the peppers, onions, celery, cayenne, and ¼ teaspoon salt and cook until the vegetables are softened, 8 to 10 minutes. Stir in the garlic and thyme and cook until fragrant, about 30 seconds. Stir in the corn, scraping up any browned bits. Stir in the broth and bring to a simmer.

4. Add the chicken with any accumulated juices and the bay leaves and bring to a simmer. Cover, place the pot in the oven, and cook until the chicken is very tender but not quite falling off the bone, about 1¼ hours.

REMOVING CORN KERNELS AND PULP FROM THE COB

1. Hold the cob on its end inside a large wide bowl and cut off the kernels using a paring knife.

2. Once the kernels are removed, firmly scrape the pulp and "milk" out of the cob using the back of a butter knife.

5. Remove the pot from the oven, transfer the chicken to a cutting board, and remove the bay leaves. When the chicken is cool enough to handle, remove the meat from the bones and shred into large pieces following the illustration on page 116; discard the bones.

6. If the sauce is too thin, continue to simmer the stew over medium-high heat as needed to thicken. Off the heat, stir in the shredded chicken, cover, and let stand for 5 minutes. Stir in the cilantro and season with salt and pepper to taste before serving.

CALAMARI STEW WITH GARLIC AND TOMATOES

STEWED CALAMARI WITH TOMATOES, GARLIC, and white wine is a classic Mediterranean dish. Unlike fried calamari, which cooks in minutes, this dish relies on low heat and a relatively long simmering time to produce moist, tender pieces of squid enrobed in a sweet, garlicky tomato sauce. And while we love the crunchy richness of fried calamari, this stewed preparation puts the calamari front and center—no deep-fried coating to mask its sweet, subtle flavor.

The ingredients for this dish are few, so we wanted to maximize the flavor of each. We decided to approach this stew's preparation as we would any other—by browning the protein to build a fond. But instead of developing a golden brown exterior, the squid merely released liquid and steamed. Changing tack, we coated the squid in flour to encourage browning, but this resulted in gummy calamari. Flummoxed, we abandoned the browning technique and instead looked to build our stew's flavor in other ways.

We started by cooking onions until tender and sweet and then, since garlic is typically a star ingredient in this dish, we added a generous eight cloves. The resulting dish had a nice garlicky punch, but tasters felt it needed more depth of flavor. Reviewing a stack of recipes we found in our

119

GARLIC TOASTS

GARLIC TOASTS ARE THE PERFECT accompaniment to a bowl of Hearty Chicken Stew (page 114), Cajun Chicken, Sausage, and Corn Stew (page 118), Mediterranean Calamari Stew with Garlic and Tomatoes (page 121), or Tuscan White Bean Stew (page 123). There are three keys to making good garlic toasts. First, use a high-quality crusty loaf of country bread and slice it into rustic, 1-inch-thick pieces; don't bother with cheap or presliced bread here. Second, toast the bread either on the grill or under the broiler in order to achieve a well-toasted flavor; a regular toaster just won't cut it. Third, gently rub one side of the toasted bread with a peeled clove of raw garlic; the warm, coarse-textured surface of the toasted bread acts like sandpaper, releasing the flavor and aroma of the garlic.

Garlic Toasts

MAKES 8 SLICES

Any rustic loaf of bread will work here, including a French baguette. If using a grill, cook the bread over medium heat until lightly charred around the edges, 1 to 2 minutes per side, before rubbing with oil and garlic.

- 8 1-inch-thick slices from a rustic loaf of country bread
- 1 large garlic clove, peeled
  Extra-virgin olive oil
  Salt and ground black pepper

Adjust an oven rack 6 inches from the broiler element and heat the broiler. Spread the bread out over a baking sheet and broil until golden brown on both sides, about 2 minutes per side. Briefly rub one side of each toast with the garlic clove. Drizzle the toasts with oil and season with salt and pepper to taste.

research, we noticed that several included celery with the aromatics. Tasters loved the added freshness and clean, vegetal flavor it brought to this stew.

To our aromatics we added some dry white wine, and settled on a generous ½ cup. We added it directly to the sautéed onion mixture and allowed it to reduce. According to our research, squid can take anywhere from 30 to 50 minutes to become tender when gently simmered, so once we added the squid and some diced tomatoes to our pot, we began testing the squid for doneness at the 30-minute mark and every five minutes thereafter. It wasn't until it hit the 45-minute mark that the squid started to become extremely tender. But when left to simmer for much longer, the squid became tough and rubbery; we realized there is about a 10-minute window for the squid to reach its ideal texture.

With our basic technique in place, we turned to examining the tomatoes. We'd used canned diced tomatoes initially, but decided to compare them to canned pureed and canned whole tomatoes. We immediately ruled out pureed tomatoes, which lacked the fresh flavor we wanted. The canned diced tomatoes were an improvement, but there wasn't enough time for the tomato pieces to sufficiently break down, leaving us with a watery stew. We had the best luck with canned whole tomatoes, which not only gave the stew a fresh tomato flavor, but broke down just enough to thicken the stew while still remaining a distinct component.

We wanted this squid stew to serve as a main course, either on its own or tossed with pasta, so we knew with about two pounds of squid we'd need a generous amount of tomatoes to balance the flavors and provide enough for a main course dinner. We settled on three 28-ounce cans of whole tomatoes. Because the tomatoes tended to lose their fresh flavor the longer they cooked, we added them to the pot after the squid had simmered for 15 minutes.

Green olives and capers lent a briny element that tasters appreciated and a teaspoon of red pepper flakes provided just the right amount of heat. Finished with chopped parsley and a drizzle of extra virgin olive oil, these ingredients perfectly showcased the flavor of the calamari.

Mediterranean Calamari Stew with Garlic and Tomatoes

SERVES 6

You can either clean the squid yourself (see below) or ask the fishmonger to clean it for you. If you cannot find pitted green olives, substitute pimiento-stuffed green olives; if the olives are particularly salty, give them a rinse. This brothy stew is often eaten over polenta or pasta, or served as a first course with Garlic Toasts (page 120). This stew cannot be reheated or made in advance.

¼	cup extra-virgin olive oil, plus extra for drizzling
2	medium onions, minced
2	celery ribs, sliced thin
8	medium garlic cloves, minced or pressed through a garlic press (about 8 teaspoons)
½	cup dry white wine
2	pounds fresh or thawed frozen squid, rinsed, bodies cut into 1-inch-wide rings and tentacles cut in half (see the illustrations below) Salt and ground black pepper
3	(28-ounce) cans whole tomatoes, drained, chopped coarse, and drained again
⅓	cup pitted Greek green olives, coarsely chopped
1	tablespoon capers, rinsed
1	teaspoon red pepper flakes
3	tablespoons minced fresh parsley leaves

1. Heat the oil in a large Dutch oven over medium-high heat until shimmering. Add the onion and celery and cook, stirring often, until softened, 5 to 7 minutes. Stir in the garlic and cook until fragrant, about 30 seconds. Stir in the wine, scraping up any browned bits, and cook until slightly thickened, 2 to 4 minutes.

2. Meanwhile, pat the squid dry with paper towels and season with salt and pepper. Stir the squid into the pot and bring to a simmer. Reduce the heat to medium-low, cover, and cook for 15 minutes.

3. Stir in the tomatoes, olives, capers, and red pepper flakes. Cover, reduce the heat to low, and continue to cook until the squid is very tender, 30 to 35 minutes.

4. Off the heat, stir in the parsley and season with salt and pepper to taste. Drizzle each portion with extra-virgin olive oil (if desired) before serving.

CLEANING SQUID

1. Reach into the body with your fingers and grasp as much of the innards as you can. Gently pull out the heart and innards.

2. You may have to make a second attempt to remove the hard, plastic-like quill; it will come out easily once you find it.

3. Cut the tentacles just above the squid's eye. Be careful of the black ink, which does stain. Discard the innards.

4. Check the tentacles for a beak. Squeeze out and discard the beak if necessary. Reserve the tentacles.

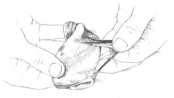

5. The thin, membrane-like skin on the squid body is edible but can be easily peeled off for a white appearance.

White Bean Stew

THE PEOPLE OF TUSCANY ARE KNOWN AS *mangiafagioli*, or "bean eaters," for the prominent role beans play in their cuisine. Cannellini (white kidney beans) are the region's most famous legume, and Tuscan cooks go to great extremes to ensure that these beans are worthy of their star status. Simmering the cannellini in rainwater to produce a creamy, almost buttery texture is not uncommon. And putting the beans in an empty wine bottle to slow-cook overnight in a fire's dying embers is not unheard of.

When we set out to make a heartier stew version of the region's classic white bean soup, we wanted the cannellini to be as memorable as any you would find in Tuscany. Collecting rainwater or cooking in the fireplace were two possibilities—but we hoped to use a more practical approach.

Our first task was to sort through all the contradictory advice we found for dried-bean cookery. We began with the most hotly contested issue: how long to soak beans before cooking. Some recipes swear that a lengthy soak leads to beans with a more tender, uniform texture. Others insist that a quick soak—an hour-long rest off the stove covered in just-boiled water—is best. In the past, our recipes have maintained that no soak at all can be the way to go.

To judge for ourselves, we cooked up batches of beans using all three approaches. To our surprise, we found relatively minor differences. The biggest difference was in cooking time: The no-soak beans took 45 minutes longer to soften fully than the other two methods. But we were seeking perfection. And since the beans soaked overnight were, in fact, the most tender and evenly cooked of the bunch and had the least number of exploded beans, that's the method we settled on.

But while the beans' interiors were creamy, their skins remained tough, and overall they were not yet what we imagined a Tuscan cook would be proud to serve. Like length of soaking, when to add salt is another much-debated topic in bean cookery. Was there something to investigate here that could help us cook up perfect beans?

TECHNIQUE: Salt-Soaking Beans

Here in the test kitchen, we've found that soaking dried beans in salt water before cooking is a good idea. The soaking slightly softens the beans and evens out the cooking time, while the salt firms up and "sets" the bean skins making the beans less prone to breaking and bursting during cooking. Don't worry if you don't have time to soak the beans (or forgot)—we've come up with a "quick salt-soak" method that works nearly as well (we still slightly prefer the overnight soak if given a choice).

Overnight Soaking Method: Pick through and rinse the beans. For every pound of beans, dissolve 2 tablespoons salt into 4 quarts cold water. Combine the beans and salt water in a large container and let the beans soak at room temperature for at least 8 hours, or up to 24 hours. Drain the beans, discarding the soaking liquid, and rinse well before cooking.

Quick Soaking Method: Pick through and rinse the beans. For every pound of beans, dissolve 3 tablespoons salt into 2 quarts boiling water. Combine the beans and hot salt water together in a large container and let the beans soak at room temperature for 1 hour. Drain the beans, discarding the soaking liquid, and rinse well before cooking.

The conventional wisdom is that salt added to beans at the beginning of cooking will prevent them from ever fully softening. Paradoxically, other advice maintains that salting beans too early can create a mushy texture. When we added salt to a batch of beans at the outset of cooking, we found it made some of the beans mealy. We checked with our science editor and learned that the seeming contradiction may be a matter of semantics. As beans cook, their starch granules swell with water, softening to a creamy texture and eventually bursting. The presence of salt in the cooking water causes the starch granules to swell less, so that fewer beans reach the point of bursting. As a result, the starch granules in the beans remain intact. To us, the texture of such beans is mealy; others may call them gritty.

Though the texture of the beans was now inferior, their skins were exactly what we wanted: soft and pliable. Was there a different way to use salt to get the same effect? Our thoughts turned to brining, which we use in the test kitchen to help meat trap water and remain moist during cooking. Over the years, we've brined everything from poultry and pork to beef and even shrimp. Why not beans? Back in the test kitchen, we made a brine by dissolving a few tablespoons of salt in water and left the beans to soak overnight in the solution. The next day, we rinsed the beans thoroughly before proceeding with the recipe. Our experiment was a success: The cannellini beans now boasted tender, almost imperceptible skins and interiors that were buttery soft. Why the change? When beans are soaked in salted water, rather than being cooked in it, not as much salt enters the beans. Its impact is confined mainly to the skins, where sodium ions interact with the cells to create a softer texture.

Although tasters were impressed with this technique, we knew that no Tuscan would stand for the number of exploded beans in the pot. Usually the culprit is an over-vigorous bubbling of cooking liquid, which disturbs the beans and causes them to blow out and disintegrate. We would need to simmer the beans very gently—with no perceptible bubbling and no stirring. Thinking back to the Tuscan technique of cooking beans overnight in a dying fire, we wondered if we might simply try cooking the beans in a 250-degree oven. In the next test, we brought the beans and water to a simmer on the stovetop, then covered the pot and placed it in the oven. This method required a little more time, but it worked beautifully, producing perfectly cooked beans that stayed intact.

With tender, creamy beans in the pot, it was time to work on the stew's other flavors. Salt-cured Italian bacon, or pancetta, is traditional in Tuscan white bean stew, lending depth and flavor, so we included it. We still needed a few more ingredients to transform the dish into a one-pot meal. We settled on chewy, earthy-tasting kale, another Tuscan favorite, along with canned diced tomatoes, carrots, celery, onion, and lots of garlic. For extra richness, we also replaced some of the water in the stew with chicken broth (low-sodium, of course, to minimize any impact on the beans).

We sautéed the vegetables (except the kale and tomatoes) with the pancetta, added the beans and water, and placed the stew in the oven. The acid in tomatoes can toughen beans, so we waited until the beans were sufficiently softened, about 45 minutes, before adding the tomatoes to the pot, along with the kale. The final touch: a sprig of rosemary, steeped in the stew just before serving, which infused the broth with a delicate herbal aroma.

Borrowing from a classic Tuscan dish called *ribollita*—leftover bean soup thickened with bread—you can make this stew even more substantial by serving it atop slabs of garlic toast. Drizzled with fruity extra-virgin olive oil, the stew is pure comfort food. And you don't need to collect rainwater or bank a fire to make it.

Tuscan White Bean Stew
SERVES 6

If pancetta is unavailable, substitute 4 ounces of bacon. For a heartier meal, place a garlic toast or two (see page 120) in the bottom of each bowl and ladle the stew over the top.

1	pound dried cannellini beans, rinsed, picked over, and salt-soaked overnight or quick salt-soaked (see page 122)
1	tablespoon extra-virgin olive oil, plus extra for drizzling
6	ounces pancetta, cut into ¼-inch pieces (see note)
1	large onion, minced
2	celery ribs, sliced ½ inch thick
2	medium carrots, peeled and cut into ½-inch pieces
8	medium garlic cloves, peeled and crushed (see the illustration on page 63)
4	cups low-sodium chicken broth
3	cups water
2	bay leaves
1	bunch kale or collard greens (about 1 pound), stems trimmed and leaves chopped into 1-inch pieces
1	(14.5-ounce) can diced tomatoes, drained and rinsed
1	sprig fresh rosemary
	Salt and ground black pepper

1. Adjust an oven rack to the lower-middle position and heat the oven to 250 degrees. Drain the beans, discarding the soaking liquid, and rinse well.

2. Cook the oil and pancetta together in a large Dutch oven over medium heat, stirring occasionally, until the pancetta is lightly browned, 6 to 10 minutes. Stir in the onion, celery, and carrots and cook, stirring occasionally, until the vegetables are softened and lightly browned, 10 to 16 minutes.

3. Stir in the garlic and cook until fragrant, about 30 seconds. Stir in the broth, water, bay leaves, and soaked beans and bring to a simmer. Cover, place the pot in the oven, and cook until the beans are almost tender (the very center of the beans will still be firm), 45 to 60 minutes.

4. Stir in the kale and tomatoes and continue to cook, covered, until the beans and greens are fully tender, 30 to 40 minutes longer.

5. Remove the stew from the oven and submerge the rosemary sprig in the liquid. Cover and let stand 15 minutes. Remove the bay leaves and rosemary sprig and season the stew with salt and pepper to taste. If desired, use the back of a spoon to press some of the beans against the side of the pot to thicken the stew before serving.

➤ VARIATION

Hearty Tuscan White Bean Stew with Sausage and Cabbage

This variation has much more meat and is made with crinkly savoy cabbage.

Follow the recipe for Tuscan White Bean Stew, substituting 1½ pounds sweet Italian sausage, casings removed, for the pancetta, ½ medium head savoy cabbage, cut into 1-inch pieces, for the kale, and 1 sprig fresh oregano for the rosemary. Cook the sausage in the oil in step 2, breaking the meat into small pieces with a wooden spoon until it loses its raw color, about 8 minutes. Transfer the sausage to a paper towel–lined plate and place in the refrigerator. Continue to follow the recipe as directed, stirring the sausage and cabbage into the stew along with the tomatoes in step 4.

HEARTY ROOT VEGETABLE AND MUSHROOM STEW

GREAT VEGETABLE STEWS MARRY HEARTY vegetables with a richly flavored broth and herbs or spices that complement the vegetables. But all too often, they are little more than a jumble of soggy vegetables devoid of color and flavor. We were after a hearty vegetable stew, one that could be as soul satisfying in the dead of winter as a beef stew. And although we love fiery Indian and Thai curries, we were looking for vegetable stew at its simplest, where the flavor of the vegetables, not the spices, take center stage.

With this in mind, we began our first order of business: selecting the veggies. Hearty root vegetables, an integral part of many meat stews, would be key, both for their earthy flavor and for their thickening properties (root vegetables are quite starchy). We really liked the flavor of parsnips, turnips, and rutabaga, as well as the more traditional carrots and potatoes. While we found that any combination of two to three root vegetables produced a flavorful, balanced stew, it was important to include potatoes, which helped balance the sweetness of the other vegetables.

Next we looked for other vegetables to serve as a contrast to the starchy ones. We wanted a hearty stew, not a soup, so delicate spring vegetables like asparagus and zucchini were immediately ruled out. Mushrooms, with their meaty flavor and texture, were an ideal choice.

Looking for the meatiest mushroom we could find, we began with portobello caps, which we halved and sliced. Tasters loved the pairing of mushroom and root vegetable, but were turned off by the portobellos' texture, which was spongy no matter how long they cooked. Simple white mushrooms provided the texture we wanted.

The main components of our stew decided on, we turned to our cooking liquid. Chicken broth would no doubt make a rich base, but we wanted a true vegetable stew. So we chose vegetable broth as our liquid.

Meat stews typically begin by browning the meat, and we began similarly, sautéing the mushrooms in oil. A little thyme and garlic deepened their flavor. Next we deglazed the pot with white wine to add flavor and some acidity. After the broth was added to the pot we tossed in the root vegetables and some bay leaves. While other stews are cooked covered, we chose to only partially cover the pot to ensure a gentle simmer; otherwise, the vegetables had a tendency to disintegrate.

After an hour of simmering the vegetables were tender and had released enough starch to thicken the sauce somewhat without falling apart, but the sauce had a disappointing canned flavor that was simply not rich enough. Clearly the store-bought vegetable broth wasn't working. Hoping to avoid the arduous route of making stock from scratch, we decided to try a hybrid technique. We tossed cubed mushrooms, onions, carrots, celery, and garlic heads in tomato paste and roasted them in the oven. We then threw them in a pot with some dried porcinis, store-bought broth, and water and simmered it on the stove for 30 minutes before straining out the solids.

The stew made with this stock was definitely good; however, it was not much easier than making stock from scratch. We wondered if we could incorporate some of the ingredients that had been used to fortify the broth into the stew itself— building flavor without a separate simmering step and without discarding any vegetables.

We made our stew again, sautéing a traditional mirepoix of minced celery, onion, and carrot along with some dried porcini (in butter, instead of oil, for more richness) before adding the fresh mushrooms. Additionally, we browned some tomato paste with the garlic and thyme before adding the liquid. Now we were getting somewhere. Tasters no longer found the stew to be "canned" tasting, and were impressed by its hearty flavor and thick

texture. Still, they found it light and wanted a richer taste.

Not wanting to lengthen our shopping list, we looked more closely at our existing ingredients to see if we couldn't eke more flavor out of them. In meat stew, much of the flavor comes from fond, the browned bits that cling to the bottom of the pan when browning the meat. In our vegetable stew, we were getting our fond from browning the mirepoix and mushrooms. We had sautéed them until they were just beginning to brown; but if browning was the key to flavor, how could we go wrong with more of a good thing? We extended the cooking time, sautéing the aromatics until they were well browned—a full 15 minutes. We then added the mushrooms and cooked them over medium-high heat until they released their liquid. Once the pot was dry we lowered the heat and continued cooking. Since mushrooms only begin browning after their liquid has evaporated, lowering the heat at this point gave us more control at the critical juncture. We were able to cook them until a dark brown fond coated the bottom of the pan, another full 15 minutes, without burning them.

This increased stovetop time for both the aromatics and mushrooms turned out to be the key—the stew now had the deep, rich flavor that we had been looking for. We finished the stew with some lemon juice and parsley for brightness, and tasters agreed—no one missed the meat.

Hearty Root Vegetable and Mushroom Stew
SERVES 6
We think this stew tastes best with a combination of two or three types of root vegetables including carrots, parsnips, turnip, rutabaga, celery root, or parsley root.

4	tablespoons (½ stick) unsalted butter
2	medium onions, minced
I	celery rib, minced
I	medium carrot, peeled and minced

<table>
<tr><td>1</td><td>ounce dried porcini mushrooms, rinsed and minced</td></tr>
<tr><td></td><td>Salt</td></tr>
<tr><td>1½</td><td>pounds white mushrooms, stems trimmed, wiped clean, and quartered</td></tr>
<tr><td>6</td><td>medium garlic cloves, minced or pressed through a garlic press (about 2 tablespoons)</td></tr>
<tr><td>1</td><td>tablespoon tomato paste</td></tr>
<tr><td>2</td><td>teaspoons minced fresh thyme leaves, or ½ teaspoon dried</td></tr>
<tr><td>½</td><td>cup dry white wine</td></tr>
<tr><td>3</td><td>cups low-sodium vegetable broth (see note)</td></tr>
<tr><td>2½</td><td>cups water</td></tr>
<tr><td>1½</td><td>pounds root vegetables, peeled and cut into 1-inch pieces (see note)</td></tr>
<tr><td>1</td><td>pound red potatoes (about 3 medium), cut into 1-inch pieces</td></tr>
<tr><td>2</td><td>bay leaves</td></tr>
<tr><td>¼</td><td>cup minced fresh parsley leaves</td></tr>
<tr><td>1</td><td>tablespoon juice from 1 lemon</td></tr>
<tr><td></td><td>Ground black pepper</td></tr>
</table>

1. Melt 2 tablespoons of the butter in a large Dutch oven over medium heat. Add the onions, celery, carrot, porcini mushrooms, and 1 teaspoon salt and cook, stirring often, until the vegetables are well browned, about 15 minutes.

2. Add the remaining 2 tablespoons butter and white mushrooms, increase the heat to medium-high, and cook, stirring often, until their liquid is released and evaporates, about 10 minutes. Reduce the heat to medium and cook, stirring often, until a dark, thick fond forms on the bottom of the pot, 5 to 8 minutes.

3. Stir in the garlic, tomato paste, and thyme and cook until fragrant, about 30 seconds. Stir in the wine, scraping up the browned bits. Stir in the broth, water, root vegetables, potatoes, and bay leaves and bring to a simmer.

4. Reduce the heat to medium-low, cover the pot partially (the lid should be just off center to leave about 1 inch open), and cook until the stew is thickened and the vegetables are tender, about 1 hour. Off the heat, remove the bay leaves and stir in the parsley and lemon juice. Season with salt and pepper to taste before serving.

BOLOGNESE SAUCE

THERE ARE SCORES OF MEAT-BASED SAUCES from Italy that get their rich flavor and unbelievably tender texture from hours of simmering, but we think Bolognese is the very best. Unlike other meat sauces in which tomatoes dominate, Bolognese sauce is about the meat, with the tomatoes in a supporting role. Bolognese also differs from many tomato-based meat sauces in that it contains butter, milk, and/or cream. The dairy ingredients give the beef an especially sweet, appealing flavor. We wanted to determine what makes a truly great version of this classic.

All Bolognese recipes can be broken down into three steps. First, vegetables are sautéed in fat. Ground meat is then browned in the pan. Finally, liquids are added and the sauce is slowly simmered over very low heat.

Using this process, a good Bolognese sauce should acquire certain characteristics. It must be quite thick in order to heighten the richness and intensity of the beef flavor. The sauce should also be smooth, with the meat disintegrated into tiny pieces, so that it will easily coat the pasta. Finally, it should be complex, with a good balance of flavors—the meat flavor should be at the fore, but there should be sweet, salty, and acidic flavors in the background.

After an initial round of testing in which we made five different styles of Bolognese, we had a recipe we liked pretty well. We preferred using only onions, carrots, and celery as the vegetables, and we liked them sautéed in butter rather than oil. We also discovered that a combination of ground beef, veal, and pork (often labeled meatloaf mix) made this sauce especially complex and rich tasting.

The liquid element of the recipe, however, proved more difficult to sort out. The secret to a great Bolognese sauce is the sequential reduction of various liquids with the sautéed meat and vegetables. The idea is to build flavor and tenderize the meat, which has toughened during the browning phase. Many recipes insist on a particular order for adding these liquids. The most common liquid choices we uncovered in our research were milk, cream, stock, wine, and tomatoes (either fresh, canned diced, crushed, or paste). We ended up testing numerous combinations to find the perfect balance.

Canned Tomato Products 101

Over the years, we've taste tested nearly every type and brand of tomato product we could lay our hands on—including whole, diced, crushed, puree, and paste. Here's our opinion on what tastes best.

DICED TOMATOES

Good for: Rustic sauces with a chunky or coarse texture, long-cooked stews, or as a substitute for crushed tomatoes (when the tomatoes are processed with their juice in a food processor).

What to buy: Sales of diced tomatoes dominate the canned tomato category. Overall, we prefer diced tomatoes packed in juice rather than those packed in puree because they have a fresher flavor. Our preferred brand, Muir Glen, garnered comments such as "sweet," "fresh tasting," and "most like fresh tomatoes."

THE BEST DICED TOMATOES
MUIR GLEN ORGANIC DICED TOMATOES

CRUSHED TOMATOES

Good for: Fresh-tasting, looser-textured sauces. (The texture of crushed tomatoes varies widely so if you can't find one of our recommended brands, we suggest crushing your own using canned diced tomatoes and a food processor for a consistent, reliable texture.)

What to buy: Crushed tomatoes have a wide range of textures. Some are thick as puree, while others are downright watery. Tasters picked Tuttorosso Crushed Tomatoes in Thick Puree with Basil as their favorite, declaring them to be "chunky, with dimensional flavor" and "very fresh-tasting." Do not confuse these with Tuttorosso's New World Style Crushed Tomatoes which rated quite poorly in our test. Tuttorosso isn't available everywhere, but Muir Glen Organic Crushed Tomatoes with Basil are available nationwide and came in a close second.

THE BEST CRUSHED TOMATOES

TUTTOROSSO CRUSHED TOMATOES IN THICK PUREE WITH BASIL

MUIR GLEN ORGANIC CRUSHED TOMATOES WITH BASIL

WHOLE TOMATOES

Good for: Dicing into bite-sized pieces and adding to dishes with a short simmering time or as a finishing ingredient added during the final few minutes of cooking.

What to buy: Whole tomatoes are peeled and packed in juice or puree. Overall, we found that those packed in juice have a livelier flavor. Our winning brand, Progresso, earned comments such as "bright, lively flavor" and "the perfect balance of acidic and fruity notes." Progresso sells whole tomatoes packed in juice and packed in puree, so be sure to read the fine print and buy the ones packed in juice.

THE BEST WHOLE TOMATOES
PROGRESSO ITALIAN-STYLE WHOLE PEELED TOMATOES WITH BASIL

TOMATO PUREE

Good for: Long-simmered, smooth, thick sauces with a deep, hearty flavor.

What to buy: We tasted eight brands of tomato puree, and although it was a very close call, Hunt's Tomato Puree edged out the other brands with tasters', comments including "nice and thick" and "tomatoey."

THE BEST TOMATO PUREE
HUNT'S TOMATO PUREE

TOMATO PASTE

Good for: Adding a slightly deeper, rounded flavor and color to nearly any soup, sauce, or stew.

What to buy: The only tomato paste packaged in a tube (invaluable for using and storing) and the only paste that contains a small amount of fat, Amore was the hands-down favorite. Tasters found its flavor to be "intense" and "fresh."

THE BEST TOMATO PASTE
AMORE TOMATO PASTE

Liquids are treated in two ways in Bolognese. In the earlier part of the cooking process, liquids are added to the pan and simmered briskly until fully evaporated, the point being to impart flavor rather than to cook the beef and vegetables. Wine is always treated this way; if the wine is not evaporated, the sauce will be too alcoholic. Milk and cream are often, but not always, treated this way. Later, either stock or tomatoes are added in greater quantity and allowed to cook off very slowly. These liquids add flavor, to be sure, but they also serve as the "cooking medium" for the sauce during the slow simmering phase.

We tested pouring wine over the browned meat first, followed by milk. We also tried them in the opposite order; milk and then wine. We felt that the meat cooked in milk first was softer and sweeter. As the bits of meat cook, they develop a hard crust that makes it more difficult for them to absorb liquid. Adding the milk first, when the meat is not crusty or tough, works better. The milk penetrates the meat, tenderizing it and making it especially sweet.

We tried using cream instead of milk, but felt that the sauce was too rich. Milk provides just enough dairy flavor to complement the meaty flavor. So we settled on milk as the first liquid for the sauce. For the second liquid, we liked both white and red wines, but we decided on white wine because it was a bit more delicate.

Now we moved on to the final element in most recipes, the cooking liquid. We did not like any of the recipes we tested with broth. Store-bought beef and chicken broths (we tried both) gave the sauce an odd chemical flavor when reduced so much, and we didn't think homemade stock was worth the effort. As for the tomato paste, we felt that it had little to offer; with none of the bright acidity of canned whole tomatoes and no fresh tomato flavor, it produced a dull sauce.

We tried tomatoes three more ways—fresh, canned crushed, and canned diced. Fresh tomatoes did nothing for the sauce and were a lot of work, since we found it necessary to peel them. (If not peeled, the skins separated during the long cooking process and marred the texture of the sauce.) Crushed tomatoes were fine but they did not taste as good as canned diced tomatoes that we pulsed in the food processor. Diced tomatoes have an additional benefit—the packing juice. Since Bolognese sauce

MAKING A FLAME TAMER

A flame tamer is a metal disk that can be fitted over a burner (electric or gas) to reduce the heat transfer. This device is especially useful when trying to keep a pot at the barest simmer. If you don't own a flame tamer, you can fashion one: Take a long sheet of aluminum foil and shape it into a 1-inch-thick ring that will fit on your burner. Make sure that the ring is an even thickness so that a pot will rest flat on it. A foil ring elevates the pot slightly above the flame or electric coil, allowing you to keep a pot of Bolognese at the merest simmer.

simmers for quite a while, it's nice to have all that juice to keep the pot from scorching.

Our recipe was finally taking shape, with all the ingredients in place. But we still wanted to know if it was really necessary to cook Bolognese sauce over low heat and, if so, how long the sauce must simmer. We found that long, slow simmering is necessary to tenderize the meat and build flavor. When we tried to hurry the process along by cooking over medium heat to evaporate the tomato juice more quickly, the meat was too firm and the flavors were not melded.

We also tried browning the meat and then simmering it in milk in a separate pan. At the same time, we browned vegetables in another and then quickly reduced the wine and tomatoes over them. When the meat had absorbed all the milk, we added it to the tomato sauce and let it finish cooking for another 30 minutes. The whole process took an hour, start to finish. The sauce was good, to be sure, but the flavor was not nearly as complex and the texture not as smooth and creamy.

We finally concluded that generations of Italian cooks have been right: Long simmering over the lowest possible heat is the only method that allows enough time for flavor to develop and for the meat to become especially tender. (A few bubbles may rise to the surface at one time but the sauce should not be simmering all over.) In fact, the meat begins to fall apart into a creamy mass when the sauce is done. There is no way to speed up this process.

As for the timing, we found that the sauce was too soupy after two hours on low heat and the meat was still pretty firm. After three to three and one-half hours, the meat was much softer, with a melt-in-the-mouth consistency. The sauce was dense and smooth at this point. We tried simmering the sauce for four hours but found no benefit. In fact, some batches cooked this long reduced too much and scorched a bit.

One final test involved browning the meat. Several sources suggest that deep browning builds flavor, a theory that makes some sense. However, other sources caution about overcooking the beef and suggest adding the first liquid to the pan as soon as the meat loses its raw color. We found this latter warning to be true. Sauces made with fully browned meat had a pleasant browned meat flavor, but the meat itself was not as tender and the sauce was not as smooth. When the first liquid was added to the pan as soon as the beef was no longer rosy, the sauce was more delicate and tender.

In the end, great Bolognese sauce is surprisingly simple to prepare—it just takes some time. The ingredients are readily available (you probably have most of them on hand) and the results are definitely worth the slow, but simple, cooking process.

Classic Bolognese Sauce

MAKES ABOUT 4 CUPS,
ENOUGH TO SAUCE 1 POUND OF PASTA

Simmering this sauce very gently is key to its super silky texture; if your stovetop runs hot, use a flame tamer (see page 128). Meatloaf mixes can be very fatty, so be sure to skim the fat from the surface of the sauce as it simmers. Serve with freshly grated Parmesan cheese.

3	tablespoons unsalted butter
¼	cup minced onion
¼	cup minced carrot
¼	cup minced celery
	Salt
1	pound meatloaf mix, or ⅓ pound each ground beef chuck, ground veal, and ground pork
1½	cups whole milk
1½	cups dry white wine
3	(14.5-ounce) cans diced tomatoes, drained, with 1½ cups of the juice reserved

1. Melt the butter in a large Dutch oven over medium heat. Stir in the onion, carrot, celery, and 1 teaspoon salt and cook until softened, 6 to 8 minutes. Stir in the ground meat and cook, breaking up the chunks with a wooden spoon, until no longer pink, about 3 minutes.

2. Stir in the milk, bring to a simmer, and cook until the milk is evaporated and only clear fat remains, about 25 minutes. Stir in the wine, bring to a simmer, and cook until it has evaporated, about 25 minutes.

3. Meanwhile, pulse the tomatoes in a food processor until slightly chunky, about 8 pulses. Stir the processed tomatoes and reserved tomato juice into the pot and bring to a bare simmer. Cook gently over low heat until the liquid has evaporated, 3 to 3½ hours. Season with salt to taste before serving.

MEAT RAGÙ

NOTHING COULD BE SIMPLER (OR MORE welcome on a cold night) than a rustic pasta sauce made from tomatoes and a richly flavored piece of meat. The meat (often pork chops) is browned, the fat drained, and the sauce built in the empty pan. The browned meat is added back to the sauce, the pan covered, and the sauce simmered slowly until the meat is fall-off-the-bone tender. The meat is then shredded and stirred into the sauce, at which point it is served over rigatoni with a good sprinkling of grated cheese.

When we began testing this sauce, it soon became clear that the choice of meat was the most important issue. We tried pork chops from the blade, loin, and sirloin. Even the fattiest chops were dry and tough after braising. We wanted the meat to almost melt when added to the tomato sauce. We clearly needed a piece of meat with more marbling so that it would not dry out during the long braising time.

We thought about a cut from the shoulder—either picnic or Boston butt—because this part of the pig has more fat than the loin, where most chops come from. The problem with these shoulder roasts was their size; the smallest at the market was 4 pounds. Nevertheless, we cut a pound of this meat into stew-like chunks and proceeded. This meat was more yielding when cooked and had a better flavor. However, the sauce tasted a bit wan; the meat had not done a really good job of flavoring the tomato sauce.

At this point, we turned to spareribs, which are fattier than roasts from the shoulder. The braised meat from spareribs was better than the Boston butt—it was tender, rich, and flavorful. Best of all, the tomato sauce really tasted meaty. The bones had flavored the sauce in a way that meat alone couldn't. But spareribs are sold in an entire rack that usually weighs 3 or more pounds. We needed only four or five ribs for a batch of sauce. That meant spending $9 on a rack of ribs and using half for the sauce and freezing the rest. Was there a more economical way to make this peasant sauce?

We paid $1.99 per pound for country-style ribs and were able to find a packet with 1½ pounds of ribs—this was just enough for one batch of sauce, with no leftovers. The sauce made with country-style ribs was similar to the spareribs sauce.

Next we wondered if this sauce could be made with beef. Short ribs are roughly equivalent to spareribs and country-style ribs. (On the cow, ribs cut from the belly, called the plate, as well as those cut from the back are called short ribs.) The sauce made with short ribs was delicious, too—remember that short ribs must be simmered longer than pork ribs because they are thicker.

Meat Ragù

MAKES ABOUT 3½ CUPS, ENOUGH TO
SAUCE 1 POUND OF PASTA

To prevent the sauce from becoming greasy, trim all external fat from the ribs and drain off most of the fat from the skillet after browning. This thick, rich sauce is best with tubular pasta, such as ziti, or penne, cooked al dente and tossed with the sauce. Serve with freshly grated Parmesan or Pecorino Romano cheese.

1½	pounds pork spareribs, country-style pork ribs, or beef short ribs, trimmed
	Salt and ground black pepper
1	tablespoon olive oil
1	medium onion, minced

½	cup dry red wine
1	(28-ounce) can diced tomatoes

1. Pat the ribs dry with paper towels and season with salt and pepper. Heat the oil in a heavy-bottomed 12-inch skillet over medium-high heat until just smoking. Add the meat and cook, turning occasionally, until well browned, 7 to 10 minutes, reducing the heat if the pot begins to scorch. Transfer the ribs to a plate.

2. Pour off all but 1 teaspoon of the fat left in the skillet. Add the onion and ¼ teaspoon salt and cook, stirring often, until softened, 5 to 7 minutes. Stir in the wine, scraping up any browned bits, and cook until the wine reduces to a glaze, about 2 minutes.

3. Add the browned ribs with any accumulated juices and the tomatoes with their juice and bring to a simmer. Reduce the heat to low, cover, and simmer gently, turning the ribs several times, until the meat is very tender and falling off the bones, 1½ to 2 hours.

4. Transfer the ribs to a clean plate. When cool enough to handle, remove the meat from the bones and shred it with your fingers; discard the fat and bones. Return the shredded meat to the sauce in the skillet. Bring the sauce to a simmer over medium heat and cook, uncovered, until heated through and slightly thickened, about 5 minutes. Season with salt and pepper to taste before serving.

➤ VARIATIONS
Meat Ragù with Rosemary and Garlic
Follow the recipe for Meat Ragù, using pork spareribs or country-style ribs. Substitute 3 medium garlic cloves, minced, for the onion, and add 2 teaspoons minced fresh rosemary to the skillet along with the garlic; sauté until softened and fragrant, about 30 seconds.

Meat Ragù with Cinnamon, Cloves, and Parsley
Follow the recipe for Meat Ragù, using beef short ribs and adding ½ teaspoon ground cinnamon, a pinch ground cloves, and 2 tablespoons minced fresh parsley leaves to the softened onion; sauté until the spices are fragrant, about 30 seconds longer.

4

BRAISES

BRAISES

BRAISING—SEARING MEAT, PARTIALLY SUB-merging it in liquid in a sealed pot, and then cooking it slowly until fork-tender—is a classic method used to render tough cuts of meat tender. Like stews, braises take time, and lots of it (our Braised Beef Brisket with Onions on page 145 spends over four hours in the oven), but the results are well worth it: You are eventually rewarded with unbelievably tender meat accompanied by a rich, flavorful sauce. And after the initial preparation, you're free to turn to other tasks, since these dishes require almost no attention during the lengthy simmering time. The technique of braising can be applied to a wide range of dishes, from satisfying comfort food like Simple Pot Roast (page 136) and Smothered Pork Chops with Spicy Collard Greens (page 165) to more refined fare perfect for enter-taining, such as Osso Buco (page 155) and Short Ribs Braised in Red Wine and Bacon (page 149).

Braising makes tough meat tender by keeping the temperature of the meat relatively low—around the boiling point of water—for a long period, which is exactly what is needed to convert the tough collagen to gelatin (the protein responsible for the tender, rich meat and thick sauces of braised dishes). In addition, the liquid in the pot creates a moist-heat environment, which helps ensure that the meat doesn't dry out.

We found that most braises work best in the oven rather than on the stovetop. The reason is simple: it is much easier to maintain a steady temperature and constant low simmer. The only exceptions to this are our chicken braises—chicken parts cook at different rates (the white meat cooks much faster than the dark) and their cooking times must be staggered. So with a dish like Chicken Provençal (page 166), we simply found it easier to do the cooking on the stovetop rather than move a pot in and out of the oven.

Building a braise is a fairly straightforward task. After the meat is seared (a step that flavors both the meat and the sauce), aromatic vegetables are sautéed, and liquid (typically wine and/or broth) is added. Once the meat is done, it is set aside to rest while the sauce is thickened, either by reducing it or by adding a small amount of flour or cornstarch.

This chapter includes a wide range of braises, from favorites like Coq au Vin (page 171) and Corned Beef and Cabbage (page 147) to less familiar fare such as Mexican Carnitas (page 159) and a Spanish classic, Braised Chicken with Almonds and Pine Nuts (page 178). We have also included a recipe for Duck Confit (page 182), in which duck legs are simmered in their own fat rather than broth. The result is meltingly tender, deeply flavorful meat.

A large heavyweight Dutch oven is the best cooking vessel for braises because it retains heat well and cooks evenly. Lightweight pots are subject to temperature fluctuations that will negatively affect stovetop cooking and oven simmering. One of the best aspects of these recipes is that they store well and the flavor even improves after a few days as the flavors continue to develop. So while low and slow may not sound as though it fits into the busy schedule of most home cooks, these dishes are designed to have long intervals of hands-off time and are a breeze to reheat.

Pot Roast

A GOOD POT ROAST BY DEFINITION ENTAILS the transformation of a tough (read cheap), nearly unpalatable cut of meat into a tender, rich, flavor-ful roast by means of a slow, moist cooking process called braising. It should not be sliceable, but rather, so tender it falls apart at the touch of a fork. And it shouldn't be pink or rosy in the middle—save that for prime rib or steak.

The meat for pot roast should be well marbled with fat and connective tissue to provide the dish with the necessary flavor and moisture. Recipes typically call for roasts from the sirloin (or rump), round (leg), or chuck (shoulder). We cooked a dozen cuts of meat to find the right one.

The sirloin roasts tested—the bottom-rump roast and top sirloin—were the leanest of the cuts and needed longer cooking to be broken down to a palatable texture. The round cuts—top round, bot-tom round, and eye round—had more fat running through them than the sirloin cuts, but the meat was chewy. The chuck cuts cooked up the most tender, although we gave preference to three of these cuts: the boneless chuck eye roast, seven-bone roast, and top blade roast. The high proportion of fat and connective tissue in these chuck cuts gave the meat much needed moisture and superior flavor, and ultimately we crowned the boneless chuck eye roast the winner because it's easy to find in supermarkets and requires minimal preparation.

But even with the right cut, we still had a problem—after four long hours of braising, the meat was precariously close to being shredded and overdone but still contained undesirable pockets of fat and connective tissue. We wondered what would happen if we split the large cylindrical roast into two sleeker halves. Dividing the roast into two fairly equal pieces was easy, as the seam of fat that runs down the center of the roast acts as a built-in guide. We trimmed the obvious pieces of fat from each lobe, leaving a thin layer of fat on top, and tied each piece to keep it from falling apart during braising. With less extraneous fat, these two roasts were definitely better than one.

With our basic preparation in place, we needed to deal with the aesthetics of the dish. Because pot roast is traditionally cooked with liquid at a low temperature, the exterior of the meat will not brown sufficiently unless it is first seared in a pan on the stovetop. High heat and a little oil were all that we needed to caramelize the exterior of the beef and boost both the flavor and the appearance of the dish.

It was time to find out what kind of liquid and how much was needed to best cook the roast and create a flavorful sauce. Using water as the braising medium, we started with a modest ¼ cup, as suggested in a few recipes. This produced a roast that was unacceptably fibrous, even after hours of cooking. After increasing the amount of liquid incrementally, we found that the moistest meat was produced when we added enough liquid to come halfway up the sides of the roast (3 to 3½ cups of liquid worked well for a 3½- to 4-pound roast). Flipping the meat every hour ensured that the roast cooked evenly and became tender throughout.

Next we tested different liquids, hoping to give both the roast and the sauce a flavor boost. In addition to the water, we tried chicken broth, beef broth, and red wine. Each broth failed to win tasters over completely when used on its own—the chicken broth was rich but gave the dish a characteristic poultry flavor, while the beef broth was a bit overpowering. We found that an equal amount of each did the job, and tasters also liked the addition of a little red wine after the roast was removed from the pot (added any earlier and its flavor penetrated the meat too deeply). Some sautéed carrot, celery, onion, and garlic added another layer of flavor to the sauce.

Some recipes thicken the sauce with a mixture of equal parts butter and flour (called a *beurre manié*); others use a slurry of cornstarch mixed with a little braising liquid. Both techniques made the sauce more gravy-like than we preferred, and we didn't care for the dilution of flavor. We chose to remove the roast from the pot once it had finished cooking, then reduced the liquid over medium-high heat until the flavors were concentrated and the sauce thickened.

Pot roast can be cooked either on the stovetop or in the oven, but after a few rounds of stovetop cooking, we felt that it was too difficult to maintain a steady temperature and constant low simmer. Turning to the oven, we began pot-roasting at 250 degrees. This method sometimes worked but, as with the stovetop method, the results were inconsistent, since it's difficult to maintain a constant simmer at this low temperature. We then tested higher temperatures to reduce the cooking time. Heat levels above 350 degrees boiled the meat to a stringy, dry texture because the exterior of the roast overcooked before the interior was cooked and tender. The magic temperature turned out to be 300 degrees—high enough to keep the meat at a bare simmer but low enough to prevent the meat from drying out.

Pot roast is well-done meat—it should be cooked to an internal temperature above 165 degrees. Up to this point, we had been bringing the meat up to an internal temperature of 200 to 210 degrees, the point at which the fat and connective tissue begin to melt. In a 300-degree oven, the roast came up to that temperature in 2½ hours, but the meat was still not fall-apart tender. We wondered what would happen if we cooked it even longer. Slowly increasing the cooking time, we found that between 3 and 3½ hours, the internal temperature of the roast was still 210 degrees, but the meat had a substantially different appearance and texture. The roast was so tender that it was starting to separate along its muscle lines. A fork poked into the meat met with no resistance and nearly disappeared into the flesh. We took the roast out of the pot and "sliced" into it. Nearly all the fat and connective tissue had dissolved into the meat, giving each bite a soft, silky texture and rich flavor. The conclusion? Not only do you have to cook pot roast until it reaches 210 degrees internally, but the meat has to remain at that temperature for a full hour. In other words, cook the pot roast until it's done—and then keep on cooking.

Building on our simple pot roast, we developed two variations. The first included root vegetables—tasters liked a combination of carrots, parsnips, and potatoes—which we added to the braising liquid as it reduced at the end. The second variation we based on *stracotto*, a rustic Italian-style pot roast, made with wine and tomatoes. We liked a single can of diced tomatoes with their juice. Many stracotto recipes also call for mushrooms and tasters felt that they added heft and depth to this dish. A final hint of rosemary (we steeped a sprig in the final sauce for 15 minutes before serving), and the flavors were perfect.

Simple Pot Roast
SERVES 6 TO 8

A $7 to $10 bottle of medium-bodied red table wine made from a blend of grapes, such as a Côtes du Rhône, will work well here. The vegetables in the braising liquid do not get strained out before serving, so be mindful to cut them into fairly even pieces. Serve with mashed or boiled potatoes.

1	(3½- to 4-pound) boneless beef chuck eye roast, pulled apart into 2 pieces, trimmed, and tied (see the illustrations below)
	Salt and ground black pepper
2	tablespoons vegetable oil
1	medium onion, diced medium
1	medium carrot, peeled and diced medium
1	celery rib, diced medium
2	medium garlic cloves, minced or pressed through a garlic press (about 2 teaspoons)
2	teaspoons sugar
1	teaspoon fresh minced thyme leaves, or ¼ teaspoon dried
1	cup low-sodium chicken broth
1	cup low-sodium beef broth
1	cup water
¼	cup dry red wine (see note)

1. Adjust an oven rack to the lower-middle position and heat the oven to 300 degrees. Pat the roasts dry with paper towels and season with salt and pepper. Heat 1 tablespoon of the oil in a

PREPARING A POT ROAST

Chuck eye roast has great flavor, but we found that the interior fat is best trimmed before cooking. Simply pull the roast apart at the natural seam and trim away large knobs of fat from each half.

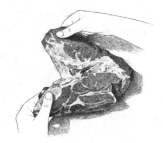

1. Pull the roast apart at its major seams (delineated by lines of fat) into two halves. Use a sharp knife as necessary.

2. Using a knife, remove the large knobs of fat from each piece, leaving a thin layer of fat on the meat.

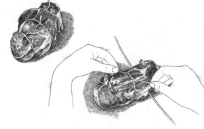

3. Tie three pieces of kitchen twine around each piece of meat to prevent them from falling apart as they cook.

large Dutch oven over medium-high heat until just smoking. Brown the roasts on all sides, 7 to 10 minutes, reducing the heat if the pot begins to scorch. Transfer the roasts to a large plate.

2. Add the remaining 1 tablespoon oil to the pot and place over medium heat until shimmering. Add the onion, carrot, celery, and ¼ teaspoon salt and cook, stirring often, until softened, 8 to 10 minutes. Stir in the garlic, sugar, and thyme and cook until fragrant, about 30 seconds. Stir in the broths and water, scraping up any browned bits, and bring to a simmer.

3. Nestle the roasts, along with any accumulated juices, into the pot and bring to a simmer. Cover, place the pot in the oven, and cook until the meat is very tender and a fork poked into it meets little resistance, 3 to 3½ hours, turning the roasts every hour.

4. Remove the pot from the oven. Transfer the roasts to a cutting board and tent loosely with foil while finishing the sauce. Defat the braising liquid following one of the methods on page 142 (if necessary, return the defatted liquid to the pot).

5. Bring the defatted liquid to a simmer over medium-high heat and cook until thickened, saucy, and measures about 1½ cups, 15 to 20 minutes. Stir in the wine and continue to simmer until the sauce measures about 1½ cups, about 2 minutes. Season the sauce with salt and pepper to taste.

6. Remove the twine, slice the roasts against the grain into ¼-inch-thick slices, and transfer to a serving platter. Spoon the sauce over the meat and serve.

➤ VARIATIONS

Pot Roast with Root Vegetables

Follow the recipe for Simple Pot Roast through step 4. Add 1½ pounds carrots, peeled and sliced ½ inch thick, 1½ pounds small red potatoes, scrubbed and cut into 1-inch pieces, and 1 pound parsnips, peeled and sliced ½ inch thick, to the defatted liquid in the pot. Cover and cook over medium heat until the vegetables are tender, about 30 minutes. Transfer the vegetables to a large bowl with a slotted spoon and cover to keep warm. Add the wine to the liquid left in the pot and continue to simmer until

the sauce measures about 1½ cups. Slice the meat as directed and serve with the vegetables and sauce.

Italian-Style Pot Roast with Mushrooms, Tomatoes, and Rosemary

This variation tastes great with polenta.

Follow the recipe for Simple Pot Roast, adding 10 ounces white mushrooms, wiped clean and quartered, to the pot with the carrot and celery in step 2. Reduce the amount of chicken and beef broths to ¾ cup each and add 1 (14.5-ounce) can diced tomatoes, with their juice, to the pot with the broths. After simmering the sauce in step 5, remove it from the heat, submerge 1 rosemary sprig in the sauce, cover, and let steep 15 minutes; remove the rosemary before serving.

EQUIPMENT: **Vegetable Peelers**

Our favorite vegetable peeler has been the OXO I-Series Swivel Peeler for its comfortably narrow grip and razor-sharp, replaceable stainless-steel blade, but we had one caveat: It weighed nearly four ounces. This isn't a problem when peeling a carrot or two, but when potatoes and apples are peeled in bulk, hand strain can become an issue. Hoping to find a lighter peeler that was just as sharp, we tested four new models.

The Zyliss Smoothglide Peeler simply wasn't sharp enough, and the stainless-steel handle on the Giannini Swivel Peeler was slippery when wet. However, the Kyocera Ceramic Perfect Peeler and Messermeister Pro-Touch Swivel Peeler passed every peeling test with flying colors, including the toughest of all: tomatoes. Although we like the adjustable blade on the Kyocera (which weighs just 2.2 ounces), testers preferred the slightly smoother motion of the 1.5-ounce Messermeister peeler, which they found comfortable even after peeling piles of apples and potatoes. It's our new favorite.

THE BEST VEGETABLE PEELER
The Messermeister Pro-Touch Swivel Peeler ($5.95) is remarkably sharp and so light that hand strain is never a problem.

MESSERMEISTER PRO-TOUCH

BEEF IN BAROLO

BEEF IN BAROLO IS AN ELEGANT DISH featuring tender, moist beef enveloped in a rich, silky red wine sauce—unlike the beefy gravy and vegetal bits characteristic of its down-home American cousin, pot roast. Most recipes utilize a tough cut of meat that is slowly braised in the famed Piedmontese wine. So what's the problem? For starters, Barolo isn't Chianti; most bottles start at a whopping $30. For that kind of investment, we wanted a lot more than a glorified pot roast. Cheap meat cooked in expensive wine? We had our doubts, but given that Italian cuisine is usually about practical home cooking, we put them aside to uncover the secret to great beef in Barolo.

Prior test kitchen efforts to perfect our Simple Pot Roast (page 136) revealed boneless chuck eye roast as the overwhelming favorite cut of meat for its moistness and flavor. Initial tests of several beef in Barolo recipes confirmed these results. In contrast, a boneless sirloin yielded what one taster called "insanely dry" meat and a watery, raw-tasting wine sauce. We also learned that taking a few extra minutes to prepare the roast before braising was well worth the effort. We split the large cylindrical roast in two, along the seam of fat that runs down the center of the roast. Doing this enabled us to trim away the large pieces of excess fat from each lobe. We left a thin layer of fat cap and seasoned and tied each piece to keep it from falling apart during braising.

Following Italian custom, we began by searing the roasts in olive oil, but the sauce needed pizzazz. We remembered seeing pancetta in some recipes and decided to give it a try. Putting the browned roast aside, we poured off all the fat and cooked the pancetta, then sautéed the aromatics in the fat rendered from this Italian bacon. This helped immensely in developing flavor. Finally we added a tablespoon of tomato paste to create a deep roasted flavor. After stirring in minced garlic, a bit of sugar, and a tablespoon of flour to help thicken the sauce during the final reduction, we were ready to add the wine.

Made from Nebbiolo grapes grown in the northern region of Piedmont, Barolo is a bold, full-bodied, often tannic and acidic red wine that is hailed as Italy's "king of wines and wine of kings." Unlike its lighter, fruitier Italian counterparts, such as Chianti, which are often better off quaffed from a glass than

INGREDIENTS: Barolo Substitutes

Not everyone has a bottle of Barolo lying around the house. Could a moderately priced wine-cabinet staple really take the place of this king of wines? We tested our recipe using five inexpensive red wines to see which was best suited to wear the crown. Our one Italian entrant, the Chianti, fell flat, as did the Merlot and Côtes du Rhône, the other medium-bodied wines in our tasting. (We do like Côtes du Rhône for other recipes where the wine isn't meant to be such a prominent flavor, as is the case with Beef in Barolo; see page 170 for more information.) These fruity wines lacked the potency of a heady Barolo. We had better luck with Zinfandel, but Cabernet Sauvignon was the most commanding and was, therefore, the better substitute.

THE BEST BAROLO SUBSTITUTES

CABERNET SAUVIGNON   ZINFANDEL

used in vigorous cooking, Barolo is very hearty and can carry the day, even after being simmered for hours. We found that in a pinch other "big reds" can be substituted (see above for more information), but this dish calls out for its namesake.

First, we focused on how and when to add the wine. Should it be reduced first to concentrate its flavors, added in two parts (at the beginning and the end), or simply dumped in with the meat? Much to our surprise and delight, dumping the whole bottle into the pot won out—this is a dish where the flavor of the wine is supposed to be prominent. But we still needed to find an ingredient to balance this big wine. Broth did not work, and neither did water. Eventually, we discovered that the sweetness of drained diced tomatoes and some fragrant fresh herbs did the trick. We gently brought the meat and braising liquid up to a simmer, covered the pot, and let the beef braise in a 300-degree oven for three hours. (When given less time, the meat was too resilient; given more, it fell apart.) Flipping the meat every hour helped to achieve perfect tenderness without dry patches.

Once the meat was tender, we removed it from the pot to rest while we concentrated on the sauce, which we felt ought to be a far cry from the typical pot roast liquid. After all, why use Barolo to start with if the sauce isn't grand? After defatting the braising liquid, we reduced the liquid over high heat to concentrate and intensify the multiple layers of flavor. Pureeing the liquid, vegetables, and herbs yielded a weak sauce that eventually separated into watery and mealy components. Straining out the vegetables proved to be key. Reduced until it measured 1½ cups, the sauce was dark and lustrous, with the body and finesse of something you might serve over a fine steak.

Worth the expense and effort? You bet. And you don't need to dip into a savings account to put this dish on the table.

Beef Braised in Barolo
SERVES 6 TO 8

Barolo is obviously the wine of choice for this stew; however, an inexpensive bottle of it may require some searching. You may substitute a Cabernet Sauvignon or Zinfandel (see "Barolo Substitutes" on page 138 for more information). Don't use thinly sliced, prepackaged pancetta here; look for pancetta at the deli counter or in an Italian market where it can be sliced ¼ inch thick to order. If pancetta is not available, substitute an equal amount of salt pork (find the meatiest piece possible), cut it into ¼-inch cubes, and boil it in 3 cups of water for about 2 minutes to remove excess salt; drain and cook as directed.

1	(3½- to 4-pound) boneless beef chuck eye roast, pulled apart into 2 pieces, trimmed, and tied (see the illustrations on page 136) Salt and ground black pepper
1	tablespoon vegetable oil
4	ounces pancetta, cut into ¼-inch cubes (see note)
2	medium onions, chopped medium
2	medium carrots, peeled and chopped medium
2	celery ribs, chopped medium
3	medium garlic cloves, minced or pressed through a garlic press (about 1 tablespoon)
2	teaspoons fresh minced thyme leaves
1	teaspoon fresh minced rosemary
1	tablespoon unbleached all-purpose flour
1	tablespoon tomato paste
½	teaspoon sugar
1	(750-ml) bottle Barolo wine (see note)
1	(14.5-ounce) can diced tomatoes, drained

1. Adjust an oven rack to the lower-middle position and heat the oven to 300 degrees. Pat the roasts dry with paper towels and season with salt and pepper. Heat the oil in a large Dutch oven over medium-high heat until just smoking. Brown the roasts on all sides, 7 to 10 minutes, reducing the heat if the pot begins to scorch. Transfer the roasts to a large plate.

2. Pour off all of the fat left in the pot, add the pancetta, and cook over medium heat, stirring often, until browned and crisp, about 8 minutes. Add the onions, carrots, celery, and ¼ teaspoon salt and cook, stirring often, until softened, 8 to 10 minutes. Stir in the garlic, 1 teaspoon of the thyme, and the rosemary and cook until fragrant, about 30 seconds. Stir in the flour, tomato paste, and sugar and cook, stirring constantly, for 1 minute. Slowly whisk in the wine, scraping up any browned bits, until smooth. Stir in the tomatoes and bring to a simmer.

3. Nestle the roasts, along with any accumulated juices, into the pot and bring to a simmer. Cover, place the pot in the oven, and cook until the meat is very tender and a fork poked into it meets little resistance, 3 to 3½ hours, turning the roasts every hour.

4. Remove the pot from the oven. Transfer the roasts to a cutting board and tent loosely with foil while finishing the sauce. Strain the braising liquid into a fat separator or bowl, discarding the solids. Defat the braising liquid following one of the methods on page 142 (if necessary, return the defatted liquid to the pot).

5. Add the remaining 1 teaspoon thyme to the defatted liquid, bring to a simmer over medium-high heat, and cook until thickened, saucy, and measures about 1½ cups, 15 to 20 minutes. Season the sauce with salt and pepper to taste.

6. Remove the twine, slice the roasts against the grain into ¼-inch-thick slices, and transfer to a serving platter. Spoon the sauce over the meat and serve.

FRENCH-STYLE POT ROAST

BOEUF À LA MODE, OR "BEEF IN THE LATEST fashion," is a classic French recipe that dates to a time when a multiple-day recipe was the rule rather than the exception. The earliest reference we found to this dish appeared in *Le Cuisinier François* (1651), an encyclopedic book that systematically catalogued French cuisine. Larding (inserting strips of marinated fat) and braising (searing the roast and simmering it partially submerged in liquid in a sealed pot) could transform an otherwise dry and chewy cut into a tender, moist, and flavorful roast. An added bonus of this cooking technique is that the braising liquid itself—red wine and beef stock—reduces into a thick, rich sauce to accompany the meat.

Although boeuf à la mode bears some similarity to American pot roast, this elegant French dish relies heavily on wine for flavor, a separately prepared mushroom-onion garnish, and a lightly thickened, silky sauce that elegantly drapes over everything. After making several classic renditions of this old-fashioned recipe, we understood its allure—and its challenges. It is to pot roast what croissants are to refrigerated crescent rolls and, as such, can require up to four days of preparation! To bring boeuf à la mode up to date for the modern home cook, some of the fussy techniques and hard-to-find ingredients would have to go.

Traditionally, this recipe starts with threading strips of seasoned, brandy-soaked salt pork or fatback through the beef roast using a long needle, or lardoir. But today's grain-fed beef gets little exercise and has much more marbling than the leaner, grass-fed beef eaten in France when this recipe was created. As long as we chose the right cut (tasters liked the flavor and texture of a boneless chuck eye roast best), there was plenty of fat in the meat and larding was just overkill. We also found that the traditional method of marinating the meat in a mixture of red wine and large-cut mirepoix (carrots, onions, and celery) for days was unnecessary as the meat picked up ample wine flavor during the three- to three-and-a-half-hour braising time. Those were two time-consuming steps we were happy to skip.

In fact, some tasters actually complained that the wine flavor was still too overpowering. The real beauty of this braise is how well the wine melds with the other ingredients—unlike Beef Braised in Barolo (page 139), the wine should have more of a supporting role. A common trick used when cooking with wine is to gently simmer and reduce it before using it as an ingredient—this intensifies its flavor but softens it at the same time. Would cooking the wine before braising the beef in it tame its strong punch? Adding the wine in the pot after the aromatic vegetables had softened, we let it cook 10 to 15 minutes until thickened and reduced to about 2½ cups, before continuing to add the broths and build the braise. Tasters were much happier with this version—the wine tasted intense, complex, and fruity, but not overpowering.

Most of the vegetable flavor in this dish comes from the garnish of glazed pearl onions and white mushrooms, which is traditionally cooked separately and added just before serving. But the sauce itself needed some vegetables to balance the wine and meat flavors. Sautéed onion and garlic helped build depth in the early stages of cooking, and tasters liked the sweetness contributed by large chunks of carrots added to the braising liquid later in the cooking process.

Salt pork is traditionally added to the sauce for richness, but tasters preferred the smoky flavor of bacon. We decided to sauté the aromatics in the bacon drippings—this sauce was improving. Compared with regular pot roast braising liquid, which is flavorful but relatively thin and brothy, the sauce that accompanies boeuf à la mode is richer and more akin to a sauce that might be found on a steak at a fine restaurant. Adding some flour to the sautéed onion and garlic helped with the overall consistency, but the sauce still lacked body. We found a quick, final simmer at the end of cooking to be just what this sauce needed to thicken to the proper consistency. Drizzled with this intense sauce and surrounded by the well-browned mushroom and onion garnish and tender carrots, this was French-style pot roast at its best.

French-Style Pot Roast

SERVES 6 TO 8

A $7 to $10 bottle of medium-bodied red table wine made from a blend of grapes, such as a Côtes du Rhône, will work well here. Serve this dish with boiled potatoes, buttered noodles, or rice.

POT ROAST

1	(3½- to 4-pound) boneless chuck eye roast, pulled apart into 2 pieces, trimmed, and tied (see the illustrations on page 136)
	Salt and ground black pepper
1	tablespoon vegetable oil
4	ounces (about 4 slices) bacon, cut into ¼-inch pieces
1	medium onion, chopped medium
3	medium garlic cloves, minced or pressed through a garlic press (about 1 tablespoon)
2	teaspoons fresh minced thyme leaves, or ½ teaspoon dried
1	tablespoon unbleached all-purpose flour
1	(750-ml) bottle dry red wine (see note)
⅔	cup low-sodium chicken broth
⅔	cup low-sodium beef broth
2	bay leaves
4	medium carrots, peeled and sliced 1½ inches thick
2	tablespoons fresh minced parsley leaves

GARNISH

2	cups frozen pearl onions
½	cup water
3	tablespoons unsalted butter
1	teaspoon sugar
10	ounces white mushrooms, wiped clean and halved if small or quartered if large
	Salt

1. FOR THE POT ROAST: Adjust an oven rack to the lower-middle position and heat the oven to 300 degrees. Pat the roasts dry with paper towels and season with salt and pepper. Heat the oil in a large Dutch oven over medium-high heat until just smoking. Brown the roasts on all sides, 7 to 10 minutes, reducing the heat if the pot begins to scorch. Transfer the roasts to a large plate.

2. Pour off all of the fat left in the pot, add the bacon, and cook over medium heat, stirring often, until browned and crisp, about 8 minutes. Add the onion and ¼ teaspoon salt and cook, stirring often, until softened, 5 to 7 minutes. Stir in the garlic and thyme and cook until fragrant, about 30 seconds. Stir in the flour and cook, stirring constantly, until golden, about 1 minute. Slowly whisk in the wine, scraping up any browned bits, until smooth and simmer until slightly thickened and the mixture measures about 2½ cups, about 15 minutes. Stir in the broths and bay leaves and bring to a simmer.

3. Nestle the roasts, along with any accumulated juices, into the pot and bring to a simmer. Cover, place the pot in the oven, and cook for 2 hours, turning the roasts after 1 hour. Stir in the carrots and continue to cook in the oven, covered, until the meat is very tender and a fork poked into it meets little resistance, 1 to 1½ hours longer, turning the roasts halfway through cooking.

4. FOR THE GARNISH: Meanwhile, bring the pearl onions, water, butter, and sugar to a boil in a large nonstick skillet over medium-high heat. Reduce the heat to medium, cover, and cook until the onions are fully thawed and tender, 5 to 8 minutes. Uncover, increase the heat to medium-high, and cook until all the liquid evaporates, 3 to 4 minutes. Add the mushrooms and ¼ teaspoon salt and cook, without stirring, for 2 minutes. Stir and continue to cook, stirring often, until the vegetables are browned and glazed, 8 to 12 minutes. Remove from the heat and set aside.

5. Remove the pot from the oven. Transfer the roasts to a cutting board and tent loosely with foil while finishing the sauce. Defat the braising liquid following one of the methods on page 142 (if necessary, return the defatted liquid to the pot).

6. Stir the garnish into the defatted liquid, bring to a simmer over medium-high heat, and cook until thickened, saucy, and the mixture measures about 3¼ cups, 15 to 20 minutes. Season the sauce with salt and pepper to taste.

7. Remove the twine, slice the roasts against the grain into ¼-inch-thick slices, and transfer to a serving platter. Spoon the sauce and vegetables over the meat, sprinkle with the parsley, and serve.

Defatting Braises 101

Through years of braising in the test kitchen, we've learned how important it is to defat the braising liquid before finishing the sauce. If you don't, the sauce winds up tasting (and looking) greasy. Unlike stews, braises aren't thickened with generous amounts of flour (the flour in stews traps the fat and emulsifies it into a thick, gravy-like sauce). Braises have very little or no flour and without it, the fat quickly rises to the surface without incorporating into the sauce.

Below are four different ways to defat a braise: Choose which one works best for you depending on the dish you are making and the equipment you have on hand. For the first three methods, it is important to let the liquid settle for 5 to 10 minutes before defatting. This allows all of the fat to separate out and float to the top.

Skim with a Ladle or Wide Spoon
1. The simplest way to defat a braise is to simply let the liquid settle in the pot for 5 to 10 minutes, then skim the fat away with a ladle or wide spoon. The advantages of this method are that it's very easy and it doesn't dirty any extra dishes; however, some fat will remain in the sauce.

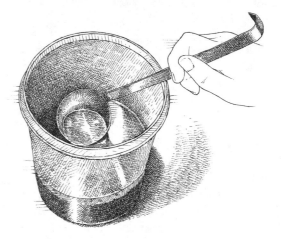

Use a Tall, Narrow Container
2. If you are using a large pot or have a large quantity of fat to skim, pour the braising liquid into a tall, narrow container before defatting. This will create a deeper layer of fat that is easier to skim and remove. Let the liquid settle for 5 to 10 minutes, then skim with a ladle or wide spoon. (Although some fat will remain in the sauce, there will be less than if you simply defat the liquid right in the pot.)

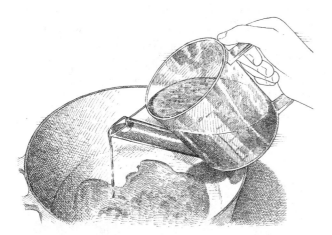

Use a Fat Separator
3. Using a fat separator is probably the most effective method for defatting a liquid; however, you will be limited by the separator's size. (We recommend that you buy the largest fat separator you can find.) To use, simply pour the braising liquid into the fat separator and let it settle for 5 to 10 minutes. Then pour the liquid back into your pot through the spout, leaving the fat behind in the separator.

Refrigerate Overnight
4. If you are making the braise the day before, you can simply refrigerate the braise without defatting— the fat will collect and solidify on top of the braise as it chills. Upon removing the braise from the refrigerator, you simply scrape the large solid pieces of fat right off the top before reheating.

BRAISED BEEF BRISKET

COOKS AROUND THE WORLD MAY NEVER SEE eye to eye on what to do with a beef brisket—Texans smoke it, the Irish pickle it, and Germans smother it in sauerkraut and prunes—but they all agree it takes time. Brisket would therefore seem an ideal cut for braising, because it takes hours of slow cooking to soften this workhorse muscle, which is otherwise as tough as leather. Sadly, this patience is usually rewarded with shreds of dry, chewy meat, as brisket tends to give up its last ounce of moisture just as it finally becomes fork tender.

Our goal was a braised brisket that was both moist and tender, with a simple sauce that complemented this naturally flavorful cut. The down-home recipes we sampled used diversionary tactics to attack the problem of dry, chewy meat, either emptying the spice rack into the pot or slathering the brisket in sticky sweet sauces made from cola, chili sauce, or powdered soup mix. More traditional recipes took a minimalist approach, braising the meat with onions in a watery broth (if not actually water). Neither strategy could disguise or remedy the basic problem: meat that was either tough or bone-dry and impossible to cut without shredding it into stringy bits.

All braises struggle with this same catch-22. For the normally tough meat to become tender, its connective tissues must be broken down, which requires hours of low-temperature, moist-heat cooking. As the meat cooks, the muscle fibers slowly contract, expelling moisture and often leaving the meat dry. The amount and distribution of the fat in the meat can make a big difference in the outcome of a braise. A chuck roast will taste succulent after a proper braise because of its relatively high and even distribution of fat. In a brisket, most of the fat is located in an exterior cap and in a few thick layers—it is not marbled throughout. As a result, fat renders into the sauce rather than basting the interior of the meat, which is rather lean. (This is especially true of flat cut brisket; see at right for more information.) For all these reasons, our typical braising technique of browning the meat on the stovetop, then braising it with wine, broth, and aromatics in a 300-degree oven until tender, delivered disappointing results. While tender, the brisket was quite dry and had an unappealing boiled flavor, and the sauce was thin and greasy. The sliced and sautéed onions we added to the pot lent a welcome sweetness, but after almost four hours they had all but disintegrated. Last, the meat appeared to cook unevenly; by the time the center of the brisket was tender, the outer layers of meat were falling apart in shreds.

BUYING BEEF BRISKET

A whole beef brisket weighs up to 12 pounds. It is usually sold in two pieces, the flat (or first) cut and the point cut. The flat cut is leaner and thinner, with a rectangular shape and an exterior fat cap. It is more commonly available at supermarkets than the point cut, which has an oblong, irregular shape and contains large interior pockets of fat.

We found the point cut to be marginally more flavorful but, more important, much less prone to drying out, thanks to all the extra fat. Unfortunately, more than a few tasters found the point cut too fatty to enjoy, and it was next to impossible to carve it into neat slices. All in all, it seemed a better cut for barbecuing than braising. The flat cut is easier to sear and to slice, provided it has cooled. Butchers usually trim away some or all of the fat cap, but try to find one with at least ¼ inch of fat in place, as it will help to keep the meat moist during cooking. (It can be hard to tell how much fat is in place because supermarkets often wrap the brisket with the fat side hidden.) If the fat cap is very thick and untrimmed in places, cut it down to a thickness of about ¼ inch.

A flat cut brisket roast usually weighs between 4 and 5 pounds, though butchers occasionally cut them into smaller 2- to 3-pound roasts. You can substitute two of these smaller cuts if that is all that is available, although the cooking time may vary.

FLAT CUT

POINT CUT

A 4- to 5-pound flat cut brisket with a decent cap of fat (top) is ideal for braising. We find its meat to be leaner and easier to slice than the highly marbled and knobby point cut brisket (bottom), but either will work in our recipe.

Looking for a better way to braise brisket, we tested an assortment of cooking vessels and techniques. To improve the flavor of the sauce, we ran a test with much less liquid than goes into a standard braise—just a half cup each of wine and broth. The resulting sauce was indeed flavorful but, in such a shallow pool of liquid, the meat cooked unevenly. (The portions exposed to the air took longer to cook.)

Not as common with beef as with pork and chicken, brining was nonetheless one way to try to reduce the moisture loss. Unfortunately, tasters found that even a mild brine resulted in meat and sauce that were unpalatably salty. Overnight marinades in wine and herbs, suggested by some traditional Eastern European recipes, left the briskets mushy and sour tasting. Some brisket recipes recommended cooking the meat fat side up and poking holes through the fat and into the meat to help the rendered fat penetrate and baste the meat. Finally some success—but while this step did make for some significant improvement in the moistness of the brisket, overall the meat was still too dry.

If we couldn't keep the moisture from leaving the meat in the first place, could we get the meat to reabsorb some of the liquid after cooking? Until this point, we had been removing the brisket from the sauce and letting it rest on a cutting board before attempting—and failing—to cut it into thin, neat slices. Next we tested letting the meat rest, and

WORTH THE WAIT

Sliced straight from the pot, brisket almost invariably shreds (left). Letting the cooked brisket rest for at least 8 hours in the braising liquid allows the meat to absorb some of these juices, and the result is meat that slices neatly and tastes better (right).

SLICED RIGHT AWAY   RESTED FOR 8 HOURS, THEN SLICED

even cool, in the sauce before slicing it, in hopes that it would reabsorb some of the flavorful liquid it had lost. Twenty minutes in the sauce had little effect on the meat, but after an hour-long rest the brisket was noticeably better. Encouraged, we let the meat cool overnight in the sauce.

The next day, cold brisket was now easy to slice without shredding. Once reheated in the sauce, the overnight brisket was dramatically improved on all counts—moist, flavorful, and meltingly tender. Weighing pieces of brisket that had rested overnight in the sauce showed that they had, in fact, gained several ounces. In effect, they had reabsorbed some of their juices from the sauce, which made the meat less dry.

Until now, our working recipe had called for equal parts red wine and beef broth as braising liquids. We tested a variety of liquids in different combinations and found that tasters actually preferred chicken broth to beef for its cleaner flavor in this dish. To boost the flavor of the sauce, we doubled the quantities of both broth and wine, then allowed them to reduce a bit before placing the braise in the oven.

As for the other ingredients in the sauce, tasters loved the sweetness of onions—sliced thick to stand up to the long cooking time—but agreed that carrots and celery were unnecessary. Brown sugar complemented the onions, while paprika and a pinch of cayenne contributed a bit of spice and heat. Garlic, tomato paste, bay leaves, and some thyme rounded out the flavors.

A debate sprang up in the test kitchen over the proper thickness of the finished sauce. Gravy enthusiasts wanted a thick sauce that would cling to the meat, while their opponents backed a thinner, more natural jus. But everyone agreed that too much flour, stirred into the skillet while building the sauce, resulted in a sauce than was overly pasty; just 2 tablespoons were enough to give the sauce the proper body. Right before serving, we added a few teaspoons of cider vinegar to brighten the flavor, and tasters unanimously approved. Now we had the best of both worlds—tender and moist—and the recipe could be made the day before serving, making it perfect for a midweek supper or even for entertaining.

Braised Beef Brisket with Onions

SERVES 6 TO 8

A $7 to $10 bottle of medium-bodied red table wine made from a blend of grapes, such as a Côtes du Rhône, will work well here. We use a 13 by 9-inch dish (rather than a Dutch oven) to ensure that the brisket can lie flat. This recipe requires some advance preparation; after cooking, the brisket must rest for at least 8 hours (or up to 24 hours) in the braising liquid in order to become moist and flavorful.

1	(4- to 5-pound) beef brisket, preferably flat cut (see page 143)
	Salt and ground black pepper
2	tablespoons vegetable oil
3	large onions (about 2½ pounds), halved and sliced ½ inch thick
1	tablespoon light or dark brown sugar
3	medium garlic cloves, minced or pressed through a garlic press (about 1 tablespoon)
1	tablespoon paprika
1	tablespoon minced fresh thyme leaves, or ¾ teaspoon dried
⅛	teaspoon cayenne pepper
2	tablespoons unbleached all-purpose flour
1	tablespoon tomato paste
1	cup dry red wine (see note)
1	cup low-sodium chicken broth
3	bay leaves
2	teaspoons cider vinegar

1. Adjust an oven rack to the lower-middle position and heat the oven to 300 degrees. Pat the brisket dry with paper towels. Place the brisket fat side up on a cutting board and poke the meat (through the fat) with a fork, about 1 inch apart. Season the brisket with salt and pepper.

2. Heat 1 tablespoon of the oil in a 12-inch skillet over medium-high heat until just smoking. Brown the brisket on both sides, 12 to 14 minutes, reducing the heat if the pan begins to scorch. Transfer the brisket to a large plate.

3. Add the remaining 1 tablespoon oil to the skillet and place over medium heat until shimmering. Add the onions, sugar, and ¼ teaspoon salt and cook, stirring often, until softened, 8 to

10 minutes. Stir in the garlic, paprika, thyme, and cayenne and cook until fragrant, about 30 seconds. Stir in the flour and tomato paste and cook, stirring constantly, for 1 minute. Slowly whisk in the wine, scraping up any browned bits, then slowly whisk in the broth until smooth. Stir in the bay leaves, bring to a simmer, and cook until thickened, about 5 minutes.

4. Pour the sauce into a 13 by 9-inch baking dish. Nestle the brisket, along with any accumulated juices, into the sauce, spooning the sauce over the meat to cover. Cover the dish tightly with foil, place it in the oven, and cook until the meat is very tender and a fork poked into it meets little resistance, 4 to 4½ hours.

5. Remove the dish from the oven. Transfer the brisket to a large plate and tent loosely with foil. Strain the braising liquid into a fat separator or bowl, reserving the onions and discarding the bay leaves. Defat the braising liquid following one of the methods on page 142.

6. Spread the onions into the baking dish, place the brisket on top, and pour the braising liquid over the meat. Let cool to room temperature, 20 to 30 minutes, then cover tightly with foil and refrigerate for at least 8 hours, or up to 24 hours.

7. About 45 minutes before serving, adjust an oven rack to the lower-middle position and heat the oven to 350 degrees. Transfer the cold brisket to a cutting board and slice it against the grain into ¼-inch-thick slices following the illustration on page 213. Drizzle the cider vinegar over the onions and sauce and return the slices of brisket to the baking dish. Cover the dish with foil and bake until heated through, 45 to 60 minutes. Season with salt and pepper to taste before serving.

➤ VARIATION

Braised Beef Brisket with Sauerkraut and Prunes

Follow the recipe for Braised Beef Brisket with Onions, substituting 3 pounds fresh sauerkraut, thoroughly rinsed and squeezed dry, for the onions, and 1 cup dry white wine for the red wine. Omit the paprika and cider vinegar and add 1 cup pitted prunes, halved, to the baking dish with the strained sauerkraut in step 6.

CORNED BEEF AND CABBAGE

CORNED BEEF AND CABBAGE, THE VENERABLE one-pot meal of boiled corned beef, cabbage, and occasionally other winter vegetables, is famous in the U.S. as the traditional St. Patrick's Day dinner, but was actually first popularized in rural Ireland as Easter Sunday dinner. Also known in parts of the U.S. as New England boiled dinner, corned beef and cabbage struck us less as a dish with big flavor and genuine dinner-table appeal than as a symbol of the stalwart Yankee ethics of hard work and thrift. That misconception, however, was the first of several to be uncovered during our testing. We came to realize that this dish needn't be mushy, overwhelmingly salty, or one-dimensional, as it had always seemed. Instead, it can be a full-flavored medley of meaty, tender, well-seasoned beef, subtle spices, and sweet, earthy vegetables, each distinct in flavor and texture.

We commenced our research and testing with the usual spate of recipes, most of which were based on a 4- to 6-pound piece of corned beef. The term "corned" refers to the curing of meat with salt, often used as a method of preservation before refrigeration became widespread. Legend has it that the salt grains were roughly the same size as corn kernels, hence the name corned beef. The cut of beef most commonly corned is boneless brisket. For retail sale, the whole brisket is usually split into two parts, called the first, or flat, cut and the second, or point, cut. Of the two, we prefer the flat cut (see "Buying Beef Brisket," page 143).

At the supermarket, we found more commercial corned beef options than we had anticipated from reading the recipes we had researched. In addition to "low-sodium" corned beef, there were regular and "gray," each in both flat and point cuts in sizes ranging from 3 to 6 pounds. The difference between regular and gray is made clear on the package. The brine for gray corned beef contains only water and salt, whereas the "regular" corned beef brine also contains sodium nitrite, which helps the meat retain its red color by reacting with purple color pigments and turning them to pink and red.

Though the color was less appealing, we far preferred the gray corned beef for its superior flavor; it tasted cleaner and beefier than the regular.

But the gray, nitrite-free corned beef is a product limited to a small region of the country (New England), so we decided to try corning our own brisket. Our research turned up two methods of corning—the wet cure and the dry cure. Both methods require close to a week, but they are also extremely easy and require very little work; all you need to do is prepare the meat and its cure.

Testing the wet method for corning beef involved tasting briskets cured in a brine of 2 cups of salt and 3 quarts of water for 14, 12, 10, seven, and five days. Among all of them, we liked the five-day brisket best, noting a pleasing saltiness alongside the distinctive flavor of beef.

At this point, we also gave the dry-cure method a go. Adapting a recipe from Julia Child's *The Way to Cook* (Knopf, 1989), we rubbed our 5-pound flat cut brisket with ¼ cup salt and a few crushed herbs and spices, placed it in a 2-gallon zipper-lock bag, weighted the meat with a brick, and let it sit for five days in the fridge. This corned beef was the best yet, with a concentrated beef flavor, an assertive yet not overpowering saltiness, and a pleasant spiciness. Curing the brisket for two extra days, seven in total, brought out the flavor of the spices a little more, without affecting the saltiness. When the beef had sufficiently cured, we simply rinsed it with water to rid the exterior of excess salt.

With the corned beef tasting just the way we wanted it, we turned our attention to the cooking method, then to the cabbage. Though most recipes call for cooking corned beef and cabbage on the stove, we did try a couple of tests in the oven. Our advice is to stick to the stove—it was easier to monitor the cooking process and we also found that adding the vegetables and adjusting the heat to compensate was easier with the pot on top of the stove.

On the stove, we noticed that the meat emerged from the pot tender and flaky if cooked at a lively simmer, as opposed to tight and tough when cooked at a full boil. We also preferred to cook the meat covered to prevent water evaporation and a resulting over concentration of salt in the broth. We experimented with different quantities of water, covering the corned beef by ½ inch to 3 inches and found that it makes no difference in terms of the meat or vegetables. The amount of water does matter to the broth, though. The broth produced from covering the meat by 1 inch and cooking it with the pot lid on was nicely seasoned.

The last, though not insignificant, variable was the cabbage and vegetables. We tested a wide variety of vegetables, from the familiar to the exotic, and settled on traditional green cabbage, as well as potatoes and carrots, which we borrowed from the New England boiled dinner. We tried cooking the vegetables along with the meat, but there were two distinct disadvantages to this approach. First, it was difficult to judge when the vegetables were properly done. Second, it would require a pot larger than any we had in the test kitchen or in our own homes.

The best method turned out to be removing the meat from the broth when done, then cooking the vegetables in the broth. This not only benefited the vegetables, giving them a full, round flavor from the salt and rendered fat in the broth, but it also allowed us time to let the meat rest before cutting it.

Corned Beef and Cabbage

SERVES 8 TO 10

You will need to allow 5 to 7 days for the curing process to take place. Be sure to leave about ¼ inch of fat on the meat for texture and flavor. Do not core the cabbage; the core helps the wedges of cabbage hold together during cooking. Serve this dish with horseradish (either plain or mixed with sour cream) and grainy mustard.

¼	cup kosher salt
2	bay leaves, crumbled
1	tablespoon black peppercorns, crushed coarse
1	tablespoon dried thyme
2¼	teaspoons ground allspice
1½	teaspoons paprika
1	(4- to 5-pound) beef brisket, preferably flat cut (see page 143)

1½	pounds (about 9 small) red potatoes, scrubbed
1½	pounds (about 9 medium) carrots, peeled and cut into thirds
1	small head green cabbage, cut into 6 or 8 wedges (see note)

1. Mix the salt, bay leaves peppercorns, thyme, allspice, and paprika together. Pat the brisket dry with paper towels. Place the brisket on a cutting board and poke both sides of the meat (through the fat) with a fork, about 1 inch apart. Rub the brisket thoroughly with the salt mixture.

2. Place the brisket in a 2-gallon zipper-lock bag, forcing out as much air as possible, and place in a pan large enough to hold it (a rimmed baking sheet works well). Cover with a second, similar-sized pan, and weight with 2 bricks or heavy cans. Refrigerate for 5 to 7 days, turning the brisket over once a day.

3. Remove the meat from the bag, pat it dry with paper towels, and place it in a large Dutch oven or stockpot. Add water to the pot until it covers the brisket by about 1 inch. Bring to a boil over medium-high heat, skimming any impurities that rise to the surface. Cover, reduce to a simmer, and cook until the meat is very tender and a fork poked into it meets little resistance, 2 to 3 hours.

4. Transfer the meat to a cutting board, ladling about 1 cup of the cooking liquid over it to keep it moist. Tent loosely with foil and let rest while cooking the vegetables.

5. Add the potatoes and carrots to the cooking liquid left in the pot and bring to a boil over medium-high heat. Cover, reduce to a simmer, and cook until they begin to soften, about 10 minutes. Add the cabbage and continue to simmer until all of the vegetables are tender, 10 to 15 minutes longer.

6. As the vegetables finish cooking, slice the meat against the grain into ¼-inch-thick slices following the illustration on page 213 and transfer to a serving platter. Transfer the vegetables to the platter with a slotted spoon and drizzle the cooking liquid over top as needed to moisten before serving.

SHORT RIBS BRAISED IN RED WINE

IN THE SUPERMARKET MEAT CASE, SHORT RIBS are often-overlooked, seldom-understood, rather intimidating hunks of meat and bone that are frequently shunned. But braise them and they become yielding, tender, and succulent. Then douse them with a velvety sauce containing all the rich, bold flavors from the braise, and they are as satisfying as beef stew, but with much more panache.

Whichever way you cut it, short ribs are just what their name says they are: short ribs cut from any part along the length of the cow's ribs. They can come from the lower belly section or higher up toward the back, from the shoulder (or chuck) area, or the forward midsection. They can be cut English or flanken style (see at right), but no matter what, they're always fatty. Of course, the fat and connective tissue are also what make them so deeply flavorful.

Our first challenge was to get them to give up their fat. The first step in most braises is browning the meat. Browning adds color and flavor, but in the case of short ribs it also presents an opportunity to render some of the fat. We browned the ribs on all sides, then carefully poured off all the fat that rendered. From there we cooked them in a simple braising liquid that consisted of chicken broth and red wine. The resulting ribs were good, but we still had some issues to work out.

Like most braises, short ribs need aromatic vegetables. A basic mirepoix of onions, carrots, and celery made a world of difference, but with the big, bold flavors of beef and red wine, we felt this braise needed more. A handful of minced garlic helped and we found nine cloves just right for this braise. A modest amount of fresh herbs, including thyme and rosemary, boosted the flavor of the meat and a couple of bay leaves rounded out the aromatics. Finally, tasters thought a little bacon added a welcome hint of smoky flavor, which we further enhanced by cooking the aromatics right in the bacon fat.

Braising liquids required only a cursory investigation. We tested water, chicken broth, beef broth,

INGREDIENTS: Short Ribs

When we started testing short ribs, we went to the local grocery store and bought out their supply. What we brought back to the test kitchen were 2- to 4-inch lengths of wide flat rib bone, to which a rectangular plate of fatty meat was attached. We also ordered short ribs from the butcher. Imagine our confusion when these turned out to be long, continuous pieces of meat about ¾ inch thick, that had been cut across the ribs and grain and that included two or three segments of rib bone. The former, we learned, are sometimes called English-style short ribs and the latter are called flanken-style ribs.

We began by braising both types of ribs. The ones from the butcher had a relatively thin, across-the-grain cut that made the meat pleasant to eat. The supermarket ribs were a bit stringier because they contained longer segments of grain. But both types were equally tender and good, so considering the cost ($3 more per pound) and effort (special order) required to procure the butcher-cut specimens, we decided to go with the supermarket variety.

ENGLISH-STYLE   FLANKEN-STYLE

and red wine, trying varying combinations of each. We eliminated the water (sticking with the wine and broths), but the sauce, despite the abundance of aromatics and herbs, remained strangely hollow and lacking. All along, we had been using a cheap, hardly potable wine. After stepping up to a good, solid one worthy of drinking, the sauce improved dramatically—it had the complexity and resonance that we were seeking. Finally, we added some diced tomatoes and tomato paste to sweeten the braise and intensify the flavors.

If the braising liquid were to transform itself into the sauce we were after, it would need some thickening. After various experiments, we found that adding just a little flour to the braise, in addition to reducing the braising liquid slightly after the meat was cooked, produced a silky sauce that cloaked the ribs gracefully. Also, we found it very important to defat the braising liquid because as browned short ribs braise, they continue to release good amounts of fat (see page 142 for more information on defatting). Straining the spent vegetables from the liquid before finishing the sauce also helped the sauce to look as refined as it tasted, along with a sprinkle of minced fresh parsley just before serving.

Short Ribs Braised in Red Wine and Bacon
SERVES 6

This recipe works with either English-style or flanken-style short ribs; see page 148 for more information on buying short ribs. A $7 to $10 bottle of medium-bodied red table wine made from a blend of grapes, such as a Côtes du Rhône, will work well here. Once cooked, the ribs can sit in the finished sauce to stay warm for up to an hour before serving. Serve with mashed potatoes or egg noodles.

6	pounds bone-in short ribs, trimmed of excess fat and silver skin (see note)
	Salt and ground black pepper
2	tablespoons vegetable oil
6	ounces (about 6 slices) bacon, cut into 1-inch pieces
3	medium onions, chopped medium
2	medium carrots, peeled and chopped medium
1	celery rib, chopped medium
9	medium garlic cloves, minced or pressed through a garlic press (about 3 tablespoons)
1	tablespoon minced fresh rosemary
1	tablespoon minced fresh thyme leaves
¼	cup unbleached all-purpose flour
1	tablespoon tomato paste
1	(750-ml) bottle dry red wine (see note)
2	cups low-sodium chicken broth
2	cups low-sodium beef broth
1	(14.5-ounce) can diced tomatoes
3	bay leaves
6	tablespoons minced fresh parsley leaves

1. Adjust an oven rack to the lower-middle position and heat the oven to 325 degrees. Pat the ribs dry with paper towels and season with salt and pepper. Heat 1 tablespoon of the oil in a large Dutch oven over medium-high heat until just smoking. Add half of the ribs and brown on all sides, 7 to 10 minutes, reducing the heat if the pot begins to scorch. Transfer the ribs to a large plate and repeat with the remaining 1 tablespoon oil and the remaining ribs; transfer to the plate.

2. Pour off all of the fat left in the pot, add the bacon, and cook over medium heat, stirring often, until browned and crisp, about 8 minutes. Add the onions, carrots, celery, and ¼ teaspoon salt and cook, stirring often, until softened, 8 to 10 minutes. Stir in the garlic, rosemary, and thyme and cook until fragrant, about 30 seconds. Stir in the flour and tomato paste and cook, stirring constantly, for 1 minute. Slowly whisk in the wine, scraping up any browned bits, then slowly whisk in the broths until smooth. Stir in tomatoes with their juice and bay leaves and bring to a simmer.

3. Nestle the short ribs, along with any accumulated juices, into the pot bone side up, and bring to a simmer. Cover, place the pot in the oven, and cook until the meat is very tender and a fork poked into it meets little resistance, 2½ to 3 hours.

4. Remove the pot from the oven. Transfer the ribs to a large plate, discarding any loose bones that have fallen away from the meat, and tent loosely with foil while finishing the sauce. Strain the braising liquid into a fat separator or bowl, discarding the solids. Defat the braising liquid following one of the methods on page 142 (if necessary, return the defatted liquid to the pot).

5. Bring the defatted liquid to a simmer over medium-high heat and cook until thickened and saucy, 5 to 10 minutes. Off the heat, season the sauce with salt and pepper to taste, then return the ribs to the sauce to warm through. Sprinkle individual portions with parsley before serving.

➤ VARIATION
Porter-Braised Short Ribs
Follow the recipe for Short Ribs Braised in Red Wine and Bacon, substituting 2 tablespoons Dijon mustard and 2 teaspoons Worcestershire sauce for the tomato paste, substituting 3 cups porter beer for the red wine, and omitting the rosemary.

CHINESE-STYLE BRAISED SHORT RIBS

BEEF SHORT RIBS AND BLACK BEAN SAUCE (made with fermented black beans) are a classic combination in Chinese cuisine and it's no wonder—the rich, meaty short ribs are perfectly suited to the musky, salty beans. Marrying these two flavors together seemed as easy as taking our favorite braised short rib recipe and tossing in some of these beans, but one batch of overly salty, inedible short ribs later, we realized we had a challenge ahead of us.

For one, our inexperience with using fermented black beans was evident. We headed into the test kitchen to find how to get this dish right, but quickly realized our first challenge was to find out more about fermented black beans. After a shopping trip and time logged in the library, we found that these small black preserved soybeans are commonly used in conjunction with garlic as a seasoning. They also are said to heighten the flavor of beef, chicken, and pork. Because they are quite pungent and salty, fermented black beans should be rinsed and soaked before cooking—and they should be used sparingly. (Although not readily available in all supermarkets, they are easy to find in Asian markets.)

Beef short ribs, on the other hand, are often hard to miss in the supermarket meat case, as they're rather intimidating hunks of meat and bone. Braising makes them tender, rich and satisfying. We knew from developing our Short Ribs Braised in Red Wine and Bacon (page 149) that browning the meat is an important step, not only to add color and flavor to the braise, but also to render some of the fat from the meat. We tried browning on the stovetop and in the oven and found that both methods accomplished our goals. The major inconvenience of oven browning is deglazing the roasting pan on the stovetop, which makes a burner-safe roasting pan a prerequisite, so we opted for browning on the stovetop. True, we needed to brown the ribs in two batches, but we didn't see this as much of an inconvenience.

With our browning method down, we moved on to building our black bean sauce. Because the flavor of the fermented beans is so strong, we didn't have to look further than water for a braising liquid. Still, since we often braise meats in a combination of chicken and beef broth, we thought we'd give that a try, too. Tasting the sauces side by side, we couldn't detect much difference, so we stayed with the water in a nod to authentic Chinese preparation.

We next turned our attention to enhancing the flavor of the sauce. We tried soy sauce, common in many recipes found in our research. Soy sauce adds not only a rich, meaty flavor to the sauce, but color as well. We tested various amounts and found that a mere 2 tablespoons was enough to heighten the flavor of the braise. At this point, we felt that the braising liquid could use a bit of brightness and rice wine did the job admirably.

Transforming the braising liquid into a sauce was a simple matter of defatting and thickening the braising liquid. In Chinese cooking cornstarch is the go-to ingredient for thickening sauces, and when added in the form of a slurry (cornstarch-water mixture) to the defatted liquid, it thickened the liquid into a silky sauce in a matter of minutes. Once poured over the ribs, the lush, flavorful sauce clung perfectly to the meaty ribs—tasters grabbed plenty of napkins before digging in.

INGREDIENTS: Fermented Black Beans

Also called salted or dried black beans, fermented black beans are actually soybeans that have been dried and fermented with garlic, salt, and other spices. It is important to rinse and soak the beans before using them or they may impart too much of a salty flavor to a dish. Fermented black beans are used sparingly and will last for months in an airtight container in the refrigerator.

Chinese-Style Braised Short Ribs

SERVES 6

This recipe works with either English-style or flanken-style short ribs; see page 148 for more information on buying short ribs. Fermented black beans can be found in Asian markets and some well-stocked supermarkets; see page 150 for more information. Because the braising liquid doesn't cover all of the ribs in the pot, be sure to move the ribs around during the cooking to ensure they are evenly cooked and flavored. Once cooked, the ribs can sit in the finished sauce to stay warm for up to an hour before serving. Serve with rice.

6	tablespoons fermented black beans, rinsed (see note)
2	tablespoons soy sauce
2	tablespoons Chinese rice cooking wine or dry sherry
4	medium garlic cloves, minced or pressed through a garlic press (about 4 teaspoons)
6	pounds bone-in short ribs, trimmed of excess fat and silver skin (see note)
	Ground black pepper
2	tablespoons vegetable oil
6	cups water
2	tablespoons cornstarch

1. Adjust an oven rack to the lower-middle position and heat the oven to 325 degrees. Soak the fermented black beans in 2 cups warm water to reduce their saltiness, about 20 minutes. Drain the beans, then toss with the soy sauce, rice wine, and garlic and set aside.

2. Meanwhile, pat the ribs dry with paper towels and season with pepper. Heat 1 tablespoon of the oil in a large Dutch oven over medium-high heat until just smoking. Add half of the ribs and brown on all sides, 7 to 10 minutes, reducing the heat if the pot begins to scorch. Transfer the ribs to a large plate and repeat with the remaining 1 tablespoon oil and the remaining ribs; transfer to the plate.

3. Pour off all of the fat left in the pot, add the fermented black bean mixture, and cook over medium heat until fragrant, about 1 minute. Stir in 5¾ cups of the water, scraping up the browned bits, and bring to a simmer.

4. Nestle the short ribs, along with any accumulated juices, into the pot, bone side up, and bring to a simmer. Cover, place the pot in the oven, and cook until the meat is very tender and a fork poked into it meets little resistance, 2½ to 3 hours, rearranging the ribs halfway through the cooking time so that all the ribs become moistened with the braising liquid.

5. Remove the pot from the oven. Transfer the ribs to a large plate, discarding any loose bones that have fallen away from the meat, and tent loosely with foil while finishing the sauce. Defat the braising liquid following one of the methods on page 142 (if necessary, return the defatted liquid to the pot).

6. Bring the defatted liquid to a simmer over medium-high heat. Whisk the cornstarch with the remaining ¼ cup water to dissolve, then whisk it into the simmering sauce. Continue to simmer the sauce, whisking constantly, until thickened, about 4 minutes. Return the ribs to the sauce to warm through before serving.

SWISS STEAKS WITH ONIONS AND MUSHROOMS

SWISS STEAK IS A DISH THAT WAS POPULAR in the early to middle part of the 20th century. Don't be fooled by the name—the term "swissing" originally referred to the process of pounding or rolling fabric or other materials in order to soften them, and has nothing to do with Switzerland at all. Swiss steak is generally made from the tougher cuts of meat, such as the round or chuck, which have been pounded with a tenderizing hammer (or run through a set of needled rollers) to produce what we know as "cube steak." Once tenderized, the meat is typically dredged in flour, browned in butter or oil, braised in liquid, and served with the resulting gravy, further tenderizing the tough cut of beef.

While this dish was somewhat familiar to us in the

test kitchen, no one actually remembered having eaten a Swiss steak since childhood. But the notion of braising steak—something we're used to pan-searing or grilling—intrigued us, so we decided to resurrect this old favorite. Perusing some recipes, we noticed a lot of variations on the theme—some Swiss steaks were braised in tomato sauce, some in stock, and others in wine. Many of the recipes also included garnishes such as onions, carrots, peppers, and mushrooms (which is why Swiss steak is also sometimes called smothered steak). Initial testing quickly narrowed our search for the ultimate Swiss steak; onions and mushrooms were a must, and tasters preferred broth as the braising liquid. With these basics determined we turned our attention to the meat.

Limiting our choices to tougher cuts that benefit from a long simmer in liquid to render them tender, we tested blade steaks, chuck steaks, cube steaks, top round steaks, and bottom round steaks. We dredged and browned each batch, added a basic braising liquid of chicken broth with onions and mushrooms, and allowed them to braise for two hours (an adequate amount of time to tenderize most any tough cut of meat). The cube steaks emerged from the oven surprisingly dry and also failed to brown properly. The top and bottom round cuts were both stringy and so dry that they were difficult to chew. The chuck steak had good flavor but all the intramuscular fat and sinew was unappealing to some. The unanimous choice for this dish was blade steak, which was praised for its meaty flavor and moist and tender texture. (There is a small line of fat that runs through this steak, but it is nearly unnoticeable after braising.)

Traditional Swiss steak recipes call for dredging the steaks in flour prior to browning them and although this disagrees with our past test kitchen experience, we felt we should at least try the traditional method. In one test we had our answer—tasters felt that the meat floured before searing was simply gummy and failed to brown properly. In addition, the flour coating peeled off during the long braising time. We turned instead to the method we use with our stews and many of our braises—adding flour to the aromatics after the meat is browned (the meat is simply seasoned with salt and pepper). This certainly worked to thicken the sauce, but with the limited amount of braising liquid that goes into Swiss steaks, we felt that flour made the resulting gravy unnecessarily thick and gloppy. We instead sought alternate ways to thicken our gravy. Cornstarch added in the form of a slurry was a consideration, but tasters ultimately liked the flavor of heavy cream to balance out the savory onion gravy that resulted with this hearty dish.

We were getting closer, but dedicated our next tests to updating the flavors of this classic dish. We started with the mushrooms. White or cremini mushrooms are an obvious and traditional choice for this dish and worked great, but we felt the addition of other mushrooms would give this dish a much-needed lift. We tried several varieties, including oyster, shiitake, portobello, and dried porcinis and finally settled on equal amounts of button and portobello mushrooms for flavor and meaty texture.

With the hearty onion flavor of the gravy and the richness of the cream, we thought this gravy could benefit from the addition of a small amount of wine—just ½ cup of dry sherry (we found that its earthy notes complemented the flavor of the onions and mushrooms) was all it needed. Sweet paprika is a spice we found in many recipes so we added that in small increments until we settled on 1½ teaspoons. Finally, we finished the sauce with lemon juice, minced fresh parsley, and an additional tablespoon of dry sherry to round out the flavors.

Swiss Steaks with Onions and Mushrooms
SERVES 4

Top blade steaks may sometimes be labeled "flat iron" steak. Make sure to buy steaks that are about the same size to ensure even cooking. Be sure to use a Dutch oven large enough to fit the steaks in a single layer.

4   (6- to 8-ounce) top blade steaks,
    ¾- to 1-inch thick
    Salt and ground black pepper
3   tablespoons vegetable oil
12 ounces cremini or white mushrooms, stems
    trimmed, wiped clean, and sliced ¼ inch thick
12 ounces portobello mushrooms caps (about
    4 medium), wiped clean and sliced ¼ inch thick
2   large onions, halved and sliced thin

1	tablespoon minced fresh thyme leaves, or 1 teaspoon dried
1½	teaspoons sweet paprika
½	cup plus 1 tablespoon dry sherry
½	cup low-sodium chicken broth
¼	cup heavy cream
2	tablespoons juice from 1 lemon
2	tablespoons minced fresh parsley leaves

1. Adjust an oven rack to the lower-middle position and heat the oven to 325 degrees. Pat the steaks dry with paper towels and season with salt and pepper.

2. Heat 1 tablespoon of the oil in a large Dutch oven over medium-high heat until just smoking. Brown the steaks on both sides, 7 to 10 minutes, reducing the heat if the pan begins to scorch. Transfer the steaks to a large plate.

3. Add 1 tablespoon more oil to the pot and place over medium-high heat until shimmering. Add the cremini and portobello mushrooms, cover, and cook until they begin to soften and release their liquid, about 5 minutes. Remove the lid and continue to cook the mushrooms, stirring often, until they are beginning to brown, 10 to 12 minutes. Transfer the mushrooms to a bowl.

4. Add the remaining 1 tablespoon oil to the pot and place over medium heat until shimmering. Add the onions, thyme, paprika, and ¼ teaspoon salt and cook, stirring often, until softened, 8 to 10 minutes. Stir in ½ cup of the sherry, scraping up any brown bits. Stir in the broth and mushrooms and bring to a simmer.

5. Nestle the steaks, along with any accumulated juices, into the pot. Spoon the sauce over the meat and bring to a simmer. Cover, place the pot in the oven, and cook until the meat is very tender and a fork poked into it meets little resistance, about 2 hours.

6. Remove the pot from the oven. Transfer the steaks to a large plate and tent loosely with foil while finishing the sauce. Stir the cream into the sauce and simmer over medium-high heat until thickened, about 1 minute. Off the heat, stir in the remaining 1 tablespoon sherry, lemon juice, and parsley and season with salt and pepper to taste. Return the steaks to the sauce to warm through before serving.

OSSO BUCO

OSSO BUCO IS A WELL-KNOWN ITALIAN DISH of braised veal shanks. The ingredients are simple: veal shanks, aromatics (onions, carrots, and celery, all sautéed), and liquids (a blend of wine, stock, and tomatoes). The shank is a robust cut of meat and the bone adds tremendous flavor to the stewing liquid. The resulting dish should be rich in flavor and color and somewhat brothy but not like a stew. Our goals for this dish were straightforward—we wanted to perfect (and simplify, if possible) the cooking technique while extracting the most flavor from its simple ingredients.

Most recipes we reviewed called for shanks from the upper portion of the hind leg, cut into pieces between 1 and 1½ inches thick. We found that purchasing shanks is tricky, even when we special-ordered them. From one market, we received perfectly butchered shanks, which were ideal except for the weight. Each shank weighed between 12 and 16 ounces—too large for individual servings. Part of the charm of osso buco is receiving an individual shank as a portion. At another market, the shanks were generally in the ideal weight range, but the butchering job was less than perfect. In the same package, shanks varied from 1 to 2½ inches thick and were occasionally cut on an extreme bias, making tying difficult and searing uneven. The first step, then, is to shop carefully. We found a thickness of 1½ inches and a weight of 8 ounces ideal. Make sure all the shanks you buy are close to these specifications. Each shank should have two nicely cut, flat sides to facilitate browning.

Preparing the meat for braising was the first step. Most recipes called for tying the shanks and dredging them in flour before searing. Though the dredging was unnecessary, we did find that tying a piece of kitchen twine around the thickest part of each shank prevents the meat from falling apart and makes for a more attractive presentation. When we skipped this step, the meat fell off the bone.

After seasoning the shanks with salt and pepper and then searing them to get a nice golden brown crust, we turned our attention to the braising liquid. Braising, by design, is a relatively inexact cooking method because the rate at which the liquid reduces can vary greatly. Some of the initial recipes we tried yielded far too much liquid, which was thin in flavor and texture. In other cases, the liquid nearly evaporated by the time the meat was tender. We needed to create a foolproof, flavorful braising liquid and cooking technique that produced a rich sauce in a suitable volume and did not need a lot of last-minute fussing.

We experimented with numerous techniques to attain our ideal liquid, including reductions before and after braising (with the aromatics and without) and a reduction of the wine to a syrup during the deglazing process. In the end, we settled on the easiest method: natural reduction in the oven. By cracking the lid on the Dutch oven, the liquid reduces as the osso buco cooks. We found further simmering on the stovetop unnecessary as long as we started with the right amount of liquid in the pot.

The braising liquid traditionally begins with a meat stock (either beef or veal) and then wine (we liked white) and tomatoes are added. As few cooks have homemade stock on hand, we tried substituting store-bought beef broth. Tasters found the beef broth too potent—it overwhelmed the delicate flavor of the veal. Instead, we turned to store-bought chicken broth for our starting point. Two cups seemed the right amount and to enrich the flavor of the broth, we used a hefty amount of diced onion, carrot, and celery. Tasters liked the large amount of garlic in one recipe, so we minced about six cloves and added them to the pot prior to the broth. We rounded out the flavors with a couple of bay leaves.

A few recipes called for an entire bottle of wine, but when we tried this amount it completely overpowered the other flavors; the resulting sauce was dominated by acidity. Some tasters also felt that when a whole bottle of wine was used, the meat was tougher than previous batches with less wine. We scaled the wine back to 2½ cups, about two-thirds of a bottle, and were happy with the results.

With the wine and broth amounts settled, we needed to figure out how to best incorporate the tomatoes. Fresh tomatoes are always a gamble outside of the summer months, so we chose canned diced tomatoes and added them with the broth.

We still needed to determine the ideal braising time. Several sources suggested cooking osso buco almost to the consistency of pulled pork. While meat cooked this way tasted good, we were after a more elegant presentation. We wanted compact meat firmly attached to the bone, so we cooked the meat until it was just fork-tender but still clinging to the bone, which took two hours. We experimented with oven temperature and found that 325 degrees reduced the braising liquid to the right consistency without any adverse effects on the texture of the meat.

Just before serving, osso buco is sprinkled with gremolata, a mixture of minced garlic, parsley, and lemon zest. We were surprised to find variations on this classic trio. A number of recipes included orange zest mixed with lemon zest or on its own. Other recipes included anchovies. We tested three gremolatas: one traditional, one with orange zest mixed in equal part with lemon zest, and one with anchovies. Tasters liked all three but favored the traditional version.

In some recipes, the gremolata is used as a garnish, and in others it is added to the pot just before serving. We chose a compromise approach, stirring half of the gremolata into the pot and letting it stand for five minutes so that the flavors of the garlic, lemon, and parsley permeated the dish. We sprinkled the remaining gremolata on individual servings for a colorful finish.

TYING VEAL SHANKS

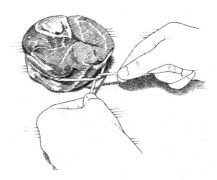

Tie a piece of twine around the thickest portion of each shank before browning to keep the meat attached to the bone while the shanks simmer.

Osso Buco

SERVES 6

To keep the meat attached to the bone during the long simmering process, tie a piece of kitchen twine around the thickest portion of each shank. The vegetables in the braising liquid do not get strained out before serving, so be mindful to cut them into tidy-looking pieces. Osso buco is traditionally served with risotto, although mashed potatoes and polenta are also good options.

OSSO BUCO

6	(8- to 10-ounce) veal shanks, 1½ inches thick, each tied once around the thickest part (see the illustration on page 154)
	Salt and ground black pepper
3	tablespoons vegetable oil
2	medium onions, diced medium
2	medium carrots, peeled and diced medium
2	celery ribs, diced medium
6	medium garlic cloves, minced or pressed through a garlic press (about 2 tablespoons)
2½	cups dry white wine
2	cups low-sodium chicken broth
1	(14.5-ounce) can diced tomatoes, drained
2	bay leaves

GREMOLATA

3	medium garlic cloves, minced or pressed through a garlic press (about 1 tablespoon)
2	teaspoons grated zest from 1 lemon
¼	cup minced fresh parsley leaves

1. FOR THE OSSO BUCO: Adjust an oven rack to the lower-middle position and heat the oven to 325 degrees. Pat the shanks dry with paper towels and season with salt and pepper. Heat 1 tablespoon of the oil in a large Dutch oven over medium-high heat until just smoking. Add half of the shanks and brown on all sides, 7 to 10 minutes, reducing the heat if the pot begins to scorch. Transfer the shanks to a large plate and repeat with 1 tablespoon more oil and the remaining shanks; transfer to the plate.

2. Add the remaining 1 tablespoon oil to the pot and place over medium heat until shimmering. Add the onions, carrots, celery, and ¼ teaspoon salt and cook, stirring often, until softened, 8 to

10 minutes. Stir in the garlic and cook until fragrant, about 30 seconds. Stir in the wine, scraping up any browned bits and cook until slightly thickened, about 5 minutes. Stir in the broth, tomatoes, and bay leaves and bring to a simmer.

3. Nestle the veal shanks, along with any accumulated juices, into the pot and bring to a simmer. Cover the pot partially (the lid should be just off center to leave about 1 inch open), place the pot in the oven, and cook until the meat is very tender and a fork poked into it meets little resistance, but is not falling off the bone, about 2 hours.

4. Remove the pot from the oven. Transfer the shanks to a large plate, remove the twine, and tent loosely with foil while finishing the sauce. Defat the braising liquid following one of the methods on page 142 (if necessary, return the defatted liquid to the pot). If the defatted liquid seems thin and watery, bring it to a simmer over medium-high heat and cook until thickened and saucy, 5 to 10 minutes.

5. FOR THE GREMOLATA: Combine all of the gremolata ingredients in a small bowl.

6. Off the heat, stir half of the gremolata into the sauce and let stand for 5 minutes. Season the sauce with salt and pepper to taste. Place the veal shanks in individual serving bowls, ladle some of the sauce over each shank, and sprinkle with the remaining gremolata before serving.

LAMB SHANKS BRAISED IN RED WINE

THERE ARE MANY TOUGH CUTS OF MEAT that are ideal for braising, but among the most richly flavored of these is the lamb shank, which is simply the bottom portion of the fore or hind leg of a lamb. Like other cuts of meat that come from the joints of animals, such as oxtails or short ribs, lamb shanks are extremely flavorful when cooked using this low, slow, moist-heat cooking method. This is because lamb shanks contain a high proportion of connective tissue and fat, which break down during the long cooking time, adding flavor to the meat and making it meltingly tender. One of our favorite lamb shank recipes is a simple Italian dish of lamb shanks braised in wine, so we headed into the kitchen to recreate this classic braise.

While we obtained satisfactory results by braising shanks on top of the stove, we quickly found we preferred braising them in the oven because of its unique heating properties. With the heat coming from all directions, the meat cooked more evenly. This is a particular advantage, given that many pans have hot spots that cause them to heat unevenly on a burner.

Because of the high fat content of this cut, several straightforward precautions are necessary to keep the level of fat in the final product to a minimum. First, if your butcher has not already done so, take the time to trim the lamb shanks of the excess fat that encases the meat. Even a long, slow braise will not successfully render all of the exterior fat on a lamb shank. Browning the shanks well before braising them also helps to render some of the exterior fat. Browning also provides a great deal of flavor to the dish, both to the lamb as well as the sauce. Finally, we found it important to defat the braising liquid after the shanks have been cooked (see page 142 for more information on this process).

With the preparation of the lamb determined, we turned our attention to the braising liquid. Stock is the traditional braising liquid because it adds textural richness as well as depth of flavor. Veal stock is one common choice, but we immediately ruled it out because almost no one has this on hand, and we were hoping to simplify things by using a store-bought broth. We preferred chicken broth to beef broth because it complemented the flavor of the lamb shanks—the beef broth, by contrast, competed with the flavor of the lamb and resulted in an overly rich sauce.

Wine is an essential component of the braising liquid for this simple dish, contributing a subtle complexity as well as a little acidity. The acid is particularly important because it balances the richness of the lamb. Too little acid creates a dull, rather flat-tasting dish. On the other hand, too much acid results in a harsh, off-putting flavor. After trying different ratios, we found that 2 parts wine to

3 parts chicken broth gave us the best flavor.

We tried both red and white wines, and while both worked well, we decided to go with red for its richer, deeper finish (we saved white wine for a variation). Our choice of aromatics was straightforward—onion, celery and carrots were all this dish needed—while a small amount of tomato paste provided another layer of flavor. A little thyme and rosemary offered a fresh herbal note. For our white wine variation, we added some mint and lemon, adding strips of lemon zest to the braise, then stirring in a tablespoon of fresh lemon juice at the end, which gave us the bright lemony flavor we were after.

Lamb Shanks Braised in Red Wine
SERVES 6
Make sure the shanks are well trimmed of fat. If your butcher has not already done this for you, take care to remove any large pockets of fat. A $7 to $10 bottle of medium-bodied red table wine made from a blend of grapes, such as a Côtes du Rhône, will work well here. If the lamb shanks are smaller than 12 ounces each, you may need to reduce the covered braising time by up to ½ hour. Serve with mashed potatoes or polenta.

6   (12- to 16-ounce) lamb shanks, trimmed (see note)
    Salt and ground black pepper
3   tablespoons olive oil
2   medium onions, minced
2   celery ribs, minced
2   tablespoons tomato paste
4   medium cloves garlic, minced or pressed though a garlic press (about 4 teaspoons)
2   teaspoons minced fresh thyme leaves
2   teaspoons minced fresh rosemary
2   cups dry red wine (see note)
3   cups low-sodium chicken broth
3   medium carrots, peeled and sliced 1 inch thick

1. Adjust an oven rack to the lower-middle position and heat the oven to 325 degrees. Pat the lamb shanks dry with paper towels and season with

salt and pepper. Heat 1 tablespoon of the oil in a large Dutch oven over medium-high heat until just smoking. Brown half of the shanks on all sides, 7 to 10 minutes, reducing the heat if the pot begins to scorch. Transfer the shanks to a large plate and repeat with 1 tablespoon more oil and the remaining shanks.

2. Add the remaining 1 tablespoon oil to the pot and place over medium heat until shimmering. Add the onions, celery, and ¼ teaspoon salt and cook, stirring often, until softened, 8 to 10 minutes. Stir in the tomato paste, garlic, thyme, and rosemary and cook until fragrant, about 30 seconds. Slowly stir in the wine, scraping up any browned bits. Stir in the broth and bring to a simmer.

3. Nestle the shanks, along with any accumulated juices, into the pot. Bring to a simmer, cover, place the pot in the oven, and cook the shanks for 1½ hours.

4. Stir in the carrots and continue to cook, uncovered, until the shank tops are browned, about 30 minutes. Turn the shanks and continue to cook, uncovered, until the other side is browned and the meat is very tender and a fork poked into it meets little resistance, 15 to 30 minutes longer.

5. Remove the pot from the oven. Transfer the shanks to a large plate and tent loosely with foil while finishing the sauce. Defat the braising liquid following one of the methods on page 142 (if necessary, return the defatted liquid to the pot).

6. Bring the defatted liquid to a simmer over medium-high heat until thickened and saucy, 10 to 15 minutes. Season the sauce with salt and pepper to taste, then return the shanks to the sauce to warm through before serving.

➤ VARIATION

Lamb Shanks Braised in White Wine with Lemon and Mint

Follow the recipe for Lamb Shanks Braised in Red Wine, omitting the rosemary, substituting 2 cups dry white wine for the red wine, and adding 4 strips lemon zest (see the illustration on page 72) with the broth in step 2. Before serving, stir 2 tablespoons minced fresh mint leaves and 1 tablespoon lemon juice into the sauce.

CARNITAS

FOR PORK LOVERS, FEW THINGS CAN TOP THE rich flavor and supple texture of Southern-style barbecued pulled pork. But to cook it, you usually have to sit outside by your smoker all day—hardly practical in the middle of winter. Having developed a successful recipe for making pulled pork indoors (see page 36), we were intrigued when we learned that *carnitas*, Mexico's version of shredded pork, is also cooked indoors. Spanish for "little meats," this *taquería* staple is used as a filling in tacos and burritos and boasts tender chunks of pork with a lightly crisped, caramelized exterior. Unlike barbecued pulled pork, where the spice rub and sauce are prominent, in carnitas, the flavor of the pork, subtly accented by earthy oregano and sour orange, takes center stage.

Most Mexican restaurants prepare carnitas by gently frying well-marbled chunks of pork in gallons of lard or oil. But home cooks often forgo all the lard in favor of a more manageable method:

SCIENCE: Using Reductive Powers

We reduce liquids all the time in recipes, particularly in braises, as a way of concentrating flavor. In our carnitas recipe, we take this process even further, reducing the braising liquid until it has the thick, syrupy consistency of a glaze. As familiar as the benefits of reducing liquids are to us, the glaze's intense taste made us wonder: Was all that flavor derived simply from evaporating the water from the braising liquid, or was there a more complex dynamic at work?

A chat with our science editor revealed the answer. The reduction's richness is in part due to the same process that makes a seared steak taste so good—the Maillard reaction. When the proteins and sugars in meat (or most any food) are subjected to a high enough temperature (around 300 to 500 degrees), they combine, leading to browning and the creation of hundreds of new flavor compounds.

In the carnitas recipe, proteins and sugars are pulled from the pork by the braising liquid, which also contains sugars from the lime and orange juices. After the meat is removed, the liquid is boiled to evaporate all the water. With the water removed, the temperature of the glaze can rise higher than water's boiling point of 212 degrees, eventually kicking off the Maillard reaction. The result: a viscous, highly concentrated glaze with exceptional depth of flavor.

simmering the meat in a seasoned broth in the oven (essentially braising it) and then sautéing it in some of the rendered fat. The latter method definitely sounded more appealing—who wants to deal with deep-frying in gallons of lard at home?—but we wondered if simmering and sautéing could possibly yield the same results. We tried it anyway, gently cooking the meat in a couple quarts of water spiked with citrus and other typical carnitas flavorings, and pulling the pork out after it was softened. We then fried the meat in the fat skimmed from the cooking liquid.

To our surprise, the pork turned out tender, with a browned exterior and reasonably good flavor. If we'd gotten these results without even trying, surely with a little work we could do even better. But we wouldn't consider this successful unless we could create carnitas with the addictive taste and texture of the deep-fried versions we've enjoyed in Mexican restaurants.

We were using a boneless Boston butt, the cut most carnitas recipes call for and the same cut American cooks use for barbecued pulled pork. Though this shoulder roast contains a good amount of fat, which can translate to deep flavor, all the liquid in the pot washed out the taste. Over the course of several tests, we went from 8 cups of liquid down to 2, the bare minimum for cooking a 3- to 4-pound roast. Braising the meat in a small amount of liquid was clearly better than completely submerging it. Still, tasters thought the pork flavor was not concentrated enough. Swapping out the water for chicken broth made little difference. And browning the meat before braising it also failed to intensify its taste. So where was the pork flavor going?

Down the drain, that's where. We'd been discarding the leftover cooking liquid after removing the meat and skimming off the fat. To capture that lost flavor, we would need to figure out how to reincorporate the liquid into the dish. Perhaps we could reduce the liquid, as the French do in their intensely flavored sauces. Back in the kitchen, we braised another batch of meat in the oven. This time, instead of pouring off the broth after we removed the pork, we left it in the pot, reducing it on the stovetop until it had the consistency of a thick, syrupy glaze.

With the glaze at hand, we were left wondering what the next step should be. If we added the pork back to the pot, we were afraid the glaze, which had no water left to evaporate, would burn and stick to the bottom. Because we needed to get the exterior of the pork to crisp, more cooking was a must. What about tossing the pork with the glaze and putting it into the oven? We spread the coated meat on a rimmed baking sheet and turned on the broiler. To ensure that neither glaze nor meat would burn, we placed the sheet on the same lower-middle rack we'd used for braising. Minutes later, the carnitas emerged from the broiler beautifully caramelized, the shredded parts of the meat transformed into crisp wisps with wonderfully rich flavor. The only problem: super-greasy meat.

The greasiness was our fault; we had not defatted the cooking liquid before reducing it. But when we did skim away some of the fat, we ended up with a reduction that was thin and sticky and didn't flavor

TECHNIQUE: Warming Tortillas

Our preferred way to warm tortillas is over the open flame of a gas burner or in a skillet, which gives them a toasted flavor; however, an oven or microwave will also work. Once they are warmed, be sure to wrap the tortillas in foil or a clean kitchen towel until ready to use or they will dry out. If your tortillas are very dry, pat each tortilla with a little water before warming them.

Gas Stove: Toast the tortillas, 1 at a time, directly on the cooking grate over a medium flame until slightly charred around the edges, about 30 seconds per side. Immediately wrap the toasted tortillas in foil or a kitchen towel to keep them warm and soft until serving time.

Skillet: Toast the tortillas, 1 at a time, in a skillet over medium-high heat until softened and speckled with brown, 20 to 30 seconds per side. Immediately wrap the toasted tortillas in foil or a kitchen towel to keep them warm and soft until serving time.

Oven: Stack 6 tortillas inside a foil packet and heat in a 350-degree oven until warm and soft, about 5 minutes. Keep the tortillas in the foil packet until serving time.

Microwave: Stack 12 tortillas on a plate, cover with microwave-safe plastic wrap, and microwave on high power until warm and soft, 1 to 2 minutes. Remove the plastic wrap and cover the tortillas with a kitchen towel to keep them warm and soft until serving time.

the meat as well. Going straight to the source, we trimmed as much fat as possible from the pork butt before cooking it. This got rid of the greasiness, but it also left the carnitas too dry. We were already broiling the meat. Why not let that work in our favor as a way to remove fat? Instead of spreading the carnitas directly on a baking sheet, we placed the meat on a rack set inside of it. The rack elevated the pieces of pork, allowing excess fat to drip down while the glaze stuck to the meat. The better air circulation under and around the pork also made for crispier shreds of meat and better texture overall.

All that was left was to refine the flavors in the braising liquid, which gives the pork its character. In traditional versions, other flavors take a back seat to the pork, and our recipe followed suit. Instead of garlic, we stuck with the mellow sweetness of onion. To emulate the Mexican sour oranges used in authentic carnitas, we used a mix of fresh lime and orange juices, adding the spent orange halves to the pot to impart floral notes. Bay leaves and oregano gave the meat aromatic accents. Cumin, though not a typical ingredient in carnitas, brought an earthy dimension that complemented the other flavors.

Tucked into warm corn tortillas and topped with minced onion, fresh cilantro, and a spritz of lime, the mouthwatering taste and texture of carnitas kept tasters coming back for more.

Carnitas

SERVES 6

Boneless pork butt is often sold as Boston butt. Trim the fat cap on the pork until it is about ⅛ inch thick. We like serving carnitas spooned into warm corn tortillas for tacos, but you can also use it as a filling for quesadillas or burritos. In addition to the traditional garnishes listed below, we recommend serving the pork with fresh guacamole, salsa, or Sweet and Spicy Pickled Onions (page 160).

PORK

1 (3½- to 4-pound) boneless pork butt, trimmed and cut into 2-inch chunks (see note)
2 cups water
1 small onion, peeled and halved
2 tablespoons juice from 1 lime

2 bay leaves
1 teaspoon ground cumin
1 teaspoon dried oregano
   Salt and ground black pepper
1 medium orange, halved

TORTILLAS AND GARNISHES
18 (6-inch) corn tortillas, warmed (see page 158)
   Minced white or red onion
   Fresh cilantro leaves
   Thinly sliced radishes
   Sour cream
   Lime wedges

1. Adjust an oven rack to the lower-middle position and heat the oven to 300 degrees. Combine the pork, water, onion, lime juice, bay leaves, cumin, oregano, 1 teaspoon salt, and ½ teaspoon pepper in a large Dutch oven. Juice the orange into a bowl and remove any seeds (you should have about ⅓ cup juice). Add the juice and spent orange halves to the pot.

2. Bring the mixture to a simmer over medium-high heat, stirring occasionally. Cover, place the pot in the oven, and cook until the meat is very tender and a fork poked into it meets little resistance, about 2 hours, flipping the pieces of meat halfway through the cooking time.

3. Remove the pot from the oven and turn the oven to broil. Using a slotted spoon, transfer the pork to a bowl. Discard the orange halves, onion, and bay leaves from the braising liquid (do not defat the liquid). Bring the liquid to a simmer over medium-high heat and cook, stirring often, to a syrupy glaze that measures about 1 cup, 8 to 12 minutes.

4. Using 2 forks, pull each piece of pork in half. Gently toss the reduced braising liquid with the pork and season with salt and pepper to taste. Spread the pork in an even layer on a wire rack set inside a rimmed baking sheet or on a broiler pan.

5. Place the baking sheet on the lower-middle rack and broil until the top of the meat is well browned (but not charred) and the edges are slightly crisp, 5 to 8 minutes. Flip the pieces of meat and continue to broil until the top is well browned and the edges are slightly crisp, 5 to 8 minutes longer. Serve with the warm tortillas and garnishes.

BRAISED RIBS WITH BLACK-EYED PEAS AND COLLARD GREENS

THERE'S A SIMPLE SOUTHERN SIDE DISH in which black-eyed peas, collard greens, and a smoked ham hock are slowly cooked together for hours until the beans are creamy, the greens are velvety soft, and the broth is suffused with the smoky sweetness of the ham. Slow simmering over low heat transforms this trio of modest ingredients into something rich, earthy, and surprisingly complex. As the beans and greens stew, the beans absorb the "pot liquor" (or "likker"), the rich broth shed by the greens and ham hock. The broth is so flavorful that, in some instances, it is served on its own as a soup course, or ladled over dry, coarse cornbread.

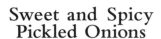

Sweet and Spicy Pickled Onions

MAKES ABOUT 2 CUPS

The onions can be refrigerated in an airtight container for up to 1 week.

I	medium red onion, halved and sliced thin (about 1½ cups)
I	cup red wine vinegar
⅓	cup sugar
2	jalapeño chiles, stemmed, seeded, and cut into thin rings
¼	teaspoon salt

Place the onion slices in a medium heatproof bowl. Bring the vinegar, sugar, jalapeños, and salt to a simmer in a small saucepan over medium-high heat, stirring occasionally, to dissolve the sugar. Pour the hot vinegar mixture over the onion, cover loosely, and let cool to room temperature, about 30 minutes. When cool, drain and discard the liquid and serve the onions.

Our goal was to capitalize on the flavors and basic technique of the recipe, but expand the dish into a full-blown meal with the addition of a heftier cut of meat. Ham hocks may be flavorful, but they yield a scant amount of edible meat (the bulk of a ham hock is skin and fat—hence the great flavor).

Our basic concept for the recipe was to brown the meat, sauté aromatics including onions and garlic, and then simmer the beans, collards, meat, and aromatics in the oven until tender. In other words, we were going to treat it like a classic braise. Looking for a ham hock substitute that would deliver a bit more meat, we first turned to boneless pork butt (or Boston butt), which is well suited to braising—the meat becomes fork-tender as it simmers. Leaner cuts from the loin, such as pork chops and pork tenderloin, tend to turn tough and dry when braised.

After cutting up 3 pounds of boneless pork butt into stew-sized pieces, we quickly realized out we had too much meat. Real estate was at a premium in the pot, which was already filled with beans and greens, and the pork butt was simply too big. Fitting a maximum of 2 pounds of the meat in the pot, we were pleased with the results—the meat added a nice pork flavor to the stew and had a tender texture.

Knowing, however, that a 2-pound boneless pork butt can be quite hard to find, we took another look at our options and decided to try country-style pork ribs. Unlike spare- and baby-back ribs, country-style ribs are cut more towards the shoulder (where the pork butt comes from), so they have more fat. Giving these ribs a whirl, we found they cooked up perfectly alongside the beans, and were tender and moist after simmering. The bonus of using these ribs is the complete lack of prep they require—you can use them straight from the package. Pitting bone-in and boneless country-style ribs against one another, we noted that both worked fine. A few tasters argued that the bones added a little extra flavor to the sauce, but the majority of the tasters thought the bones weren't worth the mild annoyance.

INGREDIENTS:
Country-Style Pork Ribs

These meaty, tender ribs are cut from the upper side of the rib cage from the fatty blade end of the loin. Butchers usually cut them into individual ribs and package several together.

The ribs lent a rich pork flavor to the beans and greens, but tasters missed the smoky backbeat laid down by the hock in the original recipe. The solution proved simple: include bacon. Rendered after the ribs were browned, a quarter pound of bacon yielded enough fat in which to cook the onions and garlic, and enough meat to deliver the same smoky flavor that the ham hock had provided.

Moving on to the black-eyed peas, we already knew that we favored a two-step bean cooking method that involves soaking the beans in salt water, then cooking the beans without salt. By soaking the beans in salt water, we are able to firm up and "set" the bean skins making the beans less prone to breaking and bursting during cooking (for more information on this technique, see page 122). Just one to one and a quarter hours of simmering is all it takes for these brined beans to turn tender. If cooked longer, the beans simply burst open and turn to mush.

According to Southern tradition, the collard greens are added to the pot at the beginning and stewed right alongside the beans and pork. We liked this method—the greens were tender and their flavor enriched the overall dish. True Southerners typically serve stewed collard greens and black-eyed peas with pepper-spiked vinegar but we developed an easy recipe for pickled onions (see page 160) that knocked tasters' socks off and added a welcome kick of fresh flavor and color.

Braised Ribs with Black-Eyed Peas and Collard Greens
SERVES 6 TO 8

We prefer to use boneless country-style pork ribs here, but bone-in country-style ribs can be substituted. Do not substitute canned or frozen black-eyed peas. Although somewhat untraditional, Sweet and Spicy Pickled Onions (page 160) add a welcome, vinegary kick of flavor to this dish.

- 1 pound (about 2⅔ cups) dried black-eyed peas, rinsed, picked over, and salt-soaked overnight or quick salt-soaked (see page 122)
- 2 pounds boneless country-style pork ribs
  Salt and ground black pepper
- 1 tablespoon vegetable oil
- 4 ounces (about 4 slices) bacon, cut into ¼-inch pieces
- 1 medium red onion, minced
- 1 large celery rib, chopped fine
- 6 medium garlic cloves, minced or pressed through a garlic press (about 2 tablespoons)
- 3½ cups low-sodium chicken broth
- 1 cup water
- 1 small bunch collard greens (about 1 pound), stemmed and sliced thin crosswise (see the illustration below)
- 2 bay leaves
- 1 recipe Sweet and Spicy Pickled Onions (optional, page 160)

SEPARATING COLLARD GREEN STEMS AND LEAVES

Hold each leaf at the base of the stem over a bowl filled with water. Use a sharp knife to slash the leafy portion from both sides of the thick stem.

1. Adjust an oven rack to the lower-middle position and heat the oven to 300 degrees. Drain the beans, discarding the soaking liquid, and rinse well.

2. Pat the ribs dry with paper towels and season with salt and pepper. Heat the oil in a large Dutch oven over medium-high heat until just smoking. Brown the ribs on both sides, 7 to 10 minutes, reducing the heat if the pot begins to scorch. Transfer the ribs to a large plate.

3. Pour off all of the fat left in the pot, add the bacon, and cook over medium heat, stirring often, until browned and crisp, about 8 minutes. Stir in the onion, celery, and ¼ teaspoon salt and cook, stirring often, until softened, 5 to 7 minutes. Stir

in the garlic and cook until fragrant, about 30 seconds. Stir in the broth, water, beans, collard greens, and bay leaves, scraping up any browned bits, and bring to a simmer.

4. Nestle the ribs, along with any accumulated juices, into the pot and bring to a simmer. Cover, place the pot in the oven, and cook until the beans are tender and the meat is very tender and a fork poked into it meets little resistance, 1 to 1¼ hours.

5. Remove the pot from the oven and discard the bay leaves. Season with salt and pepper to taste and serve, passing the pickled onions (if using) separately.

EQUIPMENT: Pepper Mills

When we tested pepper mills in 2001, we discovered two models, the Unicorn Magnum Plus and the East Hampton Industries PepperMate, that produced far more ground pepper than classic wooden, finial-topped pepper mills. We rounded up four promising newer models and one classic wooden mill and brought them into the test kitchen to see if they could compete with the Magnum Plus and the PepperMate.

To test each mill's output, we had three testers grind medium-ground pepper at a steady rate for 30 seconds, then weighed and averaged the results. To gauge the uniformity of their grinds, we compared piles of pepper from each mill ground at fine, medium, and coarse settings.

We value output efficiency, as 2 tablespoons of freshly ground pepper can take 10 wrist-wrenching minutes with ineffective mills but only about a minute with an efficient mill. But the quality of a pepper mill's grind is just as important. We regularly use fine-, medium-, and coarse-ground pepper, and we want uniformity (pepper pieces of the same size) in each setting. And we want to be able to easily adjust the mill between settings.

Uniformity of pepper ground at different settings is tied to the design and workmanship of the grinding mechanism: The best grinders have more and sharper teeth that fit together better than the teeth of inferior models. In this regard we particularly liked the William Bounds ProView and the PepperMate, both of which produced uniform grinds at all settings; this was most evident in the pristine powder of their finely ground pepper.

In the efficiency test, the Unicorn Magnum Plus again proved its mettle with a 30-second output (about 1 tablespoon) that was almost twice that of the runner-up—and it took less muscle to operate. Conversely, the Trudeau One Hand mill produced an average of only ⅓ teaspoon—nearly 10 times less than the Magnum Plus—in the same 30 seconds. Why? The Magnum Plus's grinding mechanism is not only well machined, it's also bigger than the others. The Magnum Plus and the PepperMate (still the top two mills for output) also have small, ergonomic cranks that make for wrist-friendly turning.

While they weren't as efficient as the Magnum Plus, both the William Bounds and the Peugeot mills have adjustable rings that click into fixed settings—the William Bounds has settings for fine, medium, and coarse, and the Peugeot has six settings. The ease with which you can get to your desired grind setting is a real plus.

The bottom line? The Unicorn Magnum Plus is still the pepper mill to beat: it's comfortable and easy to fill, and has exceptional grind quality, a huge capacity, and an astonishing output.

THE BEST PEPPER MILL

The Unicorn Magnum Plus ($45) is still the best pepper mill on the market, producing an abundance of perfectly ground pepper with minimal effort.

UNICORN
MAGNUM PLUS

Smothered Pork Chops

SMOTHERED PORK CHOPS, A HOMEY DISH of chops braised in deeply flavored onion gravy, are nothing fancy but when done right they are utterly satisfying. The cooking process is straightforward: you brown the chops, remove them from the pan, brown the onions, return the chops to the pan, cover them with the onions and gravy (hence the term smothered), and braise them until tender. Our initial recipe tests, however, produced bland, dry pork and near-tasteless gravies with consistencies ranging from pasty to processed to gelatinous to watery. This was not going to be as easy as we thought.

To get this recipe right, we knew we'd have to identify the best chops for this dish and the best way to cook them. And the gravy was no less important. We wanted a heady, multidimensional flavor, bold onion presence, and satiny, just-thick-enough texture.

Some of the recipes we found specified sirloin chops, which are cut from the rear end of the loin. Our tasters found this cut a little dry—and it can often be hard to find. Blade chops, cut from the far front end of the loin, were juicier but suffered the same spotty availability. Of the two remaining types of chops, center-cut loin and rib, we found the latter to be the juiciest and most flavorful because it had a bit more fat.

We tried rib chops as thick as 1½ inches and as thin as ½ inch and were surprised when tasters unanimously chose the thinner chops (½ inch to ¾ inch thick). Thick chops overwhelmed the gravy, which tasters felt should share equal billing with the meat. Thin chops also picked up more onion flavor during cooking. We also tried boneless chops, but they cooked up dry, so we decided to stick with bone-in for optimum juiciness.

Though we typically brine pork, we skipped this step for two reasons: First, the chops cook in a moist environment provided by the gravy, so dry chops weren't much of an issue. Second, no matter how we adjusted the salinity of the brine, the salt-infused meat caused the gravy to become intolerably salty.

Last we tackled the question of cooking time. Although we usually prefer to cook pork just to 150 degrees to ensure tenderness, this was one application where further cooking was necessary since we wanted to give the chops plenty of time to become infused with the flavor of the gravy and onions.

After their initial searing, the chops were nicely browned, with a rosy interior. Fifteen minutes of braising in the gravy boosted the flavor but toughened the chops, which now registered almost 200 degrees. At that temperature, the meat fibers have contracted and expelled moisture, but the fat and connective tissue between the fibers, called collagen, have not had a chance to melt fully and turn into gelatin. It is this gelatin that makes braised meats especially rich and tender. Another 15 minutes of braising time solved the problem. At this point, the chops registered 210 degrees; the extra time allowed the fat and collagen to melt completely, so the meat was very tender—and it had also absorbed a good amount of flavor from the onions and sauce.

With the timing down for cooking the pork chops, we turned our attention to the onions and gravy. The onions are an essential component to this recipe—they're what give this dish its "smothered" name. Yellow onions beat out red onions and sweet Vidalias with their deep brown hue (once cooked) and balanced flavor. We tried them minced, chopped, and sliced both thick and thin. Thin-sliced onions cooked down to a meltingly soft texture that was our favorite. We tried simply softening the onions until they were translucent versus cooking them for a few more minutes until their edges browned, a winning technique that accentuated their natural sweetness. We wanted to make sure that the onions released enough moisture to dissolve (or deglaze) the flavorful, sticky browned bits (called fond) left in the pan by the chops, so we salted them lightly. The heat and salt worked together to jump-start the breakdown of the onions' cell walls, which set their juices flowing. We also added 2 tablespoons of water to the pan at the end for insurance.

Finally we looked at the gravy. We immediately ruled out the canned condensed soup called for in many recipes, which resulted in a processed and glue-like gravy. Water produced a weak, thin gravy, but chicken broth was a vast improvement, adding much-needed flavor. To thicken the sauce we first tried cornstarch, but it resulted in a somewhat gelatinous gravy. Next we tried adding flour in three different ways. Flouring the chops before browning them turned their exteriors gummy. Flouring the onions left the gravy tasting of raw flour. Last, we tried a roux, a mixture of flour and fat (in this case, vegetable oil) cooked together. The roux was simple to make and it thickened the sauce reliably without adding the taste of raw flour, lending the gravy both a smooth finish and another layer of flavor that was slightly nutty.

The roux was good, but we wondered if we could improve it further still and eke out more flavor in the process. We fried a couple of slices of bacon and substituted the rendered fat for the vegetable oil in the roux. What a hit! The sweet, salty, smoky bacon flavor underscored and deepened all of the other flavors in the dish. Browning the roux for five minutes also enhanced its rich, toasty flavor.

SCORING PORK CHOPS

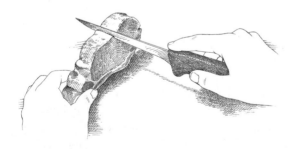

Using a sharp knife, cut two slits, about 2 inches apart, through the outer layer of fat and connective tissue. This will keep the chops from curling as they cook.

Homey, satisfying, and full of rich flavor, these smothered pork chops are sure to impress.

Smothered Pork Chops
SERVES 4

Nicking the edges of the pork chops ensures that they won't curl up during browning. Be sure to use low-sodium chicken broth in this recipe or the sauce will taste quite salty. Serve with plain egg noodles, rice, or mashed potatoes to soak up the rich gravy.

4	(6- to 7-ounce) bone-in rib pork chops, ½ to ¾ inch thick, scored (see the illustration at left)
	Salt and ground black pepper
2	tablespoons vegetable oil, plus extra as needed
2	medium onions, halved and sliced thin
2	medium garlic cloves, minced or pressed through a garlic press (about 2 teaspoons)
I	teaspoon minced fresh thyme, or ¼ teaspoon dried
2	tablespoons water
3	ounces (about 3 slices) bacon, chopped fine
2	tablespoons unbleached all-purpose flour
1¾	cups low-sodium chicken broth
2	bay leaves
I	tablespoon minced fresh parsley leaves

1. Pat the chops dry with paper towels and season with salt and pepper. Heat 1 tablespoon of the oil in a 12-inch nonstick skillet over medium-high heat until just smoking. Brown the chops on both sides, 7 to 10 minutes, reducing the heat if the pan begins to scorch. Transfer the chops to a large plate.

2. Add the remaining 1 tablespoon oil to the skillet and return to medium heat until shimmering. Add the onions and ¼ teaspoon salt and cook, stirring often, until softened and lightly browned, about 10 minutes. Stir in the garlic and thyme and cook until fragrant, about 30 seconds. Stir in the

water, scraping up any browned bits, then transfer to a bowl.

3. Add the bacon to the skillet and cook over medium heat until browned and crisp, about 8 minutes. Transfer the bacon to a paper towel–lined plate. Pour off all but 2 tablespoons of the fat left in the skillet (or add more oil if necessary). Whisk the flour into the fat left in the skillet and cook, stirring often, over medium-low heat until well browned, about 5 minutes.

4. Slowly whisk in the broth, scraping up any browned bits, until smooth. Return the chops to the skillet and cover them with the reserved onions. Add the bay leaves, cover, and bring to a simmer. Reduce the heat to low and cook until the meat is very tender and a fork poked into it meets little resistance, about 30 minutes.

5. Transfer the chops to a serving platter and tent loosely with foil while finishing the sauce. Return the sauce to a simmer and cook until thickened, about 5 minutes. Discard the bay leaves, stir in the parsley, and season with salt and pepper to taste. Spoon the sauce over the chops and sprinkle with the crisp bacon before serving.

➤ VARIATIONS

Smothered Pork Chops with Cider and Apples
Follow the recipe for Smothered Pork Chops, substituting apple cider for the chicken broth and 1 large (or 2 small) Granny Smith apples, peeled, cored, and cut into ⅓-inch-thick wedges, for one of the onions. Increase the salt to ½ teaspoon in step 2.

Smothered Pork Chops with Spicy Collard Greens
Follow the recipe for Smothered Pork Chops, omitting 1 of the onions, increasing the garlic to 4 cloves, and increasing the oil to 2 tablespoons in step 2. Before returning the browned chops to the pan in step 4, add 4 cups thinly sliced collard greens and ½ teaspoon red pepper flakes.

CHICKEN PROVENÇAL

WHEN DONE RIGHT, CHICKEN PROVENÇAL represents the best of simple French cooking—tender, moist pieces of chicken are slowly simmered with an aromatic, garlicky tomato sauce and a sprinkling of nutty niçoise olives. But order it in a restaurant and the results are often disappointing, the flavor dull and muddy and the sauce thin and practically nonexistent. We knew such a simple dish shouldn't be so difficult to prepare.

The chicken was our starting point. We already knew we had a preference for chicken pieces with the skin on—the skin helps to contribute flavor to the sauce from the browning process. The amount of browning is also important. A side-by-side taste test—one batch made with lightly browned chicken pieces, the other with deeply browned pieces—revealed that more browning renders more fat and results in more chicken flavor. Tasters were split on whether to use all dark meat, all white meat, or a combination of the two. The bottom line: use the cuts you like. As long as the thighs get a head start cooking before the breasts are added to the pot, the end result is just as good either way.

Most recipes use 3 tablespoons of oil per batch of chicken, which was too greasy. We then tried browning a batch of chicken in just 1 tablespoon of oil and found that the skin quickly rendered a couple of additional tablespoons of fat. But even with this reduced amount of fat, tasters still found the final dish to be greasy. Pouring off all but 1 tablespoon of the fat after browning the chicken eliminated the greasiness.

Our final tests with the chicken focused on the cooking method. Although many of our braises cook in a 300-degree oven, for our chicken braises we thought a simple stovetop method would work better. Because we were using chicken parts, and the cooking time was staggered when using both breasts and thighs, it seemed more practical to braise on the stovetop rather than having to go in and out of the oven.

Next, we tested the optimal braising time. Technically, thighs are considered done when they reach an internal temperature of 170 degrees, or after 30 minutes of braising. Unfortunately, 30 minutes of braising produced thighs that were somewhat bland and not quite tender. But wouldn't cooking them longer dry out the chicken? To our surprise, it didn't. After one hour, the meat reached an internal temperature of 210 degrees and was extremely moist and tender. The long stay in the oven breaks down the connective tissue in the thighs, much as it does in a pot roast, yielding more tender meat. (Because white meat contains little connective tissue, there's no benefit to cooking it longer, so breasts only need about 20 minutes.) In addition, thighs have plenty of fat that keeps them moist as they braise.

Tomatoes play a prominent role in chicken Provençal's lively sauce. Crushed and pureed canned tomatoes each produced a thick, sweet, overbearing sauce reminiscent of bad Italian restaurant food. Canned diced tomatoes, though more promising, presented the opposite problem: Even when drained, they contain a fair amount of liquid, and the resulting sauce was too thin. We added a few tablespoons of tomato paste to the diced tomatoes, as well as a bit of flour, and the texture improved dramatically—now the sauce coated the chicken without overwhelming it. Chicken broth rounded out the flavors while providing a bit more volume. Tasters also liked the addition of some onion and garlic, as well as a little wine. For a more intense flavor—and better consistency—we ended up reducing the braising liquid after removing the chicken from the pot.

Whole niçoise olives appeared in nearly every recipe, but tasters complained about the pits. No problem, we were able to find pitted niçoise olives in our supermarket.

As for seasonings, the combination of dried herbs referred to as *herbes de Provence* (lavender, marjoram, basil, fennel seed, rosemary, sage, summer savory, and thyme) seemed like the obvious choice. But tasters said that these dried herbs, when used alone, were too strong, giving the sauce a flavor that bordered on medicinal. Fresh thyme, oregano, parsley, and bay leaves were preferred (though a teaspoon of the dried blend can be added to fresh herbs for another layer of flavor). A pinch of

cayenne balanced the sweet tomatoes, while a little onion and garlic rounded out the flavors. Inspired by one of the better initial recipes tested, we tried adding a teaspoon of minced anchovies along with the garlic. Although tasters could not identify the ingredient, everyone agreed the sauce tasted richer and fuller. The final item on our list was lemon zest, a common and, as it turned out, welcome addition.

Chicken Provençal
SERVES 4 TO 6

If using both chicken breasts and thighs/drumsticks, we recommend cutting the breast pieces in half so that each serving can include both white and dark meat. The breasts and thighs/drumsticks do not cook at the same rate; if using both, note that the breast pieces are added partway through the cooking time. Herbes de Provence is a dried mixture of herbs often used in the south of France and includes basil, fennel seed, lavender, marjoram, rosemary, sage, summer savory, and thyme. You can find herbes de Provence in most large grocery stores.

4	pounds bone-in, skin-on chicken pieces (split breasts cut in half, drumsticks, and/or thighs), trimmed (see note)
	Salt and ground black pepper
2	tablespoons vegetable oil, plus extra as needed
1	medium onion, minced
6	medium garlic cloves, minced or pressed through a garlic press (about 2 tablespoons)
1	tablespoon minced fresh thyme leaves
1	teaspoon minced fresh oregano leaves
1	teaspoon herbes de Provence (optional, see note)
1	anchovy fillet, rinsed and minced (about 1 teaspoon)
⅛	teaspoon cayenne pepper
2	tablespoons tomato paste
1	tablespoon unbleached all-purpose flour
½	cup dry white wine
1½	cups low-sodium chicken broth
1	(14.5-ounce) can diced tomatoes, drained
2	bay leaves
1½	teaspoons grated zest from 1 lemon

½ cup pitted niçoise olives
1 tablespoon minced fresh parsley leaves
   Extra-virgin olive oil, for serving

1. Pat the chicken dry with paper towels and season with salt and pepper. Heat 1 tablespoon of the oil in a large Dutch oven over medium-high heat until just smoking. Add half of the chicken and brown on both sides, 7 to 10 minutes, reducing the heat if the pot begins to scorch. Transfer the chicken to a large plate and repeat with the remaining 1 tablespoon oil and the remaining chicken; transfer to the plate. (If using thighs and/or drumsticks, remove and discard the skin.)

2. Pour off all but 1 tablespoon of the fat left in the pot (or add more oil if necessary) and place over medium heat until shimmering. Add the onion and ¼ teaspoon salt and cook over medium heat, stirring often, until softened, 5 to 7 minutes. Stir in the garlic, thyme, oregano, herbes de Provence (if using), anchovy, and cayenne and cook until fragrant, about 30 seconds. Stir in the tomato paste and flour and cook, stirring constantly, for 1 minute. Slowly whisk in the wine, scraping up any browned bits, then slowly whisk in the broth until smooth. Stir in the tomatoes and bay leaves and bring to a simmer.

3. Nestle the chicken, along with any accumulated juices, into the pot and bring to a simmer. Cover, reduce the heat to medium-low, and simmer gently until the chicken is fully cooked and tender, about 1 hour for the thighs and drumsticks (170 to 175 degrees on an instant-read thermometer) or 20 minutes for the breasts (160 to 165 degrees on an instant-read thermometer). (If using both types of chicken, simmer the thighs and drumsticks for 40 minutes before adding the breasts.)

4. Transfer the chicken to a serving platter, tent loosely with foil, and let rest while finishing the sauce. Defat the braising liquid following one of the methods on page 142 (if necessary, return the defatted liquid to the pot).

5. Stir 1 teaspoon of the lemon zest into the defatted liquid, bring to a simmer, and cook until the sauce has thickened slightly, 4 to 6 minutes. Off the heat, discard the bay leaves, stir in the olives, cover, and let sit for 5 minutes. Season the sauce with salt and pepper to taste. Toss the remaining ½ teaspoon lemon zest with the parsley. Spoon the sauce over the chicken, sprinkle with the parsley mixture, drizzle lightly with extra-virgin olive oil, and serve.

CHICKEN FRICASSEE

CHICKEN CAN BE PREPARED JUST ABOUT ANY way—roasted, sautéed, grilled, fried, stir-fried, oven-fried, baked, poached, and smoked—but these days we rarely think about a simple fricassee. Why? Well, for one thing, most of us mistake it for some outdated Cordon Bleu preparation. In fact, a chicken fricassee is nothing more than chicken simmered in broth, after which a simple sauce is made from the liquid. It's simple, it's flavorful, and it's easy. So why is it also forgotten?

For many versions of this recipe, the answer is quite simple: It is either too time-consuming or no longer appeals to the modern palate. But certain recipes do deserve a second life, and it seemed high time to resurrect chicken fricassee.

The process did involve solving some problems, however. The first was to define the parameters of the recipe. The fricassee has had a long history and many different interpretations. Originally, a French fricassee was chicken (and sometimes vegetables) cooked in a white sauce. Over time, this dish evolved to become chicken cooked in a clear liquid, usually chicken stock but sometimes water and/or wine. When the chicken was done, it was removed from the pan, and then a sauce was made from the cooking liquid. This simple definition was a good starting point.

But we had other considerations as well. We did not want an extremely rich sauce, preferring instead something lighter and more modern. We also wanted to develop a recipe that could be put together simply, using the minimum number of pans and ingredients. Producing moist chicken was going to be important, as was producing a flavorful, well-balanced sauce that was neither too rich nor too acidic.

We first addressed the issue of the chicken itself. Since we like a choice of white or dark meat, we prefer chicken parts (such as thighs and breasts). Furthermore, for braises we've found we like chicken parts with the skin on, as the skin helps to contribute flavor to the sauce from the browning process. Browning our chicken in vegetable oil, rather than butter, was the way to go—we found that the chicken burned in places when browned in butter.

Many traditional French recipes simmer the browned chicken in equal amounts of chicken broth and white wine. Tasters judged a sauce made this way too acidic—a result of the generous amount of wine, we reasoned. For our next version we cut out the wine and used only chicken broth, but now the sauce tasted flat. A bit of wine was definitely in order. Adding the wine back in incremental amounts, we found that ½ cup of dry white wine combined with 1½ cups of chicken broth yielded the right balance of meaty richness and bright flavors. To this liquid base, we added vegetables—common inclusions in recipes we found were carrots, celery, mushrooms, onions, shallots, and garlic. Our favorite combination was onion and mushrooms, with a little minced garlic and thyme and a couple of bay leaves added for flavor.

With our flavors in place, it was time to get our technique down. We browned two batches of chicken first, one batch lightly and the other to a deep golden brown on both sides. The more caramelized bits that were left in the pan, the richer the sauce, so we realized that achieving a deep golden brown crust was a must. Once the chicken was nicely browned, we removed it from the pan to cook our garnish. We sautéed the onions and mushrooms together, added the aromatic flavorings, deglazed the pan with white wine, and then added the chicken broth. We were now ready to return the chicken to finish cooking.

With the chicken pieces nestled in the stewing liquid, we started our timer. Twenty minutes later the breast meat was perfectly cooked but the thighs were still undercooked and tough. Another 20 minutes later, the thighs were approaching perfect while the breasts were dry and overcooked. We were going to have to stagger the time the meat went into the pan if we wanted a perfect fricassee. This was simple enough; once our stewing liquid was simmering and ready for the chicken, we added only the thighs and cooked them, covered, for 40 minutes. At that

point we added the breast meat and cooked the entire dish for an additional 20 minutes. All the meat was perfectly cooked and it was time to finish the sauce.

Many traditional recipes finish the sauce with egg yolks and cream, but we didn't want heavy sauce, and trying to prevent the egg yolks from curdling in the pan seemed too fussy for this simple meal. We omitted the eggs and focused on the cream, adding various amounts to find the perfect balance of richness and meatiness. Tasters were stuck between ⅓ cup and ½ cup cream, some citing the more generous amount as too rich, while others felt it was just right. We went with ⅓ cup, knowing we could always add more if necessary. Either way, this chicken fricassee was everything we wanted it to be: simple, rich, and deeply flavored.

Chicken Fricassee

SERVES 4 TO 6

If using both chicken breasts and thighs/drumsticks, we recommend cutting the breast pieces in half so that each person can have some white meat and dark meat. The breasts and thighs/drumsticks do not cook at the same time; if using both, note that the breast pieces are added partway through the cooking time. Serve with rice, plain noodles, or crusty bread.

4	pounds bone-in, skin-on chicken pieces (split breasts cut in half, drumsticks, and/or thighs), trimmed (see note)
	Salt and ground black pepper
2	tablespoons vegetable oil
2	tablespoons unsalted butter
10	ounces white mushrooms, wiped clean and quartered
1	medium onion, minced
2	medium garlic cloves, minced or pressed through a garlic press (about 2 teaspoons)
2	teaspoons minced fresh thyme leaves, or ½ teaspoon dried
2	tablespoons unbleached all-purpose flour
½	cup dry white wine
1½	cups low-sodium chicken broth
2	bay leaves

⅓   cup heavy cream
2   teaspoons juice from 1 lemon
2   tablespoons minced fresh parsley leaves

1. Pat the chicken dry with paper towels and season with salt and pepper. Heat 1 tablespoon of the oil in a large Dutch oven over medium-high heat until just smoking. Add half of the chicken and brown on both sides, 7 to 10 minutes, reducing the heat if the pot begins to scorch. Transfer the chicken to a large plate and repeat with the remaining 1 tablespoon oil and the remaining chicken; transfer to the plate. (If using thighs and/or drumsticks, remove and discard the skin.)

2. Pour off all of the fat left in the pot, add the butter, and melt over medium heat. Add the mushrooms, onion, and ¼ teaspoon salt and cook, stirring often, until lightly browned, 10 to 12 minutes. Stir in the garlic and thyme and cook until fragrant, about 30 seconds. Stir in the flour and cook, stirring constantly, for 1 minute. Slowly whisk in the wine, scraping up any browned bits, then slowly whisk in the broth until smooth. Add the bay leaves and bring to a simmer.

3. Nestle the chicken, along with any accumulated juices, into the pot and bring to a simmer. Cover, reduce the heat to medium-low, and simmer gently until the chicken is fully cooked and tender, about 1 hour for the thighs and drumsticks (170 to 175 degrees on an instant-read thermometer) or 20 minutes for the breasts (160 to 165 degrees on an instant-read thermometer). (If using both types of chicken, simmer the thighs and drumsticks for 40 minutes before adding the breasts.)

4. Transfer the chicken to a serving platter, tent loosely with foil, and let rest while finishing the sauce. Defat the braising liquid following one of the methods on page 142 (if necessary, return the defatted liquid to the pot).

5. Stir the cream into the defatted liquid, bring to a simmer over medium-high heat, and cook until thickened, saucy, and measures about 1½ cups, 15 to 20 minutes. Off the heat, discard the bay leaves, stir in the lemon juice, and season with salt and pepper to taste. Spoon the sauce over the chicken, sprinkle with the parsley, and serve.

COQ AU VIN

ONE OF THE CLASSICS OF FRENCH CUISINE, coq au vin may sound fancy, but at heart it is really nothing more than a simple braised chicken dish. Chicken is cooked in a red wine sauce and finished with bacon, glazed pearl onions, and sautéed mushrooms. At its best, coq au vin is a boldly flavored dish, the acidity of the wine rounded out by rich, salty bacon and sweet caramelized onions and mushrooms. The chicken acts like a sponge, soaking up those same dark, compelling flavors. We set about creating a recipe that would satisfy our appetite for a really great coq au vin.

When doing research on this classic braise, we noticed that the recipes fell into two categories: those that were simple and rustic in character, and ones that were a bit more complicated, but promised a more refined dish. The recipes in the first category were versions of a straightforward brown fricassee. Tasting these simpler versions, we recognized them as the serviceable renditions of recent memory: The sauces were good but not extraordinary; the chicken tasted mostly like chicken.

We moved on to testing a handful of much more complicated recipes. One of them was a two-day affair with a much more elaborate sauce. The recipe began by combining red wine with veal stock and browned vegetables and reducing this mixture by about half. The chicken was then browned and the pan deglazed with the reduced wine mixture. Once the chicken was cooked, the sauce was strained, bound first with *beurre manié* (a paste of mashed butter and flour), and then with a bit of chicken liver pureed with heavy cream, and finished with flambéed cognac.

Although this particular recipe was built on the same basic model as the others, this dish was in a whole different league. It was what a good coq au vin ought to be—the sauce was beautifully textured, clean-flavored, and rich without being heavy or murky. The chicken was drenched in flavor. Though we were able to make it in just one day instead of two, the recipe unquestionably demanded more time, more last-minute fussing, and a lot more dishes than the simpler versions. Could we get the same great flavors and textures with a slightly streamlined approach?

In trying to simplify this recipe, two techniques stood out when we compared it with the others. First, this recipe used all chicken legs instead of both legs and breasts, which is traditional. It also bound the sauce differently than the others, using beurre manié and chicken liver rather than sprinkling the meat or vegetables with flour at the beginning.

Traditionally coq au vin makes use of an entire bird, so when we tasted the version that used legs only, many tasters missed the white meat. Other tasters felt all dark meat made sense for gauging the cooking time since white and dark meats cook at a different rate. The recipe works well with a mixture of white and dark meat as long as the thighs are given a head start before the breast are added to

INGREDIENTS: Red Wines for Cooking

When a recipe calls for red wine, the tendency is to grab whatever is inexpensive, close at hand, or already open on the counter. But as with any ingredient, the type of wine you cook with can make a big difference. The wrong wine can turn a good sauce bad. Yet because wines range enormously in flavor, body, and astringency, choosing a good one for the kitchen can be a shot in the dark.

What defines a good red cooking wine? It is appropriate for a wide range of recipes, easy to find at the local store, and consistent through the years. To help determine which red wines are good cookers, we set up a series of three cooking tests—a quick tomato sauce, a long-cooked beef stew, and a pan sauce for steak—through which we could test numerous bottles.

Organizing the overwhelming body of red wine into manageable groups, we assigned four categories based on flavor, body, and style: light/fruity, smooth/mellow, hearty/robust, and nondescript jug wine. Ironically, the only type of wine not represented is the "cooking wine" found on most supermarket shelves. In the past, we found that these low-alcohol concoctions have no flavor, a high-pitched acidity, and an enormous amount of salt, which renders them both undrinkable and a very poor choice for cooking.

We began by cooking with a representative from each category: a light/fruity Beaujolais, a smooth/mellow Merlot, a hearty/robust Cabernet Sauvignon, and a jug of Paul Masson Mountain Burgundy. The results were drastically different. The Beaujolais made refreshingly fruity but wimpy sauces, while the Merlot made for balanced sauces with an overcooked, jam-like flavor. The Cabernet Sauvignon proved to be too hearty for an all-purpose cooking wine, and the Paul Masson made sweet, simple sauces that neither offended nor impressed anyone.

Although none of the four groups "won" this first round of testing, what emerged were some important attributes of a good cooking wine and some characteristics of which to be wary. The light wine made weak sauces and the hearty wine made sauces that were too muscular. Oak flavors (from barrel aging) did not soften as they cooked and tasted bitter and harsh. Fruity characteristics, on the other hand, mingled well with the other sauce ingredients and complemented their flavors.

Narrowing our focus to smooth, fruity, medium-bodied wines with little oak influence, we tried four more types of wine in the trio of recipes: a Chianti, a Zinfandel, a Pinot Noir, and a Côtes du Rhône. The Chianti tasted great in the tomato sauce but made an astringent pan sauce and cardboard-tasting stews. The Zinfandel tasted overcooked and jammy in the tomato sauce and turned the pan sauce bitter. While both the Côtes du Rhône and Pinot Noir turned in impressive results across the board, the Côtes du Rhône was stellar. When compared with the sauces made with Pinot Noir (a wine made from just one type of grape), the Côtes du Rhône (made from a blend of grapes) had a fuller, more even-keeled flavor. The varietals within the blend compensated for each others' shortcomings. The resulting sauces were potent but well rounded. Besides Côtes du Rhône, there are many fruity, medium-bodied, blended wines, including wines from the greater Rhône Valley, Languedoc (near the Mediterranean), Australia, and the United States.

We found a strong correlation between price and quality when it comes to red wine. Tests demonstrated that a $5 bottle cooked much differently from bottles costing $10, $20, or $30. As a wine cooks and reduces, it becomes a more intensely flavored version of itself, and defining characteristics become unbearably obvious. The sweet, bland $5 wines cooked down to a candy-like sauce, while the $10, $20, and $30 bottles were increasingly smooth, with multiple layers of flavor. Although the higher-end wines tasted slightly more balanced and refined, none of the tasters thought the flavor difference between the $10 and $20 or $30 bottles was worth the extra money. What's more, limiting the price to around $10 does not restrict your options when shopping. We found plenty of good blends from California, Australia, and France.

the pot; the choice of cuts is up to you. Browning the chicken in the fat from the bacon gave us a rich base upon which to build the sauce.

We first tested a coq au vin bound with beurre manié and compared it with one in which the vegetables (the onions and mushrooms) were sprinkled with flour. We liked the streamlined method of sprinkling the flour over the vegetables, and decided to add a bit of tomato paste along with the flour for a rounder flavor. After that we simply added the liquid components—broth and wine—then nestled in the browned chicken and left it to simmer. The finished dish was good, but some felt the richness of the butter in the beurre manié was missing in this leaner sauce. To solve that, we whisked cold butter into the finished sauce, which rounded out the flavors with the added benefit of thickening the sauce.

This, at last, was a relatively simple coq au vin worth making.

~≈⊁

Coq au Vin
SERVES 4 TO 6

Regular bacon can be substituted for the thick-cut bacon. A $7 to $10 bottle of medium-bodied red table wine made from a blend of grapes, such as a Côtes du Rhône, will work well here. If using both chicken breasts and thighs/drumsticks, we recommend cutting the breast pieces in half so that each person can have some white meat and dark meat. The breasts and thighs/drumsticks do not cook at the same time; if using both, note that the breast pieces are added partway through the cooking time.

6   ounces (about 5 slices) thick-cut bacon, chopped medium
4   pounds bone-in, skin-on chicken pieces (split breasts cut in half, drumsticks, and/or thighs), trimmed (see note)
      Salt and ground black pepper
      Vegetable oil, as needed
10   ounces white mushrooms, wiped clean and quartered
1¼   cups frozen pearl onions, thawed
2   medium garlic cloves, minced or pressed through a garlic press (about 2 teaspoons)

1   teaspoon minced fresh thyme leaves, or ¼ teaspoon dried
3   tablespoons unbleached all-purpose flour
1   tablespoon tomato paste
1   (750-ml) bottle dry red wine (see note)
2½   cups low-sodium chicken broth
2   bay leaves
2   tablespoons unsalted butter, cut into 2 pieces and chilled
2   tablespoons minced fresh parsley leaves

1. Fry the bacon in a large Dutch oven over medium-low heat until rendered and crisp, about 10 minutes. Transfer the bacon to a paper towel–lined plate with a slotted spoon, and reserve the fat separately in a small bowl.

2. Pat the chicken dry with paper towels and season with salt and pepper. Heat 1 tablespoon of the bacon fat in a large Dutch oven over medium-high heat until just smoking. Add half of the chicken and brown on both sides, 7 to 10 minutes, reducing the heat if the pot begins to scorch. Transfer the chicken to a large plate and repeat with 1 tablespoon more bacon fat (if necessary, add oil) and the remaining chicken; transfer to the plate. (If using thighs and/or drumsticks, remove and discard the skin.)

3. Pour off all but 1 tablespoon of the fat left in the pot (or add oil if necessary), and place over medium heat until shimmering. Add the mushrooms, pearl onions, and ¼ teaspoon salt, and cook over medium heat, stirring often, until lightly browned, 10 to 12 minutes. Stir in the garlic and thyme and cook until fragrant, about 30 seconds. Stir in the flour and tomato paste, and cook, stirring constantly, for 1 minute. Slowly whisk in the wine, scraping up any browned bits, then slowly whisk in the broth until smooth. Stir in the bay leaves and bring to a simmer.

4. Nestle the chicken, along with any accumulated juices, into the pot and bring to a simmer. Cover, reduce the heat to medium-low, and simmer gently until the chicken is fully cooked and tender, about 1 hour for the thighs and drumsticks (170 to 175 degrees on an instant-read thermometer) or 20 minutes for the breasts (160 to 165 degrees on

an instant-read thermometer). (If using both types of chicken, simmer the thighs and drumsticks for 40 minutes before adding the breasts.)

5. Transfer the chicken to a serving platter, tent loosely with foil, and let rest while finishing the sauce. Defat the braising liquid following one of the methods on page 142 (if necessary, return the defatted liquid to the pot).

6. Bring the defatted liquid to a simmer over medium-high heat and cook until thickened, saucy, and measures about 2 cups, about 20 minutes. Off the heat, discard the bay leaves, whisk in the butter, and season the sauce with salt and pepper to taste. Spoon the sauce over the chicken, sprinkle with the reserved bacon and the parsley, and serve.

CHICKEN CACCIATORE

CACCIATORE, WHICH MEANS "HUNTER-STYLE" in Italian, originally referred to a simple method of cooking fresh-killed game. Game hen or rabbit was sautéed along with wild mushrooms, onions, and other foraged vegetables, then braised with wine or broth. Today, this dish is often made with chicken and often with poor results. Cacciatore has become a generic "red sauce" dish, one that tends to be greasy and overly sweet. Still, we knew there was a really good version of this dish to be found, and we were determined to discover it.

We began our work with a blind taste test. We gathered an abundance of recipes (every Italian cookbook seems to include some form of cacciatore), then selected what seemed to be the more authentic versions (no boneless, skinless chicken breasts, no jarred tomato sauces). All four of the recipes we chose started with the same basic preparation: Chicken (a whole chicken cut up in all but one of the recipes) is dredged in flour and sautéed in olive oil, then removed from the pan, which is then deglazed with either wine or broth. Vegetables—most often tomatoes, onions, and mushrooms—are added, the chicken is returned to the pot, and the dish is then left to cook until the meat is tender throughout.

From the test results, we came to a few conclusions and devised a working recipe. As we learned while developing our Chicken Provençal (page 166), chicken parts are a more convenient option than cutting up a whole chicken. We chose bone-in, skin-on parts—the bone keeps the meat moist and the skin helps to contribute flavor to the sauce from the browning process. To address the overabundance of grease in the dish (a problem in all of the recipes we tried), we browned each batch of chicken in just 1 tablespoon of oil, them poured off all the fat except for 1 tablespoon before adding the aromatics. And the vegetables needed to be kept to a minimum—a combination of onions, mushrooms (we liked meaty portobellos), and tomatoes would suffice.

Next came the braising medium. Preliminary tests suggested that red wine would prevail. Most tasters liked its bold presence, although some thought its hearty flavor was a bit too overpowering. We tried cutting the wine with small amounts of water, dry vermouth, and chicken broth and found that the latter buffered the strong presence of the wine and rounded out the flavors. (Because some tasters preferred the lighter, brothier taste of the version made with white wine, we decided to offer that as a variation on the master recipe.)

At this point, the sauce was rich in flavor but

CLEANING MUSHROOMS

Mushrooms, with their hard-to-reach spots, can be difficult to clean. We like to use a clean, soft-bristled toothbrush. It provides a comfortable handle, and the small head slips easily under the gills to capture every stray bit of dirt. You can also use a damp paper towel to wipe away the dirt.

lacking in substance. Truthfully, the consistency was more like a broth; the vegetables and chicken were lost in liquid. We solved this problem by adding a little flour directly to the pot after the vegetables had sautéed, which produced a silky and robust sauce. On a whim, we threw in a piece of Parmesan cheese rind, an option we had noticed in one of the recipes we tested earlier. The sauce, very good before, now surpassed all of our expectations. It was substantial and amply flavored. A sprinkling of sage was the perfect finish to this satisfying dish.

Chicken Cacciatore with Portobellos and Sage
SERVES 4 TO 6

A $7 to $10 bottle of medium-bodied red table wine made from a blend of grapes, such as a Côtes du Rhône, will work well here. If using both chicken breasts and thighs/drumsticks, we recommend cutting the breast pieces in half so that each serving can include both white and dark meat. The breasts and thighs/drumsticks do not cook at the same rate; if using both, note that the breast pieces are added partway through the cooking time. The addition of the Parmesan cheese rind is optional, but we highly recommend it for the robust, savory flavor it lends the dish. An equal amount of minced fresh rosemary can be substituted for the sage.

4   pounds bone-in, skin-on chicken pieces (split breasts cut in half, drumsticks, and/or thighs), trimmed (see note)
    Salt and ground black pepper
2   tablespoons olive oil, plus extra as needed
6   ounces (about 3 medium) portobello mushroom caps, wiped clean and cut into ¾-inch pieces
1   medium onion, minced
4   medium garlic cloves, minced or pressed through a garlic press (about 4 teaspoons)
2   teaspoons minced fresh thyme leaves, or ½ teaspoon dried
1   tablespoon unbleached all-purpose flour
½   cup dry red wine (see note)
1½ cups low-sodium chicken broth
1   (14.5-ounce) can diced tomatoes, drained

2   bay leaves
1   Parmesan cheese rind, about 4 by 2 inches (optional, see note)
2   teaspoons minced fresh sage leaves

1. Pat the chicken dry with paper towels and season with salt and pepper. Heat 1 tablespoon of the oil in a large Dutch oven over medium-high heat until just smoking. Add half of the chicken and brown on both sides, 7 to 10 minutes, reducing the heat if the pot begins to scorch. Transfer the chicken to a large plate and repeat with the remaining 1 tablespoon oil and the remaining chicken; transfer to the plate. (If using thighs and/or drumsticks, remove and discard the skin.)

2. Pour off all but 1 tablespoon of the fat left in the pot (or add more oil if necessary) and place over medium heat until shimmering. Add the mushrooms, onion, and ¼ teaspoon salt and cook, stirring often, until lightly browned, 10 to 12 minutes. Stir in the garlic and thyme and cook until fragrant, about 30 seconds. Stir in the flour and cook, stirring constantly, until golden, about 1 minute. Slowly whisk in the wine, scraping up any browned bits, then slowly whisk in the broth until smooth. Stir in the tomatoes and bay leaves and bring to a simmer

3. Nestle the chicken, along with any accumulated juices, and Parmesan rind (if using) into the pot and bring to a simmer. Cover, reduce the heat to medium-low, and simmer gently until the chicken is fully cooked and tender, about 1 hour for the thighs and drumsticks (170 to 175 degrees on an instant-read thermometer) or 20 minutes for the breasts (160 to 165 degrees on an instant-read thermometer). (If using both types of chicken, simmer the thighs and drumsticks for 40 minutes before adding the breasts.)

4. Transfer the chicken to a serving platter, tent loosely with foil, and let rest while finishing the sauce. Discard the bay leaves and cheese rind. Defat the braising liquid following one of the methods on page 142 (if necessary, return the defatted liquid to the pot).

5. Bring the defatted liquid to a simmer over

medium-high heat and cook until the sauce has thickened slightly, 4 to 6 minutes. Stir in the sage and season with salt and pepper to taste. Spoon the sauce over the chicken and serve.

➤ VARIATION

Chicken Cacciatore with White Wine and Tarragon

Follow the recipe for Chicken Cacciatore with Portobellos and Sage, substituting 3 large shallots, minced (¾ cup), for the onion, 10 ounces white mushrooms, wiped clean and halved, for the portobellos, ½ cup dry white wine for the red wine, and 2 teaspoons minced fresh tarragon leaves for the sage.

INDIAN-STYLE CHICKEN CURRY

THE TERM "CURRY" IS DERIVED FROM THE Tamil word *kari*, which simply means sauce or gravy. We tend to think of curry as a spiced yellow-colored meat and vegetable stew typically served over rice. But a curry can be most any type of stew, and as a result there are hundreds, perhaps thousands, of ways to make curry. We wanted to develop a recipe for yellow curry and set out to discover what separates good curry from bad curry. And while we wanted an authentic-tasting curry, we didn't want it to consist of exotic, hard-to-find ingredients; we hoped to find a way to use supermarket staples.

As we quickly found out, there are many variables when making curry, including the types of spices used and whether they are whole or ground, the amounts of the aromatics, whether or not the meat is seared, and whether the curry contains some form of dairy (such as yogurt) or coconut milk.

While some curries are made with exotic whole and ground spices (fenugreek, asafetida, dried rose petals, and so on), we decided to limit ourselves to everyday ground spices such as cumin, cloves, cardamom, cinnamon, and coriander. Our testing

dragged on for days, and it was hard to reach a consensus in the test kitchen. Frankly, most of the homemade spice mixtures we tried were fine.

We had been reluctant to use store-bought curry powder, assuming its flavor would be inferior to a homemade blend, but it seemed worth a try. We were surprised to find that tasters liked the store-bought curry powder nearly as well as a homemade mixture made with seven spices. It turns out that store-bought curry powder contains some of the exotic spices we had dismissed at the outset. As long as we used enough, our recipe had good flavor. We cooked all of our spices in oil (a process known as blooming) to develop their flavors and infuse the cooking oil. This simple step took just one minute and turned commercial curry powder into a flavor powerhouse.

Finally, we experimented with garam masala, a spice blend often sprinkled onto Indian dishes before serving. Like curry powder, garam masala varies in ingredients but it usually includes warm spices such as black pepper, cinnamon, coriander, and cardamom (its name means "hot spice blend" in Hindi). Following our success with the curry powder, we decided to buy a jar of commercial garam masala. But when we added a few pinches to the cooked curry, the result was raw and harsh-tasting. What if we first bloomed the garam masala along with the curry powder? Sure enough, the garam masala mellowed into a second wave of flavor that helped the curry reach an even more layered complexity.

With our flavor base of spices in place, we moved on to the aromatics. Garlic and ginger are an integral part of all curries (and of Indian cuisine in general) and we found that using a healthy amount of both was crucial to a well-rounded curry flavor. A little fresh minced jalapeño also boosted the flavor and added some heat. Many of the curries we tested included some form of tomato product, be it fresh chopped tomatoes, tomato sauce, or tomato paste. We tried each of these on their own and in combination with one another. Fresh tomatoes by themselves added the acidity the curry needed, but didn't offer a very deep flavor. Tomato sauce had an assertive tinny taste. Tomato paste supplied a sweet, roasted flavor when cooked with the onions. A combination of fresh tomatoes and tomato paste worked best. We added the tomato paste to the onions along with the garlic and ginger and stirred the fresh tomatoes in just before serving to preserve their texture.

As the curry was beginning to come together, we investigated whether it was essential to sear the chicken before it was simmered in the sauce—some recipes we found did this, while others did not. For most of our chicken braises, we prefer chicken pieces with the skin on, and this was no exception—the skin helps to contribute flavor to the sauce from the browning process. Furthermore, we liked the choice of white or dark meat (though you can certainly use all one or the other). Not surprisingly, the breasts cooked in a third of the time as the thighs, so we would have to stagger the cooking. Once the base curry sauce was simmering and ready for the chicken, we added only the thighs and cooked them for 40 minutes. At that point we added the breast meat and cooked the

entire dish for an additional 20 minutes. All the meat was perfectly cooked at the same time.

As for the liquid component of the sauce, we were surprised to find that water did a fine job. Typically we would reach for chicken broth in a recipe like this, but given the complexity of our curry spices, chicken broth is simply unnecessary (as well as untraditional). Most authentic curry recipes we researched also include yogurt or coconut milk in with the water. Though we had trouble with both yogurt and coconut milk at the beginning of our testing, we found that if we added one of them at the end of cooking (to prevent curdling) and used less of it (so it didn't overwhelm the other flavors) it was the perfect finish to our curry. We liked the flavor of both, so we leave the decision up to you.

Finished with some green peas, a handful of minced cilantro, and a little butter to round out the sauce, our curry is as rich and flavorful as a traditional curry, with the appeal and ease of a weeknight meal.

INGREDIENTS: Garam Masala

Though there are countless variations of garam masala, the warm flavors (garam means "warm" or "hot" and masala means "spice blend") dominating this Indian spice blend are consistent: coriander, black pepper, dried chiles, cardamom, and cinnamon are staples, while nutmeg, cloves, mace, fennel, and cumin frequently turn up as supporting players. Garam masala is commonly sprinkled on finished dishes, but we find this method results in harsh flavors. Instead, we prefer it bloomed in oil or butter at the outset of a dish.

Concocting this complex spice blend at home can add a great deal of time to recipe preparation—not to mention how it can crowd your pantry with jars of seldom-used ingredients, running up a hefty shopping tab in the process. In search of a good-tasting commercial garam masala, we tested a few of the top brands.

Tasters disliked the bitter and overwhelming flavors of Spice Islands and Zamouri garam masalas. Spice Barn garam masala was dubbed one-dimensional. Penzeys Punjabi Style garam

masala combined the basic coriander-cardamom-cinnamon-pepper-chile combination with a few exotic additions that tasters found warm, floral, and tangy.

But tasters' favorite was McCormick Gourmet Collection garam masala for its ability to both assimilate into dishes and also round out their acidic and sweet notes. Tasters also liked the slightly pungent hits of coriander and the subtle warmth of cardamom, cinnamon, and cloves. Widely available in supermarkets, McCormick won praise from tasters for adding a mellow, well-balanced aroma to most dishes.

THE BEST GARAM MASALA
Sticking with mostly core garam masala ingredients won this super market brand top ratings with tasters.

Indian-Style Chicken Curry
SERVES 4 TO 6

If using both chicken breasts and thighs/drumsticks, we recommend cutting the breast pieces in half so that each person can have some white meat and dark meat. The breasts and thighs/drumsticks do not cook at the same time; if using both, note that the breast pieces are added partway through the cooking time. We prefer the richer flavor of whole milk yogurt and regular coconut milk here; however, low-fat yogurt, nonfat yogurt, or light coconut milk can be substituted. Adjust the spiciness of this dish by including the minced ribs and seeds from the jalapeño. Serve with rice.

4	pounds bone-in, skin-on chicken pieces (split breasts cut in half, drumsticks, and/or thighs), trimmed
	Salt and ground black pepper
2	tablespoons vegetable oil, plus extra as needed
2	tablespoons sweet or mild curry powder
I	teaspoon garam masala
2	medium onions, minced
6	medium garlic cloves, minced or pressed through a garlic press (about 2 tablespoons)
I	tablespoon minced or grated fresh ginger
I	jalapeño chile, seeds and ribs reserved, chile minced (see note)
I	tablespoon tomato paste
I	cup water
2	plum tomatoes, cored, seeded, and chopped fine (about I cup)
½	cup frozen peas, thawed
½	cup coconut milk or plain whole milk yogurt (see note)
¼	cup minced fresh cilantro leaves
2	tablespoons unsalted butter

1. Pat the chicken dry with paper towels and season with salt and pepper. Heat 1 tablespoon of the oil in a large Dutch oven over medium-high heat until just smoking. Add half of the chicken and brown on both sides, 7 to 10 minutes, reducing the heat if the pot begins to scorch. Transfer the chicken to a large plate and repeat with the remaining 1 tablespoon oil and the remaining chicken; transfer to the plate. (If using thighs and/or drumsticks, remove and discard the skin.)

2. Pour off all but 2 tablespoons of the fat left in the pot (or add more oil if necessary) and place over medium heat until shimmering. Add the curry and garam masala and cook until fragrant, about 10 seconds. Stir in the onions and ¼ teaspoon salt and cook, stirring often, until softened, 5 to 7 minutes. Stir in the garlic, ginger, jalapeño, and tomato paste and cook until fragrant, about 30 seconds. Stir in the water, scraping up any browned bits, and bring to a simmer.

3. Nestle the chicken, along with any accumulated juices, into the pot and bring to a simmer. Cover, reduce the heat to medium-low, and simmer gently until the chicken is fully cooked and tender, about 1 hour for the thighs and drumsticks (170 to 175 degrees on an instant-read thermometer) or 20 minutes for the breasts (160 to 165 degrees on an instant-read thermometer). (If using both types of chicken, simmer the thighs and drumsticks for 40 minutes before adding the breasts.)

4. Transfer the chicken to a serving platter, tent loosely with foil, and let rest while finishing the sauce. Defat the braising liquid following one of the methods on page 142 (if necessary, return the defatted liquid to the pot).

5. Stir the tomatoes, peas, coconut milk, cilantro, and butter into the defatted liquid and cook over medium heat until the butter is melted and the sauce is hot, 1 to 2 minutes. Season the sauce with salt and pepper to taste, spoon it over the chicken, and serve.

➤ VARIATIONS
Indian-Style Lamb Curry
Follow the recipe for Indian-Style Chicken Curry, substituting 4 pounds round-bone lamb chops for the chicken; brown as directed in step 1, and braise as directed in step 3 until the meat is very tender and a fork poked into it meets little resistance, about 1½ hours.

BRAISED CHICKEN WITH ALMONDS AND PINE NUTS

POLLO EN PEPITORIA IS A HEARTY BRAISED chicken dish flavored with many of the quintessential ingredients of Spanish cooking: sherry, almonds, garlic, and saffron. Though it has a long history (some say it dates back to the 13th century), this dish was unfamiliar to us. But we were immediately intrigued by its savory combination of bold flavors, and so we set out to make a braised chicken dish that we hoped would be a unique alternative to the familiar French classics.

Most authentic recipes start with a whole chicken, but we already knew from other chicken braises that chicken parts work well—and simplify preparation. Using chicken parts also allowed us to customize the dish: we could use all white or all dark meat or a combination of the two. Bone-in, skin-on parts gave us the best flavor and the skin protected the meat during the browning process. Just a little trimming of excess fat and skin was all the preparation the chicken pieces needed.

To begin, we browned the chicken in a Dutch oven to develop a fond—the base of the flavorful sauce. While the chicken rested on a plate, we cooked an onion in the pan, adding tomatoes once the onion had softened. Next, we added chicken broth and wine to the mix. In our research, we found that some recipes call for a dry white wine while others call for a dry sherry. We tested them both, side by side, and tasters unanimously chose the sauce with sherry—its deep, earthy flavor made this dish unique.

Another ingredient we found that was important to this dish is a pinch of ground cinnamon—it adds a depth of flavor that isn't obvious, but is missed when omitted from the recipe. Once the broth and

---

HARD-COOKED EGGS

BECAUSE SO MANY HARD-COOKED (OR HARD-BOILED) EGG RECIPES LEAVE US WITH either cracked shells or green-tinged, sulfurous yolks (a common side effect of overcooked eggs), we wanted to develop a foolproof cooking method. The method below yields eggs with tender whites and perfectly cooked yolks every time.

Hard-Cooked Eggs

MAKES 6 EGGS

You can easily scale this recipe up or down as desired; alter the pot size as needed, but do not alter the cooking time. Fresher eggs will have more centered yolks when cooked, while older eggs will produce off-center yolks.

6   large eggs

Place the eggs in a medium saucepan, cover with 1 inch of water, and bring to a boil over high heat. As soon as the water reaches a boil, remove the pan from the heat, cover, and let sit for 10 minutes. Transfer the eggs to an ice-water bath and chill for 5 minutes, then peel.

PEELING EGGS FAST

1. After draining the hot water from the pot used to cook the eggs, shake the pot back and forth to crack the shells.

2. Add enough ice water to cover the eggs and cool. The water seeps under the broken shells, allowing them to be slipped off without a struggle.

wine were added and the fond was scraped from the bottom of the pan, we placed the chicken back in the pan and covered it, to finish cooking. When the chicken was done, we tented it with foil while we finished the sauce.

The last element to go into the pot was the *picada*, a paste stirred into the sauce as a thickening and flavoring agent. A combination of ground almonds, pine nuts, parsley, and saffron, picada adds unmistakable body and flavor to the sauce and is the heart of this dish. For further texture and richness, we added a minced hard-cooked egg (a common garnish) to the sauce with the picada. Once the sauce returned to a simmer, we cooked it until thickened, which took just a couple of minutes, then poured it directly over the chicken and we had a juicy, flavorful, and versatile chicken dish—easy enough to serve during the week and special enough for company.

EQUIPMENT: Food Processors

A food processor can make quick work out of any number of kitchen tasks, from slicing potatoes and shredding cheese to pureeing sauces and making pasta or tart doughs. After using food processors repeatedly over the years, we have found two brands that have surpassed all others. The KitchenAid 12-Cup KFP750 ($249.99) and the 11-Cup Cuisinart Pro Custom 11 ($179.95) each have a large-capacity workbowl and powerful motor that excels at any kitchen task we throw at it. The KitchenAid was the hands-down winner with vegetable prep, but the Cuisinart performs all other tasks as well (or better) and costs less.

THE BEST FOOD PROCESSORS

If vegetable prep is important to you, buy the KitchenAid 12-Cup food processor ($249.99). Otherwise, the 11-Cup Cuisinart Pro Custom 11 ($179.95) performed all other tasks as well as (or better than) its pricier competition.

KITCHENAID   CUISINART

Braised Chicken with Almonds and Pine Nuts

SERVES 4 TO 6

If using both chicken breasts and thighs/drumsticks, we recommend cutting the breast pieces in half so that each serving can include both white and dark meat. The breasts and thighs/drumsticks do not cook at the same rate; if using both, note that the breast pieces are added partway through the cooking time. The picada—a mixture of ground nuts, garlic, parsley, and saffron—is easiest to make in the food processor but it can also be combined with a mortar and pestle or by hand.

PICADA AND EGG

2	tablespoons chopped almonds
2	tablespoons chopped pine nuts
1	tablespoon minced fresh parsley leaves
2	medium garlic cloves, minced or pressed through a garlic press (about 2 teaspoons)
1/8	teaspoon saffron threads, crumbled
1	hard-cooked egg, minced (see page 177)

CHICKEN AND SAUCE

4	pounds bone-in, skin-on chicken pieces (split breasts cut in half, drumsticks, and/or thighs), trimmed (see note)
	Salt and ground black pepper
2	tablespoons olive oil, plus extra as needed
1	medium onion, minced
1/2	cup dry sherry (see note)
1 1/2	cups low-sodium chicken broth
1	(14.5-ounce) can diced tomatoes, drained
2	bay leaves
	Pinch ground cinnamon

1. FOR THE PICADA AND EGG: Process the almonds, pine nuts, parsley, garlic, and saffron together in a food processor to a finely chopped paste, 12 to 15 seconds. Transfer to a small bowl, stir in the egg, and set aside.

2. FOR THE CHICKEN AND SAUCE: Pat the chicken dry with paper towels and season with salt and pepper. Heat 1 tablespoon of the oil in a large Dutch oven over medium-high heat until just smoking. Add half of the chicken and brown on

both sides, 7 to 10 minutes, reducing the heat if the pot begins to scorch. Transfer the chicken to a large plate and repeat with the remaining 1 tablespoon oil and the remaining chicken; transfer to the plate. (If using thighs and/or drumsticks, remove and discard the skin.)

3. Pour off all but 1 tablespoon of the fat left in the pot (or add more oil if necessary) and place over medium heat until shimmering. Add the onion and ¼ teaspoon salt and cook over medium heat until softened, 5 to 7 minutes. Stir in the sherry, scraping up any browned bits. Stir in the broth, tomatoes, bay leaves, and cinnamon and bring to a simmer.

4. Nestle the chicken, along with any accumulated juices, into the pot and bring to a simmer. Cover, reduce the heat to medium-low, and simmer gently until the chicken is fully cooked and tender, about 1 hour for the thighs and drumsticks (170 to 175 degrees on an instant-read thermometer) or 20 minutes for the breasts (160 to 165 degrees on an instant-read thermometer). (If using both types of chicken, simmer the thighs and drumsticks for 40 minutes before adding the breasts.)

5. Transfer the chicken to a serving platter, tent loosely with foil, and let rest while finishing the sauce. Defat the braising liquid following the illustrations on page 142 (if necessary, return the defatted liquid to the pot).

6. Bring the braising liquid to a simmer over medium-high heat and cook until thickened and saucy, 4 to 6 minutes. Stir in the picada and continue to simmer until the sauce is thickened, about 4 minutes longer. Discard the bay leaves, spoon the sauce over the chicken, and serve.

RED-COOKED CHICKEN

RED-COOKED CHICKEN—A CHINESE DISH of chicken gently simmered in dark soy sauce, rice wine, ginger, scallions, and star anise until stained a deep mahogany—is as dramatic as it is enjoyable to eat. Red cooking is a Chinese cooking technique that is also called Chinese stewing, red stewing, or

INGREDIENTS: Dark Soy Sauce

There are many different kinds of soy sauce, but most of them fit into two categories: light and dark. Light soy sauce (aka regular soy sauce), the kind most commonly used, is the thinner and saltier of the two and is used as a condiment as much as it's used in cooking. Dark soy sauce, on the other hand, is used exclusively in cooking. It is less salty, a bit sweet, darker in color, and thicker due to a longer brewing process and the addition of molasses. It adds a fruity richness and dark brown color to dishes, such as Red-Cooked Chicken (page 180). Look for dark soy sauce in Asian markets and some well-stocked supermarkets.

red braising and is linked to Shanghai and other parts of eastern China that are known for the premium quality of their soy sauce and rice wine.

As with any braise, this dish begins with the meat. We tried using a whole bird cut into manageable pieces, but found the extra work unnecessary and ultimately decided on chicken pieces. Dark meat is the most forgiving part of the bird when braising, as it's difficult to overcook, but white meat also works well in this braise as long as it's removed from the pot when it reaches 160 degrees (otherwise it dries out).

Our biggest challenge was the sauce. Once the chicken was browned, we added our sauce ingredients—equal amounts of dark soy sauce and chicken broth formed the base of the sauce. Chinese rice cooking wine or dry sherry (we found either one works well in this dish) added a little acid and a generous 3 tablespoons of sesame oil rounded out the flavors. Unfortunately, the resulting sauce was thinner and more bitter than we wanted. Simply decreasing the chicken broth from ½ cup to ⅓ cup helped remedy that problem, but not enough. With the slightly bitter quality of the dark soy sauce, the flavor of the sauce was still not quite right—we would need something to counter the bitterness. Sugar was our most likely savior, and after trying granulated, light brown, and dark brown, we found that 3 tablespoons of light brown sugar added enough rich sweetness to bring this sauce back into balance.

Next we turned our attention to the aromatics. Ginger and garlic are typically used in recipes for red-cooked dishes and a generous 2 tablespoons of each was perfect. Five-spice powder, a blend of cinnamon, cloves, fennel seed, star anise, and Sichuan peppercorns, is traditional to the flavor of this dish. We found that the powder made the sauce a bit gritty, so instead we focused on two of the spices. Three pieces of star anise added a delicate licorice flavor to the sauce, while 1 teaspoon of Sichuan peppercorns gave the sauce an alluring heat.

With our recipe for red-cooked chicken near completion, we headed back into the kitchen for one last test. In our early research we had come across a few recipes that included hard-cooked eggs alongside the chicken. Although tasters weren't sold on the idea, just one test changed their minds. The eggs, which are hard-cooked first, cooled, and then peeled, are added to the braise with the browned chicken. In the finished dish, the outsides of the eggs are stained a deep mahogany, yet the interiors remain snowy white and bright yellow. But it was the combination of the rich, earthy eggs alongside the moist, meaty chicken that had everyone sold. This simple extra step turned this Chinese classic into a new test kitchen favorite.

Red-Cooked Chicken

SERVES 4 TO 6

The dark soy sauce is what gives the chicken and eggs their characteristic red-tinted color and deep, earthy flavor in this recipe; you can substitute regular soy sauce but the dish will be lighter in color and less flavorful. This dish is well seasoned on its own and doesn't require salt and pepper. If using both chicken breasts and thighs/drumsticks, we recommend cutting the breast pieces in half so that each serving can include both white and dark meat. The breasts and thighs/drumsticks do not cook at the same rate; if using both, note that the breast pieces are added partway through the cooking time. Serve with rice.

4	pounds bone-in, skin-on chicken pieces (split breasts cut in half, drumsticks, and/or thighs), trimmed (see note)
	Salt and ground black pepper
2	tablespoons vegetable oil, plus extra as needed
6	medium garlic cloves, minced or pressed through a garlic press (about 2 tablespoons)
2	tablespoons minced or grated fresh ginger
1	teaspoon Sichuan peppercorns (see below)
3	star anise
½	cup dark soy sauce (see note)
⅓	cup low-sodium chicken broth
¼	cup Chinese rice cooking wine or dry sherry
3	tablespoons toasted sesame oil
3	tablespoons light brown sugar
4	hard-cooked eggs, peeled (see page 177)

1. Pat the chicken dry with paper towels and season with salt and pepper. Heat 1 tablespoon of the oil in a large Dutch oven over medium-high heat until just smoking. Add half of the chicken and brown on both sides, 7 to 10 minutes, reducing the heat if the pot begins to scorch. Transfer the chicken to a large plate and repeat with the remaining 1 tablespoon oil and the remaining chicken; transfer to the plate. (If using thighs and/or drumsticks, remove and discard the skin.)

2. Pour off all but 1 tablespoon of the fat left in the pot (or add more oil if necessary) and place over medium heat until shimmering. Add the garlic, ginger, Sichuan peppercorns, and star anise and cook until fragrant, about 30 seconds. Stir in the dark soy sauce, broth, rice wine, sesame oil, and sugar, scraping up any browned bits and bring to a simmer.

3. Nestle the chicken, along with any accumulated juices, and hard cooked eggs into the pot and bring to a simmer. Cover, reduce the heat to

---

INGREDIENTS: Sichuan Peppercorns

Not familiar with Sichuan Peppercorns? It's not surprising. From 1968 until 2005, these berries of a spiny shrub indigenous to the Sichuan province of China were banned from importation into the United States—it seems they were viewed as potential carriers of a tree disease that could have harmed our citrus crops. Now that they have returned, they are working their way back into authentic Sichuan dishes here in the United States.

Sichuan peppercorns are one of the ingredients in the five-spice powder, a traditional Chinese spice blend. They have purplish-red husks and shiny black seeds. It is preferable to buy Sichuan peppercorns with the shiny black seeds removed as it's the reddish-brown husks that are used for their aromatic, gently floral fragrance and their telltale numbing effect on the tongue.

---

medium-low, and simmer gently until the chicken is fully cooked and tender, about 1 hour for the thighs and drumsticks (170 to 175 degrees on an instant-read thermometer) or 20 minutes for the breasts (160 to 165 degrees on an instant-read thermometer). (If using both types of chicken, simmer the thighs and drumsticks for 40 minutes before adding the breasts.)

4. Transfer the chicken and eggs to a serving platter, tent loosely with foil, and let rest while finishing the sauce. Defat the braising liquid following the illustrations on page 142. Spoon the defatted liquid over the chicken and eggs and serve.

DUCK CONFIT

DUCK CONFIT IS PERHAPS THE ULTIMATE braised dish. Best known as an essential component of cassoulet, the classic French stew, duck confit is also frequently served on its own with a simple salad. As with all braises, the meat (in this case, duck legs) is cooked slowly in simmering liquid until meltingly tender. But what is unique about duck confit is the braising liquid: the duck legs cook in, not wine, not broth, but their own fat. The result is a rich, luxurious dish with ultra-concentrated flavor—a true special occasion dish.

Duck or goose confit came about before the days of refrigeration as a means of preserving the meat in order to last the family through the long winter months—confit translates as "to conserve." The duck was first cured in salt (salt staves off bacteria, ensuring a longer shelf life) for up to 48 hours and then was very slowly simmered in its own fat until meltingly tender. The meat was packed in a special earthenware urn, the fat was poured on top until the meat was covered (bacteria cannot grow in fat), and the urn was buried deep into the ground to stay cool until the confit legs were removed from the urn for a meal. (Duck legs are used rather than breast meat because the dark meat stands up well to this process and is less prone to drying out.)

Food preservation has come a long way since then. These days, the duck legs are salted for flavor, not for curing. We had done some testing along

these lines in the past and found that salting meat does not dry it out; instead, it actually helps the meat retain moisture. It's simply a matter of timing. Meat naturally contains some salt and lots of water that coexist in a happy balance, but sprinkling salt on its surface throws off the balance. The water in the meat immediately starts moving toward the saltier surface to restore equilibrium. Once that happens, the exterior salt has pulled so much water to the surface that it alters the balance of the salt concentration. To restore equilibrium again, the water simply changes direction, flowing back into the meat, this time bringing the dissolved salt with it. Essentially, it's a brine without the water. It takes as much as eight hours for this entire process to happen. (Once equilibrium is restored, the balance remains indefinitely; however, the salt continues to tenderize the meat so if you let it rest too long you end up with mushy meat.) With this knowledge and a couple of tests, we found that an overnight cure with salt is the perfect amount of time to properly season the duck legs before they are cooked. Some fresh thyme leaves and dried bay leaves added to the cure gave an aromatic note to the flavor of the duck.

As for the cooking method, there's only one kind of fat we recommend cooking the duck in—its own. Most duck confit recipes we researched cooked the duck slowly in a moderately low oven, and we agree with this advice. The oven makes it easy to maintain a consistent moderate temperature with zero hot spots (as opposed to cooking it on the stovetop). After testing a variety of oven temperatures, we found that cooking the legs for two hours at 300 degrees yielded the texture we were looking for. The only tricky part of this method is getting the baking dish of duck legs and hot fat to and from the oven without spilling it. Our recommendation—use a baking dish that fits the duck legs snugly in one layer, but has tall sides, and place it on a rimmed baking sheet.

Because duck is not always that easy to find, we decided to try confit chicken legs and confit turkey legs as well. While they're not as common, we thought they would make a nice alternative. With our method in place, we simply swapped out duck legs for chicken legs, and tasters were pleased with the results. The chicken legs were incredibly tender.

Next up were the turkey legs. We split the thighs from the drumsticks, as the whole legs were rather large. Once again tasters were smiling. A note on fat used for chicken or turkey confit—duck fat definitely has more flavor, but for the sake of convenience, feel free to substitute vegetable oil.

Duck Confit

MAKES 6 CONFIT DUCK LEGS

When trimming the duck legs, simply remove any large pieces of fat around the edges and backside. Duck fat can be found at high-end butcher shops, specialty shops, or online (try www.dartagnan.com or www.hudsonvalleyfoiegras.com). The duck fat is crucial here for texture and flavor; however, if you are a little short, you can substitute vegetable oil. The duck fat can be reused again and again for up to a year if stored properly; to store, simply remelt the fat, strain it through a fine-mesh strainer, and refrigerate in an airtight container (discard the fat when it develops an off-smell). This dish is quite rich; we recommend serving it with a salad. Duck confit is also an essential component of Cassoulet (page 112).

6	whole duck legs, trimmed (see note)
1	tablespoon kosher salt
¼	teaspoon ground black pepper
10	sprigs fresh thyme
4	bay leaves, crumbled
6–8	cups duck fat, melted (see note)

1. Pat the duck legs dry with paper towels and sprinkle evenly with the salt and pepper. Toss the legs with the thyme and bay leaves in a large bowl, cover tightly with plastic wrap, and refrigerate for 8 to 24 hours.

2. Adjust an oven rack to the middle position and heat the oven to 300 degrees. Lay the legs, skin side up, in a single layer in a large baking dish and sprinkle the thyme and bay leaves over top. Place the dish on a rimmed baking sheet. Melt the duck fat in a medium saucepan over medium heat until liquefied, 5 to 10 minutes. Pour the melted duck fat over the legs until they are covered completely. Carefully transfer the dish to the oven and cook, uncovered, without moving the duck, until the skin has rendered most of its fat, the meat is very tender, and the leg bones twist easily away from the meat, about 2 hours (the oil will be bubbling gently).

3. Being very careful of the hot fat, transfer the dish to a wire rack and let cool completely, about 2 hours. (At this point, the duck legs, if encased completely in fat, can be wrapped with plastic wrap and refrigerated for up to 1 month; if necessary transfer the cooled legs to a smaller container and pour the cooled fat over the top to cover completely.

4. To serve, remove the duck legs from the fat and scrape off as much of the fat as possible. Lay the legs, skin side down, in a 12-inch nonstick skillet and cook gently over medium-low heat until the skin is crisp, 8 to 10 minutes. Gently flip the legs over and continue to cook until the legs are heated through, 4 to 6 minutes. Serve immediately.

➤ VARIATIONS

Chicken Confit
For convenience, feel free to substitute all vegetable oil here for the duck fat.

Follow the recipe for Duck Confit, substituting 6 whole chicken legs for the duck legs; cook as directed, reducing the oven time to about 1¾ hours.

Turkey Confit
For convenience, feel free to substitute all vegetable oil here for the duck fat; you will need about 8 cups of fat in order to cover the turkey completely.

Follow the recipe for Duck Confit, substituting 6 turkey thighs, turkey drumsticks, or a combination of the two, for the duck legs. Use a small roasting pan, and cook as directed, increasing the oven time to 2¼ to 2½ hours.

DAUBE PROVENÇAL **PAGE 100**

WHITE CHICKEN CHILI **PAGE 92**

184

SALMON EN COCOTTE WITH LEEKS AND WHITE WINE   **PAGE 74**

ROASTED CAULIFLOWER **PAGE 301**

CASSOULET **PAGE 112**

187

BAKED LONG-GRAIN BROWN RICE WITH PARMESAN, LEMON, AND HERBS   **PAGE 257**

ROAST BONE-IN LEG OF LAMB WITH GARLIC AND ROSEMARY **PAGE 17**

ROASTED WINTER SQUASH HALVES WITH SOY SAUCE AND MAPLE SYRUP **PAGE 325**

190

CHINESE BARBECUED PORK **PAGE 33**

SLOW-COOKER BOLOGNESE SAUCE **PAGE 248**

CARNITAS **PAGE 159**

COQ AU VIN **PAGE 171**

BEEF BRAISED IN BAROLO   **PAGE 139**

195

SLOW-COOKER CHICKEN PROVENÇAL   **PAGE 231**

SAVORY BREAD PUDDING WITH SPINACH AND FETA   **PAGE 279**

CLASSIC BEEF CHILI **PAGE 86**

5

SLOW-COOKER FAVORITES

SLOW-COOKER FAVORITES

TO SOME, PREPARING A "SLOW-COOKED" MEAL means blocking off precious weekend hours to spend time in the kitchen tending a hearty braised roast or stirring a rich, satisfying stew. To others, it means simply plugging in a slow cooker and getting dinner on the table without much labor or baby-sitting. Slow cookers promise home cooks the ultimate walk-away meal: Just put your ingredients in the pot that morning, and eight to 10 hours later a flavorful dinner will be yours. The slow cooker can make a complex-tasting dish surprisingly easy to prepare. The catch, however, is that to coax a really good dinner from your slow cooker, you can't just dump a bunch of raw ingredients in and walk away; you must commit some time to a bit of prep work, either in the early morning hours or, in some cases, the night before.

For this chapter, we were looking for hearty yet practical recipes, packed with flavor. But we also hoped to minimize, where possible, the amount of advanced prep you would need to do before the ingredients are added to the slow cooker. After all, slow-cooker recipes are meant to be a life raft, not a complicated project.

For hearty meals such as Beef Stew (page 206), Coq au Vin (page 232), Weeknight Chili (page 215), or Southwestern-Style Pot Roast (page 204), the biggest question we faced was: Is it truly crucial to brown the meat before adding it to the slow cooker? While conventional cooking wisdom screamed yes, we wondered if, after hours in a slow cooker, tasters would really notice whether the meat had been browned or not. When stews with browned meat were pitted against those with unbrowned meat, few could tell the difference—we found that there was a variety of techniques and ingredients we could employ that essentially made up for the flavor lost by not browning. Sautéing the

---

EQUIPMENT: Slow Cookers

Part of the appeal of a slow cooker has always been its modest price. But as slow cookers have gained popularity in recent years, manufacturers have added new features—and higher price tags. Does more money buy a better slow cooker? To find out, we rounded up seven models priced between $40 and $150. We chose slow cookers with oval inserts and capacities of 6 quarts or greater—features we have found to be essential for any slow cooker.

A programmable timer was deemed a real asset, especially because all the machines with timers automatically switch to a warming mode when the timed cooking is done. This means that even if you're late coming home from work, your dinner won't be overcooked (or cold).

Other features we found beneficial include an "on" light (so you don't accidentally leave it on overnight), insert handles (which make it easy to remove the insert), and a clear lid that allows you to see the food as it cooks.

The U.S. Department of Agriculture recommends that meat be brought out of the "danger zone" (that is, get above 140 degrees) within four hours. Every machine we tested was able to bring the meat up to temperature in the allotted time—even on low.

Although excess moisture is often a problem in slow-cooker dishes, most recipes are written assuming there will be little or no evaporation. The All-Clad, Hamilton Beach Stay or Go, Hamilton Beach Probe, Rival, and West Bend machines only allowed about 2 percent of their contents (3 quarts of 42-degree water) to evaporate after three hours of covered cooking on high. The two cookers that fared worst in this test, the KitchenAid and the Cuisinart, lost about 6 percent and 4 percent of their water, respectively.

All the slow cookers we tested did a good job with slow-cooking pot roast on both high and low and cooking chili and beans on high. But more important than the cooking tests were the features we deemed essential: timers that automatically shift to a "keep warm" setting at the end of cooking; a clear lid; an "on" indicator light; and handles on the insert. In the end, the All-Clad Stainless Steel Slow Cooker with Ceramic Insert came out ahead, providing slow, steady heat every time.

THE BEST SLOW COOKER

The All-Clad Stainless Steel Slow Cooker with Ceramic Insert ($149.95) aced all the cooking tests, and it has every feature we want, including insert handles and a clear lid.

ALL-CLAD

aromatics until lightly browned, along with some tomato paste, helped create the robust, roasted flavor we would have otherwise been missing, and adding soy sauce to the slow cooker made our stews taste deeper and rounder, as a fond normally would.

There were only a few recipes where we learned we couldn't skip browning the meat, particularly our Bolognese Sauce (page 248). While we were able to simplify traditional Bolognese recipes by finishing up ours in the slow cooker, the initial reduction of liquids over browned meat and vegetables proved key to getting that deep, trademark Bolognese flavor we were after.

We also found our slow cooker was the ideal appliance for making robustly flavored chicken broth at home (see page 243). While not a hearty meal unto itself, chicken broth is the foundation of numerous recipes, and though there are times when a store-bought broth will work, there are many recipes whose success depends on a rich, deeply flavored broth as the cornerstone ingredient (consider almost any broth-based soup, such as wonton or chicken noodle). Here, once again, our slow cooker came to the rescue.

You will notice that the recipes in this chapter all have a range of cooking times. Establishing cooking times for slow-cooker recipes is not an exact science, and every machine is a little different, so take our guidelines as a good approximation of how long the cooking will likely take rather than as an absolute. The bottom line is that you need to get to know your own slow cooker by trying it out on a variety of recipes.

SLOW-COOKER POT ROAST

POT ROAST RECIPES APPEAR IN EVERY COOK-book featuring slow cookers and are touted as "starter" recipes in the ubiquitous manuals that come with the appliance. And justly so, for pot roast is a natural for the slow cooker. The problem is that many slow-cooker pot roasts turn out dry and stringy, floating in a vat of greasy, flavorless, watery

liquid. Yet another issue is size. We found many recipes that called for 2½- to 3-pound roasts, but after 10 hours in the slow cooker, the catch phrase "Where's the beef?" took on new meaning. We wanted to turn this supposedly basic, "entry-level" meal into something beyond ordinary. We had our work cut out for us.

We started with the incredible shrinking roast issue. Our initial testing showed that the average beef chuck eye roast shrank by as much as 2 pounds during the prolonged cooking time, which quickly eliminated the smaller roasts. To compensate for this shrinkage, we decided to use roasts that weighed 5 to 6 pounds.

Previous pot roast tests had shown that reaching and sustaining an internal temperature of 200 to 210 degrees was necessary for a meltingly tender piece of meat. To determine how long it would take a 5- or 6-pound roast to reach that point in the slow cooker, we conducted tests using temperature probes inserted into the center of roasts cooked on both low and high. The ideal time in our 6-quart slow cooker was nine to 11 hours on low or five to seven hours on high. With the size and time set, we moved on to flavoring.

As would be the case with our other slow-cooker recipes for this chapter, we wanted to keep things simple and skip browning the meat before adding it to the slow cooker. Though we were worried that doing so would have an adverse effect with such a large cut, we were actually pleased to find that after 10 hours in the slow cooker, both the texture and the exterior color of the unbrowned roast were fine. And though the flavor was good overall, we wanted to find a way to get back that depth that comes from browning meat and deglazing the pan. We created a faux fond by sautéing our aromatics, with tomato paste to encourage browning, before adding them to the slow cooker. We also added soy sauce to the slow cooker to draw out more beefy flavor. Combined with chicken broth, red wine, and tomatoes, our braising liquid was now full flavored and was at a good jumping-off point for our final sauce, or "gravy," to accompany the roast.

We wanted our gravy to be thick enough to coat the slices of pot roast without being pasty. We tried cornstarch, flour, and even corn tortillas as thickeners. In the end, instant tapioca proved to be ideal since it could be added at the beginning of cooking without imparting an off-flavor to the dish. Finished with a hefty amount of chopped fresh parsley, this was tender pot roast and flavorful gravy that proved a "starter" recipe can go far beyond everyday expectation.

Slow-Cooker Pot Roast

SERVES 6 TO 8

In most markets, you will have to special order a large 5- to 6-pound beef chuck eye roast. Alternatively, you can use two 3-pound roasts (which are easier to find). The pot roast will shrink significantly as it cooks in the slow cooker. A $7 to $10 bottle of medium-bodied red table wine made from a blend of grapes, such as a Côtes du Rhône, will work well here. See below for make-ahead instructions.

1	(28-ounce) can diced tomatoes
2	tablespoons vegetable oil
3	medium onions, minced
¼	cup tomato paste
8	medium garlic cloves, minced or pressed through a garlic press (about 8 teaspoons)
1	tablespoon minced fresh thyme leaves, or 1 teaspoon dried
	Salt
¾	cup dry red wine (see note)
¾	cup low-sodium chicken broth
2	medium carrots, cut into 1-inch pieces
6	tablespoons Minute tapioca
⅓	cup soy sauce
1	(5- to 6-pound) boneless beef chuck eye roast, tied at 1-inch intervals (see note)
	Ground black pepper
¼	cup minced fresh parsley leaves

1. Process the tomatoes with their juice in a food processor until smooth, about 15 seconds and set aside. Heat the oil in a 12-inch nonstick skillet over medium heat until shimmering. Add the onions, tomato paste, garlic, thyme, and ¼ teaspoon salt and cook, stirring often, until the vegetables are softened and lightly browned, 10 to 12 minutes. Stir in the wine, scraping up any browned bits.

2. Transfer the mixture to the slow cooker and stir in the tomatoes, broth, carrots, tapioca, and soy sauce until evenly combined. Season the meat with salt and pepper and nestle it into the slow cooker. Cover and cook, either on low or high, until the meat is tender, 9 to 11 hours on low or 5 to 7 hours on high.

3. Transfer the roast to a cutting board, tent loosely with foil, and let rest for 20 minutes. Let the cooking liquid settle for 5 minutes, then gently tilt the slow cooker and remove as much fat as possible from the surface using a large spoon. Stir in the parsley and season with salt and pepper to taste.

4. Untie the roast and slice into ½-inch-thick pieces. Arrange the meat on a serving platter and pour 1 cup of the sauce over the top. Serve, passing the remaining sauce separately.

➤ VARIATION
Slow-Cooker Southwestern-Style Pot Roast

For a milder flavor, use a smaller amount of chipotle chiles.

Follow the recipe for Slow-Cooker Pot Roast, adding 3 tablespoons chili powder and 2 tablespoons ground cumin with the onions in step 1 and substituting 1 tablespoon minced fresh oregano (or 1 teaspoon dried) for the thyme. Omit the wine, increase the chicken broth to 1½ cups, and add 2 to 4 teaspoons minced chipotle chile in adobo sauce with the tomatoes in step 2. Substitute 3 tablespoons minced fresh cilantro leaves for the parsley.

MAKE-AHEAD TIPS FOR SLOW COOKERS

Slow-cooker recipes provide you with the ultimate make-ahead meal—all of the ingredients go into the pot in the morning and when you come home from work, a hearty, satisfying meal is waiting for you. The trick is that there is a certain amount of prep work that must be done before you can assemble everything in one pot. The good news is that if you would prefer not to spend time in the morning chopping and sautéing vegetables, much of it can be done the night before. For the recipes in this chapter, here are some things you can do the night before to save time in the morning.

1. Cook the onion mixture as described (in step 1 and/or 2 of most recipes), then transfer it to an airtight container and refrigerate.
2. Prep any vegetables (except potatoes) and refrigerate.
3. Trim and cut the meat and refrigerate (be sure to store meat separately from other ingredients).

SLOW-COOKER BEEF STEW

RECIPES FOR SLOW-COOKER BEEF STEW ARE divided into two types. In one, the meat, vegetables, and seasoning are simply dumped into a pot and left to their own devices. Effortless, yes. But flavorful? We'd have to say no. The second type of stew, the one in which the meat is browned before it goes into the slow cooker, is the more flavorful. Here the foundation for flavor is built on the browned bits left behind, which are the backbone of the stew's sauce. But in developing a recipe for slow-cooker beef stew for this cookbook, where our goal was to maximize flavor with extended cooking and minimize labor, we needed to streamline our kitchen work, not spend 45 minutes getting the stew ready before it even went into the slow cooker. Could we skip browning the meat and still end up with a richly flavored beef stew? Browning meat was so ingrained into our culinary educations that we never considered it optional until now, when convenience and simplicity dictated that we find a way around it. Needless to say, we had reservations.

To begin our testing, we decided to prepare two recipes. For one, we browned the meat (we opted for a beef chuck eye roast) as we've always done. For the other, we skipped the browning step and simply dumped everything raw into the slow cooker. Once the cooking time was up, we lifted the lids and, to our surprise, found that we couldn't tell the two stews apart, at least visually. But flavor is what really matters and, after tasting each one, we found that the stew with the browned meat was indeed beefier and richer.

We knew that in order to successfully justify jettisoning the browning step, we needed to come up with a flavor replacement for the fond. We tried an array of "browning sauces," like Gravy Master and Kitchen Bouquet, as well as bouillon cubes and different combinations of beef and chicken broth. After extensive testing, we landed on a winning solution. We used a combination of soy sauce (its salty elements reinforced the beefy flavor and added deep color) and tomato paste, which we browned along with the onions before adding them to the slow cooker. This step created additional flavor notes and also took care of the problem with throwing onions into the slow cooker raw, which tasters agreed made the stew taste vegetal and the onions sour.

There were, however, still those in the test kitchen who were having a hard time coming to grips with this unconventional, unbrowned approach to a full-flavored stew. To make sure that everyone was on board with our new technique, we conducted a blind taste test of three stews, side by side: browned beef stew, unbrowned beef stew with no flavor replacement, and unbrowned beef stew with our fond replacement of sautéed aromatics, tomato paste, and soy sauce. Unaware of the different methods used, the majority of tasters favored the third stew. We were happy that taste buds, rather than preconceived notions, settled the controversy. Our third stew was rich and full-bodied, and we were pleased with how much time we had saved. Knowing that our test cooks are a tough crowd to please, we were satisfied that we had landed on a reliable way to save valuable prep time, without sacrificing flavor.

Satisfied with our faux fond, we moved on to address one troubling issue that resulted from not browning: greasiness. Because browning helps to render fat and we were now not browning, our stew had a grease slick on top that tasters found disturbing. Up until now, we had been using a chuck eye roast that we trimmed and cut into 1½-inch pieces. Wondering if leaner roasts would solve our problem, we tested five stews made with different cuts of beef: top round, bottom round, eye round, rump roast, and top sirloin. After all that work, it turned out that none were as flavorful and tender as the chuck eye roast. All of the others were too lean, resulting in flavorless, dry meat. We decided that we didn't mind using a spoon to skim a bit of grease from the stew if that was what it would take to get maximum flavor, so we returned to the chuck eye.

The next dilemma was how to thicken our stew. Many recipes turn to a slurry (a starch stirred together with liquid) of either flour or cornstarch, which has to be stirred into the stew at the end of the cooking time. While both of these options ultimately worked to thicken the stew, they tasted starchy and required a lag time to allow the starch to fully thicken the stew. We found that instant tapioca, stirred in at the onset of cooking, worked like magic. Our stew was thick without being tacky, there was no raw, starchy aftertaste, and it required no last-minute fussing.

Moving on, we wanted to find a way to prevent the potatoes from disintegrating as they simmered away for hours in the slow cooker. Leaving them whole worked OK, but some still busted apart, which meant we had to add an extra step of cutting the potatoes up before serving. Stealing a trick often used in grilling, we made a "hobo pack" by wrapping the potatoes (and carrots, for good measure) in a foil packet. Then we placed the packet on top of the beef in the slow cooker. When we opened the packet and poured the tender vegetables and their

juices back into the stew at the end of cooking, the results were amazing. The carrots and potatoes were both perfectly cooked and the potatoes were perfectly intact. Finally, we had a slow-cooker beef stew that was easy to make and tasted great.

MAKING A FOIL PACKET

We discovered that the best way to keep vegetables from disintegrating after 10 or more hours in the slow cooker is to wrap them in a foil packet, or "hobo pack." Keeping the vegetables out of the stewing liquid slows down their cooking time and keeps their flavors distinct. Here's how you do it:

1. Place the vegetables on one side of a large piece of foil. Fold the foil over, shaping it into a packet that will fit into your slow cooker, then crimp to seal the edges.

2. Place the foil packet directly on top of the stew, pressing gently as needed to make it fit inside the cooker.

Slow-Cooker Beef Stew
SERVES 6 TO 8

Feel free to add a pound of parsnips, peeled and cut into 1-inch pieces, to the foil packet along with the carrots and potatoes. See page 204 for make-ahead instructions.

- 3 tablespoons vegetable oil
- 4 medium onions, minced
- ¼ cup tomato paste
- 6 medium garlic cloves, minced or pressed through a garlic press (about 2 tablespoons)
- 1 tablespoon minced fresh thyme leaves, or 1 teaspoon dried
  Salt
- 1½ cups low-sodium chicken broth
- 1½ cups low-sodium beef broth
- ⅓ cup soy sauce
- 2 tablespoons Minute tapioca
- 2 bay leaves
- 1 (5-pound) boneless beef chuck eye roast, trimmed and cut into 1½-inch pieces
  Ground black pepper
- 1½ pounds red potatoes, cut into 1-inch pieces
- 1 pound carrots (about 6 medium), peeled and cut into 1-inch pieces
- 2 cups frozen peas

1. Heat 2 tablespoons of the oil in a 12-inch nonstick skillet over medium-high heat until shimmering. Add the onions, tomato paste, garlic, thyme, and ¼ teaspoon salt and cook, stirring often, until the onions are softened and lightly browned, 10 to 12 minutes. Stir in the chicken broth, scraping up any browned bits.

2. Transfer the mixture to the slow cooker and stir in the beef broth, soy sauce, tapioca, and bay leaves until evenly combined. Season the beef with salt and pepper and nestle it in the slow cooker.

3. Toss the potatoes, carrots, and remaining 1 tablespoon oil together and season with salt

and pepper. Following the illustrations on page 206, wrap the vegetables in a foil packet. Set the vegetable packet on top of the stew in the slow cooker. Cover and cook, either on low or high, until the meat is tender, 9 to 11 hours on low or 5 to 7 hours on high.

4. Transfer the vegetable packet to a plate. Let the cooking liquid settle for 5 minutes, then gently tilt the slow cooker and remove as much fat as possible from the surface using a large spoon. Remove the bay leaves. Carefully open the foil packet (watch for steam), then stir the vegetables, along with any accumulated juices, into the stew. Stir in the peas and let stand until the peas are heated through, about 5 minutes longer. Season with salt and pepper to taste before serving.

➤ VARIATION

Slow-Cooker Beef Burgundy

We prefer to use Pinot Noir in this recipe, but any $7 to $10 bottle of medium-bodied red table wine made from a blend of grapes, such as a Côtes du Rhône, will work. Regular bacon can be substituted for the thick-cut bacon. See page 204 for make-ahead instructions.

8	ounces (about 6 slices) thick-cut bacon, cut into ¼-inch pieces
3	medium onions, minced
I	medium carrot, peeled and chopped fine
¼	cup tomato paste
6	medium garlic cloves, minced or pressed through a garlic press (about 2 tablespoons)
I	tablespoon minced fresh thyme leaves, or I teaspoon dried
	Salt
I	(750-ml) bottle Pinot Noir (see note)
I	cup low-sodium chicken broth
⅓	cup soy sauce
2	tablespoons Minute tapioca
2	bay leaves
I	(5-pound) boneless beef chuck eye roast, trimmed and cut into 1½-inch pieces
	Ground black pepper
2	cups frozen pearl onions
½	cup water
3	tablespoons unsalted butter
2	teaspoons sugar
10	ounces cremini mushrooms, trimmed, wiped clean, and halved if small or quartered if large

1. Cook the bacon in a 12-inch nonstick skillet over medium heat until crisp, about 8 minutes. Transfer the bacon to a paper towel–lined plate, leaving the fat in the skillet, and refrigerate until serving time.

2. Pour off all but 2 tablespoons of the bacon fat left in the skillet and heat over medium-high heat until shimmering. Add the onions, carrot, tomato paste, garlic, thyme, and ¼ teaspoon salt and cook, stirring often, until the vegetables are softened and lightly browned, 10 to 12 minutes. Stir in the wine, scraping up any browned bits, bring to a simmer, and cook until the mixture measures about 3 cups, 10 to 12 minutes.

3. Transfer the mixture to the slow cooker and stir in the chicken broth, soy sauce, tapioca, and bay leaves until evenly combined. Season the beef with salt and pepper and nestle it in the slow cooker. Cover and cook, either on low or high, until the meat is tender, 9 to 11 hours on low or 5 to 7 hours on high.

4. About 20 minutes before serving, bring the frozen pearl onions, water, butter, and sugar to a boil in large nonstick skillet over medium-high heat. Reduce the heat to medium, cover, and cook until the onions are fully thawed and tender, 5 to 8 minutes. Uncover, increase the heat to medium-high, and cook until all the liquid evaporates, 3 to 4 minutes. Add the mushrooms and ¼ teaspoon salt and cook, without stirring, for 2 minutes. Stir and continue to cook, stirring often, until the vegetables are browned and glazed, 8 to 12 minutes. Remove from the heat and set aside.

5. Let the cooking liquid settle for 5 minutes, then gently tilt the slow cooker and remove as much fat as possible from the surface using a large spoon. Remove the bay leaves, stir in the pearl onion mixture, and season with salt and pepper to taste. Reheat the bacon in the microwave on high power until heated through and crisp, about 30 seconds. Sprinkle individual portions of stew with the crisp bacon before serving.

Slow-Cooker Hungarian Beef Goulash

GOULASH IS A HUNGARIAN STEW MADE with chunks of beef and robustly flavored with Hungarian paprika. When made correctly, it's rich and satisfying. The problem is that it's not easy to get it right in the slow cooker, and our first attempts turned out watery and bland.

Beef, onions, garlic, and paprika are the constants in this dish. Other possible ingredients include potatoes, tomatoes, and bell peppers. Our goal was to create a very simple stew with tender, flavorful beef in a rich, intensely flavored sauce. The sauce would be rusty in color, both from the paprika and from the good browning that the onions would receive.

To decide what cut of meat to use, we looked to tests we had done for our Slow-Cooker Beef Stew (page 205). After testing five different cuts—top round, bottom round, eye round, rump roast, and top sirloin—none proved as flavorful and tender as the chuck eye roast. Chuck eye isn't a particularly lean cut, but we didn't mind skimming a bit of grease off our goulash with a spoon if that was what it would take to get the best flavor and texture.

We also knew from our beef stew that because the meat for the goulash went into the slow cooker unbrowned, replacing the brown fond would be important. To begin, we cooked the onions, tomato paste, and a hefty quantity of good-quality Hungarian paprika to a deep brown. This pretoasting of the tomato paste and paprika added the traditional deep rust color that we were looking for, which, to our surprise, withstood the time in the slow cooker. Then we added the unusual ingredient that had served us well in our stew recipe: soy sauce, for its salty, beef-like flavor.

Although we agreed onions were a must, the recipes we looked at were divided on the question of garlic. Tasters, however, were not. Everyone in the test kitchen liked garlic in this stew. Six cloves added depth and also balanced the sweetness of the paprika and onions. The quantity of paprika was the next problem to solve. Too much and the

INGREDIENTS: Paprika

Both sweet and hot paprika come from the dried pods of *Capsicum annuum L.*, which includes a large swath of pepper varieties ranging from sweet red bell peppers to hot chile peppers. The type of pepper used will influence the flavor, spiciness, and intensity of the paprika. Sweet paprika is made from only the middle layer of the pepper's outer wall (the mesocarp), while hot paprika also contains some of the white veins (the placenta) and seeds, where most of the heat resides. Most paprika labeled "paprika" or "mild paprika" is of the sweet variety.

Heat aside, we wanted to find out if there were any flavor differences between the two varieties and if one was better suited for a particular type of recipe than another. We took our winning brand (Penzeys Hungary Sweet Paprika) and its spicy counterpart (Penzeys Half-Sharp Paprika, the retailer's only type of hot paprika) and used each in three applications: Hungarian beef goulash, barbecue sauce, and a dry rub for baked chicken breasts. Most tasters found the sweet paprika, with its "bright," "well-balanced," and "smoky" flavors, to be a better choice in the goulash; the hot paprika was less flavorful, aside from its pronounced heat. The differences were even more apparent in the spice-rubbed chicken breasts, where the hot paprika took on an unpleasant bitter edge. In the barbecue sauce, however, tasters found both varieties perfectly acceptable, and some preferred the sauce made with the hot paprika. Here, its spiciness seemed less aggressive and was actually a virtue.

If you're just going to buy one paprika, we recommend stocking the more versatile sweet, as a pinch or two of cayenne pepper can be added to replicate the flavor of the hot stuff.

goulash tasted bitter, almost burnt. Too little and we ended up with a goulash that paled in comparison to our standard stovetop recipe. We settled on ¼ cup, which provided the perfect amount of flavor and color without being overpowering.

Recipes uncovered in our research used an assortment of liquids, including water, beef broth, and chicken broth. We found that water created a bland stew, and store-bought beef broth, in conjunction with the large volume of paprika, contributed a bitter edge to the goulash. Chicken broth proved to be the best option, lending the stew solid body and just enough richness without competing with the other flavorings. Some recipes also include wine in the mix, although authentic recipes do not. We tried varying amounts of red wine, and tasters felt that its flavor was overpowering. Goulash should be soft and mellow, and while red wine added complexity, it also made the stew acidic and a bit harsh. A few sources suggested white wine, but tasters were again unimpressed, so we stuck with tradition and left wine out. Our recipe was coming together.

Many Hungarian goulash recipes do not include sour cream, which seems more popular in German and Austrian versions, but our tasters all felt that sour cream mellowed and enriched this stew. To prevent the sour cream from curdling, we combined it with a little of the hot stewing liquid to temper it, and then stirred the mixture back into the slow cooker.

Goulash is traditionally served over buttered egg noodles or spaetzle. Egg noodles require almost no effort to cook and are our first choice. Mashed potatoes are not traditional, but they make an excellent accompaniment too.

Slow-Cooker Hungarian Beef Goulash

SERVES 6 TO 8

If you like things spicy, feel free to add a pinch of cayenne pepper or hot paprika. Serve over buttered egg noodles and garnish with some minced fresh parsley just before serving. See page 204 for make-ahead instructions.

2	tablespoons vegetable oil
3	medium onions, minced
¼	cup sweet paprika (see note)
¼	cup tomato paste
6	medium garlic cloves, minced or pressed through a garlic press (about 2 tablespoons)
1	teaspoon caraway seeds
	Salt
2	cups low-sodium chicken broth
⅓	cup soy sauce
¼	cup Minute tapioca
2	bay leaves
1	(5-pound) boneless beef chuck eye roast, trimmed and cut into 1½-inch pieces
	Ground black pepper
½	cup sour cream

1. Heat the oil in a 12-inch nonstick skillet over medium-high heat until shimmering. Add the onions, paprika, tomato paste, garlic, caraway seeds, and ¼ teaspoon salt and cook, stirring often, until the onions are softened and lightly browned, 10 to 12 minutes. Stir in the chicken broth, scraping up any browned bits.

2. Transfer the mixture to the slow cooker and stir in the soy sauce, tapioca, and bay leaves until evenly combined. Season the meat with salt and pepper and nestle it in the slow cooker. Cover and cook, either on low or high, until the meat is tender, 9 to 11 hours on low or 5 to 7 hours on high.

3. Let the cooking liquid settle for 5 minutes, then gently tilt the slow cooker and remove as much fat as possible from the surface using a large spoon. Remove the bay leaves. In a small bowl, stir 1 cup of the cooking liquid into the sour cream to temper, then stir the sour cream mixture back into the stew. Season with salt and pepper to taste before serving.

SLOW-COOKER ROPA VIEJA

THERE ARE MANY DISHES BASED ON TRADITION that have stood the test of time because they boast rich, vibrant flavors while requiring surprisingly few ingredients. Such is the case with *ropa vieja*. A Cuban Creole dish by origin, ropa vieja is a simple preparation of shredded beef with peppers and onions that are simmered in a flavorful sauce highlighted by tomatoes, garlic, cumin, and oregano. Though traditionally prepared on the stovetop, ropa vieja seemed like a natural fit for our slow cooker given its long simmering time. So we set out to see if we could utilize our favored cooking technique and still capture the many layers of flavor found in this Cuban classic.

The first decision was what type of beef to use. Most recipes call for either a beef brisket or a skirt steak. When we tasted these side by side, tasters were unanimous in their opinion: skirt steak was

EQUIPMENT:
Inexpensive Nonstick Skillets

Nothing takes the challenge out of cooking stir-fries and delicate foods, like eggs, better than a nonstick skillet. A nonstick skillet is also great for sautéing aromatics for many of our slow-cooker recipes; the slick coating makes it a breeze to scrape up the browned bits left behind that add essential flavor to these dishes. The downside is that nonstick skillets are easily damaged—the coating inevitably scratches, chips off, or becomes ineffective—so we find it best to buy inexpensive ones. We tested eight 12-inch nonstick skillets ranging in price from $8.99 to $60. Our main criticisms focused on durability (some pans were downright flimsy and beat up after just a few uses); weight (a couple were ridiculously heavy, making them difficult to maneuver); and pan construction (placement and type of handles as well as actual usable cooking space, which ranged from 9 inches to 10½ inches). The Wearever Hard-Anodized Nonstick Skillet ($29.99) was our favorite—sturdy but lightweight, it was a breeze to maneuver and has a comfortable handle that stayed cool on the stovetop.

THE BEST INEXPENSIVE NONSTICK SKILLET

WEAREVER

The Wearever Hard-Anodized Nonstick Skillet ($29.99) offers the best combination of nonstick performance and solid construction.

the clear winner. They found it to be more tender and succulent. Skirt steak shredded easily and some described it as less chewy than the brisket, and it had the added benefit of a shorter cooking time. Because skirt steak can be hard to find, we tested flank steak as well. It was a touch less tender, but still better suited to this dish than brisket, making it a good second choice. With our meat decision made, we now turned to the broth and overall cooking method.

In our research, we found that authentic recipes call for making a large batch of beef broth from the meat and then simmering the beef in a flavorful sauce with onions and peppers. The beef broth is then reduced and used in making the final dish. However, after a few long days in the kitchen making beef broth, we were left with gallons of extra broth and pounds of gray, overcooked beef. We wondered if there was a different way to approach this dish. Since we didn't need all that extra broth, could we simply braise the meat in the slow cooker and then use the braising liquid as our broth? This turned out to be a perfect solution. Using just enough water to barely cover the meat left us with a highly concentrated beef broth that we could use in the dish, and our meat was cooked until it shredded easily but still retained its juiciness.

Although meats are typically browned before being added to the slow cooker, we decided to find out if we could skip this step, as we had with several of our other slow-cooker recipes, by utilizing a fond replacement in lieu of browning. We set up two slow cookers, one with browned meat and raw aromatics and the other with raw meat and browned aromatics. By browning the aromatics with tomato paste, we replaced the flavors of the fond that we had lost by not browning the meat, and adding soy sauce to the slow cooker provided depth. In the end, tasters had trouble distinguishing between the two batches. Since it is easier to sauté aromatics than to sear meat, we went with the former. We could now turn our attention to the flavors in the sauce and the finishing touches.

The recipes we found in our research all called for sautéing onions, green peppers, and garlic together with cumin and oregano, then adding some wine, tomato sauce, homemade beef broth, and olives, and finally simmering this sauce to let the flavors combine. In these recipes, the shredded beef is prepared separately, then tossed in at the end and heated through. After a failed attempt at simply combining everything in the slow cooker, we stuck with tradition and sautéed the sauce ingredients in a Dutch oven, then added the slow-cooked, shredded meat and its broth.

In our initial tests for the sauce, tasters thought the inclusion of tomato sauce imparted an overcooked tomato flavor. We were after a fresher and brighter taste. We tried canned crushed tomatoes, canned diced tomatoes, and canned whole tomatoes. The crushed tomatoes varied significantly in taste and quality, depending on the brand. The diced tomatoes were a bit too chunky in the sauce and did not have enough time to cook down, and the whole tomatoes presented the same problem. We found that crushing the diced tomatoes in the food processor with a few quick pulses, before adding them to the sauce, was the best way to get the texture and fresh taste we were looking for.

Finally, we experimented with the peppers. Green peppers are a staple in ropa vieja, but we tried also adding some red peppers to offset the some-times bitter taste that green peppers impart. Tasters liked the red peppers and found they contributed a pleasant sweetness. With a splash of vinegar at the end to brighten the flavor and a handful of chopped parsley, we now had a ropa vieja to savor.

Slow-Cooker Ropa Vieja
SERVES 6 TO 8

This classic Cuban Creole dish combines shredded beef with bell peppers and onions in a flavorful sauce. We slightly prefer skirt steak to flank steak because it has a more tender texture, but it can be difficult to find. Serve with rice. See page 204 for make-ahead instructions.

MEAT

2 tablespoons vegetable oil
2 medium onions, minced
¼ cup tomato paste
2 medium garlic cloves, minced or pressed through a garlic press (about 2 teaspoons)
Salt
2½ cups water
¼ cup soy sauce
2 bay leaves
2½ pounds skirt or flank steak, cut into 3-inch pieces (see note)
Ground black pepper

PEPPERS AND SAUCE

1 (14.5-ounce) can diced tomatoes
2 tablespoons vegetable oil
2 large red bell peppers, stemmed, seeded, and sliced into thin strips
2 large green bell peppers, stemmed, seeded, and sliced into thin strips
1 medium onion, halved and sliced thin
Salt
3 medium garlic cloves, minced or pressed through a garlic press (about 1 tablespoon)
1 teaspoon dried oregano
¾ teaspoon ground cumin
½ cup dry white wine
½ cup pimiento-stuffed green olives, rinsed and halved
2 tablespoons fresh minced parsley leaves
1–3 tablespoons white wine vinegar
Ground black pepper

1. FOR THE MEAT: Heat the oil in a 12-inch nonstick skillet over medium-high heat until shimmering. Add the onions, tomato paste, garlic, and ¼ teaspoon salt and cook, stirring often, until softened and lightly browned, 8 to 10 minutes. Stir in the water, scraping up any browned bits.

2. Transfer the mixture to the slow cooker and stir in the soy sauce and bay leaves until evenly combined. Season the meat with salt and pepper and nestle it in the slow cooker. Cover and cook, either on low or high, until the meat is tender, 9 to 11 hours on low or 5 to 7 hours on high.

3. Transfer the meat to a platter and cool slightly. Using 2 forks, shred the meat into small pieces, discarding any fat, following the illustration on page 104. Let the cooking liquid settle for 5 minutes, then gently tilt the slow cooker and remove as much fat as possible from the surface using a large spoon. Measure out and reserve 2 cups of the cooking liquid, discarding any extra liquid.

4. FOR THE PEPPERS AND SAUCE: Pulse the tomatoes with their juice in a food processor until coarsely pureed, about 7 pulses, and set aside. Heat the oil in a large Dutch oven over medium-high heat until shimmering. Add the bell peppers, onion, and ½ teaspoon salt and cook, stirring often, until the vegetables are softened and lightly browned, 8 to 10 minutes. Stir in the garlic, oregano, and cumin and cook until fragrant, about 1 minute. Stir in the wine, scraping up any browned bits. Stir in the processed tomatoes, olives, and 2 cups reserved cooking liquid from the meat, bring to a

simmer, and cook, stirring often, until the peppers are soft and the sauce has thickened slightly, 12 to 15 minutes.

5. Stir in the shredded meat and continue to cook until the meat is heated through and the flavors have combined, about 5 minutes. Stir in the parsley and 1 tablespoon of the vinegar. Season with the remaining 2 tablespoons vinegar, salt, and pepper to taste before serving.

SLOW-COOKER BRISKET

MOST PEOPLE (TEXANS ANYWAY) WILL TELL you there's no way that good barbecue can come from a slow cooker. Traditional recipes require that you cook the brisket low and slow on a real outdoor grill, with charcoal and wood chips, and spend lots of time tending the fire. The brisket comes out tender, juicy, and full of that smoky flavor that is the essence of the real deal. But what if you want barbecued brisket in winter and you don't care much for tending a grill in the cold or snow? We wondered if this summertime favorite could be made indoors, in the slow cooker. It was worth a shot.

Classic recipes for brisket call for a spice rub that is spread over the meat, which then sits overnight in the refrigerator so that the flavors permeate it. We put together a simple rub of brown sugar, paprika, onion powder, garlic powder, cumin, and cayenne, rubbed the meat thoroughly with it, and let it sit overnight. In the morning, it was time to cook the brisket, and we moved on to choosing what kind of liquid (and how much of it) should be added to the slow cooker.

While the inside of a covered grill is similar to a sauna, the slow cooker is more like the steam room across the hall, with moisture rather than dry heat as the cooking medium. For our first test, we tried adding 2 cups of beef broth to the slow cooker, an amount that barely covered the brisket. Hours later, when we lifted the lid, we were surprised at what we found. The brisket was literally floating in liquid,

a whopping 7 cups of it. And this liquid had a very diluted beefy flavor. We wondered if we could cut back on the broth and thereby concentrate the flavor. We tested quantities all the way down to ½ cup and were still disappointed with the wateriness of the sauce. Then we wondered what would happen if we replaced the broth with something a bit more flavorful and viscous, like barbecue sauce. Unwilling to take time to make our own, we reached for our favorite store-bought brand and ladled some over the top of the brisket. We were initially concerned that we weren't adding enough liquid to the slow cooker, but when the brisket was done, we realized we needn't have worried. So much juice came out of the brisket that there was plenty of liquid in the slow cooker (about 4 cups), and it was packed with flavor. The barbecue sauce imparted just the right amount of smokiness to the brisket—a flavor that we thought could compete with that of a brisket cooked outdoors. We knew we were getting closer to a great indoor brisket, but the meat was still not as tender as we felt it should be.

All slow-cooked meat suffers from the same Catch-22 situation. For the normally tough meat to become tender, its connective tissues must be broken down, which requires hours of low-temperature cooking. But as the meat cooks, the muscle fibers slowly contract, expelling moisture and often leaving the meat dry. The amount and distribution of the fat in the meat can make a big difference. A chuck roast will taste succulent after a proper braise because of its relatively high amount and even distribution of fat. In a brisket, however, most of the fat is located in an exterior cap and in a few thick layers; it is not marbled throughout. As a result, fat renders into the sauce rather than basting the interior of the meat, which is rather lean. We knew we couldn't keep moisture from leaving the meat, but wondered if there was a way to get the meat to reabsorb some of the liquid after cooking.

Up until this point, we had been removing the brisket from the sauce and letting it rest on a carving board before attempting to cut it into thin, neat slices. (Like a flank steak, brisket has long muscle fibers and must be sliced against the grain to avoid being chewy. These same long fibers, however, turn into shreds once connective tissue has been dissolved, making the meat difficult to slice.) We decided to try letting the meat rest in the sauce before slicing it, with the hope that it would reabsorb some of the flavorful liquid it had lost. This time the brisket was noticeably better. Then it occurred to us that if we poked some holes in the brisket and covered it with a little of the sauce, even more moisture and flavor might return to the meat. This worked like a charm, and we soon realized that the longer the brisket sits in the sauce after cooking, the more tender it becomes.

However, letting the beef sit in the sauce for a long time after it is cooked isn't very convenient—one of the main reasons home cooks use a slow cooker is so that they can have dinner on the table within minutes of getting home from work. With this in mind, we determined that the minimal amount of time the brisket should rest in the sauce before serving was 30 minutes.

Now that we had successfully developed a slow-cooker version of barbecued brisket, we began to wonder if this method would work with another barbecue classic: pulled pork. Using the traditional roast used for pulled pork—a boneless pork Boston butt—we gave the recipe a whirl, with great success. After cooking, the pork roast fell apart into tender, juicy shreds. By first removing the tender, falling-apart roast from the sauce, we could easily shred the pork properly (ridding it of any gristle) and degrease and season the sauce. The tender pulled pork and flavorful sauce are a perfect pair on a hamburger bun.

SLICING BRISKET

Use a long sharp knife to cut the meat against the grain into thin slices. Slicing it with the grain will result in tough, stringy slices.

Slow-Cooker Barbecued Brisket

SERVES 6 TO 8

For our brisket, we prefer flat cut; for more information about buying brisket, see page 143. You can either make your own barbecue sauce (see Classic Barbecue Sauce on page 35), or use your favorite store-bought brand—we like Bull's Eye Original.

¼ cup packed light brown sugar,
   plus extra to taste
¼ cup paprika
I tablespoon onion powder
I tablespoon garlic powder
I tablespoon ground cumin
I teaspoon cayenne
   Salt
I (4- to 5-pound) beef brisket,
   preferably flat cut (see note)
I cup barbecue sauce (see note)
   Cider vinegar
   Ground black pepper

1. Mix the sugar, paprika, onion powder, garlic powder, cumin, cayenne, and ½ teaspoon salt together, then rub the mixture evenly over the meat. Wrap the meat tightly in plastic wrap and refrigerate for at least 8 hours, or up to 12 hours.

2. Unwrap the brisket and lay it fat side up in the slow cooker. Spread the barbecue sauce evenly over the brisket. Cover and cook, either on low or high, until the meat is very tender and meets little resistance when poked with a fork, 9 to 11 hours on low or 5 to 7 hours on high.

3. Transfer the brisket to a 13 by 9-inch baking dish and cover loosely with foil. Let the cooking liquid settle for 5 minutes, then gently tilt the slow cooker and remove as much fat as possible from the surface using a large spoon. Season the sauce with additional sugar, vinegar, salt, and pepper to taste.

4. Poke the brisket all over with a fork, pour 1 cup of the sauce over top, and let it rest, covered, for at least 30 minutes. Following the illustration at left, thinly slice the brisket across the grain. Arrange the meat on a serving platter and serve, passing the remaining sauce separately.

➤ VARIATION
Slow-Cooker Pulled Pork
Follow the recipe for Slow-Cooker Barbecued Brisket, substituting 1 (5- to 6-pound) boneless pork butt, cut in half lengthwise, for the brisket, and skipping step 4. To serve, shred the pork while still hot using two dinner forks, discarding any fat, following the illustration on page 104. Toss the shredded pork with 1 cup of the sauce, if desired adding more to taste, and serve on hamburger buns, passing the remaining sauce separately.

SLOW-COOKER WEEKNIGHT CHILI

GROUND BEEF CHILI IS A NATURAL FOR THE slow cooker but, despite the myriad recipes for it, most that we tested turned out watery and bland. We were looking for a hearty all-American chili, with rich flavors and a thick, substantial texture—perfect as a foil for all those wonderful accompaniments (which are half the reason for making chili in the first place), like a dollop of sour cream, a sprinkling of cheese, a smattering of diced onions or avocado, or the fresh touch of cilantro or chives.

Most recipes begin by cooking and draining ground meat, then sautéing onions, garlic, and peppers. Always on the lookout for ways to shorten prep time, our first order of business was to see if we needed to cook the meat before it went into the slow cooker. We learned some tricks in our beef stew testing (see page 205) that allowed us to bypass browning by creating a faux fond with sautéed aromatics and tomato paste, so we followed that method here. Pitting chili made with browned beef against one made with raw beef and the faux fond method, we found little discernable difference between the two.

Now ready to zero in on flavors, we tried varying amounts of onion, garlic, peppers, celery, and carrots. Tasters liked a hefty quantity of onion and garlic, but they put the kibosh on the peppers, celery, and carrots because they made the chili taste too vegetal and sweet. After this first step, things

became less clear. The most pressing concerns were the spices (how much and what kind) and the details concerning the meat (how much and what fat content). There was also the cooking liquid (what kind, if any) to resolve and the quantities of tomatoes and beans to consider.

Our first experiments with these ingredients followed a formula we had seen in a lot of recipes: 2 pounds ground beef, 3 tablespoons chili powder, 2 teaspoons ground cumin, and 1 teaspoon each red pepper flakes and dried oregano. Many recipes add the spices after the beef has been browned, but we knew from previous experience in the test kitchen that ground spices taste better when they have direct contact with hot cooking oil.

To see if these results would apply here, we set up a test with two pots of chili: one with the ground spices added right to the slow cooker and one with the spices sautéed with the aromatics. The batch made with untoasted spices tasted harsh and bitter, while the one made with spices toasted with the aromatics was far better, offering a more fully developed spice flavor.

Although we didn't want a chili with killer heat, we did want real warmth and depth of flavor. Commercial chili powder is typically 80 percent ground dried red chiles, with the remaining 20 percent a mix of garlic powder, onion powder, oregano, ground cumin, and salt. To boost flavor, we increased the amount of chili powder from 3 to 4 tablespoons, added more cumin and oregano, and added chipotles (smoked jalapeños) for heat and a smoky background flavor. We tried some more exotic spices, including cinnamon (which was deemed "awful"), allspice (which seemed "out of place"), and coriander. In the end, we settled on the classic combination of chili powder, cumin, and oregano.

It was now time to take a closer look at the meat. Two pounds of ground beef seemed ideal when paired with two 15.5-ounce cans of beans. Because we knew we weren't going to be able to drain any grease from the beef, we naturally started out with the leanest beef we could find, which was 90 percent lean. This chili, however, turned out dry, sandy, and largely devoid of flavor. When we tried the 80 percent lean beef, we were left with an orange pool of grease floating on top of the chili that was difficult to remove, but the chili had good flavor. Turning to 85 percent lean beef, we found our winner—it had enough fat to carry the flavor of the spices throughout the chili, and although there was a slick of grease on top, it was a manageable amount and easy enough to skim off before serving. Taking another cue from our beef stew testing, we added a little soy sauce for both flavor and color.

We then moved on to which liquid, if any, to add. We tried batches made with water (too watery), chicken broth (too chickeny and dull), beef broth (too beefy), wine (too acidic), and no liquid at all except for that in the tomatoes (beefy tasting and by far the best). Though some have made chili with beer and been satisfied with the results, when we tried it we found that it subdued that great beefy flavor. Keep the beer on ice for drinking with dinner.

We knew tomatoes were definitely going into the pot, we just had to decide on the type and amount. We first tried two 14.5-ounce cans of diced tomatoes. Definitely not enough tomatoes. What's more, the tomatoes were too chunky, and they were floating in a thin sauce. We tried two 28-ounce cans of diced tomatoes, pureeing the contents of one can in the food processor to thicken the sauce. Although the chunkiness was reduced, the sauce was still watery. Next we paired one can of tomato puree with one can of diced tomatoes and, without exception, tasters preferred this combination's thicker consistency.

Most recipes for slow-cooker chili add the beans toward the end of cooking so that they will heat through without falling apart. But this method often makes for very bland beans floating in a sea of highly flavorful chili. After testing several options, we found it best to add the beans with the tomatoes. The more time the beans spent in the pot, the better they tasted. In the end, we preferred dark red kidney beans or black beans because both keep their shape better than light red kidney beans, another common choice.

With our recipe basically complete, it was time to try some of those offbeat additions that other cooks swear by, including cocoa powder, ground coffee beans, raisins, chickpeas, mushrooms, olives,

and lima beans. Our conclusion? Each of these ingredients either tasted out of place or was too subtle to make much difference. Lime wedges, passed separately at the table, both brightened the flavor of the chili and accentuated the heat of the spices. We now had a hearty, flavorful chili, ready for all our favorite garnishes and trappings.

Slow-Cooker Weeknight Chili
SERVES 8 TO 10

Do not use beef any leaner than 85 percent or its texture will turn dry and sandy as it cooks. For a milder chili, use the smaller amount of chipotle chiles; if you like yours spicy, use the full 4 teaspoons. When the chili is done, break up any remaining large pieces of beef with the back of a spoon before serving. See page 204 for make-ahead instructions.

2	tablespoons vegetable oil
3	medium onions, minced
6	medium garlic cloves, minced or pressed through a garlic press (about 2 tablespoons)
¼	cup chili powder
¼	cup tomato paste
I	tablespoon ground cumin
½	teaspoon red pepper flakes
	Salt
I	(28-ounce) can diced tomatoes
2	(15.5-ounce) cans dark red kidney beans, drained and rinsed
I	(28-ounce) can tomato puree
3	tablespoons soy sauce
I	tablespoon minced fresh oregano leaves, or I teaspoon dried
I	tablespoon brown sugar
2–4	teaspoons minced chipotle chile in adobo sauce (see note)
2	pounds 85 percent lean ground beef
	Ground black pepper
2	limes, cut into wedges

1. Heat the oil in a 12-inch nonstick skillet over medium-high heat until shimmering. Add the onions, garlic, chili powder, tomato paste, cumin, pepper flakes, and ¼ teaspoon salt and cook, stirring often, until the onions are softened and lightly browned, 10 to 12 minutes. Stir in the diced tomatoes with their

juice, scraping up any browned bits.

2. Transfer the mixture to the slow cooker and stir in the beans, tomato puree, soy sauce, oregano, sugar, and chipotle until evenly combined. Season the meat with salt and pepper and stir it into the slow cooker, breaking up any larger pieces. Cover and cook, either on low or high, until the meat is tender and the chili flavorful, 8 to 9 hours on low or 5 to 6 hours on high.

3. Let the chili settle for 5 minutes, then gently tilt the slow cooker and remove as much fat as possible from the surface using a large spoon. Season with salt and pepper to taste and serve with the lime wedges.

SLOW-COOKER BRAISED LAMB WITH RED WINE AND CUMIN

THOUGH THE SLOW COOKER IS MOST OFTEN brought out for weeknight suppers, it is also perfect for preparing special occasion meals. Tender lamb, scented with cumin and bathed in a sweet-tart red wine sauce, is one of those company-is-coming-for-dinner meals that is sure to impress.

First, we tackled the main components of the sauce. Our goal was to create a potently flavored sauce that could hold its own against the strong flavor of the lamb itself. Building a bold braising liquid was a good start. We tested braising lamb in both white and red wine. White wine wasn't assertive enough. Red wine fared better, but dumping a bottle into the slow cooker then walking away didn't quite work either—the wine flavor was much too potent and harsh. Instead, we simmered and reduced the wine with our aromatics until it had a concentrated flavor and had lost most of its astringency.

Adding tomato paste to the sautéed aromatics gave the sauce a touch of sweetness, and we balanced the flavors in the slow cooker by adding

chicken broth. To help bring out the meaty flavor of the lamb, and avoid the hassle of having to brown the meat before adding it to the slow cooker, we turned to a proven trick we had used many times in the past—we added a dash of soy sauce. It created a deep, round flavor that tasters appreciated. We relied on another test kitchen favorite, instant tapioca, to help thicken our sauce to just the right consistency without adding any additional flavors.

Next, we zeroed in on the lamb and which cut might work best. We considered shanks, leg, and shoulder, since all three are marbled cuts that tend to do well with braising and can achieve that fall-off-the-bone tenderness we were after. However, in this recipe shanks fell short of tasters' expectations for two reasons. First, they made the sauce greasy. Second, because the sizes available at the supermarket varied, it was sometimes hard to fit six lamb shanks into the slow cooker. Boneless leg of lamb didn't fare much better, with the meat emerging somewhat dry. In the end, boneless shoulder worked the best. Both tender and succulent, it was our tasters' first choice. Tying the shoulder ensured even cooking, and thoroughly trimming it of excess fat reduced both the greasiness and gaminess of the sauce (most of the gamey flavor that lamb is known for comes from the fat).

Finally, we circled back around to seasoning and looked at the cumin, which we wanted to take an important, but not center-stage, role in the dish. When added at the end of cooking, both the meat and the spice tasted too raw. Incorporating it into the sauce in the slow cooker at the onset of cooking was a touch better. But we had the best results sautéing it with our aromatics; cooking the cumin in the intense heat of the skillet toasted and rounded out its flavor. We tried both whole and ground cumin, but tasters disliked biting into whole cumin seeds, which had taken on a bitter taste by the end of the braise. We settled on a full tablespoon of ground cumin.

Robustly flavored and short on gaminess, this lamb dish from our slow cooker was truly worthy of our next special occasion.

Slow-Cooker Braised Lamb with Red Wine and Cumin

SERVES 6 TO 8

It is important to thoroughly trim the lamb and defat the sauce in order to prevent the sauce from tasting gamey. A $7 to $10 bottle of medium-bodied red table wine made from a blend of grapes, such as a Côtes du Rhône, will work well here. See page 204 for make-ahead instructions.

2	tablespoons vegetable oil
2	medium onions, minced
8	medium garlic cloves, peeled and crushed (see the illustrations on page 63)
1	tablespoon tomato paste
1	tablespoon ground cumin
1	tablespoon minced fresh thyme leaves, or 1 teaspoon dried
	Salt
1	(750-ml) bottle dry red wine (see note)
1	cup low-sodium chicken broth
⅓	cup soy sauce
3	tablespoons Minute tapioca
1	(5-pound) boneless lamb shoulder roast, trimmed and tied (see the illustrations on page 72)
	Ground black pepper

1. Heat the oil in a 12-inch nonstick skillet over medium-high heat until shimmering. Add the onions, garlic, tomato paste, cumin, thyme, and ¼ teaspoon salt and cook, stirring often, until the onions are softened and lightly browned, 8 to 10 minutes. Stir in the wine, scraping up any browned bits, bring to a simmer, and cook until the mixture measures about 3 cups, 10 to 12 minutes.

2. Transfer the mixture to the slow cooker and stir in the chicken broth, soy sauce, and tapioca until evenly combined. Season the lamb with salt and pepper and nestle it in the slow cooker. Cover and cook, either on low or high, until the meat is tender, 9 to 10 hours on low or 5 to 6 hours on high.

3. Transfer the lamb to a cutting board, tent loosely with foil, and let rest for 20 minutes. Meanwhile, strain the sauce through a fine-mesh strainer into a fat separator, and let settle for 5 minutes. Pour the defatted juices into a small saucepan, season with salt and pepper to taste, cover, and keep warm over low heat.

4. Untie the roast and slice into ½-inch-thick pieces. Arrange the meat on a serving platter and pour 1 cup of the sauce over the top. Serve, passing the remaining sauce separately.

SLOW-COOKER PORK POT ROAST

IN OUR EARLIER RECIPE TESTING FOR THIS chapter, we had successfully created a slow-cooker beef pot roast recipe (see page 203) that gave us both a tender roast and a flavorful gravy. Could we use this recipe to come up with an equally impressive slow-cooker pork pot roast recipe? We felt like the chances were good, so we headed to the test kitchen to find out.

We started by focusing on the meat, and in particular, the cut of pork we would use. Our beef pot roast is made using a beef chuck eye roast, and because the fat content and marbling of a pork picnic shoulder are similar to that of beef chuck eye, we determined that a picinic shoulder was our best bet. Next, the size of the roast. While the slow-cooker beef pot roast calls for a 5- to 6-pound beef chuck eye roast, a 5- to 6-pound boneless pork picnic shoulder was a little more difficult to come by. Instead, we ended up using two smaller pork picnic shoulder roasts that were 2½ to 3 pounds each. Not only was it easier to find the smaller roasts in the supermarket, but they were also easier to manage in the slow cooker. Most boneless pork shoulder roasts come bound in string netting, which is difficult to remove after cooking, so we cut the netting off before cooking, trimmed the roasts, and then tied each one with cooking twine.

With our roasts ready to cook, we turned our attention to the question of browning. We wanted to find out whether we could apply to our pork roast recipe what we had learned when preparing our beef roast—that we could skip the browning and utilize a fond replacement of seared aromatics with tomato paste to make up for the lost flavors. So we pitted a seared roast against an unseared roast that was smothered in a lightly browned mixture of onions, garlic, and tomato paste (the tomato paste encouraged the flavorful browning of the aromatics). This turned out to be a worthwhile test, as tasters had trouble distinguishing between the two. We opted to go the simpler route and stick with the unseared roast with sautéed aromatics.

We now had a tender and juicy pork roast, so we turned next to the braising liquid. Our first tests for this recipe used the same braising liquids as our beef pot roast—chicken broth, red wine, tomato paste, and diced tomatoes (processed in a food processor until smooth). While well suited to our beef roast, it didn't balance well with the pork; the sauce's red wine and strong tomato flavor was too potent and overwhelmed the delicate flavor of the pork. The pork roast also released a lot of liquid, which made the sauce thin and watery.

Eliminating the broth was a good first step in the right direction, as the pork juices were plenty flavorful on their own. Using just ½ cup of red wine and draining the diced tomatoes (and not processing them) also helped the more delicate flavors of the pork shine through. But the sauce still tasted a bit harsh. Switching from red to white wine was an improvement, and reducing the amount of tomato paste to 1 tablespoon helped, too. A splash of white wine vinegar added at the end of cooking refreshed the sauce's flavor and lent a welcome brightness, and thyme provided a soft herbal note. While onions, garlic, and carrots are essential to the base flavor of this dish, we tried adding plenty of other vegetables as well. Tasters agreed on a surprising favorite, parsnips, which contributed sweetness and a heady perfume to the dish.

To thicken the sauce we initially turned to flour and cornstarch, but both gave the sauce a pasty texture and masked its flavors. Instead, instant tapioca, a thickener the test kitchen likes for its neutral flavor and ease of use, produced just the right thick, glossy texture without affecting taste. With that final step taken care of, we had successfully created a pork pot roast that was well flavored and complemented by a balanced sauce.

We then tried out a Latin American variation incorporating the flavors of fresh chiles (including fresh jalapeños and smoky chipotles), cumin, orange, and sweet potatoes with great success. To keep the sweet potatoes from breaking apart during the extended cooking, we found it necessary to wrap them in a foil packet and place the packet on top of the pork in the slow cooker. As the pork simmered in the liquid below, the potatoes steamed perfectly, retaining their shape and flavor. This brightly flavored dish is a perfect change of pace for any weeknight family dinner.

Slow-Cooker Pork Pot Roast
SERVES 6 TO 8
We use two smaller roasts for this recipe because the meat cooks more quickly, and small roasts are easier to manage in the slow cooker—and easier to find in the supermarket. See page 204 for make-ahead instructions.

2	tablespoons vegetable oil
2	onions, minced
6	medium garlic cloves, minced or pressed through a garlic press (about 2 tablespoons)
I	tablespoon tomato paste
I	tablespoon fresh thyme leaves, or I teaspoon dried
	Salt
½	cup white wine
I	(28-ounce) can diced tomatoes, drained
I	pound carrots (about 6 medium), peeled and cut into I-inch pieces
I	pound parsnips, peeled and cut into I-inch pieces
3	tablespoons Minute tapioca
2	(2½- to 3-pound) boneless pork picnic shoulder roasts, trimmed and tied
	Ground black pepper
2	teaspoons white wine vinegar

1. Heat the oil in a 12-inch nonstick skillet over medium-high heat until shimmering. Add the onions, garlic, tomato paste, thyme, and ¼ teaspoon salt and cook, stirring often, until the onions are softened and lightly browned, 8 to 10 minutes. Stir in the wine, scraping up any browned bits.

2. Transfer the mixture to the slow cooker and stir in the tomatoes, carrots, parsnips, and tapioca until evenly combined. Season the pork with salt and pepper and nestle it in the slow cooker. Cover and cook, either on low or high, until the meat is tender, 9 to 10 hours on low or 5 to 6 hours on high.

3. Transfer the pork to a cutting board, tent with foil, and let rest for 20 minutes. Let the cooking liquid settle for 5 minutes, then gently tilt the slow cooker and remove as much fat as possible from the surface using a large spoon. Stir the vinegar into the sauce and season with salt and pepper to taste.

4. Untie the roasts and slice them into ½-inch-thick pieces. Arrange the pork, carrots, and parsnips on a serving platter and spoon 1 cup of the sauce over the top. Serve, passing the remaining sauce separately.

➤ VARIATION

Slow-Cooker Pork Pot Roast with Sweet Potatoes, Orange, and Cilantro

For more heat, include some of the jalapeño seeds and ribs when mincing. See page 204 for make-ahead instructions.

3	tablespoons vegetable oil
2	medium onions, minced
3	jalapeño chiles, seeds and ribs removed, chiles minced (see note)
6	medium garlic cloves, minced or pressed through a garlic press (about 2 tablespoons)
1	tablespoon ground cumin
1	tablespoon tomato paste
1	teaspoon dried oregano
	Salt
1	cup low-sodium chicken broth
1	(14.5-ounce) can diced tomatoes
1	cup orange juice
2	tablespoons soy sauce
2	tablespoons Minute tapioca
1	strip zest from 1 orange (see the illustration on page 72)
2	teaspoons minced chipotle chile in adobo sauce
2	(2½- to 3-pound) boneless pork picnic shoulder roasts, trimmed and tied

	Ground black pepper
1½	pounds sweet potatoes (about 2 medium), peeled and cut into 1-inch pieces
6	tablespoons minced fresh cilantro leaves
1	cup sour cream
1	tablespoon juice from 1 lime

1. Heat 2 tablespoons of the oil in a 12-inch nonstick skillet over medium-high heat until shimmering. Add the onions, jalapeños, garlic, cumin, tomato paste, oregano, and ¼ teaspoon salt and cook, stirring often, until the onions are softened and lightly browned, 10 to 12 minutes. Stir in the chicken broth, scraping up any browned bits.

2. Transfer the mixture to the slow cooker and stir in the tomatoes, orange juice, soy sauce, tapioca, orange zest, and chipotle until evenly combined. Season the pork with salt and pepper and nestle it in the slow cooker.

3. Toss the sweet potatoes with the remaining 1 tablespoon oil and season with salt and pepper. Following the illustrations on page 206, wrap the sweet potatoes in a foil packet. Set the vegetable packet on top of the pork in the slow cooker. Cover and cook, either on low or high, until the pork is tender, 9 to 11 hours on low or 5 to 7 hours on high.

4. Transfer the sweet potato packet to a plate. Transfer the pork roasts to a cutting board, tent loosely with foil, and let rest for 20 minutes. Let the cooking liquid settle for 5 minutes, then gently tilt the slow cooker and remove as much fat as possible from the surface using a large spoon. Carefully open the foil packet (watch for steam), then stir the sweet potatoes along with any accumulated juices into the stew. Stir in ¼ cup of the cilantro and season with salt and pepper to taste.

5. Mix the sour cream, the remaining 2 tablespoons cilantro, and lime juice together in a small bowl and season with salt and pepper to taste. Untie the roasts and slice them into ½-inch-thick pieces. Arrange the pork and potatoes on a serving platter and pour 1 cup of the sauce over the top. Serve, passing the remaining sauce and cilantro sour cream separately.

SLOW-COOKER PORK AND HOMINY STEW

POZOLE IS THE MEXICAN NAME FOR BOTH hominy (dried field corn kernels treated with lime and boiled until tender but still chewy) and a stew made with hominy and pork. The stew is made throughout Mexico in several quite distinct incarnations: pozole blanco (white pozole) is prepared without any chiles; pozole verde (green pozole) is made with tomatillos, fresh green chiles, and cilantro; and pozole rojo (red pozole) is made with dried red chiles. With its long simmering time, pozole was a natural for our slow cooker, and after much deliberation, we decided to focus our efforts on pozole rojo.

Pozole should have a complex, richly flavored broth with lots of body. The meat, which is shredded, must be exceedingly tender, while the hominy should be chewy and sweet. Although pozole has become more popular in the United States, especially in the Southwest, most American cooks balk at preparing such traditional recipes, many of which take 12 hours or more to execute. One of the culprits in the case of pozole is the hominy. If you begin with dried field corn, you must boil it with slaked lime (calcium hydroxide powder, which loosens the hulls), then wash the corn and pinch the germ from each kernel by hand. Another concern when making pozole is the meat. In Mexico, pozole is traditionally made with cuts rarely sold in American supermarkets (unsmoked pig's feet and pig's head, for example). We would have to find an acceptable substitute. With these goals in mind, we started to work on our slow-cooker red pozole recipe. The meat seemed like the place to start.

In lieu of the unique cuts traditionally used, we settled on country-style ribs, not only because of their availability but because they require little trimming. Authentic red pozole is also made with bones, supplemented with some boneless meat from the shoulder or loin. We wondered how important bones were to this dish. We prepared one batch with boneless country-style pork ribs and another with bone-in country-style pork ribs. The liquid of the pozole prepared without bones was weak in flavor and thin in texture. The version made with the bone-in ribs had a distinctive, satisfyingly full-bodied pork flavor. It was obvious to tasters that bones are key. In addition, the bones released a significant amount of gelatin that gave the pozole a voluptuous body.

Pozole differs from other meat stews in that the meat is shredded rather than cubed. The meat is usually stewed in large chunks until it is tender enough to pull apart by hand. Leaving the ribs whole proved to be the best method—the stewing time was not excessive (5 to 6 hours on high in the slow cooker) and the meat was easy to shred.

Pozole differs from most stews in another regard. While stew meat is typically browned to enhance the flavor of both the meat and the stewing liquid, in many pozole recipes, the meat is simply added raw to the simmering liquid. The reason is simple: Browning creates a firmer, crustier texture on the outside of each piece of meat, which in turn makes the shredding process more difficult. One alternate approach is to sweat the meat with some onions, and another is to skip precooking of the meat entirely and instead sauté the aromatics with tomato paste to develop a deep roasted flavor, which happens to be a technique we've had great success with in other slow-cooker recipes. We tried all three, simmering, sweating, and sautéing the aromatics with tomato paste, and found, not surprisingly, that the latter method developed the best flavor in the liquid without firming up the texture of the meat. In addition to onions, garlic is typically added at the outset when making pozole. We found five cloves to be ample, and their presence was definitely felt, even after the extended cooking.

Next, it was time to decide on the liquid and other seasonings. We tested water and canned chicken broth. Although the water was fine, the broth was superior, adding not only depth of flavor but body to the stewing liquid. While some versions of red pozole reserve the tomatoes as part of the garnish, our tasters liked the tomatoes cooked right into the stew because the acidity of the tomatoes added a lively flavor and good texture.

Oregano is a signature ingredient in pozole. Several varieties are grown in Mexico, all of which differ from the Mediterranean oregano popular in this country. Because it does not have the anise compounds found in Mediterranean varieties, Mexican oregano's flavor is earthier and more potent. We tested pozole with dried Mexican, dried Mediterranean, and fresh Mediterranean oregano. (We were unable to purchase fresh Mexican oregano.) Although all varieties worked, we preferred the clean, authentic flavor of Mexican oregano. (Look for it in the international aisle of the supermarket.)

The next component of the pozole to examine was the chiles. The red color of the dish traditionally comes from dried chiles, so we tested several possibilities: anchos, New Mexican reds, and pasillas. We removed stems and seeds from the dried chiles, soaked them in boiling water, and then pureed the chiles and soaking liquid to create a thick paste, which we sautéed with the aromatics. We also tested toasting the chiles before soaking but found that this step added little to this dish. In the end, despite the break with tradition, tasters felt that dried chiles just weren't worth the extra effort, as their flavor began to seriously diminish throughout the hours of slow cooking. Instead, we added 2 tablespoons of chili powder to the onions at the onset of cooking. Chili powder was an easy answer to our dried chile dilemma, and sautéing it with the other aromatics helped its flavor bloom.

It was time to deal with the hominy. We started by preparing one batch of pozole with freshly rehydrated hominy, which took hours to prepare, and another batch with canned hominy, which took seconds to drain and rinse. The pozole with freshly cooked hominy was superb, but the pozole with canned hominy was still really good. The hominy was chewy (as hominy should be) and relatively sweet, so we decided it was worth using canned to save a significant amount of prep time. Canned hominy comes in white and yellow varieties, depending on the type of field corn used. We tested white and yellow hominy and found that both types are fine. Flavor isn't much of an issue, as both are sweet and "corny" tasting. We determined that adding the canned hominy at the beginning of cooking allows it to soak up some of the flavorful broth.

Our pozole recipe turned out to be remarkably simple—minimal prep and a walk-away time of up to 9 hours for a slow cooker set to low heat. We do recommend taking the extra 10 minutes needed

to prepare all the suggested garnishes, which will brighten this stew and turn it into a one-dish meal.

Slow-Cooker Mexican-Style Pork and Hominy Stew
SERVES 6 TO 8

This traditional Mexican stew features tender shredded pork and hominy in a flavorful broth and is garnished with colorful raw vegetables. If you have trouble finding canned hominy, look for it in the international aisle of your supermarket. In addition to lime wedges, we recommend preparing other traditional garnishes of shredded lettuce, diced red onion, fresh cilantro, and sliced radish. See page 204 for make-ahead instructions.

2	tablespoons vegetable oil
2	medium onions, minced
¼	cup tomato paste
2	tablespoons chili powder
2	teaspoons dried Mexican oregano, or 2 tablespoons minced fresh oregano
5	medium garlic cloves, minced or pressed through a garlic press (about 5 teaspoons) Salt
5	cups low-sodium chicken broth
3	(14-ounce) cans white or yellow hominy, drained and rinsed
1	(14.5-ounce) can diced tomatoes
⅓	cup soy sauce
5	pounds bone-in country-style pork ribs Ground black pepper
¼	cup minced fresh cilantro leaves
1	tablespoon juice from 1 lime
8	corn tortillas, warmed (see page 158)
2	limes, cut into wedges

1. Heat the oil in a 12-inch nonstick skillet over medium-high heat until shimmering. Add the onions, tomato paste, chili powder, oregano, garlic, and ¼ teaspoon salt and cook, stirring often, until the onions are softened and lightly browned, 8 to 10 minutes. Stir in 1 cup of the chicken broth, scraping up any browned bits.

2. Transfer the mixture to the slow cooker and stir in the remaining 4 cups chicken broth, hominy, tomatoes with their juice, and soy sauce until evenly combined. Season the pork with salt and pepper and nestle it in the slow cooker. Cover and cook, either on low or high, until the meat is tender, 8 to 9 hours on low or 5 to 6 hours on high.

3. Transfer the meat to a platter and cool slightly. Let the stew settle for 5 minutes, then gently tilt the slow cooker and remove as much fat as possible from the surface using a large spoon. Using 2 forks, shred the pork, discarding the bones and fat, following the illustration on page 104. Add the pork back to the slow cooker, stir in the cilantro and lime juice, and season with salt and pepper to taste. Serve with the tortillas and limes wedges.

➤ VARIATION
Slow-Cooker Mexican-Style Chicken and Hominy Stew
Follow the recipe for Slow-Cooker Mexican-Style Pork and Hominy Stew, substituting 5 pounds bone-in chicken thighs, skin removed and trimmed, for the pork. Cover and cook on low until the meat is tender, 4 to 5 hours. Shred the meat as directed, discarding the bones and fat.

SLOW-COOKER SMOTHERED PORK CHOPS

THE BEST SMOTHERED PORK CHOPS ARE FALL-off-the-bone tender, covered with caramelized onions, and enriched with a deeply flavored onion gravy. We wondered if we could slow this recipe down to an eight-hour braise in the slow cooker, starting it in the morning and having it ready by dinnertime. And if so, more importantly, could it still be as good as the original?

The test kitchen's favorite smothered pork chop recipe uses relatively thin ½- to ¾-inch rib chops, so that's where we started. It took exactly eight hours to disprove the notion that you can't over-cook anything in a slow cooker. The chops were dry and stringy. It appeared that thin was not in, so we moved to thicker chops. We were certain that huge 2-inch-thick chops, special ordered from the butcher, were going to be the answer. We just had to determine which was better, rib or center cut.

To our dismay, both of these cuts also overcooked in eight hours. We were thinking about cutting back on the cooking time when a test kitchen colleague suggested blade chops, which are cut from the shoulder end of the loin and contain a significant amount of fat and connective tissue. When we tried them, the fat melted into the meat, keeping it moist and tender, and the connective tissue all but disappeared over the course of eight hours. Best of all, there was no need to special order extra-thick chops, since ¾-inch pork blade chops worked perfectly and were readily available.

Unfortunately, the gravy and onions weren't coming together quite as smoothly. It was becoming clear that the "dump and cook" method of loading the slow cooker with raw ingredients wasn't going to produce enough flavor. We knew that searing the chops would create a deeper flavor, but we were hoping we could skip this step as we had with other slow-cooker recipes. So to make up for the loss of flavor from not browning, we turned to bacon fat to provide a smoky base for the sauce, reserving the rendered bacon as a garnish for the final dish. Deeply caramelizing the onions and garlic in the bacon fat with the help of a little brown sugar further intensified the sauce. Thyme and bay leaves gave it aroma, and a healthy shot of soy sauce acted as a fond replacement in the absence of searing the meat. Our slow-cooker smothered chops were turning a corner.

Our last challenge was to get the texture of the onions and gravy right—the sauce was still too watery. More onions thickened it, but they also threw off the balance of flavors. Our solution was buried in the back of our cabinet. Instant tapioca, though a benchwarmer most of the time, is an ideal starter for thickening sauces in the slow cooker because it thickens without breaking down or turning gloppy, and it never masks flavor as other thickeners sometimes do. The result was a thick, rich gravy that truly smothered each chop.

We finished the sauce with a splash of vinegar to brighten things up, then garnished the chops with the bacon we'd cooked earlier as well as some chopped parsley. We now had a recipe that was just as good as the original—and it practically cooked itself.

Slow-Cooker Smothered Pork Chops

SERVES 6

The pork chops are so tender after cooking that it is best to use a spoon to remove them from the slow cooker to keep them from breaking apart. See page 204 for make-ahead instructions.

4	ounces (about 4 slices) bacon, cut into ¼-inch pieces
3	medium onions, halved and sliced thin
4	teaspoons light brown sugar
3	medium garlic cloves, minced or pressed through a garlic press (about 1 tablespoon)
1	tablespoon minced fresh thyme leaves, or 1 teaspoon dried
	Salt
3	cups low-sodium chicken broth
¼	cup soy sauce
2	tablespoons Minute tapioca
2	bay leaves
6	bone-in blade-cut pork chops, about ¾-inch thick
	Ground black pepper
1	tablespoon cider vinegar
1	tablespoon minced fresh parsley leaves

1. Cook the bacon in a 12-inch nonstick skillet over medium heat until crisp, about 8 minutes. Transfer the bacon to a paper towel–lined plate, leaving the fat in the skillet, and refrigerate until serving time.

2. Pour off all but 2 tablespoons of the bacon fat left in the skillet and place over medium-high heat until shimmering. Add the onions, 1 teaspoon of the brown sugar, garlic, thyme, and ¼ teaspoon salt to the skillet and cook, stirring often, until the onions are soft and caramelized, 10 to 15 minutes. Stir in 1 cup of the chicken broth, scraping up any browned bits.

3. Transfer the mixture to the slow cooker and stir in the remaining 2 cups broth, remaining tablespoon brown sugar, soy sauce, tapioca, and bay leaves until evenly combined. Season the pork chops with salt and pepper and nestle them in the slow cooker. Cover and cook, either on low or high, until the meat is tender, 7 to 8 hours on low or 4 to 5 hours on high.

4. Transfer the pork chops to a serving platter with a large spoon, tent with foil, and let rest for 20 minutes. Let the cooking liquid settle for 5 minutes, then gently tilt the slow cooker and remove as much fat as possible from the surface using a large spoon. Remove the bay leaves, stir in the vinegar, and season with salt and pepper to taste. Reheat the bacon in the microwave on high power until heated through and crisp, about 30 seconds. Pour 1 cup of the sauce over the chops, sprinkle with the crisp bacon and parsley, and serve, passing the remaining sauce separately.

CHOOSING THE RIGHT PORK CHOP

The secret to great slow-cooked smothered pork chops is choosing the right chop. The excess fat on a blade chop melts away after eight hours in the slow cooker.

BLADE	RIB	CENTER CUT
The fat in these inexpensive chops keeps them from drying out in a slow cooker.	Our favorite for grilling and sautéing, but too lean for all-day cooking.	Our second choice for grilling and sautéing, but, again, too lean for the slow cooker.

SLOW-COOKER COUNTRY-STYLE PORK AND BEANS

RICH, MEATY PORK AND TENDER, CREAMY beans are a satisfying combination. Our goal for this dish, typically cooked low and slow in the oven, was to develop a recipe that worked in a slow cooker—and that tasted far better than the syrupy-sweet canned versions available in most supermarkets. We wanted something more like the French classic, cassoulet: not too sweet, mildly spicy, and with lots of tender meat. We wanted pork and sausage to be the dominant forces in this stew, surrounded by soft, creamy beans stewed for hours in a flavorful broth. But many of the slow-cooker versions we encountered dished up greasy, bland stews with beans that had passed their point of perfection hours before the allotted cooking time was up.

Our first question was, which type of beans would work best? Given the fact that the lucky legume would be spending hours in the slow cooker, we knew that it had to be a sturdy variety. We tested navy beans and cannellini beans and found that both types burst open during cooking, rendering them mushy and waterlogged. Great Northern beans were our next choice. Sturdier than navy and cannellini beans, great Northern beans delivered the creamy texture we wanted, and they also held their own for the duration of cooking. An overnight soak in salt water (for more information about salt-soaking beans, see page 122) gave them a head start on slowly absorbing the moisture they needed to cook evenly. It also served to ensure that the beans would not split open during the long cooking process.

Looking for a cut of pork for our stew that would be moist, tender, and flavorful, we started with pork shoulder. We peeled, boned, trimmed, and cubed this gargantuan cut of pork into stew-sized pieces, a process that took quite a bit of time and yielded quite a bit of waste. While the end-product in this stew was tender, the preparation time that was involved sent us in search of a speedier alternative. Pork butt seemed a good choice for its high fat content, but it too required a substantial amount of butchering that we weren't willing to do. We settled on country-style pork ribs, which are available bone-in and boneless. Leaving the meat on the bone added more flavor to the stew and kept the meat in recognizable portions. The meat turned out moist and flavorful.

We tested two methods of preparing the ribs prior to adding them to the slow cooker, browned and unbrowned. While searing adds deeper flavor to stews and braises, it is also is a hassle for slow-cooker recipes, which we think should be as simple and streamlined as possible. Our previous slow-cooker recipes had skipped the browning step, instead using a fond replacement technique that involves sautéing the aromatics with a dollop of tomato paste to encourage browning and caramelization. We gave this technique a shot, pitting a batch of browned ribs against an unbrowned batch. Smothering the unbrowned ribs with a flavorful mixture of onions, garlic, thyme, and fennel seeds lightly browned with tomato paste catapulted the unbrowned version to the top of tasters' lists. We deglazed the skillet with white wine (which tasters preferred over red) to pick up the browned bits; the addition of wine to the sauce also helped the other individual flavors shine through. Some diced tomatoes helped liven up the sauce.

The last important component in question was sausage. We tested Italian sausage, chorizo, and kielbasa and preferred the last choice for two reasons. Not only did it contribute a smoky flavor to the stew, but it seemed to retain its flavor throughout the cooking process. Others seemed to release their flavors into the stew and end up as rubbery, flavorless chunks of meat by the end of the long cooking time.

This stew is hearty and full flavored without being fussy to prepare. The combination of meaty ribs, spicy kielbasa, and creamy beans gives it great flavor and heft, and it's perfect for either a busy weeknight or weekend since it can be left alone to cook nearly all day.

Slow-Cooker Country-Style Pork and Beans with Sausage

SERVES 6 TO 8

See page 204 for make-ahead instructions.

1	pound dried great Northern beans, rinsed, picked over, and salt-soaked overnight or quick salt-soaked (see page 122)
2	tablespoons vegetable oil
2	medium onions, minced
6	medium garlic cloves, minced or pressed through a garlic press (about 2 tablespoons)
2	tablespoons tomato paste
1	tablespoon minced fresh thyme leaves, or 1 teaspoon dried
1	teaspoon fennel seeds
1	cup dry white wine
2	(14.5-ounce) cans diced tomatoes
1	pound kielbasa, sliced 1 inch thick
2¾	cups low-sodium chicken broth
2	bay leaves
3	pounds bone-in country-style pork ribs Ground black pepper
¼	cup minced fresh parsley leaves Salt

1. Drain and rinse the beans and transfer them to the slow cooker. Heat the oil in a 12-inch nonstick skillet over medium-high heat until shimmering. Add the onions, garlic, tomato paste, thyme, and fennel seeds and cook, stirring often, until the onions are softened and lightly browned, 8 to 10 minutes. Stir in the wine, scraping up any browned bits.

2. Transfer the mixture to the slow cooker and stir in the tomatoes with their juice, kielbasa, chicken broth, and bay leaves until evenly combined. Lightly season the pork with pepper and nestle it in the slow cooker. Cover and cook, either on low or high, until both the beans and pork are tender, 9 to 11 hours on low or 6 to 7 hours on high.

3. Let the cooking liquid settle for 5 minutes, then gently tilt the slow cooker and remove as much fat as possible from the surface using a large spoon. Remove the bay leaves, stir in the parsley, and season with salt and pepper to taste before serving.

SLOW-COOKER SWEET AND SOUR RIBS

MENTION "RIBS" AND "SLOW COOKER" IN THE same sentence and you're sure to draw incredulous looks. But when you think about it, it makes sense. Ribs are excellent when cooked in a moist, steamy environment. So we set out to see if we could create one of our favorite rib recipes—sweet and sour ribs—in the slow cooker. Their succulent meat and potent mahogany-colored sauce make them the center of attention at any gathering.

Conventional recipes roast these ribs in a hot oven, pulling them out midway through cooking to coat them in a sweet, tangy sauce. The sauce reduces in the oven, coating the ribs with concentrated flavor. Slow-cooker recipes that try to duplicate these well-lacquered beauties often fall far short of expectations. Most versions come out gray and flavorless with a watery sauce. We knew we could do better, so we headed into the kitchen and pulled out the slow cooker to prove it. We began by choosing our ribs and putting together a working sauce recipe.

There are three popular pork rib choices in the butcher's case, namely, baby back ribs, whole spareribs, and St. Louis–style spareribs. Whole spareribs, we quickly learned, were too big to fit in the slow cooker (each rack can weigh upward of 5 pounds). Both baby back and St. Louis–style spareribs, however, are smaller and worked out very well. In fact, we often found that the baby back ribs at the store were just mislabeled St. Louis–style ribs!

Most rib recipes call for removing the thin, chewy membrane from the back of the ribs, which is a great idea if you plan on grilling or roasting them. But after hours of cooking in the moist environment of the slow cooker, racks without the membrane fell apart when we tried to remove them. Leaving the membrane attached for this recipe held the ribs together during cooking.

In order to fit the ribs in the slow cooker, we initially cut them into smaller three-bone pieces and shingled them on top of each other. But stacking them against each other left us with unevenly cooked ribs. For our next test we arranged the full racks of ribs standing up around the perimeter and finally spiraling in towards the center of the slow cooker.

We poured the sauce over the top and let it drip down to slowly baste the ribs as they cooked. This time, because we had left space between the ribs, they cooked more evenly. And because the sauce was poured on top of the standing ribs, they slow-basted during cooking, absorbing more of the sauce's sweet and sour flavors. We transferred the ribs to a cutting board to rest and turned our attention to the sauce.

There were three basic components to our sauce; the sweetener, the aromatics, and the fruit. Most recipes we researched dumped sugar, honey, or even jam on top of the ribs, followed by a heaping handful of onions, peppers, and pineapple. In search of a fresher, more cohesive flavor, we started by sautéing our aromatics with a hefty amount of garlic, ginger, and tomato paste (the last of these helped with browning and flavor development). Sautéing the aromatics before adding them to the slow cooker served two purposes: It drove off the excess moisture from the vegetables and it concentrated their flavors. For sweetness we added brown sugar and jam, settling on apricot because of its bright, fruity flavor. To incorporate pineapple flavor we tried both canned and fresh pineapple. The canned was basically flavorless and added little to the sauce. Fresh pineapple's contribution was only as good as its ripeness, which was inconsistent at best. In the end we opted for pineapple juice concentrate. This gave us the intense pineapple flavor we were seeking, and it is also one-third of the price of a fresh pineapple. The last touches to the sauce were soy sauce for depth and rice vinegar for brightness. Armed with a cohesive, flavorful sauce recipe, we headed back to the slow cooker.

The basic flavors were there now, but so much moisture leached from the ribs as they cooked that the sauce was diluted and not thick enough to coat the ribs. We tried using instant tapioca, our slow cooker standby, without success. It was obvious that we would need to finish the sauce on the stove. After the ribs had cooked, reducing the sauce for about 15 minutes on the stovetop made it thick enough to stick to the ribs when the two were tossed together. The resulting ribs were tender, well seasoned throughout, and coated with a lacquer-like sauce that left tasters longing for more.

Slow-Cooker Sweet and Sour Sticky Ribs
SERVES 4 TO 6

Authentic baby back ribs weigh about 1½ pounds per rack, while St. Louis–style spareribs weigh about 3 pounds per rack. (Note that commercially packaged "baby back" ribs are often just mislabeled St. Louis–style spareribs.) Both types of ribs, however, will work well here. Pineapple juice concentrate can be found in the freezer section next to orange juice concentrate. Serve these ribs with steamed rice and sliced scallions. See page 204 for make-ahead instructions.

1	medium onion, chopped coarse
1	red bell pepper, stemmed, seeded, and chopped coarse
6	medium garlic cloves, peeled and crushed (see the illustrations on page 63)
1	(6-inch) piece fresh ginger, peeled and sliced into ¼-inch rounds
2	tablespoons vegetable oil
2	tablespoons tomato paste
1	(12-ounce) jar apricot jam
1	(6-ounce) can frozen pineapple juice concentrate
6	tablespoons soy sauce
¼	cup dark brown sugar
5	tablespoons rice vinegar
¼	teaspoon red pepper flakes
6	pounds baby back ribs or St. Louis–style spareribs (see note)
	Salt and ground black pepper
2	tablespoons minced fresh cilantro leaves

1. Pulse the onion, bell pepper, garlic, and ginger together in a food processor until finely chopped, about 8 pulses. Heat the oil in a 12-inch nonstick skillet over medium-high heat until shimmering. Add the processed vegetables and tomato paste and cook, stirring often, until the vegetables are softened and lightly browned, 8 to 10 minutes. Stir in the apricot jam, pineapple juice concentrate, soy sauce, brown sugar, ¼ cup of the vinegar, and red pepper flakes, bring to a simmer, and cook until slightly thickened, about 5 minutes.

2. Pat the ribs dry with paper towels and season with salt and pepper. Transfer the ribs to the slow cooker and arrange them standing upright with the meaty side against the interior wall. Pour the sauce over the ribs. Cover and cook on low until the meat is tender, 4 to 5 hours.

3. Transfer the ribs to a cutting board, tent with foil, and let rest for 20 minutes. Let the cooking liquid settle for 5 minutes, then gently tilt the slow cooker and remove as much fat as possible from the surface using a large spoon. Strain the sauce through a fine-mesh strainer into a medium sauce-pan. Bring the sauce to a simmer and cook until the mixture measures 2 cups, 15 to 20 minutes.

4. Stir the remaining tablespoon vinegar into the sauce and season with salt and pepper to taste. Slice the ribs between the bones and toss with the sauce and cilantro. Transfer the ribs to a large platter and serve.

➤ VARIATION
Slow-Cooker Barbecued Sticky Ribs
Authentic baby back ribs weigh about 1½ pounds per rack, while St. Louis–style spareribs weigh about 3 pounds per rack. (Note that commercially packaged "baby back" ribs are often just mislabeled St. Louis–style spareribs.) Both types of ribs, however, will work well here. You can either make your own barbecue sauce (see Classic Barbecue Sauce on page 35), or use your favorite store-bought brand—we like Bull's Eye Original.

    3   tablespoons paprika
    2   tablespoons packed light brown sugar
    I   tablespoon salt
    I   tablespoon ground black pepper
    ¼   teaspoon cayenne pepper
    6   pounds baby back ribs or St. Louis–style
        spareribs (see note)
    3   cups barbecue sauce (see note)

1. Combine the paprika, brown sugar, salt, pepper, and cayenne in a small bowl, then rub the mixture evenly over the ribs. Transfer the ribs to the slow cooker and arrange them standing upright with the meaty side against the interior wall of slow cooker. Pour the barbecue sauce over the ribs. Cover and

cook on low until the meat is tender, 4 to 5 hours.

2. Transfer the ribs to a cutting board, tent with foil, and let rest for 20 minutes. Let the cooking liquid settle for 5 minutes, then gently tilt the slow cooker and remove as much fat as possible from the surface using a large spoon. Strain the sauce through a fine-mesh strainer into a medium sauce-pan. Bring the sauce to a simmer and cook until the mixture measures 2 cups, 15 to 20 minutes.

3. Slice the ribs between the bones and toss them with the barbecue sauce. Transfer the ribs to a warmed platter and serve.

SLOW-COOKER CHICKEN WITH WINE AND TARRAGON

CHICKEN WITH WHITE WINE, TARRAGON, and cream is a sophisticated, company-worthy dish, and we wondered if it was yet another meal that could be successfully replicated in a slow cooker. We wanted chicken braised in a wine-and-herb-infused sauce that was rich and creamy enough to serve over rice. We wanted it to be simple to prepare, yet elegant enough for a special occasion.

We started our testing by making the choice between white meat and dark meat chicken. While we have a tendency to prefer chicken thighs (dark meat) over breasts (white meat) in slow-cooked dishes because thighs are less likely to dry out, we realize that many people want slow-cooker options that feature white meat. So we made chicken breasts the focus of our testing (although chicken thighs would be a fine substitute.) We discovered that bone-in chicken pieces were a must, as both the bone and skin help keep the chicken moist during the long cooking time.

Many slow-cooker chicken recipes call for browning the chicken before adding it to the slow cooker. While this helps develop a deeper flavor, we hoped we could avoid this step. After all, slow-cooker recipes should be as easy as they are tasty. We set up a side-by-side test of seared against unseared chicken to see which would prevail with tasters. Using bone-in, skinless breasts, we seared one batch, transferred it to the slow cooker, and added the cooking liquid. The other batch went in to the slow cooker cold along with the cooking liquid, and we opted to also sauté the aromatics before adding them. As it turned out, tasters had a tough time distinguishing between the two, so we moved forward with our easier, unseared version.

Next up, the sauce. Our initial sauces turned out a bit greasy, but we found we could easily fix this by removing the chicken skin before cooking. To the basic sautéed aromatics of onion and garlic, we added some white mushrooms, bay leaves, and soy sauce (we've come to depend on soy sauce to help deliver depth of flavor to slow-cooker sauces). To deglaze the skillet, we used some dry white wine, scraping up the browned bits (the fond) from the skillet. Then we added chicken broth, fresh tarragon, and heavy cream and transferred it all to the slow cooker. After four hours, the chicken was tender, but we were hardly impressed with the resulting sauce. The mushrooms had turned gray and slimy, the aromatic tarragon had all but disappeared, and the heavy cream had separated, leaving us with a curdled, watery sauce.

The mushroom and tarragon issues were easy to fix. Cremini mushrooms, which are baby portobello mushrooms, weathered the braise far better than white mushrooms. Because of their firmer, meatier texture, they were able to withstand the long cooking time without breaking down and becoming mushy. And to keep the tarragon flavor from waning, we decided to stir it into the sauce right before serving.

To address the broken sauce, we tried adding the cream after the chicken had finished cooking and had good results, but the sauce was still thin. Many recipes turn to a slurry (a starch stirred together with liquid) of either flour or cornstarch, which has to be stirred in at the end of the cooking time. While both of these options worked to thicken the sauce, the starchy taste was evident and they required extra time to allow the liquid to fully thicken. We found that instant tapioca, stirred in at the onset of cooking, worked like magic. The resulting sauce was the perfect consistency, light and creamy, with a delicate tarragon flavor.

Served over rice or polenta, this is a recipe that will impress, and it can be pulled together any night of the week.

EQUIPMENT: Kitchen Shears

A pair of kitchen shears is not an essential kitchen implement. But when you need to butterfly or trim chicken, there is no tool better suited to the task. To test their versatility, we also used kitchen shears to cut lengths of kitchen twine, trim pie dough, and cut out parchment paper rounds. We found two pairs to recommend.

Wüsthof Kitchen Shears ($34.95) made easy, smooth cuts even through small chicken bones and completed all tasks flawlessly. The size and proportion of the shears felt ideal—the blades could open wide for large jobs and to achieve more forceful cutting, but the shears were also suited to smaller, more detailed tasks, such as snipping pieces of twine. These shears boasted heft, solid construction, and textured handles that were comfortable even when wet and greasy. They were also suitable and comfortable for left-handed users.

Messermeister Take-Apart Kitchen Shears ($23.99) were also great performers, though the blades didn't have quite the spread of those on the Wüsthof. These shears, too, made clean, easy cuts and accomplished all tasks without hesitation. The soft, rubberlike handles proved extremely comfortable, but lefties take note: These scissors were clearly designed for right-handed users.

THE BEST KITCHEN SHEARS

WÜSTHOF   MESSERMEISTER

Wüsthof Kitchen Shears performed flawlessly in all tests. Messermeister Take-Apart Kitchen Shears are less expensive than the Wüsthof, and they worked nearly as well; however, left-handed testers were less enthused with this model.

Slow-Cooker Chicken with White Wine, Tarragon, and Cream

SERVES 6 TO 8

If cremini mushrooms are unavailable, substitute portobello mushroom caps, cut into 1-inch pieces. Serve with polenta or white rice. See page 204 for make-ahead instructions.

2	tablespoons vegetable oil
1¼	pounds cremini mushrooms, trimmed, wiped clean, and halved if small or quartered if large (see note)
2	medium onions, minced
4	medium garlic cloves, minced or pressed through a garlic press (about 4 teaspoons)
2	teaspoons minced fresh thyme leaves, or ½ teaspoon dried
	Salt
1¾	cups dry white wine
1½	cups low-sodium chicken broth
1	pound carrots (about 6 medium), peeled and cut into 1-inch pieces
3	tablespoons Minute tapioca
2	tablespoons soy sauce
2	bay leaves
4	pounds bone-in chicken pieces (split breasts or thighs), skin removed and trimmed
	Ground black pepper
1	cup heavy cream
¼	cup minced fresh tarragon leaves

1. Heat the oil in a 12-inch nonstick skillet over medium-high heat until shimmering. Add the mushrooms, onions, garlic, thyme, and ¼ teaspoon salt, cover, and cook, stirring often, until the mushrooms have released their liquid, 8 to 10 minutes.

2. Uncover the skillet and continue to cook until the mushrooms and onions are lightly browned, 8 to 10 minutes. Stir in the wine, scraping up any browned bits, and simmer until thickened and measures about 3 cups, about 5 minutes.

3. Transfer the mixture to the slow cooker and stir in the broth, carrots, tapioca, soy sauce, and bay leaves until evenly combined. Season the chicken

with salt and pepper and nestle it in the slow cooker. Cover and cook on low until the chicken is tender, 4 to 5 hours.

4. Transfer the chicken and carrots to a serving platter and tent loosely with foil. Let the cooking liquid settle for 5 minutes, then gently tilt the slow cooker and remove as much fat as possible from the surface using a large spoon. Remove the bay leaves, stir in the cream and tarragon, and season with salt and pepper to taste. Spoon 1 cup of the sauce over the chicken and serve, passing the remaining sauce separately.

➤ VARIATION

Slow-Cooker Chicken with Lemon and Artichokes

Follow the recipe for Slow-Cooker Chicken with White Wine, Tarragon, and Cream, substituting 1 pound frozen artichoke hearts, thawed, for the mushrooms in step 1. Stir 1 tablespoon juice from 1 lemon into the sauce with the cream and tarragon before serving.

SLOW-COOKER CHICKEN PROVENÇAL

CHICKEN PROVENÇAL MAY REPRESENT THE best of French peasant cooking—chicken on the bone is slowly simmered with tomatoes, garlic, herbs, and olives—but it is not a very well-known dish here in the United States, and even less known as a slow-cooker recipe. We soon discovered why. The handful of recipes we tested produced rubbery, dry chicken, dull and muddy flavors, and a sauce that was either too thick or too thin, too sweet or too greasy. (We even found one recipe that included ½ cup of mayonnaise!) Could we successfully create a slow-cooker version of this traditional, flavorful dish? We headed to the test kitchen to find out.

The chicken was our natural starting point. Most recipes we reviewed begin with browning a cut-up whole chicken, then removing it from the pot, sautéing some aromatic vegetables, deglazing the pot with white wine or dry vermouth, adding stock, tomatoes, olives, and herbs, and finally simmering the chicken in the slow cooker until it is cooked. When we used a whole cut-up chicken, we encountered several problems. First, the skin, although crisp after browning, turned soggy and unappealing after braising in the slow cooker. Second, the wings contained mostly inedible skin and very little meat. Finally, with all this skin in the slow cooker, we were left with a greasy sauce. We tried again, this time using bone-in chicken pieces, and only breasts and thighs. The meat came out tender, moist, and flavorful and the sauce was much less greasy, especially since we removed the skin from the chicken prior to cooking.

Next, we addressed searing the chicken, which is usually the first step in most slow-cooker recipes. When we tried searing skinless chicken pieces, they stuck to the pan the outer layer of the chicken becoming tough and dry from browning. The skin, it turns out, acts as a necessary cushion between the meat and the pan and without it searing wasn't a viable option. Our slow-cooker archives led us to a favorite test kitchen technique for replacing the fond by adding tomato paste to the sautéed

PITTING NIÇOISE OLIVES

Removing the pits from tiny niçoise olives by hand is not an easy job; if you can't find pitted olives at the supermarket, use this method.

Cover a cutting board with a clean kitchen towel and spread the olives on top, about 1 inch apart from each other. Place a second clean towel over the olives. Using a mallet, pound all of the olives firmly for 10 to 15 seconds, being careful not to split the pits. Remove the top towel and, using your fingers, press the pit out of each olive.

aromatics, which encourages browning and simulates the roasted flavor of seared meat.

Our final tests with the chicken focused on the timing. Chicken is notorious for drying out with extended cooking, even in the moist environment of a slow cooker. After several rubbery results, we found that the optimal cooking time and temperature was four to five hours on low. Any longer and the chicken overcooked, and cooking the chicken on high for half that time turned out inconsistent results and negated using a slow cooker in the first place.

With the chicken issues squared away, we turned our attention to the sauce. We were after a light, fresh taste. Onions, lots of garlic, and tomato paste were set as the foundation. Preliminary tests showed that both dry white wine and dry vermouth work well for deglazing the pan, but the wine turned out to be the favorite among tasters; the vermouth seemed to exaggerate the acidity of the tomatoes. Tomato sauce and pureed canned tomatoes each produced a thick, sweet, overbearing sauce reminiscent of bad Italian restaurant fare. Canned diced tomatoes, though more promising, presented the opposite problem: even when drained they contain a fair amount of liquid, and the resulting sauce was too thin. We found a happy medium in crushed tomatoes, which improved the sauce dramatically— the sauce coated the chicken without overwhelming it. The final addition of chicken broth rounded out the flavors while providing a bit more volume.

Whole niçoise olives appeared in nearly every recipe, but tasters complained about the pits. No problem—we were able to find pitted niçoise olives in our supermarket. As for seasonings, tasters liked a combination of fresh oregano and parsley.

We considered olive oil to be essential (after all, it's a signature ingredient of Provençal cuisine), and stirring in 2 teaspoons at the end perfumed the dish. The final item on our list was lemon zest, a common and, as it turned out, welcome addition. We found that the zest is best added at the end, sprinkled in with the parsley and olives. These last light and fresh touches of olive oil, lemon zest, and parsley showed us how far we'd come from even the thought of adding mayonnaise to this dish. We felt we had restored a classic to the status it deserves.

Slow-Cooker Chicken Provençal

SERVES 6 TO 8

If pitted niçoise olives are unavailable, see the pitting illustration on page 230. This dish is often served with rice or slices of crusty bread, but polenta is also a good accompaniment. See page 204 for make-ahead instructions.

2	tablespoons vegetable oil
3	medium onions, minced
12	medium garlic cloves, minced or pressed through a garlic press (about 4 tablespoons)
2	tablespoons tomato paste
	Salt
1½	cups dry white wine
1	(28-ounce) can crushed tomatoes
2	cups low-sodium chicken broth
1	tablespoon minced fresh oregano leaves
2	bay leaves
4	pounds bone-in chicken pieces (split breasts or thighs), skin removed and trimmed
	Ground black pepper
½	cup pitted niçoise olives, chopped coarse (see note)
¼	cup minced fresh parsley leaves
2	teaspoons extra-virgin olive oil
1½	teaspoons grated zest from 1 lemon
1	lemon, cut into wedges

1. Heat the oil in a 12-inch nonstick skillet over medium-high heat until shimmering. Add the onions, garlic, tomato paste, and ¼ teaspoon salt and cook, stirring often, until the onions are softened and lightly browned, 10 to 12 minutes. Stir in the wine, scraping up any browned bits, bring to a simmer, and cook for about 5 minutes, until the mixture measures about 2 cups.

2. Transfer the mixture to the slow cooker and stir in the tomatoes, chicken broth, oregano, and bay leaves until evenly combined. Season the chicken with salt and pepper and nestle it in the slow cooker. Cover and cook on low until the chicken is tender, 4 to 5 hours.

3. Transfer the chicken to a serving platter and tent loosely with foil. Let the cooking liquid settle for 5 minutes, then gently tilt the slow cooker and remove as much fat as possible from the surface using a large spoon. Remove the bay leaves, stir in the olives, parsley, olive oil, and lemon zest, and season with salt and pepper to taste. Spoon 1 cup of the sauce over the chicken and serve, passing the remaining sauce and lemon wedges separately.

SLOW-COOKER COQ AU VIN

IN THIS TRADITIONALLY PROVINCIAL FRENCH peasant dish, chicken is simmered for hours in red wine, allowing the meat to soak up the liquid's rich flavor. Mushrooms, herbs, and onions—and sometimes a little bit of pork fat—round out this simple yet flavorful stew. The extended simmering is what gives this dish its robust flavor, so it seemed like a natural for the slow cooker. We would, of course, have to make some changes, but we had high hopes of duplicating the rich, complex taste. Though it's often thought of as a special occasion meal, we also hoped to simplify our coq au vin recipe to the point that we wouldn't have to wait for a formal dinner party to serve it.

We carefully studied the traditionally flavored slow-cooker coq au vin recipes we found. The basic process was to cook bacon in a Dutch oven, sauté a cut-up chicken with mirepoix vegetables (carrots, celery, and onions) in the rendered fat, transfer everything to the slow cooker, and simmer the chicken in red wine, herbs, and chicken stock, adding pearl onions and mushrooms as garnish. We decided to start by focusing on the chicken.

In the test kitchen, many of our existing slow-cooker chicken recipes call for bone-in, skinless chicken thighs because they retain their moisture in the slow cooker slightly better than breasts. But we discovered that if careful attention is paid to the clock (no more than four to five hours on the low setting), bone-in breasts can retain their juiciness in the slow cooker and can be an option as well for this recipe. We had also learned through previous tests that using bone-in chicken is essential for protecting the meat from drying out, and it has the added benefit of fortifying the sauce with an even stronger chicken flavor.

While many recipes call for searing chicken to develop a hearty fond for the base of the sauce, in the past we've found ways around this process by creating a faux fond. Our technique involves sautéing the aromatics with tomato paste and adding a dash of soy sauce to the slow cooker. Since this had worked so well in the past, we stuck with it for our coq au vin. However, instead of cooking the aromatics in vegetable oil as we normally would, we opted for bacon fat for added flavor and smokiness, reserving the bacon to garnish our finished dish.

Our first attempt at putting it all together had us dumping a bottle of red wine and a splash of chicken broth into the slow cooker along with the chicken and sautéed aromatics. This version came out tasting boozy and astringent, and the chicken released juices that we hadn't accounted for. To get a rounder, less astringent flavor, we tried reducing the wine in the skillet with the aromatics and we cut back on the amount of chicken broth to compensate for the juices released from the chicken during cooking. This trick worked beautifully. By the time the wine mixture had reduced to 3 cups, its flavors had concentrated and the boozy taste had cooked off considerably. Further testing led us to remove the broth entirely, which let the concentrated wine flavor really jump out.

Some recipes call for sautéing pearl onions and mushrooms with the aromatics and adding them at the onset of cooking. However, because of the strength of the red wine sauce, we found that it was best to brown the mushrooms and pearl onions separately, then stir them in at the end just before serving. As for the type of mushrooms and onions, cremini mushrooms were favored over button for their earthier flavor, and tasters thought frozen pearl onions were nearly as good as fresh. The quicker prep time for the frozen variety gave

them the winning edge—and made our recipe that much easier.

To thicken the sauce, some classic French recipes call for whisking in chicken's blood or a *beurre manié* (a mixture of cold butter and flour). While we were intrigued, we weren't too keen on adding blood—or looking for a place that sells it—and a beurre manié seemed fussy. Instead, we opted for inauthentic (but simpler) instant tapioca, adding it to the slow cooker at the start of cooking. This produced a sauce with the thick, glossy texture we were after.

Tasters marveled at how close we'd come to matching the flavor of an original coq au vin with a fraction of the effort. Rich and brimming with the flavors of bacon, mushrooms, and red wine, this coq au vin shed the dish's haute-cuisine, labor-intensive trappings and moved it to the convenience of the slow cooker.

Slow-Cooker Coq au Vin

SERVES 6 TO 8

Regular bacon can be substituted for the thick-cut bacon. A $7 to $10 bottle of medium-bodied red table wine made from a blend of grapes, such as a Côtes du Rhône, will work well here. See page 204 for make-ahead instructions.

4	ounces (about 3 slices) thick-cut bacon, cut into ¼-inch pieces
2	medium onions, minced
8	medium garlic cloves, peeled and crushed (see the illustrations on page 63)
2	tablespoons tomato paste
2	teaspoons minced fresh thyme leaves, or ½ teaspoon dried
	Salt
1	(750-ml) bottle dry red wine (see note)
⅓	cup soy sauce
3	tablespoons Minute tapioca
2	bay leaves
4	pounds bone-in chicken pieces (split breasts or thighs), skin removed and trimmed
	Ground black pepper
2	cups frozen pearl onions, thawed

½ cup water

3 tablespoons unsalted butter

2 teaspoons sugar

10 ounces cremini mushrooms, trimmed, wiped clean, and halved if small or quartered if large

1. Cook the bacon in a 12-inch nonstick skillet over medium heat until crisp, about 8 minutes. Transfer the bacon to a paper towel–lined plate, leaving the fat in the skillet, and refrigerate until serving time.

2. Pour off all but 2 tablespoons of the bacon fat left in the skillet and place over medium-high heat until shimmering. Add the onions, garlic, tomato paste, thyme, and ¼ teaspoon salt and cook, stirring often, until the onions are softened and lightly browned, 8 to 10 minutes. Stir in the wine, scraping up any browned bits, and cook until the mixture measures about 3 cups, 8 to 10 minutes.

3. Transfer the mixture to the slow cooker and stir in the soy sauce, tapioca, and bay leaves until evenly combined. Season the chicken with salt and pepper and nestle it in the slow cooker. Cover and cook on low until the meat is tender, 4 to 5 hours.

4. About 20 minutes before serving, bring the pearl onions, water, butter, and sugar to a boil in a 12-inch nonstick skillet over medium-high heat. Reduce the heat to medium, cover, and cook until the onions are fully thawed and tender, 5 to 8 minutes. Uncover, increase the heat to medium-high, and cook until all the liquid evaporates, 3 to 4 minutes. Add the mushrooms and ¼ teaspoon salt and cook, without stirring, for 2 minutes. Stir and continue to cook, stirring often, until the vegetables are browned and glazed, 8 to 12 minutes. Remove from the heat and set aside.

5. Let the cooking liquid settle for 5 minutes, then gently tilt the slow cooker and remove as much fat as possible from the surface using a large spoon. Remove the bay leaves, stir in the pearl onion mixture, and season with salt and pepper to taste. Reheat the bacon in the microwave on high power until heated through and crisp, about 30 seconds. Sprinkle individual portions of stew with the crisp bacon before serving.

SLOW-COOKER CHICKEN POT PIE

THE IDEA OF SIMPLIFYING A TRADITIONAL chicken pot pie recipe by making the filling in the slow cooker has occurred to us on many occasions. But time after time we shied away. We just didn't think that a slow cooker could produce an up-to-par gravy, with its complex layers of flavor and its perfectly silky texture, somewhere between a soup and a stew. Not to mention the issues with the vegetables. A filling that is chock-full of bright, fresh vegetables going into the slow cooker looks completely different after four or five hours; carrots may survive, but ingredients like peas and fresh herbs fade from spring green to drab olive. Then there was poaching the chicken. Despite all the issues, we weren't going to be scared off this time; we suspected it could be done, so we set off for the test kitchen determined to succeed.

The elements we were after included a flavorful, silky sauce, one that was perfectly thickened without the extra work of making a roux, vegetables that were bright and tender-crisp even after hours of cooking, and chicken that was perfectly cooked—all done in the slow cooker. The final step of baking the finished filling in the oven with a biscuit topping would be the easy part.

We began by determining the ideal cut of chicken for our pot pie. We knew from previous slow-cooker experience that bone-in chicken thighs are the cut of choice when the meat is to be shredded before serving (which is how we prefer chicken in pot pies), because they remain more moist and tender than bone-in chicken breasts. We also knew that discarding the chicken skin before adding the meat to the slow cooker would prevent the final sauce from becoming overly greasy. We decided not to sear the chicken prior to adding it to the slow cooker; not only were the flavor benefits from doing so minimal, but searing would also cause the meat to develop a crusty exterior, a texture we did not want in the pie. Instead, we would get our depth of flavor from sautéing the aromatics, onions and garlic, prior to adding them to the slow cooker.

With the chicken's preparation decided, our next task was to develop a sauce that was flavorful, creamy, and of the proper consistency. The sauce for chicken pot pie is traditionally based on a roux (a mixture of butter and flour sautéed together briefly) that is thinned with chicken broth and often enriched with cream. However, we had mixed results in the slow cooker using a roux for this recipe. The sauce came out gloppy and heavy. Adding cream at the onset of cooking also proved troublesome, as it was fully curdled by the end. To solve these issues we did two things. First, we moved away from the traditional roux, instead using instant tapioca, which we added at the start of cooking along with the chicken broth. It gave us a velvety sauce that our tasters felt was as rich as a traditional roux-thickened sauce. To solve the curdling issue, we decided to add the cream at the end, which kept it from breaking during the long cooking process. We tested amounts of cream from ¼ to 1 cup and finally settled on ½ cup, which tasters felt was rich but not overwhelming. We found that the bones improved the flavor of the broth during the long cooking time, while deglazing the aromatics with white wine gave the sauce a touch of acidity. Adding soy sauce, which contains natural glutamates (flavor enhancers), made the sauce taste deeper and rounder.

We then moved on to the vegetables. We tested our pot pie with the classic combination of peas and carrots, using raw vegetables, sautéed vegetables, frozen vegetables, and parboiled vegetables. After comparing the pies, we found that raw carrots added a subtle sweetness to the sauce and were perfectly cooked after four to five hours. Frozen peas—the most convenient option—held their color and flavor best, especially when simply stirred into the sauce at the end. A handful of parsley added a touch of freshness to the finished filling.

With the filling complete, we turned to our biscuit topping. Drop biscuits were the simple choice. We wanted biscuits that were crisp and golden brown on the outside, with the customary drop-biscuit craggy tops and tender, fluffy insides. While oil-based biscuits are easy to work with, they lack flavor, so butter was a must. Using buttermilk, rather than milk, gave them a rich, buttery tang and made the exteriors more crispy and the interiors

fluffier. To ensure the proper rise, choosing the right leavener was an important step. An abundance of baking powder tasted metallic, but because buttermilk provides the acid that soda needs to act, we realized we could replace some of the baking powder with baking soda. This gave us the rise we needed without the metallic bitterness.

We knew that properly combining the butter and buttermilk would be one of our biggest challenges for the biscuits. If both ingredients weren't at just the right temperature, the melted butter clumped in the buttermilk. We didn't like testing and retesting temperatures, so we went ahead and made a batch with lumpy buttermilk. The result was a surprisingly well-risen biscuit with a light, fluffy texture. The water in the lumps of butter had turned to steam in the oven, helping create height.

Now we just had to marry the pot pie and the biscuits. We transferred the finished pot pie filling to a 13 by 9-inch baking dish and dropped the raw biscuit dough on top. While the top of the biscuits browned, the bottoms were gummy and doughy. To solve this problem we parcooked the biscuits until the bottoms were just set but the tops had no color. We placed these biscuits on top of the hot pot pie filling that had just been poured from the slow cooker and put the whole pie in the oven. The biscuit tops browned in about 25 minutes (and the bottoms were no longer gummy). With that, we had a chicken pot pie with a creamy, perfectly textured gravy, bright vegetables, and flavorful chicken—and we had done it successfully in the slow cooker.

Slow-Cooker Chicken Pot Pie with Biscuit Topping
SERVES 8
While we think the best pot pies are those made with homemade biscuits, you can substitute store-bought biscuit dough (such as those in pop-and-bake canisters). See page 204 for make-ahead instructions.

POT PIE FILLING
2 tablespoons vegetable oil
2 medium onions, minced
4 medium garlic cloves, minced or pressed
    through a garlic press (about 4 teaspoons)

2   teaspoons minced fresh thyme leaves, or
    ½ teaspoon dried
    Salt
½   cup dry white wine
2   cups low-sodium chicken broth
1   pound carrots (about 6 medium), peeled
    and cut into ½-inch pieces
3   tablespoons soy sauce
3   tablespoons Minute tapioca
2   bay leaves
4   pounds bone-in chicken thighs
    (about 12 medium), skin removed
    and trimmed
    Ground black pepper
1   cup frozen peas
½   cup heavy cream
¼   cup minced fresh parsley leaves

BISCUIT TOPPING

1½ cups (7½ ounces) unbleached
    all-purpose flour
1½ teaspoons baking powder
1   teaspoon sugar
¼   teaspoon baking soda
¼   teaspoon salt
¾   cup buttermilk, chilled
6   tablespoons (¾ stick) unsalted butter,
    melted and cooled

1. FOR THE POT PIE FILLING: Heat the oil in a 12-inch nonstick skillet over medium-high heat until shimmering. Add the onions, garlic, thyme, and ¼ teaspoon salt and cook, stirring often, until the onions are softened and lightly browned, 8 to 10 minutes. Stir in the wine, scraping up any browned bits.

2. Transfer the mixture to the slow cooker and stir in the chicken broth, carrots, soy sauce, tapioca, and bay leaves until evenly combined. Season the chicken with salt and pepper and nestle it into the slow cooker. Cover and cook on low until the chicken is tender and beginning to pull away from the bone, 4 to 5 hours.

3. Transfer the chicken to a serving platter and tent loosely with foil. Let the cooking liquid settle for 5 minutes, then gently tilt the slow cooker and remove as much fat as possible from the surface

using a large spoon. Using 2 forks, shred the chicken, following the illustration on page 116, discarding the bones and fat. Stir the shredded chicken back into the slow cooker along with the peas, cream, and parsley. Season the filling with salt and pepper to taste. Pour the filling into a 13 by 9-inch baking dish.

4. FOR THE BISCUIT TOPPING: About an hour before the filling is done, adjust an oven rack to the lower-middle position and heat the oven to 375 degrees. Line a baking sheet with parchment paper. Whisk the flour, baking powder, sugar, baking soda, and salt together in a large bowl. In a small bowl, stir the chilled buttermilk and melted butter together until the butter forms small clumps. Stir the buttermilk mixture into the flour mixture with a rubber spatula until just incorporated and no streaks of flour remain. Using a greased ¼-cup measure, scoop out and drop 8 mounds of dough onto the prepared baking sheet, spacing them about 1½ inches apart. Bake until the bottoms are just set, about 8 minutes.

5. Increase the oven temperature to 400 degrees. Place the parcooked biscuits on top of the pot pie filling. Bake until the tops are golden brown and the filling is bubbling, about 25 minutes. Let cool for 10 minutes before serving.

➤ VARIATION

Slow-Cooker Chicken Pot Pie with Pie Crust Topping

Follow the recipe for Slow-Cooker Chicken Pot Pie with Biscuit Topping, substituting two unbaked store-bought pie crusts for the biscuit topping. Brush half of one of the unbaked pie crusts with water, then overlap half the second pie crust on top of the moistened area (the moisture helps seal the two pieces together). Roll them together to form a 15 by 11-inch rectangle. Roll the dough loosely around the rolling pin, then gently unroll it over the casserole dish and trim, following the illustrations on page 236. Make sure the filling is hot when you do this; otherwise the topping will turn gummy. Cut four 1-inch vent holes down the center length of the dough. Bake the pot pie in a 425-degree oven until the pastry is golden and the filling is bubbly, about 25 minutes.

TOPPING POT PIE WITH PIE DOUGH

1. After overlapping two pie crusts and rolling them into a single 15 x 11-inch rectangle, roll the dough loosely over the rolling pin and unroll it evenly over the baking dish.

2. After laying the rectangle of dough over the pot pie filling, trim the dough to within ½ inch of the pan lip.

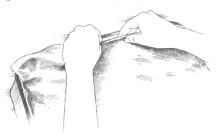

3. For a fluted edge, tuck the overhanging dough back under itself so the folded edge is flush with the lip of the pan.

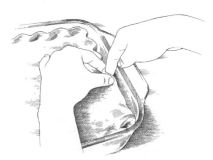

4. Holding the dough with the thumb and index finger of one hand, push the dough with the index finger of your other hand to form a pleated edge. Repeat all around the edge to flute the dough.

SLOW-COOKER CHICKEN AND SAUSAGE GUMBO

GUMBO IS A LEGENDARY STEW-LIKE DISH from Louisiana, famous not only for its complex flavor but also for its temperamental nature. Generally speaking, gumbo usually includes some type of seafood, poultry, or small game along with sausage or some other highly seasoned, cured smoked pork. Also present is the Creole and Cajun "holy trinity" of onion, bell pepper, and celery. Quite often, gumbos are thickened with okra or ground dried sassafras leaves, known as filé (pronounced fee-LAY) powder. And last, but very important, gumbos are usually flavored with a dark brown roux. This roux is the heart of a good gumbo. Unfortunately, it can be incredibly tricky to make, requiring careful attention to temperature and time to get the flavor just right. Our goal was to re-create the flavors of this legendary dish, dark roux and all, into an easier recipe that could be made in a slow cooker.

In classic French cooking, a roux is nothing more than flour cooked gently in some type of fat to form a paste that is used to thicken sauces. If the flour is just barely cooked, you have a white roux; if cooked to a light beige, you have a blond roux. When it reaches the color of light brown sugar, you have brown roux. Creole and Cajun cooks push the process to the outer limit for their gumbos. When they make roux, they keep cooking until the flour reaches a shade of very dark brown, sometimes just short of black. This breaks down the starches in the flour to the point where the roux offers relatively little thickening power. Instead, it imbues gumbo with a complex, toasty, smoky flavor and a deep, rich brown color that define the dish. The problem is that the flour can burn very easily, and the only safeguards against that are relatively low heat and constant stirring. This means that it often takes as long as an hour of constant stirring and careful attention to make a dark roux. Few cooks are willing to go to this trouble, so we had to shorten that time if we wanted a more practical recipe for our slow-cooker gumbo.

Our goals for this recipe were falling into place. Obviously, the roux was key. We wanted to feature its flavor over a cacophony of herbs and spices and to streamline its preparation. Once we mastered the roux, we would have to determine the components and flavorings of the stew. As a starting point, we knew we wanted to feature chicken over shrimp or game and to include sausage, which, in our opinion, was absolutely necessary for an authentic, richly flavorful gumbo. Finally, we would have to decide on the various ingredients and flavorings, including whether to use okra or filé as a thickener—using either would bring not only viscosity but also a distinct flavor to the gumbo.

First, the roux. The distinctive taste, color, and aroma of dark roux is a central characteristic of Creole and Cajun food. Most of the recipes we saw called for cooking the roux over low heat while stirring constantly for anywhere from 40 to 60 minutes or, as they say in Louisiana, "about the time it takes to drink two cold beers." Since the roux truly does need to be stirred constantly as it cooks to avoid burning the flour, which would give the mixture a noticeably bitter taste, time was the first issue we had to address. We decided that 20 minutes would be an acceptable time allotment for making our roux. Any longer than that, we reasoned, and most cooks would probably skip over this dish. Furthermore, and just as important, our tasters discerned little difference in flavor between gumbos made with the traditional low-heat, long-cooking roux and those with a roux that was cooked faster and hotter.

To hit that 20-minute mark, we knew we'd have to increase the heat and probably preheat the oil before adding the flour. We began with the widely used 1-1 ratio of all-purpose flour to vegetable oil, using ½ cup of each. Some cooks recommend heating the oil until it smokes and then cooking the roux over high heat. Though this method produced a very dark roux in less than 10 minutes, the sizzle and smoke was too much for us. The process felt out of control, and the specter of burned roux loomed large.

So we slowed things down a bit, preheating the oil over medium heat for only about two minutes (well below the smoke point), then added the flour and began to cook the roux. At the 20-minute stopping point, the roux had cooked to a deep reddish brown, about the color of dark chocolate. It had started to smoke once or twice, but it cooled fairly quickly when we removed it from the heat, stirred it for a minute, then returned it to the burner. In all, the process was much less nerve-wracking than the high-heat methods we had tried, and it yielded absolutely acceptable results.

We experimented with a number of fats beyond the vegetable oil—including bacon fat, sausage fat, butter, and different types of oil—but ended up preferring the flavor and ease of vegetable oil. We tried different ratios of fat to flour, varying them by as much as 6 tablespoons up and down from the ½ cup starting point, but none improved on the original 1-1 ratio in terms of either taste or performance.

We'd seen instructions for microwave roux along the way and thought it might reduce the time and effort spent even further. The microwave roux seemed vaguely promising until the day we turned the test kitchen into a scene from a *Lethal Weapon* movie by putting a superheated, microwave-safe bowl with its smoking-hot contents down on a damp counter. The bowl did not merely shatter, it exploded, literally raining glass shards and globs of fiery hot roux into every corner of the room. We were lucky no one was hurt and sure enough, a quick call to the test kitchens at Corning Consumer Products confirmed that they do not recommend heating oil in any Pyrex product for 10 minutes on high in the microwave. We crossed that method off the list.

Throughout the roux testing, another problem was cropping up: All along, we had followed the instructions in most of the recipes we'd studied to add simmering broth, which is about 200 degrees, to a hot roux-vegetable mixture, also about 200 degrees. Occasionally, the roux and broth would mix smoothly, but sometimes they wouldn't, and the result was little globs of brown flour floating in a layer of oil at the surface of the liquid. We were perplexed. But there is another, if less popular, school of thought that we had come across. A few recipes advise cooling either the roux or the broth before combining them. Sure enough, adding room-temperature broth (which was far easier than cooling the roux) did the trick. Room-temperature broth, at about 75 degrees, mixed into the hot roux beautifully; broth at about 150 degrees also mixed in very well and was only slightly less smooth than the batch tested with cooler broth. Another key to a smooth gumbo was to thoroughly mix the roux into the liquid before the starch in the flour in the roux had a chance to swell up and gelatinize.

Looking next to the sausage, we had a few options, but only one that was truly authentic. Andouille, a spicy smoked Cajun sausage, is ubiquitous in classic gumbo. Attempts to substitute andouille with kielbasa or chorizo took away from the classic gumbo taste we were after. The only modification we needed to make was the thickness of the andouille slices. Anything less than ½ inch and the sausage threatened to dry out.

The rest of the recipe development process focused on testing the wide range of ingredients and flavorings that constitute gumbo. Our two biggest flavoring questions concerned tomatoes (some say that gumbo just isn't gumbo without them) and garlic. Tasters finally agreed that gumbo was just fine without tomatoes, but they gave the thumbs up to garlic, six cloves of it, in fact. We found that other seasonings in gumbo can range from elaborate mixtures of herbs, spices, and sauces down to nothing more than salt. We tried what seemed like one hundred seasoning variations and finally settled on a simple combination of thyme and bay leaves. In our experiments with different proportions for the holy trinity of onion, bell pepper, and celery, a ratio of about ½ part celery to 1 part pepper to 1 part onion tasted best. We did, however, add red peppers to the traditional green bell pepper, on account of their sweeter, fuller flavor.

Next we considered the level of spicy heat, usually provided by cayenne pepper either alone or in combination with a hot pepper sauce. We wanted enough spice to feel a slight heat in the back of our throats after we swallowed a couple of spoonfuls. A mere ¼ teaspoon of cayenne did the trick, and tasters favored the powder over the vinegary taste of bottled hot sauce.

Last, we considered whether to thicken the gumbo with okra or filé powder. While both are probably acquired tastes, tasters preferred okra for the color, texture, and flavor it added. Adding it to the slow cooker at the onset of cooking did away with its characteristic sliminess.

By the time we had finished cranking out slow cooker after slow cooker of gumbo, its once exotic Southern flavor and aroma had become familiar, even comforting. With our early travails now just a memory, we had become hooked on this Louisiana dish's deep, smoky flavor.

DARK ROUX PRIMER

With flour just added to the oil, the roux at left is very light in color. After about 10 minutes of cooking, the mixture browns to about the color of peanut butter (center). The completed dark roux, at right, is a deep reddish brown, almost the color of dark chocolate.

Slow-Cooker Chicken and Andouille Sausage Gumbo

SERVES 6 TO 8

Making a dark roux can be dangerous because its temperature can exceed 400 degrees. Therefore, use a deep pot for cooking the roux and long-handled utensils for stirring it, being careful not to splash it on yourself. Serve with rice. You can prepare this recipe through step 2 and refrigerate the mixture in an airtight container overnight; however, it will need to be reheated before adding it to the slow cooker as the mixture will have solidified.

½	cup vegetable oil
½	cup unbleached all-purpose flour
2	medium onions, minced
1	red bell pepper, stemmed, seeded, and chopped fine
1	green bell pepper, stemmed, seeded, and chopped fine
1	celery rib, chopped fine
6	medium garlic cloves, minced or pressed through a garlic press (about 2 tablespoons)
2	teaspoons minced fresh thyme leaves, or ½ teaspoon dried
	Salt
¼	teaspoon cayenne pepper
6	cups low-sodium chicken broth, room temperature (see note)
1	pound andouille sausage, sliced ½ inch thick
12	ounces fresh okra, sliced ½ inch thick, or frozen cut okra, thawed
2	bay leaves
4	pounds bone-in chicken thighs (about 12 medium), skin removed and trimmed
	Ground black pepper
4	scallions, sliced thin
2	tablespoons minced fresh parsley leaves

1. Heat the oil in a large Dutch oven over medium heat until shimmering. Gradually stir in the flour with a wooden spoon, working out any small lumps. Cook, stirring constantly, reaching into the corners of the pan, until the mixture has a toasty aroma and is deep reddish brown, about the color of dark chocolate, about 20 minutes. (The roux will thin as it cooks; if it begins to smoke, remove it from the heat and stir constantly to cool slightly.)

2. Stir in the onions, bell peppers, celery, garlic, thyme, 1 teaspoon salt, and cayenne and cook, stirring often, until the vegetables soften, 10 to 12 minutes. Stir in the chicken broth in a slow, steady stream. Increase the heat to medium-high and bring the mixture to a simmer.

3. Once simmering, transfer the mixture to the slow cooker and stir in the sausage, okra, and bay leaves until evenly combined. Season the chicken with salt and pepper and nestle it in the slow cooker. Cover and cook on low until the chicken is tender, 4 to 5 hours.

4. Remove the chicken to a platter to cool slightly. Let the cooking liquid settle for 5 minutes, then gently tilt the slow cooker and remove as much fat as possible from the surface using a large spoon. Using 2 forks, shred the chicken, following the illustration on page 116, discarding the bones and fat. Remove the bay leaves and stir in the shredded chicken, scallions, and parsley. Season with salt and pepper to taste before serving.

SLOW-COOKER CURRIED CHICKEN WITH POTATOES

THE ROBUST FLAVOR OF CURRIES, WHETHER they are made with vegetables or meat, are central to Indian cuisine. When made well, these dishes showcase complex layers of flavor and at the same time are light and clean tasting. Curry powder, the key ingredient, is actually a blend of 20 different spices and herbs, and it is what makes these dishes complex and engaging. However, we found it was easy for curries to become overpowering, with cloyingly thick sauces. We wanted to create a chicken curry recipe that was mild but flavor-packed, with a light but substantial sauce that would hold its own when served over couscous or rice. And perhaps most importantly, we wanted to keep things simple by preparing our recipe in the slow cooker.

We began with the chicken. Based on prior test kitchen experience, we knew a few things about cooking chicken in the slow cooker. First, bone-in chicken thighs are the cut of choice when the meat is to be shredded before serving because they remain more moist and tender than bone-in chicken breasts. Second, instead of browning the chicken, we found that browned aromatics effectively simulate the flavor of searing without the headache or mess. Third, discarding the chicken skin before adding the meat to the slow cooker prevents the final sauce from becoming overly greasy. We knew we would employ these rules here as well.

Moving on to the flavors of curry, we found the hassle and expense of making our own curry powder not worth the effort or cost—store-bought yellow curry powder tastes great. To balance and round out the flavor of the store-bought curry powder, we added a small amount of garam masala. Garam masala is a mixture of "warm" spices, including coriander, black pepper, cumin, cardamom, and cinnamon, and is typically used to finish Indian dishes. In this case, however, we preferred to add it at the onset of cooking along with the curry powder. Coaxing the maximum flavor from dried spices requires blooming them in hot oil, which we accomplished by adding the curry powder and garam masala to the skillet before sautéing the aromatics. This not only added multiple layers of flavor to the curry, but it also gave us a strong foundation for our faux fond. For aromatics, we found that a traditional combination of onions, carrots, garlic, ginger, and jalapeño chiles worked well, and once they were sautéed and fragrant, we deglazed the pan with chicken broth.

These first attempts at developing a well-rounded curry were promising, but the flavors still fell a bit flat, so we turned to tomatoes, a classic curry ingredient. We tried adding diced tomatoes with their juice, but the resulting stew had a diluted flavor that tasters disliked. We tried crushed tomatoes and "stir-fried" them in the hot skillet along with the aromatics in the hopes of coaxing out more flavor. This, too, fell short of expectations. Our solution was to add tomato paste to the skillet with the aromatics and to finish the curry with fresh diced tomatoes. The tomato paste lent flavor and body to the stew and the frying process intensified the tomato flavor. The fresh tomatoes added at the end provided acidity and brightness.

Coconut milk, a star ingredient in curries of many origins, adds an incredible richness to a stew, but because of its relatively high fat content, we were reluctant to add it at the beginning of the cooking process. When exposed to high heat, the fat in coconut milk has a tendency to separate, leaving behind an oil slick. Stirring it in at the end avoided this problem and gave the sauce a creamy texture while deepening the curry's flavor. Because coconut milk is so rich and thick, we found that we needed to increase the chicken broth from 2 to 2½ cups to temper the richness.

We wanted potatoes with our curry, but in our first attempts to add them, the chicken was done before the potatoes were soft enough to be edible. Quartering red potatoes solved the problem. The cut potatoes absorbed the flavors of the stew and helped to thicken the curry with their starch. To augment the thickening process, we stirred in instant tapioca, and, finally, to brighten the flavors and enhance the muted colors, we finished this classic Indian curry with green peas and fresh cilantro leaves.

Slow-Cooker Curried Chicken with Potatoes
SERVES 6 TO 8

We prefer Penzeys curry powder and McCormick garam masala. Serve this dish with Baked Long-Grain White Rice (see page 256). For more heat, include the jalapeño seeds and ribs when mincing. We prefer the richer flavor of regular coconut milk here; however, light coconut milk can be substituted. See page 204 for make-ahead instructions.

- 3 tablespoons vegetable oil
- 2 tablespoons sweet or mild curry powder
- I teaspoon garam masala
- 2 medium onions, minced
- I jalapeño chile, seeds and ribs removed, chile minced (see note)

2   tablespoons tomato paste

4   medium garlic cloves, minced or pressed
     through a garlic press (about 4 teaspoons)

1   tablespoon minced or grated fresh ginger
     Salt

2½   cups low-sodium chicken broth

1½   pounds red potatoes (about 5 medium),
     scrubbed and cut into 1-inch pieces

4   medium carrots, peeled and cut
     into 1-inch pieces

3   tablespoons soy sauce

3   tablespoons Minute tapioca

4   pounds bone-in chicken thighs
     (about 12 medium), skin removed
     and trimmed
     Ground black pepper

1   cup frozen peas

2   plum tomatoes, cored, seeded,
     and chopped fine

½   cup coconut milk (see note)

¼   cup minced fresh cilantro leaves

1. Heat 2 tablespoons of the oil in a 12-inch nonstick skillet over medium-high heat until shimmering. Add the curry powder and garam masala and cook until fragrant, about 10 seconds. Stir in the onions, jalapeño, tomato paste, garlic, ginger, and ¼ teaspoon salt and cook, stirring often, until the vegetables are lightly browned and softened, 10 to 12 minutes. Stir in 1 cup of the chicken broth, scraping up any browned bits.

2. Transfer the mixture to the slow cooker and stir in the remaining 1½ cups chicken broth, potatoes, carrots, soy sauce, and tapioca until evenly combined. Season the chicken with salt and pepper and nestle it in the slow cooker. Cover and cook on low until the chicken is tender, 4 to 5 hours.

3. Let the cooking liquid settle for 5 minutes, then gently tilt the slow cooker and remove as much fat as possible from the surface using a large spoon. Stir in the peas, tomatoes, coconut milk, and cilantro and let stand until the peas and tomatoes are heated through, about 5 minutes longer. Season with salt and pepper to taste before serving.

INGREDIENTS: Coconut Milk

Coconut milk is not the thin liquid found inside the coconut itself; that is called coconut water. Coconut milk is a product made by steeping equal parts shredded coconut meat and either warm milk or water. The meat is pressed or mashed to release as much liquid as possible, the mixture is strained, and the result is coconut milk.

We tasted seven nationally available brands (five regular and two light) in coconut pudding, coconut rice, Thai-style chicken soup, and curry. Among the five regular brands, tasters gravitated to those with more solid cream at the top of the can (most cans recommend shaking before opening to redistribute the solids). These brands also had a much stronger coconut flavor.

In the soup and curry, tasters preferred Chaokoh because of its exceptionally low sugar content (less than 1 gram per ⅓ cup). By comparison, brands with more than twice as much sugar (Ka-Me, Goya, and Thai Kitchen) tasted "saccharine." In the sweet recipes, tasters gave velvety Ka-Me top votes for

its "fruity" and "complex" flavor. In these recipes, the extra sugar was an advantage.

The light coconut milks we tasted were not nearly as creamy—a serious flaw in desserts but less so in soup. Of the two light brands tasted, we preferred the richer flavor of A Taste of Thai.

THE BEST COCONUT MILKS

Among the full-fat coconut milks, Ka-Me (left) is best suited for sweet recipes, while Chaokoh (center) is our favorite for soup and curry. A Taste of Thai light coconut milk (right) was surprisingly good, especially in soup.

241

SLOW-COOKER CHICKEN BROTH

CHICKEN BROTH IS THE BASIS FOR COUNT-less recipes, and it is arguably the most important liquid in any cook's repertoire. Sure, there are times when a store-bought broth will do the job (think dishes with a laundry list of ingredients and flavors), but there are many other recipes whose success depends on a rich, deeply flavored broth as the cornerstone ingredient. With the help of a full-bodied chicken broth, otherwise ordinary soups become extraordinary, and with the help of the slow cooker, we thought making a recipe for a chicken broth with as much unadulterated chicken flavor as possible was absolutely doable. After all, broths are simmered long and slow to draw out maximum flavor from the meat and bones, a task well suited for the slow cooker.

We started with the most common technique for making broth: the simmering method. We placed all the ingredients (chicken, vegetables, aromatics, and water) in our slow cooker, simmered everything for hours, then strained and defatted the broth. We tested a tremendous number of ingredients—everything from thyme and parsley to carrots and parsnips—and found that we preferred stock with fewer ingredients. Onions, garlic, and salt complemented the flavor of the chicken; everything else was a distraction.

We tried making broth with a whole cut-up chicken, including whole legs and wings, as well as the more traditional neck and back. While a whole chicken yielded a decent broth, cutting it up was a little more work than we wanted, and we also thought some of the parts weren't necessary. Chicken legs alone made a broth that tasters described as "livery." Necks and backs drew the same comments. Chicken wings were the surprise winner—the resulting broth was remarkably clear, refined, and full-flavored.

When we tasted the various batches of broth at different intervals, it was clear that more time yields a better broth—up to a point. About eight hours on low or up to five hours on high was optimal. However, after that, we could not taste any improvement; evidently the meat and bones were spent, having given up all their flavor.

FREEZING BROTH EFFICIENTLY

A. Ladle cooled broth into nonstick muffin tins and freeze. When the broth is frozen, twist the muffin tin just as you would twist an ice tray. Place the frozen blocks in a zipper-lock bag and seal it tightly. Store the bag in the freezer.

B1. An alternative is to pour the stock into a coffee mug lined with a quart-size zipper-lock bag.

B2. Place the filled bags flat in a large shallow roasting pan and freeze. Once the stock is solidly frozen, the bags can be removed from the pan and stored in the freezer.

Conventional wisdom says that stocks and broths should be skimmed of impurities, the foamy gray matter that floats to the top of the pot, during cooking. While we find this to be true when making stocks (because stocks use many more bones), we found no benefits from skimming our broth made from chicken wings in the slow cooker. Because the broth never comes to a strong boil, the foam is minimal; disturbing it halfway through cooking only reincorporates it into the broth. However, we did find it important to degrease the broth before straining. When we didn't do this, we found that the agitation of straining incorporated the fat into the broth, making our final product greasy. Additionally, if you have time it is worthwhile to degrease the broth a second time. Refrigerating the broth after straining will allow the remaining fat to congeal, at which point it can be removed. With that final detail ironed out, we had a robustly flavorful broth ready to go into our next dish or to be frozen for future use.

Once we had established our ingredient list and technique, we decided to give making a broth with roasted chicken a try. Roasted-chicken broth, a great base for sauces and gravies, gets its depth of flavor from roasted chicken and aromatics. This turned out to be a relatively simple departure from our master recipe. Tossing the chicken wings and onion in a roasting pan, we roasted them in a 450-degree oven until they were golden brown. From here we added everything to the slow cooker and let it go. The resulting stock was dark in color and had a pleasant caramelized-onion flavor.

With a modicum of effort and a small shopping list, we had transformed this kitchen staple to pure liquid gold with the help of our slow cooker. This recipe is definitely good enough to make us reconsider buying our broth in the future.

Slow-Cooker Chicken Broth
MAKES ABOUT 3 QUARTS
This chicken broth is good as a base for soups and stews, or even on its own. If you have time, you can degrease the broth a second time; refrigerating it after straining will allow the fat to congeal, at which point it can be removed.

- 3 pounds chicken wings
- 3 quarts water
- 1 medium onion, chopped medium
- 3 medium garlic cloves, peeled and crushed (see the illustrations on page 63)
- 1 teaspoon salt

1. Combine all of the ingredients in the slow cooker. Cover and cook, either on low or high, until the broth is deeply flavored and rich, 8 to 9 hours on low or 4 to 5 hours on high.

2. Let the broth settle for 5 minutes, then gently tilt the slow cooker and remove as much fat as possible from the surface using a large spoon. Strain the broth through a fine-mesh strainer into a large container, discarding the solids.

➤ VARIATION
Slow-Cooker Roasted-Chicken Broth
This broth has a deeper flavor that is well suited to stews, gravies, and sauces.

Follow the recipe for Slow-Cooker Chicken Broth, first roasting the chicken wings and onion together in a large nonstick roasting pan on the lower-middle rack of a 450-degree oven until golden brown, about 40 minutes. Transfer the roasted chicken wings and onion to the slow cooker, add the remaining ingredients, and continue to cook the broth as directed.

SLOW-COOKER BEEF AND BARLEY SOUP

BEEF AND BARLEY SOUP IS THE PERFECT cold-weather comfort food—the ultimate good-for-what-ails-you soup. What could be better than tender beef married with vegetables, a flavorful broth, and hearty barley? There were problems, though, with many of the recipes we tested, including a lack of flavor, minuscule amounts of beef, and textures that were either thin and watery or overly thick. We knew we'd need to come up with a recipe that yielded lots of beef, an intensely flavored broth, and just the right amount of barley to make this a satisfying one-pot meal. What better place to do this than in our slow cooker?

We started with blade steak, which is cut from the chuck or shoulder of the cow, trimming it into ½-inch pieces. Following the technique we discovered while developing our beef stew recipe (see page 205), we built a flavorful base for our soup by sautéing onions and carrots along with tomato paste, then deglazing the pan with a good-quality dry red wine, scraping up the tasty browned bits from the bottom. Many recipes contained either tomato puree (which we thought was too sweet) or canned diced tomatoes. The texture of the soup made with diced tomatoes left us cold, since we didn't care for long-cooked, flavorless bits of tomatoes floating on the top of our soup. We opted to pulse the tomatoes in the blender first, which worked perfectly.

Next we turned our attention to the remaining liquid component, which was water in many recipes. A great soup deserves good broth, not water, but because of the time involved in making homemade broth, that was not an option. As this was a beef soup, we naturally tested canned beef broth, but found its flavor a bit overwhelming. When we combined the beef broth with an equal amount of chicken broth, the soup tasted much more balanced. Chicken broth and beef broth, together with vegetables and soy sauce (a formula we had developed in previous slow-cooker recipes to serve as a fond replacement), gave us the deep flavors we wanted.

The final component of our soup was the barley. Pearl barley, the most commonly available variety, has had its tough outer hulls removed, which makes it a fairly quick-cooking grain and a good choice for this recipe. Since pearl barley can absorb two to three times its volume of cooking liquid, we knew that we needed to be judicious in the quantity we added to the soup. After all, we were making soup, not a side dish. After some experimenting, we found that ¼ cup was the ideal amount; it lent a pleasing texture to the soup without overfilling the slow cooker with swollen grains. A final sprinkling of fresh parsley added a bright finish to this simple yet satisfying dish.

Slow-Cooker
Beef and Barley Soup
SERVES 6 TO 8

The barley, cooked over a long period of time, adds a velvety texture as well as a nutty flavor to the soup. Two tablespoons of minced fresh dill can be substituted for the parsley. See page 204 for make-ahead instructions.

1	(28-ounce) can diced tomatoes
2	tablespoons vegetable oil
3	medium onions, minced
¼	cup tomato paste
1	tablespoon minced fresh thyme leaves, or 1 teaspoon dried
	Salt
½	cup dry red wine
2	cups low-sodium beef broth

TRIMMING BLADE STEAKS

1. Halve each steak lengthwise, leaving the gristle on one half.

2. Cut away the gristle from the half to which it is still attached.

3. Cut the trimmed meat crosswise into ½-inch pieces.

2 cups low-sodium chicken broth
2 carrots, peeled and cut into ½-inch pieces
⅓ cup soy sauce
¼ cup pearl barley
2 pounds blade steak, trimmed and cut
    into ½-inch pieces
    (see the illustrations on page 244)
    Ground black pepper
¼ cup minced fresh parsley leaves

1. Process the tomatoes with their juice in a food processor until smooth, about 15 seconds, and set aside. Heat the oil in 12-inch nonstick skillet over medium-high heat until shimmering. Add the onions, tomato paste, thyme, and ¼ teaspoon salt and cook, stirring often, until the vegetables are softened and lightly browned, 10 to 12 minutes. Stir in the wine, scraping up any browned bits.

2. Transfer the mixture to the slow cooker and stir in the processed tomatoes, broths, carrots, soy sauce, and barley until evenly combined. Season the meat with salt and pepper and nestle it in the slow cooker. Cover and cook, either on low or high, until the meat is tender, 9 to 11 hours on low or 5 to 7 hours on high.

3. Let the cooking liquid settle for 5 minutes, then gently tilt the slow cooker and remove as much fat as possible from the surface using a large spoon. Stir in the parsley and season with salt and pepper to taste before serving.

Slow-Cooker Italian Sunday Gravy

NOTHING COULD BE MORE WELCOMING ON a cold night than coming home to a rustic, flavor-packed meat sauce ready to toss with some pasta for a comforting, stick-to-your-ribs meal. We wondered if this classic Sunday "gravy," made from tomatoes, meatballs, stuffed and rolled flank steak known as *braciole,* pork chops, sausage, and aromatics, could transition from the stovetop to the slow cooker. It seemed like it would be ideally suited to our favored walk-away cooking medium.

However, our initial tests proved that idea to be far from the truth. The sauce was watery and puddled on our plate, sliding off the pasta into a disappointing mess. We decided to focus first on the meat of the issue, so to speak, then deal with the consistency of the sauce.

In classic recipes, the meat is first browned and drained of fat, then set aside so that the sauce can be built in the same pan. The browned meat is then added back to the sauce, the pan is covered, and the sauce simmers, slowly, until the meat is fall-off-the-bone tender. Finally, the meat is shredded and stirred into the sauce, at which point it is served over rigatoni with a good sprinkling of grated cheese. We would still follow these steps, making just a few tweaks here and there to streamline the recipe and make it work for the slow cooker.

First, we had to look at our selection of meats. Stovetop recipes call for a large stockpot, in which case the quantity and variety of meat doesn't really matter. But in our 6-quart slow cooker, we had to be more selective. The meatballs disintegrated when we added them at the outset, and since we didn't want to commit to adding them at the half-way mark, they failed to make the cut. Braciole tasted great, but it was too unwieldy for a slow cooker so it, too, was omitted.

Without the meatballs and braciole, our sauce lacked depth. To replace their beefy flavor, we tried other cuts of beef that work well in long-cooked recipes. Tasters preferred flank steak to brisket and chuck eye roast (both of which made the sauce too greasy when used in combination with pork). For the pork, regular chops were tough and chewy, and baby back ribs didn't add enough flavor. We settled on country-style pork ribs, which provided flavorful meat that fell off the bone after eight hours in the slow cooker. In fact, both the ribs and the flank steak were tender enough to shred and stir back into the sauce. Finally, both sweet and hot Italian sausages, sliced in half, added kick and stayed juicy.

Browning the sausage on the stovetop gave us a jump-start on our sauce. We used the same skillet, and some of the flavorful drippings from cooking the sausage, to brown our aromatics (onions, a whopping 12 cloves of garlic, and oregano) with some tomato paste. We had skipped browning in other slow-cooker recipes, but here, browned meat and the drippings were key, creating a good base for our sauce. We poured the red wine into the skillet to help pick up any brown bits before adding it all to the slow cooker.

We thought the tomatoes would be the easy part, but many of our early tests were too watery. There wasn't much evaporation as the sauce cooked, so we needed to use something thicker than canned diced tomatoes, the test kitchen's first

EQUIPMENT: Garlic Presses

A defiantly sticky and undeniably stinky job, hand-mincing garlic is a chore many cooks avoid by pressing the cloves through a garlic press. The question for us was not whether garlic presses work, but which of the many available models works best. After squeezing our way through 12 different models, the unanimous winner was Kuhn Rikon's 2315 Epicurean Garlic Press. Solidly constructed of stainless steel, it has an almost luxurious feel, with ergonomically curved handles that are comfortable to squeeze and a hopper that smoothly and automatically lifts out for cleaning as you open the handles. It passed all our kitchen tests with flying colors. At $35, however, it is also quite expensive. Another that did well in our tests was the Trudeau Garlic Press—with a solid construction, it is sturdy and easy to use and is our best buy at a reasonable $11.99.

THE BEST GARLIC PRESSES

The Kuhn Rikon 2315 Epicurean Garlic Press produces a very fine mince, good yield, and great paste consistency, making it the all-around winner. The Trudeau Garlic Press is a solid and reliable choice for those looking to spend a little less and it is our best buy.

KUHN RIKON

TRUDEAU

choice for most tomato sauces. Further testing and tasting revealed that a combination of drained diced tomatoes, canned tomato sauce, and tomato paste had the best balance of flavor and texture. Finally, to brighten the finished sauce, we added fresh basil. With that, we had our own version of Sunday gravy, and it was worthy of any Italian grandmother's praise.

Slow-Cooker Italian Sunday Gravy

MAKES 14 CUPS,
ENOUGH FOR 2 POUNDS OF PASTA

We like serving this hearty sauce with short tubular pasta such as rigatoni.

1	tablespoon vegetable oil
1	pound sweet Italian sausage links
1	pound hot Italian sausage links
2	medium onions, minced
1	(6-ounce) can tomato paste
12	medium garlic cloves, minced or pressed through a garlic press (about 4 tablespoons)
2	teaspoons dried oregano
	Salt
½	cup dry red wine
1	(28-ounce) can diced tomatoes, drained
1	(28-ounce) can tomato sauce
1½	pounds bone-in country-style pork ribs
1½	pounds flank steak
	Ground black pepper
3	tablespoons chopped fresh basil leaves

1. Heat the oil in a 12-inch nonstick skillet over medium-high heat until just smoking. Add the sweet sausage and cook until well browned and the fat begins to render, about 8 minutes. Transfer the sausage to a paper towel–lined plate, leaving the fat in the skillet. Repeat with the hot sausage, leaving the fat in the skillet.

2. Pour off all but 2 tablespoons of the fat left in the skillet and place over medium-high heat until shimmering. Add the onions, tomato paste, garlic, oregano, and ¼ teaspoon salt and cook, stirring often,

until the onions are softened and lightly browned, 8 to 10 minutes. Stir in the wine, scraping up any browned bits.

3. Transfer the mixture to the slow cooker and stir in the diced tomatoes and tomato sauce until evenly combined. Season the ribs and flank steak with salt and pepper and nestle them into the slow cooker. Cover and cook, either on low or high, until the meat is tender, 9 to 10 hours on low or 5 to 6 hours on high.

4. Transfer the sausages, ribs, and flank steak to a platter and let cool slightly. Let the cooking liquid settle for 5 minutes, then gently tilt the slow cooker and remove as much fat as possible from the surface using a large spoon. Using 2 forks, shred the ribs and flank steak into small pieces, following the illustration on page 116, discarding any bones and fat. Slice the sausages in half crosswise. Stir the shredded meat, sausages, and basil into the sauce and season with salt and pepper to taste before serving.

SLOW-COOKER BOLOGNESE SAUCE

MEATY BOLOGNESE IS ONE OF THE TEST kitchen's favorite pasta sauces. Unlike other meat sauces where tomatoes dominate (think jars of spaghetti sauce with flecks of meat in a sea of tomato puree), Bolognese sauce is about the meat, with tomatoes in a supporting role. Bolognese sauce is unique in that it contains dairy, which gives the beef an especially sweet flavor. As the ingredients simmer away, tough ground meat is transformed into a silky sauce with complex flavors. Because of its naturally long simmering time (on the stovetop it can take more than 4 hours), we thought Bolognese sauce would be a perfect candidate for the slow cooker.

So why do most slow-cooker Bolognese recipes fail? One recipe simply threw all the ingredients in together and let them cook. Hours later, our test cooks dined on waterlogged hamburger soup. Another recipe simmered the liquids on the stovetop before adding them to the slow cooker, but simmering milk with acidic wine and tomatoes just made a curdled mess. Another recipe suggested using less liquid—tablespoons rather than cups—so there would be no need for evaporation. Several hours later, this sauce looked the part, but the rich flavor that comes from simmering large amounts of liquid down to a concentrated base was absent.

We had a lot of issues to tackle, and vegetables were first under the microscope. Softening the vegetables on the stovetop was a must. Most recipes called for celery, carrots, and onion, and we found all three essential. While garlic found a home, tasters thought too many herbs were distracting, and we settled on a mere teaspoon of thyme. Either butter or olive oil can be used to sauté the vegetables, and we chose butter for its richer flavor.

Next, we turned to browning the ground meat. While we had come up with methods to get around browning in our other slow-cooker recipes, the bland results from our early dump-and-cook Bolognese test had proven we couldn't make such shortcuts here. As most traditional Bolognese recipes will tell you, the sequential reduction of liquids over browned meat and vegetables is the key to getting the deep flavor the sauce is known for. So, despite the extra work, we knew it was a necessary step to get the flavor we were after. We used equal parts ground beef, pork, and veal, and again we found all three to be necessary. We were, however, able to avoid buying several packages of meat by purchasing the trusty supermarket "meatloaf mix," made from equal parts of each. (In a pinch, a combination of ground chuck and pork will suffice.) We reduced the milk over the meat until its fat had separated out, a common Bolognese technique for developing the fullest flavor and softest texture.

Tomatoes add sweetness to Bolognese sauce, and their juice is used to braise the meat. We tried all kinds—crushed, diced, sauce—and in the end liked the canned whole tomatoes best because they come packed in so much juice. We pureed them in the blender to allow the meat to take the starring role for texture. To provide a deeper, slow-cooked tomato flavor, we added some tomato paste.

We then transferred everything to the slow cooker, added the wine, and cracked the lid to allow for evaporation. So far so good, but the temperature plummeted and the sauce sat stagnant for hours. We were back to square one.

Then it dawned on us. We had assumed that the low setting on the slow cooker would work best. After all, "low and slow" is the mantra for this sauce when made on the stovetop. But when we switched the cooker to high, the mixture bubbled away, even with the lid off, which allowed for maximum evaporation. Eight hours later, we had a silky, robust Bolognese sauce.

This slow-cooker Bolognese definitely rivals any prepared by the traditional method. Hearty and flavorful—now that's our idea of good slow cooking.

Slow-Cooker Bolognese Sauce

MAKES 12 CUPS,
ENOUGH FOR 3 POUNDS OF PASTA

Because steam rises from the sauce as it cooks, it's best to place the slow cooker on a counter with no cabinetry overhead. Choose a fruity, dry white wine like Sauvignon Blanc or Pinot Gris; oaky-tasting Chardonnay is too strong and will affect the flavor of the sauce.

  2 (28-ounce) cans whole tomatoes
  3 tablespoons unsalted butter
  1 medium onion, minced
  1 small carrot, peeled and chopped fine
  ½ celery rib, chopped fine
  3 tablespoons tomato paste
  3 medium garlic cloves, minced or pressed
     through a garlic press (about 1 tablespoon)
  1 teaspoon minced fresh thyme leaves,
     or ¼ teaspoon dried
     Salt
  3 pounds meatloaf mix, or 1½ pounds ground
     chuck and 1½ pounds ground pork
     Ground black pepper

  3 cups whole milk
  1 (750-ml) bottle dry white wine

1. Process the tomatoes with their juice in a food processor until smooth, about 20 seconds, and set aside. Melt the butter in a Dutch oven over medium-high heat. Add the onion, carrot, celery, tomato paste, garlic, thyme, and ¼ teaspoon salt and cook, stirring often, until the vegetables are softened and lightly browned, 8 to 10 minutes. Add the meat, ¾ teaspoon salt, and ½ teaspoon pepper and cook, breaking up the meat, until crumbled into tiny pieces and lightly browned, about 5 minutes.

2. Stir in the milk, bring to a simmer, and cook until the milk evaporates and only the clear fat remains, 10 to 15 minutes. Stir in the processed tomatoes and wine, cover, and bring to a boil.

3. Transfer the mixture to the slow cooker, cover, set the temperature to high, and bring to a boil. Once the mixture comes to a boil, remove the lid and simmer until the sauce is very thick, 7 to 8 hours.

4. Let the cooking liquid settle for 5 minutes, then gently tilt the slow cooker and remove as much fat as possible from the surface using a large spoon. Season with salt and pepper to taste before serving.

SLOW-COOKER MEATBALLS IN MARINARA

MAKING BIG, LITTLE ITALY–SIZED MEATBALLS is easy. Making big meatballs that are also tender and moist, with enough structure to hold their shape in the slow cooker, is not so simple. Most recipes rely on two tricks: mixing the usual ground beef with ground pork (for flavor and texture) and adding a *panade*, a paste made from bread and milk. The panade adds both moisture and tenderness to the meatballs. The recipes we started testing made use of both tricks, but as soon as we made our first batch of meatballs we could see that we were in trouble. The moment the meatballs went into the slow cooker, they collapsed under their own weight and spread out like soggy hamburger patties. It was time to get down to business.

To start, we took a good look at meatball basics: the meat, the binders, and the flavorings. Most meatball recipes call for equal parts of pork and beef and use a fairly wet panade made with upward of 2 cups of milk. Cutting back on the milk was an obvious way to make the meatballs sturdier, but we quickly learned that cutting the milk out completely wasn't an option—without it, the meatballs turned rubbery and tough. Adding back the milk a tablespoon at a time, we landed on a good balance of tenderness and sturdiness by using just ⅓ cup.

Using a higher ratio of beef to pork also helped the meatballs hold together better during the long cooking time. We cut way back on the pork and wound up with a winning beef to pork ratio of 5 to 1. Without the extra pork, however, the flavor of the meatballs had turned a bit bland. Then a colleague suggested substituting raw Italian sausage for the ground pork. This turned out to be a great idea—not only were we able to boost the flavor of the meatballs a bit, but buying small amounts of sausage is often easier and more convenient than buying small amounts of ground pork. To boost the flavor of the meatballs further, we found it important to add some sautéed onion, garlic, red pepper flakes, and dried oregano. Finished with some fresh parsley and a handful of Parmesan cheese, these meatballs now had some serious flavor.

Most meatball recipes fry the meatballs first to help firm them up and rid them of excess grease, and the browned bits left in the pan after frying are used to flavor the sauce. Yet frying these huge meatballs, even in our largest pan, needed to be done in two batches, not to mention the splattery mess it created. What's more, the crust created on the exterior of the meatballs translated into a tough texture tasters didn't approve of. We thought of baking the meatballs in the oven to release some

of their fat without creating a crust, but waiting for the oven to heat up didn't make this recipe any more convenient. Frustrated, we did something unexpected, and turned to the microwave. Our reasoning was this—we needed to cook the meatballs just enough to allow them to exude most of their fat and firm up the meat without making the exterior tough, while still keeping things simple enough for a slow-cooker meal. As it turned out, this worked beautifully; it only took about five minutes on high power.

With the beginnings of a great meatball recipe in hand, we finally turned our attention to the sauce. However, without the flavorful browned bits from frying the meatballs, we knew that avoiding a bland sauce would be a challenge. To compensate for the missing fried-meatball flavor, we sautéed our aromatics with tomato paste, then deglazed our pan with red wine before pouring the mixture into the slow cooker along with tomatoes, the foundation of the sauce, and soy sauce for added depth. As it turned out, the sauce required exactly the same sautéed aromatics as the meatballs, so in order to simplify things, we sautéed a single large batch of aromatics, using half for the meatballs and half for the sauce.

We experimented with various tomato products for our sauce—diced, pureed, and crushed. Diced tomatoes didn't blend into the sauce as much as we would have liked, and everyone agreed that tomato puree was too sweet and too thick. Crushed tomatoes gave us both the fresh flavor and smooth, light texture that we were seeking. However, crushed tomatoes vary significantly in taste and quality, depending on the brand. We found that crushing diced tomatoes in the food processor was the best solution. The resulting sauce had a deep crimson color and a deep, rich flavor. Once our sauce was in the slow cooker and ready to go, we added our microwaved meatballs and let the cooking go from there.

With the pairing of our satisfying sauce and perfected meatballs, we had a dish that tasted like it was delivered straight from Little Italy—maybe even better.

Slow-Cooker Meatballs in Marinara

SERVES 6

The meatballs and sauce both use the same onion mixture, so be sure to reserve half of the mixture for the meatballs before adding the wine to the skillet. See page 204 for make-ahead instructions. In addition, the meatballs can be assembled, shaped (but not microwaved), and stored covered tightly in plastic wrap overnight.

2	(28-ounce) cans diced tomatoes
2	tablespoons vegetable oil
2	onions, minced
¼	cup tomato paste
8	medium garlic cloves, minced or pressed through a garlic press (about 8 teaspoons)
1½	teaspoons dried oregano
¼	teaspoon red pepper flakes
	Salt
½	cup dry red wine
½	cup water
2	tablespoons soy sauce
2	slices hearty white sandwich bread
⅓	cup milk
1½	ounces Parmesan cheese, grated (about ¾ cup)
¼	cup minced fresh parsley leaves
2	large eggs, lightly beaten
1¼	pounds 90 percent lean ground beef
¼	pound sweet Italian sausage, casings removed
2	tablespoons chopped fresh basil leaves
1–2	teaspoons sugar

1. Process the tomatoes with their juice in a food processor until smooth, about 15 seconds, and set aside. Heat the oil in a 12-inch nonstick skillet oven over medium-high heat until shimmering. Add the onions, tomato paste, 6 cloves of the garlic, oregano, red pepper flakes, and ¼ teaspoon salt and cook, stirring often, until the onions are softened and lightly browned, 8 to 10 minutes.

2. Transfer half the onion mixture to a large bowl and set aside. Stir the wine into the skillet with the remaining onion mixture, scraping up any browned bits. Transfer the onion–red wine mixture to the slow cooker and stir in the processed tomatoes, water, and soy sauce until evenly combined.

3. Add the bread and milk to the bowl of reserved onion mixture and mash together until smooth. Add 1 ounce of the Parmesan, parsley, eggs, remaining 2 garlic cloves, and ¾ teaspoon salt to the bowl and mash to combine. Add the ground beef and sausage and knead with your hands until thoroughly combined. Form the mixture into twelve 2-inch meatballs. Place the meatballs on a large microwavable plate and microwave on full power until most of the fat is rendered, about 5 minutes.

4. Nestle the meatballs in the slow cooker, discarding the rendered fat. Cover and cook on low until the meatballs are tender and the sauce is slightly thickened, 4 to 5 hours.

5. Let the cooking liquid settle for 5 minutes, then gently tilt the slow cooker and remove as much fat as possible from the surface using a large spoon. Gently stir in the remaining ½ ounce Parmesan and basil into the sauce and season with salt and sugar to taste before serving.

6

SIDE DISHES FROM THE OVEN

SIDE DISHES FROM THE OVEN

MANY CLASSIC SIDE DISHES, SUCH AS BAKED beans, corn pudding, and savory bread puddings, are traditionally cooked in the gentle, steady heat of the oven. But there are also numerous sides prepared on the stovetop, requiring not just a good pot but also vigilance—and often a lot of stirring—to yield perfect results. For this chapter, we naturally wanted to explore the classic baked side dishes, but we also wondered if we could test the limits on some of the recipes in the stovetop group—rice, risotto, and polenta, to name a few— and make them more convenient for the home cook, perhaps even more reliable, by finding ways to make them in the oven while retaining their texture and flavor.

The oven offers many advantages—a good amount of walk-away time (freeing up the cook, an important asset when entertaining) and it tends to be a more consistent, reliable way to cook. After all, we've all experienced the disasters that the inconsistent heat of electric stoves and thin metal pots can cause. We wanted to avoid those problems. The basic method for cooking these dishes appeared simple: toss some beans, grains, or rice in a baking dish with a liquid, cover, and bake until done. But as we tested our way through this chapter, we found that while this concept was basically true, there were exceptions, along with many secrets to getting each dish just right.

The major flaw in this overarching idea turned out to be that almost all of these dishes require at least a little stovetop time. For some, it's simply to boil water, while for others, such as Baked Rice Casserole (page 266), the dish needs to be precooked on the stovetop before going into the oven.

That said, we found numerous pluses to moving traditionally stovetop sides to the oven. For instance, our Creamy Baked Polenta (page 269) and Baked Risotto (page 264) don't need constant stirring. Once you get them into the oven, you only have to stir them once while they bake. And we found that you can have creamy baked risotto by simply stirring in 1¼ cups of warm chicken broth once it emerges from the oven. Serve these typically labor-intensive sides at a dinner party and everyone will wonder how the cook could look so relaxed.

The oven also offers the perfect solution for one of the most finicky of side dishes: rice. We mastered a foolproof technique for Baked Long-Grain White Rice (page 256), and found that the same method, with only a few tweaks, also worked beautifully for wild rice, brown rice, and barley. This was probably our simplest recipe in the chapter to nail down. We poured 2¼ cups boiling water over 1½ cups of white rice in an 8- inch square baking dish, which we then covered and placed in the oven. It was that simple. And since rice dishes are great for company, we made sure all the recipes could be doubled and could be easily spruced up for variations like Baked Long-Grain White Rice with Dates and Lentils (page 256) and Baked Wild Rice with Almonds and Cranberries (page 259).

Beans, another all-time favorite side, can seem simple at first but problems often come up: creamy beans can turn mushy and under- and overseasoning is often an issue. And of course many bean recipes can take all day. We wanted to create manageable recipes that would lead to consistent, savory results. We found that 250 degrees was the ideal oven temperature, yielding beans that were creamy and full-flavored. We also found that the bean dishes should be covered initially to keep the beans moist and promote even cooking, but toward the end the lid should be removed to allow the sauces to adequately reduce and become more intensely flavored.

Finally, to round out the chapter, we wanted a few all-American comfort food side dishes. We developed recipes for Baked Grits Casserole (page 271), Savory Bread Pudding (page 279), and Southern Spoon Bread (page 282), all of which will not only warm you up from the inside out, but will also work well for any meal, be it brunch, lunch, or dinner.

BAKED RICE AND BARLEY

COOKING RICE AND BARLEY PILAF-STYLE—sautéing the grains in a little oil with some aromatics, then adding liquid and cooking gently on the stovetop—is a favorite technique of ours in the test kitchen. It produces wonderfully clean, fragrant flavors and tender, separate grains of rice or barley in no time. But the pilaf method isn't always convenient because it requires both stovetop space and careful attention to timing and heat levels. What do you do if your stovetop is already covered in pots and pans? For a rice side dish that steers clear of the stovetop and is simple to make, let the oven come to the rescue.

Hoping to develop a universal baking technique for various types of rice as well as barley, we used long-grain white rice as our primary test subject. We began by trying out a set of instructions we found in nearly all of the recipes we looked at for baked rice: mix one part white rice and two parts water together in a baking dish, cover, and bake unattended in a moderately hot oven until the rice is tender and the water absorbed. Although these simple instructions didn't produce the greatest rice—it was wet, mushy, and unevenly cooked—the method seemed promising, particularly because it offered a good 45 minutes of walk-away time. We were confident that with just a little tweaking we could iron out these problems and find a universal method for baking rice and barley. Sticking with long-grain white rice for the bulk of our testing, we broke down the standard rice baking instructions so that we could test each of the variables—the ingredient amounts, oven temperature, assembly method, and flavorings—one at a time.

From our many experiences with the pilaf method, we knew that finding the right ratio of rice to water would be crucial, making the difference between success and the garbage can. (We also knew that various types of rice and barley would require slightly different amounts of water, but we would handle such details later.) Though most sources propose a 1-2 ratio of white rice to water,

we decided to test every possibility from a 1-1 ratio to a 1-2 ratio. We noted a substantial improvement when we used a ratio of 1 to 1¾—the rice was evenly cooked, but not wet or mushy. (Not coincidentally, this is the exact same ratio used in our own well-tested stovetop rice pilaf recipe.) Scaling up the amount of rice so that it fit nicely into an 8-inch baking dish, we found 1½ cups of rice fit perfectly and would serve 4 to 6 people.

Moving on to the oven temperature, we tested batches of white rice cooked in ovens ranging from 250 degrees to 450 degrees at 50-degree increments. Does a lower oven temperature result in better-textured rice? The answer is no. Rice baked at temperatures under 325 degrees turned out increasingly gummy, with an unpleasant mealy texture in the center of each grain. Meanwhile, rice baked at temperatures above 375 degrees was equally unpleasant—the grains near the sides of the dish were hard and crunchy, while the grains in the center had blown-out exteriors and barely cooked interiors.

We then pitted more moderate oven temperatures of 325, 350, and 375 degrees against one another. When tasted side by side, all three temperatures produced acceptable results, but the 375-degree batch was the most evenly cooked, a success we thought was probably due to the fact that it was the only batch that simmered lightly as it cooked. We then realized that bringing the cooking liquid to a boil before stirring it into the rice—another rice pilaf trick—might improve the texture even more. Bingo. The magical combination of simmering the liquid before baking and a 375-degree oven produced tender, perfectly cooked grains of rice, from the edges to the very center of the dish.

Since we were on a roll using many of our tried-and-true rice pilaf tricks, we tested two more on our baked rice: rinsing the rice before cooking and letting the rice steam after cooking. Rinsing the rice, which for our stovetop pilaf resulted in more tender, separate grains, did not work well for the baked version. When rinsed, raw rice takes on a wet, clumpy texture, which is fine for the stovetop rice pilaf since these clumps separate when sautéed in hot oil. They don't get this opportunity in the baked version. When we poured the hot cooking liquid over raw, clumpy rice in baking dish, the rice refused to separate into distinct grains. As it baked, we watched the wet rice clumps stick together and dry out. The unrinsed rice, on the other hand, produced distinct, separate grains when baked. We decided to let well enough alone. Meanwhile, letting the rice steam by leaving it covered for 10 minutes after baking produced a more fragrant rice that was tender but still had a slight texture to the interior.

We added a small amount of butter and a little salt to the cooking liquid to enhance and round out the rice's natural nutty flavor. For more exotic flavor variations, we found it easy to add spices and aromatics to the cooking liquid when bringing it to a simmer, or to add garnishes such as herbs, dried fruit, and nuts during the already baked rice's steaming time or just before serving.

Finally, with a successful baked white rice under our belts, we turned our attention to adapting the recipe to other types of rice and barley. In our previous experiences, long-grain brown rice required a ratio of water to rice similar to that

required for preparing long-grain white rice, and this recipe was no exception. We fine-tuned the amounts, finally settling upon 2⅓ cups of water to 1½ cups of rice. The main difference between the two types of rice was the baking time—the brown rice took 60 to 70 minutes to absorb all of the water and fully bake, 10 to 20 minutes longer than the white rice.

Wild rice, we felt, would be more of a challenge. We were skeptical that we could cook it the same way we had the brown and white rice because we usually don't pilaf wild rice, but rather boil it. However, curious to see what would happen if we went ahead and baked it, we gave our white-rice method a whirl, settling on one part wild rice to two parts water. We had to bake the rice for 70 to 80 minutes before it was fully cooked, but to our great pleasure and surprise, it worked beautifully. The rice was nutty in flavor with the desired chewy texture. The only complaint was that it tasted a bit too salty. That was a quick fix—we lowered the amount of salt from 1 teaspoon to ¾ teaspoon.

In addition to our various types of rice, we also wanted to find out if we could bake barley

---

INGREDIENTS: Long-Grain Rice

The beauty of white rice resides in its neutral flavor, which makes it good at carrying other flavors. But is all long-grain white rice created equal? We set up a taste test to find out. We rounded up a converted rice, three standard supermarket options, and an organic white rice available in bulk from a natural foods store. The most noticeable difference was an unpredictable variance in cooking time. According to the U.S. Rice Producers Association, the age of the rice, its moisture content, and the variety used can affect the rate of water uptake. Inconsistent cooking times are barely noticeable in plain rice, but they can become more apparent when other ingredients—such as aromatics and vegetables—are added to the pot. All rices but one were noted for being "clean" and "like rice should be." The exception was Uncle Ben's, a converted rice that failed to meet our standards on all fronts. Converted rice is processed in a way that ensures separate grains, a firm texture, and more pronounced flavor. Those "round," "rubbery" grains and the telltale yellowish tint

immediately brought back not-so-fond memories of "dining hall rice." Tasters agreed that some "stickiness" and minor "clumping" make for more natural-looking and better-tasting rice. The recommended brands were universally liked.

THE BEST LONG-GRAIN RICE
The flavor of Canilla Extra Long (left) was likened to that of jasmine rice, and tasters found Carolina Extra Long Grain Enriched Rice (center) to have a good, clean slate on which to add flavor. Sem-Chi Organically Grown Florida Long Grain Rice (right) was rated the chewiest, with roasted and nutty flavors.

successfully in the oven. The nutty flavor of this hearty, nutrient-rich grain offers a great alternative to rice, and it can be similarly flavored, with herbs, toasted nuts, or dried fruits. For this recipe we decided to use pearl barley (barley that has had the bran removed and has been steamed and polished), since it is the most widely available. To begin, we tried baking 1½ cups barley in 3 cups water. But barley can absorb two to three times its volume in cooking liquid, and the water disappeared before fully cooking the grains. So we increased the water ¼ cup at a time, finally landing on 3½ cups of water as the perfect amount for 1½ cups of barley. With the water amount determined, we were ready to really put the baking method to the test. After giving it 70 minutes in the oven (20 minutes longer than the white rice) and a 10-minute rest on the counter, we peeled back the foil cover to reveal perfectly cooked barley. The grains were separate, fully cooked without being soggy, and had the rich nuttiness we were after. Our easy-to-prepare baked barley, an excellent accompaniment for a range of entrées, proves barley isn't just for soups or stews.

Baked Long-Grain White Rice
SERVES 4 TO 6

Basmati rice also works well here. You cannot substitute medium- or short-grain white rice. Be sure to cover the pot when bringing the water to a boil in step 2; any water loss due to evaporation will affect how the rice cooks. If doubling the recipe, use a 13 by 9-inch baking dish; the baking time need not be increased. Feel free to add chopped fresh herbs, grated lemon zest, or grated fresh Parmesan to the rice before serving, if desired.

1½	cups long-grain white rice (see note)
2¼	cups water
2	teaspoons unsalted butter
1	teaspoon salt

1. Adjust an oven rack to the middle position and heat the oven to 375 degrees. Spread the rice in an 8-inch square glass baking dish.

2. Bring the water, butter, and salt to a boil in a covered medium saucepan over high heat. Once boiling, stir the mixture to combine, then immediately pour it over the rice.

3. Cover the baking dish tightly with a double layer of aluminum foil. Bake the rice until it is tender and no water remains, 40 to 50 minutes.

4. Remove the baking dish from the oven, uncover, and fluff the rice with a fork. Re-cover the dish with foil and let the rice stand for 10 minutes before serving.

➤ VARIATIONS
Baked Long-Grain White Rice with Dates and Lentils

Basmati rice also works well here. You cannot substitute medium- or short-grain white rice. Be sure to cover the pot when bringing the water to a boil in step 2; any water loss due to evaporation will affect how the rice cooks. We prefer using green lentils in this recipe, but brown lentils will also work. If doubling the recipe, use a 13 by 9-inch baking dish; the baking time need not be increased.

1½	cups long-grain white rice (see note)
3	tablespoons unsalted butter
1	medium onion, minced
1	teaspoon salt
¼	teaspoon ground cinnamon
	Pinch ground cloves
¼	cup green lentils, picked over and rinsed (see note)
2⅓	cups water
½	cup dates, chopped fine

1. Adjust an oven rack to the middle position and heat the oven to 375 degrees. Spread the rice in an 8-inch square glass baking dish.

2. Melt the butter in a medium saucepan over medium heat. Add the onion and salt and cook, stirring often, until softened, about 5 to 7 minutes. Stir in the cinnamon and cloves and cook until fragrant, about 30 seconds. Stir in the lentils and water. Cover the pot, increase the heat to high, and bring the mixture to a boil. Once boiling, stir the mixture to combine, then immediately pour it over the rice.

3. Cover the baking dish tightly with a double layer of aluminum foil. Bake the rice until it is tender and no water remains, 40 to 50 minutes.

4. Remove the baking dish from the oven, uncover, and fluff the rice with a fork. Stir in the dates, re-cover the dish with foil, and let the rice stand for 10 minutes before serving.

Baked Long-Grain White Rice with Saffron, Apricots, and Almonds

Basmati rice also works well here. You cannot substitute medium- or short-grain white rice. Be sure to cover the pot when bringing the water to a boil in step 2; any water loss due to evaporation will affect how the rice cooks. If doubling the recipe, use a 13 by 9-inch baking dish; the baking time need not be increased.

1½	cups long-grain white rice (see note)
3	tablespoons unsalted butter
1	medium onion, minced
1	teaspoon salt
	Pinch saffron
2¼	cups water
½	cup dried apricots, chopped fine
¼	cup sliced almonds, toasted (see page 309)

1. Adjust an oven rack to the middle position and heat the oven to 375 degrees. Spread the rice in an 8-inch square glass baking dish.

2. Melt the butter in a medium saucepan over medium heat. Add the onion and salt and cook, stirring often, until softened, about 5 to 7 minutes. Stir in the saffron and cook until fragrant, about 30 seconds. Stir in the water. Cover the pot, increase the heat to high, and bring the mixture to a boil. Once boiling, stir the mixture to combine, then immediately pour it over the rice.

3. Cover the baking dish tightly with a double layer of aluminum foil. Bake the rice until it is tender and no water remains, 40 to 50 minutes.

4. Remove the baking dish from the oven, uncover, and fluff the rice with a fork. Stir in the apricots, re-cover the dish with foil, and let the rice stand for 10 minutes. Stir in the sliced almonds before serving.

Baked Long-Grain Brown Rice
SERVES 4 TO 6

You can substitute either medium- or short-grain brown rice here, but the grains will fall apart a bit as they cook. Be sure to cover the pot when bringing the water to a boil in step 2; any water loss due to evaporation will affect how the rice cooks. If doubling the recipe, use a 13 by 9-inch baking dish; the baking time need not be increased.

1½	cups long-grain brown rice (see note)
2⅓	cups water
2	teaspoons unsalted butter
1	teaspoon salt

1. Adjust an oven rack to the middle position and heat the oven to 375 degrees. Spread the rice in an 8-inch square glass baking dish.

2. Bring the water, butter, and salt to a boil in a covered medium saucepan over high heat. Once boiling, stir the mixture to combine, then immediately pour it over the rice.

3. Cover the baking dish tightly with a double layer of aluminum foil. Bake the rice until it is tender and no water remains, 60 to 70 minutes.

4. Remove the baking dish from the oven, uncover, and fluff the rice with a fork. Re-cover the dish with foil and let the rice stand for 10 minutes before serving.

➤ VARIATIONS

Baked Long-Grain Brown Rice with Parmesan, Lemon, and Herbs

You can substitute either medium- or short-grain brown rice here, but the grains will fall apart a bit as they cook. Be sure to cover the pot when bringing the water to a boil in step 2; any water loss due to evaporation will affect how the rice cooks. Feel free to substitute other fresh herbs such as mint or tarragon for the basil. If doubling the recipe, use a 13 by 9-inch baking dish; the baking time need not be increased.

1½	cups long-grain brown rice (see note)
2	tablespoons unsalted butter
1	medium onion, minced
1	teaspoon salt
2⅓	cups water

1   ounce Parmesan cheese, grated
    (about ½ cup)
¼   cup minced fresh parsley leaves
¼   cup chopped fresh basil leaves
1   teaspoon grated zest plus ½ teaspoon
    juice from one lemon
⅛   teaspoon ground black pepper

1. Adjust an oven rack to the middle position and heat the oven to 375 degrees. Spread the rice in an 8-inch square glass baking dish.

2. Melt the butter in a medium saucepan over medium heat. Add the onion and salt and cook, stirring often, until softened, about 5 to 7 minutes. Stir in the water. Cover the pot, increase the heat to high, and bring the mixture to a boil. Once boiling, stir the mixture to combine then immediately pour it over the rice.

3. Cover the baking dish tightly with a double layer of aluminum foil. Bake the rice until it is tender and no water remains, 60 to 70 minutes.

4. Remove the baking dish from the oven, uncover, and fluff rice with a fork. Stir in the Parmesan, parsley, basil, lemon zest, lemon juice, and pepper. Re-cover the dish with foil and let the rice stand for 10 minutes before serving.

Baked Long-Grain Curried Brown Rice with Tomatoes and Peas

You can substitute either medium- or short-grain brown rice here, but the grains will fall apart a bit as they cook. Be sure to cover the pot when bringing the water to a boil in step 2; any water loss due to evaporation will affect how the rice cooks. If doubling the recipe, use a 13 by 9-inch baking dish; the baking time need not be increased.

1½ cups long-grain brown rice (see note)
2   tablespoons unsalted butter
1   medium onion, minced
1   teaspoon salt
1   tablespoon minced or grated fresh ginger
1½ teaspoons curry powder
1   medium garlic clove, minced or pressed
    through a garlic press (about 1 teaspoon)

1   (14.5-ounce) can diced tomatoes, drained
2⅓ cups water
½   cup frozen peas, thawed

1. Adjust an oven rack to the middle position and heat the oven to 375 degrees. Spread the rice in an 8-inch square glass baking dish.

2. Melt the butter in a medium saucepan over medium heat. Add the onion and salt and cook, stirring often, until softened, about 5 to 7 minutes. Stir in the ginger, curry powder, and garlic and cook until fragrant, about 30 seconds. Stir in the tomatoes and cook until heated through, about 2 minutes. Stir in the water. Cover the pot, increase the heat to high, and bring the mixture to a boil. Once boiling, stir the mixture to combine, then immediately pour it over the rice.

3. Cover the baking dish tightly with a double layer of aluminum foil. Bake the rice until it is tender and no water remains, 60 to 70 minutes.

4. Remove the baking dish from the oven, uncover, and fluff the rice with a fork. Stir in the peas, re-cover the dish with foil, and let the rice stand for 10 minutes before serving.

INGREDIENTS: Frozen Peas

In the test kitchen, we have come to depend on frozen peas. Not only are they more convenient than their fresh, in-the-pod comrades, but they taste better. Test after test, we found frozen peas to be tender and sweet while fresh peas tasted starchy and bland. Trying to understand this curious finding, we looked to the frozen food industry for some answers.

Green peas lose a substantial portion of their nutrients within 24 hours of being picked. This rapid deterioration is the reason for the starchy, bland flavor of most "fresh" peas found at the grocery store. These not-so-fresh peas might be several days old, depending on where they came from and how long they were kept in the cooler. Frozen peas, on the other hand, are picked, cleaned, sorted, and frozen within several hours of harvest, which helps preserve their delicate sugars and flavors. Fittingly enough, when commercially frozen vegetables first began to appear in the 1920s and 1930s, green peas were among them. So unless you grow your own or know a reputable local farm stand, you're better off buying frozen peas.

Baked Wild Rice

SERVES 4 TO 6

Be sure to cover the pot when bringing the water to a boil in step 2; any water loss due to evaporation will affect how the rice cooks. If doubling the recipe, use a 13 by 9-inch baking dish; the baking time need not be increased.

1½	cups wild rice
3	cups water
2	teaspoons unsalted butter
¾	teaspoon salt

1. Adjust an oven rack to the middle position and heat the oven to 375 degrees. Spread the rice in an 8-inch square glass baking dish.

2. Bring the water, butter, and salt to a boil in a covered medium saucepan over high heat. Once boiling, stir the mixture to combine, then immediately pour it over the rice.

3. Cover the baking dish tightly with a double layer of aluminum foil. Bake the rice until it is tender and no water remains, 70 to 80 minutes.

4. Remove the baking dish from the oven, uncover, and fluff the rice with a fork. Re-cover the dish with foil and let the rice stand for 10 minutes before serving.

➤ VARIATIONS

Baked Wild Rice with Almonds and Cranberries

Be sure to cover the pot when bringing the water to a boil in step 2; any water loss due to evaporation will affect how the rice cooks. Finely chopping the cranberries ensures that they will soften in the steaming rice. Dried cherries can be substituted for the cranberries. If doubling the recipe, use a 13 by 9-inch baking dish; the baking time need not be increased.

1½	cups wild rice
3	tablespoons unsalted butter
1	medium onion, minced
¾	teaspoon salt
3	cups water
¼	cup dried cranberries, chopped fine
¼	cup sliced almonds, toasted (see page 309)

1. Adjust an oven rack to the middle position and heat the oven to 375 degrees. Spread the rice in an 8-inch square glass baking dish.

2. Melt the butter in a medium saucepan over medium heat. Add the onion and salt and cook, stirring often, until softened, about 5 to 7 minutes. Stir in the water. Cover the pot, increase the heat to high, and bring to a boil. Once boiling, stir the mixture to combine, then immediately pour it over the rice.

3. Cover the baking dish tightly with a double layer of aluminum foil. Bake the rice until it is tender and no water remains, 70 to 80 minutes.

4. Remove the baking dish from the oven, uncover, and fluff the rice with a fork. Stir in the cranberries, re-cover the dish with foil, and let the rice stand for 10 minutes. Stir in the sliced almonds before serving.

Baked Wild Rice with Porcini Mushrooms

Be sure to cover the pot when bringing the water to a boil in step 2; any water loss due to evaporation will affect how the rice cooks. If doubling the recipe, use a 13 by 9-inch baking dish; the baking time need not be increased.

1½	cups wild rice
3	tablespoons unsalted butter
1	medium onion, minced
¾	teaspoon salt
½	ounce dried porcini mushrooms, rinsed and minced
1	teaspoon minced fresh thyme leaves
3	cups water
1	tablespoon minced fresh parsley leaves

1. Adjust an oven rack to the middle position and heat the oven to 375 degrees. Spread the rice in an 8-inch square glass baking dish.

2. Melt the butter in a medium saucepan over medium heat. Stir in the onion and salt and cook,

INGREDIENTS: Wild Rice

Wild rice and traditional cultivated rice are both members of the grass family (as are wheat, corn, oats, barley, and rye). Truly "wild" wild rice is native to the northern Great Lakes, where it is still harvested. But most so-called wild rice is now cultivated on farms in California. Cultivated wild rice grown in man-made paddies costs between $3 and $5 per pound, while hand-harvested rice from lakes and streams in Minnesota and Canada costs about $9 per pound.

stirring often, until softened, about 5 to 7 minutes. Stir in the mushrooms and thyme and cook until fragrant, about 1 minute. Stir in the water. Cover the pot, increase the heat to high, and bring the mixture to a boil. Once boiling, stir the mixture to combine, then immediately pour it over the rice.

3. Cover the baking dish tightly with a double layer of aluminum foil. Bake the rice until it is tender and no water remains, 70 to 80 minutes.

4. Remove the baking dish from the oven, uncover, and fluff the rice with a fork. Stir in the parsley, re-cover the dish with foil, and let the rice stand for 10 minutes before serving.

Baked Barley

SERVES 4 TO 6

Don't substitute hulled barley for the pearl barley. Be sure to cover the pot when bringing the water to a boil in step 2; any water loss due to evaporation will affect how the barley cooks. If doubling the recipe, use a 13 by 9-inch baking dish; the baking time need not be increased.

1½	cups pearl barley (see note)
3½	cups water
2	teaspoons unsalted butter
1	teaspoon salt

1. Adjust an oven rack to the middle position and heat the oven to 375 degrees. Spread the barley in an 8-inch square glass baking dish.

2. Bring the water, butter, and salt to a boil in a covered medium saucepan over high heat. Once

boiling, stir the mixture to combine, then immediately pour it over the barley.

3. Cover the baking dish tightly with a double layer of aluminum foil. Bake the barley until it is tender and no water remains, 70 to 80 minutes.

4. Remove the baking dish from the oven, uncover, and fluff the barley with a fork. Re-cover the dish with foil and let the barley stand for 10 minutes before serving.

➤ VARIATION

Baked Barley with Porcini Mushrooms

Don't substitute hulled barley for the pearl barley. Be sure to cover the pot when bringing the water to a boil in step 2; any water loss due to evaporation will affect how the barley cooks. If doubling the recipe, use a 13 by 9-inch baking dish; the baking time need not be increased.

1½	cups pearl barley (see note)
3	tablespoons unsalted butter
1	medium onion, minced
1	teaspoon salt
¼	ounce dried porcini mushrooms, rinsed and minced
1	teaspoon minced fresh thyme leaves
3½	cups water

1. Adjust an oven rack to the middle position and heat the oven to 375 degrees. Spread the barley in an 8-inch square glass baking dish.

2. Melt the butter in a medium saucepan over medium heat. Add the onion and salt and cook, stirring often, until softened, about 5 to 7 minutes. Stir in the mushrooms and thyme and cook until fragrant, about 1 minute. Stir in the water. Cover the pot, increase the heat to high, and bring the mixture to a boil. Once boiling, stir the mixture to combine, then immediately pour it over the barley.

3. Cover the baking dish tightly with a double layer of aluminum foil. Bake the barley until it is tender and no water remains, 70 to 80 minutes.

4. Remove the baking dish from the oven, uncover, and fluff the barley with a fork. Re-cover the dish with foil and let the barley stand for 10 minutes before serving.

BAKED MEXICAN RICE

IN MEXICO, RICE PILAF, OR *ARROZ A LA Mexicana,* often stands on its own as a separate course, in the manner that Italians serve pasta. On the American table, it can make a unique side dish, one that is great to serve with chili or any kind of spicy- or smoky-flavored entrée. Mexican rice is usually cooked pilaf-style: The rice grains are sautéed in oil, along with onions, garlic, tomatoes, and chiles, and then simmered on the stovetop in broth until done. It is a basic dish with a reasonable ingredient list, yet we often find it vexing. When we put a selection of recipes from respected Mexican cookbook authors to the test, variable ingredient quantities and cooking techniques produced disparate results. Two of these recipes turned out soupy and greasy; a third was simply burnt. These oily and scorched versions were clearly off track. Though we knew we would need to stick to first sautéing the rice in oil on the stovetop to get the flavor right, we hoped we could then move the dish to the oven to finish cooking. Our goal was to not only prevent scorching but to make a more foolproof recipe.

We first looked at sautéing methods. While some recipes call for only a quick sauté, taking the time to cook the rice until it was golden brown proved crucial in providing a mild, toasted flavor and satisfying texture. As for the amount of oil, we experimented with a wide range, from 3 tablespoons to 1¼ cups. When we essentially deep-fried the rice in copious amounts of oil, as more than one recipe suggested, the rice was, not surprisingly, much too oily; even straining off excess oil from the rice as directed didn't help, and it was a messy process. Insubstantial amounts of oil made rice that was dry and lacking richness. One-third cup of oil seemed just right—this rice was rich but not greasy.

Now it was time to look into baking the rice. Though we were introducing some recipe-specific ingredients in this rice dish, we thought it could probably be cooked like our Baked Long-Grain White Rice (page 256). So we stirred the rice into a mixture of chicken broth, tomatoes, and onions (the essential flavors of Mexican rice) and popped it in the oven. Initial testing proved that our hunch was right. Still, as we baked batch after batch, we were frustrated by cooking times that were inconsistent, a problem we hadn't had with the white rice. Most batches of our Mexican rice contained a smattering of crunchy grains mixed in with tender ones. Prolonged cooking didn't solve the problem; what did was stirring the rice partway through cooking to reincorporate the thick tomato mixture that was settling on the top. We also dropped the oven temperature by 25 degrees to 350 degrees. With this practice in place, every last grain cooked evenly.

With a foolproof baking method under our belts, our attention turned to the cooking liquid and the flavoring. The cooking liquid traditionally used in Mexican rice is a mixture of chicken broth and pureed tomatoes. Experiments with a variety of ratios helped us to settle on equal parts of each. With too much tomato puree, the rice tasted like warm gazpacho; with too little, its flavor waned.

Each and every recipe we consulted called for fresh tomatoes and when we pitted rice made with canned tomatoes against rice made with fresh, the reason for using the latter was clear. Batches made with fresh tomatoes tasted, well, fresh. Using fresh tomatoes was the difference between having rice that was scented with tomatoes and rice that was overtaken by them. The batches made with canned tomatoes tasted overcooked and too tomatoey. Pureeing our fresh tomatoes with the onion produced the balanced yet fresh flavor we were after; it also saved us a step, by allowing us to process the onion in the food processor rather than having to chop it by hand. To capture the one benefit of canned tomatoes—an intense, tomato-red color—we stirred in an untraditional ingredient: tomato paste. It gave the rice an appealing red hue while also adding an extra lift in flavor.

To get the additional flavors we were after, we sautéed a generous amount of garlic and jalapeños in the oil with the rice before mixing in the puree of tomato and onion. After stirring in the tomato paste and chicken stock and bringing the whole mixture to a boil, all we had to do was pour it in the dish and bake it.

While many traditional recipes consider the addition at the end of fresh cilantro and minced jalapeño optional, in our opinion they were mandatory. The raw herbs and pungent chile complemented the richer tones of the cooked tomatoes, garlic, and onions. Lime wedges were the final touch; a squeeze of acidity illuminated the flavors even further. With that, we had a flavorful, authentic-tasting Mexican rice recipe that we could rely on, batch after batch.

Baked Mexican Rice

SERVES 6 TO 8

Rinsing the rice produces more distinct, separate grains. To rinse the rice, you can place it in a fine-mesh strainer and rinse under cool water, or place it in a medium bowl and repeatedly fill the bowl with water while swishing the rice around, then carefully drain off the water. In either case, you must rinse until the water runs clear. Vegetable broth can be substituted for the chicken broth.

2	medium ripe tomatoes (about 12 ounces), cored and quartered
I	medium white onion, peeled, trimmed, and quartered
3	medium jalapeño chiles
⅓	cup vegetable oil
2	cups long-grain white rice, rinsed (see note)
4	medium garlic cloves, minced or pressed through a garlic press (about 4 teaspoons)
2	cups low-sodium chicken broth
I	tablespoon tomato paste
I½	teaspoons salt
½	cup minced fresh cilantro leaves
I	lime, cut into wedges

1. Adjust an oven rack to the middle position and heat the oven to 350 degrees. Process the tomatoes and onion in a food processor until smooth and thoroughly pureed, about 15 seconds, scraping down the bowl as needed. Transfer the mixture to a liquid measuring cup; you should have 2 cups (if necessary, spoon off and discard any excess).

2. Remove and discard the ribs and seeds from 2 of the jalapeños, then mince. Mince the remaining jalapeño with its ribs and seeds and reserve separately.

3. Heat the oil in a large Dutch oven over medium-high heat for 1 to 2 minutes. Drop 3 or 4 grains of the rinsed rice in the oil; if the grains sizzle, the oil is ready. Stir in the rice and cook, stirring frequently, until the rice is light golden and translucent, 6 to 8 minutes.

4. Reduce the heat to medium, stir in the garlic and seeded minced jalapeños and cook, stirring constantly, until fragrant, about 1½ minutes. Stir in the 2 cups pureed tomato-onion mixture, chicken broth, tomato paste, and salt. Cover the pot, increase the heat to high, and bring the mixture to a simmer. Place the pot in the oven and bake the rice until it is tender and no water remains, 30 to 35 minutes, stirring well halfway through the cooking time.

5. Remove the rice from the oven, uncover, and fluff the rice with a fork. Stir in the cilantro and add the reserved minced jalapeño with ribs and seeds to taste. Re-cover the pot and let the rice stand for 10 minutes before serving with the lime wedges.

➤ VARIATION

Baked Mexican Rice with Charred Tomatoes, Chiles, and Onion

In this variation, the vegetables are charred in a cast-iron skillet, which gives the finished dish a deeper color and a slightly toasty, smoky flavor; don't use a traditional or even a nonstick skillet here or you will be left with burnt spots that are difficult to remove, even with vigorous scrubbing. Rinsing the rice produces more distinct, separate grains. To rinse the rice, you can place it in a fine-mesh strainer and rinse under cool water, or place it in a medium bowl and repeatedly fill the bowl with water while swishing the rice around, then carefully drain off the water. In either case, you must rinse until the water runs clear. Vegetable broth can be substituted for the chicken broth.

3 medium jalapeño chiles

2 medium ripe tomatoes (about 12 ounces), cored

1 medium white onion, peeled and halved

6 medium garlic cloves, unpeeled

⅓ cup vegetable oil

2 cups long-grain white rice, rinsed (see note)

2 cups low-sodium chicken broth

1 tablespoon tomato paste

1½ teaspoons salt

½ cup minced fresh cilantro leaves

1 lime, cut into wedges

1. Cut 2 of the jalapeños in half lengthwise, then remove and discard the ribs and seeds. Mince the remaining jalapeño with its ribs and seeds and reserve separately.

2. Heat a large cast-iron skillet over medium-high heat for about 2 minutes. Add the tomatoes, onion, garlic, and seeded halved chiles and toast the vegetables, using tongs to turn them frequently, until softened and almost completely blackened, about 10 minutes for the tomatoes and 15 to 20 minutes for the other vegetables. When cool enough to handle, trim the root ends from the onion and halve each piece. Remove the skins from the garlic and mince. Mince the jalapeños.

3. Adjust an oven rack to the middle position and heat the oven to 350 degrees. Process the toasted tomatoes and onion in a food processor until smooth and thoroughly pureed, about 15 seconds, scraping down the bowl if necessary. Transfer the mixture to a liquid measuring cup; you should have about 2 cups (spoon off and discard any excess).

4. Heat the oil in a large Dutch oven over medium-high heat for 1 to 2 minutes. Drop 3 or 4 grains of the rinsed rice in the oil; if the grains sizzle, the oil is ready. Stir in the rice and cook, stirring frequently, until the rice is light golden and translucent, 6 to 8 minutes.

5. Reduce the heat to medium, stir in the 2 cups pureed tomato-onion mixture, toasted minced garlic, toasted minced jalapeños, chicken broth, tomato paste, and salt. Cover the pot, increase the heat to high, and bring the mixture to a boil. Place

the pot in the oven and bake the rice until it is tender and no water remains, 30 to 35 minutes, stirring well halfway through the cooking time.

6. Remove the rice from the oven, uncover, and fluff the rice with a fork. Stir in the cilantro and add the reserved minced jalapeño with ribs and seeds to taste. Re-cover the pot and let the rice stand for 10 minutes before serving with the lime wedges.

BAKED RISOTTO

THOUGH RISOTTO, ONE OF THE HALLMARKS of northern Italian cooking, has become increasingly popular, nobody ever said it was easy. Preparing this classic dish the traditional way, on the stovetop, requires vigilance, constant stirring, and patience. But that's something not all of us have the time for. That is why there is room for a less demanding version: baked risotto. Baked risotto uses an appealingly simple technique for creating this otherwise labor-intensive dish, and we found a solid dozen recipes that rely on the following basic steps: Onions are sautéed in butter, Arborio rice is stirred in and briefly toasted, hot broth and flavorings are added, and the rice is baked in the oven until tender. The first half of the recipe mirrors traditional risotto; the second half is downright heretical. Isn't risotto defined by its intensive stirring?

Our biggest concerns going in were oven temperature and liquid volume. On the stovetop, risotto is cooked at a reasonable clip, simmering rapidly but not quite boiling. How could we replicate this in the oven? Baked at too high a temperature, the rice would boil and cook unevenly; too low, and the rice would stew. We tried temperatures ranging from 300 degrees to 450 degrees and found that 400 degrees yielded the best results. The temperature kept the rice at a steady simmer but below a full-blown boil.

We also knew that the liquid volume was critical to getting the right texture. In classic risotto, liquid is added in small increments, but for baking it must be added all at once. In our first batches, we added too much liquid and the grains of rice blew out and turned mushy. We decreased the volume of liquid (we were using a combination of chicken broth and wine) in subsequent tests until we had perfectly cooked rice using 4½ cups. But at this point another problem cropped up: while this amount yielded creamy risotto, it only stayed creamy for about 5 minutes once it emerged from the oven.

We were stumped. We thought that perhaps baked risotto is just a drier version of the original. Then a test kitchen colleague suggested adding more liquid after the rice emerged from the oven. We were a bit skeptical since we had already tried cooking the rice with more liquid with poor results. But, much to our surprise, when we stirred an extra ½ cup of hot chicken broth into the fully cooked risotto, it was absorbed, making the dish a bit creamier. We felt that we were on the right path, so we kept adding broth until tasters were satisfied with an additional 1¼ cups.

While our baked risotto would not be mistaken for the more classically made version (ours was still a little drier and firmer textured), we decided

that amplifying its flavors could help make up for any textural discrepancies. A few cloves of garlic, minced and sautéed with the onions, added an extra dimension that tasters liked. We felt that we were still falling a little short in creaminess, but a generous amount of Parmesan solved that problem.

True, our baked risotto had a different sort of unctuous texture than the velvety classic, but it certainly was a close second. And since it didn't require vigilance and incessant stirring, leaving us free to turn to other tasks, we were more than happy with the final results.

Baked Risotto

SERVES 6 TO 8

Avoid buying Arborio rice from bulk bins or in old-looking packages. Old or stale rice does not cook as well as fresher rice and may require substantial amounts of additional liquid—a real problem with this recipe since it is baked out of sight in the oven. If you cannot find Arborio rice, standard medium- or short-grain rice will do in a pinch, though the texture will not be as creamy. This risotto is best served immediately because it begins to firm up as it sits.

3	tablespoons unsalted butter
1	medium onion, minced
	Salt
3	medium garlic cloves, minced or pressed through a garlic press (about 1 tablespoon)
	Large pinch saffron (optional)
2	cups Arborio rice (see note)
4¾	cups low-sodium chicken broth
1	cup dry white wine
2	ounces Parmesan cheese, grated (about 1 cup)
	Ground black pepper

1. Adjust an oven rack to the middle position and heat the oven to 400 degrees.

2. Melt the butter in a large Dutch oven over medium heat. Add the onion and ¼ teaspoon salt and cook, stirring often, until softened, about 5 to 7 minutes. Stir in the garlic and saffron, if using, and cook until fragrant, about 30 seconds. Stir in the

INGREDIENTS: Arborio Rice

The stubby, milky grains of Arborio rice, once grown exclusively in Italy, are valued for their high starch content and the subsequent creaminess they bring to risotto. But does the best Arborio rice have to come from Italy?

To find out, we cooked up batches of Parmesan risotto with two domestically grown brands of Arborio rice and four Italian imports; all brands are widely available in supermarkets. To our surprise, the winning rice hailed not from Italy, but from the Lone Star State.

THE BEST ARBORIO RICE

RiceSelect, a Texas-grown rice, won tasters over with its "creamy, smooth grains" and "good bite."

RICESELECT ARBORIO RICE

INGREDIENTS:
Supermarket Parmesan Cheese

The buttery, nutty, slightly fruity taste and crystalline crunch of genuine Parmigiano-Reggiano cheese is a one-of-a-kind experience. Produced using traditional methods for the past 800 years in one government-designated area of northern Italy, this hard cow's-milk cheese has a distinctive flavor that is touted as coming as much from the region's geography as from the production process. But is all of this regional emphasis for real, or can really good Parmesan be made anywhere?

Recently, many more brands of shrink-wrapped, wedge-style, American-made Parmesan have been appearing in supermarkets. They're sold at a fraction of the price of authentic stuff, which can cost up to $33 a pound. To see how they stacked up, we bought eight nationally distributed brands at the supermarket: six domestic Parmesans and two imported Parmigiano-Reggianos. These supermarket wedges ranged from $8.49 to $17.17 per pound. Twenty testers tasted the eight brands of Parmesan cheese three ways: broken into chunks, grated, and cooked in polenta. Boar's Head Parmigiano-Reggiano was the tasters' favorite, with a pleasingly nutty flavor.

THE BEST SUPERMARKET PARMESAN CHEESE
Tasters like the good crunch and tangy, nutty flavor of this rich, complex cheese.

BOAR'S HEAD
PARMIGIANO-REGGIANO

rice and cook until the grain edges are transparent, about 4 minutes.

3. Stir in 3½ cups of the chicken broth and the wine. Cover the pot, increase the heat to high, and bring to a simmer. Place the pot in the oven and bake the rice until it is tender and no water remains, about 20 minutes.

4. Just before removing the risotto from the oven, microwave the remaining 1¼ cups broth in a covered microwave-safe bowl on high power until hot. Remove the risotto from the oven and stir in the hot broth and Parmesan. Season with salt and pepper to taste and serve immediately.

BAKED RICE CASSEROLE

BAKED RICE CASSEROLES HAVE ALWAYS promised a solution to the vexing problem of how to easily serve a rice side dish to a large crowd and keep it warm. A rice casserole, baked in a serving dish, is ready for the table or buffet, and while there are other baked rice options that can be easily doubled to serve a crowd, a rice casserole often makes a stronger choice for long stints on the buffet table since it retains its heat much longer, thanks to a protective topping and a creamy sauce. But with these advantages come numerous challenges, as we discovered when we tested several of the dozens of recipes we found. A dry, pasty texture plagued some, while others were overloaded with cheese and other fatty ingredients. Either way, swallowing more than a mouthful was a trial. The texture of the rice never failed to disappoint. "Blown out" grains were commonplace, as were pockets of crunchy, undercooked rice. All the recipes were sorely in need of a fundamental technique for cooking the rice thoroughly and evenly. We set out to develop a basic, more-than-barely-edible recipe for a rice casserole, one with a simple cheese sauce that could be easily varied by adding or substituting any number of ingredients.

Many recipes call for cooked rice, which we found unhelpful: the amount of rice needed to fill a casserole dish precluded using leftovers, and in any event, starting with fully cooked rice guaranteed that the grains would overcook in the oven, at least around the edges. Others suggest parboiling the rice in salted water, then draining and adding it to a sauce made separately. We objected to this method for two reasons: the extra pot and the wasted opportunity to flavor the rice by cooking it together with aromatics and the sauce.

For our first attempt we tried the easiest option—we poured a hot, cheesy, liquid mixture over the rice, stirred to combine, and baked it in the oven just like we did for our baked rice recipes (see page 254). It was a complete disaster. The rice was undercooked and hard in the center, and the few grains that cooked through were gummy. We tried cooking at both higher and lower heat, and for shorter and longer periods of time—all to no avail, as the rice was always inedible. Why had this cooking method worked so beautifully for plain rice, but so miserably for creamy rice casserole?

The reason this dish was different from our other baked rice, we discovered, was that flour had been added to help bind the sauce. Rice cooks more slowly in a flour-bound sauce because swollen starch granules (the flour) trap much of the water, making it impossible for the rice grains to absorb it. We thought precooking the rice in the liquid on the stovetop before baking it might help cook the rice more evenly. Our hunch was right. We tested a variety of cooking times and were surprised to learn that the best results were obtained by cooking the rice for a full 20 to 25 minutes on the stovetop in the liquid ingredients of our sauce prior to stirring in the cheese and pouring the mixture into the baking dish. Under normal circumstances, 20 minutes in boiling liquid would be enough to overcook rice, yet ours was just tender. Any less than 20 minutes and the rice came out of the oven chalky and underdone, especially at the center; in these cases, simply increasing the oven time only worsened the discrepancy in doneness between edges and center, and also dried out the dish. Any longer than 25 minutes and the rice grains blew out in the oven, making a mushy mess.

Next we tested the types and proportions of liquids to use. Our options were water, milk, chicken broth, and cream. Tasters found that cream, in addition to the butter and cheese in the sauce, made the dish too rich. Even whole milk, in the volume necessary to cook the 3 cups of raw rice needed to fill a casserole dish, made for a heavy sauce. But the casserole made entirely with broth was, not surprisingly, too "chickeny," overwhelming the other flavors of the dish. Tasters found the right balance of flavor and richness with an even mixture of milk and chicken broth, diluted with a couple cups of water.

We moved on to consistency. Even with only ¼ cup of flour to thicken 10 cups of liquid, our casseroles were turning out a little pasty, thanks to all the extra starch released from the rice grains as they cooked. We tried rinsing the rice to remove some of this starch, but this was only marginally effective. Much better results were obtained by reducing the flour even further, down to a mere 2 tablespoons.

The sauce started out very thin—perfect for cooking the rice—then thickened as the rice absorbed water and leached starch.

We had only to adjust the flavors and make a topping and our recipe would be complete. Tasters favored sharp cheddar over milder cheeses, as it contrasted with the rich starchiness of the dish; a dash of cayenne pepper was approved for the same reason.

As for the topping, we immediately canned the idea of using store-bought bread crumbs, finding their flavor stale and lifeless. Instead, we preferred the fresh, somewhat sweet flavor of sliced sandwich bread, ground into crumbs using a food processor. Mixed with a little melted butter, these crumbs browned nicely, providing just the right amount of crunch. And finally, the fresh flavors of lemon and parsley sprinkled on the finished dish contributed a welcome brightness. With that, we had a perfected rice casserole, one certain to disappear at the next neighborhood gathering.

Baked Rice Casserole
SERVES 8 TO 10

Stir the sauce frequently for the first few minutes after adding the rice, as this is when the rice is most likely to clump and stick to the bottom of the pan.

TOPPING

4	slices high-quality white sandwich bread, torn into quarters
2	tablespoons unsalted butter, melted

RICE

4	tablespoons (½ stick) unsalted butter
1	medium onion, minced
3	medium garlic cloves, minced or pressed through a garlic press (about 1 tablespoon)
2	tablespoons unbleached all-purpose flour
4	cups low-sodium chicken broth
4	cups whole milk
2	cups water
3	cups long-grain white rice
1½	teaspoons salt
¼	teaspoon ground black pepper
⅛	teaspoon cayenne pepper

8 ounces sharp cheddar cheese, shredded
   (about 2 cups)
2 tablespoons minced fresh parsley leaves
1 lemon, cut into wedges

1. FOR THE TOPPING: Pulse the bread and butter together in a food processor until coarsely ground, about 6 pulses; set aside.

2. FOR THE RICE: Adjust an oven rack to the middle position and heat the oven to 400 degrees. Melt the butter in a large Dutch oven over medium heat. Add the onion and cook, stirring often, until softened, 5 to 7 minutes. Stir in the garlic and cook until fragrant, about 30 seconds. Stir in the flour and cook, stirring constantly, until golden, about 1 minute.

3. Slowly whisk in the broth, milk, and water until smooth and bring to a simmer, whisking often. Stir in the rice, salt, pepper, and cayenne and return to a simmer. Cover the pot, reduce the heat to medium-low, and cook, stirring often, until the rice has absorbed much of the liquid and is just tender, 20 to 25 minutes. Off the heat, stir in the cheddar.

4. Pour the rice mixture into a 13 by 9-inch baking dish and sprinkle with the bread crumb topping. Bake until the topping is browned and the casserole is bubbling, 20 to 25 minutes.

5. Remove the dish from the oven and let rest for 10 minutes. Sprinkle with the parsley and serve with the lemon wedges.

➤ VARIATIONS

Coconut–Cardamom Baked Rice Casserole

We prefer the fragrant flavor of jasmine rice in this variation, but you can substitute conventional long-grain white rice. For more heat, include the jalapeño seeds and ribs when mincing. The sauce for this variation does not require any flour.

TOPPING
1 cup roasted, unsalted cashews
4 slices high-quality white sandwich bread, torn
   into quarters
2 tablespoons unsalted butter, melted

RICE
2 tablespoons unsalted butter
1 medium onion, minced
2 jalapeño chiles, seeds and ribs removed,
   chile minced (see note)
1 tablespoon minced or grated fresh ginger
2 medium garlic cloves, minced or pressed
   through a garlic press (about 2 teaspoons)
1 teaspoon ground cardamom
4 cups low-sodium chicken broth
4 cups coconut milk
2 cups water
3 cups jasmine rice
1½ teaspoons salt
¼ teaspoon ground black pepper
2 tablespoons minced fresh cilantro leaves
1 lime, cut into wedges

1. FOR THE TOPPING: Process the cashews in a food processor until coarsely ground, 5 to 10 seconds. Add the bread and butter and pulse until coarsely ground, about 6 pulses; set aside.

2. FOR THE RICE: Adjust an oven rack to the middle position and heat the oven to 400 degrees. Melt the butter in a large Dutch oven over medium heat. Add the onion and jalapeños, and cook, stirring often, until softened, 5 to 7 minutes. Stir in the ginger, garlic, and cardamom and cook until fragrant, about 30 seconds.

3. Whisk in the broth, coconut milk, and water until smooth, and bring to a simmer. Stir in the rice, salt, and pepper and return to a simmer. Cover the pot, reduce the heat to medium-low, and cook, stirring often, until the rice has absorbed much of the liquid and is just tender, 20 to 25 minutes.

4. Pour the rice mixture into a 13 by 9-inch baking dish and sprinkle with the bread crumb topping. Bake until the topping is browned and the casserole is bubbling, 20 to 25 minutes.

5. Remove the rice from the oven and let rest for 10 minutes. Sprinkle with the cilantro and serve with the lime wedges.

267

Baked Rice Casserole with Butternut Squash

This variation replaces some of the rice with butternut squash. Because of the moisture from the squash, this recipe does not require additional water to dilute the cooking liquid. If the ricotta you purchase is very grainy, pulse it in a food processor until smooth before using.

TOPPING

1	cup pecans
4	slices high-quality white sandwich bread, torn into quarters
2	tablespoons unsalted butter, melted

RICE

2	tablespoons unsalted butter
1	pound butternut squash, peeled and cut into 1-inch cubes
1	medium onion, minced
2	medium garlic cloves, minced or pressed through a garlic press (about 2 teaspoons)
3	tablespoons chopped fresh sage leaves
2	tablespoons unbleached all-purpose flour
4	cups low-sodium chicken broth
4	cups whole milk
2	cups long-grain white rice
1/8	teaspoon ground nutmeg
1 1/2	teaspoons salt
1/4	teaspoon ground black pepper
12	ounces ricotta cheese (about 1 1/2 cups, see note)
1	ounce Parmesan cheese, grated (about 1/2 cup)
1	lemon, cut into wedges

1. FOR THE TOPPING: Process the pecans in a food processor until coarsely ground, 5 to 10 seconds. Add the bread and butter and pulse until coarsely ground, about 6 pulses; set aside.

2. FOR THE RICE: Adjust an oven rack to the middle position and heat the oven to 400 degrees. Melt the butter in a large Dutch oven over medium heat. Add the squash and cook, stirring occasionally, until just beginning to soften, about 5 minutes. Stir in the onion and cook until softened, 5 to 7 minutes. Stir in the garlic and sage and cook until fragrant, about 30 seconds. Stir in the flour and cook, stirring

constantly, until golden, about 1 minute.

3. Slowly whisk in the broth and milk until smooth and bring to a simmer, whisking often. Stir in the rice, nutmeg, salt, and pepper and return to a simmer. Cover the pot, reduce the heat to medium-low, and cook, stirring often, until the rice has absorbed much of the liquid and is just tender, 20 to 25 minutes. Off the heat, stir in the ricotta and Parmesan.

4. Pour the rice mixture into a 13 by 9-inch baking dish and sprinkle with the bread crumb topping. Bake until the topping is browned and the casserole is bubbling, 20 to 25 minutes.

5. Remove the rice from the oven and let rest for 10 minutes. Serve with the lemon wedges.

BAKED POLENTA

POLENTA, HAILING FROM THE NORTHERN regions of Italy, is simply coarse-ground cornmeal cooked in water to form a soft mush. Often served with roasted meats, stews, and braises, it can also be served as a hearty first course or light entrée when topped with sautéed cherry tomatoes or sausage and Swiss chard. Ideally, its texture should be smooth, creamy, and soft, but still stiff enough to be eaten with a fork and hold its shape when dolloped onto a plate.

The ingredients may be few, but the traditional Italian method for cooking polenta is a lot of work. The cornmeal must be slowly added to boiling salted water and stirred constantly (to prevent scorching) during the entire 30- to 40-minute cooking time. Thirty minutes of this constant stirring can seem like an eternity. We thought that was an awful lot of time to spend hovering over a side dish, so we set out to see if we could simplify the method.

We wanted to find a cooking method that would produce a rich corn flavor and velvety texture—and wouldn't wear us out in the process. We thought that slow, very gentle heat, not vigilant stirring, might be the key to unlocking cornmeal's smooth texture. Because the oven offers just such an environment, we had high hopes that baking could be our solution.

EQUIPMENT: Cheese Graters

Whether you are dusting a plate of pasta or grating a full cup of cheese to use in a recipe, a good grater should be efficient and easy to use. After grating more than 10 pounds of Parmesan, we concluded that success is dependent on a combination of sharp grating teeth, a comfortable handle or grip, and good leverage for pressing the cheese onto the grater. Our favorite model was a flat grater based on a small maneuverable woodworking tool called a rasp. Shaped like a ruler, but with lots and lots of tiny, sharp raised teeth, the Microplane grater can grate large quantities of cheese smoothly and almost effortlessly. The black plastic handle, which we found more comfortable than any of the others, also earned high praise. Other flat graters also scored well. What about box graters? They can deliver good results and can do more than just grate hard cheese—but if grating hard cheese is the task at hand, a box grater is not our first choice.

THE BEST GRATER

The Microplane grater has very sharp teeth and a solid handle, which together make grating cheese a breeze. This grater also makes quick work of ginger and citrus zest.

MICROPLANE

To test baking polenta, we knew we would still need to start on the stovetop, since the initial step of adding the polenta gradually to boiling salted water is important in preventing clumping. We boiled some water, along with some salt, in a Dutch oven on the stovetop, stirred in the polenta, covered the pot, and put it in the oven. The hope was that the low, steady heat of the oven would shield the polenta from cooking too rapidly and gradually allow the starches to be released and the flavor of the cornmeal to develop. We kept the cover on the pot the entire time, to hold in moisture and reduce the risk of drying out the top layer of the polenta as it baked. It might be polenta heresy, but we only stirred the polenta once while it cooked (halfway through). After an hour the polenta emerged from the oven fluffy, creamy, and full of rich corn flavor. Baking had once again worked its magic.

After fine-tuning the critical proportions and determining that a ratio of 7 cups water to 1½ cups cornmeal delivers the right consistency, we moved on to testing different types of cornmeal. While good for making spoon bread, finely ground cornmeal, such as the Quaker brand sold in many supermarkets, is too powdery and makes gummy, gluey polenta. Stone-ground cornmeal also produces lousy polenta because the grind is too uneven. The best polenta, we confirmed, is that which is actually labeled as "polenta" and is made with evenly ground, medium- to coarse-ground cornmeal.

Finally, to complement the corn flavor we stirred in some garlic and Parmesan cheese right before serving. This baked polenta was flavorful and creamy—good enough to mistake for any batch that had been stirred for an eternity.

Creamy Baked Polenta
SERVES 6

Do not substitute instant polenta here. Coarse or medium-ground cornmeal that is not labeled as "polenta" can be substituted for the polenta as long as it is evenly ground and has no fine, floury bits. In order for the Parmesan to melt completely we found it best to use finely grated fresh Parmesan rather than pregrated cheese, which has a coarse, granular texture; finely grating the Parmesan is easy to do using a rasp-style grater or the smaller holes of a box grater.

- 7 cups water
- Salt
- 1½ cups (9 ounces) polenta (see note)
- 2 ounces Parmesan cheese, finely grated (about 1 cup, see note)
- 4 tablespoons (½ stick) unsalted butter
- 1 medium garlic clove, minced or pressed through a garlic press (about 1 teaspoon)
- Ground black pepper

1. Adjust an oven rack to the middle position and heat the oven to 350 degrees.

2. Bring the water to a boil in a large covered Dutch oven over high heat. Remove the lid and stir in 1½ teaspoons salt. Very slowly pour the polenta into the boiling liquid while stirring constantly in a circular motion with a wooden spoon, following the illustration on page 270.

3. Cover, place the pot in the oven, and bake until the polenta no longer has a raw cornmeal taste and all of the liquid has been absorbed, about 1 hour, stirring well halfway through the cooking time.

4. Remove the polenta from the oven and stir in the Parmesan, butter, and garlic. Season with salt and pepper to taste before serving.

MAKING POLENTA

When the water comes to a boil, add the salt, then pour the polenta into the water in a very slow stream from a measuring cup, all the while stirring in a circular motion with a wooden spoon to prevent clumping.

BAKED GRITS

A STAPLE OF THE SOUTHERN TABLE, GRITS can be a nutritious and substantial start to the day, or a good addition to the dinner plate as a side. There are myriad options for preparation: grits can be quickly and easily made on the stovetop and enhanced with a little maple syrup or molasses, or, like polenta, grits can be cooked to a thick consistency, cooled, sliced, and fried. But our favorite way to cook grits is to bake them. Sadly, we have found that baked cheese grits are often far from perfect. They are either bland and watery or too thick and gluey. We set out to develop a foolproof recipe for baked grits, a dish that would be rich, hearty, and full of corn flavor.

We started by looking at the varieties of grits available in our local grocery store. There were two kinds: instant, which cook in five minutes, and old-fashioned, which cook in 15 minutes. In a side-by-side tasting, most tasters thought the instant grits were too creamy and tasted overprocessed. The old-fashioned grits were creamy yet retained a slightly coarse texture that tasters liked—after all, they are called "grits" for a reason.

While our grits would eventually be baked, we determined that their cooking had to start on the stovetop to achieve the right consistency. We found that 15 minutes over medium heat did the trick.

To add richness without relying solely on butter, as many recipes do, we decided to try cooking the grits in milk rather than water. The grits tasted good, but more in a hot-breakfast-cereal way, and the subtle flavor of the grits themselves disappeared behind the milk flavor. We then tried a small amount of heavy cream and water mixed together. We were surprised to find that the cooked cream did not develop the same strong "cooked" flavor as milk. This is because the extra fat in cream keeps the milk proteins from breaking down when heated. Everyone liked this batch—the grits were rich but without an overwhelming dairy flavor. After a few more batches of varying proportions, we found that 1 part cream to 3 parts water was best.

To further improve on things, we tried a few simple additions that would enhance the flavors without being overpowering. Diced onion cooked in the saucepan before adding the cream and water brought depth and a touch of sweetness. Though many tasters liked a little garlic as well, others thought the garlic overwhelmed the other flavors, so we decided to leave it out. A touch of hot sauce added a piquancy that cut through the richness.

Next we looked at cheese options. Monterey Jack made the grits taste sour, so it was out. Regular cheddar was bland, but we felt the flavor was getting there. Extra-sharp cheddar proved to be the winner. The flavor was assertive yet complemented the subtle corn flavor of the grits without being overwhelming.

Finally, we wanted to fine-tune the texture. We knew we wanted the dish to be dense, somewhere between baked polenta and custardy spoon bread, but closer to the former. We started off by adding three lightly beaten eggs to the grits before baking, but this just created an airy, soufflé-like texture that tasters found unpleasant. We needed more eggs to bind the grits and give the dish the density we desired. Five eggs made the grits too heavy and eggy. The happy medium of four eggs provided just enough structure without making the grits taste overly eggy.

Forty-five minutes in a 350-degree oven (with a little more cheese sprinkled on top) finished the grits perfectly. We had attained our ideal for baked grits: rich and robust, with a clear corn flavor shining through.

Baked Grits Casserole

SERVES 6 TO 8

Do not substitute instant grits; they do not offer enough texture or body and will make the casserole gluey. Feel free to substitute other cheeses such as smoked cheddar or smoked Gouda for the extra-sharp cheddar.

3	tablespoons unsalted butter
1	medium onion, minced
4½	cups water
1½	cups heavy cream
¾	teaspoon hot sauce
1	teaspoon salt
1½	cups old-fashioned grits (see note)
8	ounces extra-sharp cheddar cheese, shredded (about 2 cups)
4	large eggs, lightly beaten
¼	teaspoon ground black pepper

1. Adjust an oven rack to the middle position and heat the oven to 350 degrees. Grease a 13 by 9-inch baking dish with 1 tablespoon of the butter.

2. Melt the remaining 2 tablespoons butter in a large Dutch oven over medium heat. Add the onion and cook, stirring often, until softened, 5 to 7 minutes. Stir in the water, cream, hot sauce, and salt. Cover the pot and bring to a boil.

3. Remove the lid and slowly whisk in the grits. Reduce the heat to low and cook uncovered, stirring often, until the grits are thick and creamy, about 15 minutes. Off the heat, whisk in 1 cup of the cheese, the eggs, and pepper.

4. Pour the mixture into the prepared baking dish and smooth the top with a rubber spatula. Sprinkle the remaining cup of cheese over the top. Bake the grits until the top is browned and the grits are hot, 35 to 45 minutes. Remove the grits from the oven and let rest for 10 minutes before serving.

➤ VARIATION

Baked Grits Casserole with Pepper Jack Cheese and Bell Pepper

Follow the recipe for Baked Grits Casserole, adding 1 medium red bell pepper, stemmed, seeded, and chopped fine, to the pot with the onion in step 2 and increasing the cooking time to 8 to 10 minutes. Substitute 8 ounces pepper Jack cheese, shredded (about 2 cups), for the cheddar.

INGREDIENTS: Extra-Sharp Cheddar

What is extra-sharp cheddar? The U.S. Department of Agriculture's only requirement regarding cheddar is that the final product contain at least 50 percent milk-fat solids and no more than 39 percent moisture by weight. As for what distinguishes different varieties of cheddar—mild, medium, sharp, extra-sharp, and beyond—that is left in the hands of the cheese makers. Our research revealed that most extra-sharp cheddars are aged from nine to 18 months. As cheddar ages, new flavor compounds are created, and the cheese gets firmer in texture and more concentrated in flavor—and it gets sharper.

Our tasters generally liked the older, sharper cheeses best. Our three top-rated cheeses—Cabot Private Stock, Cabot Extra Sharp, and Grafton Village—are all aged for at least 12 months, and tasters rated them the sharpest. Tasters praised the Cabot Private Stock's well-rounded sharpness and depth of flavor; it was not, however, as sharp as the Grafton Village, whose sharpness was described by some tasters as "overwhelming."

As for texture, tasters preferred the older cheeses for their denser, more crumbly bite. Younger cheeses had more moisture and a springier, more rubbery texture—fine in a young cheese, but not what we wanted in extra-sharp cheddar. As for melting ability, tasters didn't mind a little greasiness (older cheddars separate when melted, because they contain less water and thus have less insulation against some of their fat melting out) as long as there was big flavor to back it up.

THE BEST EXTRA-SHARP CHEDDARS
Cabot Private Stock Cheddar Cheese and Cabot Extra Sharp Cheddar Cheese were tasters' favorites for their sharpness and well-balanced flavors.

BOSTON BAKED BEANS

HEADY WITH SMOKY PORK AND BITTERSWEET molasses, authentic Boston baked beans are both sweet and savory, a unique combination of the simplest ingredients, unified and refined during a long simmer. They are a fine example of the whole being greater than the sum of the parts.

A close reading of recipes—and there are thousands out there—made it clear that authentic Boston baked beans are not about fancy seasonings. They are about developing intense flavor by means of the judicious employment of canonical ingredients (beans, pork, molasses, mustard, and sometimes onion) and slow cooking. Testers quickly rejected recipes with lengthy lists of untraditional ingredients and short cooking times.

The most important item on the shopping list is, of course, the beans, the classic choice being standard dried white beans in one of three sizes: small white beans, midsize navy or pea beans, or large great Northern beans. While the latter two choices were adequate, tasters preferred the small white beans for their dense, creamy texture and their ability to remain firm and intact over the course of a long simmer. (The two larger sizes tended to split.)

When cooking dried beans, we usually favor a two-step method that involves soaking the beans in salt water prior to cooking them—this method worked for this recipe as well. By soaking the beans in salt water, we were able to firm up and "set" the bean skins, making the beans less prone to breaking and bursting during cooking.

Next came the meat. For Boston baked beans, some type of cured pork is essential for lush texture and depth of flavor, though it should never dominate. Although traditionalists swear by salt pork, we decided to first try its meatier version, pork brisket. While its flavor was enjoyable, tasters felt that the beans made with pork brisket lacked richness—the brisket was too lean. Not surprisingly, salt pork scored high with tasters, though some felt the flavor was too mild. We then tried bacon, a more modern choice, but alone it was deemed "too smoky and overwhelming" by most, even though the heartier pork flavor was appreciated. On a whim, we put both salt pork and bacon into the pot and found the perfect middle ground. The bacon brought the desired depth to the beans, and the salt pork muted the bacon's hickory tang. Twice as much salt pork as bacon proved to be the right balance.

In traditional recipes, the salt pork is cast raw into the beans (often as a large piece) and melts into the sauce, but during tests it failed to render completely. Gelatinous chunks of fatty pork bobbing among the beans left even the most carnivorous tasters cold. We tried dicing the pork into smaller bits, but this was only a partial success; some unmelted fat remained. Next, we tried browning the pork in the Dutch oven prior to adding the beans, and the results were surprising. This simple step (and one not recommended in any of the recipes we'd found) made the flavor of the beans significantly fuller and better than anything we had yet tasted. Apparently, the melted fat more readily flavored the cooking liquid, and the browned bits of meat tasted richer.

While yellow onion was a controversial ingredient in classic recipes, we sensed its flavor could be important. Our intuition proved right. Tasters loved its sweetness and the full flavor it lent the beans, especially once sautéed in the rendered pork fat. Tasters favored a fine dice so that the onion all but disappeared by the time the beans were ready.

Next we tackled the final two ingredients: mustard and molasses. Dry mustard, the classic choice, had worked fine, but most of the test kitchen felt home cooks were more likely to have prepared mustard on hand and that it provided a perk—vinegar—to cut the beans' sweetness. We tested several varieties, including Dijon, German whole grain, yellow, and brown. They all brought a unique flavor to the beans, but brown mustard—Gulden's brown mustard, in particular—was best, imparting a pleasant sharpness without calling attention to itself. Even with the mustard's tang, though, we found it necessary to add vinegar for acidity. Most classic recipes add cider vinegar at the start of the cooking time, but we found the acidity stayed sharper when it was added to the finished beans. A scant teaspoon proved enough to cut the molasses's sweetness and accent the other flavors.

The molasses, we discovered, would take some finessing, as its brutish flavor and intense sweetness dominated the beans when added carelessly. After tasting batches made with mild, full-flavored (also known as "robust"), and blackstrap varieties, most tasters preferred the subtler tones of the mild. We settled on just ½ cup baked with the beans for a balance of moderate sweetness and palate-cleansing bitterness, and a tablespoon added after cooking to gently reemphasize its character.

All that was left to do now was look at the cooking time and temperature. We knew that, to a certain extent, flavor and texture were in opposition. The longer the beans cooked, the better the sauce's flavor, but past a certain crucial moment of equilibrium, time worked against the beans, turning them to mush.

We tested oven temperatures in increments of 25 degrees between 200 and 350 degrees. At 200 degrees, the beans took upward of eight hours to cook and even then, they were still on the crunchy side. At 350 degrees, the beans percolated vigorously and exploded. We found that the best temperature was 250 degrees, which, after 3½ hours, yielded beans that were creamy-textured and a sauce that was full-flavored.

While pleased with the beans' texture and the overall flavor, we still wanted a thicker sauce—soupy beans were not acceptable. We discovered that it was

not simply a matter of reducing the volume of water, however, as this led to unevenly cooked beans. The problem was rooted in the method: We had been cooking the beans start to finish covered with a lid, which had prevented the cooking liquid from reducing effectively. When we removed the lid for the last hour of cooking, we got the results we were looking for—the sauce had reduced to a syrupy, intensified liquid that perfectly coated the beans.

Boston Baked Beans
SERVES 6

We prefer the texture of small white beans here; they are actually labeled and sold as "small white beans." Midsize beans such as navy or pea beans, or large beans such as great Northern beans, will also work, but they are more likely to split open during cooking.

1	pound (about 2½ cups) dried small white beans, rinsed, picked over, and salt-soaked overnight or quick salt-soaked (see page 122)
4	ounces salt pork, trimmed of rind and cut into ½-inch cubes
2	ounces (about 2 slices) bacon, cut into ¼-inch pieces
1	medium onion, minced
4	cups water
½	cup plus 1 tablespoon mild molasses
1½	tablespoons prepared brown mustard, such as Gulden's
1	teaspoon cider vinegar
	Salt and ground black pepper

1. Adjust an oven rack to the middle position and heat the oven to 250 degrees. Drain the beans, discarding the soaking liquid, and rinse well.

2. Cook the salt pork and bacon in a large Dutch oven over medium heat, stirring occasionally, until lightly browned and most of the fat is rendered, about 7 minutes. Stir in the onion and cook, stirring often, until softened, 5 to 7 minutes. Stir in the water, ½ cup of the molasses, and the mustard to combine, then stir in the drained beans. Cover the pot, increase the heat to high, and bring to a simmer.

BUYING SALT PORK

The salt pork shown at top has a high ratio of fat to meat and is preferable in this recipe to leaner, meatier salt pork, like the piece shown at bottom.

FATTY

LEAN

3. Place the pot in the oven and bake until the beans are tender, about 2½ hours, stirring halfway through the cooking time. Remove the lid and continue to bake until the liquid has thickened to a syrupy consistency, about 1 hour longer, stirring halfway through the cooking time.

4. Remove the beans from the oven and stir in the remaining 1 tablespoon molasses and the vinegar. Season with salt and pepper to taste before serving.

➤ VARIATION
Barbecued Baked Beans

Barbecued beans, with their brasher flavor, stand up better than Boston baked beans to the big flavors of grilled and barbecued foods. We prefer the texture of small white beans here; they are actually labeled and sold as "small white beans." Midsize beans such as navy or pea beans, or large beans such as great Northern beans, will also work, but they are more likely to split open during cooking. You can either make your own barbecue sauce (see Classic Barbecue Sauce on page 35), or use your favorite store-bought brand—we like Bull's Eye Original.

I	pound (about 2½ cups) dried small white beans, rinsed, picked over, and salt-soaked overnight or quick salt-soaked (see page 122)
4	ounces (about 4 slices) bacon, cut into ¼-inch pieces
I	medium onion, minced
4	medium garlic cloves, minced or pressed through a garlic press (about 4 teaspoons)
4	cups water
I	cup strong black coffee
½	cup plus I tablespoon barbecue sauce (see note)
¼	cup packed dark brown sugar
I½	tablespoons prepared brown mustard, such as Gulden's
I	tablespoon mild molasses
½	teaspoon hot sauce
	Salt and ground black pepper

1. Adjust an oven rack to the middle position and heat the oven to 250 degrees. Drain the beans, discarding the soaking liquid, and rinse well.

2. Cook the bacon in a large Dutch oven over medium heat stirring occasionally, until lightly browned, about 7 minutes. Stir in the onion and cook, stirring often, until softened, 5 to 7 minutes. Stir in the garlic and cook until fragrant, about 30 seconds. Stir in the water, coffee, ½ cup of the barbecue sauce, the brown sugar, mustard, molasses, and hot sauce until combined, then stir in the drained beans. Cover the pot, increase the heat to high, and bring to a simmer.

3. Place the pot in the oven and bake until the beans are tender, about 2½ hours, stirring halfway through the cooking time. Remove the lid and continue to bake until the liquid has thickened to a syrupy consistency, about 1 hour longer, stirring halfway through the cooking time.

4. Remove the beans from the oven and stir in the remaining 1 tablespoon barbecue sauce. Season with salt and pepper to taste before serving.

CUBAN-STYLE BAKED BLACK BEANS

CUBAN CUISINE FOR THE MOST PART IS AN amalgamation of the flavors of many cultures—Spanish, African, Caribbean, and even Chinese—and has evolved over the years into what is known as Cuban Creole. At the heart of any typical Cuban meal are black beans, but this dish is hardly your ordinary staple. The many layers of flavor—earthiness, with a smoky depth and a touch of brightness—make these black beans a great addition to almost any plate, and they offer a complexity that makes them hard to tire of.

The perfect black beans should be tender without being mushy, with just enough resistance to make a satisfying chew. More often than not, black beans are unevenly cooked, or cooked until they turn into a grey mush. We knew we could do better. We wanted to create a recipe for full-flavored, creamy black beans that kept their color and cooked evenly. To achieve this, we looked to our Boston Baked Beans (page 273) for inspiration. In that recipe, baking resulted in evenly cooked beans with creamy centers and intact exteriors.

First, we looked at soaking methods. We usually prefer beans that have been soaked in a salt-water solution for 8 to 24 hours before cooking them, as this firms up and "sets" the bean skins, making them less prone to breaking and bursting during cooking. We figured this would be the case with our black beans as well. Just to be sure, we compared beans that had been salt-water soaked overnight with a batch of unsoaked beans. We also tried a batch using a quick-soak method, in which the beans are brought to a boil in salted water, briefly simmered, and then covered for one hour off the heat.

The unsoaked beans had tough skins and a tough interior, so we nixed that method. We found that the quick-soak method caused a slightly larger than average percentage of the beans to burst during cooking, but was still deemed acceptable. The clear winner was the overnight salt-water soaked batch. The beans were tender and creamy but didn't fall apart.

With a soaking method established, we turned to water amounts. We had discovered during our soaking tests that it was important to cook the beans in enough water; too little water and the beans on top cooked more slowly than the beans underneath. We found that the ideal proportions for our salt-soaked beans, which require far less water than regularly soaked beans, was 3½ cups of water to 1 pound of beans. To ensure that the beans cooked evenly, we stirred them once during the cooking time.

SORTING DRIED BEANS WITH EASE

It is important to rinse and pick over dried beans to remove any stones or debris before cooking. To make this task easier, sort dried beans on a white plate or cutting board. The neutral background makes any unwanted matter easy to spot and discard.

Now that we had beans that emerged from the oven intact, evenly cooked, and with great texture, it was time to determine the best way to build layers of flavor without drowning out the earthiness in the beans. We first tried adding pork. A typical addition in many of the recipes we found, meat gives the dish a necessary depth of flavor. We tested cooking beans with a ham hock, bacon, ham, and pork loin. We liked all four, and each gave the beans a slightly different flavor. Bacon and ham produced an assertive flavor, while pork loin was the subtlest. We ultimately decided to go with the ham hock, which provided a smooth background flavor without taking over.

In many Latin recipes, a *sofrito* (the Latin American answer to the French mirepoix of carrots, onions, and celery) is added to the cooked beans for flavor. Chopped vegetables—usually onion, garlic, and green bell pepper—are sautéed in olive oil until soft and then stirred into the beans. Incorporating this mixture into our beans added another layer of fresh flavor without overwhelming them.

We then ran several experiments with additional flavorings. We tested whether sugar was necessary and found that we didn't like the added sweetness. For an acidic component, we tested red wine vinegar against balsamic and cider vinegars, as well as lime and lemon juices. Lime juice was the best fit, and when we paired it with a sprinkling of cilantro, we knew we had the taste of tradition.

We were finally satisfied, save for the beans' unappealing grayish brown color. We knew there had to be a way to keep the beans black, and with great determination we set out to find it. It was our science editor who suggested that we try adding a little baking soda to the beans. Black beans' coating contains pigments that change color with changes in pH: the addition of an acidic component to the beans would make them lighter, whereas the alkaline nature of baking soda causes the beans to retain their dark color. We experimented by adding various amounts of baking soda to the beans both during and after cooking. Larger quantities created a soapy aftertaste; a mere ⅛ teaspoon produced great-tasting beans with a darker, more appetizing color than unadulterated beans. Problem solved.

Cuban-Style Baked Black Beans

SERVES 6

Serve with sour cream, minced red onion, and hot sauce.

1	pound (about 2½ cups) dried black beans, rinsed, picked over, and salt-soaked overnight or quick salt-soaked (see page 122)
2	tablespoons extra-virgin olive oil
1	medium onion, minced
1	small green bell pepper, stemmed, seeded, and minced
9	medium garlic cloves, minced or pressed through a garlic press (about 3 tablespoons)
2	teaspoons dried oregano
1½	teaspoons ground cumin
3½	cups water
1	smoked ham hock
2	bay leaves
⅛	teaspoon baking soda
½	cup minced fresh cilantro leaves
1	tablespoon juice from 1 lime
	Salt and ground black pepper

1. Adjust an oven rack to the middle position and heat the oven to 250 degrees. Drain the beans, discarding the soaking liquid, and rinse well.

2. Heat the oil in a large Dutch oven over medium heat until shimmering. Stir in the onion and bell pepper and cook until the vegetables are softened, 8 to 10 minutes. Stir in the garlic, oregano, and cumin and cook until fragrant, about 30 seconds. Stir in the water, ham hock, bay leaves, and baking soda until combined, then stir in the drained beans. Cover the pot, increase the heat to high, and bring to a simmer.

3. Place the pot in the oven and bake until the beans are tender, about 2 hours, stirring halfway through the cooking time. Remove the lid and continue to bake until the liquid has thickened to a syrupy consistency, about 30 minutes longer, stirring halfway through the cooking time.

4. Remove the beans from the oven, discard the ham hock and bay leaves, and stir in the cilantro and lime juice. Season with salt and pepper to taste before serving.

BAKED LENTILS

THOUGH OFTEN RESERVED FOR HO-HUM lentil soup or salads found in natural foods cafés, earthy lentils are an ideal foil to other flavors, making them a perfect base for myriad side dishes to pair with everything from fish to meat. Here in the test kitchen our favorite way to prepare them is by braising. Cooking them in liquid in a covered pot results in rich flavor, but if they cook even a little bit too long or over a heat level that is too high, they can burst and turn to mush. Our goal was to make a baked lentil dish—flavorful with aromatics, spices, and sausage—that would emerge from the oven with the lentils intact.

Before we looked at cooking the lentils, we had to determine which type of lentils to use. Brown, green, and red are the most common choices on supermarket shelves. At specialty markets and natural food stores, you can also find black lentils and French green lentils (lentilles du Puy), the latter being the darling of chefs around the globe. In addition to color differences, lentils can be divided according to their size—large or small—and to whether they are split (like peas) or not. Ordinary brown and green lentils are large, while red, black, and lentilles du Puy are small. Red lentils are often sold split and are used most frequently in Indian dishes such as dal.

To finalize our choice, we made five batches, each one using a different-colored lentil. Red lentils were quickly disqualified—they disintegrated before the ingredients in the dish had enough time to meld. Though the black lentils remained intact, their flavor was unimpressive. The larger green and brown lentils fared reasonably well, exceeding test kitchen expectations, but the favored choice in the end was lentilles du Puy. They were highly praised for their hearty flavor and firm texture, and they retained their shape better than all of the others.

Next, it was time to look at the details of baking. Using our baked beans cooking method (see page 272) as a guide, we sautéed some aromatics in a Dutch oven on the stovetop, added the lentils and liquid to the pot, covered the mixture, and brought it to a boil before transferring it to a 250-degree oven. These lentils, however, were overcooked and falling apart. We tried simply cooking them for less time, but that didn't solve the problem. Since lentils take far less time to cook than beans, we thought bringing the water to a boil before putting the pot in the oven, as we had with our baked beans, might be an unnecessary step. So we sautéed the aromatics, added the lentils and water, and covered the pot before transferring it directly to the oven (no bringing the liquid to a boil). Success! These lentils stayed intact and were evenly cooked.

Next, we fine-tuned the dish's texture by looking at oven temperatures, testing temperatures ranging from 250 to 400 degrees. Our initial testing temperature of 250 degrees took too long and the resulting lentils were too soft. Meanwhile, the 400-degree oven brought the mixture to a rapid simmer, resulting in broken lentils. The best temperature was 300 degrees, which yielded lentils that were intact and creamy in about 80 minutes. The only problem was that there was too much cooking liquid left in the pot. We couldn't reduce the amount of cooking liquid because then the lentils wouldn't be completely covered, which would leave us with hard, undercooked lentils on top and perfectly cooked ones underneath, even if we were using a lid. We didn't want to serve soupy lentils, so we borrowed another trick we learned while baking batch after batch of beans—finishing the baking without the lid. We removed the lid for the final 20 minutes, which was just long enough to get the liquid to the right consistency and solve the problem.

With our cooking technique down, we next looked to flavoring. We knew the lentils would be properly complemented by aromatics and herbs like onions, garlic, and thyme. Their addition lent sweetness and depth. We also liked the addition of canned diced tomatoes, which provided fruitiness and a balancing acidity.

As for spices, smoked paprika gave this dish all the punch it needed. Produced only in the Vera region of Spain, smoked paprika (known as *pimentón*) is made from peppers that are slowly smoked over oak prior to crushing. The flavor is intensely smoky and comes in three grades: sweet, hot, and bittersweet. For this dish, we favored bittersweet paprika, as sweet was too mild and hot numbed the palate. For the best flavor, we found it

was important to toast the smoked paprika briefly in the skillet before adding liquid.

To give the dish an even fuller flavor, we added diced sausage. We tried a wide range of readily available varieties, including chorizo, linguiça, both hot and sweet Italian sausage, and kielbasa. The last type won out for its smoky-sweet flavor, compact texture, and ability to stay incredibly moist and juicy throughout a long cooking time.

For our final touch, a scattering of thinly sliced scallions on top added both a piquant punch and visual appeal.

Baked Lentils with Sausage
SERVES 4

Lentilles du Puy, sometimes called French green lentils, are our first choice for this recipe, but brown or regular green lentils will work fine, too; cooking times may vary depending on the type of lentils used. Despite its localized Spanish production, smoked paprika is widely available in specialty stores and large markets. However, you can substitute regular paprika. Serve this dish warm or at room temperature with a drizzle of lemon juice or sherry vinegar.

2	tablespoons extra-virgin olive oil
1	medium onion, minced
	Salt
4	ounces kielbasa, cut into ¼-inch pieces
4	medium cloves garlic, peeled and sliced thin (following the illustration on page 71)
1¼	teaspoons smoked paprika (see note)
1	teaspoon minced fresh thyme leaves
1	(14.5-ounce) can diced tomatoes, drained
1½	cups low-sodium chicken broth
1½	cups water
1	cup lentilles du Puy, picked over and rinsed (see note)
2	scallions, sliced thin
	Ground black pepper

1. Adjust an oven rack to the middle position and heat the oven to 300 degrees. Heat the oil in a large Dutch oven over medium heat until shimmering. Add the onion and ½ teaspoon salt and cook, stirring often, until softened, 5 to 7 minutes. Stir in the sausage, garlic, paprika, and thyme and cook until

fragrant, about 30 seconds. Stir in the tomatoes, broth, water, and lentils.

2. Cover, place the pot in the oven, and bake until the lentils are tender, about 1 hour, stirring halfway through the cooking time. Remove the lid and continue to bake until the liquid has evaporated, about 20 minutes longer.

3. Remove the lentils from the oven and scatter the scallions over the top. Season with salt and pepper to taste before serving.

BREAD PUDDING

WHAT'S EASIER THAN QUICHE, STURDIER than soufflé or strata, and combines the best qualities of all of them? The answer is savory bread pudding. The best savory bread puddings have a rich, scoopable custard and enough of the bread sticking out for some of the edges to crisp up during cooking. Made properly, savory bread puddings offer a crunchy toasted bread topping that perfectly contrasts the rich, cheesy custard beneath.

But bread pudding is not without its issues. First, it is easy to go overboard and add too much of a good thing. Many of the savory bread puddings we sampled in the test kitchen were simply too rich, with a belly-busting overabundance of custard. The bread should not get lost among the other ingredients, but rather should be balanced and complemented by them. A good bread pudding should have a restrained filling with a few additional components chosen to accent the bread and custard.

In essence, then, we wanted to scale bread pudding back, keeping it just rich enough to be satisfying, with just enough complementary flavors to add to the picture without stealing the show. We also wanted a cohesive casserole rather than a bunch of stray ingredients baked together in a dish. All the principal parts and steps—custard, bread, fillings, and how and when they were assembled and cooked—were subject to review.

Naturally, bread is the foundation of bread pudding and was a logical place for us to begin.

Though sliced white sandwich bread was the type specified in many recipes, we also saw some that called for Italian, French, sourdough, multigrain, rye, pumpernickel, challah, focaccia, and even hamburger and hot dog buns. We tried them all, and in the end tasters preferred French baguettes for their strong crumb and neutral flavor. We also tested bread puddings made with and without the crust. Tasters thought that the crust gave the bread pudding a better texture, so we left it on.

Some recipes cube the bread and stale it overnight, but these bread puddings looked more like the cobblestone streets in the French Quarter than something we'd like to eat with dinner. We wanted a more rustic look and had much better results tearing the baguette into ragged pieces. Toasting the torn pieces to a deep golden brown enriched their flavor and gave the bread a crispness that helped to prevent the finished dish from turning soggy.

We then turned our attention to the custard that binds the pieces of bread together. In a battery of custard tests, we looked at different dairy products. Recipes commonly call for low-fat milk, whole milk, or half-and-half, and sometimes even heavy cream (the last option usually in combination with another dairy liquid). We tried each one of these alone as well as in every conceivable combination, and most tasters preferred a mixture of 3 parts cream to 2 parts milk. It was rich but not over the top.

Though the question of the liquid was settled, we still had some egg testing to do—our custard kept curdling on us. We tested whole eggs, yolks only, whites only, and various combinations. Because whites set faster than yolks, we found that replacing the traditional whole eggs with just egg yolks helped stave off curdling. Plus, it yielded a flavorful custard that tasters favored.

The last major adjustment we made to the custard was its overall quantity in relation to the amount of bread. Too little made for a dry bread pudding, while too much made it too rich. Our final balance between custard and bread made a pudding that was moist yet sturdy enough to hold together.

Though our basic bread pudding was very good, we knew the flavorings and fillings would be what would catapult it to glory. We added garlic, fresh thyme, and a healthy dose of Parmesan cheese, all of which added dimensions of flavor without taking over. As for salt and pepper, we learned that a heavy hand is best; a teaspoon of salt and ¾ teaspoon pepper brought the flavors into focus.

For baking our casserole, we found that a wide, shallow baking dish allowed the bread pudding to bake much more evenly than the deep soufflé dish recommended in many recipes (a standard 13 by 9-inch Pyrex dish works great). Lowering the baking temperature from the frequently recommended 375 degrees to 350 degrees was another tactic we adopted to even out the cooking and to help curdle-proof our pudding. The result was a savory and versatile dish—great served alongside roast pork or chicken, and perfect for brunch or a light dinner when served with a salad.

Savory Bread Pudding

SERVES 6 TO 8

We prefer the flavor and texture of a high-quality French baguette here, but a conventional supermarket baguette will also work.

1	(18- to 20-inch) French baguette, torn into 1-inch pieces (about 10 cups)
1	tablespoon unsalted butter
8	large egg yolks
3	cups heavy cream
2	cups whole milk
2	ounces Parmesan cheese, grated (about 1 cup)
2	teaspoons minced fresh thyme leaves
2	medium garlic cloves, minced or pressed through a garlic press (about 2 teaspoons)
1	teaspoon salt
¾	teaspoon ground black pepper

1. Adjust an oven rack to the middle position and heat the oven to 450 degrees. Arrange the bread in a single layer on a baking sheet and bake until crisp and browned, about 12 minutes, turning the pieces over halfway through baking. Remove the bread from the oven and let cool.

2. Reduce the oven temperature to 350 degrees. Grease a 13 by 9-inch baking dish with the butter.

3. Whisk the yolks, cream, milk, ½ cup of the Parmesan, the thyme, garlic, salt, and pepper together in a large bowl. Add the toasted bread and toss until evenly coated. Let the mixture sit until the bread softens and begins to absorb the custard, about 30 minutes, tossing occasionally. (If the majority of the bread is still too hard after 30 minutes, let it soak for another 15 to 20 minutes.)

4. Pour half of the bread mixture into the prepared baking dish and sprinkle with ¼ cup more Parmesan. Pour the remaining bread mixture into the dish and sprinkle with the remaining ¼ cup Parmesan. Bake until the custard is just set, about 60 minutes, rotating the dish halfway through the baking time.

5. Remove the bread pudding from the oven and let rest for 10 minutes before serving.

➤ VARIATIONS

Savory Bread Pudding with Spinach and Feta

Follow the recipe for Savory Bread Pudding, omitting the Parmesan cheese. Stir 1 (10-ounce) package frozen chopped spinach, thawed and squeezed dry, and 4 ounces feta cheese, crumbled (about 1 cup), into the yolk mixture in step 3.

Savory Bread Pudding with Bacon and Onion

Cook 6 ounces (about 6 slices) bacon, cut into ¼-inch pieces, in a 12-inch nonstick skillet over medium heat until well browned, about 10 minutes. Transfer the bacon to a paper towel–lined plate, leaving the fat in the skillet. Stir 1 medium onion, halved and sliced thin, and ½ teaspoon salt into the fat left in the skillet, cover, and cook over medium heat, stirring occasionally, until the onion softens and releases its juices, about 10 minutes. Uncover and continue to cook, stirring often, until the onion begins to brown, about 6 minutes. Follow the recipe for Savory Bread Pudding, sprinkling the bacon and onion slices over the first layer of bread with the Parmesan in step 4.

CORN PUDDING

CORN PUDDING IS A COMBINATION OF EGGS, milk, and cream graced with a generous helping of fresh-off-the-cob corn. In essence, it is a savory corn custard. We set out to develop a recipe for a tender, creamy custard that surrounded and showcased the sweet, subtle flavor of the corn.

We originally thought that this baked custard would be a no-brainer. Many American cookbooks include recipes for corn pudding, and they all invariably boil down to varying combinations of the four main ingredients. Given this agreement among recipes, we were quite surprised to find that our first puddings were all failures. Each and every one curdled and wept, producing an unwanted pool of watery liquid on the surface.

Puddings cooked in a water bath fared better than those exposed directly to the oven heat. But the water bath alone was not enough to produce smooth, tender custard. It seemed obvious that the corn in the pudding was the source of the escaping liquid; the question was how to get rid of the moisture in the corn without losing the fresh corn flavor.

After experimenting with various options, we settled on a simple two-step approach. First, we cooked the corn kernels in a little butter on the stovetop until the moisture in the pan had almost evaporated. Then we drew out a bit more of the kernels' liquid by simmering them in heavy cream. (Because heavy cream, unlike milk or even light cream, can be cooked at a boil without curdling, we reasoned that it would be safe to simmer the corn together with the required cream.) After simmering, we had a thick mixture that, once baked, made for a dish with great flavor and without any seeping liquid.

Now we were ready to move on to the final steps of balancing ingredients and flavors. The first thing we noticed about our now smooth and creamy custard was the corn—there was too much of it, interfering with the smooth texture. To reduce the corn-to-custard ratio, we cut back from 4 cups of corn to 3 cups. This helped, but there still seemed

to be too many intruding kernels. We thought that perhaps pureeing some of the corn would smooth out the texture without sacrificing any of the corn flavor. Pureeing turned out to be overkill; we wanted the pudding to have some texture, and now it didn't have enough. As an in-between solution, we tried grating some of the corn directly off the cobs on the coarse side of a box grater. This method gave us just what we were looking for in terms of flavor as well as texture. A touch of sugar drew out the sweetness of the corn, while cayenne pepper added the final kick.

Creamy Corn Pudding
SERVES 6

Fresh corn is crucial for the flavor of this savory pudding; do not substitute frozen corn.

4	tablespoons (½ stick) unsalted butter
6	ears fresh corn, husks and silk removed
⅔	cup heavy cream
1½	teaspoons salt
1	teaspoon sugar
¼	teaspoon cayenne pepper
1⅓	cups whole milk
4	large eggs, room temperature
1	tablespoon cornstarch

1. Adjust an oven rack to the middle position and heat the oven to 350 degrees. Grease an 8-inch square baking dish with 1 tablespoon of the butter. Place a kitchen towel on the bottom of a large roasting pan and place the prepared baking dish on the towel. Bring a kettle of water to a boil.

2. Following the illustrations on page 119, cut the kernels from 5 of the ears of corn into a large bowl, reserving the cobs. Grate the remaining ear of corn over the large holes of a box grater into the same bowl, then use the back of a butter knife to scrape the milk from all of the cobs into the bowl.

3. Melt the remaining 3 tablespoons butter in a large skillet over medium heat. Stir in the corn mixture and cook, stirring occasionally, until the

corn is bright yellow and the liquid has almost evaporated, about 5 minutes. Stir in the cream, salt, sugar, and cayenne and continue to cook until the mixture is thickened and a spoon leaves a trail when dragged across the bottom of the pan, about 5 minutes.

4. Transfer the cooked corn mixture to a medium bowl. Whisk in the milk, then the eggs and cornstarch, until thoroughly combined. Pour the mixture into the prepared baking dish.

5. Place the roasting pan in the oven and carefully pour the boiling water into the pan to reach halfway up the sides of the baking dish. Bake the pudding until the top has lightly browned in spots and the center is soft but set, 20 to 25 minutes.

6. Remove the roasting pan from the oven and carefully remove the baking dish from the water bath. Let the pudding cool for at least 10 minutes before serving. Serve hot or warm.

SOUTHERN SPOON BREAD

SPOON BREAD IS A SOUTHERN SPECIALTY made from a cornmeal batter that is poured into a baking dish and cooked until set. The texture is somewhere between rich cornbread and a soufflé (because it is on the softer side—and must be served with a spoon—it is probably closer to the latter). Spoon bread can be served as a side dish in place of rice or potatoes, and it works well for any meal of the day.

To make spoon bread, you first whisk cornmeal into a simmering liquid (such as water, milk, or half-and-half) and let it thicken to a "mush," as if you were cooking oatmeal. Once the mush has cooled, the other ingredients, including eggs, salt, and butter, are added. The mixture is then poured into a baking dish and baked for 35 to 45 minutes. The results should be light as air, with a tender, rich crumb. However, as with many traditional dishes,

ingredients and cooking techniques for spoon bread vary enormously. We began to develop the recipe for our ideal spoon bread by first tackling the best way to make the cornmeal mush.

The proportion of liquid to solids differed wildly in the recipes we consulted. We tried various ratios and learned that heavier mushes baked up, not surprisingly, somewhat heavy. Meanwhile, lighter versions simply did not gel adequately. We settled on a medium-thick batter, using 3 cups liquid to 1 cup cornmeal.

The act of stirring cornmeal into simmering milk can be tricky; the meal can separate from the liquid and turn into a bunch of lumps rather than a smooth mush if you aren't diligent. Plenty of recipes call for the use of a double boiler to prevent lumping, but because going this route requires 20 to 30 minutes of gentle stirring, we preferred to just focus intently on the job at hand—start whisking like crazy and don't stop until the mush is thickened, two to four minutes later. It's not much work when you consider the alternative time investment. We also noted that it was important to keep the cooking temperature low to ensure that the cornmeal would soften as it cooked.

Having settled on the mush-making method, we moved on to consider the individual ingredients of the dish. Spoon bread made with water is like cornbread made with water: lean. Because spoon bread is often an accompaniment to a special meal, we prefer to splurge on the real article and cut fat and calories somewhere else. Half-and-half was our liquid of choice, as it supplied the essential richness.

The oldest recipes for spoon bread call for incorporating eggs whole, while a later trend is to separate the eggs and incorporate beaten whites to produce a lighter, more soufflé-like dish. These days we are beginning to see other alternatives, with chemical leaveners compensating for the work the eggs would do. After tasting several dozen versions, we found that those spoon spreads made with baking powder or baking soda tasted plainly of chemicals. Beaten whites, we confirmed, remain the best leavener.

Lastly, we considered the important question of what type of cornmeal to use. Yellow corn is more common in the North and more often the choice in that region, while Southerners choose white for the same reason. We found that both worked well, the major difference being that the white produced a slightly milder flavor. A more important variation came with grinds. We found we preferred a fine grind because it produces a considerably smoother texture. Yellow Quaker cornmeal has a texture akin to table salt and is the proper grind for spoon bread. If you can't get fine-ground cornmeal in your local store, it's no problem. You can approximate a fine grind by putting a medium-ground cornmeal in the food processor or, even better, the blender. The processing will take several minutes, but eventually you will have little clouds of powder-fine meal in the bottom of the work bowl or blender jar, ready to make a batch of perfectly textured spoon bread.

Southern Spoon Bread
SERVES 6 TO 8

For a smooth-textured spoon bread, be sure to use finely ground cornmeal. Both yellow and white cornmeal will work fine here; white cornmeal will have a milder flavor. Spoon bread deflates fast, so serve it as quickly as possible.

3	tablespoons unsalted butter
3	cups half-and-half
1	teaspoon salt
1	cup (5 ounces) fine-ground cornmeal (see note)
3	large egg yolks, room temperature
2	teaspoons water
3	large egg whites, room temperature
¼	teaspoon cream of tartar

1. Adjust an oven rack to the middle position and heat the oven to 350 degrees. Grease a 1½-quart soufflé dish with 1 tablespoon of the butter.

2. Bring the half-and-half and salt to a simmer in a large saucepan. Reduce the heat to low and slowly whisk in the cornmeal. Continue to cook, whisking constantly, until the cornmeal thickens, 2 to 4 minutes. Transfer the mixture to a medium bowl and stir in the remaining 2 tablespoons butter. Set the mixture aside to cool slightly.

3. Whisk the egg yolks and water together in a small bowl until lemon-colored and very frothy, about 1 minute. Stir the egg yolks into the cooled cornmeal mixture.

4. In a large bowl, whip the egg whites and cream of tartar together with an electric mixer on medium-low speed until foamy, about 1 minute. Increase the mixer speed to medium-high and continue to whip the egg whites until stiff peaks form, 2 to 4 minutes.

5. Fold one-quarter of the whipped egg whites into the cornmeal mixture until almost no white streaks remain. Fold in the remaining whipped egg whites until just incorporated. Gently pour the mixture into the prepared soufflé dish, wiping any drips from the rim. Bake the spoon bread until golden brown and risen above the rim of the dish, about 45 minutes. Serve immediately.

➤ VARIATION
Southern Spoon Bread with Cheddar Cheese

Follow the recipe for Southern Spoon Bread, stirring 2 ounces sharp cheddar cheese, shredded (about ½ cup), into the cooked cornmeal mixture with the yolks in step 3.

7

SLOW-COOKED VEGETABLES AND FRUITS

SLOW-COOKED VEGETABLES AND FRUITS

MANY VEGETABLES CAN BE EATEN RAW OR cooked quickly (think steaming or stir-frying), but when we want to add serious flavor to vegetables, we usually like to slow things down. Classic slow cooking techniques such as roasting and braising are great for coaxing big, long-cooked flavor from vegetables. In this chapter we set out to discover which cooking methods best concentrate the flavor and improve the texture of a variety of vegetables, from artichokes to winter squash. What we learned is that "slow" is a relative term; while some vegetables are naturally slow cooking, for others, slow is about the best cooking method for drawing out flavors or creating new ones.

In some cases, we wanted to refine and improve the techniques for well-known slow-cooked vegetable recipes such as Roasted Beets (page 293), Baked Potatoes (page 315), and Roasted Root Vegetables (page 320). Here, the dry heat of the oven caramelizes the natural sugars in these vegetables, creating an incredibly flavorful side dish. And roasting is simple—after a little trimming and cutting, the vegetables need just a quick toss with oil, salt, and pepper. Once in the oven, the vegetables need only occasional supervision. It's important to keep in mind that too much moisture inhibits browning; if the vegetables are crowded they will steam instead of roast. Placing them in a single layer on a rimmed baking sheet (or roasting pan) ensures that moisture can evaporate. (In most cases, we recommend lining the baking sheet with aluminum foil for easy cleanup.)

Braising is another slow cooking technique that we've found is ideal for certain vegetables—especially those that are fibrous or bitter. Southern-Style Collard Greens (page 302), for instance, become tender and lose their assertive bitter flavor when cooked this way. As a bonus, vegetables cooked this way gain flavor from the braising liquid; likewise, the braising liquid is flavored by the vegetable and can be turned into a sauce that you can serve with the vegetable.

Though many of the vegetables in this chapter naturally take a long time to cook, we found that the techniques of roasting and braising work for quicker-cooking vegetables as well. Braised Brussels Sprouts (page 295) and Braised Leeks (page 310)

take less than 20 minutes, but you'd never guess it—the sprouts' rich, nutty flavor and the leeks' tender, creamy texture belie their relatively quick cooking time.

At the other end of the spectrum, we found that cooking some vegetables for an unexpectedly long time produces entirely new flavors and textures. Artichoke Confit (page 291), Slow-Braised Carrots (page 299), and Baked Sweet Potatoes (page 318) all take an hour or two to cook, but the results—unbelievably sweet and tender vegetables—are worth the wait.

We also aimed to streamline some otherwise fussy recipes. Gratins traditionally involve multiple steps—cooking the vegetable, making a sauce, and browning the casserole—and we wondered if there wasn't a way to simplify this process. By creating just the right sauce (a béchamel), we discovered we could simply toss the raw vegetables together with the sauce and let the dish come together in the oven—no parcooking the vegetables required. Sure, our Potato Gratin (page 327) takes longer than a traditional one (ours spends about two hours in the oven), but who cares when all you have to do is put it in the oven and walk away?

Most of the recipes in this chapter are side dishes, but we were also really excited to develop some recipes that use slow cooking to transform vegetables into a new condiment or flavoring agent with intense, concentrated flavor. The wonderful thing about Oven-Caramelized Onions (page 311), Roasted Garlic (page 305), and Oven-Dried Tomatoes (page 323) is how versatile they are; we'll show you how to incorporate them into everything from dips and dressings to pesto and aioli.

Finally, we looked at fruit. Most fruit, of course, is eaten raw, but we found that a little heat can transform an ordinary piece of fruit into something extraordinary, as with our Skillet-Roasted Pears with Caramel Sauce (page 337). Roasting or baking fruit also allows you to use a moderate oven temperature and extended cooking time to turn out-of-season fruit flavorful and tender; a perfect example is our Pan-Roasted Peaches (page 334), which makes an unexpected side dish or simple, elegant dessert.

SLOW-COOKED ARTICHOKES

FOR A GOOD NUMBER OF PEOPLE, THE mention of artichokes brings to mind the canned, marinated, or frozen ones. If you are cooking the fresh variety—you know, the big, green flower-like globes—the most common approach is to steam them whole (with minimal trimming before cooking) and let your dinner guests eat them leaf by leaf. But steaming isn't your only option; artichokes are wonderful when cooked slowly. Slow cooking concentrates their delicate, earthy flavor and yields tender leaves and a succulent heart. We wanted to explore this less familiar approach to cooking artichokes and decided to develop recipes using two different slow methods—braising and slow roasting in oil (a method known as *confit*).

Artichokes are commonly marketed in three sizes: baby (2 to 4 ounces each), medium (8 to 10 ounces each), and large (12 ounces or more each). Surprisingly, different-sized artichokes simultaneously bud on the same plant; the artichokes that grow on the plant's center stalk are the largest, and the smallest artichokes grow at the juncture between the plant's leaves and the stem. After preparing, cooking, and eating all three sizes, we found that we preferred the baby and medium artichokes to the large ones, which can be tough and fibrous.

When selecting fresh artichokes at the market, we find it best to follow a few rules of thumb. The artichokes should be tight and compact, like flower buds (which they are), and have an unblemished, bright green hue. They should "squeak" when you rub the leaves together—evidence that the artichoke still retains much of its moisture. If you tug at a leaf, it should cleanly snap off; if it bends, it's old. Also be on the lookout for leaves that appear dried out and feathery about the edges—a sure sign of an over-the-hill artichoke.

Because of their size, baby artichokes don't need a lot of trimming to get to the heart. Whether you are working with baby or medium artichokes and leaving them whole or trimming them to the heart, artichokes will turn brown almost as soon as they are cut. It is crucial to submerge them in acidulated water, which neutralizes the enzymes responsible for oxidation. We tried a variety of acids to prevent oxidation, including white wine vinegar, apple cider vinegar, and lemon juice, and were most pleased with lemon juice because of its bright yet neutral flavor.

We focused our attention first on braising artichokes. Braising is an excellent option for medium artichokes that have been trimmed of all inedible portions before cooking. The artichokes become extremely tender and the braising liquid turns into a rich, flavorful sauce. But what is the best liquid for braising artichokes? We tested three obvious choices: wine, broth, and water. It was no surprise to discover that water diluted the artichoke flavor, making a dull, flat-tasting sauce. Using either wine or broth alone was better, but a combination of the two was best, providing just the right balance of flavors without overwhelming the delicate artichokes. The acidity of the wine gave the finished dish a bright flavor, while the broth added depth and richness. As for herbs, we found rosemary to be too pungent for the master recipe (but quite promising for a variation), and parsley contributed little. We liked the subtle yet earthy flavor of thyme the best.

Next, we moved on to our artichoke confit. In French, the term *confit*—which translates as "to conserve"—refers to foods, usually meat, that are salted and slowly cooked, then stored, in fat. This preparation was traditionally a means of preservation, but these days everything from fish to vegetables can be found prepared this way. In fact, in restaurants, the term "confit" now refers to most anything cooked low and slow in fat, which gives the food a velvety, unctuous texture and concentrates its flavor. We found that baby artichokes are well suited to this cooking method, because it intensifies their sweet, nutty flavor and there is no choke to remove—the inedible outer portions must be trimmed, but otherwise, baby artichokes can be cooked as is.

We found that pure olive oil was best for this recipe because of the fruity flavor it contributes. It is imperative that the artichokes be completely submerged in the oil; if any leaves are sticking out, they will become dry and tough (if this happens, simply remove them before serving). A few thyme sprigs, lemon zest strips, and garlic cloves were all we needed to round out the flavors, providing bright, clean background notes. When it came to oven temperature and time, cooking the artichokes in a low, 250-degree oven for up to two and a half hours provided gentle, even cooking and enough time for the artichokes to become tender and infused with flavor. Finally, we determined that a large saucepan, with its relatively tall, narrow shape, was the best vessel for this cooking method, since it allowed us to get away with just 3 cups of oil to surround the artichokes. (If this seems like a lot of oil, don't worry—it is really flavorful and can be refrigerated and saved for later uses, such as a salad dressing or a dipping sauce for bread.)

While our artichoke confit is great as is, it also provides the perfect base for a couple of quick, easy recipes such as Marinated Artichokes (page 292), which can be used as part of an antipasto plate, or Artichoke Tapenade (page 292), which can be tossed with pasta or spread on baguette slices.

PREPARING ARTICHOKES FOR BRAISING

1. Holding the artichoke by the stem, bend back and snap off the thick outer leaves, leaving the bottom portion of each leaf attached. Continue snapping off the leaves until the light yellow inner leaves are exposed.

2. Using a paring knife, trim away the dark skin where the leaves were snapped off.

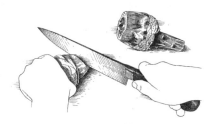

3. Cut the dark, purplish tip off the top of the choke.

4. Using a vegetable peeler, peel away the dark, tough skin covering the stem, then trim the bottom ½ inch off the stem.

5. Cut the artichoke in half lengthwise.

6. Scrape out the small purple leaves and the fuzzy choke in the center with a melon baller or grapefruit spoon.

Braised Artichokes

SERVES 4

Be sure to drain the artichokes well before cooking. You will need a skillet with a tight-fitting lid for this recipe. We found that a nonstick skillet works best here, but a traditional skillet can also be used. We recommend using a medium-bodied dry white wine, such as Sauvignon Blanc or Chardonnay, in this recipe. These are especially good with chicken and fish.

1	lemon
4	medium artichokes (8 to 10 ounces each)
3	tablespoons olive oil
1	medium shallot, minced
	(about 3 tablespoons)
	Salt
¾	cup dry white wine (see note)
¾	cup low-sodium chicken broth
2	teaspoons minced fresh thyme leaves
	Ground black pepper

1. Cut the lemon in half and squeeze the juice into a large bowl of cold water. Drop the spent lemon halves into the water.

2. Following the illustrations on page 289, snap off the thick outer leaves of each artichoke, trim away any dark skin with a paring knife, and cut off the tip off the choke. On the stem, peel away the dark, tough skin and trim the bottom. Cut the artichoke in half, scrape out the small purple leaves and fuzzy choke, and drop the artichoke halves into the bowl of lemon water until ready to cook.

3. Drain the artichokes thoroughly, discarding the lemon water. Heat the oil in a 12-inch nonstick skillet over medium heat until shimmering. Add the shallot and ¼ teaspoon salt and cook until softened, about 2 minutes. Add the drained artichokes, wine, broth, thyme, and ⅛ teaspoon pepper. Bring to a simmer, cover the pan, and cook the artichokes until a fork inserted into the center meets little resistance, 25 to 35 minutes.

4. Uncover and continue to cook until the liquid is slightly thickened, about 2 minutes. Season with salt and pepper to taste and serve.

EQUIPMENT: Large Saucepans

A large saucepan is an essential piece of cookware. In the test kitchen, we use our large saucepans for making rice and oatmeal, blanching vegetables, and cooking small amounts of pasta, soup, stew, and all kinds of sauces. Which begs an obvious question: does the brand of pan matter? In order to answer this question, we tested eight models, all between 3.3 and 4 quarts in size.

The tests we performed were based on common cooking tasks and designed to highlight specific characteristics of the pans' performance. To determine the relative cooking speed of each saucepan, we sautéed onions over medium heat. Cooking white rice provided a good indication of a pan's ability to heat evenly. Making pastry cream showed us how user-friendly the pan was—was it shaped such that a whisk could reach into the corners without trouble, and could we pour liquid from it neatly?

We found that the most important quality for a saucepan is even and slow heating. The best pans for slow and steady cooking were either very heavy or had relatively thick bottoms. An aluminum core throughout the pan also ensures even heating

and minimal scorching. Finally, we liked pans with long handles; a few of the pans we tested had small handles on either side, which tend to get hot quickly and can be difficult to hold with one hand while scraping out the contents with the other.

So which pan should you buy? With its heft and aluminum core, the All-Clad saucepan excelled at every test.

THE BEST LARGE SAUCEPAN

With its solid feel and perfectly proportioned shape, the All-Clad Stainless 4-Quart Saucepan ($184) passed every test with flying colors.

ALL-CLAD

➤ VARIATION

Braised Artichokes with Tomatoes and Rosemary

Follow the recipe for Braised Artichokes, substituting 4 medium garlic cloves, minced or pressed through a garlic press (about 4 teaspoons), for the shallot and cooking the garlic for 30 seconds. Reduce the amount of wine to ½ cup, substitute 1 (14.5-ounce) can diced tomatoes with their juice for the chicken broth, and substitute 2 teaspoons minced fresh rosemary for the thyme.

Artichoke Confit

MAKES ABOUT 4 CUPS,
OR 32 ARTICHOKE HALVES

Don't waste expensive extra-virgin olive oil in this recipe; you can use a blend of equal parts olive oil and less expensive vegetable oil if desired. If the artichokes are not completely covered by the oil when cooking, the outer leaves exposed to the heat of the oven will become tough and dry—simply remove and discard these before serving. Serve the artichokes as a side dish or appetizer, or use in one of the recipes on page 292. The reserved confit oil will have a slight artichoke flavor and can be refrigerated in an airtight container for up to 2 weeks; use the oil to make Marinated Artichokes (page 292), Artichoke Tapenade (page 292), salad dressing, or for dipping bread.

1	lemon
16	baby artichokes (2 to 4 ounces each)
3	cups olive oil (see note)
6	medium garlic cloves, peeled and crushed (see the illustration on page 63)
2	sprigs fresh thyme
	Salt and ground black pepper

1. Adjust an oven rack to the middle position and heat the oven to 250 degrees. Remove 6 strips of zest from the lemon, following the illustration on page 72, and set aside. Cut the lemon in half and squeeze the juice into a large bowl of cold water. Drop the spent lemon halves into the water.

2. Cut the top quarter off each artichoke and, following the illustrations at right, snap off the outer leaves and trim away the dark skin. Peel and trim the stem, then cut the artichoke in half lengthwise. Drop the artichoke halves into the bowl of lemon water until ready to cook.

3. Drain the artichokes thoroughly, discarding the lemon water, and transfer to a large saucepan. Add the strips of lemon zest, oil, garlic, thyme, ½ teaspoon salt, and ¼ teaspoon pepper. Place the pot, uncovered, in the oven and cook the artichokes until a fork inserted into the center meets little resistance, 2 to 2½ hours, stirring occasionally as needed to make sure the artichokes are covered by the oil.

4. Remove the saucepan from the oven and let the artichokes cool in the oil for at least 15 minutes, or up to 4 hours. To serve, remove the artichokes from the oil with a slotted spoon (reserving the oil separately if desired, see note) and season with salt and pepper to taste. (The cooled artichokes can be refrigerated in the confit oil in an airtight container for up to 2 weeks; return the artichokes and oil to room temperature before serving.)

PREPARING BABY ARTICHOKES FOR CONFIT

1. After cutting off the top quarter from the artichoke, snap off the outer leaves until the light yellow inner leaves are exposed.

2. Using a paring knife, trim away the dark skin where the leaves were snapped off and the dark, tough skin covering the stem. Trim away the very end of the stem, then cut the artichoke in half lengthwise.

Artichoke Tapenade
MAKES ABOUT 1½ CUPS

Either warm or room-temperature artichokes will work fine here. Toss this tapenade with pasta or serve as a spread with crackers or good bread.

½	recipe (16 artichoke halves) Artichoke Confit (page 291)
¼	cup reserved oil from Artichoke Confit or extra-virgin olive oil
2	tablespoons chopped walnuts, toasted (see page 309)
1	teaspoon minced fresh thyme leaves
1	small garlic clove, minced or pressed through a garlic press (about ½ teaspoon)
¼	teaspoon grated zest plus 1 tablespoon juice from 1 lemon
⅛	teaspoon cayenne pepper Salt and ground black pepper
1	ounce Parmesan cheese, grated (½ cup)

Process the artichokes, reserved confit oil, walnuts, thyme, garlic, lemon zest, lemon juice, cayenne, ¼ teaspoon salt, and ⅛ teaspoon pepper together in a food processor until smooth, about 30 seconds, scraping down the bowl as needed. Transfer the mixture to a medium bowl and stir in the Parmesan. Season with salt and pepper to taste.

Marinated Artichokes
MAKES ABOUT 2 CUPS

Either warm or room-temperature artichokes will work fine here. These marinated artichokes are great as an antipasto with shaved Parmesan cheese, tossed with pasta, or served in a salad.

2	tablespoons reserved oil from Artichoke Confit (page 291) or extra-virgin olive oil
2	tablespoons minced fresh mint leaves
1	small garlic clove, minced or pressed through a garlic press (about ½ teaspoon)
¼	teaspoon grated zest plus 1 tablespoon juice from 1 lemon Salt and ground black pepper
½	recipe (16 artichoke halves) Artichoke Confit

Combine the reserved confit oil, mint, garlic, lemon zest, lemon juice, ¼ teaspoon salt, and ⅛ teaspoon pepper in a medium bowl. Gently fold in the artichokes. Cover and refrigerate until the flavors meld, at least 1 hour or up to 2 days. Season with salt and pepper to taste before serving.

ROASTED BEETS

BEETS ARE SLOW COOKING BY NATURE— because they're hard and quite dense, they take a long time to become tender. Unfortunately, the beets most of us remember from childhood are the canned or pickled kind (the ones nestled among pink pickled eggs in giant jars). Tart and mushy, these beets leave much to be desired. No wonder a whole generation raised on these sorts of beets won't give them a second chance. Freshly cooked beets, however, are altogether different, with a sweet, earthy flavor and firm, juicy texture. These days you'll find them served in the fanciest of restaurants, as a side dish or as the star of a composed salad.

We wanted to find the best way of cooking beets to extract their natural sugars and develop a firm-yet-tender texture, so we tried three methods: boiling, steaming, and roasting. Boiling beets diluted their flavor. Looking at the pink water, we knew that some of that flavor had escaped into the cooking water. Steaming was a slightly better method, but the flavors weren't as concentrated as we would have liked. Roasting was the next option. We tried wrapping the beets in foil as well as leaving them unwrapped. The unwrapped beets dried out and became leathery, but the wrapped beets were juicy and tender with the concentrated sweetness we were looking for. There was another significant advantage with the wrapped beets: The roasting pan remained stain free.

We found that an oven temperature of 400 degrees delivered good results—we found no benefit to cooking them at a lower temperature and at higher temperatures the beets tended to shrivel up and dry out. Medium beets become tender in 45 minutes to an hour. Smaller beets take less time. We don't recommend roasting very large beets, because they can be woody. Beets are easiest to peel after cooking, when the skins can simply be rubbed off with paper towels.

The best part about roasted beets is that the long cooking time brings out their natural sweetness, and they don't really need much more adornment than a little olive oil, salt, and pepper, or perhaps a sprinkling of fresh herbs to turn them into a flavorful side dish. Cooled to room temperature, they make a great addition to a salad, with toasted nuts and blue cheese, goat cheese, or feta.

Roasted Beets

SERVES 4

When buying beets, look for bunches that have the most uniformly sized beets so that they will roast in the same amount of time. If the beets are different sizes, remove the smaller ones from the oven as they become tender. Roasted beets can be served warm, at room temperature, or chilled. These beets taste great as is, or try tossing them with fresh herbs, toasted nuts, or crumbled cheese, such as blue cheese, feta, or goat cheese.

1½ pounds beets (about 6 medium), trimmed and greens discarded
2 tablespoons extra-virgin olive oil
Salt and ground black pepper

1. Adjust an oven rack to the middle position and heat the oven to 400 degrees. Trim all but about 1 inch of the stems from the beets. Wash the beets well and remove any dangling roots. Wrap the beets individually in foil and place on a rimmed baking sheet. Roast the beets until a skewer inserted into the center meets little resistance (you will need to unwrap the beets to test this), 45 to 60 minutes.

2. Remove the beets from the oven and carefully open the foil packets (make sure to keep your hands and face away from the steam). When the beets are cool enough to handle, carefully rub off the skins using a paper towel. Slice the beets ¼ inch thick.

3. Toss the sliced beets with the oil and season with salt and pepper to taste. Serve warm or at room temperature.

➤ VARIATION
Harvard Beets
Follow the recipe for Roasted Beets through step 2, cooking, peeling, and cutting the beets as directed (do not toss with oil as directed in step 3). Bring ¼ cup sugar, ¼ cup cider vinegar, and 1 teaspoon cornstarch to a simmer in a medium saucepan over medium heat, whisking often. Add the cooked, sliced beets and continue to simmer until the mixture is slightly thickened, about 5 minutes. Stir in 1 tablespoon unsalted butter and serve warm or at room temperature.

REMOVING BEET STAINS

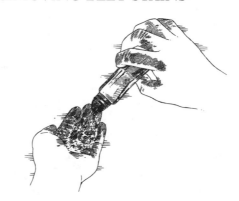

When cut, beets can stain everything they touch, including hands and cutting boards. To help remove these stains, sprinkle the stained area with salt, rinse, and then scrub with soap. The salt crystals help lift the beet juices away.

ROASTED AND BRAISED BRUSSELS SPROUTS

BRUSSELS SPROUTS PROBABLY HAVE THE WORST reputation of any vegetable—kids and adults alike flee at the sight of them. But we think this is simply because they are almost always poorly prepared; overcooking turns them limp and bitter. When done right however, Brussels sprouts are crisp, tender, and nutty-flavored. Wanting to rid this vegetable of its notoriety, we decided to develop a couple of foolproof techniques for cooking it.

Our favorite approaches for cooking Brussels sprouts—roasting and braising—are very different, but equally successful. With roasting, the dry heat from the oven concentrates the flavors of the vegetable, resulting in tender sprouts with toasty exteriors. Braising involves simmering the sprouts in a small amount of liquid, which has the added bonus of creating a flavorful sauce to accompany them.

The best Brussels sprouts are available in late fall through early winter, peaking in late November. They are often associated with the holidays because of their short season. When buying Brussels sprouts, choose those with small, tight heads, no more than 1½ inches in diameter, for the best flavor. Larger sprouts can often be trimmed of loose leaves along the stem and still be quite good. Look for firm, compact, bright green Brussels sprouts. Yellow or brown-tipped leaves usually indicate that they are older. Once purchased, sprouts can be stored in the refrigerator for no longer than four to five days.

First, we tried roasting the Brussels sprouts. As for most roasted vegetables, our goal was to achieve the perfect ratio of crisp, intensely flavored exterior to tender interior. After a few tests, we found that with Brussels sprouts, the simplest approach was the best. We tossed the Brussels sprouts with oil, spread them in an even layer on a large rimmed baking sheet, and roasted them in a 350-degree oven. The sprouts cooked up tender, but we wanted more of the caramelized exterior. We increased the oven temperature to 400 degrees and cut the sprouts in half to increase the contact with the hot baking sheet. This did the trick, yielding perfectly browned, crisp-tender sprouts with a clean flavor.

Happy with our roasted Brussels sprouts, we tried braising. We braised 1 pound of sprouts on top of the stove in a 12-inch skillet, using 1 cup of water. We cooked the Brussels spouts, which we cut in half, until they were just tender. We then removed the lid and reduced the cooking liquid down to a sauce. These Brussels sprouts met all the criteria we had established—they were tender, nutty flavored, and bright green—but the sauce needed a little more depth.

For our next test, we substituted chicken broth (which we'd had success with in other braised vegetable recipes) for the water. This was a winner, adding more flavor to both the vegetable and the sauce. We wondered if the addition of a little wine would further enhance the flavor of the dish. However, unlike more delicately flavored vegetables, sprouts braised in wine and chicken broth didn't taste much different from the ones braised in just broth, so we decided to skip the wine. We then developed a couple of simple variations, one with bacon and one with currants. For our final variation we braised the sprouts in heavy cream, a classic French technique for cooking vegetables. Lightly seasoned with salt, pepper, and nutmeg, the finished sprouts absorbed most of the cream, creating a slightly sweet, nutty flavor. Rich and creamy, this version of braised Brussels sprouts is perfect for the holidays.

Roasted Brussels Sprouts

SERVES 6 TO 8

When trimming the Brussels sprouts, be careful not to cut too much off the stem end or the leaves will fall away from the core.

2 pounds small Brussels sprouts, stem ends trimmed, discolored leaves removed, and halved through the stems
2 tablespoons olive oil
   Salt and ground black pepper

1. Adjust an oven rack to the middle position and heat the oven to 400 degrees. Line a large rimmed baking sheet with foil.

2. Toss the sprouts with the oil, ½ teaspoon salt, and ¼ teaspoon pepper. Arrange the sprouts in a single layer on the prepared baking sheet and roast until golden brown, 25 to 30 minutes, shaking the pan every 10 minutes to redistribute the vegetables.

3. Remove the sprouts from the oven and season with salt and pepper to taste before serving.

Braised Brussels Sprouts

SERVES 4

When trimming the Brussels sprouts, be careful not to cut too much off the stem end or the leaves will fall away from the core. You will need a skillet with a tight-fitting lid for this recipe. We found that a nonstick skillet works best here, but a traditional skillet can also be used.

2 tablespoons unsalted butter
I medium shallot, minced
   (about 3 tablespoons)
   Salt
I pound small Brussels sprouts, stem ends
   trimmed, discolored leaves removed, and
   halved through the stems
I cup low-sodium chicken broth
   Ground black pepper

1. Melt the butter in a 12-inch nonstick skillet over medium heat. Add the shallot and ¼ teaspoon salt and cook until softened, about 2 minutes. Add the sprouts, broth, and ⅛ teaspoon pepper and bring to a simmer. Cover and cook until the sprouts are bright green, about 9 minutes.

2. Uncover and continue to cook until the sprouts are tender and the liquid is slightly thickened, about 2 minutes. Season with salt and pepper to taste and serve.

➤ VARIATIONS

Brussels Sprouts with Bacon
Do not use maple-flavored bacon here; it will give an unpleasant flavor to this dish.

Cook 3 ounces (about 3 slices) bacon, cut into ½-inch pieces, in a 12-inch nonstick skillet over medium heat until crisp, about 5 minutes. Transfer the bacon to a paper towel–lined plate, leaving the fat in the pan. Follow the recipe for Braised Brussels Sprouts, substituting the bacon fat for the butter. Sprinkle with the reserved bacon before serving.

Curried Brussels Sprouts with Currants
If currants are unavailable, substitute an equal amount of coarsely chopped golden raisins.

Follow the recipe for Braised Brussels Sprouts, adding 1½ teaspoons curry powder with the shallot and 3 tablespoons currants with the chicken broth.

Brussels Sprouts Braised in Cream
This rich dish is perfect for holidays.

Follow the recipe for Braised Brussels Sprouts, substituting 1 cup heavy cream for the chicken broth and adding a pinch freshly grated nutmeg with the salt and pepper. Sprinkle with 2 tablespoons minced fresh parsley leaves or chives before serving.

BRAISED CABBAGE

CABBAGE CAN BE PREPARED IN A VARIETY OF ways, though often it is cooked quickly (as part of a stir-fry) or not cooked at all (as part of a slaw) to preserve its crisp crunch. But slowly cooking cabbage transforms it into something entirely new, bringing out a sweetness and silky richness that can only come with time. One of our favorite slow-cooked cabbage dishes is German-style red cabbage that has been slowly braised with sweet and sour flavorings. Though it is a simple recipe, it is one that requires a careful balancing act between the sweet and sour elements. We hoped to strike that balance and develop an ideal side dish to accompany a hearty main course of roasted meat.

Most of the recipes we researched seemed strikingly similar: they included shredded cabbage, onions, some sort of liquid such as broth, wine, or juice, and a few seasonings. But once we got into the kitchen and prepared these recipes, the similarities among

SHREDDING CABBAGE

1. Cut the cabbage into quarters and cut away the hard piece of core attached to each quarter.

2. Separate the cored cabbage into stacks of leaves that flatten when pressed lightly.

3a. Use a chef's knife to cut each stack diagonally (this ensures long pieces) into thin shreds.

3b. Or roll the stacked leaves crosswise to fit them into the feed tube of a food processor fitted with the shredding disk.

them ended. Some of the braised cabbage dishes tasted raw and oddly seasoned while others were overcooked and had an overpowering aroma. We needed to break this recipe down to the basics and start from the ground up.

Starting with the cabbage, we found the pre-shredded variety to be useless because it was either shredded much too thin or the shreds were uneven within the package, resulting in uneven cooking—some bites were fine, while others were raw or overcooked. Shredding your own cabbage by hand isn't difficult and you can make the task even easier by using a food processor.

Next, we examined the cooking method. Braising is a cooking method in which liquid is added to the pot and covered to create a gentle, moist heat environment. Some recipes we looked at covered the pot from the outset and others did not. The uncovered cabbage looked slightly bleached out at the edges, and had less flavor compared to the cabbage that was cooked underneath a lid. Finally, we tested cooking times. When the cabbage was cooked for less than 30 minutes it tasted raw and crunchy, while cabbage cooked for an hour tasted mushy and overcooked. The ultimate braising time proved to be 30 to 40 minutes, at which point the cabbage was softened but retained a slight bite.

Taking a closer look at the braising liquids from the recipes we researched, we tried them all: orange juice, chicken broth, vinegar, apple cider, red wine, and even port. Tasting them side by side, we picked the sweet and fruity (but not overwhelmingly so) apple cider as our favorite. Just 1½ cups of cider was plenty to provide some steam to help the cabbage wilt and braise, without leaving a lot in the bottom of the pan at the end to make the cooked cabbage too wet. A final splash of cider vinegar before serving helped perk up the flavors and balance the sweet with a little tart.

With the basics down, we refined the flavors in our cabbage. Tasters complained that the cabbage was a little lean tasting, so we decided to add some bacon, which lent a smoky depth and richness to the finished dish. Sugar helped to pump up the flavor further, and brown sugar added a bit more flavor than white. Moving on to the spices, we tried everything from peppercorns and juniper berries to pumpkin pie spice and finally settled on a combination of cinnamon, caraway seeds, allspice, bay leaves, and thyme. At last, we had found the perfect balance of sweet and sour.

Sweet and Sour Red Cabbage

SERVES 6 TO 8

This cabbage tastes even better the next day.

4	ounces (about 4 slices) bacon, chopped fine
1	medium onion, minced
1	cinnamon stick, or ¼ teaspoon ground cinnamon
½	teaspoon caraway seeds
¼	teaspoon ground allspice
	Salt
1	medium head red cabbage (about 2 pounds), cored and shredded into ¼-inch-thick pieces (see the illustrations on page 296)
1½	cups apple cider
3	bay leaves
3	tablespoons light brown sugar
1	teaspoon minced fresh thyme leaves, or ½ teaspoon dried
3	tablespoons cider vinegar
	Ground black pepper

1. Cook the bacon in a large Dutch oven over medium heat until the fat is just beginning to render, about 2 minutes. Add the onion, cinnamon stick, caraway seeds, allspice, and ¼ teaspoon salt and continue to cook until the onion is softened and lightly browned, about 10 minutes.

2. Stir in the cabbage, cider, bay leaves, 1 tablespoon of the sugar, thyme, and ½ teaspoon salt. Cover and cook the cabbage, stirring often, until wilted and tender, 30 to 40 minutes.

3. Discard the cinnamon stick and bay leaves. Stir in the vinegar and remaining 2 tablespoons sugar. Season with salt and pepper to taste and serve.

SLOW-BRAISED CARROTS

ROASTING IS OUR GO-TO METHOD FOR bringing out the rich, sweet flavor of carrots. But we were intrigued by a number of recipes we have seen for braised carrots, in which carrots are cooked very slowly with a little bit of fat and a little bit of liquid. One that particularly caught our attention added the liquid (in this case, water) little by little over the course of an hour, using just enough to keep the pan from burning. The method seemed a bit meticulous but we had to try it. One bite was all it took to convert us—the carrots were unbelievably sweet and rich, more so than any roasted carrots we had ever had. They had the nutty, caramelized edges that we prize roasted carrots for, but more intense carrot flavor and an unbelievably tender, almost creamy, interior. While tasters loved them, we were not as enthusiastic about the constant attention to the skillet they required. We decided to see if we could develop a streamlined method for braising carrots without sacrificing flavor and texture.

The first order of business was determining the best way to prep the carrots. The original recipe cut them into ⅜-inch disks and spread them in a single layer in the pan. This shape maximized the browning surface, but flipping the softened disks without crushing them (or burning our fingers) was tricky and time-consuming. Additionally, carrots often taper dramatically, and cutting narrow slices yielded disks of wildly different sizes. We thought about using whole bagged "baby" carrots (which are actually trimmed regular carrots) to address the size issue as well as streamline the prep, but tasters found them to be a bit dull-tasting and disappointing.

Regular carrots were the clear choice. Instead of slicing the carrots crosswise into skinny discs, which are tedious to flip over during cooking, we found it best to cut them into 2-inch lengths. To make the carrot lengths more uniform, we found it necessary to slice the thicker pieces (from the stem end) in half lengthwise.

Next we addressed the cooking method. Looking for a fuss-free approach, one that didn't require constant monitoring, we threw the ingredients into an uncovered, preheated skillet and then transferred it to the oven, adding the water all at once (rather than doling it out a little at a time). These carrots weren't awful, but the oven had noticeably withered them and they were inferior to the original in both flavor and texture. Clearly, we would have to move back to the stovetop, but we wondered if we could keep our streamlined technique of adding the water all at once.

We did just that, then covered the skillet and cooked the carrots gently until they had softened.

EQUIPMENT: Cutting Boards

Buying a cutting board starts with deciding on its material. Until recently, there were just two good options: wood and plastic. But recently, eco-friendly bamboo boards and lightweight composite boards (fashioned from laminated wood fiber) have appeared in kitchen stores everywhere. Do these newcomers offer anything better than the old standbys? We gathered a lineup made from all four materials to find out. We whacked at them with a cleaver, subjected them to hundreds of cuts with a new, factory-sharpened knife, and repeatedly knocked them off the counter. When we were done, we chopped chipotle chiles in brick-red adobo sauce to see how easily they would clean up.

Maple boards that were too heavy were uncomfortable to set up, wash, and put away. In this category we preferred the lighter yet still substantial maple board from J.K. Adams, which was roomy but not unwieldy or heavy, felt great under the knife, and took all the abuse we could dish out.

In the plastic category, gimmicky boards failed to measure up, but the Architec Gripper board was a solid choice, with a durable surface and hundreds of rubber feet, which make the board a pleasure to cut on by keeping it rock-solid on the counter. Any stains on this board were blasted clean in the dishwasher.

We were most skeptical about the wood-composite boards and they did indeed disappoint. Despite their purported resemblance to real wood, these boards looked like the thin, hard particleboard they were. The Epicurean model (a product we see everywhere) immediately lived down to our low expectations, making a nasty clack under the knife and giving off sawdust under repeated cuts. As for the Snow River Grand Epicure Pro, it was noticeably curved fresh out of the box and was warped dramatically by the end of testing. Cutting on it felt hard and unpleasant under the knife, and our cuts left raggedy fissures and deep scars on the maple surface.

Bamboo boards are lightweight and attractive, but we wondered about their endurance (bamboo is a kind of grass). However, the butcher block–style Totally Bamboo Congo Board turned out to be a pleasant surprise, matching the outstanding comfort and ease of cutting on a classic maple butcher block (and practically impervious to abuse).

In the final analysis, our top-rated boards cut across material distinctions, displaying similar features of comfort, durability, and solid construction.

THE BEST CUTTING BOARDS

If you're willing to wash by hand and do occasional maintenance to keep your board in peak form, the top-performing Totally Bamboo Congo board ($39.99) and J.K. Adams's Takes Two maple board ($22) are good choices. If you prefer washing your board in the dishwasher, we recommend the plastic Architec Gripper Nonslip board ($14.99).

TOTALLY BAMBOO   J.K ADAM'S   ARCHITEC

At this point we removed the lid and continued to cook the carrots slowly as excess moisture evaporated and the carrots browned. This approach of adding all the water at the outset of cooking and then covering the carrots for half of the cooking time worked beautifully; we could now jump-start cooking without sacrificing caramelization. With this streamlined approach we now had carrots that were just as good as the original—caramelized on the outside, creamy on the inside, and bursting with sweetness.

Slow-Braised Carrots

SERVES 4

It may seem like these carrots take a long time to cook, but it's worth the wait for their sweet, caramelized flavor and creamy interior. You will need a skillet with a tight-fitting lid for this recipe. If the carrots are getting too dark too quickly in step 2, reduce the heat as needed. Serve with freshly grated Parmesan cheese, if desired.

2	tablespoons unsalted butter
1½	pounds carrots (about 9 medium), peeled, cut into 2-inch lengths, and cut in half lengthwise if thick
⅓	cup water
¾	teaspoon sugar
	Salt and ground black pepper

1. Melt the butter in a 12-inch nonstick skillet over low heat. Lay the carrots in the pan in a single layer (cut side down if halved). Pour the water into the pan and sprinkle with the sugar and ½ teaspoon salt. Cover and cook the carrots until tender, about 30 minutes.

2. Uncover, increase the heat to medium-low, and continue to cook the carrots until browned on one side, 10 to 15 minutes. Flip the carrots and continue to cook until the water has evaporated and the carrots are browned on the second side, 10 to 15 minutes longer. Season with salt and pepper to taste and serve.

ROASTED CAULIFLOWER

MOST COOKS BOIL CAULIFLOWER, WHICH WE simply can't understand. When things go wrong (and they often do), the cauliflower is smelly (from overcooking) and mushy. Even when you avoid overcooking, boiled cauliflower is bland. No wonder it often gets served with a creamy, flavorful cheese sauce. But when properly prepared, cauliflower is great, with a nutty, slightly sweet flavor. So what's the secret? Roasting is a great technique for coaxing big, long-cooked flavor from vegetables—the dry heat caramelizes their natural sugars. We had never roasted cauliflower (we typically braise it), but given the success of roasting other vegetables it seemed worth a try.

We found three basic techniques in our research: roasting cauliflower that has been blanched, roasting cauliflower that has been steamed, and roasting raw cauliflower. Each method separated a cauliflower head into florets before roasting on a baking sheet in a very hot oven (around 475 degrees), but we found that cutting the cauliflower into wedges allowed maximum surface area to come into contact with the hot pan. Each simple preparation coated the cauliflower florets with oil, salt, and pepper at some point in the procedure.

When all three versions were sampled side by side, the blanching-and-roasting technique was the loser of the bunch. The florets were soggy and pale, with little flavor. The steam-roasted cauliflower emerged with creamy, evenly cooked florets but so-so browning and flavor. Finally, the straight-up roasted cauliflower was well liked for its caramelized exterior; however, it cooked unevenly and had some dried-out, gritty florets.

Our goal was to combine the last two methods and produce nicely caramelized cauliflower with a creamy texture. While testing the straight-up roasting technique, we noticed that the cauliflower was shedding its moisture in the first minutes of roasting. We were pretty sure that covering the baking

Soy-Ginger Sauce with Scallion

MAKES ENOUGH FOR 1 RECIPE
ROASTED CAULIFLOWER

If using this sauce, use vegetable oil to roast the cauliflower instead of olive oil.

2	teaspoons vegetable oil
1	tablespoon minced or grated fresh ginger
2	medium garlic cloves, minced or pressed through a garlic press (about 2 teaspoons)
¼	cup water
2	tablespoons soy sauce
2	tablespoons mirin
1	tablespoon rice vinegar
1	teaspoon toasted sesame oil
1	scallion, sliced thin

Cook the oil, ginger, and garlic together in a small skillet over medium-high heat until fragrant, 1 to 2 minutes. Reduce the heat to medium-low, stir in the water, soy sauce, mirin, and vinegar and simmer until slightly syrupy, 4 to 6 minutes. Drizzle the sauce and sesame oil over the roasted cauliflower and sprinkle with the scallion before serving.

Curry-Yogurt Sauce

MAKES ENOUGH FOR 1 RECIPE
ROASTED CAULIFLOWER

If using this sauce, use vegetable oil to roast the cauliflower instead of olive oil.

1	tablespoon vegetable oil
1	large shallot, minced (about ¼ cup)
	Salt
2	teaspoons curry powder
¼	teaspoon red pepper flakes
⅓	cup water
¼	cup plain yogurt
2	tablespoons minced fresh cilantro leaves
1	teaspoon juice from 1 lime
	Ground black pepper

Heat the oil in a small skillet over medium-high heat until shimmering. Add the shallot and ¼ teaspoon salt and cook until softened, about 2 minutes. Stir in the curry powder and red pepper flakes and cook until fragrant, about 30 seconds. Off the heat, whisk in the water, yogurt, cilantro, and lime juice. Season with salt and pepper to taste. Drizzle the sauce over the roasted cauliflower before serving.

Sherry Vinegar–Honey Sauce with Almonds

MAKES ENOUGH FOR 1 RECIPE
ROASTED CAULIFLOWER

Both regular and golden raisins taste great here.

1	tablespoon olive oil
¼	cup raisins (see note)
3	medium garlic cloves, minced or pressed through a garlic press (about 1 tablespoon)
¼	cup water
3	tablespoons sherry vinegar
2	tablespoons honey
¼	cup sliced almonds, toasted (page 309)
2	tablespoons minced fresh parsley leaves
	Salt and ground black pepper

Cook the oil, raisins, and garlic together in a small skillet over medium-high heat until fragrant, 1 to 2 minutes. Reduce the heat to medium and stir in the water, vinegar, and honey. Simmer until slightly syrupy, 4 to 6 minutes. Stir in the almonds and parsley and season with salt and pepper to taste. Drizzle the sauce over the roasted cauliflower before serving.

sheet would trap this moisture and add just enough steam to cook the cauliflower properly.

After some tinkering, we discovered that 10 minutes was the perfect amount of time to leave the foil on. The steam kept the florets moist enough to withstand the next 20 minutes of roasting and prevented them from turning dry and gritty. Served with a drizzle of extra-virgin olive oil or a quickly prepared sauce, roasted cauliflower is a revelation—sweet, creamy, and packed with flavor.

Roasted Cauliflower

SERVES 4 TO 6

This dish stands well on its own, or drizzled with extra-virgin olive oil or any of the sauces on page 300. Alternatively, you can make a spiced version with either curry powder or chili powder. Simply stir 2 teaspoons of either spice into the oil before seasoning the cauliflower in step 2.

I	medium head cauliflower (about 2 pounds)
¼	cup extra-virgin olive oil
	Salt and ground black pepper

1. Adjust an oven rack to the lowest position and heat the oven to 475 degrees. Line a large rimmed baking sheet with foil. Trim the outer leaves of the cauliflower and cut the stem flush with the bottom of the head. Following the illustration below, cut the cauliflower into 8 equal wedges through the core.

CUTTING CAULIFLOWER FOR ROASTING

Cut the head of cauliflower into 8 large wedges through the center core. The core will help the wedges of cauliflower hold together and make them easy to flip over during cooking.

2. Lay the cauliflower wedges, cut side down, on the prepared baking sheet. Drizzle the cauliflower with 2 tablespoons of the oil and sprinkle with salt and pepper. Gently rub the oil and seasonings into the cauliflower. Gently flip the cauliflower and repeat on the second cut side with the remaining 2 tablespoons oil, salt, and pepper.

3. Cover the baking sheet with foil and roast the cauliflower for 10 minutes. Remove the foil and continue to roast until the bottoms of the cauliflower pieces are golden, 8 to 12 minutes.

4. Working quickly, remove the baking sheet from the oven and carefully flip the wedges. Continue to roast until the cauliflower is golden all over, 8 to 12 minutes longer.

5. Remove the cauliflower from the oven and season with salt and pepper to taste before serving.

COLLARD GREENS

ANY SOUTHERNER WILL TELL YOU THAT collard greens require long cooking and the smokiness of cured pork to be edible. We tend to agree—slowly cooking the greens in a sweet, smoky broth goes far in tempering the assertive bitterness of collards. When the greens and pork are done boiling, the remaining cooking liquid is called "pot liquor" (or "likker") and is often used to cook a second batch of greens, or served as an accompaniment or gravy. We wanted to cook collard greens in the traditional way and maintain that deep, Southern flavor and meltingly tender texture that can only come from low, slow cooking.

We first addressed the greens. While more tender greens (such as spinach) can simply be wilted in a hot pan, tough greens like collards don't have enough moisture to withstand this cooking technique; they scorch before they wilt. We knew that we would need to simmer our greens in enough water to render them tender, but not wash out their flavor.

We tested cooking the greens in an abundant 3 quarts of water, a moderate 6 cups, and a mere 2 cups. We found that cooking the greens in 3 quarts of water diluted their flavor. Plus, we were left with too much pot liquor. In 2 cups of water the greens cooked unevenly because a good portion of them wasn't in contact with the water. Six cups of water was perfect. This amount removed enough bitterness to make these assertive greens palatable, but not so much as to rob them of their character. And it produced just enough pot liquor to make our Southern friends happy.

Some cooks will tell you that you have to cook the greens for upward of two hours. Greens cooked this long were bland and mushy. We then tested cooking the greens for shorter amounts of time and found that 45 minutes was enough for the greens to become tender. This cooking time further mellowed their flavor without causing them to lose too much of their signature bite.

Lastly, we focused on the seasoning. In the South greens are typically cooked in water or a pork broth. Pork broth seemed fussy for our recipe, but we wondered if chicken broth, the test kitchen's go-to broth, might boost the flavor and add depth to our greens and pot liquor. Indeed it did, so we made the switch. Next, we knew our recipe needed pork, and we liked the smoky, potent flavor of bacon in our greens. We used the rendered fat from the bacon to sauté some aromatics. We found that onion and garlic rounded out the flavor of the greens. Tasters were split on whether or not they wanted hot pepper sauce or vinegar drizzled over their greens, so we made both optional—the choice is up to you.

Southern-Style Collard Greens
SERVES 6

The leftover cooking liquid, traditionally called pot liquor, can be sopped up with corn bread or biscuits, or used to cook a second batch of collard greens, as is traditionally done in the South. Serve with hot pepper sauce or vinegar, if desired.

4   ounces (about 4 slices) bacon, cut into ¼-inch pieces
1   medium onion, minced
     Salt
3   medium garlic cloves, minced or pressed through a garlic press (about 1 tablespoon)

6   cups low-sodium chicken broth
2   pounds collard greens (about 2 bunches), stemmed and chopped coarse
     Ground black pepper

1. Adjust an oven rack to the lower-middle position and heat the oven to 350 degrees.

2. Cook the bacon in a large Dutch oven over medium heat until the fat is just beginning to render, about 2 minutes. Stir in the onion and ¼ teaspoon salt and cook until softened, 5 to 7 minutes. Stir in the garlic and cook until fragrant, about 30 seconds. Add the broth and bring to a simmer over medium-high heat.

3. Stir in the greens, a handful at a time, until wilted. Cover, place the pot in the oven, and cook until the greens are tender and the broth is flavorful, about 45 minutes.

4. Remove the pot from the oven and season with salt and pepper to taste before serving.

CREAMED CORN
LATE SUMMER CORN IS OFTEN SIMPLY BOILED in water for a quick and flavorful side dish. But when we really want to emphasize corn's clean, sweet flavor, we like to make creamed corn—the time the corn spends gently simmering in fresh cream allows its full range of flavors and sweetness to shine through. But if you don't handle the corn and cream correctly, you wind up with an abysmal overcooked, just-out-of-the-can flavor.

Many recipes start by boiling the corn on the cob, then cutting the kernels off the cob and mixing them with a cream sauce. This technique, however, loses much of the sweet, delicate corn flavor to the cooking water. We quickly rejected this method in favor of recipes that simmer the corn kernels (which are first cut free from the cobs) directly in the cream. This technique releases their sugary, summery flavor into the sauce, which is where you want it to be.

Simply simmering fresh corn kernels in cream, however, wasn't enough. This method produced a thin, lumpy mixture that lacked the thickened, spoonable texture we desired. Scraping the pulp out of the spent cobs helped a bit, but we wanted the sauce a bit thicker. Flour just made the sauce gummy and overwhelmed the flavor of the corn. We then tried grating a few of the ears, which broke down some of the kernels into smaller pieces. This did the trick. By grating half of the raw kernels off the cob, we were able to release more of the corn's natural thickener.

After making a few batches of this recipe with different types of corn, we realized that the cooking times can differ, depending on the corn's variety and age. While some corn cooked in only 10 minutes, other corn needed five minutes longer. We also found that as the corn and cream cook and thicken, the heat needs to be adjusted to keep the mixture at a simmer to prevent the bottom from burning.

As for the other ingredients, we tried using half-and-half instead of heavy cream, but tasters missed the luxurious flavor and heft provided by the latter. A little shallot, garlic, and fresh thyme complemented the delicate flavor of the corn, while a pinch of cayenne added a little kick.

MINCING A SHALLOT

1. Place the peeled bulb flat side down and make several slices parallel to the work surface, almost to (but not through) the root end. Then make a number of very closely spaced parallel cuts through the top of the shallot down to the work surface.

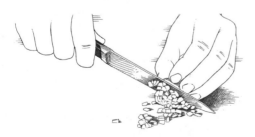

2. Finish the mincing by making very thin slices perpendicular to the lengthwise cuts.

Creamed Corn

SERVES 6 TO 8

For best texture and flavor, we like a combination of grated corn, whole kernels (cut away from the cobs with a knife), and corn pulp (scraped from the ears with the back of a butter knife).

5	ears corn, husks and silk removed
2	tablespoons unsalted butter
I	medium shallot, minced (about 3 tablespoons)
	Salt
I	medium garlic clove, minced or pressed through a garlic press (about I teaspoon)
I ½	cups heavy cream
½	teaspoon minced fresh thyme leaves
	Pinch cayenne pepper
	Ground black pepper

1. Following the illustrations on page 119, cut the kernels from 3 ears of the corn into a large bowl, reserving the cobs. Grate the remaining 2 ears of corn over the large holes of a box grater into the same bowl, reserving the cobs. Using the back of a butter knife, scrape the milk from all of the cobs into the bowl.

2. Melt the butter in a medium saucepan over medium heat. Add the shallot and ¼ teaspoon salt and cook until softened, about 2 minutes. Stir in the garlic and cook until fragrant, about 30 seconds. Stir in the corn mixture, cream, thyme, cayenne, and ⅛ teaspoon pepper. Bring the mixture to a simmer and cook, stirring occasionally, until the corn is tender and the mixture is thickened, 10 to 15 minutes. Off the heat, season with salt and pepper to taste and serve.

➤ VARIATION
Creamed Corn with Red Pepper, Chipotle, and Lime
Follow the recipe for Creamed Corn, omitting the thyme and cayenne. Add ½ red bell pepper, stemmed, seeded, and cut into ¼-inch pieces with the shallot, and add 1 teaspoon minced chipotle chile in adobo sauce with the cream. Before serving, stir in 1 tablespoon minced fresh cilantro leaves and 2 teaspoons juice from 1 lime.

ROASTED GARLIC

GARLIC IS AS FUNDAMENTAL TO COOKING as salt. Whether the cloves are minced, chopped, sliced, or smashed, garlic can be found in almost every cuisine across the globe. Raw garlic is distinguished by its pungency, but slow roasting turns garlic incomparably flavorful, nutty, and sweet. Roasted garlic has a soft, buttery consistency, which is perfect to spread on bread or to flavor and thicken sauces and dressings.

Why does roasting mellow garlic's flavor? When raw garlic is cut, a pungent compound is produced that gives garlic its typical aroma and bite. (That's why minced garlic is more strongly flavored than sliced—the more it is cut, the more compound is produced). Because heat breaks down an enzyme necessary for this compound, roasting garlic cloves will pretty much eliminate the development of any harsh garlic flavor.

Roasting garlic is fairly simple, but we thought it was worth some tests to find the best method. Most recipes call for wrapping a whole head of garlic in foil and then cooking it in the oven until very soft. A few sources suggest poaching the garlic first (in chicken stock, wine, or milk) and then roasting it, but we quickly dismissed this notion because poaching tended to weaken the garlic flavor too much.

Some recipes coat the head of garlic with oil before it is wrapped in foil and others omit this step. We roasted two heads of garlic, each in a separate foil pack, one with oil and one without. The garlic roasted without the oil was pale and steamy. Using a small amount of extra-virgin olive oil helped to caramelize the garlic and gave the cloves a deeper, toasty flavor. Don't go overboard with the oil. Too much oil (one head needs just ½ teaspoon of oil) makes the garlic greasy and unappetizing.

Next, we wondered if separating the cloves would result in a shorter cooking time. It did, but the separated cloves dried out and became leathery. Keeping the head intact helped to keep the cloves juicy and cooked them evenly. The last thing to test was the oven temperature. We tried temperatures from 300 to 500 degrees and found that 425 degrees produced the best results, with

garlic that was slightly caramelized on the outside and creamy on the inside.

This roasted garlic is great simply spread on bread, but we also took it a step further and developed two recipes that use our roasted garlic as the base—a creamy salad dressing in which the garlic actually thickens the dressing, making it silky smooth and incredibly sweet and flavorful, and a roasted garlic aioli that's perfect for spreading on sandwiches or dipping vegetables.

ROASTING GARLIC

1. Cut ½ inch off the top of each garlic head to expose most of the tops of the garlic cloves.

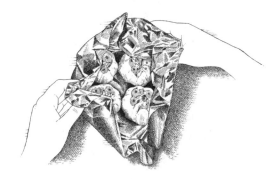

2. Place the garlic heads, cut side up, in the center of a large piece of aluminum foil. Drizzle each head with ½ teaspoon olive oil and sprinkle with a pinch of salt, then gather the corners of the foil over the garlic and twist to seal.

3. To remove the garlic from the roasted and cooled heads, use your hand or the flat edge of a chef's knife to squeeze the garlic from the skins, starting from the root end and working up.

Roasted Garlic

MAKES ABOUT ½ CUP

This recipe can be adjusted for as many or as few garlic heads as you want. Serve the garlic alongside bread, or use in one of the recipes below.

4   large garlic heads
2   teaspoons olive oil
    Salt

1. Adjust an oven rack to the middle position and heat the oven to 425 degrees. Following the illustrations on page 304, cut ½ inch off the top of each garlic head to expose most of the tops of the garlic cloves. Place the garlic heads, cut side up, in the center of a large piece of aluminum foil. Drizzle each with ½ teaspoon of the oil, sprinkle with a pinch of salt, and gather the foil up around the garlic tightly to form a packet.

2. Place the packet directly on the oven rack and roast the garlic for 45 minutes. Carefully open just the top of the foil to expose the garlic and continue to roast until the garlic is soft and golden brown, about 20 minutes longer.

3. Remove the garlic from the oven and let it cool for 20 minutes. When cool, squeeze the garlic from the skins into a bowl. (The roasted garlic can be refrigerated in an airtight container for up to 1 week.)

Roasted Garlic Aioli

MAKES ABOUT I CUP

If you do not have regular olive oil, use a blend of equal parts extra-virgin olive oil and vegetable oil. This aioli cannot be made in a blender because it is too thick. Use this sauce as a condiment for meat, fish, or vegetables, or as a spread on sandwiches.

2   large egg yolks
4   teaspoons juice from I lemon
⅛   teaspoon sugar
    Salt and ground black pepper
¾   cup olive oil
½   recipe (¼ cup) Roasted Garlic (above)

Process the egg yolks, lemon juice, sugar, ¼ teaspoon salt, and ⅛ teaspoon pepper together in a food processor until combined, about 10 seconds. With the machine running, gradually add the oil in a slow, steady stream, scraping down the bowl as needed. After the oil is added, process for 5 seconds longer until thick and creamy. Add the garlic and pulse until incorporated, about 5 pulses. Season with salt and pepper to taste. (The aioli can be refrigerated in an airtight container for up to 3 days.)

Creamy Roasted Garlic Dressing

MAKES ABOUT ⅔ CUP

The pureed garlic gives this flavorful dressing a thick and creamy consistency that is naturally lower in fat than other creamy dressings.

½   recipe (¼ cup) Roasted Garlic (above)
3   tablespoons extra-virgin olive oil
2   tablespoons water, plus extra as needed
2   tablespoons cider vinegar
I   tablespoon Dijon mustard
½   teaspoon minced fresh thyme leaves
    Salt and ground black pepper

Puree the roasted garlic, oil, water, vinegar, mustard, thyme, ½ teaspoon salt, and ⅛ teaspoon pepper together in a blender (or food processor) until thick and smooth, about 1 minute. (If the dressing is too thick, puree in additional water, 1 tablespoon at a time, as needed.) Season with salt and pepper to taste. (The dressing can be refrigerated in an airtight container for up to 4 days.)

BRAISED AND ROASTED GREEN BEANS

DELICATE AND SLENDER, GARDEN-FRESH haricots verts need only a few minutes of steaming, a pat of butter, and a sprinkle of salt and pepper to be ready for the table. In fact, they are so sweet, crisp, and tender that it's not uncommon to eat them raw. Take the same route with mature supermarket green beans, however, and you'll regret it. Unlike their lithe cousins, overgrown store-bought beans are often tough and dull, demanding special treatment.

One way to solve this problem is with braising: gentle, moist cooking in a covered pot has a tenderizing effect, and the braising liquid flavors the beans as they cook. (The bright green color of the beans is a casualty of this method, but the flavor is well worth the sacrifice in color). We wanted to develop a simple recipe for braised green beans with a basic but flavorful sauce.

Starting with the sauce, we first tried a combination of white wine and chicken broth (a pairing commonly used in vegetable braises), but tasters thought the wine was a bit out of place. Switching to all chicken broth was an improvement, and we rounded out the flavors with some red pepper flakes, fresh thyme, a fair amount of garlic, and a dash of lemon juice at the end. This was a bold but clean-flavored sauce.

Some of our other vegetable braises thicken the cooking liquid into a sauce by simmering with the lid off after the vegetable is cooked. However, when it came to green beans, tasters wanted a sauce with a little extra clinginess that would allow it to actually coat the beans. Flour seemed like the best way to achieve this, but we wondered if we could avoid cooking the flour in an extra step. We tried adding 2 teaspoons of flour to the pan with the aromatics and letting it cook with the green beans, and we were pleased with the results. We had a velvety, clingy sauce by the time the green beans were cooked through.

As for the cooking time, we found that the beans need at least 15 or 20 minutes to pick up enough flavor to make this method worthwhile.

More time (we tried all the way up to 45 minutes) added little in terms of flavor but did hurt both color and texture.

Cream and tomato sauce are also classic braising liquids for green beans, and with our method established, it was easy to modify the master recipe to include them in variations. For the first variation, we substituted cream for some of the broth and toned down the garlic. Dried minced porcinis added an earthy depth of flavor and paired well with the cream. For our tomato sauce we went with Italian flavorings, substituting olive oil for the butter and using fresh oregano in place of the thyme.

We were happy with the success of braised green beans, and wondered if there were other means of cooking out-of-season green beans. Our thoughts immediately turned to roasting. Would a stint in a dry, hot oven have a positive effect on these tough green beans?

We had our answer when an embarrassingly simple test produced outstanding results. Roasted in a hot oven with only oil, salt, and pepper, an entire baking sheet of beans disappeared faster than French fries. Repeated tests confirmed that roasting consistently transforms geriatric specimens into deeply caramelized, full-flavored beauties. Here's why: As green beans mature, their fibers toughen and their sugars are converted to starch. The hot, dry heat of the oven helps to reverse the aging process. Fibers break down and an enzymatic reaction causes the starch to turn back into sugar, restoring sweetness. Roasting also encourages browning—a benefit lost with moist cooking methods.

The technique needed a few refinements. Those rare roasted-green-bean recipes that we found called for at least 2 tablespoons of oil per pound of beans, but we favored a more restrained approach. A single tablespoon of oil encouraged browning without making the beans slick and greasy. And after testing multiple time and temperature combinations, 20 minutes (with a quick stir at the halfway point) in a 450-degree oven proved optimal. As we had found when roasting other vegetables, lining the baking sheet with aluminum foil prevented burning and made cleanup easy.

We now had beans that tasted great straight up, and it was time to experiment with some flavor variations. But their development was not without missteps: Aromatics (garlic and ginger) scorched when added at the beginning. The solution wasn't to lower the heat (the beans didn't brown well enough) but rather to add these ingredients halfway through cooking. And when liquid seasonings like vinegar and sesame oil slid right off the beans onto the baking sheet, we included a spoonful of sticky sweetener (honey or maple syrup) to create an appealing glaze, a move that incidentally incited even more caramelization. Last, a smattering of raw ingredients (toasted nuts or seeds, or fresh herbs) when the beans finished cooking provided complexity and textural interest.

Garlic-Lemon Braised Green Beans

SERVES 4

Braised green beans lose their bright green color but gain flavor from the braising liquid. You will need a skillet with a tight-fitting lid for this recipe. We found that a nonstick skillet works best here, but a traditional skillet can also be used.

2 tablespoons unsalted butter
I medium shallot, minced (about 3 tablespoons)
  Salt
6 medium garlic cloves, minced or pressed through a garlic press (about 2 tablespoons)
2 teaspoons unbleached all-purpose flour
I teaspoon minced fresh thyme leaves
⅛ teaspoon red pepper flakes
I¼ cups low-sodium chicken broth
I pound green beans, trimmed
I tablespoon juice from I lemon
  Ground black pepper

1. Melt the butter in a 12-inch nonstick skillet over medium heat. Add the shallot and ¼ teaspoon salt and cook until softened, about 2 minutes. Stir in the garlic, flour, thyme, and red pepper flakes and cook until fragrant, about 30 seconds.

2. Stir in the broth and add the green beans. Cover, reduce the heat to medium-low, and simmer, stirring occasionally, until the green beans are tender, 15 to 20 minutes.

3. Off the heat, stir in the lemon juice and season with salt and pepper to taste before serving.

➤ VARIATIONS

Green Beans Braised in Porcini Cream
Follow the recipe for Garlic-Lemon Braised Green Beans, reducing the amount of garlic to 2 cloves (about 2 teaspoons) and reducing the amount of chicken broth to ½ cup. Substitute ⅛ ounce dried porcini mushrooms, rinsed and minced, for the red pepper flakes. Add ¾ cup heavy cream with the chicken broth and beans in step 2.

Green Beans Braised in Tomatoes
Process 1 (14.5-ounce) can diced tomatoes with their juice in a food processor until smooth, about 10 seconds. Follow the recipe for Garlic-Lemon Braised Green Beans, substituting 2 tablespoons olive oil for the butter, 1 teaspoon minced fresh oregano leaves for the thyme, and the pureed tomatoes for all of the chicken broth. Omit the lemon juice and season the beans with ¼ teaspoon sugar before serving.

TRIMMING GREEN BEANS QUICKLY

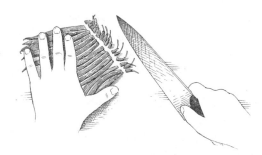

Instead of trimming the end from one green bean at a time, line up the beans on a cutting board and trim all the ends with just one slice.

Roasted Green Beans

SERVES 4

A pair of tongs is the tool best suited to redistributing the green beans on the hot baking sheet.

1 pound green beans, trimmed
1 tablespoon olive oil
Salt and ground black pepper

1. Adjust an oven rack to the middle position and heat the oven to 450 degrees. Line a large rimmed baking sheet with foil.

2. Toss the green beans with the oil, ½ teaspoon salt, and ¼ teaspoon pepper. Arrange the green beans in a single layer on the prepared baking sheet. Roast the green beans for 10 minutes.

3. Working quickly, remove the baking sheet from the oven and carefully redistribute the green beans in a single layer. Continue to roast until the green beans are dark golden brown in spots and have begun to shrivel, 10 to 12 minutes longer.

4. Remove the beans from the oven, season with salt and pepper to taste, and serve.

➤ VARIATIONS

Roasted Green Beans with Red Onion and Walnuts

Combine 1 tablespoon balsamic vinegar, 2 medium garlic cloves, sliced thin, 1 teaspoon honey, and 1 teaspoon minced fresh thyme leaves in a small bowl and set aside. Follow the recipe for Roasted Green Beans, roasting ½ medium red onion, cut into ½-inch-thick wedges, along with the beans. After roasting the beans and onion for 10 minutes in step 2, toss the beans and onions with the vinegar-honey mixture before redistributing them and continuing to roast as directed in step 3. Before serving, sprinkle with ⅓ cup toasted chopped walnuts (see page 309).

Roasted Sesame Green Beans

Combine 3 medium garlic cloves, minced or pressed through a garlic press (about 1 tablespoon), 2 teaspoons honey, 1 teaspoon minced or grated

EQUIPMENT: Tongs

It is hard to imagine cooking or grilling without the benefit of kitchen tongs. A large fork pierces foods and causes some loss of fluids. A spatula is useless with flank steak or chicken parts. A pair of tongs, however, is ideal for turning foods as they cook. But today it's possible to find tongs in a wide array of styles. The handles may be ergonomic or the tongs may telescope or fold in half. Are these newfangled versions any better than basic, old-school models?

Testing all manner of tongs, we groped and grabbed kebabs, asparagus, chicken drumsticks, and 3-pound slabs of ribs and found that tong performance differs dramatically. The business end of a pair of tongs, the pincers, can be smooth or scalloped, and we found that those with scalloped edges get a better grip on food. But that's not the end of the story. The shape of the scalloping can vary. Our tests showed that pincers with deep, sharp scalloping were more likely to break delicate foods, rip thin-skinned items, or shred meat fibers. We preferred the gentler touch of wide, shallow scalloping. And pincers that were slightly concave, or cupped, did a good job of grasping hard, irregularly shaped, and large objects.

The winner was a pair of 12-inch locking tongs made of stainless steel and Santoprene by OXO. They missed a perfect score only because one picky tester thought the pincers bruised cooked asparagus. A minor complaint indeed—and a flawless performance otherwise.

THE BEST TONGS

The OXO Good Grips 12-inch Locking Tongs ($10.99) have soft cushioning on the arms, keeping hands comfortable, firmly planted, and cool.

OXO GOOD GRIPS

fresh ginger, ½ teaspoon toasted sesame oil, and ¼ teaspoon red pepper flakes in a small bowl and set aside. Follow the recipe for Roasted Green Beans. After roasting the beans for 10 minutes in step 2, toss the beans with the garlic-ginger mixture before redistributing them and continuing to roast as directed in step 3. Before serving, sprinkle with 4 teaspoons toasted sesame seeds (see page 309).

TECHNIQUE : Toasting Nuts and Seeds

The best way to maximize the flavor of nuts and seeds, no matter if you are baking with them, using them in a sauce, or sprinkling them over a salad or pasta, is to toast them. To toast a small amount of nuts or seeds (less than 1 cup), put them in a dry skillet over medium heat and cook, shaking the pan often, until fragrant and lightly browned, 3 to 8 minutes. To toast large quantities of nuts, spread the nuts in a single layer on a rimmed baking sheet (or two baking sheets if necessary) and toast in a 350-degree oven, shaking the pan often, until fragrant and lightly browned, 5 to 10 minutes. Be sure to watch the nuts closely as they toast—they can go from golden to burnt very quickly.

BRAISED LEEKS

LEEKS ARE OFTEN UNDERRATED AS vegetables in their own right, usually reserved for soup or building a flavor base for other dishes. But their unique, onion-like sweetness makes them a delicious side dish, especially when slowly braised, which enhances their delicate flavor.

Our first action was to better acquaint ourselves with the best leeks for braising. Leeks come in all sizes, but in most stores they are bundled together without regard to size. To ensure even cooking times, we made our own bundles of same-size leeks. We also tried to buy the leeks with the longest white stems, the most tender and useable part of a leek; the white parts can vary from 4 to 8 inches so it pays to be discriminating when selecting them.

Don't be fooled by supermarkets that sell leeks that are already trimmed down to the lighter base part. While this may seem like a good deal because you aren't paying for the upper leaves, which are discarded anyway, the truth is that the actual purpose of this procedure is to trim away aging leaves and make tough, old leeks look fresher to the unwary consumer. The bottom line: hand select your leeks and try to find a store that sells them untrimmed. Once you get them home, trimming is essential because it is the only way to expose the many layers of the leek and clean it properly. Instead of following the often-recommended technique of slicing off the leaves right where they lighten into the white base of the leek, we found we could move about 2 inches upward into the leaves, to the point at which the light green part turns dark green, without any ill effect.

The next step is to clean the leeks. Since leeks grow underground, during the process of pushing upward they collect dirt between their layers. We've come across leeks that had only a few grains of dirt between the layers, but we've also found leeks with mud jammed in the crevices. We found that the best way to clean the leeks for this recipe is to halve them lengthwise, leaving the root end intact, but trimming off the dangling roots. Under running water, gently pull the layers apart to wash away the dirt nestled inside (see the illustration below). Once cleaned, the halved leeks are ready to be braised.

Next we focused on technique. Since braises often start with browning, we followed suit. We found that browning the leeks on the cut side only kept the leeks together and made them easier to serve, but the flavor wasn't quite as intense as those browned on both sides. To compensate for only browning one side, we tried sprinkling a little sugar into the pan before adding the leeks to help the caramelization and this worked—the leeks

CLEANING LEEKS FOR BRAISING

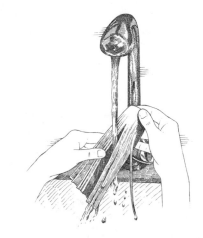

When braising leeks, we like to cut the leeks lengthwise in half, but we always find dirt nestled between the layers. To clean them, hold each leek under cold, running water, carefully pulling the leaves apart to allow the dirt to wash away. Then gently pat dry with a paper towel.

caramelized to a deeper brown, which resulted in a sauce with richer flavor.

We continued our testing by exploring braising liquids. After testing water, cream, white wine, and chicken broth—both alone and in different combinations—we settled on equal parts white wine and chicken broth, which produced deep yet brightly flavored leeks that retained a hint of onion flavor—something we wanted to preserve. To make the most of the braising liquid, we removed the leeks once they were finished cooking and tented them with foil to keep them warm, then we cranked up the heat and reduced the braising liquid. A tablespoon of butter and a little lemon juice rounded out the flavors of the sauce and minced parsley added color. Simple yet satisfying, these leeks make an elegant side dish.

Braised Leeks

SERVES 4

You will need a skillet with a tight-fitting lid for this recipe. We found that a nonstick skillet works best here, but a traditional skillet can be used. We prefer to use large leeks for this recipe; the diameter of each leek should be about 1 inch and it should be trimmed to be about 6 inches in length in order to fit easily in the skillet. When prepping the leeks, be sure to trim only the dangling roots from the root end, leaving the base of the leek intact to hold the layers together. The leeks can fall apart easily when cooking if not handled gently.

3	tablespoons unsalted butter
½	teaspoon sugar
	Salt
4	large leeks, white and light green parts only, root ends trimmed, halved lengthwise, and rinsed thoroughly (see the illustration on page 309)
¼	cup dry white wine
¼	cup low-sodium chicken broth
½	teaspoon minced fresh thyme leaves
1	tablespoon minced fresh parsley leaves (optional)
1	teaspoon juice from 1 lemon
	Ground black pepper

1. Melt 2 tablespoons of the butter in a 12-inch nonstick skillet over medium-high heat. Sprinkle the sugar and ¼ teaspoon salt evenly over the bottom of the skillet and add the leeks, cut-side down, in a single layer. Cook, shaking the pan occasionally, until golden brown, about 5 minutes, adjusting the heat as needed if the leeks are browning too quickly.

2. Add the wine, broth, and thyme. Reduce the heat to low, cover, and simmer until the leeks lose their vibrant color, turn translucent, and a fork inserted into the root end meets little resistance, about 10 minutes.

3. Gently transfer the leeks to a serving platter, cover, and set aside, leaving the liquid in the skillet. Return the liquid to a simmer over medium-high heat and cook until slightly thickened, about 2 minutes. Off the heat, whisk in the remaining 1 tablespoon butter, the parsley (if using), and lemon juice and season with salt and pepper to taste. Spoon the sauce over the leeks and serve.

OVEN-CARAMELIZED ONIONS

AS AN AROMATIC, ONIONS PLAY A SUPPORTING role in countless recipes, deepening the flavor of the other ingredients. A brief sauté to soften and lightly brown is the most common treatment for onions, but when gently coaxed far beyond this point, this everyday pantry staple is transformed into something remarkable. Sweet and glossy, with complex flavor, caramelized onions easily play a wide range of culinary roles, from a condiment for burgers to a sauce for roast chicken. Caramelized onions can also team up with bacon and sour cream to make a classic dip or be used on their own as a topping for steak.

Although the ingredients needed are minimal, most recipes for caramelizing onions require a watchful eye and constant stirring on the stovetop. We were hoping to find a more hands-off and foolproof method allowing the heat do the work—and us to walk away.

Looking for a way to streamline this process, we began by reviewing conventional recipes for caramelizing onions. Most start by heating butter and/or oil in a skillet or saucepan, adding sliced onions (and sometimes sugar) and cooking over low to medium-low heat, stirring frequently, for up to 2 hours. Through experience we knew that impatiently trying to shorten this stirring time by cranking up the heat results in burnt onions. Instead we tried keeping the heat as low as possible and simply stirring the onions less frequently. Unfortunately, without continual attention, these onions burned as well.

We needed steady heat that wouldn't cause scorching—the stovetop was concentrating too much heat at the bottom of the pot. Why not use the oven? We spread oiled sliced onions on a baking sheet and roasted them at 450 degrees. Instead of caramelizing, however, they simply dried out. Lower temperatures caused the onions to steam. Next, we cooked as many sliced onions as we could squeeze into a Dutch oven (4 pounds), with far more promising results—the onions cooked slowly and evenly, building flavor all the while. Lightly coating the pot with vegetable oil spray ensured the onions wouldn't stick, and helped prevent the onions around the edge of the pot from burning.

After some trial and error, we finally settled on a method in which we cooked the onions covered in a 400-degree oven for an hour, then continued cooking with the lid ajar for another hour and a half. Covering them for the first hour kept the heat even and onions moist, allowing us to leave them unattended. After the onions have released their moisture, browning can begin. Cracking the lid at this point evaporated any excess moisture, encouraged browning, and prevented a "stewed" flavor. Once the browning began, we only had to stir the onions every half hour.

With our new hands-off method, the onions emerged from the oven golden, soft, and sweet, and a nice fond had begun to collect on the bottom of the pot (which we scraped up to further enhance the flavor of the onions). Even better, we'd only had to tend to them a handful of times in two and a half hours.

Oven-Caramelized Onions
MAKES ABOUT 2 CUPS

Be sure to use yellow onions here; sweet onions, such as Vidalia or Walla Walla, will make this recipe overly sweet and somewhat gummy. Serve these onions alongside a wedge of cheese as an appetizer, as a side dish for steak, or as a sandwich topping. You can also use them in one of the recipes on page 312.

3   tablespoons unsalted butter
4   pounds yellow onions (about 8 medium), halved and sliced ¼ inch thick
      Salt and ground black pepper

1. Adjust an oven rack to the lower-middle position and heat the oven to 400 degrees. Coat the inside of a heavy-bottomed large Dutch oven with vegetable oil spray.

2. Melt the butter in the prepared Dutch oven over medium-low heat. Stir in the onions and 1 teaspoon salt. Cover, place the pot in the oven, and cook for 1 hour (the onions will be moist and slightly reduced in volume).

EQUIPMENT: Wooden Spoons

Is there any real difference between one wooden spoon and another? In a word, yes. We used 10 models to caramelize onions and stir pots of thick vegetable curry. To test durability, we also tried snapping each in half. Here's what we liked: thin edges (which scrape more effectively than thick); a handle that's strong but not too bulky; and a broad bowl that covers a lot of surface area and can reach into the corners of a pot.

THE BEST WOODEN SPOON

Strong but lightweight, with a comfortable grip and a broad, thin-edged bowl, the Mario Batali 13-Inch Wooden Spoon ($4.95) scraped and stirred its way to the top.

MARIO BATALI

Bacon, Scallion, and Caramelized Onion Dip

MAKES ABOUT I CUP

Half a recipe of Oven-Caramelized Shallots can be substituted for the onions. Serve this dip with potato chips or baguette slices.

3	ounces (about 3 slices) bacon, cut into ¼-inch pieces
¼	recipe (½ cup) Oven-Caramelized Onions (page 311), chopped fine
⅓	cup mayonnaise
⅓	cup sour cream
2	scallions, minced
2	teaspoons cider vinegar
	Salt and ground black pepper

1. Cook the bacon in a small skillet over medium heat until crisp, about 5 minutes. Transfer to a paper towel–lined plate and set aside.

2. Combine the cooked bacon, caramelized onions, mayonnaise, sour cream, scallions, and vinegar. Season with salt and pepper to taste. Transfer the dip to a small bowl, cover with plastic wrap, and refrigerate until the flavors meld, at least 1 hour, or up to 2 days, before serving.

Caramelized Onion Jam

MAKES ABOUT I CUP

One recipe of Oven-Caramelized Shallots can be substituted for the onions. This jam tastes great on toast or sandwiches or served with cheese and crackers.

½	recipe (1 cup) Oven-Caramelized Onions (page 311), minced
1	tablespoon cider vinegar
2	teaspoons minced fresh thyme leaves
	Salt and ground black pepper

Pulse the onions, vinegar, and thyme together in a food processor to a jam-like consistency, about 5 pulses. Season with salt and pepper to taste. (The jam can be refrigerated in an airtight container for up to 1 week.)

3. Working quickly, remove the pot from oven and stir the onions, scraping the bottom and sides of the pot. Partially cover, return the pot to the oven, and continue to cook until the onions are deep golden brown, 1½ to 1¾ hours longer, stirring the onions and scraping the bottom and sides of the pot every 30 minutes.

4. Remove the onions from the oven, stir to scrape up any browned bits, and season with salt and pepper. Serve warm or at room temperature. (The onions can be refrigerated in an airtight container for up to 1 week.)

➤ VARIATIONS

Oven-Caramelized Shallots

MAKES ABOUT I CUP

Because shallots are somewhat expensive and time-consuming to prepare, we scaled this variation down.

Follow the recipe for Oven-Caramelized Onions, reducing the amount of butter to 2 tablespoons, substituting 2 pounds shallots (16 large), peeled and quartered, for the onions, and reducing the amount of salt to ½ teaspoon. Reduce the covered cooking time in step 2 to 45 minutes, and the partially covered cooking time in step 3 to 1 hour.

PORTOBELLO MUSHROOMS

WHEN IT COMES TO COOKING MUSHROOMS, you might think—since they can be eaten raw—that a quick sauté would do the trick. But it takes time to really bring out their deep, rich, earthy flavors. Mushrooms are composed of 80 percent water, and it stands to reason that to avoid rubbery, flavorless, colorless mushrooms, some of the water has come out. What better way to draw out moisture and concentrate flavor than by roasting?

Since white mushrooms are inexpensive and

SCORING MUSHROOMS

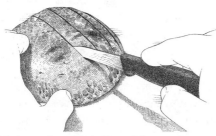

1. With the tip of a pairing knife carefully score the smooth (non-gill) side of the mushroom in one direction, ⅛ inch deep, spaced about ½-inch apart.

2. Score the mushroom again in the opposite direction to make a crosshatch pattern.

almost always available (they are the only choice in some markets), we started our testing with them. After just one test, however, we changed gears. The mushrooms filled the baking sheet in a nice, even layer going into the oven, but only a measly 1½ cups of roasted mushrooms emerged. If we wanted to make enough for a side dish, we would have to use two baking sheets or cook the mushrooms in batches. Instead, we turned to larger portobello mushrooms—their meaty texture meant we could use less and fit them all on one sheet.

Since their introduction into the U.S. from Italy in the 1980s, dark-brown portobellos have joined white button mushrooms as a "go-to" variety. And it's little wonder. Their bowl-sized caps and dense, meaty texture make them versatile and satisfying.

We were able to fit eight portobello mushroom caps comfortably on a rimmed baking sheet. We started by roasting the mushrooms in a 400-degree oven on a baking sheet for 40 minutes. Unfortunately, the mushrooms emerged tough and a little rubbery. The long and intense exposure to the dry heat of the oven was to blame. Our next thought was to

place them on a wire rack to allow the most surface area exposure; however, this left us with wet, soggy mushrooms, as the moisture from the mushrooms dripped onto the hot baking sheet and essentially steamed them.

Running out of options, we tried scoring the mushrooms with shallow cuts on their surface before cooking them in the oven. It worked—the mushrooms were no longer rubbery and had lost enough moisture to intensify their flavor. The only problem was that the mushrooms weren't actually caramelized. What if we preheated the tray? The results were just what we were looking for; a beautiful caramelized exterior, with profound mushroom flavor.

Although these roasted mushrooms are great simply tossed with a vinaigrette of olive oil, balsamic vinegar, thyme, and garlic, we also like the addition of chopped olives and oregano. These intensely flavored mushrooms make a truly spectacular side dish or an excellent antipasto option.

Roasted Portobello Mushrooms
SERVES 4 TO 6
Scoring the mushrooms maximizes the evaporation of moisture during cooking, resulting in a concentrated mushroom flavor.

8	medium portobello mushroom caps (4 to 5 inches each), wiped clean
¼	cup extra-virgin olive oil
	Salt
1	tablespoon balsamic vinegar
1	tablespoon minced fresh parsley leaves
2	teaspoons minced fresh thyme leaves
1	small garlic clove, minced or pressed through a garlic press (about ½ teaspoon)
	Ground black pepper

1. Line a large rimmed baking sheet with foil. Adjust an oven rack to the upper-middle position, place the prepared baking sheet on the rack, and heat the oven to 400 degrees.

2. Following the illustrations above, cut ⅛-inch-deep slits in a ½-inch crosshatch pattern on the top of each mushroom cap. Brush both sides of the caps

with 2 tablespoons of the oil and sprinkle evenly with 1 teaspoon salt.

3. Working quickly, remove the baking sheet from the oven. Carefully arrange the caps, gill side up, on the preheated baking sheet. Roast the mushrooms until they have released some of their juices and are beginning to brown around the edges, 10 to 12 minutes.

4. Flip the caps over and continue to roast until the liquid has completely evaporated and the caps are golden brown, 10 to 12 minutes longer. Meanwhile, make a vinaigrette by combining the remaining 2 tablespoons oil, vinegar, parsley, thyme, garlic, and ¼ teaspoon pepper in a medium bowl.

5. Remove the mushrooms from the oven, and let cool slightly. When cool enough to handle, slice the mushrooms into ½-inch strips, toss with the vinaigrette, and season with salt and pepper to taste. Serve warm or at room temperature.

➤ VARIATION

Roasted Portobello Mushrooms with Greek Flavors

Follow the recipe for Roasted Portobello Mushrooms, substituting 2 tablespoons juice from 1 lemon for the vinegar and 2 teaspoons minced fresh oregano leaves for the thyme. In step 5, add 12 kalamata olives, pitted and chopped coarse, to the mushrooms with the vinaigrette.

BAKED POTATOES

IN THE WORLD OF JUNE CLEAVER, POTATOES were baked at 350 degrees because they were put into the oven along with the roast, which cooked at 350 degrees. The world has changed a lot since Wally and the Beav sat down to dinner, and the evening meal has become a hastier project—using the microwave to cook potatoes is not uncommon. We wanted to slow things back down, so we decided to find the best way to make a good, old-fashioned baked potato.

Along the way, we baked all-purpose potatoes, Yukon Golds, and Idaho-grown russets. While all the potatoes we tried baked just fine, the high-moisture boiling potatoes and the Yukon Golds did not produce the desirable fluffy, dry texture we got from russets. We then tried baking them poked and unpoked—although a potato has never exploded in our oven, we've heard of it happening. Poking the potato before baking will prevent this, but we found it does not measurably affect the amount of moisture retained by the potato; the flesh of poked and unpoked potatoes were equally dry, so we leave the choice up to you. Greasing the potatoes with oil had no positive effect on browning so we skipped it. And, against the wishes of all the potato experts in the world, we also tried baking them in foil, but it turns out the experts are right—foil only trapped steam, resulting in limp, damp skins and dense flesh.

OPENING A BAKED POTATO

To ensure that the flesh does not steam and become dense, it's imperative to open a baked potato or sweet potato as soon as it comes out of the oven. This technique maximizes the amount of steam released and keeps the potato fluffy and light.

1. Use the tines of a fork to make a dotted X on the top of each potato.

2. Press in at the ends of the potato to push the flesh up and out. Besides releasing steam quickly, this method helps the potato trap and hold on to bits of butter.

SCRUBBING POTATOES

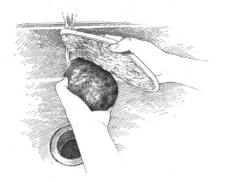

Buy a rough-textured bathing or exfoliating bath glove exclusively for use in the kitchen. The glove cleans dirt away from potatoes and other root vegetables, but it's relatively gentle and won't scrub away the skin.

After all this experimentation, what we discovered was that the traditional slow baking is best, mainly because of the effect it has on the skin. The skin of a potato baked at 350 degrees for an hour and fifteen minutes simply has no peer. Just under the skin, a well-baked potato will develop a substantial brown layer. This is because the dark skin absorbs heat during cooking, and the starch just inside the skin is broken down into sugar and starts to brown. All good cooks know that browning adds flavor to everything from layer cakes and bread to roasted meat and onions. If you love baked potato skin, this is definitely your method. In addition, we found that cooking the potatoes right on the oven rack was the best way to promote even browning and skin that was perfectly cooked all the way around, not just on top.

Potatoes cooked at 400 and 450 degrees will obviously cook faster—at 450 they may even cook in 45 minutes—but because they cook for a shorter time, the inner browned layer isn't as even or as flavorful as it is with the slower, lower method. In addition, the skin isn't quite as thick and chewy. Cooked long enough to develop chewy skin at these higher temperatures, the inner, browned layer becomes thick and unpleasant.

We also tried starting potatoes at 500 degrees for 10 minutes and then turning the oven down to 350 degrees to see if this would crisp the skin even more, but this method failed to promote even browning.

Thus, the perfect potato takes the longest to cook. Also, be forewarned: The most important step to a fluffy potato is opening it wide when it's hot and letting the steam escape rather than being trapped in the potato. Letting the potato sit a while after baking, or providing a too-small opening, will steam the potatoes and cause their flesh to become dense.

Baked Potatoes

SERVES 4

You can cook as many potatoes as you like without altering the cooking time.

4   medium russet potatoes
    (7 to 8 ounces each), scrubbed

1. Adjust an oven rack to the middle position and heat the oven to 350 degrees. Place the potatoes directly on the rack and bake until a skewer inserted into the center meets little resistance, about 1¼ hours.

2. Remove the potatoes from the oven and, following the illustrations on page 314, pierce them with a fork on top to form a dotted X. Press on the ends of each potato to open it up and release the steam before serving.

ROASTED POTATOES

ROASTED POTATOES TAKE TIME—ESPECIALLY if you are after the perfect roasted potatoes, which are crisp and deep golden brown on the outside, with moist, velvety, dense interior flesh. The potatoes' slightly bitter skin provides a contrast to the sweet, caramelized flavor that their flesh develops during the roasting process. They are rich but never greasy, and are often accompanied by the heady flavors of garlic and herbs.

To start, we roasted several kinds of potatoes. We liked high-starch/low-moisture potatoes (such as russets) the least. They did not brown well and their dry, fluffy texture was more appropriate for baked potatoes. The medium-starch all-purpose potatoes (such as Yukon Golds) produced a beautiful golden crust, but the interior flesh was still rather dry. The best roasting potatoes came from the low-starch/high-moisture category (we used red potatoes). These potatoes emerged from the oven with a light, delicate crust, an interior that was more moist than any of the others, and a complex, nutty flavor with hints of bitterness and tang.

After choosing the red potatoes, we began to test oven temperatures. At 425 degrees, the result was an even-colored, golden-brown potato with a thin, crisp crust and an interior that was soft and dense, although still slightly dry.

While researching, we came across some recipes that called for parboiling the potatoes before roasting them. Hoping that this approach would produce a texturally superior potato that retained more of its moisture after cooking, we tried boiling the potatoes for seven minutes prior to roasting. This produced a potato closer to our ideal, but preparation required considerable attention owing to the additional step.

We then tried covering the potatoes for of the first 20 minutes of their roasting time. We were especially drawn to this technique because it provided a way to steam the potatoes in their own moisture that required little extra effort on the cook's part. The results were perfect. The crisp, deep golden-brown crust was perfectly balanced by a creamy, moist interior. These potatoes had a sweet and nutty caramelized flavor, with just a hint of tang from the skin. This simplest of methods produced the very best roasted potatoes.

The next step in the process was figuring out how to add garlic flavor, which makes a good variation on the standard roasted potatoes. If we added minced garlic during the last five minutes of cooking, it burned almost instantly. Coating the potatoes with garlic-infused oil failed to produce the strong garlic flavor that we were after, and roasting whole, unpeeled garlic cloves alongside the potatoes and squeezing the pulp out afterward to add to the potatoes was too tedious. Whole peeled cloves roasted alongside the potatoes were sweet and soft, but tasters wanted garlic flavor in every bite, not just when they were eating a garlic clove. The best method turned out to be both simple and flavorful. We mashed raw garlic into a paste, placed it in a large stainless steel bowl, put the hot roasted potatoes in the bowl, and tossed them together. This method yields potatoes with a strong garlic flavor yet without the raw spiciness of uncooked garlic. The garlic tasted great in a classic pairing with rosemary, and also with other aromatics, herbs, lemon, and olives.

Roasted Red Potatoes

SERVES 4 TO 6

If using very small potatoes, cut them in half instead of into wedges and flip them cut side up during the final 10 minutes of roasting.

- 2   pounds red potatoes (about 6 medium), scrubbed and cut into ¾-inch wedges
- 3   tablespoons olive oil
       Salt and ground black pepper

1. Adjust an oven rack to the middle position and heat the oven to 425 degrees.

2. Toss the potatoes with the oil, ½ teaspoon salt, and ¼ teaspoon pepper. Arrange the potatoes

FLIPPING ROASTED POTATOES

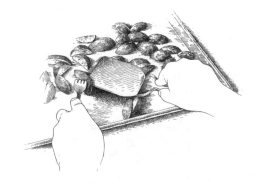

Press the metal spatula against the roasting pan as you slide it under the potatoes to protect the crisp crust. Flip the potatoes so that the other cut sides come into contact with the hot pan.

in a single layer on a large rimmed baking sheet, cut side down. Cover the baking sheet with foil and roast the potatoes for 20 minutes.

3. Carefully remove the foil and continue to roast the potatoes until the sides touching the pan are crusty and golden, about 15 minutes. Following the illustration on page 316, flip the wedges over and continue to roast until crusty and golden on both sides, about 8 minutes longer.

4. Remove the potatoes from the oven and season with salt and pepper to taste before serving.

➤ VARIATIONS

Roasted Red Potatoes with Garlic and Rosemary

Following the illustrations on page 27, mince 1 medium garlic clove to a paste with ⅛ teaspoon salt. Follow the recipe for Roasted Red Potatoes, sprinkling 2 tablespoons minced fresh rosemary over the potatoes during the final 3 minutes of roasting. Toss the roasted potatoes with the garlic paste before serving.

Roasted Red Potatoes with Shallot, Lemon, and Thyme

Following the illustrations on page 27 mince 1 medium garlic clove to a paste with ⅛ teaspoon salt, then mix with 1 medium shallot, minced (about 3 tablespoons), 1 teaspoon minced fresh thyme leaves, and ½ teaspoon grated zest and 1 teaspoon juice from 1 lemon. Follow the recipe for Roasted Red Potatoes, tossing the roasted potatoes with the garlic paste mixture before serving.

Roasted Red Potatoes with Feta, Olives, and Oregano

Following the illustrations on page 27, mince 1 medium garlic clove to a paste with ⅛ teaspoon salt, then mix with 2 ounces feta cheese, crumbled (about ½ cup), 12 kalamata olives, pitted and chopped, and 1 tablespoon juice from 1 lemon. Follow the recipe for Roasted Red Potatoes, sprinkling 1 tablespoon minced fresh oregano over the potatoes during the final 3 minutes of roasting. Toss the roasted potatoes with the garlic paste mixture before serving.

SLOW-COOKED SWEET POTATOES

THE HIGH SUGAR CONTENT OF SWEET potatoes makes them a perfect candidate for slow cooking—time in the oven caramelizes the sugars, drawing out the unique, earthy sweetness of the sweet potato. Two of our favorite ways to cook sweet potatoes are to bake them and to slowly simmer them in a combination of butter and brown sugar (a holiday favorite known as candied sweet potatoes).

The culinary magic of the baked sweet potato is largely unsung, but we're not sure why: When baked slowly, a whole sweet potato almost candies itself, and the natural sugars create an ultra-flavorful deep brown layer just underneath the skin. While it's easy enough to throw a sweet potato in the oven until it is cooked through, we wanted to find the best method to fully exploit the sweet potato's high sugar content for ultimate caramelization.

Sweet potatoes come in countless varieties, but there are two distinct types: white-fleshed and orange-fleshed. Though sweet potatoes are often mislabeled "yams" in grocery stores, neither the orange nor the white sweet potatoes have any relation to a true yam, which is covered with a thick, fibrous skin and is starchy and fairly bland tasting. Though there are many wonderful varieties of white and purple sweet potatoes, they are generally starchy and drier than orange-fleshed sweet potatoes. Orange-fleshed sweet potatoes are dense, watery, and more easily caramelized, and are essential for these recipes.

Armed with piles of sweet potatoes, we first addressed time and oven temperature. We tested cooking times from 45 minutes to five hours as well as oven temperatures ranging from 200 to 450 degrees. We also tried cooking the potatoes in foil, which was not a good idea as it resulted in steamed, wet potatoes and little caramelization. A 350-degree oven turned out to be the best—at lower temperatures, the flesh under the skin didn't caramelize and brown. At higher temperatures the sugars began to burn and imparted a bitter flavor to the potatoes. Just two hours at 350 degrees resulted in the best caramelization and the creamiest, most flavorful flesh.

Next we tested how best to treat the potatoes after baking. One recipe we came across advocated turning the oven off after baking but leaving the potatoes in the oven for an hour. We didn't find this did anything for the flavor. In fact, letting them rest in the oven or on the counter kept moisture locked in the potato and tended to make the flesh wet and dense. The texture and flavor of the potatoes was best when they were split open right from the oven to release as much steam as possible. These potatoes were fluffy and moist, without being soggy.

We also did a number of tests to find the best way to handle the skin. When sweet potatoes bake, they ooze syrup, sometimes a significant amount. For this reason, baking the potatoes directly on the oven rack was not an option, but an aluminum foil–lined baking sheet was perfect. We also tested pricking the skin with a fork before baking, but found this did not affect how much syrup the potato exuded. Flipping the potatoes every half hour during the roasting time insured that no side sat in the syrup long enough to burn.

Unlike a regular baked potato, the skin of the sweet potato is often discarded because of its often leathery, unappealing texture. Although this was a fact we were prepared to accept, we decided to try rubbing the skin with oil before baking. This simple step made a huge difference, preventing the skin from drying out and becoming too chewy. We now had it all: ideal caramelization, creamy flesh, and moist, flavorful skin.

Next we turned to that traditional Thanksgiving favorite, candied sweet potatoes. Chunks of sweet potato, slowly simmered in a sauce of sugar and butter, are delectable when done right. Unfortunately, many renditions of this dish lose the flavor of the sweet potato itself, resulting in an overly sweet and overly seasoned dish that tastes more like a loose, crustless pumpkin pie than a savory side dish. We wanted a recipe that would accentuate the natural flavor of the sweet potato rather than covering it up in a saccharine goo.

The method employed by many candied sweet potato recipes is to boil peeled pieces of potato before tossing them with a brown sugar and butter sauce. Despite the popularity of the method, we found these sweet potatoes to be watery and bland. Boiling the sweet potatoes washed away vital flavors and added moisture that was difficult to get rid of. Looking for a more gentle approach, we turned to the oven. We tossed raw, peeled pieces of sweet potato with brown sugar and butter and baked them in a covered casserole dish. Unfortunately, this method also produced a watery sauce as well as unevenly cooked potatoes. As the brown sugar and butter began to melt, the potatoes leached some of their liquid, making a watery cooking medium in which the potatoes began to float.

We had better luck once we tried cooking the potatoes on the stovetop. When we slowly cooked the potatoes in a Dutch oven with butter, brown sugar, and a small amount of water, the flavors of the potatoes and the sauce melded. The potatoes cooked perfectly in about 50 minutes, resulting in the ultimate candied sweet potatoes, with a rich and complex sauce. Although the sauce was still a bit watery when we removed the lid, it was easy to crank up the heat and reduce it quickly to a thicker consistency.

We then tested adding chicken broth, wine, and cider in place of the water, but tasters felt these flavors interfered with the clean taste of the sweet potatoes. While a few tasters liked the flavor of dark brown sugar, most found it overpowering. White sugar, on the other hand, was unanimously deemed too bland, so we stuck with light brown sugar. We also tried all sorts of spices and herbs, but tasters once again preferred the simple flavors of the sweet potatoes themselves, seasoned only with salt and pepper.

Baked Sweet Potatoes
SERVES 4

This recipe is designed to work with orange sweet potatoes and doesn't work well with white or purple sweet potatoes. Flipping the potatoes several times during cooking will ensure even browning and prevent any leaking juices from burning. You can cook up to six potatoes at the same time with this method without altering the cooking time.

4   small sweet potatoes (about 8 ounces each), scrubbed (see note)

4   teaspoons olive oil

1. Adjust an oven rack to the middle position and heat the oven to 350 degrees. Line a large rimmed baking sheet with foil.

2. Rub the sweet potatoes with the oil, then arrange them on the prepared baking sheet, spaced about 3 inches apart. Bake the sweet potatoes until the skin is deep brown, about 2 hours, giving the potatoes a quarter turn every 30 minutes.

3. Remove the potatoes from the oven and, following the illustrations on page 314, pierce them with a fork on top to form a dotted X. Press on the ends of each potato to open it up and release the steam before serving.

Candied Sweet Potatoes

SERVES 8 TO 10

For a more intense molasses flavor, use dark brown sugar in place of light brown sugar.

8   tablespoons (1 stick) unsalted butter

3¾ pounds sweet potatoes (about 6 medium), peeled and cut into 1-inch chunks

1   cup packed light brown sugar

½   cup water
    Salt and ground black pepper

1. Melt the butter in a large Dutch oven over medium-high heat. Add the sweet potatoes, sugar, water, 1 teaspoon salt, and ¼ teaspoon pepper and bring to a simmer. Cover, reduce the heat to medium-low, and cook, stirring occasionally, until the sweet potatoes are tender, 45 to 55 minutes.

2. Uncover, increase the heat to medium-high, and cook until the sauce has reduced to a glaze, about 10 minutes. Season with salt and pepper to taste before serving.

ROASTED ROOT VEGETABLES

ROASTING IS AN IDEAL METHOD FOR COOKING root vegetables because it evaporates much of their water, concentrating their natural sugars and yielding a rich, sweet taste and hearty texture. Roasting also gives the vegetables a caramelized, golden skin that is a wonderful contrast to their soft, moist interior.

The test kitchen has a favorite method for roasting potatoes (see page 315), the most common root vegetable, but what do you do when you want to roast a few different root vegetables at once? Is there a one-size-fits-all treatment that can produce beautifully browned and evenly cooked root vegetables? We were after a technique that was simple, un-fussy, and would work with a variety of root vegetables.

After assembling a preliminary combination of root vegetables—we liked potatoes, carrots, parsnips and an onion—we were ready to address the cooking method. The test kitchen's technique for roasting potatoes seemed a good place to start. We chopped our vegetables, tossed them with oil, and roasted them in a 425-degree oven, covered with foil for the first portion of the cooking time. This method produces ideally crisped skin and creamy flesh when cooking potatoes alone, but none of the vegetables in our test, not even the potatoes, browned well. Additionally, the flavors of the individual vegetables were somewhat muted and indistinct.

Why did this recipe work with well with just potatoes but not with the combined root vegetables? Covering the potatoes preserves their moisture and prevents them from drying out before cooking through. But the other vegetables—the carrots, parsnips, and onion—have a higher moisture content than potatoes, so we reasoned that covering them was trapping too much moisture.

Forgoing the foil and roasting the vegetables uncovered the whole time proved more successful. There was good caramelization and the flavors were developed and distinct. But the skin of the carrots and parsnips were unpleasantly shriveled and the onions were a bit burned. However, the ease of throwing the vegetables in the oven was exactly what we were looking for. Overall the approach was promising, it just needed some tweaking.

Oven temperature seemed like it could be the key so we decided to experiment. Would dramatically reducing the temperature produce tender, evenly caramelized vegetables? The answer was no: at 250 and 300 degrees the vegetables barely browned. We tested higher temps, but 450 and 500 did worse than shrivel some of the vegetables: they burned before cooking through. In the end, a modest adjustment proved the answer: 400 degrees produced the best and most consistent browning for the potatoes, carrots, parsnips, and onion, as well as turnips, rutabaga, and sweet potatoes (peeled or unpeeled worked great). (Beets dyed the other vegetables pink, and were a pain to peel raw, so we did not include them in our mix.) This recipe works with any combination of these vegetables, but we recommend being judicious in your selection—too many in the mix can really muddy their flavors. We prefer sticking to two or three different root vegetables, in addition to onion.

Our basic technique down, we homed in on some of the finer points of roasting a combination of root vegetables. It is important, and well worth the few extra minutes, to be diligent about cutting the vegetables to uniform size for even cooking. In order to achieve even browning, we found it necessary to stir the vegetables every 15 or so minutes during roasting.

Up until now, we had simply been roasting the vegetables in a roasting pan. Testing a variety of other pans, we found both the surface type and size of the pan to be important. A nonstick surface is ideal because the browning that develops during roasting sticks to the vegetables rather than the pan. When roasting other vegetables, we often advocate lining a baking sheet with aluminum foil for easy cleanup, but root vegetables (potatoes in particular) tend to stick to the foil, making them hard to stir. As for pan size, you need to use a pan that is large enough to accommodate the vegetables without

crowding—crowded vegetables won't brown well. In the end, we found that either a nonstick rimmed baking sheet or a large nonstick roasting pan was ideal here.

For variations, tasters liked rosemary and the mild, nutty flavor of whole garlic cloves roasted with the vegetables (raw garlic competed too much with the medley). Another favorite was bacon and thyme, and for something a little different, we glazed the warm vegetables with spicy maple syrup and orange zest.

Roasted Root Vegetables
SERVES 4 TO 6

Feel free to substitute equal amounts of sweet potatoes, rutabagas, or turnips for the carrots, parsnips, and/or red potatoes; be sure to cut all of the vegetables into 1¼-inch pieces before cooking. Slicing the onion into wedges through the root end helps keep the pieces intact during cooking. These vegetables can be served warm but also taste great at room temperature.

1   pound carrots (about 6 medium), peeled and cut into 1¼-inch pieces
1   pound parsnips (about 6 medium), peeled and cut into 1¼-inch pieces
1   pound red potatoes (about 3 medium), scrubbed and cut into 1¼-inch chunks
1   medium onion, halved and sliced into 1¼-inch wedges through the root end
3   tablespoons olive oil
    Salt and ground black pepper

1. Adjust an oven rack to the middle position and heat the oven to 400 degrees.

2. Toss all of the vegetables together with the oil, ½ teaspoon salt, and ¼ teaspoon pepper. Arrange the vegetables in a single layer in a large nonstick roasting pan or rimmed baking sheet.

3. Roast the vegetables until tender and golden brown, 1 to 1¼ hours, shaking the pan every 15 minutes to redistribute the vegetables.

4. Remove the vegetables from the oven and season with salt and pepper to taste before serving.

Spicy Maple-Glazed Roasted Root Vegetables

This variation is best served warm.

Combine 3 tablespoons maple syrup, ½ teaspoon grated zest from 1 orange, and ⅛ teaspoon cayenne pepper in a small bowl. Follow the recipe for Roasted Root Vegetables, tossing the vegetables with the maple syrup mixture before serving.

Roasted Root Vegetables with Garlic and Rosemary

Follow the recipe for Roasted Root Vegetables, tossing 12 medium garlic cloves, peeled, and 1 tablespoon minced fresh rosemary with the vegetables and oil in step 2.

Roasted Root Vegetables with Bacon and Thyme

Cook 6 ounces (about 6 slices) bacon, cut into ½-inch pieces, in a 12-inch skillet over medium heat until crisp, about 5 minutes. Transfer the bacon to a paper towel–lined plate and reserve 3 tablespoons of the fat. Follow the recipe for Roasted Root Vegetables, substituting the reserved bacon fat for the oil and adding 1 tablespoon minced fresh thyme leaves. Sprinkle with the reserved bacon before serving.

SLOW-ROASTED AND OVEN-DRIED TOMATOES

A PERFECTLY RIPE, FRESHLY PICKED AUGUST tomato needs no more preparation than slicing and sprinkling with salt. Unlike, say, an artichoke, cooking is not an outright necessity for tomatoes. However, if you are lucky enough to have an abundance of garden tomatoes, or you're just looking for ways to improve average supermarket tomatoes, then slow-roasted and oven-dried tomatoes are a great option. We love the sweet, concentrated flavor that develops from slowly cooking tomatoes—an easy-to-achieve distillation of summer.

CORING TOMATOES

Place the tomato on its side on the work surface. Holding the tomato stable with one hand, insert the tip of a paring knife about 1 inch into the tomato at an angle just outside of the core. Move the paring knife with a sawing motion, at the same time rotating the tomato toward you until the core is cut free.

Focusing first on slow-roasted tomatoes, we determined that in the best versions, the tomato's juices are concentrated by the slow, steady heat of the oven and become one with the olive oil in which it is roasted. We were after tomatoes with a sweet, intense tomato flavor and a juicy, melt-in-your-mouth texture. Most recipes use tomato slices, and we did the same—½-inch-thick slices proved ideal. We explored different options for tomato types that would yield round, robust, juicy slices. After a few tests, we settled on the ever-present, large, round, ruby-red tomato, but really any color of large round tomato will do.

For flavoring the tomatoes, we needed aromatics that would stand up to the long cooking time. Basil and mint were too delicate and shriveled in the oven; more robust herbs like oregano, thyme and rosemary fared better but tasters felt they seemed out of place in this dish. Garlic slices were ideal—the fine slivers practically melted during the slow bake, reduced to sweet and slightly chewy bits.

As for the type of oil to use, extra-virgin olive oil was the unanimous winner. It perfumed the tomatoes with an herbaceous, peppery aroma. Like the tomatoes, the olive oil gains flavor during roasting, so any oil left over in the pan can be saved for flavoring a vinaigrette or brushing on bruschetta.

Preparation takes mere moments, but the roasting takes some time. These are not oven-dried tomatoes, which can take upward of five hours in a tepid oven, but they are also not classic oven-roasted tomatoes, cooked at high heat for less than an hour for a near candy-like sweetness and intensity. Aiming for something in between, we set the temperature parameters at 300 and 400 degrees and began testing.

In a 400-degree oven, the garlic browned too quickly and turned acrid, ruining the dish. Erring on the side of caution, we lowered the temperature to 325 degrees and were pleased with the results. Within one and a half hours, the tomatoes were slightly wrinkled and browned but, more important, their juices had largely evaporated, leaving the flavor of the olive oil at the forefront. A lower temperature yielded no better-tasting results and took longer, so we stuck with 325 degrees.

These plump, sweet, juicy slow-roasted tomatoes make an unexpected and impressive side dish. However, they can also be used almost anywhere you would use raw tomatoes: as a sauce for pasta, grilled meats, a topping for bread, even a chopped salsa. Using our slow-roasted tomatoes, we developed simple recipes for a pasta sauce and a salsa.

Next, we turned our attention to making oven-dried tomatoes, our version of the ubiquitous sun-dried tomato. We were not interested in making a completely dry, shelf-stable product like store-bought sun-dried tomatoes. Rather, we wanted something plumper and moister. Although this partially dried tomato would have to be refrigerated and used quickly, it would have different uses—as a condiment and a sandwich ingredient.

When we began to research the subject, we found that the proper preparation of the tomatoes was a matter of some debate. Various authors claimed to have success with peeled and unpeeled, cored and uncored, seeded and unseeded, and sliced and halved tomatoes. One of the only factors that everyone agreed on was that plum tomatoes are the best choice for drying, as they offer more meat and less moisture than round tomatoes.

Dehydrators are typically used to make sun-dried tomatoes these days, and they generally work at 125 to 135 degrees. But most home ovens cannot be set this low, so we started our testing with a 200-degree oven. We began with the easiest preparation procedure—halving the tomatoes lengthwise and placing them cut-side down on racks set on baking sheets. Unfortunately, this approach did not work. The combination of low oven temperature

and the amount of moisture held within the seeds and cores of the tomatoes prevented the tomatoes from giving off their moisture easily and evenly. As a result, it took nearly 12 hours to dry them.

We tried propping the oven door open for increased ventilation, cutting the tomatoes in slices, coring them, and cutting across the tomatoes rather than lengthwise. In most cases, the tomatoes dried fairly well up to a point, but there always seemed to be a pocket of moisture in the middle that never dried out. We tried peeling and seeding the tomatoes and finally got our first good results. However, peeling the tomatoes was a bit laborious. Alternatively, piercing the skin of halved, cored, and seeded tomatoes with the tip of a sharp paring knife seemed promising. There were still unwanted pockets of moisture in the middle, but we were getting closer.

We then wondered if placing the tomatoes on a wire rack (set directly on the oven rack, with the baking sheet on the rack below to catch any drippings) would help increase air circulation, resulting in drier tomatoes. After three hours for smaller tomatoes and up to six hours for larger ones, they were perfect. The tomatoes were consistently dry with a nice texture and intense flavor.

These tomatoes can be used where you would sun-dried tomatoes—in a sandwich, on a pizza, or to make a salad dressing. If you lack inspiration, we've included recipes for a zesty pesto, and a creamy, basil-infused dip.

~

Slow-Roasted Tomatoes
SERVES 4

These tomatoes can be served as a side dish or used to make either of the recipes on page 323. When finished, the cooking oil will have a slight tomato flavor and can be refrigerated in an airtight container for up to 2 weeks; use the oil to make Slow-Roasted Tomato Sauce (page 323), a homemade salad dressing, or a dipping sauce for bread.

½   cup extra-virgin olive oil

4   medium garlic cloves, sliced thin

2   pounds ripe tomatoes (about 5 medium), cored and cut crosswise into ½-inch-thick slices (see the illustration on page 321)
     Salt and ground black pepper

1. Adjust an oven rack to the middle position and heat the oven to 325 degrees.

2. Grease the bottom of a 13 by 9-inch baking dish with 2 tablespoons of the oil and sprinkle half of the garlic across the bottom of the dish. Arrange the tomato slices in the pan, overlapping the edges as needed to fit. Pour the remaining 6 tablespoons oil over the tomatoes and sprinkle with salt and the remaining garlic. Roast the tomatoes until they are slightly shriveled and most of their juices have been replaced with oil, 1½ to 2 hours.

3. Remove the dish from the oven and let the tomatoes cool in the oil for at least 15 minutes, or up to 4 hours. To serve, remove the tomatoes from the oil with a slotted spoon (reserving the oil if desired; see note), and season with salt and pepper to taste. (The cooled tomatoes and oil can be refrigerated together in an airtight container for up to 2 weeks; return to room temperature before serving.)

Oven-Dried Tomatoes
MAKES 16 TOMATO HALVES

The drying time of these tomatoes varies depending on the desired texture. For tomatoes with a moist, slightly plump texture—perfect for sandwiches and salads—dry them in the oven for 3 to 4 hours. For a well-dried texture and more intense flavor—perfect for chopping and adding to sauces, pestos, and dips—dry the tomatoes in the oven for 5 to 6 hours.

2 pounds plum tomatoes (about 8 medium), cored, halved lengthwise, and seeded (see the illustration on page 324)

1. Adjust the oven racks to the middle and lower-middle positions and heat the oven to 200 degrees. Grease a large wire rack with vegetable oil spray and line a large rimmed baking sheet with foil.

Slow-Roasted Tomato Salsa
MAKES ABOUT 2 CUPS

This recipe is a great way to make salsa when you can't get flawlessly ripe tomatoes. For more heat, include the jalapeño seeds and ribs when mincing.

1 recipe Slow-Roasted Tomatoes (page 322), chopped coarse
¼ cup minced red onion
1 jalapeño chile, seeds and ribs removed, chile minced (see note)
2 tablespoons minced fresh cilantro leaves
1–2 tablespoons juice from 1 lime
Salt and ground black pepper

Combine the tomatoes, onion, jalapeño, cilantro, and 1 tablespoon of the lime juice in a medium bowl. Season with salt, pepper, and additional lime juice to taste. Let sit at room temperature until the flavors meld, about 30 minutes, before serving. (The salsa can be refrigerated in an airtight container for up to 2 days; return to room temperature before serving.)

Slow-Roasted Tomato Sauce
MAKES ABOUT 2 CUPS

Serve over pasta with grated Parmesan cheese. This sauce is also great as a topping for chicken, fish, or bread.

1 recipe Slow-Roasted Tomatoes (page 322), chopped coarse
¼ cup reserved tomato cooking oil, or extra-virgin olive oil
¼ cup chopped fresh basil leaves
1 small garlic clove, minced or pressed through a garlic press (about ½ teaspoon)
Salt and ground black pepper

Combine the tomatoes, reserved oil, basil, and garlic in a medium bowl. Season with salt and pepper to taste and serve. (The sauce can be refrigerated in an airtight container for up to 2 days; return to room temperature before serving.)

2. Prick the skin of each tomato about 7 times using the tip of a sharp knife. Arrange the tomatoes, cut-side down, on the prepared wire rack. Set the wire rack with tomatoes on the middle rack and place the prepared baking sheet on the lower-middle rack. Dry the tomatoes for 3 to 6 hours, depending on the tomatoes' size and the desired texture.

3. Remove the tomatoes from the oven. (The tomatoes can be refrigerated in an airtight container for up to 1 week.) Serve warm, at room temperature, or chilled.

SEEDING PLUM TOMATOES

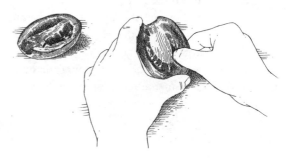

Halve the cored tomatoes lengthwise, cutting through the core end. Break through the inner membrane with your finger and scoop out the seeds and gelatinous material.

Oven-Dried Tomato Pesto

MAKES ABOUT I CUP

This recipe will work with both textures of Oven-Dried Tomatoes (moist and well dried); however, we slightly prefer the more intense flavor of well-dried tomatoes here. This pesto is great on pasta or sandwiches.

1	recipe Oven-Dried Tomatoes (page 323), chopped coarse
6	tablespoons extra-virgin olive oil
¼	cup walnuts, toasted (page 309)
1	small garlic clove, minced or pressed through a garlic press (about ½ teaspoon)
	Salt and ground black pepper
1	ounce Parmesan cheese, grated (½ cup)

Pulse the tomatoes, oil, walnuts, garlic, ½ teaspoon salt, and ⅛ teaspoon pepper together in a food processor until smooth, about 15 pulses, scraping down the bowl as needed. Transfer the mixture to a small bowl, stir in the cheese, and season with salt and pepper to taste. (The pesto can be refrigerated in an airtight container for up to 3 days.)

Oven-Dried Tomato and Basil Dip

MAKES ABOUT I CUP

This recipe will work with both textures of Oven-Dried Tomatoes (moist and well-dried), however, we slightly prefer the more intense flavor of well-dried tomatoes here. Serve this dip with a variety of crudités or baguette slices.

½	recipe (8 tomato halves) Oven-Dried Tomatoes (page 323), chopped fine
⅓	cup mayonnaise
⅓	cup sour cream
2	tablespoons minced fresh basil leaves
2	teaspoons juice from 1 lemon
1	small garlic clove, minced or pressed through a garlic press (about ½ teaspoon)
	Salt and ground black pepper

Stir all of the ingredients together in a small serving bowl and season with salt and pepper to taste. Cover the bowl with plastic wrap and refrigerate until the flavors meld, at least 1 hour or up to 2 days, before serving.

ROASTED WINTER SQUASH

WINTER SQUASHES, SUCH AS ACORN AND butternut, with their tough skin and dense interior, are ideal for slow cooking. Unlike some vegetables that are best cooked until just done, winter squash must be cooked until well done to develop the sweetest flavor and smoothest texture. Though varieties of winter squash vary significantly in size and texture, we were hoping to develop a one-recipe-fits-all approach.

First, some tips about the squash itself. Over the years, we have halved, seeded, and cooked a lot of squash, and have noticed significant differences in quality, depending on where we purchased the squash, how we stored it, and how long we kept it. Some were richly flavored, with deep, golden orange flesh, while others were spongy and pale. We learned that all varieties of domestically grown winter squash are in season from July through November. Squash purchased in the off-season is usually imported from Mexico and is likely to be more expensive. Squash that had spent weeks in transit cooked up dehydrated, fibrous, and pasty in the test kitchen.

Squash should be hard and heavy for its size, an indication that it contains a lot of moisture and has not been sitting on the supermarket produce shelf for weeks. Winter squash should be stored at cool room temperature, not in the refrigerator. When we stored squash for a few weeks in the refrigerator, chill damage set in, causing the flavor and texture to deteriorate.

As for the cooking method, the best approach for our recipe turned out to be both the most traditional and the simplest: roasting halved squash. After some experimentation, we found that roasting the unpeeled and seeded halves cut-side down gave a slightly better texture than roasting them cut-side up. We found it best to cook the squash on a foil-lined baking sheet that had been oiled. The oil promoted better browning and reduced the risk of sticking, and the foil made cleanup easy.

When it came to flavoring the squash, we kept the master recipe simple—just salt and pepper—and then came up with some variations. For one version, we brushed a soy sauce and maple syrup glaze over the squash and continued roasting until it caramelized. Next, we made a classic sauce of brown butter and sage, which we simply spooned over the roasted squash halves before serving.

~⚬~

Roasted Winter Squash Halves

SERVES 4

This recipe can be made with butternut, acorn, buttercup, kabocha, or delicata squash. The cooking time will vary depending on the kind of squash you use. Start checking for doneness after the first 30 minutes.

- 2 tablespoons olive oil
- 2 pounds winter squash (1 medium or 2 small), halved lengthwise and seeded (see note)
  Salt and ground black pepper

1. Adjust an oven rack to the middle position and heat the oven to 400 degrees. Line a large rimmed baking sheet with foil and grease the foil with 1 tablespoon of the oil.

2. Brush the cut sides of the squash with the remaining 1 tablespoon oil. Place the squash, cut-side down, on the prepared baking sheet and roast until a fork inserted into the center of the squash meets little resistance, 30 to 50 minutes.

3. Remove the squash from the oven and turn cut side up. If necessary, cut large pieces in half to yield 4 pieces. Season with salt and pepper to taste and serve.

➤ VARIATIONS

Roasted Winter Squash Halves with Soy Sauce and Maple Syrup

Combine 3 tablespoons maple syrup, 2 tablespoons soy sauce, and ½ teaspoon minced or grated fresh ginger in a small bowl. Follow the recipe for Roasted Winter Squash Halves, substituting 2 tablespoons vegetable oil for the olive oil. In step 3, turn the squash cut side up, brush with the maple mixture, and continue to roast until golden and caramelized, 5 to 10 minutes longer.

Roasted Winter Squash Halves with Brown Butter and Sage
Melt 6 tablespoons (¾ stick) unsalted butter in a small skillet over medium heat. Add 6 medium sage leaves, sliced thin, and cook, swirling the pan occasionally, until the butter is golden brown and the sage is crisp, 4 to 5 minutes. Follow the recipe for Roasted Winter Squash Halves, drizzling the browned butter over the squash before serving.

VEGETABLE GRATINS

VEGETABLE GRATINS ARE THE ULTIMATE slow-cooked side dish. The vegetables—usually cauliflower, potatoes, or other root vegetables—are coated with heavy cream, topped with cheese, and baked in a shallow dish until a golden brown casserole of tender vegetables bound by a creamy, flavorful sauce emerges from the oven. Unfortunately, vegetable gratins can be difficult to make successfully. More often than not, they contain mushy or undercooked vegetables and an unappetizing, curdled sauce. We set out to fix these problems and create a foolproof gratin.

Potatoes are perhaps the most traditional vegetable to cook in this style, so we started there. Taking a cue from several published potato gratin recipes, we rubbed shallow dishes with garlic, sliced potatoes and laid them in rows, topped them with heavy cream and cheese, and placed them in the oven to bake. We also made recipes that parboiled the sliced potatoes in cream on top of the stove before dumping the mixture into a shallow casserole dish, sprinkling it with cheese, and finishing it in the oven. Both versions presented problems.

We liked the ease of simply slicing and baking the vegetables, but in two out of three of the recipes that took this approach, the sauce broke, leaving us with cottage cheese–like curds floating in a watery

sauce. On the other hand, the recipes in which the potatoes were precooked were coated with a rich, creamy sauce (it turns out that the potatoes release some of their starch into the cooking liquid and act as a natural thickening agent that keeps the sauce from breaking). But precooking the potatoes also meant they had to be stirred, which required constant attention and can also cause the potatoes to break apart. Could we have it all—the ease of letting the oven do the work and a smooth, creamy sauce?

We knew that we needed a sauce that was stable enough to withstand a long cooking time without breaking. We thought of baked macaroni and cheese, which is bound together with béchamel—the classic French sauce of milk thickened with flour—before going into the oven. We made a quick sauce on the stovetop, tossed it with potatoes to coat, and transferred the mixture to a shallow dish to bake. The gratin came out of the oven with a silky smooth, creamy sauce. Tasters' only complaint was that the sauce wasn't quite rich enough, so we went back to using heavy cream and made everyone happy.

With the sauce in place, it was time to tweak its flavor. The delicate flavor of shallots and a little garlic worked wonders. Some fresh thyme contributed an herbaceous flavor that was neither showy nor distracting. Cayenne pepper added a little heat, and some ground nutmeg was welcome for its nutty sweetness.

Next, we focused on the potatoes. We cooked russet, all-purpose, and Yukon Gold varieties side by side in our basic gratin fashion. While Yukon Gold and all-purpose potatoes weren't bad, tasters found them a bit waxy. The traditional russets, with their tender bite and earthy flavor, were the unanimous favorite. The russets also formed tighter, more cohesive layers owing to their higher starch content.

Up until now, we had been using the tiresome technique of carefully layering the sauce-coated, raw potatoes slices, one at a time, in a shallow dish. Instead, we found that we were able to simply pour the potatoes into the dish, and gently press them to remove any air pockets. We covered the dish with foil and baked it in a 350-degree oven for one and a half hours, after which we sprinkled the potatoes with a handful of Gruyère and let the gratin cook uncovered for another half hour. The potatoes emerged from the oven as a bubbling inferno with a golden crown. Although the casserole was quite loose straight out of the oven, a 10-minute rest was all it needed to cool off a bit and become a cohesive dish. With our basic technique down, we came up with three variations by swapping sweet potatoes, parsnip, and fennel for some of the potatoes.

EQUIPMENT: Measuring Spoons

Every cook knows that measuring spoons are essential when it comes to baking, and we consider them very useful for most other cooking applications as well. But which brand is best?

After filling nine spoons to level, then carefully weighing the contents, we concluded that every brand was sufficiently accurate. So preferences came down to design. We measure dry ingredients by scooping a heaping spoonful, then sweeping a flat knife or other tool across the spoon to level (a method we call "dip and sweep"). Easy enough—unless the shape of the spoon hinders either the dipping or the sweeping. Fat spoons, spoons with short handles, overly bulky spoons, and spoons with raised handles all made this task more difficult. When measuring out liquid ingredients, shallow spoons posed a higher risk of spillage than deep spoons.

Where did we end up? The sturdy Cuisipro spoons ($13.95) feature an elongated, oval shape that proved optimal for scooping ingredients from a narrow jar. In addition, the ends of the handles curl down, putting them level with the spoon's base and thereby allowing a full measure to be set down on the counter with no tipping and no mess. Perfection is in the details.

THE BEST MEASURING SPOONS
The oval shape of the Cuisipro Measuring Spoons ($13.95) makes for easy scooping into tall, narrow jars.

CUISIPRO

The success of the potato gratin transitioned us into cauliflower. Following the technique we used for the potatoes, we made a cauliflower gratin, cutting the florets into 1-inch pieces. We quickly learned that since cauliflower has more moisture and less starch than potatoes, we would have to make a thicker sauce. We tossed the florets with a sauce so thick it was paste-like, but as the cauliflower cooked in the oven, covered with foil, it released its moisture, loosening the sauce to the perfect creamy consistency. As we did with the potatoes, we held off until the final 30 minutes of cooking to add the cheese. This way we were able to stir the cauliflower to coat it evenly with the sauce without compromising the beautiful, golden brown top.

Potato Gratin
SERVES 6 TO 8

We like to use a shallow 2-quart gratin dish, which allows for the most surface area (and browned crust), but a 13 by 9-inch Pyrex baking dish also works. Prep and assemble all of the ingredients before slicing the potatoes or the potatoes will begin to brown (do not store the sliced potatoes in water; this will make the gratin bland and watery). Slicing the potatoes ⅛ inch thick is crucial for the success of this dish; use a mandoline, a V-slicer, or a food processor fitted with a ⅛-inch-thick slicing blade. Parmesan cheese can be substituted for the Gruyère, if desired.

3	pounds russet potatoes (about 6 medium), peeled and sliced ⅛ inch thick
2	tablespoons unsalted butter
2	medium shallots, minced (about 6 tablespoons)
1½	teaspoons salt
3	medium garlic cloves, minced or pressed through a garlic press (about 1 tablespoon)
2	teaspoons minced fresh thyme leaves
¼	teaspoon ground black pepper
⅛	teaspoon ground nutmeg
⅛	teaspoon cayenne pepper
1	tablespoon unbleached all-purpose flour
1½	cups heavy cream
3	ounces Gruyère cheese, grated (¾ cup)

1. Adjust an oven rack to the middle position and heat the oven to 350 degrees. Coat a 2-quart casserole dish with vegetable oil spray. Place the potatoes in a large bowl and set aside.

2. Melt the butter in a small saucepan over medium heat. Add the shallots and salt and cook until softened, about 2 minutes. Stir in the garlic, thyme, black pepper, nutmeg, and cayenne and cook until fragrant, about 30 seconds. Stir in the flour and cook until incorporated, about 1 minute. Whisk in the cream and bring to a simmer until thickened, about 2 minutes.

3. Pour the sauce over the potatoes and toss to coat thoroughly. Transfer the mixture to the prepared dish and gently pack the potatoes into an even layer, removing any air pockets. Cover the dish with foil and bake until the potatoes are almost tender, about 1½ hours.

4. Remove the foil and sprinkle with the Gruyère. Continue to bake, uncovered, until the potatoes are lightly browned on top and a fork inserted into the center meets little resistance, 20 to 30 minutes. Let the potatoes sit for 10 minutes before serving.

➤ VARIATIONS

Potato Gratin with Sweet Potatoes
Follow the recipe for Potato Gratin, substituting 1 pound sweet potatoes (about 2 small), peeled and sliced ⅛ inch thick, for 1 pound of the russet potatoes.

Potato Gratin with Parsnips
Follow the recipe for Potato Gratin, substituting 1 pound parsnips (about 6 medium), peeled and sliced ⅛ inch thick, for 1 pound of the russet potatoes.

Potato Gratin with Fennel
Follow the recipe for Potato Gratin, substituting 1 large fennel bulb (about 1 pound), trimmed, halved, cored, and sliced thin, for 8 ounces of the russet potatoes. Add ¼ teaspoon fennel seeds, crushed, to the saucepan with the garlic in step 2.

~≫

Cauliflower Gratin
SERVES 4 TO 6

We like to use a shallow 2-quart gratin dish, which allows for the most surface area (and browned crust), but a 13- by 9-inch Pyrex baking dish also works. Parmesan cheese can be substituted for the Gruyère, if desired.

1	medium head cauliflower (about 2 pounds), cored and florets cut into 1-inch pieces (see the illustrations below)
2	tablespoons unsalted butter
1	medium shallot, minced (about 3 tablespoons)
1	teaspoon salt
1	medium garlic clove, minced or pressed through a garlic press (about 1 teaspoon)
1	teaspoon minced fresh thyme leaves

PREPARING CAULIFLOWER

1. Start by pulling off the outer leaves and trimming off the stem near the base of the head.

2. Turn the cauliflower upside down so the stem is facing up. Using a sharp knife, cut around the core to remove it.

3. Using the tip of a chef's knife, separate the florets from the inner stem.

4. Cut the florets in half, or in quarters if necessary, so that individual pieces are about 1 inch square.

⅛ teaspoon ground black pepper
 Pinch ground nutmeg
 Pinch cayenne pepper
1 tablespoon unbleached all-purpose flour
¾ cup heavy cream
3 ounces Gruyère cheese, grated (¾ cup)

1. Adjust an oven rack to the middle position and heat the oven to 350 degrees. Coat a shallow 2-quart gratin dish with vegetable oil spray. Place the cauliflower in a large bowl and set aside.

2. Melt the butter in a small saucepan over medium heat. Add the shallot and salt and cook until softened, about 2 minutes. Stir in the garlic, thyme, black pepper, nutmeg, and cayenne and cook until fragrant, about 30 seconds. Stir in the flour and cook until incorporated, about 1 minute. Whisk in the cream and bring to a simmer until thickened, about 1 minute.

3. Pour the sauce over the cauliflower and toss to coat thoroughly. Transfer the mixture to the prepared dish and gently pack the cauliflower into an even layer. Cover the dish with foil and bake until the cauliflower is almost tender, about 35 minutes.

INGREDIENTS: Gruyère Cheese

Though its fame derives mainly from its use in fondue and French onion soup, Gruyère is also a table cheese revered for its creamy texture and savory flavor. Both Switzerland and France make authentic versions that are crafted from raw cow's milk and aged for the better part of a year in government-designated regions (the French cheese is called Gruyère de Comté). Though labeled "Gruyère," domestic cheeses of this type bear little resemblance to the real thing. Made from pasteurized cow's milk, they are aged for fewer months and have a rubbery texture and bland flavor. In fact, in a blind taste test of nine brands, tasters overwhelmingly panned the two domestic versions, likening one (from Boar's Head) to "plastic." Imported Gruyères, on the other hand, received raves. The top picks in the lineup were three reserve cheeses, aged 10 or more months to develop stronger flavor: the Gruyère Reserve carried by Whole Foods Market, Emmi Le Gruyère Reserve, and a Gruyère Salé from a Boston area cheese shop.

4. Remove the foil, stir the cauliflower to coat with the sauce, and sprinkle with the Gruyère. Continue to bake, uncovered, until the cauliflower is lightly browned on top and tender, 20 to 30 minutes. Let the cauliflower sit for 10 minutes before serving.

SLOW-COOKED RATATOUILLE

RATATOUILLE, WITH ITS ROOTS AS A SIMPLE farmer's dish, can be described as French soul food. A vegetable stew featuring eggplant, zucchini, red pepper, tomatoes, and fresh herbs, a well-made ratatouille embodies the essence of flavors from a summer garden. Fantastic eaten warm as a side dish with roasted meat or with crusty bread or rice as a light main course, it only gets better the next day, drizzled with olive oil and eaten cold, tossed with pasta, or used as a filling for omelets. Ratatouille may be a rustic dish but that doesn't mean it is easy to prepare. Judging from the numerous bad ratatouilles we've had, ratatouille is not an easy dish to get right. The flavors of a well-made ratatouille are light and multilayered; the flavor of each vegetable remains distinct, heightened by the presence of the others. Bad ratatouilles are a soggy mess of vegetables indistinguishable from one another in taste and texture, often sitting in a watery tomato bath.

The name ratatouille is derived from the French *touiller,* meaning "to stir"—a forewarning, perhaps, of the work involved in the classical French preparation, where each vegetable is painstakingly sautéed separately and then combined at the last minute. In addition to this traditional recipe, we also found recipes that toss all the ingredients together in one pot and slowly stew them until tender. Although we wanted to avoid the labor of the classical version, we were skeptical that multiple raw vegetables, stewed together, would retain their individual character. But we were intrigued by the possibility of this streamlined approach, so we headed into the kitchen with the goal of making a really good ratatouille that did not require constant hands-on attention.

We started with the fundamentals: preparing the vegetables. Eggplant, zucchini, onion, bell peppers and tomatoes are what typically compose ratatouille. Tasters wanted some contrast in texture, so we sliced the onions and peppers into strips and cut the zucchini and eggplant into 1-inch pieces, leaving the skin on. Ideally we would use fresh, ripe tomatoes, but outside the peak summer months they have little flavor and poor texture. Picked at the height of the season, canned, diced tomatoes are guaranteed to be ripe and sweet.

Our key players in place, we could now address cooking technique. Despite our skepticism, we thought it made sense to start with the simplest method first—the one-pot version. We cooked the onions and peppers until they had started to release some of their moisture, then tossed in the rest of the vegetables and simmered them on the stove until tender. The resulting product was mushy and one-dimensional. We concluded that precooking the eggplant and zucchini before combining them with the onions and peppers was a necessity, both to evaporate excess moisture and to develop flavor. But what was the best way to precook them?

Eggplant is often salted to draw liquid out of it before cooking, but we wanted to be able to dry the eggplant and zucchini in one step. Roasting the zucchini and eggplant in the oven seemed promising. We tossed the cubed vegetables with oil, spread each on a baking sheet, and cooked them in the oven until browned. Meanwhile, we sautéed the onions and peppers in a Dutch oven, added the tomatoes, and brought it all to a simmer. The roasted vegetables then went into the Dutch oven and everything was heated through before being finished with fresh herbs. .

This ratatouille was finally headed in the right direction—the vegetables remained distinct and the flavors were less muddied—a vast improvement to the soupy mess we'd made earlier. However, the zucchini and eggplant had now lost too much moisture from their long roasting in the dry heat of the oven. We wondered if we could brown them instead on the stovetop, which would allow us to

cook the vegetables over higher heat in a shorter amount of time. We sautéed the eggplant and zucchini in batches in a large skillet with olive oil. Since we weren't looking to cook them through but just sear the outside, each batch only took four minutes over medium-high heat. Using a nonstick skillet, we found that we only needed 1 tablespoon of oil per batch.

Once all of the eggplant and zucchini were browned, we transferred them to the Dutch oven with the onions, peppers, and tomatoes and placed the pot in the oven. Partially covering the pot allowed some liquid to reduce but also prevented the vegetables from drying out, and an oven temperature of 325 kept the stew at a gentle simmer. We cooked the ratatouille for about an hour, until it had thickened somewhat and the vegetables had cooked through but still retained their shape. We found it was best to stir only once —very gently, halfway through cooking. The short blast of high heat from the stovetop and the slow, low heat of the oven had proven the right combination. We achieved a medley of vegetables with distinct textures and flavors that harmonized but still retained their own voice.

As for the seasonings, a light hand with the garlic was all the dish needed. While herbes de Provence (a combination of dried herbs) are often used in ratatouille, tasters preferred the clean flavor of fresh thyme, along with fresh basil or parsley to accentuate the fresh garden flavors.

Slow-Cooked Ratatouille

SERVES 6 TO 8

Using fresh herbs is important here; 2 teaspoons minced rosemary can be substituted for the thyme. It is important to cook the eggplant and zucchini (in batches) until they are brown, but to stir them as little as possible to prevent them from turning mushy.

6   tablespoons olive oil
2   medium onions, halved
     and sliced ¼ inch thick
2   red bell peppers, stemmed, seeded,
     and sliced into ¼-inch strips

Salt

2 medium eggplants (about 2 pounds), cut into 1-inch pieces

3 medium zucchini (about 1½ pounds), cut into 1-inch pieces

2 medium garlic cloves, minced or pressed through a garlic press (about 2 teaspoons)

2 teaspoons minced fresh thyme leaves

1 (28-ounce) can diced tomatoes

¼ cup chopped fresh basil leaves or minced fresh parsley leaves

Ground black pepper

1. Adjust an oven rack to the lower-middle position and heat the oven to 325 degrees. Heat 2 tablespoons of the oil in a large Dutch oven over medium-low heat until shimmering. Add the onions, peppers, and 1 teaspoon salt, cover, and cook, stirring occasionally, until the vegetables are softened and have released their liquid, about 10 minutes. Uncover, increase the heat to medium, and cook, stirring occasionally, until the onions are golden brown, 5 to 10 minutes longer.

2. While the onions and peppers cook, heat 1 tablespoon more oil in a 12-inch nonstick skillet over medium-high until shimmering. Add half of the eggplant and cook, stirring occasionally, until browned, about 4 minutes. Transfer the eggplant to a medium bowl. Repeat with 1 tablespoon more oil and the remaining eggplant, then transfer to the bowl. Working in two batches, repeat again with the remaining 2 tablespoons oil and the zucchini, transferring each batch to the bowl with the eggplant.

3. When the onions are golden brown, stir in the garlic and thyme and cook until fragrant, about 30 seconds. Add the tomatoes with their juice, scraping up any browned bits. Gently stir in the browned eggplant and zucchini and bring to a simmer. Partially cover, place the pot in the oven, and cook the ratatouille until slightly thickened but the vegetables still retain their shape, about 1 hour, gently stirring halfway through cooking. Stir in the basil, season with salt and pepper to taste, and serve.

BAKED APPLES

HOMEY AND COMFORTING, BAKED APPLES have been forgotten over the years. But when looking for recipes for slow-cooked fruit, it was hard to pass up an opportunity to perfect a recipe for this simple dessert. We soon found, however, that despite their simplicity there were some pitfalls to overcome before finding the best recipe.

The most common problem during testing was that the apples split or became too mushy when baked. The ideal baked apple holds its shape during baking and softens and remains moist without becoming mushy. We tested nine apple varieties to see how they would hold up and taste when baked. Among common varieties, only Golden Delicious apples rated well. McIntosh apples were mushy and Red Delicious and Granny Smith were too dry. Several lesser-known varieties also baked up nicely, including Baldwin, Cortland, Ida Red, and Northern Spy.

After further testing we surmised that steam was causing the apple skin to split open. To allow the steam to escape and to keep the apples from bursting in the oven, we found it helpful to remove a strip of skin around the stem with a vegetable peeler. To fill the apples we hollowed out the core without puncturing the blossom end of the apple. The easiest way to core a whole apple thoroughly is with a melon baller. Start at the stem end and use the melon baller to scoop out and remove the core.

When it came to baking, we found that the apples required a moderate oven heat of 350 degrees; higher temperatures caused the apples to split. To keep the apples moist, we found it best to bake them surrounded by a pool of cider, which also reinforced their flavor. However, there was one drawback to this baking method: the sauce was always too watery. Our solution was to take the liquid remaining in the pan after the apples finished cooking and reduce it on the stovetop. After a brief simmer, we had a super-concentrated sauce that clung to the apples.

Now that we had perfected the technique for baking the apples, we directed our attention to the flavorings. A half cup of sugar sprinkled over the apples before they went in the oven helped to tame their inherent tartness and a bit of ground cinnamon helped bring forth the apples' flavor.

Cider-Baked Apples with Cinnamon Sugar

SERVES 4

Golden Delicious, Cortland, and Baldwin are our favorite apples to use here. A melon baller is the best tool to use to core the apples. Take care not to puncture the blossom end (opposite the stem end) of the apples when coring them. Do not to overbake, or the skins will split, causing the apples to lose their shape. Serve these baked apples warm with whipped cream, ice cream, vanilla yogurt, or crème fraîche.

4	large apples (about 8 ounces each)
½	cup sugar
½	teaspoon ground cinnamon
1	cup apple cider

1. Adjust an oven rack to the middle position and heat the oven to 350 degrees. Following the illustration below use a vegetable peeler to remove a strip of skin from around the stem of each apple, then use a melon baller to scoop out the core, being careful not to puncture the blossom end.

PREPARING APPLES FOR BAKING

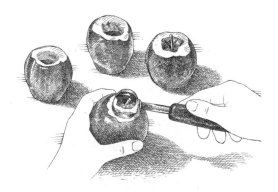

Using a vegetable peeler, remove a strip of skin from around the stem end of the apple. Using a melon baller, scoop out the core, being careful not to puncture the blossom end.

2. Combine the sugar and cinnamon in a small bowl. Arrange the apples upright in an 8-inch baking dish and sprinkle the cinnamon sugar in and around the apples. Pour the cider into the dish.

3. Bake the apples until a fork inserted into the center meets little resistance, 45 to 55 minutes, brushing with the cider several times during baking. Transfer the apples to a serving platter and loosely tent with aluminum foil while making the sauce.

4. Pour the cooking liquid into a small saucepan. Bring to a simmer over medium-low heat and cook until the liquid is syrupy, about 10 minutes. Spoon some of the sauce over each apple and serve, passing the remaining sauce separately.

➤ VARIATIONS

Honey-Baked Apples with Crème Fraîche

Follow the recipe for Cider-Baked Apples with Cinnamon Sugar, substituting ½ cup honey for the sugar and 1 cup water for the cider. Omit the cinnamon. Place a strip of lemon zest (see page 72) in each apple cavity, then squeeze the juice of 1 lemon evenly over the apples. Bake the apples as directed and serve with a dollop of crème fraîche.

Walnut-Raisin Baked Apples with Maple Syrup

Mix ¼ cup raisins, ¼ cup chopped walnuts, and 4 tablespoons (½ stick) unsalted butter, softened, together in a small bowl. Follow the recipe for Cider-Baked Apples with Cinnamon Sugar, substituting ½ cup maple syrup for the sugar and dividing the raisin mixture evenly between each apple cavity. Bake the apples as directed.

Rum-Baked Apples with Almond Paste and Mascarpone

Mix 3 ounces almond paste, 3 tablespoons sugar, 2 tablespoons dark rum, and 1 tablespoon unsalted butter, softened, together in a small bowl. Follow the recipe for Cider-Baked Apples with Cinnamon

SLOW-COOKED VEGETABLES AND FRUITS

Sugar, omitting the cinnamon, reducing the amount of sugar to 5 tablespoons, and dividing the almond paste mixture evenly between each apple cavity. Bake the apples as directed. Before serving, mix ½ cup mascarpone cheese with 1 tablespoon sugar and 1 teaspoon dark rum, and dollop the mixture over the apples.

BAKED BANANAS

A BANANA SEEMS LIKE A FAIRLY ORDINARY fruit—until you eat one that's been slowly baked. It's warm and sweet, the color of honey. Paired with a buttery brown sugar sauce, it is pure bliss. Because a medium-ripe banana is already tender and sweet, we knew we wouldn't have to work hard to coax out its natural sweetness even further.

We peeled some bananas, cut them in half, and arranged them in a baking dish with just a sprinkling of brown sugar and a few dots of butter. After one hour in a moderate oven (350 degrees), a mess of mushy bananas emerged. We quickly switched gears—for the next test, we decided to leave the bananas whole. This was a huge improvement. They were definitely soft, but they held their shape beautifully. And they made for an impressive presentation.

Up until now we had been baking the bananas uncovered for the entire time, but the portions that were exposed to the heat of the oven were drying out a bit. We wondered what would happen if we covered the bananas for part of the baking time? Covering the baking dish created a moist, butter-and-sugar-scented environment for the bananas to start cooking. After 30 minutes, we removed the foil and baked the bananas uncovered for an additional 30 minutes. This allowed the bananas to become golden and the butter, sugar, and juices from the bananas to reduce, making a rich, syrupy sauce. We decided to gently flip the bananas halfway through the uncovered baking time to give all sides of the bananas a chance to stay moist and brown.

We drizzled the sauce over the browned bananas and took a bite; ordinary bananas never tasted so good. When served with vanilla ice cream, this makes an excellent and easy dessert—and the oven does all the work!

Baked Bananas
SERVES 8

Very ripe plantains (the skin will be almost black) can be substituted for the bananas; do not, however, use very ripe bananas or they will become too mushy in the oven. Serve with sour cream or vanilla ice cream.

8	ripe but firm bananas, peeled (see note)
½	cup packed light or dark brown sugar
4	tablespoons (½ stick) unsalted butter, cut into ½-inch cubes

1. Adjust an oven rack to the middle position and heat the oven to 350 degrees. Arrange the bananas in a single layer in a 13 by 9-inch baking dish. Sprinkle with the sugar and dot with the butter. Cover the dish with foil and bake for 30 minutes.

2. Uncover and continue to bake until the bananas are softened and golden brown, about 30 minutes longer, flipping the bananas over with a wide spatula halfway through baking. Serve.

➤ VARIATION
Baked Pineapple
We find it easiest to buy a fresh pineapple that has already been peeled and cored. If you are peeling and coring your own, you will need 1 pineapple for this recipe. Do not substitute canned pineapple.

Follow the recipe for Baked Bananas, substituting 1 pound peeled and cored fresh pineapple (see note), sliced into ½-inch-thick rings, for the bananas, and reducing the butter to 2 tablespoons.

ROASTED PEACHES

WHEN PEACHES ARE SOFT AND RIPE, THEY are best eaten out of hand or perhaps sliced and served with a drizzle of balsamic vinegar. Ripe peaches that are still a bit firm are better suited to roasting, where the heat of the oven can work its magic, caramelizing the exterior of the peaches and rendering them soft, not mushy, and incredibly sweet and juicy. And they make an unexpected side dish or an easy dessert.

We started out in the kitchen by halving and pitting the peaches. We then sprinkled the cut sides of the peaches with sugar and roasted them on a baking sheet in a 400-degree oven. Right from the start, our tasters said they wanted more caramelization on each peach. Achieving this in the oven was not possible though, because the peaches became tender before they had a chance to properly brown. And worse, any browning that did occur stuck to the pan, not the peaches. Perhaps we would have better luck if we started by cooking the peaches on the stovetop in a nonstick skillet.

As we do for many pan-roasted recipes, we melted a little butter in the skillet, then added the sugar-sprinkled peaches, cut side down. After just two minutes, the peaches were beginning to caramelize and we transferred them to the oven to roast until tender. The peaches benefited from the richness of the butter, which also helped glaze them nicely and promoted browning.

Some tasters suggested adding more butter and sugar to the pan to make a caramel sauce for the peaches, but most preferred the simplest route. The peaches had plenty of flavor on their own and they remained versatile—we suggest drizzling them with balsamic vinegar and serving them alongside roasted chicken or pork, or if you want to serve them with dessert just add a scoop of vanilla, ginger, or cinnamon ice cream. We think these pan-roasted peaches are so flavorful and beautiful that you'll go out of your way to buy peaches that aren't perfectly ripe, just so you can make them.

Pan-Roasted Peaches
SERVES 4

Do not use either rock-hard or overly ripe peaches when making this recipe. These peaches can be served savory or sweet—they are great drizzled with balsamic vinegar and served with chicken or pork, or served with vanilla ice cream or whipped cream for dessert.

- 4 ripe but firm peaches (7 to 8 ounces each), halved and pitted
- 1 tablespoon sugar
- 2 tablespoons unsalted butter

1. Adjust an oven rack to the middle position and heat the oven to 400 degrees.

2. Sprinkle the cut side of each peach with sugar. Melt the butter in a 12-inch ovensafe nonstick skillet over medium heat. Add the peaches, cut side down, and cook until beginning to brown, about 2 minutes.

HALVING AND PITTING PEACHES

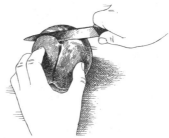

1. Locate the crease that marks the pointed edge of the pit. Position the knife at a 90-degree angle to the crease and cut the fruit in half, pole to pole.

2. Grasp both halves of the fruit and twist apart. The halves will come apart cleanly, so the pit can be easily removed.

3. Transfer the skillet to the oven and roast the peaches until the cut sides are caramelized and a fork inserted into the center meets little resistance, 25 to 35 minutes. Using potholders (the skillet handle will be hot), remove the skillet from the oven. Remove the peaches from the skillet and serve.

➤ VARIATIONS

Pan-Roasted Plums

Follow the recipe for Pan-Roasted Peaches, substituting 4 ripe but firm plums (6 to 7 ounces each), halved and pitted, for the peaches and reducing the cooking time in step 3 to 15 to 25 minutes.

SKILLET-ROASTED AND OVEN-POACHED PEARS

PEARS TASTE GREAT STRAIGHT FROM THE market, but they are also excellent when cooked, since they hold their shape and texture well. We wanted to take this ordinary fruit and develop two uncomplicated recipes—one for caramelized pears and one for poached—that would allow the inherent flavor of the fruit to remain intact, while improving its tenderness and enhancing, rather than masking, its flavor.

Here in the test kitchen, we have tried cooking pears in varying states of ripeness. Perfectly ripe fruit cooks quickly and easily. But we have found that cooking is also a perfect remedy for underripe or bland fruit, rendering it immediately edible. Rock-hard pears, however, never attain a tender texture no matter how long they cook, and if the pears are too ripe, they are difficult to handle and easily cook to mush. Moderately ripe pears, then, are our favorites to work with; the pears should give slightly when pressed with a finger.

Before developing our recipes, we focused our attention on which pear to use and immediately narrowed it down to the readily available pear varieties: Bosc, d'Anjou, Comice, and Bartlett. The favorites were the Bartlett, for its floral, honeyed notes, and the Bosc, because it tasted like a sweet, ripe pear should taste. The other two varieties were unremarkable in flavor and unattractive in appearance, as they experienced some discoloration during cooking.

We first tried our hand at caramelized pears—we wanted soft, golden pears with an accompanying caramel sauce that would cling to the fruit. While it would be easy enough to make the sauce and cook the pears in separate pans, we found it more efficient to cook the pears right in the caramel sauce. We brought water and sugar (the basis for caramel sauce) to a boil in a skillet, slid halved pears into the hot mixture, and let them cook in the slowly browning caramel. We noted it was easiest to trim the bottom of the pears before cooking them, rather than after, so that they would stand upright on the plate.

With our first batch, we tried removing the pears from the pan before finishing the caramel with heavy cream. This didn't work so well: the

CORING PEARS

1. Using a melon baller or teaspoon measuring spoon, scoop out the seeds and core in the center of each pear half.

2. Using the tip of a paring knife, cut out the blossom end (bottom) of each pear half.

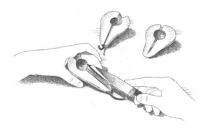

3. Remove the thin core and stem by making a V-shaped incision along both sides of the core, leaving the stem attached if desired.

pears turned unappetizingly sticky as they cooled, having been essentially cooked in sugar candy. For our next batch, we tried adding the cream to the pan around the pears as they finished caramelizing, which transformed the sticky sugar syrup into a smooth sauce that slid right off the pears. We let the pears drain for a few minutes on a wire rack set over a rimmed baking sheet and then drizzled them with the caramel sauce before serving.

Changing gears, we moved on to our poached pears, with the goal of soft, tender pears that could be served with the poaching liquid as the sauce. Most recipes use upward of one bottle of wine to poach pears on the stovetop, but we took a different approach. By using the oven, we were able to reduce the amount of wine needed to just ½ cup. We cut the pears in half and arranged them in a baking dish, then added the wine along with some sugar. We covered the baking dish with foil to keep all the liquid from evaporating and baked the pears in a 300-degree oven for one and a half hours. The resulting pears were tender and brightly flavored, and an added bonus was that the liquid had reduced to form a syrupy sauce.

Tasters were happy with the texture of the pears and the consistency of the sauce, but they wanted both to be infused with aromatics for more depth. A combination of fragrant lemon zest strips, warm cinnamon sticks, herbaceous thyme sprigs, and floral vanilla bean hit all the right notes.

EQUIPMENT: Spatulas

Hardly anyone spends time thinking about spatulas. But the fact is, every spatula has its issues. Old-fashioned rubber spatulas melt in high heat. Newfangled kinds made from heat-resistant silicone are sometimes more gimmicky than useful. Some are too stiff or too flexible. Why can't manufacturers come to the rescue and design a better spatula?

We chose 10 silicone contenders, all of which were dishwasher-safe. Testers put each one through a series of nine tests that included everything from delicate mixing to high-heat cooking and heavy-duty stirring—we even tried to stain, melt, and destroy them. After all, what good is a great spatula if it isn't going to last?

The business end of a spatula, the head, is its single most critical feature. We liked silicone heads, which are heat-resistant and inert (they don't release chemicals into the air or your food). Our favorite spatulas had heads that were not only soft and flexible enough to sweep all traces of batter out of a mixing bowl but stiff enough to remove fond from a skillet. We also decided that the top edge of the head had to be flat, fairly rigid, and squared off. The edge of the tip and sides had to be thin enough to maneuver into hard-to-reach corners.

We liked long handles that kept our hands a safe distance from the food, and were rigid enough to provide leverage. And while flat handles are the classic choice in a rubber spatula, we broke with tradition by preferring rounded handles. We also liked our spatula handle to be as heat-resistant as the head—one handle actually melted as it rested on the edge of a hot skillet.

After all the flipping, folding, scraping, and stirring was done, we declared a pair of winners—the Rubbermaid Professional 13½-Inch Heat Resistant Scraper ($18.99) and the Tovolo Silicone Spatula ($8.99). Both designs feature heads large enough to move volumes of food, with tips rigid enough to lift fond from a skillet. Their handles were easy to manipulate at any angle and didn't dip your fingers in the food. Neither showed signs of melting or discoloring, even when we left them in a hot pan at higher-than-recommended temperatures. The Tovolo's good looks and nice price make it hard to resist, but, in the end, the larger overall size and sturdiness of the Rubbermaid won our highest accolades.

THE BEST SPATULAS
The Rubbermaid Professional 13½-Inch Heat Resistant Scraper ($18.99) is a workhorse with an extra-long handle and a generously sized head. The Tovolo Silicone Spatula ($8.99) boasts a snazzy blue head and a brushed stainless steel handle that never got hot and proved remarkably comfortable to hold; it is our best buy.

RUBBERMAID   TOVOLO

Skillet-Roasted Pears with Caramel Sauce

SERVES 6

This dish is quite rich, so plan on serving just half of a pear per person. For the best texture, try to buy pears that are neither fully ripe nor rock-hard; choose those that yield just slightly when pressed. Trimming ¼ inch off the bottom of each pear half allows them to stand up straight when serving, making a beautiful presentation.

3	ripe but firm Bosc or Bartlett pears (about 8 ounces each)
⅓	cup water
⅔	cup sugar
⅔	cup heavy cream
	Salt

1. Line a large rimmed baking sheet with foil, set a wire rack inside the prepared baking sheet, and set aside. Halve and core the pears, following the illustrations on page 335. Trim ¼ inch off the bottom of each pear half.

2. Add the water to a 12-inch nonstick skillet, then pour the sugar into the center of the pan (don't let it hit the pan's sides). Gently stir the sugar with a clean spatula to moisten it thoroughly. Bring to a boil over high heat and cook, stirring occasionally, until the sugar has dissolved completely and the liquid is bubbling, about 2 minutes.

3. Add the pears to the skillet, cut side down, cover, reduce the heat to medium-high, and cook until the pears are almost tender (a fork inserted into the center of the pears meets slight resistance), 13 to 15 minutes, reducing the heat as needed to prevent the caramel from getting too dark.

4. Uncover, reduce the heat to medium, and cook until the sauce is golden brown and the cut sides of the pears are beginning to brown, 3 to 5 minutes. Pour the heavy cream around the pears and cook, shaking the pan until the sauce is a smooth, deep caramel color and the cut sides of the pears are golden brown, 3 to 5 minutes.

5. Off the heat, transfer the pears, cut side up, to the prepared wire rack and let cool slightly. Season the sauce left in the pan with salt to taste, then transfer it to a small bowl. Carefully (the pears will still be hot) stand each pear half upright on individual plates or a serving platter, drizzle with the caramel sauce, and serve.

➤ VARIATION

Skillet-Roasted Pears with Caramel-Pepper Sauce and Blue Cheese

Follow the recipe for Skillet-Roasted Pears with Caramel Sauce, adding ¼ teaspoon whole black peppercorns, coarsely crushed following the illustrations below, to the sauce with the salt in step 5. Serve the pears and sauce with 3 ounces strong blue cheese (such as Stilton), cut into 6 attractive wedges.

CRUSHING PEPPERCORNS

If your peppermill can't produce coarsely crushed peppercorns, you have two alternatives.

A. Chefs frequently use the back of a heavy pan and a rocking motion to grind peppercorns.

B. Or you can spread the peppercorns in an even layer in a zipper-lock plastic bag and whack them with a rolling pin or meat pounder.

Oven-Poached Pears

SERVES 4

For the best texture, try to buy pears that are neither fully ripe nor rock hard; choose those that yield just slightly when pressed. When removing strips of zest from the lemon in step 2, take care to avoid the white, bitter-tasting pith beneath the skin. We recommend using a medium-bodied dry white wine such as Sauvignon Blanc or Chardonnay.

1	lemon
4	ripe but firm Bosc or Bartlett pears (about 8 ounces each)
½	cup dry white wine (see note)
¼	cup sugar
2	sprigs fresh thyme
1	vanilla bean, halved lengthwise, seeds scraped out and reserved (see the illustrations below)
½	cinnamon stick
	Pinch salt

REMOVING SEEDS FROM A VANILLA BEAN

1. Use a small knife to cut the vanilla bean in half lengthwise.

2. Place the knife at one end of one bean half and press down to flatten the bean as you move the knife away from you and catch the seeds on the edge of the blade. Add the seeds as well as the pods to the liquid ingredients.

1. Adjust an oven rack to the middle position and heat the oven to 300 degrees.

2. Remove 6 strips of zest from the lemon following the illustration on page 72 and set aside. Cut the lemon in half and squeeze the juice into a large bowl of cold water. Drop the spent lemon halves into the water.

3. Peel, halve, and core the pears, following the illustrations on page 335, then drop the pears into the bowl of lemon water until ready to cook. Combine the reserved lemon zest strips, wine, sugar, thyme, vanilla seeds and pod, cinnamon, and salt in a 13 by 9-inch baking dish.

4. Drain the pears, discarding the lemon water, and arrange cut side down in the baking dish on top of the wine mixture. Cover the dish with aluminum foil and bake the pears until a fork inserted into the center meets little resistance, 1½ to 1¾ hours.

5. Transfer the pears to a serving platter. Remove and discard the zest, thyme, vanilla pod, and cinnamon stick. Pour the sauce over the pears before serving.

SCIENCE: Ripening Pears

In developing our recipe for Oven-Poached Pears we discovered that the ripeness of the pears affects the poaching time. Ideally, the pears should be ripe, but still firm. But getting those ripe-but-firm pears from the grocery store turned out to be difficult. We wondered why. According to the Pear Bureau Northwest, pears are an uncommon type of fruit that do not ripen successfully on the tree. They must be harvested at maturity, but before they ripen, lest their texture turn gritty and granular. This explains why virtually all pears at the grocery store are rock-hard. We tested three methods for ripening: uncovered at room temperature, in a paper bag on the counter, and in the refrigerator. The pears went into their respective corners on a Monday, and we tasted them each day to gauge their ripeness. By the end of the week, there was a clear loser. The pears kept in the fridge were only slightly riper and softer than when purchased. Those stored in a bag and those put in a basket on the counter ripened at the same speed; by Friday they were both ready for oven-poaching.

INDEX

A Note on Conversions

SOME SAY COOKING IS A SCIENCE AND AN art. We would say that geography has a hand in it, too. Flour milled in the United Kingdom and elsewhere will feel and taste different from flour milled in the United States. So we cannot promise that the loaf of bread you bake in Canada or England will taste the same as a loaf baked in the States, but we can offer guidelines for converting weights and measures. We also recommend that you rely on your instincts when making our recipes. Refer to the visual cues provided. If the bread dough hasn't "come together in a ball," as described, you may need to add more flour—even if the recipe doesn't tell you so. You be the judge. For more information on conversions and ingredient equivalents, visit our website at www.cooksillustrated.com and type "conversion chart" in the search box.

The recipes in this book were developed using standard U.S. measures following U.S. government guidelines. The charts below offer equivalents for U.S., metric, and Imperial (U.K.) measures. All conversions are approximate and have been rounded up or down to the nearest whole number.

EXAMPLE:

1 teaspoon = 4.9292 milliliters, rounded up to 5 milliliters

1 ounce = 28.3495 grams, rounded down to 28 grams

Volume Conversions

U.S.	METRIC
1 teaspoon	5 milliliters
2 teaspoons	10 milliliters
1 tablespoon	15 milliliters
2 tablespoons	30 milliliters
¼ cup	59 milliliters
⅓ cup	79 milliliters
½ cup	118 milliliters
¾ cup	177 milliliters
1 cup	237 milliliters
1¼ cups	296 milliliters
1½ cups	355 milliliters
2 cups	473 milliliters
2½ cups	592 milliliters
3 cups	710 milliliters
4 cups (1 quart)	0.946 liter
1.06 quarts	1 liter
4 quarts (1 gallon)	3.8 liters

Weight Conversions

OUNCES	GRAMS
½	14
¾	21
1	28
1½	43
2	57
2½	71
3	85
3½	99
4	113
4½	128
5	142
6	170
7	198
8	227
9	255
10	283
12	340
16 (1 pound)	454

Conversions for Ingredients Commonly Used in Baking

Baking is an exacting science. Because measuring by weight is far more accurate than measuring by volume, and thus more likely to achieve reliable results, in our recipes we provide ounce measures in addition to cup measures for many ingredients. Refer to the chart below to convert these measures into grams.

INGREDIENT	OUNCES	GRAMS
I cup all-purpose flour*	5	142
I cup whole wheat flour	5½	156
I cup granulated (white) sugar	7	198
I cup packed brown sugar (light or dark)	7	198
I cup confectioners' sugar	4	113
I cup cocoa powder	3	85
Butter†		
4 tablespoons (½ stick, or ¼ cup)	2	57
8 tablespoons (I stick, or ½ cup)	4	113
16 tablespoons (2 sticks, or I cup)	8	227

* U.S. all-purpose flour, the most frequently used flour in this book, does not contain leaveners, as some European flours do. These leavened flours are called self-rising or self-raising. If you are using self-rising flour, take this into consideration before adding leavening to a recipe.

† In the United States, butter is sold both salted and unsalted. We generally recommend unsalted butter. If you are using salted butter, take this into consideration before adding salt to a recipe.

Oven Temperatures

FAHRENHEIT	CELSIUS	GAS MARK (IMPERIAL)
225	105	¼
250	120	½
275	130	1
300	150	2
325	165	3
350	180	4
375	190	5
400	200	6
425	220	7
450	230	8
475	245	9

Converting Temperatures from an Instant-Read Thermometer

We include doneness temperatures in many of our recipes, such as those for poultry, meat, and bread. We recommend an instant-read thermometer for the job. Refer to the table above to convert Fahrenheit degrees to Celsius. Or, for temperatures not represented in the chart, use this simple formula:

Subtract 32 degrees from the Fahrenheit reading, then divide the result by 1.8 to find the Celsius reading.

EXAMPLE:

"Roast until the juices run clear when the chicken is cut with a paring knife or the thickest part of the breast registers 160 degrees on an instant-read thermometer." To convert:

$160° F − 32 = 128°$
$128° ÷ 1.8 = 71° C$ (rounded down from 71.11)